Nicaragua:
Unfinished Revolution

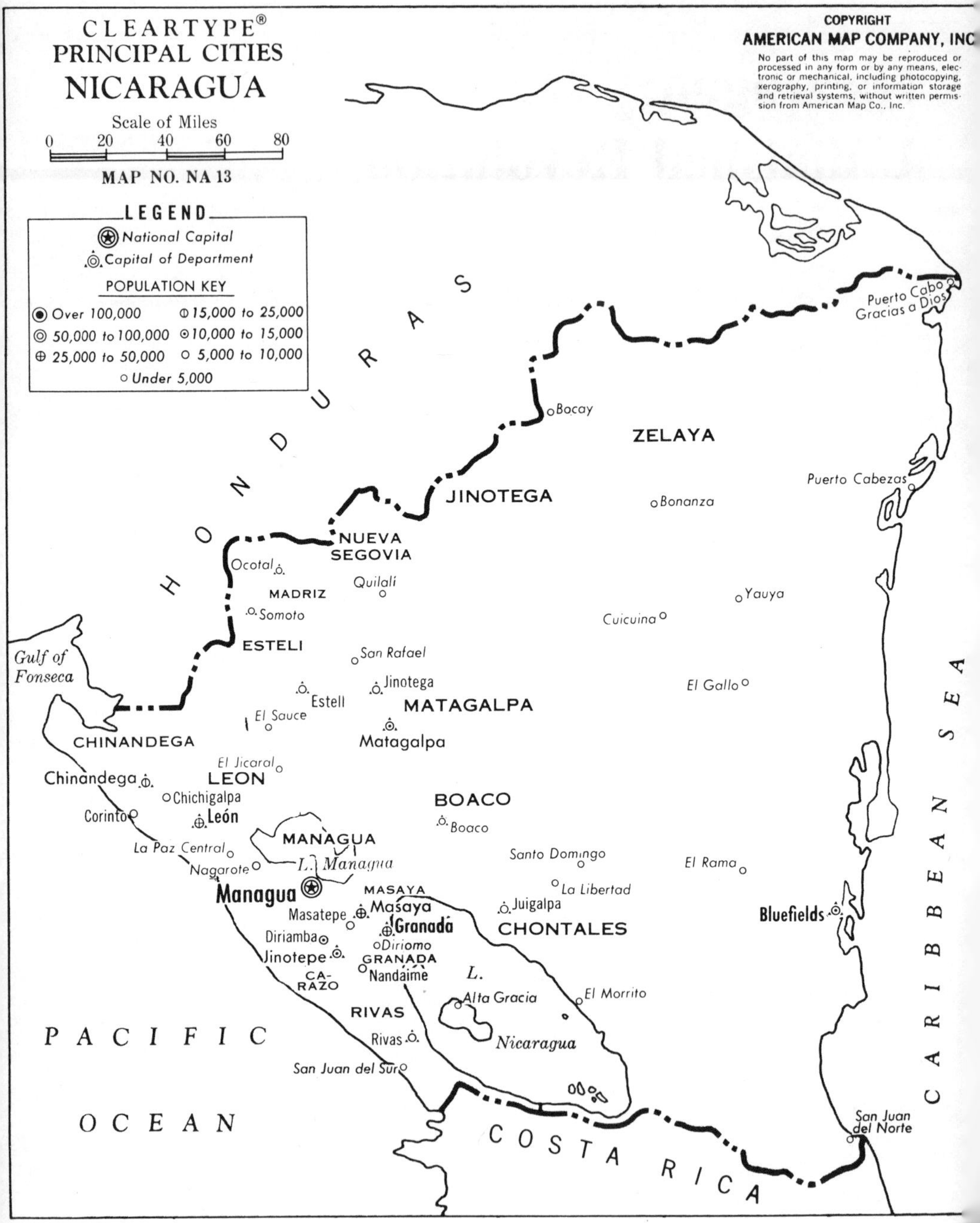

CLEARTYPE®
PRINCIPAL CITIES
NICARAGUA
Scale of Miles
0 20 40 60 80
MAP NO. NA 13
LEGEND
National Capital
Capital of Department
POPULATION KEY
Over 100,000
50,000 to 100,000
25,000 to 50,000
15,000 to 25,000
10,000 to 15,000
5,000 to 10,000
Under 5,000
COPYRIGHT
AMERICAN MAP COMPANY, INC
No part of this map may be reproduced or processed in any form or by any means, electronic or mechanical, including photocopying, xerography, printing, or information storage and retrieval systems, without written permission from American Map Co., Inc.
HONDURAS
Puerto Cabo Gracias a Dios
Bocay
ZELAYA
Puerto Cabezas
JINOTEGA
Bonanza
NUEVA SEGOVIA
Ocotal
Quilali
MADRIZ
Somoto
Yauya
Cuicuina
ESTELI
San Rafael
Gulf of Fonseca
Jinotega
Estell
MATAGALPA
El Gallo
El Sauce
Matagalpa
CHINANDEGA
El Jicaral
Chinandega
LEON
Chichigalpa
BOACO
Corinto
León
Boaco
MANAGUA
La Paz Central
L. Managua
Santo Domingo
El Rama
Nagarote
Managua
MASAYA
La Libertad
Masatepe
Masaya
Juigalpa
Bluefields
Granada
CHONTALES
Diriamba
Diriomo
Jinotepe
GRANADA
CA-RAZO
Nandaime
L.
Alta Gracia
El Morrito
RIVAS
PACIFIC
Rivas
Nicaragua
CARIBBEAN SEA
San Juan del Sur
OCEAN
San Juan del Norte
COSTA RICA

Nicaragua: Unfinished Revolution

The New Nicaragua Reader

Edited by
Peter Rosset
and
John Vandermeer

Grove Press, Inc./New York

First Grove Press Edition 1986
First Printing 1986
ISBN: 0-394-55242-3
Library of Congress Catalog Card Number: 86-372

First Evergreen Edition 1986
First Printing 1986
ISBN: 0-394-62143-3
Library of Congress Catalog Card Number: 86-372
Library of Congress Cataloging-in-Publication Data

Rosset, Peter.
Nicaragua, unfinished revolution.
Bibliography: p.
1. Nicaragua—Politics and government—1979–
2. Nicaragua—Foreign relations—1979–
3. Nicaragua—Foreign relations—United States.
4. United States—Foreign relations—Nicaragua.
5. Counterrevolutions—Nicaragua. I. Vandermeer, John.
II. Title.
F1528.R67 1986 972.85′053 86-372
ISBN 0-394-55242-3
ISBN 0-394-62143-3 (pbk.)

Printed in the United States of America

Grove Press, Inc., 920 Broadway, New York, N.Y. 10010

5 4 3 2 1

''Nicaragua's View of Nicaragua,'' by Daniel Ortega. Reprinted by permission of the Institute for National Strategy. ''Changing Course: Blueprint for Peace in Central America,'' by Policy Alternatives for the Caribbean and Central America. Reprinted by permission. ''Nicaragua's Untold Stories,'' by Robert Leiken. Reprinted by permission from *The New Republic,* October 8, 1984. ''Nicaragua and the Disenchanted Liberals,'' by Peter Marchetti. Reprinted by permission. ''How the U.S. Should Handle Nicaragua,'' by Edgar Chamorro, copyright © 1985 by The New York Times Company. Reprinted by permission. ''Hiding the War in the White House,'' by The New York Times, copyright © 1985 by The New York Times Company. Reprinted by permission. ''Nicaraguan Army: 'War Machine' or Defender of a Besieged Nation?'' by Joel Brinkley, copyright © 1985 by The New York Times Company. Reprinted by permission. ''Arms to El Salvador?'' by David C. MacMichael, copyright © 1984 by The New York Times Company. Excerpts from an article entitled ''Democrats Can Seize Central America Issue.'' Reprinted by permission. ''The Electoral Process in Nicaragua: Domestic and International Influences,'' by the Latin American Studies Association. Reprinted by permission. ''The Issue of Censorship,'' by John Spicer Nichols, from *Nicaragua: The First Five Years,* edited by Thomas Walker. Copyright © 1984 by Praeger Publishers. ''Human Rights in Nicaragua: Reagan, Rhetoric and Reality,'' by *Americas Watch,* July 1985, pp. 2–16. Reprinted by permission. ''Sandinistas Aren't the Worst,'' by Raymond Bonner, copyright © 1984 by The New York Times Company. Reprinted by permission. ''We Are Sandinistas,'' by Deirdre English, copyright © 1985 by *Mother Jones Magazine.* Reprinted by permission. ''The Nicaraguan Background,'' by Henri Weber from *Nicaragua: The Sandinist Revolution,* pp. 1–7. Reprinted by permission of Verso Editions. ''The Eagle Rises,'' by Jenny Pearce from *Under the Eagle.* Reprinted by permission of South End Press, 302 Columbus Ave., Boston, Mass., 02116. ''Play It Again Ron,'' by Ilene O'Malley in *The Alternative Review of Literature and Politics,* Sept. 1981. Reprinted by permission of Dan Morris, founder and editor of *The Alternative Review of Literature and Politics.* Ilene O'Malley thanks Michael Poln for helping research this article. ''A Dictatorship 'Made in the USA','' by Edmundo Jarquin C. and Pablo Emilio Barreto in *Nicaragua: A People's Revolution,* pp. 3–8. Reprinted by permission of the EPICA Task Force, 1470 Irving Street, N.W., Washington, D.C. 20010. ''The Historic Program of the FSLN,'' by the Sandinista National Liberation Front (FSLN). Copyright © 1982 and reprinted by permission of Pathfinder Press. ''The 1972 Earthquake and after: Somocismo in Crisis,'' by George Black. Reprinted by permission of Zed Press, 57 Caledonian Road, London N1. ''The Struggle for Power,'' by Henri Weber in *Nicaragua: The Sandinist Revolution.* Reprinted by permission of Verso Editions. ''U.S.–Nicaraguan Relations Since 1979,'' by Judy Butler. Reprinted by permission. ''Aiding the Contras,'' by David Ignatius and David Rogers. Reprinted by permission of *The Wall Street Journal,* copyright © 1985 by Dow Jones & Company, Inc. All rights reserved. ''U.S. Found to Skirt Ban on Aid to Contras,'' by Alfonse Chardi, Miami Herald Staff Writer, June 24, 1985. Reprinted by permission of the *Miami Herald.* ''Notes and Comment on the Moral Equivalent of Our Founding Fathers,'' by The New Yorker. Reprinted by permission; copyright © 1985 by *The New Yorker Magazine, Inc.* ''Nicaragua 1984: Human and Material Costs of War,'' by The Central American Historical Institute, from *Update* Jan. 29, 1985, Vol. 4, No. 1. Reprinted by permission. The Central American Historical Institute is an independent research group based in Washington, D.C. It works closely with the Instituto Histórico Centroamericano in Managua, Nicaragua. ''Beware of Aiding the 'Contras','' by McGeorge Bundy, copyright © 1985 by The New York Times Company. Reprinted by permission. ''Readying the Troops,'' by Eva Gold. Eva Gold is on the staff of NARMIC, the research, publications and audiovisual unit of American Friends Service Committee. This chapter is excerpted from a longer study entitled *INVASION: A Guide to the U.S. Military Presence in Central America 1985,* available from AFSC/NARMIC, 1501 Cherry Street, Phila., PA 19102, for $2.00. ''Honduras Changed into a U.S. Fortress,'' by Richard Beene, Nov. 26, 1984, the *Dallas Times Herald.* Reprinted by permission. ''The Road from Switzerland to Honduras: The Militarization of Costa Rica,'' by Alan Hruska. Reprinted by permission. ''Blueprint for Disaster,'' by Rear Adm. Gene R. LaRocque and Lt. Col. John H. Buchanan. Reprinted by permission. ''World Court Evasion,'' by Richard H. Ullman, copyright © 1984 by The New York Times Company. Reprinted by permission. ''Possible Violations of Law,'' by the Institute for Policy Studies. Excerpted from *In Contempt of Congress,* by the Institute for Policy Studies, 1985. Reprinted by permission. ''U.S. Economic Policies as Economic Aggression,'' by Michael E. Conroy, *New Perspectives,* May 20, 1986. Copyright © 1986 by Sage Publications, Inc. ''Nicaragua Eases into New Export Markets,'' by Tim Coone, May 8, 1985. Reprinted by permission of The Financial Times of London. ''Reagan's Brezhnev Doctrine,'' by John B. Oakes, copyright © 1985 by The New York Times Company. Reprinted by permission. ''Behind Reagan's Propaganda Blitz,'' by Robert Borosage and Peter Kornbluh, *The Nation,* April 13, 1985. Reprinted by permission. ''The Contadora Initiative,'' by Phillip Berryman, copyright © 1985 by Phillip Berryman. Reprinted by permission of Pantheon Books, a division of Random House, Inc. ''Document Describes How U.S. 'Blocked' a Contadora Treaty,'' by Alma Guillermoprieto and David Hoffman, copyright © 1984 by *The Washington Post.* Reprinted by permission. ''The War at Home,'' by Debra Reuben. Reprinted by permission. Debra Reuben is National Coordinator of the Nicaragua Network. ''Under Construction: Nicaragua's New Polity,'' by Andrew Redding. Reprinted by permission; *Christianity and Crisis,* Vol. 45, No. 12, July 22, 1985. ''Building Democracy Through Mass Organizations,'' by the *Central America Bulletin,* Nov. 1984, pp. 7–10. Reprinted by permission of The Central America Research Institute, *Central America Bulletin,* P.O. Box 4797, Berkeley, CA 94704. ''Toward a New Constitution,'' by the Institute Histórico Centro Americano. Reprinted by permission from *ENVIO,* Vol. 4, issue 53, Nov. 1985. The Instituto Histórico Centroamericano is a Jesuit-affiliated research institution based in Managua, Nicaragua. ''The Structure of the Electoral System,'' by the Latin American Studies Association. Reprinted by permission. ''Fraud in Nicaragua,'' by John B. Oakes, copyright © 1984 by The New York Times Company. Reprinted by permission. ''Labor, Democracy, and the Struggle for Peace,'' and ''Nicaraguan Trade Unions and Confederations,'' from *Labor, Democracy and the Struggle for Peace.* Report of the West Coast Trade Union Delegation to Nicaragua, Nov. 1984. Reprinted by permission of the Labor Network on Central America, P.O. Box 28014, Oakland, CA 94604, tel. (415) 531-6534. ''The Private Sector and the Mixed Economy,'' by Xablier Gorostiaga, excerpted from ''Dilemmas of the Nicaraguan Revolution,'' pp. 48–51, from *The Future of Central America: Policy Choices for the U.S. and Mexico,* Richard R. Fagen and Olga

Acknowledgments

Many people and organizations helped, in one way or another, to make this volume possible. We wish to thank, in particular, Judy Butler, Rev. Don Coleman, Joseph Collins, Mary Frances Doyle, Benita Kaimowitz, David Kaimowitz, Peter Kornbluh, Ivette Perfecto, Debra Reuben, Lisa Rosset, Barney Rosset, Hannelore Rosset, and Kathryn Savoie. We would also like to thank the Nicaragua Network, the Central American Historical Institute, the U.S. Department of State, and the White House Office of Media Relations and Planning. Laurie Russman provided research assistance, for which we are grateful. Finally, we thank Rep. Carl Pursell (R., Michigan), whose stubborn refusal to educate himself on this issue gave us the inspiration necessary to complete this book.

List of Tables

Contents

General Introduction

Since publication of the first *Nicaragua Reader* in 1983, the pattern of tension and hostility between the governments of the United States and Nicaragua has intensified. Nicaragua has continued to occupy the front pages of North American newspapers: We have read about the mining of Nicaragua's harbors, the attack on oil storage facilities, the release of "humanitarian" aid to the *contras,* a U.S. trade embargo, a case before the International Court of Justice, and Nicaragua's first elections since the 1979 revolution. The "secret war" is no longer secret, negotiated solutions slip out of reach, Nicaragua's war-torn economy has begun to deteriorate, and the United States inexorably increases its military and economic commitment in the region, prompting many to point out parallels to the early days of U.S. involvement in Indochina. While many in the Reagan administration and the Pentagon confidently proclaim that America has learned lessons from Vietnam, others speak of the new "Reagan Doctrine" of low intensity warfare as "Oh, oh, here we go again!"

As U.S. citizens who have spent considerable time in Nicaragua, we can attest that lively debate and controversy abound in both countries. At either a New York cocktail party or in a Managua slum, it is never difficult to engage in discussions about Nicaragua. Having done both, we are struck by the near total difference in the content of those discussions. It is almost as though what passes for Nicaragua here in the United States is a different country altogether from the Nicaragua discussed down there; likewise, what is a major issue here, is all too often just not an issue for most Nicaraguans.

In the United States we are accustomed to debating Nicaragua's insertion in the East-West conflict, and to arguing for or against the proposition that Nicaragua has become a totalitarian state (in our first edition, the phrase was "drifting toward totalitarianism"). Nicaraguans, on the other hand, complain about the quality of beans at the government's ENABAS outlets, and argue about who's responsible for the shortage of toilet paper and why the "imperialist" United States attacks them. It seems that never the twain shall meet. In the United States, one never hears the word *imperialism,* except in jest or in describing actions of the Soviet Union, yet in Nicaragua it is perhaps the most common word used in political discussions. And for most Nicaraguans the issue of East-West tension is pretty foreign—although constant exposure to North American journalists has taught some the use of this terminology.

We think it is unfortunate that the boundaries of the debate in the respective countries hardly overlap. Like all governments, that of Nicaragua is neither angel nor devil. It is, rather, one doing its best to promote change in a small, very poor country, drawn by historical factors into the arena of East-West tensions. Because the United States is so intimately involved, it is vital for U.S. citizens to understand what is happening in Nicaragua, and in doing so to go beyond the conventional limits of the debate, and see beyond the parameters set by each side.

It is in this spirit that we offer the readings collected in this book. Of course, we begin with the conventional opinions expressed by the leaders of both nations, Presidents Reagan and Ortega. But we make every possible attempt to go beyond those positions, and include a variety of material ranging from articles by the neoliberal/conservative Robert Leiken to former *New York Times* editor John Oakes, from documents of the U.S. Department of State to those of the Americas Watch human rights organization and the Jesuit-affiliated Central American Historical Institute. We feel confident that we have covered what are regarded as responsible opinions from left to right, even though we know that we might be considered too anti-Nicaragua by one side and too pro-Nicaragua by the other. But this is inevitable in any attempt to present all sides of a controversial issue.

The organization of this book follows the logic of the controversies surrounding Nicaragua. The first section, presenting the positions of all sides, includes official statements from the governments of the United States and Nicaragua. The second section focuses less on controversy and more on the historical background to the present situation in Nicaragua. Part 3 covers the war—certainly the central preoccupation of Nicaraguans, though often ignored here in the United States. The fourth and final section covers internal developments in Nicaragua, the successes and the failures, the planned and the unplanned. This section presents some of the lesser-known aspects of Nicaragua in documents, some of which appear in English for the first time.

In reviewing the material collected in this volume, the reader should keep in mind two things about Nicaragua. The first is Nicaragua's historical role in the world as a poor third world country, formerly a Spanish colony and until recently firmly rooted within the U.S. sphere of influence. Nicaragua's statistics have always placed it, along with Haiti and Honduras, among the poorest nations of the Western Hemisphere. It is important to understand that most Nicaraguans—rightly or wrongly—view the United States as responsible for much of that poverty because of its some fourteen-odd military interventions in Nicaragua, its more than two decades of occupation of that country during this century, and its former active maintenance of the

Somoza dynasty. For Nicaraguans, independence and sovereignty are issues greater than that of East-West tensions.

The second important point to keep in mind in reading this book is that in a very real sense the eyes of the world are focused on Nicaragua, and by association, the United States. Evidence of children starving in most of the Third World has told us that something is not working right; many people are now looking to Nicaragua to see what sort of alternative their experiment might offer. Those of all opinions should agree then, on how important it is to carefully scrutinize United States policy toward Nicaragua. Anyone interested in understanding different points of view should attempt to read these materials through different eyes—those, for instance, of one of Nicaragua's poor majority, or those of a resident of another poor third world country, and of course those of a citizen of the United States responsible to some degree for U.S. policy in Nicaragua.

Part One

THE DEBATE

Chapter I:

Overview—Setting the Terms

Editors' Introduction

The questions asked in any debate are often as important as the participants. Boss Tweed of Tammany Hall is reported to have said, "I don't care who does the voting, as long as I do the nominating." The participants of both sides in the ongoing debate about Nicaragua and the United States might well paraphrase that famous quote and say, "I don't care who does the answering as long as I choose the questions." The kinds of questions posed by policymakers and analysts tell a great deal about their viewpoints and the information they choose to present.

At the risk of stereotyping the various U.S. and Nicaraguan positions, it seems useful to characterize the general questions to which each party would like to confine discussion. The Reagan administration, for instance, would clearly like to define the principal issue with the question, "How should the United States respond to the threat of a Soviet-style terrorist state so close to our borders?" On the other hand, Nicaraguan President Ortega would like to focus the discussion around such questions as, "How has the Nicaraguan revolution remained true to the poor majority while maintaining principles of political pluralism, a mixed economy, and nonalignment?"

Each side would like to leave certain tacit assumptions unchallenged. Despite lack of evidence, for instance, the Reagan administration continues to allege that the Nicaraguan government is "totalitarian" in nature and that it supports terrorist groups in the hemisphere. And Nicaragua's Sandinista leadership, while refusing to reveal figures on the extent to which Nicaragua has received Soviet military aid, nevertheless asserts that Nicaragua presents no military threat to the region.

President Ortega asks how Nicaragua can normalize relations with the United States, while insisting that Nicaragua be free to choose its allies as if it were not in the geographic sphere of influence of a superpower. And President Reagan bases his position on the assumption that the United States cannot live with the "present structure" of the Nicaraguan government.

During the past six years there has been a veritable explosion in the number of essays seeking to define the debate over U.S.–Nicaraguan relations. From hundreds of possibilities, eight articles have been chosen here to outline the major positions.

The first two readings give Presidents Reagan and Ortega the opportunity to present the drastically different viewpoints of their respective administrations. Both talks took place in 1985 and represented the most up-to-date and comprehensive statements available. While neither statement responds to all of the major questions surrounding the U.S.–Nicaragua crisis, they do represent the essence of each president's goals for Nicaragua.

The next two selections present alternative policies that a U.S. administration could realistically follow with respect to Nicaragua. The first is from the widely reported Kissinger Commission report of 1984 that has provided the blueprint for Reagan administration policy in Central America during the last two years. The Policy Alternatives for the Caribbean and Central America (PACCA) report, prepared by prominent Latin American scholars, responds to the Kissinger Commission report by offering a different policy approach that would simultaneously preserve legitimate U.S. security interests in Central America and maximize the chances for peace and self-determination in the region.

The next reading, "Nicaragua's Untold Stories," by Robert Leiken, is typical of what might be called the "cold war liberal" position on Nicaragua. It has been an extremely influential article, quoted by President Reagan in the opening piece in this volume, and used by Democratic and Republican members of Congress alike to determine how to vote on aid to the anti-Sandinista *contras*.* Responding to the Leiken essay is the next reading by Father Peter Marchetti, a prominent American Jesuit economist serving as an advisor to the Nicaraguan government. Together, these essays define what may be termed the "center" position on Nicaragua.

These two are followed by a remarkable essay written by Edgar Chamorro, a former member of the civilian directorate of the major *contra* organization, the FDN. Despite his clearly anti-Sandinista viewpoint, he broke with the FDN over the issue of human rights violations by the *contras*, becoming a spokesperson for that portion of the opposition-in-exile that no longer supports armed counterrevolution. His recommendations for U.S. government policy are based on considerable first-hand knowledge of that policy.

Closing this section is the editorial position of the *New York Times*, which both defines and lends an ominous note to the terms of this most crucial debate.

---

*Another notable work within the same political vein is Shirley Christian, *Nicaragua: Revolution in the Family* (New York: Random House, 1985).

*1. Nicaragua's View of Nicaragua**

By Daniel Ortega

Former California governor Jerry Brown and the editors of New Perspectives *journeyed to Nicaragua last autumn to meet Sandinista leader Daniel Ortega, who shortly afterwards was elected the nation's president.*

New Perspectives: What kind of political system do you envision for Nicaragua? What country comes closest to being what you hope for Nicaragua?

Daniel Ortega: We're struggling to establish a regime that is of a democratic and pluralistic nature. We're not imitating any country in particular, but we have sought the contribution of the experiences of other countries.

Perhaps the Nicaraguan revolution is something that can be compared to the Algerian revolution. In the context of Latin America, we would see it as being close to what the Mexican process has been.

NP: What do you mean by pluralism? What is the relationship in your system between the political party and the military?

DO: The Sandinista National Liberation Front was the organization, the party, that carried out revolutionary change. The people took up arms under the Sandinista Front. Later, an army had to be constituted. That army was constituted by the same people. Therefore, the army was politicized because it was formed by the men and women who fought against the Somoza dictatorship under the banner of the Sandinista Front.

We seek pluralism in the sense that even though the Nicaraguan revolution is a very profound process, it does give room for participation by diverse groups. The revolution has established a framework within which different political, economic, and social forces can be active, can move about. Let me explain.

Remember that in Chile, in 1970 under Allende, democracy was put to a test of whether or not it was possible to alter the system with profound changes through the electoral process. The Popular Unity Party of Allende reached power through elections, but because the party presented a challenge to the system itself, the interests of the established system destroyed the Popular Unity.

Now within some Latin American democracies there is pluralist participation. For example, in Costa Rica, Venezuela, and now in Argentina, contending political forces are permitted to participate in the electoral process so long as they don't alter the system. The Communists, for example, do participate in the elections in Venezuela. They are part of the pluralist scheme, as long as they do not represent a threat to the system. They have some influence on the political decisions, and they have some influence on public opinion.

In the case of Nicaragua, where a profound revolution has taken place and where

---

*Excerpts from *New Perspectives,* Fall–Winter, 1984–1985. From an interview with former California governor, Jerry Brown.

we have not sought the classic alternative of a one-party state, we have established a framework, a new system. It is, logically, not similar to that of Chile under Allende, which was unable to defend itself; nor is it similar to that of Cuba or others within the socialist community. It has its own characteristics.

Now, of course, in the United States, if some political force were to attempt to alter the political system, that force would be destroyed by the system. In the United States, other political forces can participate, they can present opinions, and they can dissent so long as there is no attempt against the system itself. In Nicaragua, we are doing something similar. That is what I mean by pluralism in Nicaragua.

Now about the role of the military. There is an army which has the function of defending the system, which is the function of armies in all parts of the world. The North American army will defend the North American system. The Soviet army will defend the Communist system. The Sandinista army will defend the Sandinista system.

NP: In the U.S. border region, where we are concerned with security, there have been two different revolutionary histories—Mexico and Cuba. In Mexico, the role and importance of the army have diminished over the years. In Cuba, the army continues to play a major role in society. How do you analyze this situation and how might the lessons apply to Nicaragua?

DO: Cuba has an army such as it has not because of the internal situation, but because they are confronting the United States. I really don't believe the Cubans are all that interested in investing enormous amounts of resources in their army; but until they reach a situation where they are at peace with the United States, it will be very difficult for them to reduce that force. Nicaragua is an even clearer case of the same problem. We need not so much an army, but a people that is prepared to defend itself.

What you say about Mexico is correct, but Mexico was able to diminish its army to the degree that it was no longer threatened by the United States. Despite the very serious problems Mexico has had with the United States, particularly in the earlier stage of their revolution comparable to where we are now, it now has a most stable relationship. But when the Mexican system has been threatened, as was the case during the rebellion of the students in 1968, then the army has come out to repress.

NP: The U.S. government overthrew President Francisco Madero during the Mexican revolution, but as you mentioned, ultimately the United States and Mexico came to a pragmatic accommodation. Can the Nicaraguan revolution make the same sort of accommodation?

DO: There is a proposal presented by the Latin American countries that are allies of the United States. This proposal has also been supported by all of the U.S. allies in Europe. It is a proposal that has been presented after almost two years of effort. This is the proposal of the Contadora Group—Mexico, Venezuela, Colombia, and Panama.

This proposal has been accepted by Nicaragua after much reflection and analysis. For us, it represents concessions. The situation we would be in after implementing these accords is very risky because we do not belong to any military pact, while the other Central American governments are supported by the U.S. government. To accept this proposal is to put Nicaragua's security in the hands of the international community, especially of the European and Latin American countries.

Although the draft also represents concessions for the United States, the United States' power to affect and influence policies in Central America is far greater than any other country's, and Nicaragua would have to confront that power if its interests are threatened.

We accept the Contadora draft with a pragmatic end in mind, in favor of peace and accommodation, and with a sense of responsibility, conscious that our security is going to depend on a political and moral commitment of the Latin American and European friends of the United States. That is what counts above all.

Nicaragua would be placing its security on a certain political, moral commitment because we are not a part of any military bloc or alliance, nor do we aspire to be. We are in a zone where the influence of the United States is very heavy. We cannot have our security depend on what the United States says, because the Central American region will continue to be a region controlled by the United States.

NP: You acknowledge the fact, then, that Nicaragua is within the "sphere of influence" of the United States.

DO: Yes.

NP: It is obvious that conservative forces are in the ascendancy in the United States. Whether that is good or bad, it's an objective reality. How do you deal with that?

DO: I am very conscious of the new strength and force that the conservative forces have gained in the United States, and the role that the U.S. defeat in Vietnam and the hostage situation in Iran have played in helping to create this new conservatism.

Now, what is the problem we Nicaraguans confront? Our crime has been that we have made a revolution. We changed a system that was created by the United States, and this administration does not want to accept our revolution. Every day Nicaragua is being looked at through an enormous magnifying glass. All the propaganda resources the government of the United States has are deployed against us.

In Nicaragua, for example, there is a much more open society, a more pluralistic society, more liberty, more freedom of the press than in Chile, for example, or Paraguay or Haiti—just to mention the most crude examples. But the United States is not concerned about democracy in those countries. There are no comparisons made concerning those countries' totalitarianism.

I believe that in Nicaragua there is more democracy than in El Salvador. Human rights are not being violated in the way that they are in El Salvador with the uncontrollable death squads and so on. Nicaragua is being accused of religious persecution, and it is the only country in Latin America that is being accused of religious persecution by the U.S. government. But after five years of revolution, not even one priest has been assassinated in Nicaragua. In many Latin American countries, dozens of priests and religious figures have been assassinated.

It is true that in Nicaragua we don't have complete freedom of the press. There are restrictions regarding military information, and sometimes the censors make mistakes censoring certain information that doesn't have to be censored. But the mass media continues to express itself against the Sandinista government. There is right now opportunity of expression through the newspapers and on the radio. But every time a piece of information is censored in Nicaragua, this seems to be a scandal. In certain supposedly democratic countries in Latin America, the mass media have been closed down. But that's not news.

The problem is that there is an attitude on the part of the U.S. government to destroy the Nicaraguan revolution. Regardless of the efforts to establish a pluralist regime, the government of the United States does not want to take these efforts into account. The great concern of the administration is a reflection of the historical policy of the United States toward Latin America. The U.S. government is concerned that this revolution may be able to consolidate itself and thus become a very dangerous example for Latin America. It would be proof that nationalist revolutions can take place that move toward democracy and pluralism.

In one way of looking at it, the greatest favor we could perform for this administration would be if we were to define ourselves as a regime such as Cuba's. If we were to declare a Marxist-Leninist socialist revolution, if we were to declare ourselves allies of the Soviet Union, then the U.S. government would be able to say, "Do you see that it is impossible to have democratic revolutions in Latin America? Do you see that everything leads to communism? Do you see that everything is promoted by Russia and Cuba?"

In the final analysis, the United States would prefer to deal with a regime of that type. That would automatically isolate the struggle of the Salvadoran people. It would reflect a retreat, a step backward in the struggle for Latin American democracy. The Latin American governments together with the European governments would then change their attitude about the phenomenon of change in Latin America. Then the U.S. government could say to the Europeans, "Do you not see that they are a silly bunch of fools? Do you see that you are a silly bunch of fools to think it is possible to have democratic revolutions in Latin America?"

NP: Wouldn't you describe yourself as a Marxist-Leninist?

DO: I believe this is secondary. We define ourselves as Sandinistas. The Sandinista leadership has proposed to carry out a type of revolutionary leadership which believes in what is appropriate for Latin America. We believe that this is a revolution that belongs to Latin America and that it should take into account the historical conditions and characteristics of the region. We have to start from the premise that Nicaragua is not a country where there are conditions for a class struggle. It is a country with a peasant population and a working population and small commercial class. The conditions simply do not exist for the "Marxist" polarization between the working class and the bourgeoisie which takes place in the industrially developed countries.

NP: But you can't dismiss this concern with whether or not you are a Marxist-Leninist as secondary since it is regarded as a central issue by those in the administration who oppose the Sandinistas. Administration strategists say that the revolution has been betrayed, that the Arturo Cruz-type democratic elements are all gone, and that we can't trust the remaining Marxist-Leninists. At a forum sponsored by our Institute in Washington last March, Fred Iklé, the undersecretary of defense for policy, argued that "revolutionary regimes that call themselves Marxist or Communist and follow the Bolshevik approach to power have particularly undesirable features. They are irreversible, and they want to expand their type of rule into neighboring countries, if need be, by force."

DO: How can anyone with even a minimum of intelligence believe that Nicaragua would want to invade its neighbors? What possible benefit could accrue to Nicaragua by so doing? Wouldn't the United States love to see us do that? Then they could invade; but not only that, they could invade with applause from the world! Wouldn't we, deservedly so, be the object of repudiation from the entire international community?

NP: If you are not a threat to your neighbors, then why did even the Carter administration, which had originally aided the revolution, withdraw support?

DO: On the contrary, Carter continued to defend aid to Nicaragua until he left office. There was opposition to this aid, and even we at a certain point were tempted to say, "well, okay, let them keep their money," because there was hope and expectation by the Nicaraguan people, and the people were becoming indignant when they heard how the discussion was taking place in the United States. At last the aid was approved. Perhaps $55 million of that $75 million was disbursed. The rest of the aid was canceled by the Reagan government. It wasn't the Carter government.

NP: Why do you have the largest army in Central America?

DO: According to U.S. figures, the largest army is that of El Salvador—I'm talking about armies, not militias. But why would anyone doubt why we have a large army, or why we need effective weapons when the Americans are doing what they are doing to Nicaragua?

NP: Your government has been increasingly criticized by the bishops in Nicaragua. . . .

DO: Not all of the bishops criticize the government, but some of them do because the government is promoting a revolutionary process. Even in the United States, the bishops criticize the government for some of its policies in the nuclear arms arena. But, of course, your country is a big country, a powerful country which cannot be the victim of effective propaganda from other countries.

In Nicaragua, when the bishops criticize the government it does have great implications. However, in other Latin American countries, we also see that there are bishops who for various reasons criticize different governments—but that is not news. What is news is everything that happens in Nicaragua.

2. *President Reagan's View of Nicaragua**

By Ronald Reagan

As you know, the Sandinista dictatorship has taken absolute control of the government and the armed forces. It is a Communist dictatorship. It has done what Communist dictatorships do: created a repressive state security and secret police organization assisted by Soviet, East German, and Cuban advisers; harassed, and in many cases expunged, the political opposition; and rendered the democratic freedoms of speech, press, and assembly punishable by officially sanctioned harassment and imprisonment or death.

But the Communists are not unopposed. They are facing great resistance from the people of Nicaragua, resistance from the patriots who fight for freedom and their unarmed allies from the prodemocracy movement.

There is growing evidence of Sandinista brutality. We've recently learned that ten or eleven members of the Social Christian Party have been rounded up and jailed. The Sandinistas are trying to get them to confess to being counterrevolutionaries. And you might be interested in knowing one way the Communists are coercing these confessions. They have also arrested more than a hundred relatives of the political prisoners. And according to our most recent information, the Social Christian Party members are being held in the dark in small, overheated cells. Prisoners are served meals at irregular intervals—after twelve hours, for instance, and then the next in another two. The purpose is to disorient them and wear them down. Where do they get that idea? This same method has been used against political prisoners in Cuba.

Now, we do not know the exact number of political prisoners in Nicaragua today, but we get an indication from the testimony of José Gonzalez, a former vice-president of the Social Democratic Party. Gonzalez told Pope John Paul II there were about 8,000 political prisoners in 1981. He also told the Pope the Sandinistas practice repression and torture. Gonzalez, as you know, was arrested when he returned from Rome. He left Nicaragua and now lives in exile.

But the most compelling evidence of Sandinista brutality and of why people are fleeing is the Sandinistas' scorched-earth policy. We know the Sandinistas have ordered and are carrying out the forced relocation of tens of thousands of peasants. We have reports that 20,000 peasants have been moved in the past two months from their homes to relocation camps. Peasants who have escaped call themselves hostages and call the relocation camps concentration camps. The Communists themselves had admitted they're engaged in the forced resettlement of an estimated 65,000 people. Peasants and journalists tell of entire villages, homes, stores, and churches being

---

*Excerpts from President Reagan's address at a fund-raising dinner for the Nicaragua Refugee Fund, April 15, 1985.

burnt to the ground. They tell of animals slaughtered, crops burned, and villagers taken away at gunpoint in government trucks.

Why are the Communists doing this? Massed forced relocations are a common feature of modern Communist tyrannies, but there are other purposes here. For the people of many villages are actively supporting the freedom fighters, and so the Communists have decided to put more and more of the people of Nicaragua into closely guarded pens, and that way it will be easier for the regime to stalk the freedom fighters in the countryside. A Sandinista security chief has explained, "Anyone still in the hills is a guerrilla."

While all this is terrible, it can hardly come as a surprise to those who know what was done to the Miskito Indians. As you know, the Miskitos supported the Sandinistas against Somoza. But shortly after taking power, the Sandinistas attempted to indoctrinate the Miskitos in Marxist dogma, and the Indians resisted. The Sandinistas tried to put their own people in as leaders of the Miskito community, and the Indians resisted, so much that the Sandinistas labeled them "bourgeois" and, therefore, enemies of the people. They began to arrest Indian leaders. Some were murdered; some were tortured. One Miskito leader told our AFL-CIO that Tomás Borge and other leaders of the Sandinistas "came to my cell and warned me that Sandinismo would be established on the Atlantic coast even if every single Miskito Indian had to be eliminated."

Well, the Sandinistas came close. There were massacres. Eyewitnesses said some Miskitos were buried alive. Ten thousand Indians were force-marched to relocation camps. Miskito villages were burned down; they're still being burned down. Miskito villages were bombed and shelled, and they are still being bombed and shelled. In the name of humanity, these atrocities must be stopped.

Twenty thousand Indians are known to be incarcerated in relocation camps. About half are currently being held at the Tasba Pri Relocation Camps. *Tasba Pri,* by the way, means "free land." Well, above one "free land" camp, a *New York Times* reporter noted a sign that said, "Work that unites us is a revolutionary force."

In all, tens of thousands of Miskitos have been forced to flee Nicaragua, to flee the land they lived on for over a thousand years. Many now live as refugees in Honduras.

Unfortunately, it's widely believed outside Nicaragua that the Sandinistas enjoy the support of the people inside, but you know this is completely untrue. We know this from many sources, even recently the American press.

A few months ago, the *New Republic* carried a report by Robert Leiken, who had long been sympathetic to the Sandinistas and who had formerly testified in Congress against aid to the *contras*. He wrote. "One of the most common means of sustaining the myth of popular support is the Sandinistas' use of the rationing system as a lever—ration cards are confiscated for nonattendance at Sandinista meetings." And talk of inflation is branded as "counterrevolutionary plot." Sympathy with the *contras,* he said, is more and more pervasive. In fact, the peasants now call them *Los Muchachos,* the affectionate term they once used exclusively for the Sandinistas. And what do they now call the Sandinistas? Well, the latest worker's chant is "the Sandinistas and Somoza are the same thing."

In spite of all this, the Sandinista government retains its defenders in this country and in the West. They look at all the evidence that the Sandinistas have instituted a Communist regime: all the pictures of dictator Ortega embracing Castro and visiting Moscow, all the Soviet-bloc advisers, and all the Sandinista votes in the UN, such as their decision in line with the Soviet bloc to refuse the credentials of Israel. They look at this, and they say: "The Sandinistas aren't Communists, or aren't real Communists. Why, they're only nationalists, only socialists."

But these defenders admit there is a problem in Nicaragua. The problem, they say, is the freedom fighters. Well, just a few weeks ago, the whole world was treated to a so-called independent investigation of charges that the freedom fighters have committed atrocities. It spoke of these so-called atrocities in a rather riveting manner. And the report received great attention on television and in leading newspapers and publications. The report ignored Communist brutality, the murder of the Indians, and the arrest, torture, and murder of political dissidents. But we really shouldn't be surprised by that because, as our State Department discovered and *Time* magazine reported, this so-called independent investigation was the work of one of dictator Ortega's supporters, a sympathizer who has openly embraced Sandinismo and who was shepherded through Nicaragua by Sandinista operatives.

The truth is, there are atrocities going on in Nicaragua, but they're largely the work of the institutionalized cruelty of the Sandinista government. This cruelty is the natural expression of a Communist government, a cruelty that flows naturally from the heart of totalitarianism. The truth is Somoza was bad, but so many of the people of Nicaragua know the Sandinistas are infinitely worse.

We have here this evening many individuals who know these truths firsthand. Some of you may know of Bayardo Santaeliz. He is a twenty-nine-year-old Nicaraguan refugee and a former lay preacher of the Pentecostal Missionary Church in Nicaragua. And this is his story, a story told in sworn testimony before a Honduran civil rights commission. A few years ago, the Sandinistas began pressuring Bayardo to stop preaching and start fighting for the revolution. And one night after holding a prayer session in a home on the slopes of the Momotombo Volcano, Bayardo went to bed. He was awakened by Sandinista soldiers who asked if he was an evangelical preacher; Bayardo said yes. The Sandinistas arrested him, accused him of counterrevolutionary activity, verbally abused him, and then tied him and two others to a pillar. Then the Sandinistas doused the house with gasoline and threw in a match. The room went up in flames, but they burned the rope that bound Bayardo, and he escaped with his clothes in flames and his body burned. He hid in the countryside and was rescued by *campesinos* who got him to a hospital, where he lied about the causes of his injuries. And not long after, he left Nicaragua.

Bayardo, I wonder if you could rise for a moment, wherever you are here in the room.

You know, I was going to ask all of you fellows with the cameras if you wouldn't kind of turn them off me and on him, but then he came up here; so I didn't ask you that. He's just one of the many who've suffered. He knows things and has experienced things that many of us in this country can barely imagine. And I think America has to see the true face of Nicaragua. Thank you, Bayardo.

Some people say this isn't America's problem. Why should we care if Nicaragua is a democracy or not? Well, we should care for a whole host of reasons.

Democracy has its own moral imperatives, as you well know, but it also has advantages that are profoundly practical. Democratic states do not attack their neighbors and destabilize regions. Democratic states do not find it easy to declare and carry out war. Democratic states are not by their nature militaristic. Democracies are traditionally reluctant to spend a great deal of money on arms. Democratic states have built-in controls on aggressive, expansionist behavior because democratic states must first marshal wide popular support before they move.

None of these characteristics applies to totalitarian states, however. And so, totalitarian Nicaragua poses a threat to us all.

The Sandinistas have been engaged for some time in spreading their Communist revolution beyond their borders. They're providing arms, training, and a headquarters to the Communist guerrillas who are attempting to overthrow the democratically elected Duarte government of El Salvador. The Sandinistas have been caught supporting similar antidemocratic movements in Honduras and Costa Rica; Guatemala, too, is threatened. If these governments fall, as Nicaragua has fallen, it will send millions of refugees north, as country after country collapses. Already, the refugee situation is building to unacceptable levels. More than a quarter of a million refugees have fled Nicaragua since the Sandinistas took control. Some weeks, a hundred Nicaraguans a day stream into Costa Rica alone. It must be noted here that many of these refugees carry no papers, register in no official camps, and wind up on no one's official list of those who've fled. They simply cross the border of one country or another and settle where they can.

And let me emphasize a very important point: These refugees are not simply people caught in the middle of a war. They're people fleeing for their lives from the Sandinista police state. They are fleeing from people who are burning down their villages, forcing them into concentration camps, and forcing their children into military service.

The refugees come into camps in Honduras with no food and no money. Many are sick with parasites and malaria. And the great tragedy is that these people are the innocents of the war—people without politics, people who had never presumed to govern or to tell the world how to turn. They are both innocents and victims.

If the Communists continue unfettered by the weight of world opinion, there will be more victims, victims of a long march north. We've seen this before. We've seen the boat people leaving Southeast Asia in terror. We saw the streams of refugees leave East Berlin before the wall was built. We've seen these sad, lost armies fleeing in the night. We *cannot* allow it to happen again.

Some claim that the freedom fighters are simply former *Somocistas* who want to reimpose a dictatorship. That is simply not true. Listen to the roll call of their leaders: Adolpho Calero, a Nicaraguan businessman who was imprisoned by Somoza;

Alfonso Robelo, a member of the original Sandinista government, now leading freedom fighters in the south; Arturo Cruz, another former member of the Sandinista government who is supporting the freedom fighters; Edén Pastora, the famed Commander Zero, a hero of the anti-Somoza revolution.

These men are not putting their lives on the line to restore a dictatorship of the past; these men are fighting for freedom. Already they control large sections of the countryside. And as for their level of support, there are now three times as many freedom fighters fighting the Sandinistas as there were Sandinistas fighting Somoza.

There are those who say America's attempt to encourage freedom in Nicaragua interferes with the right of self-determination of the Nicaraguan people. Self-determination—you wonder what the ghosts of the Miskito Indians would say to that; you wonder what the journalists who cannot print the truth and the political prisoners who cannot speak it would say about self-determination and the Sandinistas. I think they would say that when a small Communist clique seizes a country, there is no self-determination and no chance of it.

I truly believe the history of this century forces me to believe that to do nothing in Central America is to give the first Communist stronghold on the North American continent a green light to spread its poison throughout this free and increasingly democratic hemisphere.

No evil is inevitable unless we make it so. We cannot have the United States walk away from one of the greatest moral challenges in postwar history. I pledge to you that we will do everything we can to win this great struggle.

And so, we're hopeful. We will fight on. We'll win this struggle for peace. Thank you for inviting me.

Viva Nicaragua libre. Thank you, and God bless you.

*3. The Kissinger Commission on Nicaragua**

By Henry Kissinger, *et al.*

In Nicaragua the revolution that overthrew the hated Somoza regime has been captured by self-proclaimed Marxist-Leninists. In July of 1979 the Sandinistas promised the OAS that they would organize "a truly democratic government" and hold free elections, but that promise has not been redeemed. Rather, the government has been brought fully under the control of the Sandinista National Directorate. Only two months after giving their pledge to the OAS and while successfully negotiating loans in Washington, the Sandinistas issued Decree No. 67, which converted their movement into the country's official political party and laid the foundation for the monop-

*Excerpts from the *Report of the National Bipartisan Commission on Central America,* Office of the President, January 1984.

oly of political power they now enjoy. The Sandinista Directorate has progressively put in place a Cuban-style regime, complete with mass organizations under its political direction, an internal security system to keep watch on the entire population, and a massive military establishment. This comprehensive police and military establishment not only ensures the monopoly on power within Nicaragua, it also produces an acute sense of insecurity among Nicaragua's neighbors.

From the outset, the Sandinistas have maintained close ties with Cuba and the Soviet Union. There are some 8,000 Cuban advisers now in Nicaragua, including at least 2,000 military advisers, as well as several hundred Soviet, East European, Libyan, and PLO advisers. Cuban construction teams have helped build military roads, bases, and airfields. According to intelligence sources, an estimated 15,000 tons of Soviet-bloc arms and equipment reached the Sandinista army in 1983. This military connection with Cuba, the Soviet Union, and its satellites internationalizes Central America's security problems and adds a menacing new dimension.

Nicaragua's government has made significant gains against illiteracy and disease. But despite significant U.S. aid from 1979 to 1981 (approximately $117 million), its economic performance has been poor, in part because of the disruptions caused by the revolution, in part because of the world recession, and in part because of the mismanagement invariably associated with regimes espousing Marxist-Leninist ideology. National income per capita is less than $1,000, about equal to that of the early 1960s, and Nicaragua is plagued by shortages of food and consumer goods, with the result that extensive rationing has been instituted.

Under military pressure from Nicaraguan rebels who reportedly receive U.S. support, and under diplomatic pressure from the international community, especially from the Contadora Group, the Sandinistas have recently promised to announce early this year a date and rules for 1985 elections; have offered a partial amnesty to the anti-Sandinista guerrillas; have claimed a relaxation of censorship of *La Prensa,* the only opposition newspaper; have entered into talks with the Roman Catholic hierarchy; and have issued proposals for regional security agreements. In addition, reports from Sandinista sources in Managua have hinted at a permanently reduced Cuban presence and of diminished support to other Marxist-Leninist revolutionary groups in Central America—although we have no confirmation that either has taken place or is likely to take place. Whether any one of these moves reflects a true change of course or merely tactical maneuvers remains to be seen. . . .

The Sandinista military forces are potentially larger than those of all the rest of Central America combined. The government in Managua volunteered to this Commission an intelligence briefing which left no reasonable doubt that Nicaragua is tied into the Cuban, and thereby the Soviet, intelligence network. The Commission encountered no leader in Central America, including democratic and unarmed Costa Rica, who did not express deep foreboding about the impact of a militarized, totalitarian Nicaragua on the peace and security of the region. Several expressed the view that should the Sandinista regime now be consolidated as a totalitarian state, their own freedom, and even their independence, would be jeopardized. In several countries, especially those with democratic traditions, we met leaders who expressed regret and outrage that the revolution against Somoza—which their own governments had supported—had been betrayed by the Sandinistas.

For all of these reasons, the consolidation of a Marxist-Leninist regime in Managua would be seen by its neighbors as constituting a permanent security threat. Because of its secretive nature, the existence of a political order on the Cuban model in Nicaragua would pose major difficulties in negotiating, implementing, and verifying any Sandinista commitment to refrain from supporting insurgency and subversion in other countries. In this sense, the development of an open political system in Nicaragua, with a free press and an active opposition, would provide an important security guarantee for the other countries of the region and would be a key element in any negotiated settlement.

Theoretically, the United States and its friends could abandon any hope of such a settlement and simply try to contain a Nicaragua which continued to receive military supplies on the present scale. In practical terms, however, such a course would present major difficulties. In the absence of a political settlement, there would be little incentive for the Sandinistas to act responsibly, even over a period of time, and much inducement to escalate their efforts to subvert Nicaragua's neighbors. To contain the export of revolution would require a level of vigilance and sustained effort that would be difficult for Nicaragua's neighbors and even for the United States. A fully militarized and equipped Nicaragua, with excellent intelligence and command and control organizations, would weigh heavily on the neighboring countries of the region. This threat would be particularly acute for democratic, unarmed Costa Rica. It would have especially serious implications for vital U.S. interests in the Panama Canal. We would then face the prospect, over time, of the collapse of the other countries of Central America, bringing with it the spectre of Marxist domination of the entire region and thus the danger of a larger war.

The notion that the United States should cope with a Marxist-Leninist Nicaragua, militarily allied to the Soviet Union and Cuba, through long-term containment assumes an analogy between conditions in postwar Europe and the present circumstances of Central America. The experience of the postwar period, however, shows that containment is effective as a long-term strategy only where U.S. military power serves to back up local forces of stable allies fully capable of coping with internal conflict and subversion from without. In such circumstances, the United States can help to assure the deterrence of overt military threats by contributing forces in place, or merely by strategic guarantees.

On the other hand, where internal insecurity is a chronic danger and where local governments are unable to deal with externally supported subversion, a strategy of containment has major disadvantages. It would risk the involvement of U.S. forces as surrogate policemen. Any significant deployment of U.S. forces in Central America would be very costly not just in a domestic political sense but in geostrategic terms as well. The diversion of funds from the economic, social, medical, and educational development of the region into military containment would exacerbate poverty and encourage internal instability in each of the countries that became heavily militarized.

Furthermore, the dangers facing the other Central American countries might actually grow if each side perceived that the other was tempted to use its increased military power. And the creation of garrison states would almost certainly perpetuate the armies of the region as permanent political elites. The hopes of true democracy would not be enhanced.

Therefore, though the Commission believes that the Sandinista regime will pose a continuing threat to stability in the region, we do not advocate a policy of static containment.

Instead, we recommend, first, an effort to arrange a comprehensive regional settlement. This would elaborate and build upon the twenty-one objectives of the Contadora Group. Within the framework of basic principles, it would:

- Recognize linkage between democratization and security in the region.
- Relate the incentives of increased development aid and trade concessions to acceptance of mutual security guarantees.
- Engage the United States and other developed nations in the regional peace system.
- Establish an institutional mechanism in the region to implement that system.

The original peace initiatives of Nicaragua have given little cause for optimism that we could move toward these objectives. The latest of the Sandinistas' formal proposals were presented to the United States government and to the United Nations in October 1983, as four draft treaties purportedly prepared "within the framework of the Contadora process." The treaties would bind the parties to refrain from sending arms from one country to another in the region, and otherwise to end intervention, "overt or covert," in the internal affairs of other nations of the region. Significantly, these Sandinista proposals would prohibit exercises and maneuvers of the type United States and Honduran forces have carried out, while deferring the question of foreign advisers for later discussion.

More recently, after the U.S. actions in Grenada, Managua has hinted at some accommodations in its external and internal policies. The commission is not in a position to judge the sincerity and significance of these various signals. But clearly they would require extensive elaboration and more concrete expression before they could give solid grounds for hope.

The commission believes, however, that whatever the prospects seem to be for productive negotiations, the United States must spare no effort to pursue the diplomatic route. Nicaragua's willingness to enter into a general agreement should be thoroughly tested through negotiations and actions. We must establish whether there is a political alternative to continuing confrontation in the region. Every avenue should be explored to see if the vague signals emanating from Managua in recent weeks can be translated into concrete progress. Our government must demonstrate to the people of the United States and the peoples of the region that the United States earnestly seeks a peaceful settlement.

It is beyond the scope of this commission's responsibilities to prescribe tactics for the conduct of these negotiations. As a broad generality, we do not believe that it would be wise to dismantle existing incentives and pressures on the Managua regime except in conjunction with demonstrable progress on the negotiating front. With specific reference to the highly controversial question of whether the United States should provide support for the Nicaraguan insurgent forces opposed to the Sandinistas now in authority in Managua, the commission recognized that an adequate examination of this issue would require treatment of sensitive information not appropriate to a public report. However, the majority of the members of the commission, in their respective individual judgments, believe that the efforts of the Nicaraguan insurgents represent one of the incentives working in favor of a negotiated settlement and that the future role of the United States in those efforts must therefore be considered in the context of the negotiating process. The commission has not, however, attempted to come to a collective judgment on whether, and how, the United States should provide support for these insurgent forces.

4. *Changing Course: Blueprint for Peace in Central America**

By Policy Alternatives for the Caribbean and Central America (PACCA)

Policy Alternatives for the Caribbean and Central America (PACCA) is an association of scholars, development specialists, and policymakers with long-term experience in the region. PACCA analysts were drawn from some thirty universities and research institutions.

A Response to the Report of the National Bipartisan Commission on Central America

> You come here speaking of Latin America, but this is not important. Nothing important can come from the South. History has never been produced in the South. The axis of history starts in Moscow, goes to Bonn, crosses over to Washington, and then goes to Tokyo. What happens in the South is of no importance.
>
> Henry Kissinger to Gabriel Valdes,
> Foreign Minister of Chile, June 1969

THE COMMISSION'S RECOMMENDATIONS

On January 11, 1984, the National Bipartisan Commission on Central America released its report. The 132-page document, prepared by a twelve-member commission

*Excerpts from Policy Alternatives for the Caribbean and Central America (PACCA), *Changing Course: Blueprint for Peace in Central America and the Caribbean* (Washington, D.C.: Institute for Policy Studies, 1984).

chaired by former Secretary of State Henry Kissinger, charts a policy course to deal with the unrest and instability of the region.

The Kissinger Report acknowledges that the violent upheavals in Central America are rooted in poverty and repression: "Discontents are real, and for much of the population conditions of life are miserable; just as Nicaragua was ripe for revolution, so the conditions that invite revolution are present elsewhere in the region as well." But the report charges—with an argument built on assertion rather than evidence—that the Soviet Union is the manipulator of indigenous revolution in the region. "The Soviet-Cuban threat is real," the report emphasizes, because "the conditions which invite revolution . . . have been exploited by hostile forces."[1]

The prescriptions flow directly from this misplaced diagnosis. The Kissinger Commission recommends a $400 million "emergency stabilization program," substantial increases in military assistance to El Salvador, Honduras, and even Guatemala, as well as implicitly condoning a continuation of the "covert" war against Nicaragua, which the report euphemistically terms an "incentive" for negotiation. To attack the root causes of revolution and thwart future Soviet machinations, the report proposes an $8 billion five-year aid program with unprecedented U.S. involvement in and responsibility for the economies of Central America.

The commission's recommendations are alarming in two regards. First, the military prescriptions would lead to a deepening of U.S. military involvement in a widening war in Central America. Second, the economic prescriptions would serve narrow private interests in the United States at a heavy cost to U.S. taxpayers as a whole. All historical evidence would suggest that the recommended economic aid program, managed by the current elites in power, would have a negative impact on the great majority of the people in Central America and would not serve the long-term interests of U.S. citizens either. Moreover, as the widespread negative response to the Kissinger Report indicates, adherence to its recommended course will increase political division in the United States. . . .

By not clearly condemning the secret war against Nicaragua, the commission lent its voice to the continuation of that war. Aware that more than 10,000 *contras* financed by the United States are attacking Nicaragua, the commissioners evidently believe that military pressure either will cause the Nicaraguan government to change its internal policy in "desirable" directions, or will cause the overthrow of the Sandinistas. Neither is likely.

As one of the commissioners, Mayor Henry Cisneros of San Antonio, indicated in his dissent, the attempt to support domestic opposition by enlisting it in covert operations backfires. The government has little incentive to negotiate and compromise with domestic political forces that are perceived as acting in concert with a hostile foreign power in the region, particularly when that power seems committed to its very overthrow.

The Nicaraguan revolution faces domestic opposition, but there is nothing to suggest that a military force operating from Honduras and Costa Rica can overthrow a government that retains wide popular support and national legitimacy. In more than three years of attacks, the *contras* have been unable to occupy and hold any Nicaraguan territory. The Sandinista government has armed a large part of its population and apparently can rely on it to fight forces that are viewed as agents of the United States committed to restoration of the old order. U.S. tax coffers are supporting a campaign of terrorism, murder, and sabotage. Regrettably, the Kissinger Commission did not identify what vital interests of the United States are served by these activities which the administration subsidizes but cannot acknowledge because they violate our laws, ideals, and values.

Ironically, no coherent argument is presented for the assumption that the revolutions represent a threat to U.S. national security. Lacking in evidence and analysis, the report's case is reduced to the assertion that there is a "Soviet-Cuban thrust to make Central America part of their geostrategic challenge" to the United States.[2] As Senator Daniel Moynihan suggested, this is a "doctrinal position," divorced from reality.[3] The Nicaraguan government has stated that it will not accept a Soviet base (nor has the Soviet Union indicated any interest in bearing the economic burdens necessary to gain one). Having struggled for national independence, it is inconceivable that postrevolutionary governments would elect to become Soviet bases, particularly since their economies are highly dependent upon Western aid and trade. The Soviets do not need a missile base in Central America and are not likely to risk exploring whether the United States will permit one.

The report makes much of a domino theory that suggests that revolutions spread like communicable diseases. Ideas and examples do travel. It is hard to understand why the United States should be opposed to the spread of models that work, such as health and literacy programs, no matter who develops them. U.S. influence in the region depends not on quarantining ideas and programs of other countries, but on demonstrating a genuine interest in development and democracy in the region, rather than viewing the countries as so many pawns in a geopolitical chess game. It is noteworthy that the principal "dominoes" of the region for whose sake the security policy is ostensibly pursued—Mexico and Panama—oppose the military course of U.S. policy in Central America. The commission report eschews analysis, however, relying on reiteration of a Communist peril: "No nation is immune from terrorism and the threat of armed revolution supported by Moscow and Havana."[4] Such extreme language," as Senator Edward Kennedy commented, "raises the stakes of the contest to such a level that anything short of total military victory becomes unthinkable."

An Alternative Policy

> Our government is the potent, the omnipresent teacher. For good or for ill, it teaches the whole people by its example. If the government becomes a lawbreaker, it breeds contempt for the law; it invites every man to become a law unto himself; it invites anarchy.
>
> U.S. Supreme Court Justice Louis Brandeis

A PROGRAM FOR PEACE

Over the past three years, U.S. policy has had the effect of aggravating conflicts in Central America instead of mitigating them. The immediate priority of U.S. policy must be to move back from the brink of the war that now threatens the entire region. The following is a set of concrete steps towards this end.

The Reagan administration bears the primary responsibility for the war against Nicaragua. The *contra* forces operating against Nicaragua from base camps in Honduras and Costa Rica have been armed and trained by the United States. On several occasions, administration spokesmen, including the president himself, have implied that the interests of the United States require the removal of the current government of Nicaragua.

The secret war does not exhaust the administration's policy of hostility towards Nicaragua. It has been reinforced by a large-scale military buildup in Honduras, including the indefinite deployment of U.S. combat forces under the pretext of military exercises. Finally, the United States has used its considerable leverage in the international financial community to enforce a credit embargo designed to strangle the war-torn Nicaraguan economy.[5]

The war against Nicaragua is both illegal and counterproductive. It exacerbates tensions between Nicaragua and its neighbors, fuels the regional arms race, and thereby increases the danger of regional conflict. It erodes civilian democratic institutions in Honduras, and places greater pressure on Costa Rica's financially strapped democracy. Within Nicaragua, it increases domestic polarization by identifying the internal opposition with the *contras,* and justifies limitations on political freedoms. With their nation under external attack, Nicaragua's leaders are forced to seek military aid. Successful U.S. efforts to deny them access to Western European arms markets leaves Nicaragua with no alternative but to turn to Cuba and the Soviet Union for military support.[6] Instead of encouraging the new government to remain outside the East-West conflict, U.S. policy forces it into that conflict. No country can long remain nonaligned if it is under attack by a superpower.

Although all of these activities represent a clear violation of the UN and OAS charters, the Reagan administration has justified its policy of hostility towards Nicaragua on the grounds that the United States seeks only to prevent Nicaragua from exporting revolution and endangering the security of its neighbors. But if the preservation and strengthening of democratic institutions is understood as an essential element of Costa Rican and Honduran security, then the security of these countries is today more endangered by their role as military staging areas for the war against Nicaragua than by anything Nicaragua itself has done.

Moreover, Nicaragua has offered to negotiate verifiable accords covering all the security concerns of its neighbors. It has made these offers bilaterally, multilaterally through the Contadora process, and has even offered similar negotiations to the United States.[7] As of January 1984, the United States has disparaged and dismissed all Nicaraguan initiatives.

If the real concern of the United States is that Nicaragua live in peace with its neighbors, now is the time for the United States to test the Nicaraguans' sincerity at the bargaining table.

A new policy towards Nicaragua must begin with recognition that the 1979 revolution was an overwhelmingly popular insurrection against a hated dictatorship, and was supported by all sectors of Nicaraguan society. The way in which the domestic revolutionary process has unfolded subsequently, and how it proceeds in the future, is a matter for the Nicaraguan people to decide. This is a fundamental issue of self-determination.

The United States has every right to express its criticism of Nicaragua when internal developments there run contrary to our own values. But we do not have the right to dictate how Nicaraguans organize their own political and economic affairs—especially in view of the long support accorded to the corrupt and brutal Somoza dynasty by the United States.

The United States does, however, have a legitimate interest in how Nicaragua conducts relations with its neighbors. These are issues which can and should be addressed at the negotiating table.

A new policy towards Nicaragua should begin with the following practical steps:

1. Cease support for the paramilitary exile groups attacking Nicaragua from Honduras and Costa Rica, and discourage other nations from providing such support.
2. Cut back the military force the United States has assembled around Nicaragua, including an end to military exercises in Honduras and off the Nicaraguan coast, and the withdrawal of U.S. combat forces currently deployed in Honduras.
3. End the effort to strangle Nicaragua's economy by blocking international credits.
4. Fully support and encourage a negotiated reduction of tension and the normalization of relations between Nicaragua and Costa Rica and Honduras. Such negotiations can take place either bilaterally or under the auspices of the Contadora Group, but should follow the basic outlines of the security proposals made thus far under Contadora's auspices, and should include provisions for adequate verification of compliance. They should also include provisions for a humane resettlement plan for those who were recruited to fight the covert war.
5. Accept Nicaragua's offer to negotiate bilateral security concerns.

Notes

1. *Report of the National Bipartisan Commission on Central America,* January 1984, p. 4.
2. Ibid., p. 12.
3. *New York Times,* January 13, 1984.
4. *Report of the National Bipartisan Commission on Central America,* January 1984, p. 14.
5. For a discussion of the Reagan administration's economic war against Nicaragua, see John Cavanagh and Joy Hackel, "Nicaragua: Making the Economy Scream," *Economic and Political Weekly,* Novem-

ber 5–12, 1983. According to the article's authors, the United States is waging an economic war against Nicaragua that parallels the Nixon administration's economic sanctions against Chile which contributed to the coup which overthrew the democratically elected government of leftist President Salvador Allende.

Nicaraguans estimate the U.S. pressure had deprived them of $354 million in lost trade and loans in 1983, while U.S. pressure internationally has resulted in a loss of $112.5 million in multilateral loans since 1980.

In addition, anti-Sandinista paramilitary forces supported by the United States inflicted damage on Nicaragua's productive apparatus and infrastructure amounting to $130 million in 1982, equal to over 6 percent of the country's gross national product. The authors note the damage on an equivalent scale to the U.S. economy would surpass $92 billion, roughly the amount that the U.S. federal government spends yearly on health and education combined.

6. According to the Department of State, between July 1979 and December 1983, Nicaragua received $175 to $200 million in military aid from the Soviet Union, and $50 to $70 million from Cuba, East Germany, Czechoslovakia, Poland, Bulgaria, North Korea, and Vietnam. (Telephone interview, U.S. Department of State, January 19, 1984).
7. On October 20, 1983, Nicaraguan Foreign Minister Miguel D'Escoto submitted to the Reagan administration a package of four binding accords under which the Nicaraguan government would pledge to stop the flow of arms traffic across their territory to the Salvadoran guerrillas if the United States would stop supporting anti-Sandinista rebels based in Honduras and Costa Rica. The proposed accords also would permit on-site inspections of Nicaragua and its neighbors and provide for fines and international legal penalties against any country violating the terms of the agreement. See *Washington Post,* October 21, 1983.

5. *Nicaragua's Untold Stories**

By Robert Leiken

Robert S. Leiken is a senior associate at the Carnegie Endowment and the editor of Central America: Anatomy of Conflict *(Pergamon-Carnegie, 1984).*

The seventy-two-year-old señora lives in a solid stone house constructed by the Sandinista government. Her son, Germán Pomares, was a founder of the Sandinista National Liberation Front (FSLN) who perished leading the final offensive against Somoza in 1979. Set off by a well-kept garden from the shacks of the cotton field workers of El Viejo, Mrs. Pomares's home appears comfortable. But inside, the mother of the nationally revered martyr sleeps on a cot covered with rags, and she hobbles through bare, unfurnished rooms. She lives on a pension equivalent to $10 a month. She has made four trips to the local hospital, but has yet to succeed in getting a doctor's appointment. Three times she has requested an audience with *Comandante* Tomás Borge, now the sole surviving founder of the FSLN. Each time, her son's old comrade has refused to receive her.

For one who has sympathized with the Sandinistas, it is painful to look into the

*From *The New Republic,* October 8, 1984.

house they are building, but it is unwise not to. I spent ten days in Nicaragua in August, accompanied by my brother, a trade unionist from Boston. It was my sixth visit since the revolution, and my longest since 1981. I have testified in Congress against aid to the *contras* and have supported (and continue to support) negotiations to end the civil war in El Salvador. Yet each succeeding trip to Nicaragua drains my initial reservoir of sympathy for the Sandinistas. Last year I wrote in my introduction to a book treated by the press as the "Democratic alternative to the Kissinger Report" that the Sandinistas' "failure to preserve the revolutionary alliance with the middle class and small producers as well as sectarian political and cultural policies [had] polarized the country, led to disinvestment, falling productivity and wages, labor discontent, and an agrarian crisis." This visit convinced me that the situation is far worse than I had thought, and disabused me of some of the remaining myths about the Sandinista revolution.

Everywhere we went we confronted the disparity between these myths and the unpleasant truth. The Sandinistas blame Nicaragua's economic crisis on the *contra* war and U.S. economic sanctions. Yet the standard of living in Nicaragua was deteriorating well before the U.S.-backed *contras* turned to economic sabotage in the spring of 1983. A December 1981 internal staff memorandum of the International Monetary Fund found that real wages had fallen 71 percent since July 1979. They have continued to decline in succeeding years. And even with the U.S. "economic boycott," over 25 percent of Nicaragua's exports still go to the United States, not much less than under Somoza. Nicaragua can no longer sell sugar at subsidized prices to the United States, but what it has lost in this market it has sold to Iran at prices above those of the world market. The war and U.S. sanctions have compounded a mess created by the Sandinistas themselves.

Nicaraguans themselves do not seem to accept Sandinista claims that *Yanqui* aggression is responsible for the general scarcity of consumer goods. Peasants are obligated to sell their goods to the Ministry of Commerce and Industry, and contend that its prices are too low to enable them to make ends meet. A large portion of the peasantry is now producing only for its own consumption, and the resulting shortages have dramatically driven up prices. The marketplace, once the bustling center of Nicaraguan life, is now a daunting experience for buyers and sellers alike. As shoppers make the rounds looking for rice, beans, milk, toilet paper, soap, or light bulbs, the shopkeepers' constant reply is *"No hay"* (There isn't any). For anyone unable to afford the inflated prices or without the foreign exchange to shop at the new foreign currency stores, Eastern European-style queuing is now routine.

One of the most depressing aspects of our trip was to hear from so many that their lives are worse today than they were at the time of Somoza. Before the revolution Nicaraguans ate well by Central American standards. Thanks to the country's fertile soil and its small population, even poor Nicaraguans were accustomed to beef and chicken. Now consumer goods available to the masses in other Central American countries are no longer obtainable. Barefoot children are hardly uncommon in the region, but I had never seen so many completely naked. As we encountered them, their distended stomachs displaying the telltale signs of malnutrition, Nicaraguans would bitterly recall the government slogan, *Los niños son los mimados de la revolucion* (Children are the spoiled ones of the revolution).

The shortage of basic necessities is also breeding pervasive corruption. When we asked a rural storekeeper why he was able to sell Coca-Cola while many restaurants in Managua were not, he said that he had obtained the soft drink with a bribe. We later met Ramiro, a Coca-Cola deliveryman in León and a former member of the FSLN, hitchhiking home from the city of Chinandega. He was returning from his five-hour weekly excursion after work to procure the three bottles of milk his children need. The milk cost him 150 córdobas, 30 percent of his weekly wages. (The official exchange rate is 28 córdobas to the dollar; the real, or black market, exchange rate is 250 to 1.) To get the money, he told us, he accepts bribes from some of his customers for extra cases of Coke. "This system is corrupting me against my will," he said.

Ramiro's desperate measures hardly merit censure. But others, especially high-ranking Sandinistas, are turning big profits from the scarcity. Members of a leather workers cooperative in Masaya told us that they are officially allotted 10,000 meters of leather a month; they receive between 5,000 and 7,000 meters. The cooperatives' Sandinista directors sell the remainder in Managua's Eastern Market and pocket the money. It is now a general practice for coordinators of the neighborhood Sandinista Defense Committees (CDS) to sell part of the provisions allotted to them by the government on the private market. The people are then informed that provisions have run out.

In the village of El Transito, two hours northwest of Managua, most of the people belonged to the CDS at the outset of the revolution. Now there is but one member, the coordinator, formerly the village's leading *Somocista.* (The transformation of *Somocistas* into Sandinistas and of Sandinistas into oppositionists is very common. In every town we visited we were told that former Somoza officials are now running CDSs.) The coordinator enriches himself by selling CDS foodstuffs and supplies in the Eastern Market. As we passed his house, we were able to peer through the window and see him standing there in his dark glasses, isolated and reviled.

The life-styles of the new rich contrast vividly with that of the rest of the country, and with official rhetoric. A Sandinista *nomenklatura* has emerged. Party members shop at hard-currency stores, dine at luxury restaurants restricted to party officials, and vacation in the mansions of the Somoza dynasty, labeled "protocol houses." Vans pull up daily at government and party offices, to deliver ham, lobster, and other delicacies unavailable elsewhere. In a private state dining room, I ate a sumptuous meal with a *comandante* at a long table, attended by five servants. The image of the protruding stomachs of the "spoiled ones of the revolution" intruded while we consumed our lemon meringue pie.

Intellectuals and former officials claim that decadence is endemic in upper government and party echelons. A former Sandinista diplomat recounted tales of high jinks and extravagance by Sandinista officials on foreign junkets, and women state employees complained of the same sexual harassment and blackmail that is common elsewhere in Central America. The swinging Sandinista leadership cynically presents an image of revolutionary asceticism to the outside world while being addicted to the very vices that it routinely denounces in "degenerate bourgeois society."

The widespread corruption from the lowest to the highest levels of government makes it hard for Nicaraguans to accept the notion that their problems originate from abroad, or that they should endure further sacrifices "to confront the imperialist enemy." A jobless worker in the Indian town of Monimbo complained, "The CDS insists that we unscrew the street lights to conserve energy in the fight against imperialism. People are falling in holes while the Sandinistas get rich on our misery. What are their sacrifices?"

Those Sandinistas who have refused to be corrupted recognize that their dreams have turned into a nightmare. One government official, a good friend, told me, "We have given birth to a freak. But we must keep him alive." Yet what is to be done when the freak becomes a menace to its people and neighbors? There is a general impression among those in the United States properly aghast at the CIA mining of ports and U.S. support for the professional torturers among the *contras* that the Sandinistas are the victims, not the victimizers. Inside Nicaragua, however, the image is reversed.

The word Nicaraguans employ the most frequently to describe the Sandinista government is *engaño* (hoax or trick). In the city of Chinandega, we talked with transport workers from an opposition union who on their own time and with their union dues had painted road signs to make the city safer for driving. The Sandinista government took credit for the improvement. The national literacy campaign is one of the most vaunted achievements of the revolution, praised even by many of the government's critics. Yet two "graduates" of the literacy program in a peasant village told us they could not read their diplomas. We couldn't find one student from the campaign there or in the neighboring village who had learned to read. The campaign did somewhat better in the larger cities such as León, where, we were told, some had learned to read in follow-up courses. But most had forgotten the little they had learned, and at best could now only sign their name for election registration.

The most outrageous *engaño* occurred during Pope John II's visit to Managua in March 1983. According to Sandinista accounts, the Pope's mass had been "spontaneously" interrupted by the crowd, offended by the Pope's failure to heed the request of mourning mothers who wanted him to pray for their sons killed in the battle against the *contras*. Two former government officials, who are still Sandinista supporters, told us a different story. They had been appalled at the interruptions made by cadre from the Sandinista women's organization, furnished with microphones and loudspeakers. After the Pope left, the crowd departed in disgust and the Sandinista leadership was left awkwardly standing on the platform. The two officials, depressed by the spectacle, retired to a bar located next to the offices of the FSLN radio station. They overheard a group of Sandinista radio employees at an adjoining table bragging about how they had played prerecorded tapes of crowds chanting Sandinista slogans into the sound system.

The Sandinista *engaño* has been most successful among the resident foreign press. Journalists familiar with the atrocities of the right-wing tyrannies of Central America wish to believe, quite understandably, that the Sandinistas present an alternative. In today's Nicaragua it is easy to confuse desire with reality. The resident press also frequently merges with the larger population of "internationalists," a term which embraces all those foreigners expressing solidarity with the Sandinistas, from Bulgarian and Cuban *apparatchiks* to idealistic North Americans and West Europeans. It is the general feeling among Nicaraguans that the foreign press in Managua strongly sympathizes with the government, and that it is dangerous to speak openly with them. Disaffected Sandinista intellectuals, friends of friends, who poured their hearts out to me in Managua were afraid to meet with reporters from the U.S. press. We spoke with a resident of Monimbo, where a spontaneous insurrection had ignited the revolution against Somoza in February 1978. We had spent an evening together a year before with a mutual friend, yet initially he was still distrustful. He told us that the revolution had produced "many advances for the people"; two hours later, he was saying, "Monimbo appears to be sleeping, the way it was during the time of Somoza, but the people are united. One day soon they will stand up again."

One of the most common means of sustaining the myth of popular support is the Sandinistas' use of the rationing system as a lever. In numerous villages and cities, we learned that ration cards are confiscated for nonattendance at Sandinista meetings. In Masaya we were told that before one of the "Face-the-People" meetings (in which *comandantes* meet with local residents) the ration cards of the members of cooperatives were collected; their return was made conditional on attendance. At one such meeting in Chinandega, Ortega branded talk of inflation "a counterrevolutionary plot." A pound of beans could still be purchased for five córdobas, he claimed. A man in the audience stood up and shouted, "*Comandante,* here's ten córdobas. Please get me a pound of beans." According to his neighbors, he was imprisoned later that day.

Although Nicaraguans still for the most part bow to government pressure, they do sullenly and without conviction. We witnessed two Sandinista demonstrations, one in Masaya and the other in Chinandega, two historically pro-Sandinista cities. The Chinandega rally, held at ten on a Wednesday morning, celebrated the fifth anniversary of the literacy campaign. It was attended entirely by students obligated to go by school authorities. As they marched through the streets chanting slogans distributed to them on small pieces of paper by their Sandinista instructors, pedestrians did not so much as turn their heads. None of the presumably grateful, presumably literate, people came to greet the *comandante* sent from Managua.

In Masaya the demonstration did not even benefit from student participation. As we approached the gathering in the fading afternoon, a large group of students stood on the steps of the Catholic school. They had refused to join the demonstration because the Sandinistas had removed several of their Catholic teachers. The small group of demonstrators had glazed looks in their eyes as the last speeches wound down. I asked a *campesino* in attendance whether any of the *comandantes* had come. He answered, "I don't know. I slept through it."

The Nicaraguan populace has been saturated with Sandinista bombast which issues from radio, television, newspapers, local and national political meetings, and block committees, and which is propagated in the schools, the factories, and the cooperatives. The people resist in different ways: with the indifference and boredom we saw in Chinandega and Masaya; with a resurgence in religious feelings which has filled churches and Catholic schools; with suspiciousness and bitter humor.

Jokes and wisecracks against the Sandinistas are proliferating. The two pro-Sandinista newspapers, *Barricada* and *Nuevo Diaro,* are referred to as *Burricada* (as in bore) and *Nuevo Diablo.* The FSLN is "the Somocista National Liberation Front." "Why do people prefer *Tona* [one of the two Nicaraguan beers]? Because the other, *La Victoria,* is bitter." Suspicions of the government are so deep that families of the war dead no longer believe that the government coffins shipped back from the front contain the bodies of their sons. (The coffins are sealed as a matter of policy.) People believe, improbably, that the coffins hold rocks or banana tree trunks. In Monimbo we were told that when a family and friends tried to open a coffin with a hammer and chisel, they were carried off by the police.

Nor is popular discontent restricted to these forms of passive resistance. Sympathy with the *contras* is becoming more open and more pervasive. I was stunned to hear peasants refer to the *contras* as *"Los Muchachos,"* the boys—the admiring term used to describe the Sandinistas when they were battling the National Guard. It was apparent that many Nicaraguans are listening to the "15th of September," the *contra* radio station. It must be noted, however, that the *contras* do not operate in the areas we visited, and sympathy toward them may well be proportionate to absence of direct contact.

Draft resistance has become a mass movement in Nicaragua. The government passed legislation last September under which Nicaraguan men between the ages of sixteen and forty can be drafted for two years. When we were in Nicaragua, four hundred women gathered outside the draft board in La Paz Centro, a trading town thirty-five miles northwest of Managua, to protest forced recruitment of their sons. The demonstration was the latest in a string of antidraft demonstrations in cities and towns throughout Nicaragua. *New York Times* correspondent Stephen Knizer, one of the few resident reporters to sniff out the *engaño* of Sandinista policies, reported on June 26 that "draft evasion is widespread," and found that high school attendance in six major provincial capitals had declined by as much as 40 percent. A student in León said that his high school class of forty-five had fallen to fourteen during the past year. Honduran researchers say Nicaraguan draft evaders pay 25,000 córdobas to be transported across the border, part of the money going to Nicaraguan army officials in bribes. The demand is so great that border smugglers are now requiring groups no smaller than five. Draft resistance strikes a powerful blow at the myth of widespread popular support for the government. Young people have historically been the mainstay of Sandinista support.

Perhaps the most illuminating political event in the five years of Sandinista rule was a rally held for opposition presidential candidate Arturo Cruz in Chinandega on August 5. On that Sunday morning, Sandinista chicanery, censored domestic and lackadaisical international press coverage, and the growing vigor of the opposition converged.

Chinandega, a city of approximately 60,000, was historically the heart of Sandinista organizing efforts and support. These efforts radiated out to the surrounding cotton and sugar fields, to the country's two largest sugar refineries nearby, to the stevedores at Corinto, Nicaragua's largest port, and down to León, another center of anti-Somoza resistance. One would have expected that here the opposition would be weakest, the government strongest.

The Chinandega demonstration was the last series of six held in support of Cruz. Each rally had been larger than the last. The organizers were denied access to Sandinista-controlled TV stations. They were able to place an ad on the one local non-Sandinista radio station, but they relied chiefly on two vehicles with loudspeakers, and on word-of-mouth. Two days before the rally three "angels," as members of the state security are commonly known, called on the organizers of the demonstration and accused them of being CIA agents. The *turbas divinas,* "divine mobs" of Sandinista supporters, circled their houses at night beating sticks against cans and chanting until the small hours of the morning. (Somoza's version of the *turbas*—the *Nicolasa*—used to employ the very same method against the opposition.) Meanwhile, Sandinista newspapers and television branded the opposition as consisting of *contras* and agents of American imperialism, and announced that further "aggressions" by them would not be permitted. Local authorities implied that the demonstration would be declared illegal. The day before the rally, Daniel Ortega, the head of the Sandinista government and the Sandinista presidential candidate, spoke to two hundred youths in El Viejo, a village three miles away. El Viejo's residents later claimed that the youths had been incited against the demonstration's leaders.

Fearing an attack by the *turbas,* organizers did not put up the banners or placards until early on the morning of the demonstration. But as they were working, fifty *turbas* burst into the soccer field, tearing down the banners and dispersing the organizers. They returned later during the day to try to repair the damage.

We spoke with two organizers—middle-class, professional women who had belonged to the FSLN before the revolution. (According to one, "the FSLN says that the opposition is *Somocista.* But most of the old *Somocistas* are working with the government. The opposition has remained the same. It is the FSLN that has changed.") They told us that after the *turbas'* night-time serenading, they went to complain to the offices of the party representative, the chief of police, and the chief of state security, and to the Sandinistas. They were assured that the *turbas* would be controlled and that the demonstration would not be obstructed. After the early-morning attack, the two women went to the house of the local party leader. The door was open, and they entered. In the next room they heard the *turbas* informing him of the success of their mission.

There is no question that many who wished to go to the Cruz rally stayed at home. On the day of the rally, local authorities impeded traffic from outlying areas into Chinandega. As Cruz marched through the city, many people opened their doors, gave him the "V" for victory sign, and then ducked back into their homes to avoid the ever-present eyes of the CDS. One woman said she did not go to the demonstration because she lived too close to the Sandinista youth office. She told of others who received threatening phone calls. Two weeks after the demonstration, a gas station attendant in Managua told us he had gone to the rally and that three friends who had accompanied him were in jail.

As might be expected, estimates of the turnout vary. Opposition figures soared as high as 20,000; local newsmen said 7,000. Given Sandinista efforts to reduce attendance, even 7,000 seems an impressive number, especially since three months before, the FSLN only managed to get 2,500 to Chinandega for the country's principal May Day rally. NBC taped the entire Cruz demonstration. Should this tape ever be shown publicly, experts will be able to make an accurate judgment about the number of demonstrators. When I viewed the tape it was evident that these thousands of demonstrators were hardly "bourgeoisie," as the Sandinistas claimed. They were overwhelmingly workers, peasants, and young people. I learned later that workers had hired their own trucks to come from the San Antonio Refinery and from the port of Corinto. They chanted slogans like *"El frente y Somoza son la misma cosa."* ("The Sandinistas and Somoza are the same thing.")

When Cruz began to speak, dozens of *turbas* armed with sticks, stones, and machetes surrounded the field. They came in on what appeared to be army trucks chanting, "Power to the people." They proceeded to break the windows and puncture the tires of demonstrators' cars. The police seemed to make no serious effort to restrain them. When the *turbas* attacked the demonstrators themselves, opposition youths dispersed, only to return wielding their own sticks and stones. Outnumbered, the *turbas* were routed.

The almost complete absence of foreign and domestic press coverage enabled Sandinista officials to characterize the demonstration their own way. We encountered a Sandinista official drunk at mid-day on the streets at El Viejo. He told us that the demonstration had taken place at the private home of a bourgeois and was attended only by a handful of plutocrats. In Managua, the Sandinistas told us that there had been several hundred demonstrators. The following day the Nicaraguan press carried no mention of the events except for one photograph in the official newspaper *Barricada* which purported to show the *turbas* attacked by "fascist" demonstrators. *La Prensa* had devoted several articles and photographs to the demonstration and the clashes, but these were all censored, and the paper did not appear. This was the very day that Daniel Ortega had announced the lifting of press censorship.

The demonstrations for Cruz's candidacy tested the popular mood and the prospects for "the first free elections in Nicaragua," as the Sandinistas' slogan puts it. Among the conditions that Cruz and his supporters have laid down as indispensable for participation are guarantees of freedom of movement, assembly, and equal access to the press and television; sufficient time to campaign; international observers; and, most importantly, guarantees that if he won the election he would be allowed to take office. What happened at Chinandega strongly suggests that neither a genuine election nor a genuine campaign can take place.

Chinandega also exposed the Sandinistas' electoral stratagem. Their decision to hold elections in November was based on a rudimentary political calculation. They judged that the external legitimacy provided by elections would more than compensate for their internal cost. They knew that power does not often change hands in Central America through elections. Somoza's elections had proven that, and the Sandinistas are in a far better position to control elections than Somoza ever was.

Yet their calculations were wrong on two counts. First, they failed to account for the Nicaraguan people. High-level Sandinista officials to whom I have spoken seem to live, along with their international supporters, in a dream world. They deem that the "anti-imperialist sentiments" of the Nicaraguan people allow them to bear any sacrifice even when their "anti-imperialist" leaders bear none. They receive favorable reports from lower-level cadre whose jobs depend on the perception of success. The Sandinistas knew that after five years of enforced political paralysis, the opposition was poorly organized, divided, and amateurish. The spontaneous popular reception for Cruz took them by surprise. Second, they failed to recognize the degree to which they have alienated progressive opinion in Latin America and Western Europe. Cruz's recent highly successful trip to Costa Rica, Venezuela, and Colombia, and his support from European Social Democrats like Spanish Socialist Prime Minister Felipe Gonzalez, has confounded the FSLN's electoral plans.

Thus the Sandinistas find themselves in a quandary. Will they back down and permit Cruz to run under reasonable conditions, or will they go ahead with a discredited election? Thus far at least, the Sandinistas seem unwilling to pay the price of submitting their rule to a popular test. One Sandinista official, whom I have always considered a moderate, told me privately that they would prefer a U.S. intervention because it would "vastly accelerate the Latin American revolution against U.S. imperialism." He told me that the Nicaraguan army would immediately invade Honduras and Costa Rica and be greeted as "liberators" by the people.

One can only hope that cooler Sandinista heads will prevail. Authentic elections may be the last chance to avert full-scale civil war. If democratic channels cannot be opened, the civilian opposition will be forced to link up with the armed opposition—which is exactly what happened in the 1970s in El Salvador after fraudulent elections. The United States, which has a monstrous record in Nicaragua, can do something to help. What is needed now most urgently is a bipartisan effort in support of authentic elections in Nicaragua.

As we pulled out of Managua in the fading light of a Sunday afternoon, we found ourselves directly behind an army convoy made up of about twenty vehicles. But unlike the army convoys I have seen in El Salvador, Honduras, and elsewhere, it would not permit traffic to pass. A large vehicle with a blinking light occupied the left lane, forcing vehicles coming toward us off the road. A soldier with a machine gun was poised on the rear truck. It took us four hours to cover the fifty miles to León. It was a grueling microcosm of Nicaragua today: the Sandinistas in the "vanguard" preventing the normal flow of traffic, whether out of real fear, paranoia, or bullying. Behind them the rest of the population followed, inconvenienced, irritated, and enduring another pointless "sacrifice" for the Sandinistas' militarism. Our inconvenience was only four hours: the Nicaraguan people experience this twenty-four hours a day. Their patience has worn thin.

*6. Nicaragua and the Disenchanted Liberals**

By Peter Marchetti

Peter Marchetti is an American Jesuit priest who received his doctorate from Yale and has taught at Marquette University. He has studied agrarian reform in Chile and in Nicaragua, where he has lived for the last several years.

The purpose of this article is to examine a particular American ideology which might be dubbed "disenchanted liberalism," and how this ideology influences U.S. foreign policy by filtering information from Third World countries undergoing national liberation processes. Robert S. Leiken's *New Republic* essay, "Nicaragua's Untold Stories," serves as a case study.

Leiken's article was received with easy acceptance in liberal circles with no particular investment in the Nicaraguan revolution and with resigned anger by those who support the Nicaraguan revolution but are fearful that Leiken might be right. The reaction to the article demands some attention to set the record straight, and to see how disenchanted liberal ideology projects distorted information into U.S. political culture. What concerns me more than Leiken and his article is the fact that most American politicians are predisposed by this same ideology to believe what Leiken wrote about Nicaragua. Disenchantment with welfare programs, Carter's human rights program, New Deal politics, and the Democrats are all part of the contemporary milieu. The ideological mood is, in a word, very congenial for articles like Leiken's.

Disenchanted liberalism's response to Third World revolutions has been to swing from an acritical and idealistic acceptance of the revolution in its early days to an acritical and bitter rejection of the revolution once it is forced to stake out its national sovereignty in this world so fractured with East-West tensions. From 1950 to 1960 Fidel Castro was a liberal idol, before becoming liberalism's leading satanic figure. The Sandinistas could do no wrong in their struggle against Somoza and for about nine months after they took power. Reactions to African revolutions are similar and one could feel safe in betting that disenchanted liberalism will treat the crisis brewing in the Philippines in the same way it has understood Nicaragua. Aquino has already been projected as a virtually flawless martyr of democracy; whatever new govern-

*From an unpublished manuscript.

ment replaces Marcos's dictatorship will never match up to Aquino's now other-worldly perfection.

Disenchanted liberalism loves the revolution but detests the revolutionaries who make them. Revolutionaries ruin the economy, create "Eastern European-style queuing" for scarce consumer goods, repress religion, run sham elections, and worst of all become even more corrupt and tyrannical than the dictators they replace. The motor force in this ideology is the sense of betrayal and the feeling that one's highest ideals have been tarnished by those who fail to understand what a real revolution and real democracy must be. The disenchanted liberal is in search of a salvation through politics that he finds nowhere. The disenchantment is thus with our own political order as well as with that of new nation states. The disenchanted liberal has lost his or her faith in American political culture. The hunger for political salvation leads to serial affairs with Third World revolutions. When it is salvation that is at stake, politics becomes a very personal thing.

Leiken begins his article with an intense image of betrayal. Sandinista leader Tomás Borge refuses to even talk to the mother of his old comrade Germán Pomares. The old woman "has yet to succeed in getting a doctor's appointment . . . sleeps on a cot covered with rags, hobbles through bare, unfurnished rooms . . . [and] lives on a pension equivalent to $10 a month."

Friends of mine who reside in El Viejo, the small town where Señora Pomares lives, were outraged with Leiken's account. Instead of in the gloom of Leiken's bare unfurnished rooms, Señora Pomares lives with her son, her daughter-in-law, and eleven grandchildren in a home that is well appointed by Nicaraguan standards. Instead of betraying his old comrade, Tomás Borge has adopted Germán Pomares's son and Señora Pomares frequently visits her grandchild at Borge's home. When Señora Pomares fractured her collarbone, she received immediate attention in León and daily rehabilitation treatments in Chinandega. It was another member of the family who has had a problem in getting an appointment with a particular neurologist-psychiatrist. Señora Pomares's pension is the same as all the mothers of dead Sandinistas—1,500 córdobas a month. Leiken's use of black market rates to calculate the U.S. dollar value makes the pension sound like a starvation wage. Actually, it is the minimum salary that all rural workers receive.

How could Leiken distort all this so thoroughly? The logic at work here is the sense of betrayal in the eye of the beholder. The cot covered with rags was enough to touch off Leiken's own sense of having been betrayed by the Sandinistas and enough to confirm for him that the testimony concerning Borge and Señora Pomares was true. The real ideological key here is that the disenchanted liberal identified himself with Germán Pomares who heroically gave his life for a revolution that now supposedly despises his mother.

There are countless senators and congresspeople in Washington who feel that they heroically risked votes at home by going out on a limb and defending the Sandinista revolution. The real hero for the disenchanted liberal is the ex-Sandinista, the person who has had to separate himself from the revolution because it went sour—people such as Arturo Cruz, Edén Pastora, Miguel Bolaños Hunter, and Edgar Macías.

The personal drama of betrayal and ethical option seems to eliminate the need for facts or for examining any given Third World revolution in its own particular context. This is what happened with U.S. media coverage of Nicaragua's elections. A high percentage of U.S. articles concentrated on Arturo Cruz, the hero who, after being a member of the ruling junta, refused to run in the elections. The American public received almost no information about the opposition parties that decided to take part in the electoral process nor about the figure the Sandinistas feared most, Virgilio Godoy, whose Independent Liberal Party (PLI) claimed credit for the assassination of the first Somoza. *New York Times* correspondent Stephen Kinzer, who according to Leiken is "one of the few resident reporters to sniff out the *engaño* subterfuge of Sandinista policies," only began to report on Godoy and his party once the ex-minister of labor had pulled out of the elections. As a matter of fact, Kinzer did not report anything about the conflict in the PLI over the decision to run or not, nor that the vice-presidential candidate and other important leaders left the party and ran in the elections. The only story was that Godoy and the PLI had now joined Cruz and were not going to be part of the "sham elections."

In any Third World country where social change takes place, the privileged tend to lose out because there isn't enough wealth around to benefit the poor without playing some type of zero sum economics or politics. The disenchanted liberal identifies himself immediately with those who lose out. Economic indicators such as the shortage of luxury consumer goods and the dissatisfaction of some entrepreneurs were enough to convince Leiken that the Sandinistas' "failure to preserve the revolutionary alliance with the middle class and small producers as well as sectarian political and cultural policies [has] polarized the country, led to disinvestment, falling productivity and wages, labor discontent, and an agrarian crisis."

As a United Nations advisor to the Nicaraguan government who has worked in Nicaragua for five years, one of my most frequent criticisms of Sandinista economic policy has been *overinvestment,* not disinvestment as Leiken reports. Undoubtedly some of Leiken's contacts have stopped investing, but dinner table case studies hardly substitute for a look at microeconomic data. In 1981, the economy showed an extremely high investment rate of 23 percent of its GNP. The truth is that a Sandinista Nicaragua is investing more than Somoza Nicaragua ever did. The investment rate under Somoza from 1972 to 1978 was 17.8 percent; under the Sandinista administration (1980–1984) the rate was 19.3 percent, according to Ministry of Planning figures.

The Nicaraguan government has changed its investment priorities from the city to the countryside. While capital investment in agriculture dropped by 57 percent in Guatemala and by 73 percent in Costa Rica between 1978 and 1982, capital investment in Nicaraguan agriculture grew by 149 percent between 1978 and 1980, by 34 percent in 1981, and by 126 percent in 1982. Figures are from the UN's Economic Commission for Latin America (ECLA) and the International Development Bank (IDB).

In carrying out this type of investment the Sandinistas are swimming against the stream. The rest of the Latin American countries are divesting—a normal response to the international recession which, according to ECLA, has caused a 3.3 percent drop in the continent's GNP in 1983 (Nicaragua's growth in 1983 was 5.1 percent). While I agree with the Sandinistas' investment policy, they may be pushing too much investment in a period when the costs are high. Leiken tells us productivity is falling. Quite to the contrary, a recent study I completed indicated that although productivity for the industrial sector as a whole dropped by 8 percent between 1980 and 1981, the Sandinista rationalization and austerity plan in 1982 resulted in a 13 percent increase in productivity. This is hardly the nose-dive in productivity that Leiken reports.

Despite Leiken's claim that Nicaragua is suffering an agrarian crisis, the real untold story about Nicaragua is the successful agrarian reform. What Leiken takes for a crisis is nothing more than the birth pangs of a new land tenure system. Over 51,000 of the 110,000 farmers who lacked secure tenure and access to sufficient land have now received titles from the government. In contrast to all other significant land reforms in Latin America, in which production fell by 20–50 percent, the Sandinista-designed reform has been accomplished with a constantly expanding agricultural growth. Crop production grew by 38.6 percent between 1981 and 1983 for a 12.5 percent average growth. Such performance would not have been possible without an extremely prudent land reform law which guarantees private ownership to any and all direct producers. That is, the land reform has managed to maintain the confidence of the small and medium producers as well as that of many big growers. That alliance is what gave Nicaragua an overall GNP growth in 1983 of 5.1 percent. In order to maintain that alliance with the private sector real wages have declined, but not as much as Leiken cites (71 percent from June 1979 to December 1981, according to "an internal staff memo of the International Monetary Fund"). Published data from Nicaragua's Ministry of Planning showed a much less severe decline of 22.3 percent in real wages between 1979 and 1981. As the chart shows, the drop was less severe between 1981 and 1982.

Evolution of Real Wages
(in 1977 córdobas)

	1977	1979	1980	1981	1982
Average monthly wages	1,211	1,133	960	887	849
Index base year 1977	100	94	79	73	71

One of the extraordinary things about Leiken's article is the power of his impressions and the lack of hard information. Mr. Leiken refused or canceled appointments with several people who could have given him more facts as well as a distinct perspective on the negative economic information he was hearing from his sources. He could have met with the minister of labor, but turned down that opportunity. He was uninterested in meeting with the regional governors who control day-to-day decisions in Nicaragua or with political candidates, other than those of the *Coordinadora,* who refused to enter the election. He was equally uninterested in seeing the health program in Estelí or any rural cooperatives. When the Ministry of Foreign Affairs did not get him an appointment with any of the commanders, he canceled his interviews with alternative spokespeople. The ministry responded in kind by canceling his interview with Sergio Ramírez, the vice-presidential candidate of the FSLN.

It would seem to me that if one's longest stay in Nicaragua since 1981 was only ten days, one should at least balance sources. So biased were Leiken's sources that he arrives at the conclusion that the Nicaraguan literacy campaign was a total failure. Of the 400,000 people who became literate during Nicaragua's internationally acclaimed literacy campaign, Leiken could find no one who could still read. This is strange because even though Leiken was not interested in visiting any of the country's 13,000 Popular Education Centers he should have been able to find at least one of the 161,371 people still receiving follow-up in an adult education program run by 12,211 volunteer teachers. Similarly, his judgment that the *contra* war has had little impact on the economy is suspect. Defense, which took 7 percent of the national budget in 1980, now drains 45 percent of the budget. Leiken ends up exonerating the U.S.-backed military strategy designed to disrupt the Nicaraguan economy because it is a "mess created by the Sandinistas themselves."

Leiken's treatment of the "Eastern-style queuing" is hardly more felicitous than his treatment of the overall economy. He writes: "As shoppers make the rounds looking for rice, beans, milk, toilet paper, soap, or light bulbs, the shopkeepers constant reply is *'No hay'* (There isn't any)." What Leiken doesn't tell his readers is that the prices for basic goods are even lower to the consumer than they are to the producer. The peasant producers whose "prices are too low to enable them to make ends meet" can buy their beans as a consumer for half the price they sold them as a producer. These high subsidies have caused incentive problems for certain crops, but not of the type reported by Leiken. His prototypical stereotype just doesn't fit Nicaragua. Because of the high subsidies to consumers, the rising agricultural output, and the steep increases in food imports, Nicaraguans actually ate more per capita during the first four years of the revolution (1980–1983) than they did during the last normal years of the Somoza regime (1976–1978).

The democratization of demand through food and other subsidies means that the poor not only eat more staples but are now able to buy toilet paper and use more soap. The fact that imported nonessential goods like light bulbs are hard to find doesn't mean that the market, which in Leiken's words was "once the bustling center of Nicaraguan life," is now Soviet dull as it comes off in Leiken's stereotype. The Nicaraguan government has built four new markets (bazaars where small merchants gather to sell their wares) in the hope that the huge *Mercado Oriental* would decline in size and it would be easier for people to get to the markets. What happened was that the *Mercado Oriental* continued to grow even though the new markets were thriving. The government thus discovered that one of its biggest problems is the ever-

Per Capita Food Consumption
Nicaragua 1979–1983

Products	Units	1976–78	1980–83	% Increase
Corn	lbs.	181	189	4.4
Beans	"	39.7	44.4	11.8
Rice	"	40.3	66.8	65.8
Flour	"	31.4	39.7	26.4
Cooking oil	"	17.1	24.2	41.5
Sugar	"	98.1	97.6	− 0.5
Eggs	dozens	5.0	6.5	30.0
Chicken	lbs.	4.6	8.8	91.3
Pork	"	5.2	6.4	23.1
Pasteurized milk	gallons	4.7	5.6	19.1
All milk*	"	10.8	9.1	−18.7
Beef	lbs.	25.7	19.7	−30.4

*Includes consumption of pasteurized and nonpasteurized milk. The per capita levels drop in both beef and milk because 25 percent of Nicaragua's herd was lost during the war against Somoza.

expanding number of small merchants and peddlers in Managua. Leiken's key example is even less well chosen than his overall portrayal of market conditions. He depicts a Coca-Cola deliveryman involved in corruption in order to be able to afford "three bottles of milk his children need. The milk cost him 150 córdobas, 30 percent of his weekly wages." First, there are no milk bottles in Nicaragua. Second, milk is highly subsidized. Even at black market prices, three liters of milk in plastic bags cost 9 córdobas, ten times cheaper than milk in San José, Costa Rica.

Leiken skips from corruption to the next important theme of disenchanted liberalism: the golden rule of how the attempt to create a more just society leads to the hypocritical repetition of old evils. In his extreme formulation,

> high ranking Sandinistas are turning big profits from the scarcity. . . . The transformation of *Somocistas* into Sandinistas and of Sandinistas into oppositionists is very common. In every town we visited we were told that former Somoza officials are now running CDSs [Sandinista Block Committees].

The evidence Leiken adduces for these affirmations is that a leather goods cooperative has sold some of the leather it was alloted in the market place instead of producing leather goods with all of it and that CDS block leaders have been known to sell goods on the black market. All this proves to me is that Nicaragua's thousands of new cooperatives are free to profit as they want in the market and that a significant number of block leaders are not saints but real, live human beings living in what

Leiken calls "degenerate bourgeois society." Here is disenchanted liberalism at its best. If the revolution is not perfect, if market phenomena and humanity clash with somewhat successful attempts to lessen the crush of poverty on the poor, then that revolution is more degenerate than the old order it seeks to replace because it is hypocritically "addicted to the very vices that it routinely denounces in 'degenerate bourgeois society.' " The disenchantment with attempted innocence is usually so strong that disenchanted liberalism often drops into a key that would seem to be plain, old-fashioned anticommunism.

Leiken charges the Sandinistas with widespread corruption, increasing privilege, and even sexual harassment. In a passage which is typical of how disenchanted liberal ideology twists the facts ever so deftly or exaggerates them to create an effect, Leiken writes:

> Party members shop at hard-currency stores, dine at luxury restaurants restricted to party officials, and vacation in the mansions of the Somoza dynasty, labeled "protocol houses." Vans pull up daily at government and party offices to deliver ham, lobster, and other delicacies unavailable elsewhere. In a private state dining room, I ate a sumptuous meal with a *comandante* at a long table, attended by five servants.

There is only one hard-currency store, not many as Leiken indicates. That store was set up to serve international functionaries and journalists. These places were not exclusively for Sandinistas as Leiken's text would lead us to believe. The private state dining room was a dining room for public officials and visitors of the national legislature, the Council of State. In this type of passage, Leiken seems to demand that the revolutionary state behave like St. Francis of Assisi. If it doesn't reach that level of austerity, it is then judged as profoundly corrupt. For the disenchanted liberal there is nothing in the middle, there is little balance: either idealistic support for the revolution or righteous denunciation of yet another betrayed revolution. This either/or approach is hardly helpful to either the American public or to our elected officials. As Congress edges its way to yet another fight over whether or not to finance the *contras* with our tax dollars, disenchanted liberal ideology will play a major role in the outcome, whether or not any of the representatives read Leiken's article. In the words of F. D. Maurice, "Men are generally right in what they affirm and wrong in what they deny." The amount of negativism and denial at work in the disenchanted liberal does not help any of us sort out the events in Nicaragua.

*7. How the United States Should Handle Nicaragua**

by Edgar Chamorro

Edgar Chamorro served as a director of the anti-Sandinista contra *organization, the Nicaraguan Democratic Force, from 1982 to 1984. He now lives in Key Biscayne, Florida.*

Once again, United States policy toward Nicaragua has failed at a critical juncture. Congress recently voted $27 million in "humanitarian aid" to the *contras* fighting the Sandinista regime. This will not end the conflict; it will only make matters worse.

Rather than engage itself further, economically or militarily, the best course for the United States is to distance itself from the conflict, encourage political dialogue, and support Latin American countries in their effort to prevent a regional war.

My experience as a former rebel leader convinced me that the Nicaraguan Democratic Force cannot contribute to the democratization of Nicaragua. The rebels are in the hands of former national guardsmen who control the *contra* army, stifle internal dissent, and intimidate or murder those who dare oppose them. The rebels have been subject to manipulation by the Central Intelligence Agency, which has reduced it to a front organization.

For example, in January 1984 after the CIA mined Nicaragua's harbors, I was awakened at my "safe house" in Tegucigalpa at 2 A.M. by an anxious CIA agent. He handed me a press release written in perfect Spanish by CIA officials. I was surprised to read its claim that the Democratic Force had laid these mines. I was instructed to read this announcement on our clandestine radio station before the Sandinistas broke the news.

Of course, we had no role in mining the harbors. Ironically, two months later, when a Soviet ship struck a mine, the same agent appeared. Out of fear of creating an international incident, he ordered us to deny that one of "our" mines had done the damage.

Nonetheless, President Reagan has pursuaded Congress to aid the *contras*. The message Congress sends is that a political solution is not possible and that the Sandinistas will respond only to military pressure.

But the legislators who voted for the aid are mistaken; there is still time for a political resolution, but not much. These steps should be taken:

• A political dialogue should be the first priority. Past proposals for dialogue have been delivered as ultimatums and were therefore unacceptable. The first step toward national reconciliation and dialogue must be abolition of the *contra* army.

By urging the rebels to lay down their guns, the United States could support a

---

*From the *New York Times*, June 24, 1985.

policy of national reconciliation that would strengthen the moderates and pragmatists and weaken the extremists and ideologues on both sides. Moderate political leaders should not be encouraged to leave Nicaragua to join the "freedom fighters." It is the moderates who are most capable of engaging in dialogue.

What's more, applying military pressure inflicts suffering and pain on the people of Nicaragua, leads to further political polarization, and increases the danger of military escalation. The present policy of applying pressure to the Sandinistas until they "cry uncle" grossly underestimates Nicaraguan pride and self-esteem. A revolution based on national pride and dignity will never "cry uncle."

• The Reagan administration should give more than lip service to the Contadora initiative—sponsored by Mexico, Colombia, Venezuela, and Panama—which still presents the best option for achieving a lasting political solution. Nicaragua is a Latin American problem best solved by Latin American leaders.

The funds voted by Congress are simply another vehicle to prolong this war. The only assistance worthy of the name "humanitarian aid" is help for victims on both sides.

What we must do is to recognize the good that has come from the revolution in Nicaragua. It has brought a sense of dignity and independence to the Nicaraguan people. The Sandinistas' concern for the poor cannot be faulted. Likewise, there are some democratic leaders associated with the *contras*. The challenge is to bring together the good on both sides with minimal foreign interference.

Nicaraguans must find their own solution. We are the ones who ultimately must live together. But the Sandinistas will not talk to the *contras* as long as they are perceived as Mr. Reagan's army.

Finding a solution to the conflict in Nicaragua requires patience in spite of the apparent urgency; wisdom in the midst of complexity; tolerance and magnanimity in accepting the stumbling steps of a young nation finding its own way. Such qualities are the privilege of a great power and the most important contribution that the United States can make toward resolving the crisis in Nicaragua.

*8. Hiding the War in the White House**

By the *New York Times*

When war comes, warned Senator Hiram Johnson in 1919, truth is the first casualty. The maxim applies to Nicaragua. America's covert war there has filled a whole hospital—and yet more evasion and deception came to light just last week.

When it began in 1981, this war was described as strictly an internal affair. When CIA complicity could no longer be denied, the administration explained it was nec-

*From an editorial in the *New York Times,* August 11, 1985.

essary to cut off an alleged arms flow from leftist Nicaragua to El Salvador. That story began to totter in 1984 when Nicaragua's harbors were mined to scare away neutral shipping. Even that mining was falsely ascribed to *contra* rebels; its authors were American.

Then followed the infamous *contra* manual, ghostwritten by a CIA operative, counseling political murder. This ugly business, at first denied, was finally blamed on overzealousness. Next came the scary report that Soviet ships were carrying high-performance MIGs to Nicaragua, a false alarm attributed to a faulty leak.

Now comes the news that for a year, the overt covert war has been supervised by a military aide on the president's National Security Council staff. The officer met frequently in Central America with rebel leaders, exerted "tactical influence" on their operations, and directed private donors to them. At the least these responsibilities make him a coordinator; at the most, a field marshal.

To understand why this news carries such a pungent odor, recall that Congress—the Republican Senate as well as the Democratic House—tried urgently to end covert American management of this war. It ordered a cutoff last November of all CIA funding or involvement in the *contra* insurgency.

That ban was partly lifted in June. While still barring a CIA role, Congress ambivalently approved $27 million in "humanitarian aid," to keep the *contra* effort alive. Meanwhile, supervision had already been shifted to the NSC to give President Reagan "plausible deniability" of continued CIA involvement, as one insider explained to Joel Brinkley and Shirley Christian of the *Times*.

Plausibly deniable or not, the president insists that no laws have been broken. That's true, but only in the most technical sense. Congress said no to the secret war. To shift conduct of these activities to the National Security Council is a sly, even a cynical evasion. The arrangement, says Adm. Stansfield Turner, President Carter's director of central intelligence, is "most improper."

A government that routinely deceives its people invariably winds up deceiving itself. Does the White House really know what is being done in America's name in Nicaragua? Only last week, one overzealous rebel group seized and then liberated twenty-nine American peace activists near the Costa Rican frontier.

Ducking the truth about Nicaragua has become habitual. Witness the devastating memoir of a former *contra* leader, Edgar Chamorro, in the *New Republic*. He was recruited in 1982 by an American who claimed to speak "in the name of the United States." He quit two years later feeling he had been used and misled. By Mr. Chamorro's account, the rebel leadership was handpicked by the CIA and coached in how to give deceptive testimony to Congress. He found it "was standard *contra* practice to kill Sandinista prisoners and collaborators," a practice he did his best to change.

What's most dismaying about all these deceptions is that they distract from the hard choices in dealing with Managua's provocations. Instead of a reasoned case for a plausible policy, the administration has chosen to mask war with whoppers, all the while condemning the Sandinistas as liars.

The administration intends now to move supervision of the secret war into the State Department, not for reasons of face but space. The bureau overseeing this White House war will be called—what else?—the Agency for Humanitarian Assistance.

Chapter II:

A Threat to Its Neighbors?

Editors' Introduction

Since the inauguration of President Reagan in 1980, his administration has maintained that Nicaragua is a military threat to its neighbors. Initially, members of his administration offered as evidence Nicaragua's alleged shipments of arms to the rebels in El Salvador. They gradually shifted emphasis to the claim that the Nicaraguan arms buildup was out of proportion to its legitimate defense needs, and therefore must be an offensive capability clearly ''destabilizing'' the region. Nicaragua counters that it is not shipping arms to El Salvador, that its admitted arms buildup is defensive in nature and represents a legitimate response to the U.S.-backed *contra* war and the threat of a U.S. invasion, and that it wants a negotiated solution to the region's problems. In sum, Nicaragua claims that it is not interested in threatening anyone. The Reagan administration responds that Nicaragua began stockpiling arms *before* the *contra* war began. It further claims that it has no aggressive designs toward Nicaragua, that it supports a negotiated solution, and that Sandinista ''intransigence'' has so far blocked any sort of negotiated solution. This section attempts to unravel some of these competing claims.

The first reading, a U.S. State Department report that meticulously details the Nicaraguan military buildup, presents the best description of the Nicaraguan military available. This is followed by a *New York Times* investigative piece by Joel Brinkley which seeks to evaluate the competing U.S. and Nicaraguan claims about the purpose of the buildup. While space did not permit inclusion of Nicaragua's side of this issue directly, Mr. Brinkley's article presents both sides.

Following this is an excerpt from an essay by David MacMichael, a former Central Intelligence Agency contract analyst who for two years had security clearance to see all intelligence reports and cable traffic on the Central American region. Mr.

MacMichael resigned from the agency, saying that his classified reports had been publicly misrepresented by the Reagan administration. In the excerpt he addresses the question of alleged Nicaraguan arms shipments to El Salvador.

The last two readings give the U.S. and Nicaraguan positions on attempts to find a negotiated solution for the region's problems. First is a State Department report on U.S. peace efforts, followed by the Nicaraguan embassy's summary, from their point of view, of the major negotiating efforts that both sides have undertaken. It is worth noting here that a qualitative shift has taken place in the U.S. position on negotiations. While originally claiming that Nicaragua simply refused to negotiate, the Reagan administration now uses Nicaragua's conciliatory overtures as evidence that U.S. pressure is "working." Nicaragua counters by saying that it has been making such overtures all along.

9. The Sandinista Military: 1979–1985*

By the U.S. Department of State and Department of Defense

The Buildup Begins

Once in power, the Sandinistas quickly set about building their armed forces and transforming their rag-tag guerrilla army into a well-equipped professional military. The *comandantes* realized from the outset that they would need a large, politicized military to pursue their revolutionary objectives and to maintain themselves in power once the bloom of the revolution had worn off and their true political orientation was exposed. In the fall of 1979, they initiated a military buildup without precedent in Central America. In less than six years, the Sandinistas have developed a military establishment with firepower and mobility unmatched in the region. This expansion has been made possible only with massive assistance from Cuba and the Soviet Union. Indeed, only the militarization of Cuba itself in the 1960s is comparable to what has occurred in Nicaragua since 1979.

The Sandinistas' plans called for a steady increase in the number of men under arms, first through "voluntary" enlistment and later through mandatory conscription. By early 1985, they had amassed an active duty force of more than 62,000. The Sandinistas' total strength, including all regular, reserve, and militia units and security forces, now exceeds 119,000.

Ground Forces

The Sandinista Popular Army (*Ejercito Popular Sandinista*—EPS), the full-time, regular army of the FSLN, has grown to 30,000. The EPS has systematically moved

---

*Excerpts from *The Sandinista Military Buildup* by the Department of State and the Department of Defense. Department of State Publication 9432, Inter-American Series 119, May 1985.

toward developing a combined arms capability, augmenting its conventional infantry forces with mechanized infantry, armored, and artillery brigades. The Sandinistas also have emphasized the formation of reserve and militia forces; currently, these units total some 79,000 men, of which over 27,000 are on active duty at any one time. Dozens of new military bases have been constructed throughout Nicaragua, and the Sandinistas now have some forty major garrisons and numerous smaller posts throughout the nation.

INFANTRY

The EPS has formed 10 regular infantry battalions. A special airborne battalion was inaugurated in 1982. The following year, special counterinsurgency battalions (*Battallon de Lucha Irregular*—BLI) were trained and equipped to engage anti-Sandinista forces. Units along Nicaragua's frontiers were organized as a special border guard force (*Tropas Guarda Fronteras*—TGF). The bulk of the Sandinistas' infantry forces consists of the roughly 160 reserve and militia battalions. These infantry units are equipped primarily with Soviet-bloc arms, such as the AK–47 assault rifle.

The Interior Ministry, which controls the Sandinista Police (*Policia Sandinista*—PS) and the General Directorate of State Security (*Direccion General de Seguridad del Estado*—DGSE), the Sandinista secret police, has direct command of its own brigade of 2,000 highly trained infantry troops *(Tropas Pablo Ubeda).*

ARMOR

The Sandinista army has adhered closely to Soviet-Cuban military doctrine in the development of its armed forces. When the Sandinistas seized power in July 1979, they inherited the hodgepodge collection of armor that had belonged to Somoza's National Guard, including some obsolete World War II vintage tanks, only three of which were operational. The remainder of Somoza's armor consisted of twenty-five antiquated Staghound armored cars.

The Sandinistas set about building an armored force of a size and firepower without precedent in Central America. Crews and mechanics for tanks and other vehicles were sent to Cuba for training. Facilities to support the forthcoming arsenal were built. The first Soviet-built T–55 tanks arrived in mid-1981. The T–55, weighing 36 metric tons and armed with a 100-millimeter gun, can outgun any tank previously seen in Central America. Formerly the Soviets' main battle tank, it is still being used by Warsaw Pact armies. The Sandinistas used the T–55s to form a new armored battalion stationed near Managua.

Over the next three years, ships from the Soviet bloc continued to transport tanks to Nicaragua. By 1982, the Sandinistas had obtained a sufficient number of T–55s to organize another armored battalion. By the end of 1984, they had acquired a total of more than 110 T–55 tanks, enough to form five armored battalions of 22 tanks each.

In 1984, the Soviets provided the Nicaraguans with about thirty PT–76 light tanks. This amphibious tank, armed with a 76-millimeter gun, fords rivers easily and can maneuver in some of the difficult terrain found in parts of Nicaragua.

The Soviets, through their allies, have also equipped the Sandinista army with more than 200 armored vehicles, mostly BTR–60 and BTR–152 armored personnel carriers. These vehicles are armed with a machine gun and can carry a squad of infantry. The first BTR–60s began arriving in mid-1981. The EPS has also received Soviet-made command vehicles and BRDM–2 amphibious armored reconnaissance vehicles. The Sandinistas have now formed at least one mechanized infantry brigade.

The terrain in certain parts of Nicaragua is well suited to armored operations, while in other parts of the country, the terrain imposes some constraints. Tanks can operate easily in the flat plains of the west, which encompass the principal population and economic centers of the nation. On the other hand, the mountains and rugged terrain of the northern departments limit off-road maneuverability. Nevertheless, the EPS has deployed armored units in the north, particularly in such missions as escorting convoys and guarding fixed installations. The lowlands of the Atlantic Coast region inhibit off-road use of the heavy T–55s, but the Sandinistas could deploy the amphibious PT–76s in this region. While some observers have argued that the terrain in Central America renders tanks of only marginal military value, the Sandinistas—and their Soviet suppliers—do not share this view; indeed, they have continued the rapid increase in the size of their tank force, doubling it in 1984 alone.

ARTILLERY

The growth of EPS's artillery force has been equally dramatic. During the revolution, the Sandinistas' fire-support weapons consisted of nothing larger than mortars. When they defeated Somoza's National Guard, they inherited three 105-millimeter howitzers.

During their first year in power, the Sandinistas began receiving ZIS–2s, Soviet-made 57-millimeter antitank guns. By 1981, they were obtaining D–30s, Soviet-made 122-millimeter howitzers far surpassing in range and firepower all other artillery in Central America. That same year, they began acquiring D–20s, Soviet-made 152-millimeter howitzers, which represented a further qualitative increase in their artillery capability. In 1982, Soviet-made BM–21s, capable of launching a barrage of forty 122-millimeter rockets, arrived, greatly increasing the Sandinistas' area bombardment capability. In 1983, the Sandinistas formally inaugurated a special artillery brigade, based in Managua. Currently, the EPS's inventory includes twenty-four D–30s, twenty-four D–20s, twenty-four BM–21 multiple rocket launchers, and scores of antitank guns, as well as hundreds of mortars.

SUPPORT UNITS

The Sandinistas have begun to build an elaborate infrastructure to support their combat forces. They have created a special engineering battalion and communications units. The East Germans alone have provided the Sandinistas with more than 1,000 IFA W–50 trucks since 1980. Large numbers of other vehicles have been delivered by the Soviet Union and its allies. These include more than 800 jeeps, 40 flatbed trucks capable of transporting T–55 tanks, 6 tank ferries to shuttle the T–55s across rivers, numerous communications vans, and about 75 tanker trucks for fuel. The Soviets and Soviet-bloc states have also provided a multitude of other materiel ranging from mobile maintenance workshops and field kitchens to chemical warfare decontamination equipment. In 1982, they furnished the Sandinistas with the equipment to build a communications intercept facility at Santa Maria near Managua. Subsequently, additional intercept facilities have been built at Puerto Cabezas, San Francisco, and Santa Rosa.

Air Force and Air Defense

The 2,000-troop Sandinista Air Force and Air Defense Force (*Fuerza Aerea Sandinista/Defensa Anti-Aerea*–FAS/DAA) has been undergoing substantial improvements since 1979. The Sandinistas began with the remnants of the National Guard's small air force, which included a handful of AT–33A jets, Cessna 337 push-pull aircraft, transport aircraft, trainers, and helicopters. The Sandinistas placed a high priority on developing a more powerful air arm. Early on, they sent personnel to Cuba and Soviet-bloc countries to be trained as pilots and mechanics, and they made plans to expand existing airfields and to build new ones.

Because of the long lead time associated with the acquisition of aircraft—i.e., the need for lengthy pilot training and the construction of airfields—the FAS grew slowly in its early years. The first fixed-wing aircraft added to the inventory were older and unsophisticated models such as Soviet-made AN–2s. In 1982, they aquired four Italian-made SF–260 trainer/tactical support aircraft from Libya. Two Soviet-made AN–26 medium transports added in 1983 significantly improved the Sandinistas' logistics support capabilities.

The Sandinistas' helicopter inventory has grown more rapidly. Some of these helicopters have been obtained from Western nations, such as two Alouettes received from France in 1982. The great majority of these craft have been obtained from the Soviets and their allies, however. In 1981, the first two Soviet Mi–8/HIP medium-lift helicopters arrived. The following April, the Soviets formally donated the Mi–8s to the Sandinistas, alleging that they were to be used to help develop the Atlantic Coast region of Nicaragua. In fact, the Mi–8 is one of the Soviet Union's front-line combat helicopters and can be armed with a machine gun and rocket pods. The Sandinistas have received more than a dozen Mi–8s and have used them extensively in military operations. In 1982, the Sandinistas also acquired Polish-built Mi–2/HOPLITE cargo helicopters.

In late 1984, the Sandinistas received the first of a new generation of helicopter gunships, the Mi–24/HIND D. This is the Soviets' principal attack helicopter, and it has been used extensively by the Soviets in Afghanistan. One of the most highly sophisticated attack helicopters in the world, it holds the helicopter speed record and can be armed with a multiple-barrel machine-gun, guided missiles, rocket pods, and bombs. The HIND's heavy armor, coupled with its high speed, greatly reduces its vulnerability to small arms fire. Acquisition of the HIND D adds a new dimension to warfare in Central America. Key targets in Honduras, Costa Rica, and El Salvador are all within the reach of this flying "tank." Some five to eight Mi–24s had been delivered to Nicaragua by early 1985.

The Sandinistas have three AT–33A jets, and in 1984 top FSLN leaders repeatedly proclaimed their desire to acquire additional jet fighters. Nicaraguan pilots and mechanics reportedly have been undergoing training in Cuba and the Soviet bloc since the early 1980s. In 1982, with Cuban and Soviet assistance, the Sandinistas began constructing the Punta Huete airfield in an isolated area northeast of Managua. The principal runway at Punta Huete is 10,000 feet in length, making it the longest military runway in Central America. When completed, it will be able to accommodate any aircraft in the Soviet-bloc inventory. Sixteen revetments of the size and design appropriate for jet fighters already have been constructed. In addition to Punta Huete, the Sandinistas have been upgrading their principal airbase at Sandino Airport in Managua as well as other airfields at Montelimar, Puerto Cabezas, Estelí, La Rosita, and Bluefields.

Soviet air warfare doctrine calls for aircraft to operate in a "controlled air environment," that is to say, the aircraft are controlled by command elements on the ground which monitor their actions via radar. In 1983, the first Soviet-made Early Warning/Ground Control-Intercept (EW/GCI) facility in Nicaragua was assembled near Masaya. During 1984, additional radar sites were established at Toro Blanco and Estelí. Early in 1985, a fourth radar system was emplaced at San Juan del Sur. A temporary site at El Bluff has provided coverage of the Atlantic Coast as well. A coastal surveillance radar was emplaced at El Polvon in late 1984. The Sandinistas now have radar coverage over most of Nicaragua and can monitor aircraft movements deep into Honduras, El Salvador, and Costa Rica as well. There is no other comparable radar system anywhere in the region.

The early warning capability of the radar net also is associated with the Sandinista air defense forces. As early as 1980, the Sandinistas began acquiring ZPU–4, ZU–23, and M–1939 antiaircraft guns and SA–7 surface-to-air missiles. The S–60, a 57-millimeter cannon with fire control radar, was added in 1984. Nearly 200 pieces of antiaircraft artillery and over 300 SA–7 missile launchers now ring major installations.

Navy

The 1,000-troop Sandinista Navy (*Marina de Guerra Sandinista*—MGS) has similarly undergone both a qualitative and quantitative transformation since 1979. Somoza's "navy" consisted of a handful of old patrol boats. The Sandinistas set out to acquire a fleet of more modern vessels. In 1983, they acquired two French Vedette patrol boats and two Soviet ZHUK patrol boats. In 1983–84, North Korea supplied two KIMJIN and two SINHUNG patrol boats. In 1984, Cuba delivered a third ZHUK and two YEVGENYA inshore minesweepers. In November 1984, the Soviet merchant ship *Bakuriani* delivered four Polish-built K–8 minesweeping boats.

*10. Nicaraguan Army: "War Machine" or Defender of a Besieged Nation?**

By Joel Brinkley

The threat that Nicaragua's army may pose to other Central American countries has become a central issue in the debate over renewed United States financing for the rebels fighting to topple the government.

The administration says the army is a juggernaut, far larger than the other Central American militaries and poised to attack its neighbors. But Democrats in Congress and some officials in the administration say they believe the White House has overstated its case. . . .

Mr. Reagan has accused the Nicaraguans of building "a war machine" that "dwarfs the forces of all their neighbors combined."

In February, Vice-President Bush belittled "some who still insist" that "these Marxists have no extraterritorial ambitions."

In interviews with more than two dozen officials in the White House, the Defense and State Departments, Congress, and private organizations involved with Central American affairs, these were some of the main findings:

- The Salvadoran and Guatemalan regular armies, with 48,000 and 40,000 troops, are each nearly as large as the Nicaraguan Army, which has 40,000 regular troops and another 20,000 militia members on active duty, according to Defense Department figures. When all the other Central American armies are combined, they are far larger than Nicaragua's. On the other hand, when army troops and militia are lumped together, Nicaragua's military forces are larger than those of any other Central American country, although Guatemala claims to have a 900,000-member rural civil guard.
- Senior administration officials, in speeches and in public reports, have frequently said Nicaragua intends to attack its neighbors. But State and Defense Department officials say unofficially that they do not believe Nicaragua has any such intention.
- President Reagan has said that "the Sandinista military buildup began two and a half years before" the United States-backed Nicaraguan rebels took up arms and was not a result of rebel attacks. But Defense Department records show that the first shipment of heavy Soviet-made arms to Nicaragua came many months after the first reports of rebel attacks.
- Nicaraguan officials have said one reason for their buildup is that they fear an American invasion. Administration officials confirmed that since at least 1983, the United States had used a "perception management" program, as a classified Defense Department document called it, to keep the Nicaraguans concerned that the United States might attack.

---

*Excerpts from the *New York Times,* March 30, 1985.

- White House and State Department officials were unable to verify the accuracy of several quotations that the president and others have attributed to Nicaraguan leaders in support of their assertions about Nicaragua's intentions. In one case, the State Department acknowledged that it knew of no Sandinista official who ever used an often-quoted phrase that Nicaragua seeks a "revolution without frontiers."

Even the administration's critics agree with several of the president's fundamental assertions about Nicaragua.

Many of them say they are convinced that Nicaragua has supplied arms and other assistance to El Salvador's leftist rebels, although there is disagreement about the scope of that assistance and whether it continues.

Representative Michael D. Barnes, Democrat of Maryland, the chairman of the House Subcommittee on Western Hemisphere Affairs, said that "there is no doubt" about Nicaragua's "support to the left in El Salvador."

Administration critics also agree that many of Nicaragua's leaders are Marxist-Leninists with close ties to Cuba. To some administration supporters, that fact alone is sufficient evidence of aggressive intent.

There also is widespread concern that Nicaragua could become a Soviet military base. "There's a possibility for air bases and submarine pens," and Senator Richard G. Lugar, Republican of Indiana, the chairman of the Foreign Relations Committee. Soviet and Nicaraguan officials have denied such assertions.

Army's Size and Ability Is a Matter of Dispute

A White House spokesman said Otto J. Reich, ambassador for Latin American public diplomacy, was the official best suited to outline the administration's concerns about Nicaragua and the evidence to support them.

In an interview, Mr. Reich described the Nicaraguan army as "enormous in relation to its immediate environment" and added that "invasion is one of the things we are concerned about."

The Defense Department estimates that the Nicaraguan army includes about 40,000 regular, active-duty troops and another 20,000 civilian militia members on active duty, for a total troop strength of about 60,000.

The department also estimates that El Salvador has 48,000 troops on active duty, Honduras has 21,000, and Guatemala has about 40,000, for a combined troop strength of about 109,000. Costa Rica has no army but does have a 9,500-man civil guard.

Nicaragua also has a civilian militia of 50,000, in addition to those on active duty, and administration officials sometimes include the militia in their public statements about the size of the Nicaraguan army.

Carlos Tunnerman Bernheim, the Nicaraguan ambassador to the United States, said the militia included "all types of people; factory workers, students, women, children, and old people."

All of them, he said, "have had some minimal training," adding that they would be issued weapons if Nicaragua were invaded.

A Defense Department official, acknowledging that the militia includes some women and children, said that "we don't know how well trained they are" or how many have arms.

Costa Rica has a 10,000-member civilian militia, Honduras has a 4,500-member "public security" force, and Guatemala claims to have a 900,000-member rural defense force.

Of the assertions of a possible Nicaraguan invasion of its neighbors, Foreign Minister Miguel d'Escoto Brockman of Nicaragua said, "To believe that is to believe that in addition to being evil, we are also insane."

A senior Defense Department official directly involved with Central American affairs agreed, saying that "we don't expect an attack" because "we don't think they would be that stupid."

"That would be the solution" to the Nicaragua problem, he added, because the United States would "most certainly" attack.

Administration officials frequently point to Nicaragua's armor as evidence of aggressive intent. Nicaragua has more tanks than any other country in the region.

In a speech last month, Vice-president Bush said Nicaragua had "over 150 tanks." And government white papers describing a Nicaraguan threat point out that Nicaragua has "heavy ferries to give additional amphibious mobility" to the tanks, as one white paper said. It also noted that Nicaragua's borders with Honduras and Costa Rica are "largely defined by rivers."

Defense Department officials say the Nicaraguans have 110 Soviet-built T–54 and T–55 tanks that are twenty-five to thirty years old. Col. Lawrence L. Tracy, the State Department's military adviser for Latin American public diplomacy, said the tanks "couldn't survive against modern antitank weaponry." Colonel Tracy is one of the authors of the government's most recent white paper, issued in March.

Since most of Nicaragua is too hilly for tanks, to be used against Honduras they would probably have to be loaded on flatbed trucks and driven up the Pan-American Highway, Colonel Tracy and others said.

That could be "suicidal," Colonel Tracy said. The Honduran air force, which includes more than two dozen jet fighters and bombers, "could easily take them out," a senior Defense Department official said, since Nicaragua has "no significant air force to speak of."

Mr. Reagan, in a 1983 session with reporters, said Nicaragua had "fighter planes, bombers, and so forth."

Defense Department officials say Nicaragua has no jet fighters or bombers or other modern combat aircraft, except about ten sophisticated Soviet helicopter gunships.

Mr. Reich said, "If all the Nicaraguan tanks were to simply occupy a plain in southern Honduras, they could humiliate the Honduran army, and the government could collapse."

But Mr. Reich also acknowledged that the "Sandinista military hasn't shown us much so far" in its war against the rebels.

Nicaraguan Buildup: Origin Is Debated

Ambassador Tunnerman, like other Nicaraguan officials, said that "we had to increase our military because we are facing aggression from the *contras,*" as the rebels are often called.

But a senior State Department official contended that "they announced their intentions and were rushing pell-mell to buy tanks long before the *contras* were a threat." Nicaragua denies that.

The first clear statement of Nicaragua's intent was a government paper called "the 72-hour document." Published in Managua in the fall of 1979, a few months after the Sandinistas came to power, it reported "in detail on an extraordinary meeting September 21 to 23" of the Sandinista leadership, a State Department cable from Managua said. The United States ambassador called the document "remarkably frank," and Reagan administration officials frequently cite it.

Of military plans, the document said, "Though we do not wish to downplay the need for a strong military to take care of national defense, we would like to point out that at the present time there is no clear indication of an armed counterrevolution" and "what merits our attention is domestic factors."

At the same time, in 1979 Cuba was sending a variety of specialists to Nicaragua, including military advisers, and a Defense Department official said that showed that the Nicaraguans "had this buildup planned all along."

Bosco Matamoros, an official in the largest rebel group, the Nicaraguan Democratic Force, said recently that armed rebels began attacks in Nicaragua in 1980. That is also when Sandinista officials began complaining of attacks. And in recent interviews, rebel leaders have said they began receiving training and assistance from the Argentine military in 1980.

In February 1981, Nicaragua announced it would form a large citizen militia. By then, sixty-seven Nicaraguan soldiers had been killed in attacks by several hundred rebels, many of them former Nicaraguan national guardsmen who had been operating out of Honduras for more than a year, press reports of the time said.

Also in February 1981, Defense Minister Humberto Ortega Saavedra asserted that Nicaragua needed a large militia because "there is a danger that the thousands of former national guardsmen abroad" could find support from the United States.

Months later, in mid-1981, a senior Defense Department official said, Nicaragua acquired its first Soviet-made tanks. Until then, another Defense Department official said, they had been receiving "small arms and light artillery, mostly."

Late that year, President Reagan authorized the Central Intelligence Agency to begin aiding the Nicaraguan rebels.

U.S. Has Stirred Fears of Invasion

Nicaraguan officials have repeatedly said they are worried about a United States invasion, and since at least 1983 the Reagan administration has intentionally reinforced those fears, senior administration officials confirmed.

A 1983 Defense Department document on "Central American initiatives" mentioned a "perception management program" to be "coupled with the activities of" the Big Pine II military maneuvers held that August in Honduras. The Defense Department "will take the lead" in the program, the document said, with help from the CIA and the State Department.

A senior State Department official confirmed this week that the program was still in place and said its purpose was to gain concessions from the Nicaraguan government. "Every time there's an invasion scare, they make some concessions," he said. Another senior official said, "We do our best to keep them concerned."

Statements from the president and other senior officials in Washington raise invasion concerns in Managua. But the most important element of the program, officials said, has been a series of large-scale American military maneuvers in Honduras, beginning in early 1983. From the start administration officials have said the maneuvers were intended to intimidate Nicaragua.

"One of the central purposes is to create fear of an invasion," a senior administration official said. The American troops "push very close to the border, deliberately, to set off all the alarms," he added.

Ambassador Tunnerman said that "with 12,000 troops on our border" and a "corresponding escalation of statements from the government" in Washington, "we have reason to be concerned."

The Defense Department is preparing for large-scale maneuvers along the Nicaraguan-Honduran border that will begin within a few weeks.

The administration intentionally scared the Nicaraguans in another manner last November, when officials in Washington said a ship docking in Nicaragua might be carrying Soviet fighter planes.

Administration officials said later that no planes had been unloaded. But during the MiG crisis, as Nicaraguans now call it, American surveillance aircraft flying over Managua caused a series of sonic booms, further alarming the Nicaraguans at a time when tensions were already high.

Such planes frequently fly over Nicaragua and other countries without causing sonic booms.

Mr. Reich confirmed that the booms were intended to scare the Nicaraguans. Another senior State Department official said that "there is talk about doing the same thing again."

*11. Arms to El Salvador?**

By David MacMichael

David MacMichael was a contract analyst for the Central Intelligence Agency in 1981 and 1982, when he was one of only a few people with a security clearance allowing him to see all intelligence and cable traffic from Central America. When he left the CIA he said that he was disillusioned with the "distortion" of intelligence data by the Reagan administration.

The present policy is the result of four years of hyperbole and deception. The administration has steadfastly maintained that the insurgency in El Salvador is supported and controlled by the Sandinistas. Nicaraguan arms and munitions are said to be the Salvadoran insurgency's "life-blood." It is from this central deception—that the Salvadoran rebels must depend primarily upon Nicaraguan arms—that the administration's dangerous policy grows. Thus, the evidence of this arms flow becomes, for many of us, the key question about current policy.

The Reagan hard-liners have succeeded in silencing most of those in the State Department, the military, the intelligence agencies, and elsewhere who doubted the information upon which this policy was based. This silencing of dissent has been the administration's only Central America policy success. The insurgency in El Salvador is stronger and several times larger than in 1980. The Sandinistas are bloodied but unbowed.

As an analyst for the Central Intelligence Agency's National Intelligence Council, which coordinates the intelligence community's work, from 1981 to 1983, I became convinced that intelligence on the crucial question of the arms flow from Nicaragua to the Salvadoran rebels was being badly misused to support administration policy. In my experience, analysis was strained and even distorted in the effort to convince those in Congress, the public, and the press who might have doubted the foundation of the policy. Administration officials went far beyond the data provided by intelligence sources in their public statements. Intelligence resources that could have been used to develop and present an accurate view of the Central American situation were instead used to incriminate the Nicaraguan government in accordance with preconceived notions and ideologies. After I began to question the evidence publicly, so did many others.

Now, the administration has shot itself in the foot. Amid the questions of evidence comes a new justification for the proxy war being waged against Nicaragua. The advance copies of a Defense Department and State Department *Background Paper: Nicaragua's Military Buildup and Support for Central America Subversion,* distributed to members of Congress, concludes that the "massive arms flow" from Nicaragua to the Salvadoran insurgency has consisted merely of "sporadic" deliv-

---

*Excerpts from an article entitled "Democrats Can Seize Central America Issue," *New York Times,* July 17, 1984.

eries since early 1981, and those principally of medicine, clothing, and ammunition. With this perhaps inadvertent admission, the rationale for the *contra* war disappears.

*12. The Search for Peace**

By the U.S. Department of State

U.S. support for regional diplomatic peace efforts is strong, consistent, and undiminished. We have repeatedly made clear in private communications and public statements our willingness to support and abide by a comprehensive and fully verifiable implementation of the Contadora Document of Objectives of September 9, 1983.†

During 1984, U.S. diplomacy pursued the commission's recommendations that we test ''Nicaragua's willingness to enter into a general agreement'' and support efforts of the Contadora Group to find a comprehensive, reciprocal, and verifiable approach to the Central American crisis.

The office of the ambassador at large and special envoy for Central America has proven to be an effective means for implementing this diplomacy. The incumbent, Ambassador Harry W. Shlaudeman, made twenty-seven trips to Latin America between March 1984 and March 1985, holding 139 meetings with chiefs of state and senior Foreign Ministry officials.

The Contadora Process

The Contadora process has been the centerpiece of diplomacy among the regional countries since early 1983. Although negotiations were stalled in February 1985 by a dispute over political asylum between Nicaragua and Costa Rica, the Contadora Group scheduled a new round for April.

Three drafts of a final agreement were prepared in 1984. A draft ''Contadora Act for Peace and Cooperation in Central America'' was prepared by the Contadora Group in June. After initial discussions, the Contadora Group prepared a second draft which it presented to the five Central American states on September 7. Nicaragua announced on September 21 that it would sign this draft provided it was not modified and called on the United States to adhere to an additional protocol.

The other Central American governments welcomed this draft as a positive step but cited the need to strengthen provisions for verification and control and to provide for a more balanced and orderly implementation of its security provisions in particular.

---

*Excerpts from U.S. Department of State Special Report #124.

†The nine countries participating in the Contadora process formally agreed to this document as containing the objectives of their negotiations. These countries are the four members of the Contadora Group (Colombia, Mexico, Panama, and Venezuela) and the five Central American countries (Costa Rica, El Salvador, Guatamala, Honduras, and Nicaragua).

U.S. spokesmen noted that the September 7 draft was much improved and that its elaboration was a positive step in the negotiating process. We also stated our view that provisions for verification needed to be strengthened. In consultations with Contadora participants, we stressed that our textual reservations are in no way to be equated with opposition to an effective treaty, which we would support.

On October 20, El Salvador, Costa Rica, and Honduras proposed another draft, incorporating the specific changes they felt necessary. Extensive consultations among the Contadora participants as to how the September and October versions might be reconciled took place on the margins of the OAS General Assembly in Brasilia November 12–16 and have continued through normal diplomatic channels.

The elaboration of several drafts in 1984 suggests that the Contadora process could make rapid progress in 1985. With negotiations about to resume, the key question is whether Nicaragua is willing to negotiate.

Bilateral Conversations with Nicaragua

We also have supported the Contadora process in bilateral talks with Nicaragua held in Manzanillo, Mexico. These discussions were begun at the request of the president of Mexico, acting on behalf of the Contadora Group. Secretary Shultz visited Managua on June 1, 1984, to begin the process. Since then, there have been nine rounds of talks between Special Envoy Harry W. Shlaudeman and Nicaraguan Vice-Minister of Foreign Affairs Victor Hugo Tinoco. To give the talks the maximum chance to succeed, the two sides agreed not to discuss publicly their specific content. Although the Nicaraguans have publicly characterized the talks in a general way, they have largely abided by this rule of confidentiality, as have we.

In mid-January we decided not to schedule further bilateral talks due to concern that Nicaragua was using them to avoid comprehensive negotiations within Contadora's multilateral framework. The Manzanillo talks have been useful in permitting each side to present its concerns fully to the other, but they have made no substantive progress. We undertook the Manzanillo talks in hopes of facilitating a successful outcome of the multilateral Contadora process. Any bilateral agreement necessarily would be incomplete with respect to all elements of the regional crisis. Arms and troop-level reductions, for example, can only be negotiated between Nicaragua and its neighbors. Nicaragua, however, appears to prefer a bilateral agreement, in lieu of Contadora.

On February 27, 1985, in a move that appeared designed primarily for public relations impact, President Ortega announced Nicaragua's intention to send home 100 Cuban military advisers; to suspend, for the time being, acquisition of new armaments, including "interceptor aircraft"; and to invite a U.S. congressional delegation to visit Nicaragua. The moratorium on new armaments systems is potentially significant, but only if it proves more far-reaching and permanent. The offer to send home 100 of the 2,500–3,500 Cuban military advisers could be significant, provided that it would be the beginning of a continuing withdrawal to be undertaken in the near term as part of an overall settlement.

We have communicated to all concerned our willingness to resume bilateral talks if that would contribute to a comprehensive agreement within Contadora. On March 2, Secretary of State Shultz met with Nicaraguan President Daniel Ortega in Montevideo, Uruguay, to explore such possibilities. We are looking to the Contadora negotiations for evidence of Nicaragua's willingness to negotiate seriously. Normal diplomatic channels remain open to continue this dialogue.

*13. Nicaragua's Peace Initiatives with the United States**

By the Nicaraguan Embassy to the United States
Washington, D.C.

Nicaragua has consistently attempted to negotiate all real and even imagined points of conflict with the United States. It has proposed many different solutions; it has never refused to dialogue at any bilateral or multilateral level; and it has cooperated fully with third party nations to facilitate a negotiated peace and an improved climate in Central America.

These efforts have spanned almost four years. For purposes of convenience, the different negotiations in which Nicaragua has participated can be delineated by seven phases:

1. The Enders Round (August 1981–October 1981);
2. The Mexican Initiative/Ambassadorial Talks (December 1981–August 1982);
3. The Mexican-Venezuelan Peace Initiative (September 1982–March 1983);
4. The Stone Visits (June 1983–April 1984);
5. The Motley/Shlaudeman Visits (October 1983–June 1984);
6. The Contadora Peace Initiative/Nicaragua's Draft Treaty Proposals (September 1983–?); and
7. The Shultz/Manzanillo Talks (June 1984–January 1985).

It is important to point out that Nicaragua's efforts in these negotiations:

- *preceded* U.S. support of military and paramilitary actions intended, according to U.S. officials, as a method of forcing concessions from Nicaragua;
- have been *open-ended* and *flexible,* while the U.S. unilaterally ended, suspended, or blocked each of the above processes;
- have included consideration of and respect for *all* the *legitimate security concerns* that the U.S. has raised either in regard to itself or to the region.

*From a Nicaragua Fact Sheet, March 1985.

The Enders Round (August 1981–October 1981)

Nicaragua made repeated requests for talks with the United States about improving relations soon after the inauguration of President Reagan's first term, early in 1981. However, it was not until August that Reagan sent Assistant Secretary of State for Latin America Thomas O. Enders to Managua. He arrived on August 12 for a series of six meetings.

It was during this series that Honduras granted permission to the United States to build a military base in the Gulf of Fonseca, a body of water shared by Nicaragua, Honduras, and El Salvador. Also, the United States began joint military exercises in Honduras with "Ocean Adventure 81."

Enders had promised to present Nicaragua with five "illustrative drafts" that would cover the broad range of issues to negotiate bilaterally. The first was the draft of a unilateral statement of the U.S. citing laws that forbid paramilitary training and intervention in the internal affairs of another nation. The second was a bilateral statement on noninterference and nonintervention in the internal affairs of another nation. These were to be issued consequent upon the progress of negotiations.

The other drafts on human and cultural exchanges, bilateral technical and economic assistance, and "a security proposal" were never delivered.

The United States did not follow up or even formally end the Enders Round. But in December 1981 President Reagan authorized a $19 million CIA–directed plan for paramilitary and terrorist operations against Nicaragua.

The Mexican Initiative/Ambassadorial Talks (December 1981–August 1982)

In December 1981, Nicaraguan Foreign Minister Miguel d'Escoto attempted to meet with U.S. Secretary of State Alexander Haig at the OAS meeting in St. Lucia to explore possible solutions to the tense situation between the United States and Nicaragua. Haig reacted in a rage with almost hysterical verbal accusations, thus closing the door on any possible dialogue.

In February 1982, Mexican President Lopez Portillo proposed a regional peace plan with these main points:

- the United States should cease its threats and military actions against Nicaragua;
- if the paramilitary units operating from Honduras were disbanded, Nicaragua should reduce the size of its armed forces; and
- the various affected countries should enter into mutual nonaggression pacts.

Nicaragua accepted these main points, but the U.S. response was ambiguous.

Mexican Foreign Minister Jorge Castaña then arranged for further talks between d'Escoto and Enders. However, the State Department reduced its representation to the ambassadorial level.

Nicaragua then agreed to meet with Ambassador Anthony Quainton at the Foreign Ministry in Managua. He presented Nicaragua with an eight-point proposal for negotiations.

This was followed by Nicaragua's then Ambassador to the U.S., Francisco Fiallos, presenting to the State Department a thirteen-point proposal, noting Nicaragua's willingness to discuss the eight points and any others that the United States might wish to include.

In July 1982, after a two-month delay, Quainton delivered to Deputy Foreign Minister Victor Tinoco comments on the thirteen points and a list of "suggestions" that Nicaragua should follow in order to improve the climate for negotiations.

On August 13, Nicaragua answered the Quainton communiqué and again urged that a meeting be held in Mexico between the foreign minister and the secretary of state using the combined twenty-one points as the agenda along with any other concerns that either side would have wished to discuss.

The United States never responded to the August 13 letter.

The Mexican-Venezuelan Peace Initiative (September 1982–March 1983)

The presidents of Mexico and Venezuela sent an appeal to the heads of state of Nicaragua, Honduras, and the United States in September 1982. They called for an "exploration of ways that remain open to halt the worrying escalation" of the crisis. The proposal was endorsed by 106 members of the U.S. Congress.

However, in an apparent attempt to blunt the Mexican-Venezuelan peace initiative, the Reagan administration backed a "Forum for Peace and Democracy" in San José, Costa Rica. Nicaragua was excluded from the forum, while Mexico and Venezuela declined to attend.

That same month, October 1982, Foreign Minister d'Escoto saw Secretary of State Shultz at the United Nations and suggested a conversation. The latter said he was too busy and declined.

In December 1982, junta member Sergio Ramírez pointed out that U.S. diplomats were refusing to see high-level Sandinista officials. The United States still had not responded to Nicaragua's last diplomatic note of August urging peace talks. Meanwhile, the United States continued to oppose peace talks between Honduras and Nicaragua.

In March 1983, Acting Foreign Minister Nora Astorga sent two more notes to Secretary Shultz denouncing *contra* actions. The United States did not respond.

The Stone Visits (June 1983–January 1984)

Daniel Ortega received a visit in June 1983 from U.S. Special Ambassador Richard Stone. Although Stone insisted that his mission was "to listen and to learn," he brought up charges of Nicaraguan support of Salvadoran insurgents. This allegation had been made against Nicaragua since the Enders Round, but the Reagan administration never came forth with evidence proving complicity of the Sandinista government in arms trafficking to Salvadoran rebels.

Stone met again in August with d'Escoto and Ortega, returning another time in September to meet with Ortega. His final visit with Ortega was in January 1984. In these meetings be began to insist that Nicaragua negotiate directly with the *contra* terrorists.

The Motley/Shlaudeman Visits (October 1983–June 1984)

On October 13, 1983, Assistant Secretary of State Langhorne Motley met in Managua with d'Escoto, Ortega, and Commander Julio Ramos. Motley brought up for the first time the U.S. warning that any agreement allowing for a greater Soviet presence would be unacceptable, that the importation of sophisticated warplanes would be unacceptable, that economic cooperation would be necessary on a regional level, and that democratic elections would be critical to insure a long-term peace.

With this visit it became clear the U.S. policy and demands were inconsistent. Motley made no reference to support of Salvadoran rebels.

Motley returned to Managua in April 1984, this time accompanying Stone's successor Harry W. Shlaudeman. They met with d'Escoto and Ortega and issued a veiled threat that if Nicaragua did not act concretely to lessen Soviet-Cuban ties, its alleged support of Salvadoran guerrillas and its military buildup, and provide for broad democratic participation in its government, the United States would have to take necessary measures.

The Contadora Peace Initiative/Nicaragua's Draft Treaty Proposals (September 1983–?)

ORTEGA'S SIX-POINT PROPOSAL

On July 19, 1983, Daniel Ortega, commemorating the fourth anniversary of the triumph of the revolution, issued a six-point peace proposal that included:

1. a nonaggression pact between Nicaragua and Honduras;
2. a freeze of all arms shipments to El Salvador;
3. an end to sponsorship of forces fighting against Central American governments;
4. respect for the Central American peoples' self-determination and noninterference in their internal affairs;
5. a cessation of economic aggression; and
6. a halt to the establishment of military bases and the holding of military exercises in any country in the area.

Nicaragua made known its willingness to discuss these points bilaterally and/or multilaterally within the Contadora process.

In September 1983, Nicaragua and the Central American countries signed Contadora's twenty-one-point proposal.

NICARAGUA'S TREATY PROPOSALS

In October 1983, Nicaragua presented three separate draft treaties and an accord on El Salvador to Contadora, the only country to comply with Contadora's request for concrete proposals. Among the draft treaties was a bilateral agreement with the United States that attempted to address both Nicaraguan and U.S. concerns. The United States never responded to this proposal, although Foreign Minister d'Escoto personally delivered it to the State Department.

Three clauses in that document go straight to the heart of professed U.S. security concerns:

- the first prohibits the installation of any foreign military bases in Central America and forbids military maneuvers with any foreign armed forces;
- the second prohibits the acquisition of arms of whatever type and point of origin by any country of Central America;
- the third clause calls for the immediate commencement of withdrawal of foreign military advisers and personnel in the region and requires the withdrawal process to be completed within thirty days.

NICARAGUA ACCEPTS CONTADORA PROPOSAL

In September 1984, Nicaragua became the first nation to agree to the Contadora treaty proposal. The United States, as admitted in a National Security Council document leaked to the *Washington Post*, successfully pressured the other Central American states not to sign.

The United States also was instrumental in effecting a boycott by Costa Rica, El Salvador, and Honduras of the February 1985 Contadora meeting. The Contadora nations were to submit their study of a system of verification and control. This boycott has effectively placed the Contadora process in limbo.

The Shultz/Manzanillo Talks (June 1984–January 1985)

On very brief notice, Secretary of State Shultz arrived in Managua June 1, 1984, and met with Daniel Ortega. He expressed the same concerns as Motley but he and Ortega agreed to continue discussion through their deputies, with Vice-Minister Tinoco representing Nicaragua and Shlaudeman the United States.

Shultz insisted that the talks not include Mexico or a third party. Nicaragua preferred a third party presence but conceded to Shultz's conditions.

Tinoco and Shlaudeman began their meetings in Manzanillo, Mexico, on June 25, 1984, and met there each month thereafter until the United States unilaterally suspended the talks in January 1985.

In late February, Nicaragua asked for a meeting between Shultz and Ortega during the inauguration ceremonies of President Sanguinetti of Uruguay. The United States accepted and the meeting took place in Montevideo on March 2, 1985. President Ortega briefed Secretary Shultz on the new unilateral initiatives of Nicaragua that included: a) a moratorium on the importation of any new weapons systems into Nicaragua; b) the withdrawal of 100 Cuban military advisers as an initial step toward the removal of all foreign military from the region; and c) the open invitation for a bipartisan delegation of U.S. congressmen to visit Nicaraguan military facilities to confirm that Nicaragua's armed forces and military structure are purely defensive in nature. Mr. Shultz left open the possibility that the bilateral talks of Manzanillo could resume in the future if they contributed to the Contadora process. However, he responded negatively to the above initiatives.

Chapter III:

Nicaragua: A Totalitarian State?

Editors' Introduction

As documented in the previous chapter, the Reagan administration has repeated the theme that Nicaragua is a threat to its neighbors. A second, equally common theme of those in the White House is that the initial democratic promises of the Nicaraguan revolution have been broken, and that under the Sandinistas Nicaragua has become a Soviet-style totalitarian state. The Reagan administration relies on three "proofs" that Nicaragua is a totalitarian state: delayed, unfair elections, censorship of the press, and allegations of human rights abuses committed by the Nicaraguan government.

Until the 1984 elections were announced in February of that year, the Reagan administration had repeatedly claimed that the Sandinistas reneged on their original promise to hold such elections. Subsequent to that announcement the administration sought to discredit the planned elections with charges that they would be a "sham." To date, the administration has not released any detailed statement analyzing these elections. Therefore, the only State Department view of the elections included in this section is a pre-election analysis of the prospects for a "fair" election in Nicaragua, in which serious charges are raised. This is followed by the report of a delegation sent by the Latin American Studies Association to observe the elections—the most thorough and objective coverage available—which includes evaluation of the specific charges made by the State Department.

In the next reading, former State Department contract analyst John Spicer Nichols examines the Nicaraguan media and the question of freedom of the press.

The reading which follows, the State Department's *Country Reports on Human*

Rights, caused considerable controversy among human rights organizations in the United States. In the next reading Americas Watch presents its response to that report. "Sandinistas Aren't the Worst," by former *New York Times* Central American reporter Raymond Bonner then compares the human rights records of Nicaragua and U.S. ally El Salvador.

Finally "We Are Sandinistas" presents what many Central America analysts feel is the "real" reason for the Reagan administration's belligerence toward Nicaragua: the fear that the example of a successful Nicaraguan experiment in independent development would provide an impetus to nationalist and revolutionary movements throughout Latin America.

*14. Sandinista Elections in Nicaragua**

By the U.S. Department of State

The Sandinistas hail the Electoral Law as the basis for the first free elections in Nicaragua's history. In fact, however, the Sandinistas have exploited their power to such an extent that the elections as now planned will have no more validity than those held by Somoza.

Shortly after the Electoral Law was decreed in late March, the Supreme Electoral Council was convened. As opposition leaders had feared, it was staffed entirely by members of the FSLN or Sandinista sympathizers. The Supreme Electoral Council originally proposed scheduling a two-month campaign, the minimum allowed by the Electoral Law. Following the outcry that two months was inadequate by all the parties except the FSLN, the Supreme Electoral Council announced on May 24 that the campaign would be of three months' duration. At the same time, it established a two-month period for candidate registration, May 25–July 25, and a four-day period for voter registration, July 27–30.

During June and July, Nicaragua's political parties held conventions and meetings to select their candidates. All the non-FSLN parties delayed registering their candidates, awaiting the July 19 celebration of the fifth anniversary of the revolution when the state of emergency was due to elapse. To the disappointment of these parties, Daniel Ortega announced that the state of emergency was being extended and that only certain modifications would be made to facilitate the electoral process.

On July 23, just two days before the close of the registration period, the FSLN became the first party to submit its list of candidates. Six other parties filed their lists with the Supreme Electoral Council by the July 25 deadline:

- Nicaraguan Socialist party (PSN): A Moscow-line Communist party with probably fewer than 1,000 members. Allied with the FSLN since 1980 in the Pa-

*Excerpts from a U.S. Department of State *Resource Book,* undated.

triotic Front of the Revolution, it is broadly supportive of Sandinista programs although it has disagreed with the implementation of some policies.

- Communist Party of Nicaragua (PCDEN): A hard-line Communist party with perhaps a few hundred members. It was founded by radicals who bolted from the PSN claiming that the PSN's leaders were not sufficiently revolutionary. It has criticized the FSLN for not moving fast enough to turn Nicaragua into a Marxist-Leninist state.
- Popular Action Movement—Marxist/Leninist (MAP–ML): An ultraleft Communist party so small that it could not name candidates for all ninety seats to the National Assembly. It also has criticized the FSLN for moving too slowly toward communism.
- Popular Social Christian Party (PPSC): A leftist democratic party with perhaps a few hundred members. It was founded in the 1970s by dissidents from the left wing of the Social Christian Party, and since 1980 has been allied with the FSLN in the Patriotic Front of the Revolution. It supports the goals of the revolution but is uneasy with the FSLN's drive toward a militarized Marxist state.
- Independent Liberal Party (PLI): A leftist democratic party claiming 6,000 members, PLI was allied with the FSLN in the Patriotic Front of the Revolution from 1980 until February 1984 when it withdrew to prepare for the elections. Since that time, it has become increasingly critical of the FSLN. (On October 21, PLI announced that it was withdrawing from the campaign because the existing conditions made a fair election impossible.)
- Democratic Conservative Party (PCD): One faction of what traditionally was Nicaragua's largest opposition party. In late 1983, a dispute arose among the leadership of the PCD, and the FSLN-controlled National Council of Political Parties installed one of the factions as the PCD's legal leadership. Many PCD members quickly abandoned the party and organized the new Nicaraguan Conservative Party. The PCD has been critical of the Sandinistas, but it has benefited from official favoritism. For example, the leaders of the PCD were embarrassed when more than a dozen of the party's candidates for the National Assembly declared that they had never agreed to appear on the PCD's ticket and petitioned to have their names removed. The Supreme Electoral Council decided to favor the PCD's leaders and ruled that the names would remain on the ballot, irrespective of the wishes of the candidates themselves.

The Democratic Coordinating Board *(Coordinadora)*—composed of the Social Christian (PSC), Social Democratic (PSD), and Liberal Constitutionalist (PLC) parties; two independent labor confederations; and various private sector and professional organizations; and supported by the PCD faction reorganized as the Nicaraguan Conservative Party—refused to register, claiming that the conditions necessary for free elections did not exist.

Control over the media exemplifies the advantages the Sandinistas enjoy over their opponents. Nicaragua's only television system, two of its three newspapers, and many of its radio stations are run directly by the FSLN. The Sandinistas have used the state of emergency imposed in 1982 to muzzle the independent daily *La Prensa* and all non-Sandinista radio stations. For more than two years, they have censored thousands of *La Prensa* reports on the activities of non-FSLN parties and articles which reflected unfavorably on the FSLN. Frequently, *La Prensa* failed to publish because 80–90 percent of the day's hard news was censored by the government and the paper did not have sufficient material to fill out its pages (the Sandinistas do not permit *La Prensa* to leave blank spaces). As the controversy between the Sandinistas and the Catholic Church intensified, the government even banned the broadcast of live Masses over the Church's radio station. Throughout this period, the Sandinistas bombarded Nicaraguans with revolutionary propaganda via television, radio, and the press. Concurrently, bookstores were inundated with material from Cuba and the Soviet bloc, while literature from Western sources dried up.

In response to external pressure and the unanimous demand of all the other political parties, the government announced on July 19 that it would ease censorship. While *La Prensa* subsequently was able to publish many articles which previously would have been forbidden, the government still required prior censorship of all articles and continued to cut several articles every day. When *La Prensa* reported on demonstrations against forced conscription into the Sandinista Army in the northern town of Chinandega, the Sandinistas confiscated the entire *La Prensa* allotment to the region. Government censorship of numerous articles concerning the PLI's decision to withdraw from the campaign forced *La Prensa* not to publish on October 22.

The Sandinistas' abuse of the state-run television system shows how they have exploited their control of the government to benefit the FSLN as a party. Under the Electoral Law, all parties are entitled to equal time on television. The Sandinistas originally proposed that all parties share one hour of air time per week during the campaign; under this formula, each of the ten eligible parties would have been allowed less than one minute of television time per day. Reluctantly, the Sandinistas acceded to the unified demand by all other parties for additional time; the Electoral Law as amended allows each participating party roughly 4½ minutes of air time per day. While an improvement, this concession does not begin to balance the FSLN's access via its highly politicized daily news broadcast (the only news program in the country), as well as numerous special "documentaries" and other "public interest" telecasts prepared by the government.

Television coverage of the various parties' nominations of their candidates illustrates how the Sandinistas have manipulated this system. The non-FSLN parties were mentioned on television only briefly, if at all, and then usually in derogatory terms. In contrast, the Sandinista Television System broadcast live the entire two-hour session of the Sandinista Assembly on July 17 when the FSLN's candidates were named. Interior Minister Tomás Borge, one of the nine members of the National Directorate, delivered the keynote speech, ignoring Article 63 of the Electoral Law which expressly forbids members of the Sandinista armed forces on active duty from engaging in political proselytization. Rene Nuñez, secretary of the National Directorate, then read the names of the FSLN's presidential and vice-presidential candidates and those of each of the ninety candidates to the National Assembly and their alternates. Presidential candidate Daniel Ortega then made a lengthy speech describing the FSLN's platform. In this one program, the Sandinistas used as much air time as the other participating parties were allowed in the entire first month of the campaign. Since technically the campaign had not yet commenced, this television time was not even charged against the Sandinistas' allotment.

The six non-FSLN parties have encountered great obstacles in their efforts to campaign against the FSLN. Although they received state financing under the Electoral Law, they have found it extremely difficult to purchase even minimal supplies of needed campaign materials such as paper, ink, and paint. The mobility of the parties has been restricted by the GRN's gasoline ration system which allocates only twenty gallons per vehicle per month. In contrast, the FSLN suffers no shortage of campaign materials and has blanketed whole neighborhoods with flashy billboards, swaths of red and black paint (the FSLN party colors), and Sandinista leaflets. Government trucks transport party activists, oblivious to the gas rationing. While the registered parties have been hard pressed to obtain even the most basic campaign materials, the FSLN has adorned the major streets of Managua with lighted revolving signboards.

A more serious problem for the registered parties has been harassment of their activists and interference with their campaign activities. The Sandinista army, police, and security forces have frequently detained members of these parties for performing routine campaign activities that are specifically authorized by the Electoral Law. The Sandinista military has drafted the leadership of the local youth chapters of these parties. The Sandinista Defense Committees (CDS), which exercise the quasi-governmental function of issuing ration cards, have denied ration cards to non-FSLN party activists. The CDS and other Sandinista mass organizations have harassed and intimidated the members of these parties and even resorted to physical violence.

Independent Liberal Party (PLI) candidate Virgilio Godoy protested to the Supreme Electoral Council that on the very first day of the campaign, August 1, the Sandinista military detained fifteen youths for distributing PLI propaganda. Godoy noted that his party's secretary general for the Matagalpa department had been violently taken from his home on July 27 simply for having hired a car with loud speakers to urge citizens to register to vote. Elsewhere, Sandinista authorities interrogated two PLI leaders and confiscated their campaign materials. Godoy charged on August 7 that PLI activists in Estelí, Malpaisillo, Nagarote, Jinotega, and León had been victims of attacks by members of the Sandinista army and that there had been a systematic destruction of campaign materials which the party had obtained with great difficulty. In September, PLI again protested to the Supreme Electoral Council the way the electoral process was being carried out, noting both the failure of the government to make sufficient campaign supplies available and the Supreme Electoral Council's failure to prevent FSLN activists from committing campaign abuses. The PLI charged that government-run radio stations were violating the Electoral Law by refusing to carry PLI advertisements and accused the FSLN of using its control of the armed forces and educational institutions to intimidate and indoctrinate the Nicaraguan people.

The Democratic Conservative Party (PCD) has encountered similar problems and has been equally critical of the electoral process. In a letter to the Supreme Electoral Council, the PCD charged that the FSLN usurped government goods and supplies for its political purposes and that it was denying the opposition proper access to the media. Later that month, the Coordinator of the PCD threatened that the party would pull out of the election unless 150 of his party's activists were freed from detention: those listed included the president and national secretary of the PCD youth, two members of the PCD's National Executive Council, and various PCD farm worker leaders. (Subsequently, the government did release some 25 PCD activists.) On October 7, a Sandinista *turba* (mob) armed with sticks, chains, and rocks broke up the ceremonies marking the opening of the PCD's headquarters in Jinotepe, wounding several party members and destroying the party's rented bus. The party coordinator charged that vehicles belonging to the government and the FSLN ferried the *turba* to the PCD's headquarters. While some Sandinista leaders urged their supporters not to resort to violence, the FSLN official organ *Barricada* printed an editorial by Onofre Guevara, an FSLN delegate to the Council of State, justifying the *turba*'s actions; Guevara asserted that the registered parties had provoked this violent reaction by offending the political dignity of the Nicaraguan people with their claims that they offered a genuine alternative to the revolution.

The Popular Social Christian Party (PPSC), technically an ally of the FSLN, also has been critical of the Sandinistas. In a declaration published August 7, the PPSC declared that it had "not found any sign on the part of the ruling party or its organizations that they meant to honor in practice the guarantees they have offered." The PPSC condemned the FSLN's exploitation of its control of the media for its own benefit. The declaration stated that "repressive organisms of the state" had begun to send "shock forces" out to interfere with the campaign process and added that PPSC activists in Matagalpa had been directly threatened by members of the government's state security apparatus.

The Marxist parties running in the election have fared little better. The Nicaraguan Socialist Party (PSN), the FSLN's closest ally, protested in August that party members had had their ration cards revoked by the local Sandinista Defense Committee (CDS) because of their involvement in the political campaign and that four PSN activists had been arrested by Sandinista authorities for distributing campaign materials. The Popular Action Movement—Marxist/Leninist also sent a letter to the Supreme Electoral Council in August protesting Sandinista interference with its campaign activities.

The registered parties have attempted to work together in order to offset the FSLN's dominant position. In early August, a PSN leader disclosed that his party had joined PLI, PPSC, PCD, and the PCDEN in signing a letter to the FSLN which insisted that the minimal conditions for free elections did not exist in Nicaragua and appealed for the lifting of the state of emergency and the reinstatement of civil liberties. The six parties repeatedly met as a group with the FSLN seeking to resolve problems concerning the acquisition of campaign materials and to curb FSLN abuses, but each time the talks broke down when the Sandinistas refused to take corrective action.

As the election date neared, several parties faced the hard choice of continuing to participate in an electoral process which was seriously flawed or pulling out of the campaign. Accordingly, they appealed for a "national summit" meeting of political parties in which the conduct of the electoral process would be a central issue. The first of these meetings was held on October 9, but the Sandinistas steered the discussions away from campaign issues toward the nature of the postelection political environment. Many of the registered parties interpreted this as a transparent attempt to keep them in the elections while doing nothing to address their concerns. On October 20, the Sandinistas announced that at a "national summit" meeting on the same day, a comprehensive agreement had been reached. The following day, however, the PLI decided to withdraw completely from the November 4 election. Other registered parties are considering following the PLI's lead.

The Democratic Center

The four political parties that represent Nicaragua's political spectrum from the center-left to the right are not participating in the Sandinistas' elections. Three of these parties, the Social Christians (PSC), the Social Democrats (PSD), and the Liberal Constitutionalists (PLC), belong to the Nicaraguan Democratic Coordinating Board, Ramiro Sacasa Guerrero *(Coordinadora).* Also members of the Democratic Coordinating Board are two independent labor confederations and six private-sector organizations of businessmen, merchants, farmers, ranchers, and professionals. The Nicaraguan Conservative Party, the restructured mainline faction of the Democratic Conservative Party, works closely with the Democratic Coordinating Board although it is not formally a member.

The parties of the Democratic Coordinating Board differ widely in their political orientation, but they share a common belief in the democratic system and have consistently advocated free and fair elections. On December 24, the Democratic Coordinating Board issued a document entitled *A Step Toward Democracy: Free Elections* which called for elections and listed nine points essential for meaningful elections:

- separation of state and party;
- repeal of laws that violate human rights;
- suspension of the State of Emergency;
- promulgation of an amnesty law;
- respect for freedom of worship;
- respect for freedom of organized labor;
- autonomy of the judicial branch;
- reinstatement of habeas corpus;
- a national dialogue on elections with participation by all sectors, including the armed opposition.

Throughout 1984, the parties of the Democratic Coordinating Board reiterated their desire to participate in fair and honest elections, but they declared that until these nine points were addressed, the conditions for honest elections simply did not exist. In February, they participated in the initial Council of State debate on the Electoral Law and then withdrew when the Sandinista-dominated body repeatedly rejected their proposals. The Democratic Coordinating Board stressed that the state of emergency with its censorship and restrictions on political activity precluded the possibility of an open campaign. Like the other parties, they waited anxiously for the state of emergency to elapse and were disappointed when Daniel Ortega announced on July 19 that it was being extended throughout the campaign period.

On July 20, the Democratic Coordinating Board announced that it would nominate Arturo Cruz as its presidential candidate. Cruz had been one of *Los Doce,* a group of twelve prominent Nicaraguans whose open opposition helped to undermine Somoza's regime. Following the revolution, he had served as president of the Central Bank, a member of the junta, and finally as Nicaraguan ambassador to the United States. Disillusioned by the Sandinistas failure to remain nonaligned and to promote a pluralistic society, Cruz resigned his government post and later participated in the *Rescate* (rescue) effort to restore the revolution to its original democratic course. In announcing Cruz's candidacy, the Democratic Coordinating Board emphasized that it would not register with the Supreme Electoral Council until the proper conditions for free elections existed.

On July 23, Cruz returned to Nicaragua after more than two years in exile. At a news conference the following day, Cruz voiced his support for the Democratic Coordinating Board's nine points and announced that the leaders of the three armed opposition groups had informed him that if the Sandinistas were prepared to create the conditions for free elections, they would lay down their arms. On July 25, the final day of the candidate registration period, the Democratic Coordinating Board requested an extension of the deadline to allow additional time for conditions to improve and leave the door open to elections in which all parties could compete fairly.

Daniel Ortega flatly rejected Cruz's proposals as unacceptable. Ortega vowed that the FSLN would never agree to a dialogue that included the armed opposition. Bayardo Arce announced that, at a meeting of all of Nicaragua's political parties on July 25, he had stated that the FSLN was willing to lift the state of emergency, but only if all the parties signed a declaration to the United States government and the United States Congress expressing a desire for free elections and demanding an end to aggression and the withdrawal of counterrevolutionary forces from their external sanctuaries. Arce downplayed the significance of the Democratic Coordinating Board's refusal to register Cruz. He added that the Democratic Coordinating Board could still participate in the election if it entered into an alliance with one of the registered parties by the August 4 deadline for the formation of coalitions.

On August 2, the president of the National Council of Political Parties, Hugo Mejia, proclaimed that parties that had not registered their candidates, i.e. the Democratic Coordinating Board, were barred from engaging in campaign activities. He warned that if they had not entered into an alliance by August 4, they would lose all their rights under the Political Parties Law, and they would forfeit their seats in the Council of State and in the National Assembly of Political Parties. On August 4, the Supreme Electoral Council extended by one day the period for the formation of alliances.

The Democratic Coordinating Board concluded that the conditions that had led it not to register on July 25 were unchanged. Rather than try to form an alliance with a registered party, it decided to take its message to the people outside the capital. On August 4, Cruz presided over a rally at a movie theater in Matagalpa. A Sandinista *turba* harassed those attending the rally, chanting threats and throwing stones, but Cruz's supporters held their ground. (Democratic Coordinating Board members later disclosed that some who attended the meeting subsequently were denied ration cards by the Sandinista Defense Committees.) The following day, Cruz held a much larger rally at a baseball stadium in Chinandega. Once again, a Sandinista *turba* attempted to disrupt the proceedings, but the crowd of 7,000–10,000 drove them away. On August 6, junta member and FSLN vice-presidential candidate Sergio Ramírez denounced Cruz's two rallies as illegal "aggressive acts" that would not be tolerated. Daniel Ortega labeled Cruz "an emissary of the counterrevolution and of imperialism" and rejected Cruz's proposal for a debate.

On August 7, Interior Minister Tomás Borge, a member of the FSLN National Directorate, summoned several leaders of the Democratic Coordinating Board to his Managua office. Borge informed them that the Sandinistas were willing to reach an understanding and that, although the registration period had passed, the FSLN could arrange to have it reopened. Borge assured the opposition leaders that they would be treated like any other party and warned that the consequences of abstention would be political limbo. Two days later, the Democratic Coordinating Board responded in a communiqué reconfirming that the requisite conditions for free elections still did not exist. The communiqué added that one of the "nine points," that calling for a national dialogue, might be achieved in stages, and that the Democratic Coordinating Board had formed a committee to study the steps that could lead to such an exchange.

In early August, the leaders of the armed opposition groups publicly declared that they would not insist on participating in a national dialogue. On August 15, the Democratic Coordinating Board directed a letter to Daniel Ortega noting that the armed opposition's voluntary withdrawal removed the FSLN's objection to a national dialogue and asking when such talks might begin.

One week later, the National Council of Political Parties formally stripped the three political parties in the Democratic Coordinating Board—the PSC, the PSD, and the PLC—of their legal standing. Council President Mejia declared that these "groups" no longer had the right to hold public meetings or issue public statements in connection with the electoral process. Mejia said that the parties would be allowed to retain their property and their seats on the Council of State.

With the Democratic Coordinating Board's efforts to achieve the conditions for a free election stymied, Cruz went abroad to solicit assistance in breaking the deadlock. In late August and early September, Cruz met with Costa Rican President Luis Alberto Monge, Venezuelan President Jaime Lusinchi, Colombian President Belisario Betancur, and Ecuadorean President Leon Febres-Cordero as well as many other Latin political leaders. President Betancur in particular assumed an active role in attempting to facilitate negotiations between the Sandinistas and Cruz. During these discussions, Cruz redefined the Democratic Coordinating Board's position and listed six essential points:

- full freedom of the press;
- full freedom to hold meetings and rallies;
- full access to voter registration lists and election returns;
- international observation of the elections;
- security of voting places and ability to campaign in military bases;
- postponement of the elections to allow at least ninety days for campaigning.

On September 13, Cruz returned to Nicaragua. The Democratic Coordinating Board leaders planned a large reception, but protested that the Sandinista authorities in several towns prevented busloads of Cruz supporters from traveling to the airport. At a press conference later that day, Cruz expressed his gratification for having been received at so high a level everywhere he went, and he stressed that the Democratic Coordinating Board's position was unchanged: it fervently desired to participate in free and open elections, but it would not register until the Sandinistas created the conditions necessary for free elections. Two days later, Council of State President Carlos Nuñez, one of the members of the FSLN National Directorate, responded by proclaiming that the FSLN would not accept a dialogue, nor would it discuss even one of the Democratic Coordinating Board's points.

Cruz resumed his trips to the interior on September 19, starting with a meeting with 150 political leaders in León. A *turba* composed of hundreds of members of the Sandinista Youth—19th of July—descended on the meeting site, beating drums and chanting Sandinista slogans. For two hours, the *turba* blocked the entrance to the building, threatening those inside. When Cruz and his followers attempted to leave, the Sandinistas pelted them with stones. Cruz himself sustained a head wound. The official version of the incident, as reported in an Interior Ministry communiqué, claimed that the violence was a result of provocations by Cruz and his supporters.

On September 21, Cruz held a meeting in Boaco and was again attacked by a *turba*. As Cruz attempted to leave the restaurant where the meeting was being held, the *turba* stoned his car, breaking the windows. The Sandinista police were present throughout the incident, but they failed to provide Cruz adequate protection.

That same day, the FSLN issued a communiqué stating that it would ask the National Council of Political Parties to formally request the Supreme Electoral Council to reopen the candidate registration period until September 30. Cruz attributed this suddenly flexibility to the efforts of Colombian President Betancur. Cruz stressed that since the election date was only a few weeks off, the Democratic Coordinating

Board would require that the election be postponed so that it could have at least three months to mount its campaign. The FSLN immediately rejected any possibility of postponing the elections.

The next morning, September 22, Cruz attempted to hold a meeting in Masaya. Hundreds of members of the Sandinista Youth and the Sandinista Defense Committees (CDS) armed with sticks and metal pipes marched through the streets near the meeting site, accompanied by a jeep with sound equipment. The Sandinistas' chants drowned out Cruz's speech, and *turba* members began hurling stones at the building where the meeting was taking place. Ultimately, the Interior Ministry was called on to evacuate some of Cruz's supporters from the area. As Cruz attempted to leave, the *turba* stoned the car in which he was riding, smashing the windows and inflicting considerable damage. Once again, the Sandinistas blamed the violence on provocative acts by Cruz.

Three days after the clash in Masaya, the Supreme Electoral Council authorized a new candidate registration period of September 25–October 1. The following day, the Supreme Court ruled that the National Council of Political Parties' decision to strip the parties of the Democratic Coordinating Board of their legal standing had been rendered null and void by the Supreme Electoral Council's action. These decisions made it again legally possible for the opposition parties to register. The Democratic Coordinating Board reiterated that it would not register "out of desperation or anxiety" and would only file its candidates once the conditions necessary for free elections were established. Daniel Ortega retorted that the Democratic Coordinating Board was "the political arm of the counterrevolution" and that its actions were "part of the policy of military aggression against Nicaragua." Ortega categorically refused to consider any delay of the elections.

During the Rio de Janeiro meeting of the Socialist International at the beginning of October, Cruz met with Bayardo Arce in yet another effort to reach an agreement. Arce said that the government would agree to the Democratic Coordinating Board's six demands if it would register for the election and then call on the armed opposition groups to agree to a cease-fire. If the armed opposition groups complied, the FSLN would postpone elections until January 13. If peace were not restored by October 25, the Democratic Coordinating Board could withdraw from the electoral process. Cruz accepted these terms, subject to the approval of the full Democratic Coordinating Board in Managua. At this point, however, Arce broke off the negotiations and publicly rejected any further discussion; he insisted that the elections would take place as scheduled on November 4. When Cruz returned to Managua on October 12, the Democratic Coordinating Board released a communiqué clarifying that all of its component organizations were prepared to accept the agreement which had been outlined in Rio de Janeiro.

Conclusion

If, as now seems likely, the parties representing Nicaragua's political spectrum from the center-left to the right are not on the ballot, it will be because, despite their strong and sincere efforts, they could not obtain the conditions that would allow a genuinely free and competitive election. The most significant of the non-Marxist parties which registered to run in the election, the PLI, has withdrawn for precisely the same reason. On November 4, Nicaraguan voters will have to make their choice among: the FSLN; three Communist parties of different shadings (the PSN, PCDEN, and the MAP-ML); a party of the democratic left which is allied with the FSLN (the PPSC); and a conservative party faction (PCD) which has benefited from FSLN favoritism. By election day, even this list may have become shorter if additional parties pull out. For many Nicaraguans, the Sandinista elections will offer no real choice at all. On November 4, the promise of a free election which the Sandinistas made to the Nicaraguan people and the world before they seized power will remain unfulfilled.

The United States government has consistently been a proponent of the democratic process in Nicaragua, as elsewhere in Central America. The U.S. government supports the demands of the opposition parties that the elections be free and fair, and it sympathizes with their decision not to participate unless the Sandinistas offer the necessary guarantees.

*15. The Electoral Process in Nicaragua: Domestic and International Influences**

By the Latin American Studies Association

The Latin American Studies Association (LASA) is the professional society for North American faculty members and researchers specializing in Latin America.

For the first time in LASA's history an official LASA delegation was sent, in 1984, to observe an election in Latin America. The Executive Council believed that in light of the unusual international circumstances surrounding this particular election, and the paucity of information from academic (rather than journalistic and governmental) sources concerning these matters that was available to LASA members and to the general public in the United States, a LASA-sponsored fact-finding mission could perform a valuable service. Accordingly, the delegation was charged with conducting a wide-ranging investigation of the Nicaraguan electoral process and the various political and economic forces—both domestic and international—that impinged upon it. The delegation was to write a detailed report based on its observations, interviews, and documentary research, for publication as quickly as possible in the *LASA Forum*, with wide dissemination of the findings in a variety of formats to public officials and other non-academic groups.

---

*Excerpts from *The Electoral Process in Nicaragua: Domestic and International Influences. The Report of the Latin American Studies Association Delegation to Observe the Nicaraguan General Election of November 4, 1984*. (Published November 19, 1984.)

The delegation to Nicaragua included the LASA President-elect and one former President, several members of the LASA Executive Council, several members of the LASA Task Force on Scholarly Relations with Nicaragua, and other members of the Association with special expertise on Central America. Half of the delegation members had had substantial field research experience in Nicaragua. In forming the delegation, special care was also taken to insure that a wide range of views regarding the Nicaraguan Revolution were represented.

The members of the LASA delegation received credentials from the Supreme Electoral Council of Nicaragua as official international election observers, but we were not guests of the Nicaraguan government. All expenses incurred by delegation members were covered by themselves personally, their home institutions, or by LASA. This was deemed essential to maintain the delegation's independence and neutrality. . . .

We determined our own itinerary and spoke with anyone whom we chose to approach (as well as numerous people who spontaneously approached us). During the last days of the electoral campaign and on election day, we travelled throughout the city of Managua and to provincial cities (Masaya, Matagalpa, Granada) and smaller localities (e.g., an agricultural cooperative near Matagalpa). We visited two war zones (Matagalpa, Puerto Cabezas) where counterrevolutionary forces (the "*contras*") are active.

The delegation sought information from representatives of all of the key political and economic actors in Nicaragua today, as well as "grass-roots" organizers and development practitioners. We conducted detailed (one- or two-hour) interviews with a total of 45 "key informants," including national and regional leaders of all of the political parties participating in the November 4 elections and two of the parties that boycotted or withdrew from the election.

The Domestic Context of the Election

The general elections held in Nicaragua on November 4, 1984, were the first since the overthrow of Anastasio Somoza Debayle on July 19, 1979. The intention to hold elections was part of the platform of the Sandinista National Liberation Front even before Somoza's fall. On July 20, 1979, the day after the Sandinistas took power, the government junta promulgated a "Fundamental Statute" which specified that "to the extent that the conditions of national reconstruction permit it, general elections will be held for the constitution of a National Assembly . . . in accordance with the Electoral Law which shall be promulgated at an opportune time." In a speech on August 23, 1980, celebrating the end of the FSLN government's national literacy campaign, Comandante Daniel Ortega pledged that elections would take place within five years (i.e., sometime in 1985), with the formulation of electoral laws and other preparatory activities in 1983.

Discussion of various drafts of a law on political parties commenced in March, 1981. The debate on this law continued into 1982 but was suspended in March of that year, when the ruling Junta declared a state of emergency in response to an upsurge in acts of sabotage and other counterrevolutionary activity financed by the U.S. Government. (In December, 1981, President Reagan approved an initial expenditure of $19 million for the "secret war" against the FSLN government.) The Political Parties Law was finally approved by the Council of State on August 17, 1983.

On February 21, 1984, the Government Junta issued Decree No. 1400 which set November 4, 1984, as the date for elections. Thus the 1984 elections had been in the making for more than five years, and the Sandinistas had essentially adhered to their own publicly announced schedule for holding them. Yet the issue of scheduling and guaranteeing the freedom of these elections has increasingly become a focus of controversy for the FSLN government, on both the domestic and the international front.

HISTORICAL BACKGROUND

The 1984 elections represent a major departure in Nicaragua's political history. The Nicaraguan people effectively have had no democratic tradition. In fact, the country had a tradition of non-democratic, militarized politics with rampant human rights violations. While the Nicaraguan people have long desired democratic rule, for most of them the 1984 electoral process was their first experience with participatory democracy.

In this century the most constant feature of Nicaragua's electoral history was the fact that the incumbent party was almost never voted out of office. Up to 1932, the changes from Liberal to Conservative party governments (and vice versa) were usually accomplished by armed revolt, because electoral manipulation assured the party in office more votes than its competitor. Fraudulent vote counting was the standard practice. The buying of votes was another method commonly used to insure reelection, especially during the Somoza years. The Somozas routinely bought votes for their Liberal Party with allotments of rum and food. (This explains Article 45-b of the 1984 electoral law, which prohibits the distribution of basic foodstuffs, drugs, and alcoholic beverages during the electoral campaign "for purposes of [political party] propaganda.") Still another means used by incumbent parties to perpetuate themselves in power was the frequent rewriting of the constitution or electoral laws. The Somoza family relied on such measures prior to several different elections, when existing laws would have otherwise prevented their reelection.

There were exceptions to this pattern. The presidential elections of 1928 and 1932, organized and supervised by the United States, are generally accepted as having been free of fraudulent vote counting, but even then the leading contender was not permitted to run. The United States had maintained an occupying military force in Nicaragua almost without interruption since 1912, and during this period four elections were organized and conducted under U.S. military supervision, including the posting of a U.S. Marine at every polling place.

In fact, one of the hallmarks of Nicaraguan electoral politics in this century is the central role played by the U.S. government. Beginning with its participation in the ouster of Jose Santos Zelaya in 1909, the United States has participated actively in determining who would fill the presidency. During the 1909–1933 period Nicaraguan presidential candidates actively sought U.S. endorsement in order to insure their success. Anastasio Somoza García—the first of three Somozas to rule Nicaragua—was especially successful in consolidating his political position through U.S. endorsement, first as head of the National Guard and then as founder of a political dynasty that lasted until 1979. For most Nicaraguans, therefore, elections prior to the present year meant little more than automatic ratification of candidates chosen by the incumbent party and the U.S. government.

THE DOMESTIC POLITICAL CONTENDERS

The main contender in the Nicaraguan elections of 1984 was, of course, the incumbent party, the FSLN. The elections were, inevitably, a referendum on the performance of the FSLN-dominated government of the previous five years, as well as an opportunity for opposition parties to define more sharply their differences with the FSLN and to demonstrate that there was a mass constituency for their ideas.

The party used the five years following Somoza's removal to build up its base of support throughout the country, especially through the numerous mass organizations that are linked to it. In addition to these mass organizations (CDSs, youth and women's groups, etc.), the FSLN as a political party has established thousands of community or neighborhood-level organizing committees *(comités de base)* through which its campaign and other mobilizing activities are conducted.

This nationwide organizational infrastructure gives the FSLN a powerful advantage over all other political parties. In the Matagalpa region, for example, where 200 FSLN *comités de base* were functioning during the 1984 electoral campaign, the FSLN claimed to have 3,000 FSLN militants working in the campaign. According to the regional FSLN leader in Matagalpa, these party workers visited 15,000 homes, reaching an estimated 64,000 people, in the region during the three months preceding the 1984 elections. While the vast majority of the FSLN's activists are volunteers, the party's regional committees are staffed by full-time professional organizers. There is no other political party or movement in Nicaragua that can even begin to approach the FSLN in terms of organizational breadth and capacity to mobilize people.

As in other Latin American political systems with a dominant (''hegemonic''), government-sponsored party, there is a high degree of fusion between the FSLN as a political party and the post-Somoza state in Nicaragua. For example, we were told that most FSLN members are also leaders of mass organizations (youth groups, labor unions, CDSs, etc.) which are not formally part of the FSLN structure. In fact, to become an FSLN member, one must have a record of service in one of the mass organizations and be nominated for FSLN membership by one of them. In addition, FSLN militants who serve as government officials give the party *de facto* control over the public bureaucracy, the military, and police forces. All of this is true of the government party in countries like Mexico, of course, and it goes largely unchallenged both at home and abroad. However the ''official'' party-state fusion evident in Nicaragua was one of the key issues in the 1984 elections, and it was seized upon by the United States and other foreign critics of the Sandinistas as evidence of egregious "abuse of incumbency" which allegedly made it impossible for legitimate elections to be held.

In addition to the FSLN, there were 11 other political parties legally registered in Nicaragua during 1984. Six of these opposition parties registered candidates to stand for election (although one of these, the Independent Liberal Party, PLI, later tried to withdraw from the election); three parties affiliated with the Democratic Coordinating Committee ("La Coordinadora") refused to register candidates for the election; and two other parties applied too late to register candidates, according to the Supreme Electoral Council.

Among the opposition parties that contested the elections, three could be considered to the right of the FSLN ideologically and programmatically, and three to the left. Parties to the right included:

Democratic Conservative Party (PCD), with Clemente Guido as its presidential candidate. Founded in 1979, the PCD has roots in the Conservative party tradition of Nicaragua. It is regarded by many as the "pro-Sandinista" wing or faction of the Conservative movement; one of its leaders, Rafael Córdoba Rivas, is a member of the ruling Sandinista junta. The PCD has positioned itself as a center-right party, arguing for negotiations with the *contras,* separation of the FSLN party from the state, and a complete lifting of the emergency decrees imposed in March, 1982. At the PCD's October 28 party convention there seemed to be significant support for withdrawal from the November 4 elections, but presidential candidate Guido dissolved the meeting before any vote was taken.

Independent Liberal Party (PLI), with Virgilio Godoy as presidential candidate. The PLI was founded in 1944, to challenge the dominance of the Somozas within the Liberal Party organization, and its adherents participated actively in the armed struggle to remove Anastasio Somoza Debayle. The PLI has a substantial popular base. Prior to the November 4 elections it was regarded as the only party, other than the FSLN, with a nationwide organization; and until its presidential candidate withdrew from the contest the PLI was generally expected to finish second in the balloting. Affiliated with the Liberal International, the PLI originally formed part of the Popular Revolutionary Front, the coalition of parties that were in basic agreement about the revolutionary process during the first four years of Sandinista rule. The PLI's current leader, Virgilio Godoy, served as Labor Minister in the Sandinista government until February, 1984. When Godoy resigned from the cabinet (still on good terms with the FSLN leadership, by his own report), the PLI withdrew from the "Revolutionary Front" alliance and adopted a more conservative position vis-à-vis the Sandinistas' revolutionary *proyecto.* The PLI still argues for social transformation, but with greater moderation. At least some of its leaders remain critical of private capitalists (both domestic and foreign) and see the parties affiliated with the "Coordinadora" as being tied too closely to U.S. interests. On October 21, Virgilio Godoy announced that he and his party would not be participating in the November 4 election because "minimum conditions" for free elections did not exist.

Popular Social Christian Party (PPSC), with Mauricio Díaz Dávila as presidential candidate. The PPSC developed from a split in the Social Christian Party (PSC) in 1976. Like the PLI, it was a member of the Popular Revolutionary Front from the Front's creation in 1980; unlike the PLI, it has remained in basic agreement with the Sandinistas' revolutionary *proyecto*. The PPSC characterizes itself as the "Christian Democrats of the left," while the Parent Social Christian Party represents "Christian Democrats of the right." Its program stresses "democratic socialism," but differs strongly with the FSLN in two key areas: relations between the Catholic Church and the state, and Sandinista foreign policy. The PPSC criticizes the FSLN for having acrimonious relations with the Church hierarchy, and it considers FSLN foreign policy to be aligned too closely with the Soviet Union. The PPSC leadership believes that unjust international criticism—especially from the United States—has discredited the November 4 elections and "ruined" them as a device for reducing external pressure on the Nicaraguan revolution; therefore, the party favors a new, externally legitimating election for seats in the National Assembly, to be held within a year or two.

The opposition participating in the November 4 elections also included three parties that stand to the left of the FSLN:

Nicaraguan Socialist Party (PSN), with longtime trade union leader Domingo Sánchez as its presidential candidate. The PSN is the oldest leftist party in Nicaragua, having been founded in 1944. It is aligned with and has the official recognition of the USSR. Prior to 1979 it was somewhat discredited for having collaborated with the Somoza government during the 1940s. During the war against Somoza in the 1970s, the PSN criticized the FSLN as being "adventurist," but after Somoza's ouster it joined the Popular Revolutionary Front. The PSN's social base is concentrated in the urban working class.

Nicaraguan Communist Party (PCdeN), with Allan Zambrana Salmerón as presidential candidate. The PCdeN is a traditional Latin American communist party, aligned with the Soviet Union although not recognized by it. A left-wing breakaway from the Nicaraguan Socialist Party in 1971, the PCdeN regards the FSLN as a party of petty-bourgeois reformers. The PCdeN initially opposed the idea of holding elections this year, arguing that they were premature (given the need for a "*mano dura*" to deepen the revolutionary process) and an unnecessary concession to external forces, including the "capitalist" Contadora nations. Eventually the party decided to participate in the elections because, as one of its leaders told our delegation, "We approve of some of the things that the FSLN government is doing, and we didn't want to give aid and comfort to the right, whose strategy is abstentionism and sabotage of the electoral process."

Marxist-Leninist Popular Action Movement (MAP-ML), with Isidoro Téllez as presidential candidate. By far the smallest of the parties contesting the November 4 elections, the MAP-ML also stands the farthest to the left of the FSLN. Like the PCdeN, the MAPistas consider the FSLN to be a bourgeois party. They oppose granting any political role to the Nicaraguan business community, and consider the elections and the Contadora agreement to be concessions to domestic reactionary interests and to the United States. They also oppose any accommodation with the Catholic Church and call for an officially "atheistic" state. The MAP-ML is ridiculed by the FSLN for taking such unrealistic positions "in a Catholic, Christian country like this," as FSLN vice-presidential candidate Sergio Ramírez told our delegation. Leaders of the MAP-ML were jailed by the Sandinistas in 1980 when they pressed too hard for an acceleration of the revolutionary process. The MAP-ML today is the Nicaraguan equivalent of the MIR movement in Chile under Allende.

Throughout the 1984 electoral campaign in Nicaragua, international attention focused not on the participating opposition parties just described, but upon the abstentionist opposition, led by Arturo Cruz. The abstentionist forces included several small political parties (three legally registered, one with no legal status), the Superior Council of Private Enterprise (COSEP), much of the Catholic Church hierarchy, the newspaper *La Prensa,* and two small trade union federations. In 1984 the four most conservative opposition parties (the Social Christian Party, PSC, the Liberal Constitutionalist Party, PLC; the Social Democratic Party, PSD; the Nicaraguan Conservative Party, PCN—not legally recognized as a party) joined with COSEP and the two above-mentioned labor federations to form the "Ramiro Sacasa Democratic Coordinating Committee," popularly known as "La Coordinadora." The Social Christian Party, affiliated with the international Christian Democratic movement, is the oldest (founded in 1957) and largest of the four parties belonging to the Coordinadora; but its influence within the coalition is generally believed to be second to that of COSEP, the business council.

The Social Democratic Party (PSD), founded in 1979, is the vehicle of Pedro Joaquín Chamorro, co-director of *La Prensa,* the newspaper that has served as the organ for both the PSD and the Coordinadora generally. Our delegation found *La Prensa* to be a virulently partisan newspaper, intensely opposed to the FSLN government and to the holding of the 1984 elections, and supportive of Reagan Administration policy toward Nicaragua. (The other two daily newspapers that circulate in Managua, *Barricada* and *Nuevo Diario,* are equally ardent partisans of the FSLN government.)

While the Catholic Church hierarchy did not formally participate in the activities of the Coordinadora, the Church's principal leaders—Archbishop Miguel Obando y Bravo and Bishop Pablo Antonio Vega—strongly supported the positions taken by the Coordinadora, and their views were extensively reported by *La Prensa.* In early August, *The New York Times* reported that Archbishop Obando y Bravo, in a meeting with U.S. businessmen, acknowledged that he and his diocese had been actively involved in efforts to secure the removal of the FSLN government. During 1984, public statements by Church leaders criticized the military draft, questioned the legitimacy of the FSLN government, and called for direct negotiations between the government and the *contras*—an idea strongly resisted by the Sandinistas.

Shortly after the FSLN came to power, the Church hierarchy published a pastoral letter endorsing a transition to socialism in Nicaragua, so long as individual rights were preserved. The bishops, particularly Archbishop Obando y Bravo, had been prominent in the opposition to Somoza. Despite this initial appearance of harmony between the Church and the FSLN, serious tensions developed in subsequent years. In retrospect, it seems that Church leaders like Obando y Bravo were anti-Somoza, but never accepted the *proyecto politico* of the FSLN. The bishops have viewed the Sandinistas' promotion of mass organizations as an ominous step toward totalitarianism. They have also shown growing concern over the fate of private education, despite the fact that 50 percent of the country's secondary schools remain private (mostly church-run). The hierarchy now sees the Marxist, mass-mobilization elements of the Sandinista revolution as a threat both to individual liberty of conscience and to the institutional integrity of the Church. As a member of an independent religious order reminded our delegation, "There is no historical precedent for a collaborative, conciliatory relationship between a leftist, revolutionary state and the Catholic Church, and there is skepticism that Nicaragua will produce such an innovation. It is easier to accept the thesis that they will be incompatible, sooner or later."

But the Catholic Church in Nicaragua is a complex institution composed of ideologically diverse groups and functioning at more than one level. Groups more closely associated with the grassroots level of the Church—the "Christian Base Communities" and the independent religious orders such as Maryknoll and the Jesuits—work actively in support of government programs. Priests serving in the Sandinista government have become identified with the grassroots or "popular Church," which is viewed by the hierarchy as a direct threat to its authority. Sandinista leaders, on the other hand, accuse the Church hierarchy of utilizing religious symbolism and abusing its religious authority for purely political purposes (e.g., promoting the candidates and positions of the Coordinadora).

COSEP, the prime mover in the abstentionist opposition during 1984, represents many of Nicaragua's largest business firms. It is not necessarily representative of the private sector as a whole, half of which consists of small and medium-sized producers. At one point in the struggle against Somoza, COSEP represented virtually all of the businessmen and farmers who were not tied to the Somoza family. It objected to the Somozas' efforts to monopolize business opportunities and profits. After the Sandinistas took power, COSEP was awarded five seats in the Council of State, but it withdrew its representatives in November, 1980, and has not participated since that time. Since December, 1983, COSEP has exerted its political influence primarily through the Coordinadora. Within the Coordinadora, it has strongly opposed participation in the electoral process; opposed any accommodation between the FSLN government and its domestic opposition; and aligned itself with the *contras* and external forces seeking the removal of the Sandinista regime. COSEP's leadership blames the country's economic problems on Sandinista mismanagement, claiming that the economy was in decent shape even through the war against Somoza and that production did not collapse until the FSLN began to socialize the economy and undermine private business confidence.

The Sandinistas respond that, since the beginning of their rule, they have shown a willingness to compromise with private sector interests in order to maintain a functioning mixed economy. Subsidized loans, access to scarce foreign exchange and voluntary labor have been among the incentives offered to the private sector to enhance production levels and profits. Nationalization of property has been limited to clearly defined areas of the economy (primarily banking, insurance, foreign commerce, mining, and part of the agricultural sector), and the process has not been implemented arbitrarily.

The Sandinista leaders and advisors interviewed by our delegation uniformly asserted that the FSLN government is committed to the survival of the mixed economy, as a matter of internal and geopolitical necessity, and because it is so deeply ingrained in Nicaraguan society ("almost a folkloric thing," as Comandante Jaime Wheelock put it). They emphasized that in what Wheelock characterized as "the second phase of the Revolution, beginning in January, 1985," one of the key objectives of government policy will be to provide incentives and security to the private sector.

Nevertheless, resistance to the FSLN government from the private sector continues to harden. Many businessmen argue that they have no incentive to invest, since in their view, the socialization of the economy is likely to continue. The fundamental source of tension seems to be the private sector's lack of influence over public policymaking, and the disparity between their still formidable economic power (60 percent of the economy is still in private hands) and their much diminished political influence.

The government now negotiates with private producers on a sectoral basis (as groups of coffee producers, cotton producers, etc.), rather than as members of COSEP, which the Sandinistas view as primarily a political action group. The FSLN government has also stepped up capital investment by the public sector (now 22 percent of the national budget vs. about 5 percent under Somoza), to compensate for lack of investment by private businesses. Three-quarters of new investment in productive facilities now comes from the public sector.

ELECTION DAY OBSERVATIONS AND RESULTS

The members of our delegation observed the voting process at more than thirty different polling places, chosen at random, in five different localities (the cities of Managua, Granada, and Masaya; the town of Nindirí; and a rural community, El Crucero). We were able to observe freely at all the polling places that we visited, and at most of them we also talked with election officials and poll-watchers.

The voting that we observed was very orderly, with no sense of commotion nor tension. Everyone, however, appeared to be taking the process very seriously. There was no cheerleading, no campaigning near polling places, no political materials being distributed. All party propaganda had been scrupulously removed or painted over in the vicinity of polling places. All soldiers who approached the polls to vote were unarmed or handed over their arms before entering the lines of voters. Only the electoral police responsible for security at each polling place were armed. Polling places functioned in an extremely formal, bureaucratic manner. We observed no evidence of irregularities in the voting process, at any of the polling places visited.

At most polling places, only poll-watchers representing the FSLN were present, although a few from other parties (PCD, PSN) were also observed, and we were told at several polling places that "circulating" opposition party poll-watchers had spent some time at those places. Given their manpower constraints, some opposition parties apparently relied upon rotating poll-watchers who did not attach themselves to any particular polling place for the entire day.

In some parts of the country, voting was interrupted or prevented by the presence of the *contras*. According to CSE President Mariano Fiallos, 11 polling places in the northern regions could not function because of *contra* activities. Two polling places were attacked by the *contras*, and an electoral policeman was killed in one of these mortar attacks. Several days before, *contra* leaders had announced a cease-fire for election day; but apparently some rebel units did not get the word, or the cease-fire was not, in fact, observed.

Voter turnout was heavy. By the opening of the polls at 7:00 a.m., over 100 people—10 percent of the total registered voters in the precinct—were lined up to vote in one low-income neighborhood of Managua that we visited. Lines there and elsewhere had begun to form at 4:00 a.m. In general, we observed heavier turnout and more enthusiasm among voters in low-income areas than in more affluent neighborhoods. Throughout election day, the Supreme Electoral Council preempted all programming on all of the country's radio stations. The message "Your vote is secret, your vote decides" was broadcast continuously, alternating with popular music and explanations of voting procedures.

Not surprisingly, the highest rates of abstention were in areas most affected by the war. While not quite meeting the FSLN government's own expectations, the rate of participation in Nicaragua's November 4 elections compares very favorably with the rates achieved in 11 other recent Latin American elections, as well as the 1984 U.S. presidential election.

Sandinista officials had stressed the need for a high turnout, to demonstrate the validity of the electoral process and to "send a message to Washington." "Turnout is the most important thing," Comandante Jaime Wheelock told our delegation the day before the election. "It doesn't matter how the vote is divided." Some FSLN leaders had predicted that their party would receive 80 percent of the votes. In fact, the FSLN received 67 percent; 29 percent was divided among three opposition parties to the right of the FSLN (the PCD, PLI, and PPSC); and less than 4 percent was divided among three parties to the left of the FSLN (PCdeN, PSN, and MAP-ML). The opposition parties together won 35 seats in the National Assembly (36.5 percent), including six seats for their losing presidential candidates. The detailed breakdown of votes won by each party is shown in the table on page 83. Invalid ballots comprised only 6.1 percent of the total votes cast. These include completely unmarked (blank) ballots, ballots on which more than one party or presidential candidate had been selected, and ballots improperly marked or spoiled in some other way. Before the election some anti-Sandinista voters had said that they would cast a protest vote by defacing their ballots or submitting blank ballots. But even if 100 percent of the invalid ballots tallied in the November 4 election were considered votes against the FSLN, a large protest vote did not materialize.

Election Results by Political Party

Party	Number of Votes (Presidential)	% of Valid Votes Cast	Seats Won in Assembly
FSLN	735,967	67.0%	61
PCD	154,327	14.0	14
PLI	105,560	9.6	9
PPSC	61,199	5.6	6
PCdeN	16,034	1.5	2
PSN	14,494	1.3	2
MAP-ML	11,352	1.0	2
(null)	71,209	—	
Total	1,170,142	100.0	96

Interpretations of the election results will vary. Critics of the Sandinistas will claim that the FSLN's "poor" showing—"only" two out of three Nicaraguans voted for the Frente—demonstrates its weakness, even in the face of "token" opposition. Could the FSLN have polled even a bare majority, they will ask, if the "real" opposition had run? Defenders of the FSLN will interpret the results as evidence not only of the FSLN's strength—despite the country's severe economic difficulties and the FSLN's identification with unpopular policies like conscription—but of the free and competitive character of the elections. A 33-percent share of the vote going to opposition parties, in their view, represents meaningful opposition, which the FSLN government had the political courage to recognize through a clean vote count and accurate reporting of results.

We find greater merit in this second view of the results. Prior to the election, a Nicaraguan social scientist had expressed to us his concern that the credibility of the elections would be diminished by the inability of the combined opposition parties to garner more than 20–25 percent of the vote, due to their lack of an attractive alternative program and poor organization. His concerns proved unfounded. However, the Independent Liberal Party's share of the November 4 vote was probably diminished to some extent by the confusion surrounding the attempt of its presidential candidate, Virgilio Godoy, to take the party out of the elections, just two weeks before election day. Since the ballots had already been printed and distributed by that time, Godoy's attempt to have the names of himself and other PLI candidates withdrawn from the ballot was disallowed by the CSE. Therefore, the PLI was among the seven choices offered to voters on November 4. All ballots marked for the PLI were recognized and counted by election officials as valid votes.

As to the potential strength of what FSLN critics term the "real" opposition—i.e., the parties affiliated with the Coordinadora—any assessment must be highly speculative. There were no pre-election political opinion polls to demonstrate the relative strength of opposition parties. However, there is no evidence that the Coordinadora parties possessed a mass base comparable to that of such parties as the PLI and the PCD, which were tested in the November 4 election. Even if the Coordinadora alliance had participated and received 15 percent of the votes—more than any of the opposition parties that actually competed in the election—the FSLN would still have won a majority.

What the results did demonstrate is that the opposition parties continue to command the loyalty of a significant portion of the population, and that in the unlikely event that they choose to run against the FSLN as a united front, the election could be a close contest. Despite its much-discussed "coercive" capabilities, the FSLN garnered 63 percent of the total votes cast and 67 percent of the valid votes. This is a far cry from a totalitarian political system that has frozen out all legitimate opposition—the kind of regime that some U.S. officials profess to see in Nicaragua today. It is also far removed from the Cuban system, which in the last quarter-century has never come close to having the kind of competitive elections that Nicaragua had on November 4.

Without question, the November 4 election was the cleanest held in Nicaragua since 1928, when U.S. marines were organizing and supervising the balloting. The *New York Times'* correspondent, Stephen Kinzer, reported on November 6: "Representatives of several parties and their supporters had reported irregularities at various polling places, but none produced serious evidence of large-scale fraud." The *Miami Herald*'s reporter on the scene, Juan Tamayo, observed on election day: "Though some people said that they felt pressured by the Sandinistas to vote, most said they were voting for the first time in their lives because they perceived the balloting as clean. 'Under Somoza you voted once, and someone else voted two more times in your name,' said Manuel Antonio González, 67, a carpenter in a poor Managua barrio. 'These elections have a different air.' "

La Prensa, the FSLN government's most vociferous media critic, could come up with only two reports of alleged irregularities, both in Managua: At polling place No. 451, 34 votes for the PLI allegedly were recorded by precinct-level officials, but at higher levels the PLI tally for this precinct was allegedly reduced first to 33 votes and finally to 23 votes. At polling place No. 262, a mentally ill person allegedly voted, with the assistance of another person. The rather unlikely (for the conservative *La Prensa*) source for both of these uncorroborated reports was a poll-watcher representing the Nicaraguan Socialist Party (PSN). As of the close of business on November 7, not a single formal complaint about voting or vote count irregularities had been presented at the Supreme Electoral Council, by any party. Spokesmen for several of the participating opposition parties attested to the cleanness of the elections. "It was an honorable process," a PPSC representative told *The New York Times* (November 6, 1984). "We received the vote we expected," he added.

Issues Raised by the Election

SCOPE OF THE ELECTORAL CHOICE

One of the most controversial aspects of the Nicaraguan elections of 1984 was the range of choices available to the voter. The range-of-choices question is separable from the issues of competitiveness and "free access" to campaign media (and ultimately to the voter), which also figured prominently in the debate over the Nicaraguan elections. It should also be disaggregated into two component issues: (1) Why did some opposition parties abstain from the elections? (2) How did their abstention affect the range of alternatives (programmatic, ideological, etc.) presented on the ballot?

External critics of the Nicaraguan electoral process have argued that, because legitimate opposition groups (especially Arturo Cruz and his Coordinadora coalition) were *excluded* from the process, the elections were illegitimate and uncompetitive. However, the facts simply do not support this notion of "exclusion." No major political tendency in Nicaragua was denied access to the electoral process in 1984.

The only exception to this generalization was the armed counterrevolutionaries *(contras)* who have been trying for three years to topple the Sandinista government by force. The estimated 14,000 *contras* were excluded, at the insistence of the FSLN, from direct participation in the elections and in the National Dialogue that began in October, 1984. We know of no election in Latin America (or elsewhere) in which groups advocating the violent overthrow of an incumbent government have themselves been incorporated into the electoral process, particularly when these groups have been openly supported by a foreign power. The *contras* nevertheless had a voice in the 1984 election campaign. Two of the Coordinadora-affiliated parties, the PSD and the PLC, supported their inclusion in the elections. And while denying that they represented the *contras,* Arturo Cruz and the Coordinadora seemed to endorse and promote their cause, both within Nicaragua and abroad. For example, after a one-hour meeting with U.S. Secretary of State George Shultz in Washington on October 30, Cruz emerged to tell reporters that "the *contras* are our esteemed fellow citizens who chose the route of war."

As far as legally recognized political parties are concerned, the only ones that did not appear on the ballot on November 4 were absent by their own choice, *not* because of government exclusion. This is an uncontroversial point, at least in Nicaragua. Controversy arises, however, over the motivations of the parties which chose to abstain. Determining motivations is necessarily a delicate issue for foreign observers and must be approached with some caution and respect for the internal dynamics of Nicaraguan politics. Nevertheless, it was possible for our delegation to reach some conclusions regarding the non-participation of the Coordinadora group, whose absence from the elections caused the greatest concern among most observers in the United States.

The following chronology of events is important to an understanding of the Coordinadora's behavior:

December, 1983: After the FSLN government announces that elections would take place, as promised in 1979 and 1980, the Coordinadora publishes a list of nine points, characterized as requirements for "authentic elections." Several of these demands address conditions for free elections: abolition of press censorship, access to state-owned mass media, and suspension of the emergency restrictions on freedom of assembly, political mobilization, and union activity which had been imposed by the government in March, 1982. But other demands call for major changes in the political system and reorientation of the FSLN government's policies, *before* the elections—i.e., as a condition for the Coordinadora's participation in the electoral process. The proposed changes include separation of the FSLN party from the state (especially the armed forces, the police, state-run television stations, and various mass organizations), repeal of certain laws providing for nationalization of private property, and direct negotiations between the FSLN government and representatives of the *contras*.

July 21, 1984: The Coordinadora parties name Arturo Cruz as their presidential candidate for the 1984 elections. Adán Fletes, who had already been nominated by one of the Coordinadora parties (the PSC) as its presidential candidate, steps aside and becomes Cruz's vice-presidential running mate. At this time, Cruz is still in Washington, D.C., where he is an officer of the Inter-American Development Bank. Neither Cruz nor Fletes has yet been registered by the Coordinadora as candidates to stand for election in November.

July 22, 1984: Arturo Cruz arrives in Nicaragua, as presidential candidate of the Coordinadora. He warns that he and the Coordinadora will abstain from the elections unless the FSLN government complies with the Coordinadora's "nine points" of December, 1983, and emphasizes the demand for inclusion of the *contra* leaders in the national political dialogue as the Coordinadora's "basic condition" for participation.

July 25, 1984: Cruz announces, in Managua, that the Coordinadora will boycott the 1984 elections, but that he will continue to campaign as if he had registered as an official candidate.

July 25–August 5, 1984: Cruz and the Coordinadora hold a series of campaign rallies, in Managua, Masaya, León, Chinandega, and Matagalpa. At several of these rallies there are serious disturbances involving both Cruz's supporters and FSLN militants.

August 1, 1984: The electoral campaign officially begins.

Late September, 1984: The FSLN asks the Supreme Electoral Council to extend the period for registration of candidates (the previous deadline was July 25), and reopens negotiations with Arturo Cruz and the Coordinadora, using Colombian President Belisario Betancur as mediator.

September 30–October 2, 1984: In Rio de Janeiro, at a meeting of the Socialist International, negotiations between Cruz and the FSLN (represented by Bayardo Arce) continue, with Willy Brandt serving as mediator. A provisional agreement is reached, but cannot be finalized, with each side blaming the other for blocking final approval. The FSLN government announces that the November 4 elections will be held on schedule.

November 2, 1984: Electoral campaign officially ends.

November 3, 1984: On election eve, Arturo Cruz returns to Nicaragua from Washington. In arrival remarks to the press, he pronounces the November 4 election "totally ridiculous and illegitimate . . . a farce."

Several observations can be made about this chain of events. First, there is no hard evidence that Arturo Cruz and the Coordinadora (at least the dominant elements within that coalition) ever intended to participate in elections this year or next, regardless of whether their conditions for participation were met by the Sandinistas. There is, in fact, circumstantial evidence that a decision to boycott the elections was made quite early (December, 1983, when the "nine points" were issued), and subsequent public statements notwithstanding, that decision was never seriously reconsidered. This was the conclusion drawn by a senior U.S. diplomat in Central America who was interviewed by our delegation:

> When the Coordinadora issued their nine-point statement [in December, 1983], the content of that statement showed that they had already decided not to participate. These were things that the Sandinistas would never accept. . . . Cruz himself wasn't even on the scene at that point.

In fact, the Sandinistas did accept many of the Coordinadora's "nine points," particularly those having to do with creating appropriate conditions for free elections. Most of the restrictions on political activity imposed in March, 1982, when a state of emergency was declared to deal with counterrevolutionary activities were lifted at the beginning of the electoral campaign, in early August. There was a notable relaxation of press censorship, except for military matters and some economic issues (e.g., shortages of basic goods). However, the Sandinistas did not budge on the Coordinadora's key demand—to initiate direct talks with the *contras*—and they also took the position that the Coordinadora's proposals for major changes in political structure and public policies should constitute the Coordinadora's party platform for the elections, rather than conditions for the Coordinadora's entry into the electoral process.

Judging by the agenda under discussion at the Rio de Janeiro talks in October, it seems that a significant narrowing of differences between the Coordinadora and the FSLN had been achieved in the preceding weeks. The Coordinadora dropped its demand for a direct dialogue with the *contras,* as well as its insistence upon pre-election changes in government policy and the FSLN-state relationship. In return, according to Adán Fletes, the Coordinadora's vice-presidential candidate who was present at the Rio talks, "the FSLN had agreed to all our other conditions," including a large increase in free media time to compensate for the Coordinadora's late entry into the campaign, complete abolition of press censorship ("except for military matters and national security matters"), permission to disseminate party propaganda at all government offices and military installations, an absolute guarantee against FSLN-organized disruptions of opposition-party rallies, and a ban on movement of public transportation vehicles and state-owned vehicles on election day. The key provision of the draft agreement would have postponed the date of the elections to January 13, 1985, in return for a cease-fire by the *contras,* to be negotiated by the Coordinadora. A copy of the provisional accords between the FSLN and the Coordinadora was supplied to our delegation by the Coordinadora's Adán Fletes.

There have been many different explanations for the failure to reach a final agreement in Rio de Janeiro. Adán Fletes told our delegation that the draft agreement was never signed because the FSLN's negotiator walked out of the talks. The FSLN claims that, once the draft accords had been initialed, Coordinadora leaders in Managua insisted on a delay of several days to reconsider the agreement, which the FSLN was unwilling to grant. Some independent journalistic reports corroborate this version. Other observers believe that negotiators for both sides may have exceeded their authority in Rio, and upon checking with their colleagues in Managua, they were urged to seek any pretext for getting out of the agreement. The Sandinistas clearly wanted and needed an agreement, to enlist the Coordinadora's participation and prevent the November 4 elections from being discredited internationally. Arturo Cruz, according to several key informants interviewed by our delegation, may also have wanted to run; but the more conservative elements of his Coordinadora coalition (especially the businessmen represented by COSEP), encouraged by hardliners within the Reagan Administration, vetoed any agreement.

The weight of the evidence available to us suggests that the Coordinadora group made a policy decision to pursue its political goals in 1984 outside of the electoral process. Its abstention from the elections was not the result of FSLN intransigence. The government was still negotiating with the Coordinadora over the election date in mid-October; clearly it had not yet made up its mind to proceed with elections regardless of whether the Coordinadora participated. Given the terms for campaigning and holding the elections to which the FSLN had agreed by October 2 in Rio de Janeiro, it is evident that the FSLN *was* willing to "take specific steps to create an environment conducive to genuine electoral competition," as the Coordinadora and the U.S. State Department insisted that it do.

Assuming that both sides were negotiating in good faith, it could be argued that both erred tactically: Cruz and his coalition partners, in not taking the important concessions they had extracted from the Sandinistas and standing for election in January; the FSLN in not extending itself a bit more, either to strike a deal or to call Mr. Cruz's bluff. What is unquestionable is that both sides were damaged by the failure of the Rio talks.

The breakdown of negotiations between the FSLN and the Coordinadora left six political parties on the ballot for November 4, in addition to the FSLN. During the last two weeks of the campaign, considerable confusion developed with regard to the participation of two of these parties. First, a split occurred in the Democratic Conservative Party (PCD), in which the presidential candidate, Clemento Guido, affirmed his own and his party's intention to participate in the elections, while other party leaders called for abstention. The PCD stayed in, and the internal dissension caused no significant change in the party's platform.

In the case of the Independent Liberal Party (PLI), when presidential candidate Virgilio Godoy withdrew from the election, claiming that the FSLN government had failed to provide "minimum guarantees" for free elections, his vice-presidential running mate and many of the party's candidates for the National Assembly continued in the campaign. The division within the PLI was genuine and deep. A regional PLI leader in Matagalpa told our delegation that he had argued strongly for continuing in the campaign, "despite all the inconveniences" resulting from FSLN control of the governmental apparatus, "because to withdraw would increase the risk of a U.S. invasion" by robbing the November 4 elections of legitimacy in the eyes of the world. However, the division of the PLI into abstentionist and participatory factions did not alter its basic program; and on election day, voters had the same range of choices as before Godoy's withdrawal.

A close inspection of the platforms of the seven parties listed on the November 4 ballot reveals that the Nicaraguan voter had a wide range of options on major issues—considerably wider, for example, than in recent elections in El Salvador and Guatemala. With regard to foreign policy, the FSLN government was flanked by one party attacking it for aligning Nicaragua too closely with Soviet foreign policy (the PPSC), and another party attacking it for not bringing the country closer to the Soviet camp (the PCdeN). On economic strategy, the PCD called for greater latitude for the private sector, while the MAP-ML advocated complete nationalization of private enterprise. People concerned about the military draft could also choose several alternative policies to the right of the FSLN, including that of the PCD, which wants to abolish conscription altogether. While none of the parties to the left of the FSLN called for the overthrow of the Sandinistas or a reversal of the revolutionary process, they did have significant policy differences with the incumbent government.

A senior U.S. diplomat in Central America offered our delegation the opinion that such programmatic diversity among the parties competing in the November 4 elections was of little consequence. With Arturo Cruz and the Coordinadora absent, in this official's view, the elections were totally one-sided, since the Nicaraguan voter is "not sophisticated enough" to express his disapproval of the FSLN by casting a vote for an "obscure splinter party" like the PCD or the PPSC. "The level of political awareness in this country is not high enough," the diplomat told us.

But there are some glaring inconsistencies in the official U.S. analysis of Nicaraguan voter behavior. On the one hand, we were told that Nicaraguans are profoundly unhappy with the FSLN because of the military draft, shortages of consumer goods, and other issues. On the other hand, the same U.S. official seemed to be arguing, these concerns would not determine the way Nicaraguans voted on November 4. We find it difficult to reconcile these arguments. In any case, given the impressive political maturity which the Nicaraguan people exhibited during the 1984 campaign and elections, we would hesitate to pass such a negative judgment on their ability to choose meaningfully among the alternatives presented to them on election day.

THE ISSUE OF ABUSE OF INCUMBENCY

Another argument widely used to discredit the Nicaraguan electoral process this year focused attention upon the overwhelmingly dominant role of the FSLN in the country's political system, and the Sandinistas' alleged propensity to abuse their position of incumbency. Essentially, the argument is that even if the electoral rules were not rigged to favor the FSLN, the rules would still operate unfairly to the FSLN's advantage, because of its dominant position and the lack of separation between the state and the Sandinista party. Alleged abuses of incumbency by the FSLN were the most common subject of complaints (18 percent of the total) submitted to the Supreme Electoral Council by opposition parties during the 1984 campaign.

There is little question that the FSLN is, in fact, the dominant force in the present Nicaraguan political arena. Part of its strength, like that of the PRI in Mexico, derives from its historical identification with the revolution that toppled a hated dictatorship. As FSLN vice-presidential candidate Sergio Ramírez reminded our delegation. "The FSLN is not just an electoral party. It won the revolution." Another legacy of the struggle against Somoza is the FSLN's extensive network of local-level activists. As a party, the FSLN operates primarily at the local level, and it is the only political organization in Nicaragua with the capacity to operate at that level throughout the country.

Over the past five years, the FSLN has also consolidated its control over the governmental apparatus. It has monopoly control over both the police and the military. The civilian bureaucracy presents a mixed picture, however, with supporters of the PLI and other non-Sandinista parties holding positions in many government agencies. As described in an earlier section of this report, there is a high degree of fusion between the FSLN and the various mass organizations *(Organizaciones Populares)* which have been set up or refurbished since the fall of Somoza, including the Sandinista Defense Committees (CDSs) which theoretically operate in all neighborhoods throughout the country. Finally, the FSLN has control over a substantial portion of the country's mass media, via the two state-run television stations (the only television stations in Nicaragua), 16 state-owned radio stations (out of a total of 39 in the country), and two of the nation's three daily newspapers (*Barricada,* the official government organ, and *Nuevo Diario,* which is closely aligned with the Sandinistas).

In spite of the fact that the FSLN is the dominant political force in Nicaragua today, it was obvious to our delegation that it does not have total control over the society. And there continues to be a substantial amount of "noise" in the political system, from the top level on down. The image of tight, centralized FSLN control over society and polity which the Sandinistas' critics at home and abroad have cultivated is greatly exaggerated. This applies even to the conduct of official censorship of the media. A particularly striking example occurred late in the electoral campaign: On the same evening when the government heavily censored the issue of *La Prensa* devoted to coverage of Virgilio Godoy's withdrawal from the electoral contest, Godoy was announcing his decision on national television (completely uncensored), and several days later *La Prensa*'s front page (uncensored) featured the story of Godoy's withdrawal.

Many of the "abuses of incumbency" which could be witnessed in Nicaragua during the 1984 electoral campaign are common occurrences in U.S. political campaigns: the use of government vehicles and government buildings for campaign activities, dedications of public works by incumbent party candidates, giving public employees time off from normal duties to work in campaign activities, and so forth. More serious are the frequent accusations by some opposition politicians and U.S.

officials that the FSLN has utilized its "institutional hold" on the Nicaraguan people to induce their support for FSLN candidates.

The most commonly cited channel or vehicle for such abuses is the neighborhood-level CDSs, which allegedly use their control over the distribution of food ration books to compel political obedience. We could find no evidence to support these allegations, however. The ration booklets in use in Nicaragua enable the holder to buy several basic products (e.g., rice, sugar, beans, cooking oil, soap) at state-subsidized prices through local privately-owned stores. They are distributed through the CDSs, once a year—not on a weekly or monthly basis. Our interviews with neighborhood social workers and individual residents revealed that everyone automatically receives a ration card, whether or not they participate in CDSs activities, and regardless of their political views. Community development practitioners told us that while some CDS officers may occasionally abuse their authority and "act as lord and master" over their neighbors, such abuses are neither widespread nor systematic; and they are usually motivated by personal feuds rather than political considerations. In our conversations with average citizens, we found no instances of withholding or threatened withholding of ration cards by CDS officials.

The only abuse involving the CDSs which we found to be common was the use of these organizations by the FSLN to distribute its campaign materials and to help mobilize residents to attend FSLN rallies. In the neighborhoods which we checked, CDS leaders had distributed only the materials of the FSLN. However, opposition parties were free to campaign in these areas, and their campaign posters and graffiti were quite visible. We were also informed by an official of the Supreme Electoral Council that there had been some cases of CDSs telling their members not to attend opposition party rallies.

A more troublesome area is that of official censorship. There was relatively little press censorship in Nicaragua until March, 1982, when the government declared a state of emergency in response to the escalation of *contra* activities. On August 1, 1984, restrictions on media coverage of all subjects except for military developments (e.g., attacks by the *contras*) and some economic matters (e.g., food shortages) were lifted, as part of the implementation of the 1984 Electoral Law. However, censorship of some explicitly political news occurred intermittently during the electoral campaign. The most egregious case was the initial censorship of *La Prensa*'s coverage of Virgilio Godoy's withdrawal from the election; but news about disruptions of Arturo Cruz's political rallies by FSLN sympathizers in the pre-campaign period was also suppressed.

Most acts of censorship are justified by government officials as a reflection of wartime conditions. "A country at war," FSLN leader Sergio Ramírez told us, "can't allow a newspaper which is the instrument of the enemy to publish its opinions freely." *La Prensa* is generally viewed by Sandinista officials and FSLN supporters in the general population as a mouthpiece for both the *contras* and the Reagan Administration. Our reading of *La Prensa* during the nine days we spent in Nicaragua revealed a newspaper which, while not openly subversive, is unremittingly hostile to the incumbent government in virtually every article it publishes and which self-censors any news which reflects favorably upon the FSLN. For example, on the day after the FSLN's massive end-of-campaign rally in Managua, at which the head of the FSLN junta, Daniel Ortega, delivered his most urgent warning to date of an imminent U.S. invasion of Nicaragua, not a word about this event appeared in *La Prensa*.

The official explanation for censoring news of Godoy's electoral withdrawal was legalistic: ''It's illegal to promote abstentionism, and *La Prensa*'s issue of October 22 was full of absentionist propaganda,'' Comandante Jaime Wheelock told our delegation. He was technically correct: the 1984 electoral law does prohibit advocacy of abstentionism. But the material censored from *La Prensa* on October 22 (a photocopy of which was obtained by our delegation), while politically embarrassing to the government, did not contain an explicit call for voter abstention.

Independent observers of the FSLN interviewed by our delegation concurred that press censorship is probably the weakest point in the Sandinistas' style of governance. In their view, the initial imposition of press controls in 1982 was a major error, not justified by the military circumstances at that time, and probably counterproductive. Virgilio Godoy, for example, in his televised announcement of withdrawal from the electoral campaign, used the government's censorship of this news in *La Prensa* as one of the justifications for his decision to withdraw. But these observers believe it will be very difficult for the government to extricate itself from the censorship business, especially so long as Nicaragua is under intense diplomatic and military pressure from the United States.

For purposes of this report, it is important to ask whether the press censorship practiced by the government seriously restricted the electoral candidates' freedom of speech or prevented them from getting their party's message to the electorate. Our delegation concluded that it did not. Apart from the obvious fact that censorship of *La Prensa*'s coverage of the opposition parties was far from complete (indeed, each day's edition during the last week of the campaign was full of anti-FSLN and pro-Coordinadora propaganda), there was no censorship of the country's 39 radio stations, including two stations run by the Church hierarchy and others in neighboring countries run by the *contras*. Television stations carried a series of uncensored debates involving the presidential or vice-presidential candidates of all seven parties participating in the elections. Also uncensored was the formal campaign programming of each party, broadcast free of charge on state-run television and radio stations under a provision of the 1984 Electoral Law. By the end of the campaign, each party had been given access to a total of 22 hours (15 minutes per day) of free, uninterrupted television time, in prime early evening hours, on both channels; and 44 hours (30 minutes per day) of free radio time on all state-run radio stations.

To summarize from both our discussions with various political groups and our observations, it seems clear that the FSLN took substantial advantage of its incumbent position and, in some ways, abused it. However, the abuses of incumbency do not appear to have been systematic; and neither the nature of the abuses nor their frequency was such as to cripple the opposition parties' campaigns or to cast doubt on the fundamental validity of the electoral process. While censorship of *La Prensa* continued, on a selective basis, throughout the campaign, the Sandinistas made no attempt to "shut down" their opposition. Generally speaking, in this campaign the FSLN did little more to take advantage of its incumbency than incumbent parties everywhere (including the United States) routinely do, and considerably *less* than ruling parties in other Latin American countries traditionally have done.

Some critics of the November 4 elections have argued that, even if the Sandinistas scrupulously avoided abusing their incumbency, the elections were meaningless because of the FSLN's overwhelming domination of Nicaragua's political life. The "skewed" political climate resulting from the FSLN's hegemonic role was a matter of concern to our delegation, and we probed this issue in all of our interviews with Sandinista leaders as well as independent observers. We found the comments of Sergio Ramírez, the FSLN's vice-presidential candidate and one of the three members of the current Sandinista government junta, particularly candid and useful in putting the issue into proper perspective:

> We [the FSLN] do have an advantage over our opposition: We are in power. It *is* more difficult for an opposition party to get an air force helicopter to go to campaign in Bluefields [an isolated town on the Atlantic coast of Nicaragua]. But it's like in the United States. Your President can command prime time whenever he wants it. It's certainly easier to run for President from the White House; but nobody accuses Ronald Reagan of anything illegal because he takes advantage of all that apparatus. We haven't used all the propaganda capacity that we possess. We have tried to run a limited campaign. . . .
>
> There *is* a dominant party here—the FSLN. We can't change that overnight. Political equilibrium cannot be created artificially. We are having elections here, hardly five years after a revolution; a true political earthquake. By contrast, in Mexico, the leadership introduced multi-party competition *(pluripartidismo)* including the left only six years ago. I can't say that we have a balanced political equation here. These [opposition] parties are very small parties. To us, the real danger was that these parties would not poll enough votes to gain a seat in the National Assembly, and would simply disappear. That's why we chose a proportional representation system. . . . Our goal is to open a political space, for the future.

A similar perspective was offered by Stephen Kinzer, the *New York Times'* correspondent in Managua:

> Are the elections [in Nicaragua] meaningful? If the only object of an election is to choose a president and a policy course for the country, then the answer is 'no.' But assume that you can't use the election to affect these kinds of choices. Is there still some value [to the opposition] in staying in? They are creating a political space for themselves in the future, and the government has made a commit-

ment to hold regular elections. A standard has been set, by which [the government's] future conduct can be judged.

GOVERNMENT INTERFERENCE IN OPPOSITION CAMPAIGNING

Undoubtedly the single most highly publicized issue raised by the Nicaraguan elections of 1984 was the question of FSLN harassment or interference in the campaign activities of its opponents. Specifically, it has been charged that the FSLN systematically disrupted the campaign rallies of opposition candidates, often violently, using gangs of young toughs known as *turbas*. These attacks allegedly were orchestrated by FSLN-controlled state agencies (the Interior Ministry, police forces, Sandinista youth organizations, etc.) Given the seriousness of these charges, our delegation devoted considerable effort to investigating them.

We turned first to the files of the Supreme Electoral Council, which contained documentation on formal complaints lodged by the political parties participating in the November 4 election concerning disruptions of rallies and other alleged campaign irregularities. We found only eight written complaints about *turba* activities, most of them filed by the Independent Liberal Party (PLI). Five of these complaints were substantiated through investigation by the CSE staff; three could not be substantiated upon investigation.

CSE President Mariano Fiallos told us that, in addition to the five substantiated cases of disruptions by *turbas* which occurred during the official, three-month campaign period (August 1–November 2), there had been four other cases during the pre-campaign period. Most of these cases involved Arturo Cruz and the Coordinadora-affiliated parties. It was generally agreed among our informants that these were the most serious altercations of the entire political year in Nicaragua, and they received extensive publicity abroad. Moreover, the FSLN's presidential candidate, Daniel Ortega, made a public statement on the anti-Cruz disturbances, noting that they demonstrated the frustration and anger of the Nicaraguan people, upset by the counterrevolutionary activities which Cruz and his party seemed to condone. Ortega's statement could have been construed by some as an endorsement of *turba* activity, although neither he nor any other Sandinista official directly advocated such disruptions.

There is evidence that on at least one occasion, a *turba* attack was precipitated not by the FSLN but by supporters of Arturo Cruz and the Coordinadora. On August 4, in the city of Matagalpa, a group of Cruz supporters emerged from a theater where Cruz had given a speech and assaulted a group of approximately 200 women carrying placards that protested the Coordinadora's call for direct talks with the *contras*. Three of the women protesters were wounded in the melee. The group of women reportedly included numerous widows of men killed by the *contras* or during the insurrection against Somoza.

Reports published in the United States have implied that all of the Coordinadora's rallies were violently disrupted by FSLN thugs, while the Sandinista police stood by doing nothing to restrain them. An eyewitness account of a Cruz rally held in Masaya on September 22, 1984, contradicts this generalization. A U.S. citizen who was living in Nicaragua during this period recalled the incident this way:

> Dr. Arturo Cruz . . . arrived, unannounced, and addressed about 50 of his supporters at the headquarters of the Social Democratic Party. Within minutes, several thousand Masayans gathered and began chanting anti-counterrevolutionary slogans. I had the opportunity to talk with several of the people opposing Dr. Cruz and found that they were housewives, students, artisans, teachers, and shopkeepers. They had one thing in common: they believed that Arturo Cruz is collaborating with the Reagan Administration's effort to destabilize and ultimately overthrow the Nicaraguan Government. Many of the 'thugs' had brothers, fathers or sons who had been killed by the U.S.-backed counterrevolutionaries, or *contras*. Because of the protection of the Sandinista police, Dr. Cruz delivered his speech unmolested. Among the crowd, Sandinista Front activists used their loudspeaker and credibility with the people to call for restraint and discipline.

Our conclusions concerning the problem of the *turbas* can be summarized as follows:

- The total number of incidents reported, including those which occurred in the pre-campaign period, was quite small, in the context of a thirteen and one-half week campaign, which included more than 20 political rallies or demonstrations throughout the country in any given week.
- The most serious incidents of this type occurred *before* the formal campaign even began (on August 1). Only five alleged disturbances of this type occurred during the campaign itself, and apparently none occurred during the last six weeks of the campaign.
- Whenever the Supreme Electoral Council had advance warning that disruptions of campaign rallies might occur, preventive measures were taken. In addition, the CSE placed paid advertisements in the press urging citizens to respect the right of all political parties to hold rallies without interference.
- In spite of Daniel Ortega's unfortunate statement on these disruptions, there is no evidence that the FSLN had a coherent strategy of stimulating or orchestrating them.
- At the time of all disturbances involving Arturo Cruz, Cruz and his party were not legally registered as participants in the electoral campaign (indeed, they had just announced their decision to *abstain* from the elections), and the Cruz rallies which were disrupted were held in violation of Article 38 of the 1984 electoral law, which requires all organizations seeking to conduct public campaign rallies to apply to the CSE for a permit at least one week in advance. The same article promises police protection against any groups which try to disturb public rallies or demonstrations which have been duly authorized by the CSE, but specifies that this and other rights and protections for political parties established in that

chapter of the electoral law "shall only be exercised by those who have registered to participate in the elections." In other words, given their decision not to register, Cruz and the Coordinadora were deliberately campaigning outside of the legal framework of protections which had been created by the electoral law.

- Disruptions of the campaign activities of other opposition groups were sporadic and followed no systematic pattern. There was no organized, "brown shirt" phenomenon.
- The *legally registered* opposition parties were able to hold the vast majority of their rallies unimpeded by pro-FSLN demonstrators or by other kinds of government interference. National or regional leaders of several different opposition parties (PPSC, PSN, PLI) told our delegation that they had been able to run their campaigns relatively unhindered by the FSLN, and that after the initial *turba* disruptions in late July and early August, the FSLN had made efforts to gain better control over its own supporters. PPSC leaders attributed the initial disturbances to "lack of discipline" among some of the FSLN's younger enthusiasts.

The table on page 97 summarizes the complete set of complaints regarding campaign irregularities which were presented by all legally registered parties participating in the elections to the Supreme Electoral Council, during the official campaign period.

These data were compiled through our own inspection of the CSE's complaint files. It is not possible to determine the total number of complaints made during the campaign, since some were presented to the regional Electoral Councils rather than to the Supreme Electoral Council in Managua. The political parties had been instructed by the CSE to lodge their complaints initially with the Regional Councils. However, according to the CSE's executive secretary, these instructions were generally disregarded, and most complaints ("95 percent," according to the CSE officer) were sent directly to the CSE in Managua. Based on our interviews with opposition party leaders, it seems likely that the most serious alleged incidents were reported to the CSE, and would therefore fall into the subset of complaints which are recorded in the CSE's files. Those files contain records of the investigations undertaken by the CSE in order to verify the complaints, as well as communications from the CSE to other government agencies (the military, police, etc.) and to the political parties (both plaintiffs and defendants) seeking or reporting remedial actions.

We independently verified the number of complaints filed by the opposition parties, through our interviews with leaders of these parties. However, some parties (particularly the Communist Party) informed us that they had declined to submit complaints to the CSE, either because they questioned the CSE's independence and impartiality or because they had no confidence in its ability to solve the problems that bothered opposition party leaders.

The number of complaints being received by the CSE peaked during the first two weeks of September (11 complaints in the week of September 5; 12 in the week of

Complaints of Campaign Irregularities

Subject of Complaint	Number of Alleged Incidents	%	Sustained	Number of Complaints Not Sustained	Inconclusive
Disturbances by *turbas*	8	13.0	5	3	0
Destruction of electoral propaganda, illegal painting	7	11.4	5	1	1
Slandering candidates	3	5.0	2	1	0
Verbal threats	6	10.0	4	2	0
Unfair treatment by the mass media	5	8.0	2	3	0
Small fist-fights and other coercive behavior	5	8.0	4	1	0
Political discrimination by employers against their workers	3	5.0	2	1	0
Gunshot incidents	1	1.0	0	1	0
Government abuse of its incumbency, powers	11	18.0	3	6	2
Illegal arrests of campaign workers by police	5	8.0	4	1	0
Failure to provide campaign materials (paper, etc.) as required by law	1	1.0	0	1	0
CDSs or police intimidating people (threatening to take away ration cards, etc.)	5	8.0	0	5	0
Other	1	1.0	0	1	0
Total	61	100.0	31	27	3

September 12), with only two letters of complaint received during the last month of the campaign. The Independent Liberal Party (PLI) registered the largest number of complaints (14) during the campaign, followed by the Communist Party (PCdeN) (10 complaints). Even the FSLN presented two complaints, one of which described an incident in which an FSLN candidate was allegedly stabbed by a PLI supporter, in the course of an "unauthorized" PLI demonstration. But not one person lost his life as a result of campaign violence—a remarkable record in a country experiencing its first open electoral campaign in any Nicaraguan's lifetime, at a time of armed conflict and high emotions.

When the 61 alleged incidents reported to the CSE were investigated, 50 percent were validated, 44 percent were shown to be untrue (or the events reported in the complaints were found to be different than alleged), and 5 percent remained ambiguous (the evidence was inconclusive), according to the CSE records which we examined. In the single largest category of allegations—concerning governmental abuses of power—specifics were often lacking in the complaints, making investigation difficult. Only three of the eleven allegations were sustained upon investigation; six were refuted; and no determination could be made in two cases.

At times, complaining about campaign irregularities seems to have been a campaign tactic, used by certain parties to gain attention in the media. For example, the CSE on its own initiative pursued several complaints aired in radio speeches by Socialist Party candidates, inviting the party to submit the complaints in writing; but none were forthcoming. In another instance, PLI presidential candidate Virgilio Godoy told a reporter for the *Wall Street Journal* that all members of the PLI youth committee in one city had suddenly been drafted. The committee was reconstituted, according to Godoy, but then the replacements were drafted, too. However, upon reviewing the CSE's file of complaints received from the PLI during the entire campaign period, we found that no formal complaint was ever lodged by the PLI concerning this serious allegation. By contrast, the PLI did not hesitate to file a formal complaint alleging that rooms in a government-owned hotel in Bluefields had been denied (ostensibly for political reasons) to a visiting PLI delegation.

In summary, while all the opposition parties had some valid complaints about the government's management of the 1984 elections, no party was prevented from carrying out an active campaign. The opposition leaders with whom we spoke indicated that they did, in fact, receive their legal allotments of campaign funds; were given access to paper, paint, gasoline and other necessary campaign materials (although not as quickly as some would have preferred); and were given their legal allotment of free media time. Even the casual observer could not fail to be impressed by the profusion of prominently displayed opposition-party billboards, posters, wall paintings, and graffiti which in some cities seemed to occupy every available square inch of space. The opposition could, and did, get its message out.

A CLIMATE OF FEAR AND INTIMIDATION?

An even more fundamental issue raised by the Nicaraguan elections relates to the psychological climate in which they were held. Critics have charged that "minimum conditions for free elections'' did not exist because of a generalized climate of fear and intimidation, created by the Sandinista regime. Most often mentioned in this context is the alleged use of the neighborhood-level CDS apparatus to coerce and intimidate through ''spying'' on potential dissidents, threats of retaliation in the form of denial or withdrawal of ration cards, peer pressure in the schools, and arbitrary use of the military draft to silence opponents.

This was one of the most difficult issues for our delegation to assess, given the time limitations and our inability to observe systematically such institutions as the CDSs in action. However, based on our interviews, observations, and casual conversations with individual citizens, we would characterize the situation in Nicaragua in the immediate preelection period as follows:

Complaints by opposition leaders and foreign critics of the Sandinistas cannot, in our opinion, be taken as evidence of a climate of fear and intimidation. However, our delegation interviewed some individuals who clearly *felt* intimidated by the Sandinista government. It was impossible to estimate how large a stratum of the population such individuals represent, nor in most instances to ascertain whether their fears were well-grounded. For some low-income persons whom we interviewed, fear takes the form of a generalized sense that ''something will happen'' to them if they don't do what the government wants (e.g., vote in the November 4 elections). Others have more specific concerns, such as fear of losing their ration cards. Some parents feel that their children must participate in FSLN-sponsored youth organizations.

Especially among low-income people, it is difficult to disentangle such fears from the legacy of *somocismo*. Under Somoza, opposition to the government was frequently cause for dismissal from employment, imprisonment, or death. The National Guard commonly beat up residents of poor *barrios* and extorted money from parents of boys who had been rounded up and taken to jail. ''There are still people who have the old fears,'' one resident of Ciudad Sandino, a low-income neighborhood of Managua, told us. But would this affect whether they voted on November 4, or how they would vote? Our informant responded this way:

> No, some people won't vote, but it's not because they are afraid. It's because they are opposed to the Frente [FSLN], and they don't care for any of the opposition parties. They think it was their civic duty to register, but they don't feel compelled to vote. So they will stay home. People who go along with the government will do so because they appreciate the things being done by the government for the poor. Most of them are not FSLN members or *militantes*.

Whatever their role as ''the eyes and ears of the revolution'' in the struggle against Somoza and the first years of FSLN rule, the Sandinista Defense Committees (CDSs) do not currently seem to be functioning as a heavy-handed domestic ''spying'' network. A community development worker interviewed by our delegation who has lived in one of Managua's low-income neighborhoods continuously since 1979 reported that she had not heard ''a single complaint'' about such spying in her neighborhood. While such information is anecdotal, we have no reason to question its veracity. Individual citizens with whom we talked seemed to view the CDSs primarily as groups of community activists (each block has a six-person committee elected by residents of the block, with no fixed term of office) which represent the residents before higher-level authorities and mobilize residents for public health campaigns (e.g., vaccinations), street cleaning, nightly street patrols *(vigilancia),* and other routine functions. The CDSs are also responsible for distributing ration cards, helping eligible residents (e.g., nursing mothers) to obtain free food supplements from local health clinics, and civic education (e.g., for the voter registration campaign of July, 1984).

The CDSs' control of ration cards is viewed by critics of the Sandinista government as the key to their coercive capacity; yet in our interviews in many neighborhoods in several cities, we found no evidence that ration cards were being held back or withdrawn by CDS officers, for *any* reason. Among the complaints lodged with the Supreme Electoral Council by opposition parties, there were five reports that CDSs had been intimidating people by threatening to take away their ration cards, but none of these allegations was sustained upon investigation. As noted above, the only concrete cases of governmental abuse involving CDSs during the pre-election period which we encountered was their use in at least some neighborhoods to distribute FSLN campaign propaganda (exclusively), and to mobilize people to go to FSLN campaign rallies.

We observed that the CDSs are a more complex, less centrally directed phenomenon than is commonly believed. They seem to be most active in the poorest neighborhoods and in rural areas, where they may constitute the principal mode of civic organization. In middle and upper-class neighborhoods, the CDSs are much less visible (if not *in*visible), and residents are indifferent to them. Some residents perceive them to be extensions of the FSLN political machine, and may cooperate with CDS leaders only to avoid problems with routine service delivery. We also observed that many people in Nicaragua are not reluctant to criticize the Sandinista government, in public, and often in the harshest possible terms. Every member of our delegation was approached at least once by an irate citizen, as we walked around Managua and other cities. Several of these encounters turned into heated arguments between the individual who had approached us and passers-by who joined the discussion. Frequently the people who complained to us about the incumbent government identified themselves as fervent anti*somocistas* who felt that the Sandinistas had "betrayed" the revolution through their embrace of "Communism." These people did not feel intimidated. They were, however, intensely opposed to the FSLN's *proyecto de transformación,* which they had not anticipated.

Outspoken criticism of government policy may, however, become a casualty of the atmosphere of crisis and invasion fears prompted by increased U.S. pressure on the FSLN government. In his closing speech of the 1984 campaign, FSLN presidential candidate Daniel Ortega essentially equated voter abstention from the election with "aid and comfort" to the enemy—the United States and domestic "fifth column" elements seeking to undermine Nicaragua's democratic process. We view this as a disturbing sign that the siege mentality resulting from intense U.S. military and psychological pressures on Nicaragua may begin to blur the lines between legitimate dissent and "treason."

Should this come to pass, it would be a large step backward for a government that, having replaced a regime with a brutal record on civil liberties and human rights, has made major efforts to control abuses. Reports by human rights organizations published since 1979 confirmed an early elimination of torture and political kidnappings ("disappearances"). Significant human rights abuses did occur during the FSLN government's removal of the Miskito Indians from combat zones near the Honduran border, although Amnesty International concluded that "reports of shootings and other deliberate brutality during the transfer were later shown to be false." More recently, charges by opposition parties of politically motivated arrests and detention suggest the possibility of civil rights abuse under the state of emergency declared by the government in March, 1982. Nevertheless, compared to other nations in the region and in the face of the war against the *contras,* such abuses are on a very small scale.

However, in one area—university autonomy—there seems to have been a significant deterioration in recent years. This has been a major point of dispute between the FSLN and the Popular Social Christian Party (PPSC), which tends to agree with the Sandinistas on other issues of domestic policy. The PPSC accuses the government of "killing university autonomy" in Nicaragua. Several well-informed sources consulted by our delegation expressed concern about what they termed a "serious erosion" of university autonomy—one of the objectives of the struggle against Somoza—which has occurred since 1979. Now, the rectors of the two divisions of the National University are appointed by the government rather than elected by their faculties; and the activities of at least one other academic research center have been heavily politicized. It is not clear, however, whether reduced institutional autonomy has been translated into less freedom of expression for individual scholars.

Finally, in assessing the psychological climate for the November 4 elections, it is important to differentiate between the "climate of fear and intimidation" that some FSLN policies and actions allegedly have created, and the fear generated by the activities of the *contras* and the U.S. military, which during the week before the election began daily supersonic overflights of Nicaragua which have caused loud sonic booms across much of the national territory and a sense of near panic among the population.

We found the war-induced climate of fear to be most intense in the Atlantic coast region, in and around the town of Puerto Cabezas, which was visited by two members of our delegation and our videotape crew. This area is the home of 54,000 Miskito Indians, a people who have become a symbol of international concern over indigenous rights and national responsibilities in guaranteeing such rights. Today, the Miskito and their neighbors in the Atlantic coast region suffer the consequences of an economic system paralyzed by armed conflict. Agricultural production, fishing, and local commerce have all been seriously disrupted.

Because of the armed conflict, fifteen Miskito communities could not be included in the national voter registration effort in late July, and nine polling places in the region were closed on election day due to *contra* activities. During the last weeks of the electoral campaign, the *contras* operating in this area focused their efforts upon convincing the local population to boycott the elections. From a radio station in Costa Rica, the *contras* were broadcasting a very clear message: people who vote, and their families, would be marked for killing by the *contras*. People of the region who discussed the situation with our delegation emphasized the ''high price of dying'' that might have to be paid by those who turned up at the polls on November 4. But a few persons also suggested, obliquely, that *failure* to vote might place individuals and communities in a situation of potential jeopardy, with regard to Sandinista troops stationed in the region. In short, people who live in the Puerto Cabezas area felt both a fear of voting and a fear of abstention, and spoke of the negative consequences of doing either.

International Influences on the Electoral Process

International actors had a profound impact on the Nicaraguan electoral process. They influenced the timing of the elections, the institutional structure of the electoral process, the number of electoral contenders (and therefore the range of choice for voters), the environment in which the process occurred, and even the amount of attention which the election outcome received internationally.

Throughout the three-year period prior to February 21, 1984, when the FSLN government announced the date of this year's elections, the Reagan Administration had cited the absence of elections in Nicaragua since the overthrow of Somoza in 1979 as one of the principal justifications for the Administration's policy of hostility toward the Sandinistas. Not only had the Sandinistas ''betrayed'' their promises of 1979–1980 to hold free elections; the failure to hold elections was proof, in the Administration's view, that the FSLN was bent on constructing a totalitarian regime. But when the Sandinistas made their announcement on February 21 of this year, the U.S. administration changed its position, now arguing that conditions for a truly democratic election did not exist in Nicaragua. CSE President Mariano Fiallos recalls that ''within a matter of days'' after the February 21 announcement, ''pressure began to build [from the U.S.] to postpone the elections.''

In a recent policy statement on ''Democracy in Latin America and the Caribbean,'' the U.S. State Department attributes the Sandinistas' decision to hold elections on November 4, 1984, to ''widespread internal pressures and disillusionment abroad.'' But all Nicaraguan political leaders whom we interviewed, irrespective of their feelings toward the FSLN, told us that internal pressures, whether from opposition parties or individual citizens, were *not* a factor in the decision to call for elections this year. In their view, the pressures were all external.

By 1983, the Reagan administration's criticisms of the failure to hold elections had seriously eroded international support for the Sandinista government, particularly among the West Europeans on whom the government depends for most of its foreign economic assistance, as well as among key members of the Democratic Party in the

United States. The Sandinistas clearly understood that the continued lack of elections reduced their ability to defend themselves abroad.

As a senior official of the Nicaraguan Foreign Ministry told us, the November 4 elections were "a key element in our national defense strategy. Our internal legitimacy is not in question. What *is* in question is our international legitimacy." The date of November 4 was selected so that Nicaragua would have a legitimate, elected government in place *before* the anticipated re-election of Ronald Reagan in the United States on November 6. The Sandinistas expected (correctly, as subsequent events have demonstrated) that the Reagan administration would sharply increase military and political pressure on Nicaragua once the U.S. elections were over. They hoped that a competitive election with heavy turnout would help to shield Nicaragua against this anticipated onslaught.

Thus in the official Nicaraguan view, holding elections this year (rather than in 1985, as originally promised) would help the FSLN's friends abroad, and "our friends will help us." The key "friends" referred to in this context include the Contadora nations and the Socialist International, as well as the individual leaders associated with these movements (e.g., Willy Brandt, Carlos Andres Pérez, Belisario Betancur), who had been pressing the Sandinistas to reach an agreement with their domestic opposition. Even so, most groups both within and outside of Nicaragua were caught off guard by the Sandinistas' decision to set an election date in 1984. Several opposition party leaders told us that they had not been expecting elections until 1985.

The FSLN government made extensive efforts to obtain Western input as it structured the electoral process. A delegation of Nicaraguan officials made two tours of democracies in Latin America, Western Europe, and the United States in search of information on electoral procedures. Special attention was devoted to the European systems of proportional representation that maximized the role of minority parties. In the end, the Nicaraguans selected key components of the French, Italian, Austrian, and Swedish electoral systems.

The Sandinistas also sought material support from abroad to mount the elections. Substantial contributions came from Norway ($800,000 for paper for campaign activities and the election itself), Sweden ($400,000, also for paper, as well as technical assistance from the Swedish Electoral College), and Finland ($450,000 for 50 electronic calculators, 500 rolls of calculator paper, 700 tons of newsprint, and hundreds of gallons of printer's ink). France also provided technical assistance and modest financial aid. It should be noted that foreign assistance for the electoral process came exclusively from countries with vigorous Western democratic traditions. None of the donors subsequently complained that its aid had been misused.

THE U.S. ROLE

The role of the United States in the Nicaraguan electoral process was quite different. Within three months after the Sandinistas' announcement that elections would be held this year, a new U.S. policy on elections in Nicaragua had crystallized. According to a report by *New York Times* correspondent Philip Taubman, based on statements by unnamed "senior Administration officials," that new policy line was as follows:

> Since May, when American policy toward the election was formed, the Administration has wanted the opposition candidate, Arturo Cruz, either not to enter the race, or, if he did, to withdraw before the election, claiming the conditions were unfair, [senior Administration] officials said. 'The Administration never contemplated letting Cruz stay in the race,' one official said, 'because then the Sandinistas could justifiably claim that the elections were legitimate, making it much harder for the United States to oppose the Nicaraguan Government.'

The principal instrument for implementing this policy, according to Taubman's official sources, was COSEP, the Superior Council of Private Enterprise, "which was in frequent contact with the C.I.A. about the elections," and whose mission was to prevent Mr. Cruz from reaching an agreement with the Sandinistas.

A senior U.S. official in Central America, interviewed at length by our delegation, declined to respond specifically to the statements made in the October 21 *New York Times* article, although he denied, in general terms, that the U.S. had attempted to prevent opposition candidates from participating in the November 4 election.

Nevertheless, in the six-month period leading up to the election, the Reagan Administration used a combination of diplomatic, economic, and military instruments in a systematic attempt to undermine the Nicaraguan electoral process and to destroy its credibility in the eyes of the world. Within Nicaragua, the behavior of U.S. diplomats was clearly interventionist. This behavior included repeated attempts to persuade key opposition party candidates to drop out of the election, and in at least one case, to bribe lower-level party officials to abandon the campaign of their presidential candidate, who insisted on staying in the race.

Apparently one of the first steps taken to implement the new, post-February 21 U.S. policy toward the Nicaraguan elections was the elevation of Arturo Cruz and his Coordinadora coalition to the status of the country's "strongest" opposition group. The Reagan Administration effectively focused media attention on the participation or nonparticipation of Cruz as the litmus test of free elections in Nicaragua. While there was never any credible evidence that Cruz and the Coordinadora had a broad popular following in Nicaragua (Cruz himself had lived in Washington, D.C. since 1970, returning to Nicaragua for only a year, in 1979–80), the Administration successfully portrayed them as *the* significant opposition force, without whose participation any election in Nicaragua would be meaningless.

The senior U.S. official in Central America interviewed by our delegation claimed that "the U.S. didn't *need* to pressure the Coordinadora and Cruz not to participate" in the November 4 election, since, judging by the Coordinadora's provocative "nine points" statement of December, 1983, "they had already decided not to participate." Nevertheless, the Reagan Administration continued to focus public attention on the controversy generated by the Coordinadora's refusal to register for the elections, and Cruz's on-again, off-again negotiations with the Sandinistas which continued almost until the eve of the election. Even liberal Democrats in Washington who are usually critical of Reagan Administration policy toward Nicaragua were swept up in the crusade to have the November 4 elections postponed until January 15, 1985, ostensibly to give Arturo Cruz and the Coordinadora sufficient time to campaign.

With Arturo Cruz and his followers definitely out of the electoral contest, attention shifted to Virgilio Godoy, leader of the Independent Liberal Party. Godoy was, until February of this year, the Minister of Labor in the FSLN government. His anti-Somoza credentials were impeccable, and it was widely believed in Nicaragua that of all the opposition parties, the PLI had the broadest social base and the only nationwide organization.

Godoy was one of several opposition party leaders in Managua with whom U.S. officials maintained virtually continuous contact during the six months preceding the election. There was a well-beaten path to his door. Godoy told our delegation that his headquarters, located in a tiny, run-down private house, had been visited several times during this period by the U.S. Embassy's Political Counselor, who met with both Godoy and his vice-presidential running mate. Other visitors, according to Godoy, included Langhorne Motley, the U.S. Assistant Secretary of State for Inter-American Affairs, and Harry Shlaudeman, the Administration's special envoy for Central America. On October 20, U.S. Ambassador to Nicaragua Harry Bergold and the Embassy's Political Counselor, J. Michael Joyce, visited Godoy again. The next day, just two weeks before the election, Godoy announced that he was withdrawing from the elections, claiming that the Sandinistas had failed to provide "minimum conditions" for conducting a political campaign. (By that time, the PLI had been actively campaigning for two and one-half months.) When our delegation asked Godoy what had been discussed in his October 20 meeting with the U.S. diplomats, the timing of which he described as "unfortunate, in retrospect," Godoy replied: "The Ambassador wanted to express the point of view of his government regarding the elections; that this was not the best time to hold elections."

The senior U.S. official in Central America whom we interviewed described the October 20 meeting with Godoy as follows: "We were not pressuring him. We only wanted to know what he was going to do. Godoy voted along with the majority of his party's leadership to withdraw from the election." When members of our delegation expressed amazement that Godoy had been approached on October 20 only to ascertain his opinions about the election, the senior U.S. official responded: "The U.S. Government has made it adequately clear that we do not consider these elections to be a valid expression of the popular will in Nicaragua."

Virgilio Godoy denied that his party's decision to quit the election had been influenced by his conversations with U.S. officials, but when asked whether his personal views on participation in the election had been influenced, he declined comment, saying only that "my party has expressed its collective will." When our delegation asked one of Godoy's oldest friends to suggest an explanation for his late withdrawal from the elections, he responded: "I can't explain his behavior. He would not just sell himself to the U.S. Embassy. I think he was subject to terrible pressure from the Embassy."

While at least one U.S. diplomat has admitted that Embassy officials did, in fact, pressure opposition politicians to withdraw from the elections ("It was really very light pressure." the unnamed diplomat told *The New York Times*), the senior U.S. official in Central America whom we interviewed denied that Godoy or other opposition politicians had been pressured in this way.

However, the preponderance of evidence from several independent sources casts considerable doubt on such assertions. Mauricio Díaz, the presidential candidate of the PPSC, was also visited by the U.S. Embassy's Political Counselor, on October 24. A PPSC leader told *The New York Times'* Managua correspondent, Stephen Kinzer, that the U.S. diplomat's visit was "clearly related to the American desire that as few parties as possible participate in the campaign." Díaz and the PPSC were not persuaded to drop out.

Clemente Guido, the presidential candidate of the Democratic Conservative Party (PCD), also opted to stand for election. However, according to Guido, the U.S. Embassy made very large financial offers to several other PCD leaders. "Two weeks before the election," Guido told *The New York Times,* "a U.S. Embassy official visited my campaign manager and promised to help him with money to succeed me as party leader if he withdrew from my campaign. He did." Guido confirmed this bribery attempt in a tape-recorded interview with Professor Martin Diskin of the Massachusetts Institute of Technology, which was made available to our delegation. "Your government," he told Diskin, "has an interest in making sure that these elections are not recognized as legitimate." The *New York Times* correspondent, Stephen Kinzer, also learned that senior U.S. diplomats had been in regular contact with "influential members" of Guido's party, "including several who urged the party at a convention [on October 28] to drop out of the campaign." Still another opposition party leader interviewed by Kinzer recalled "very clear pressure" from the United States to withdraw from the election.

U.S. efforts to induce the withdrawal of the PCD and the PLI from the elections provoked a major split in each party. PLI dissidents charged that U.S. officials had offered Virgilio Godoy $300,000 not to run. The PLI's vice-presidential candidate announced his intention to continue in the elections, as did a number of the PLI's candidates for the National Assembly. The majority faction led by Godoy condemned their candidacies and threatened reprisals. In the PCD, Clemente Guido's decision to continue as a candidate was publicly denounced and declared "totally invalid" by another top PCD leader. As a result, during the last week of the campaign both of these key opposition parties were embroiled in bitter conflicts between their abstentionist and non-abstentionist factions.

The final results of Nicaragua's election were not even reported by most of the international media. They were literally buried under an avalanche of alarmist news reports, based on secret intelligence information deliberately leaked to the U.S. television networks by Reagan administration officials, which portrayed a massive, Soviet-supplied offensive arms build-up in Nicaragua, allegedly aimed at giving the Sandinistas the capacity to invade neighboring countries. While most of the leaked information was soon proven false, and U.S. officials were forced to admit that there was no evidence that Nicaragua was planning to invade its neighbors, the uproar over the initial leaks helped the administration's hardliners on Nicaragua to further two important objectives: (1) to build public and congressional support for a renewal of direct U.S. aid to the *contras,* which had been suspended by Congress earlier this year; and (2) to distract attention from the Nicaraguan elections, with their heavy turnout, absence of irregularities, and competitiveness (a 33-percent opposition vote). At least the second of these objectives was fully realized. The outcome of the Nicaraguan elections was virtually ignored in the United States and Western Europe.

Upon reviewing the whole course of U.S. conduct in relation to the Sandinista government since 1981, as well as the specific actions taken this year to discredit an electoral process which by Latin American standards was a model of probity and fairness (at least to all candidates who chose to register and submit themselves to a popular test), we must conclude that there is *nothing* that the Sandinistas could have done to make the 1984 elections acceptable to the United States Government.

In dealing with the FSLN regime, the Reagan administration, by its own admission, applies a double standard. When asked by our delegation why the United States enthusiastically endorsed the 1984 elections in El Salvador (where all political groups to the left of the Christian Democrats were unrepresented) yet condemned the more inclusionary electoral process in Nicaragua (seven parties, three to the right and three to the left of the FSLN), a senior U.S. official in Central America explained that

> The United States is not obliged to apply the same standard of judgment to a country whose government is avowedly hostile to the U.S. as for a country, like El Salvador, where it is not. These people [the Sandinistas] could bring about a situation in Central America which could pose a threat to U.S. security. That allows us to change our yardstick.

*16. The Issue of Censorship**

By John Spicer Nichols

John Spicer Nichols is associate professor of journalism at the Pennsylvania State University and a specialist in international communication and comparative foreign journalism.

All societies limit the range of public discussion during times of conflict,[1] and revolutionary Nicaragua has been no exception. The Sandinista government, which was under attack from domestic and foreign opponents since 1979, steadily assumed control over the public communication system in Nicaragua and limited debate on a variety of sensitive political, religious, and economic matters. Therefore,

*Excerpts from an article entitled "The Media," in Thomas W. Walker, ed., *Nicaragua: The First Five Years* (New York: Praeger, 1985).

the important questions in studying the Nicaraguan media are not whether the media were controlled or should be controlled. Rather the issue is whether the conditions existed (or might eventually exist) under which a wide range of information and opinion could be exchanged among a wide range of people if and when the level of conflict in Nicaragua is eventually reduced.

Background

Understanding the important role of the newspaper *La Prensa* in the Nicaraguan revolution is essential to answering this question. The newspaper's longtime editor Pedro Joaquín Chamorro Cardenal was first and foremost a political activist. As the descendant of one of Nicaragua's most prominent political families, which included four Conservative presidents, Chamorro dedicated his entire life to the overthrow of the Liberal Party regime of the Somoza family. In his early years, Chamorro was arrested, jailed, or exiled on a variety of charges, including organizing violent political demonstrations, running guns, leading an invasion force to overthrow the government and participating in the assassination of Anastasio Somoza García, the first of the Somoza family dynasty. In his later years, Chamorro reverted to less overt opposition to the Somoza dictatorship through the family-owned newspaper *La Prensa* and conventional party politics.[2]

Chamorro's venomous editorial attacks enraged Somoza, who responded by repeatedly censoring or otherwise repressing *La Prensa*. The censorship of *La Prensa* earned this previously obscure political combatant a reputation among regional press organizations and human rights groups, which placed pressure on the regime to end the repression. When Somoza periodically succumbed to international pressure and ended the censorship, Chamorro renewed his harsh attacks, provoking a new round of censorship. Somoza was never able to escape from this downward cycle, which contributed to his demise.

Of particular importance was Chamorro's relationship with the Inter-American Press Association (IAPA), a Miami-based organization of publishers of privately owned newspapers in the hemisphere. The major function of the conservative publishers' association has been to classify the countries of the hemisphere according to its narrow definition of press freedom and to censure those not practicing Western libertarianism.[3] Chamorro served as an IAPA director, member of the executive committee, and vice-president of its powerful Freedom of the Press Committee. In the 1960s and early 1970s, a time when most North Americans thought references to Central America meant Iowa, Chamorro was winning regional media awards, was a popular speaker to U.S. media groups, and was well known among U.S. media opinion leaders. It is important to note that Chamorro's awards and popularity were not for anything he wrote (or, for that matter, anything he was prevented from publishing). His influence was based largely on the simple fact that he was the object of repression by one of the hemisphere's more repugnant dictators.

In short, the Somoza regime could not have picked a better target for assassination if it had a masochistic desire to earn the enmity of the foreign press. The January

1978 killing of Chamorro by assassins believed to be sympathetic to Somoza (if not under the direction of Somoza or his lieutenants) not only rallied the North American press against the regime and helped to bring Nicaragua to the top of the U.S. foreign policy agenda, but it also enlarged the domestic opposition. Probably more than any other single event, this assassination solidified the opposition of the moderate business community, the Church, and the urban middle class, which were already disgruntled by Somoza's gross corruption, and led the group into an uneasy alliance with the dissimilar opposition forces of the FSLN. That coalition was instrumental in the overthrow of Somoza.[4]

After the assassination, *La Prensa,* under the direction of the Chamorro family, removed its mask as a news medium and engaged in overt sedition. The newspaper's offices were used to coordinate much of the urban opposition, and a sizable number of the staff, including the slain editor's youngest son, Carlos Fernando Chamorro, were Sandinista fighters or supporters. The Somoza National Guard responded by destroying the newspaper plant in the final days of the insurrection.

Although the Chamorro family was united in its opposition to the Somoza regime, it was badly divided over what it supported. When *La Prensa* resumed publication in August 1979 after the fall of Somoza, the family split into two factions. Xavier Chamorro, who replaced his slain brother as editor, argued that *La Prensa* should support the new Sandinista government as long as it represented the needs of the Nicaraguan people. The other faction of the family, led by Pedro Joaquín Chamorro Barrios, Jaime Chamorro Cardenal, and Pablo Antonio Cuadra (respectively, the oldest son, another brother, and a longtime associate of the murdered editor), favored a closer alliance with business and Church leaders, who were emerging as opposition to the Sandinistas. The intense family squabble was resolved when Xavier Chamorro was given 25 percent of the newspaper's assets to start a competing daily, *El Nuevo Diario,* in May 1980. While the vast majority of the technical and editorial staff joined *El Nuevo Diario, La Prensa* retained its facilities, a small minority of the staff, and, most important, its name. Compounding the family division, Carlos Chamorro had become editor of *Barricada,* the official voice of the FSLN and the only other daily newspaper in the country.

Purged of its progressive faction, the unified leadership of *La Prensa* resumed its traditional stance as arch-critic of the government. The newspaper attacked the increasingly Marxist orientation of the Sandinista-dominated ruling junta and editorialized in support of Church and business leaders, who struggled with the Sandinistas for power. As foreign and domestic opposition to the Sandinistas escalated and Nicaragua's economic problems worsened, the government became increasingly sensitive to *La Prensa*'s criticism and correspondingly promulgated stringent regulations for the nation's media. In September 1980 the junta issued decrees 511, 512, and 513 to supplement the 1979 General Provisional Law on the Media of Communication. The decrees provided for temporary suspension of a news medium for wrongful publication of information that compromised national security or the fragile national economy. The Directorate of Communication Media, a division of the Ministry of Interior, was designated to interpret and enforce the decrees. Next, in September

1981, the junta issued the Laws of Maintenance of Public Order and Security and Economic and Social Emergency, which provided for jail terms of up to three years for those found guilty of disseminating false economic information or other forms of "economic sabotage."[5] Finally, on March 15, 1982, after a series of skirmishes with counterrevolutionary forces and sabotage acts, the Sandinista government, citing the threat of a U.S.-backed invasion, declared a state of emergency. Under the decree, all radio newscasts were suspended, all radio stations were required periodically to join a government network, and all radio and print media were subject to prior censorship.[6] Other rights guaranteed by the Statute on the Rights of Nicaraguans, issued by the new government in 1979, were not affected by the state of emergency.

La Prensa was closed by the Directorate of Communication Media for the first time on July 10, 1981. In the first five years of the revolution, the newspaper was closed a total of seven times and failed to publish nearly two dozen times because of heavy censorship, delays caused by censorship, or in protest against government restrictions.[7] The official censorship of *La Prensa* was accompanied by violent demonstrations in front of the newspaper's offices, alleged harassment of some staff members, vandalism of the homes of Chamorro family members, and increasingly ugly exchanges between *La Prensa* and the Sandinista leadership. The few privately owned radio stations that broadcast news or opinion critical of the government suffered similar and in some cases worse fates, but foreign and domestic attention was focused on *La Prensa,* the only opposition print medium in Nicaragua. Except for a brief thaw in late 1983 when the government greatly reduced (but did not eliminate) censorship of *La Prensa* and made a special allocation of scarce foreign exchange so that *La Prensa* could purchase the newsprint necessary to continue publication, strict Sandinista control of the media continued at this writing. The control was closely correlated to the deterioration of relations with the domestic opposition, primarily sectors of the Church and the business community, and to intensified foreign pressure by counterrevolutionaries sponsored by the United States.

Censorship of **La Prensa** *in Context*

"So long as there continues to exist a vast plan for military aggression and economic, political, and ideological destabilization originating in the United States government, the Nicaraguan state has a legitimate right to establish censorship . . ." said Carlos Chamorro, editor of the Sandinista newspaper *Barricada.* "Personally, as a journalist, I am not in agreement with censorship," he added, "but I do agree that necessary measures must be taken to prevent the news media from being used to destabilize the country. . . ."[8]

During its entire existence, *La Prensa* primarily had been a political weapon intended to overthrow the existing government. In the tradition of the newspaper's slain editor, many of *La Prensa* staff engaged in overt revolutionary or counterrevolutionary activity. For example, two top Sandinista commanders, Bayardo Arce and William Ramírez, worked as *La Prensa* reporters while attempting to overthrow the

Somoza regime. Similarly, two reporters working for the postrevolutionary *La Prensa* were tried and convicted of counterrevolutionary activity, and a few members of the Chamorro extended family were active counterrevolutionaries.[9]

"We know *La Prensa* is conspiring against us," said Commander Ramírez. "I used to be a conspiring journalist myself. What they are trying to do at *La Prensa* we have already done. We know all the tricks."[10]

Aside from overt political activities, the editorial function of *La Prensa* was decidedly different from that of U.S. media. The United States theoretically prizes political criticism in the media, but that criticism is hardly (if ever) intended to overthrow the existing system. Rather, criticism in the U.S. media is seen as a means of maintaining the existing political system in functional balance. For example, the reporting of Watergate by the U.S. media protected the political system from manipulation and thereby perpetuated the governmental status quo. While the U.S. media may express a preference for one political party over another, most people would be hard pressed to think of a daily newspaper in the United States that openly advocates a change in the country's form of government. In contrast, the traditional goal of *La Prensa* always was to overthrow the existing political order.

Just as the ends of *La Prensa* were different from those of the U.S. media, so too were the means. The U.S. media derive their power from their ability to disseminate information and opinion to mass audiences. However, *La Prensa*'s power was not rooted in its content or audience. By any reasonable journalistic standard, *La Prensa* was a newspaper of unusually low quality. Before and after the revolution, it was consistently irresponsible, sensational, poorly written and edited, and frequently inaccurate.[11] For example, during early 1982, *La Prensa* gave extensive coverage to the so-called Sweating Virgin, a religious statue in a Managua *barrio* that supposedly exuded drops of water. *La Prensa*'s articles, written by codirector Pedro Joaquín Chamorro himself, implied that the "apparition" was sweating for Nicaragua.[12] Not exactly the stuff that wins Pulitzer prizes.

Further, most of the material censored from *La Prensa* was readily available from other sources. Stories banned from *La Prensa* frequently appeared in *Barricada* and *El Nuevo Diario*,[13] and most important information or opinion that did not appear in the dailies was heard from the church pulpit or foreign radio, including Voice of America and clandestine broadcasts from the *contras*.

Even if *La Prensa*'s content were of higher journalistic quality and unavailable elsewhere, its influence still would have been limited. In a country where the majority of the population was newly and/or marginally literate, no newspaper was particularly influential beyond the urban upper and middle classes. Even though *La Prensa* had the largest circulation, it printed only about 55,000 copies daily for a nation of nearly three million people. Even with a significant pass-along relationship, *La Prensa* reached only a small elite. The vast majority of the Nicaraguan people rarely (if ever) came in contact with a copy of *La Prensa*. But paradoxically, almost everybody in the country and every foreign observer with a passing knowledge of Nicaragua knew of the existence of the newspaper and its plight. In short, *La Prensa*'s power was not derived from bringing news and opinion to mass audiences. Rather, its sizable international and domestic reputation was based almost entirely on the fact that it was censored by the government.

Therefore, it was in the best interests of *La Prensa* to provoke continued censorship. Without censorship, it would be judged on its dubious editorial quality by a very limited audience. Consequently, a cat-and-mouse game between *La Prensa* and the government emerged. The editors almost gleefully baited the government in print and, in turn, the censors, made paranoid by wartime pressures and *La Prensa*'s seditious tradition, searched for hidden meanings in every line of copy. As a result, innocuous and sometimes silly content was censored from the paper. "*La Prensa* now . . . has increased its level of provocation," said Nelba Blandón, head of the Directorate of Communication Media and the chief government censor. "Its objectives are very simple: to force us to censor as much of the information as possible for their later appearance in front of the world as victims of the totalitarians."[14] The Sandinistas seemed to be caught in the same dilemma regarding *La Prensa* as was the Somoza regime.

Range of Debate in Nicaragua Compared to United States

The various press associations, human rights groups, and other organizations that evaluate freedom of expression around the world have a tendency to compare the conditions in a given country with a nonexistent media utopia in the United States. When compared to the libertarian *theory* of the United States, the *reality* of any media system comes up short. But when realities are matched, it becomes evident that all nations severely curtail dissent during times of national crisis. During every U.S. war, most of them fought to protect the world from dictators or totalitarians, the government tightly controlled the range of public discussion. Take for example World War I.[15] The declaration of war in April 1917 quickly led to an anti-German hysteria in the United States. Federal, state, and local governments passed numerous laws restricting dissent, and the courts, as a rule, interpreted them as broadly as possible. Thousands—perhaps tens of thousands—of U.S. citizens were prosecuted under these laws for uttering "antiwar" remarks.[16] The most notorious of those laws was the federal Espionage Act of 1917. One of the many provisions of the law made interference with military or recruiting activities a crime punishable by up to twenty years in prison, and another made it illegal to mail printed material that violated any other section of the act. By conservative estimates, at least 2,000 people were indicted under the law and at least 877 of them were convicted, almost all for what they said or wrote. In addition, more than 100 publications were banned from the mails.[17]

None of the laws was found unconstitutional, and the use of the Espionage Act to limit dissent was specifically upheld by the U.S. Supreme Court in *Schenck* vs. *United States*. Schenck had been convicted of distributing a circular that opposed the conscription law and called on the public to resist the law in an unspecified way. In that landmark decision, Justice Oliver Wendell Holmes wrote for the court:

> We admit that in many places and in ordinary times the defendants in saying all that was said in the circular would have been within their constitutional rights. But the character of every act depends upon the circumstances in which it is done. The most stringent protection of free speech would not protect a man in falsely shouting fire in a theatre and causing a panic. It does not even protect a man from an injunction against uttering words that may have all the effect of force. The question in every case is whether the words used are used in such circumstances and are of such a nature as to create a clear and present danger that they will bring about the substantive evils that Congress has a right to prevent. It is a question of proximity and degree. When a nation is at war many things that might be said in times of peace are such a hindrance to its effort that their utterance will not be endured so long as men fight and that no Court could regard them as protected by any constitutional right.[18]

Given that the United States was a relatively mature and homogeneous political system during World War I and was not particularly threatened by the fighting, the range of public discussion tolerated in Nicaragua during the first five years of the revolution was remarkable.

Despite assertions by President Reagan, IAPA and others[19] that the control of the Nicaraguan media was virtually totalitarian, the diversity of ownership and opinion was unusual for a Third World country, particularly one at war. In the summer of 1984, two of the three daily newspapers were privately owned. *El Nuevo Diario,* while supportive of the revolution, criticized specific programs and operations of the government, and censors permitted *La Prensa* to publish, for example, manifestos of opposition political groups and a pastoral letter critical of the regime.[20] The official FSLN paper *Barricada* also engaged in tactical criticism of the government and established several features designed to encourage feedback from a broader range of Nicaraguans.[21] Also books, periodicals, and other publications were printed by political parties, university groups, and other nongovernment organizations. Billboards with messages from opposition political parties were commonplace around the country.

Radio was without question the most important medium of entertainment and information in Nicaragua. In 1984, the majority of the approximately fifty stations on the air were privately owned. Two of the private stations produced their own news programs, and four other independent producers supplied news programs to other private and government radio stations. None of them was subject to prior censorship.[22] The People's Radio Broadcasting Corporation, an entity of the government, owned fifteen radio stations, most of them expropriated from the Somoza family and its supporters, and owned shares of several other privately owned stations.[23]

Radio Sandino, the official station of the FSLN, and the Voice of Nicaragua, the official station of the junta, subscribed to the Leninist principle of constructive criticism and regularly aired programs, such as "Direct Line," which were intended to facilitate a dialogue between the listeners and public officials or other guests on the program. Similarly the country's only two television channels, both operated by the

FSLN, regularly aired public feedback programs, such as "Face the People." However, only about 10 percent of the TV programming was locally produced. The largest portion of the programming came from the United States and Mexico.[24]

The New Nicaraguan Agency, a national and international news service, operated under the mixed ownership and management of *El Nuevo Diario,* the People's Radio Broadcasting Corporation, and the junta and was not subject to prior censorship.[25] In addition, the Nicaraguan news media subscribed to a wide variety of other international news services, ranging from the Associated Press of the United States to Tass of the Soviet Union.

Prognosis for Wider Range of Debate

Would a wider range of public discussion emerge in Nicaragua if and when the level of conflict was reduced? According to censor Nelba Blandón, the answer was yes. "When the danger to Nicaragua from armed attacks by ex-Somoza guardsmen disappears, *La Prensa* would again be allowed to commit the sin of publishing lies," she said.[26] However, the issue was far more complex than a simple administrative decision. Three interrelated ideological, economic, and social factors were sure to influence to a large extent the evolution of the mass communication system in Nicaragua and the degree and nature of controls exercised over public debate:

1. *Ideology.* Much of the Sandinista rhetoric was classic Third World socialism, but the actual media policy that was emerging during the fifth year of the revolution was uniquely Nicaraguan. Various speeches, interviews, and writings of the FSLN leadership and other media policymakers emphasized: (a) the rights of society to receive important and useful information instead of the rights of the individual or a social class to send information, (b) the definition of news as a social good rather than an economic commodity, and (c) the use of the media for the mobilization of society toward common goals, such as national defense, literacy, or economic development.[27] "Revolutionary journalism should be the machete, the rifle, the grenade, and the cannon in the firm and calloused hands of our workers and peasants, for we are at war . . . ," Commander Luis Carrión Cruz, member of the FSLN National Directorate and Deputy Interior Minister, told the Union of Nicaraguan Journalists. "We cannot waste energy in this war on anything that does not contribute to the rapid and effective material, political, and ideological destruction of the people's enemies."[28]

However, to the extent that ideology is manifest in a nation's laws, the new Nicaraguan media policy was not consistent with Marxist doctrine and was a clear concession not only to Nicaragua's history and culture but also to the special role of *La Prensa.* In its fifth and final session, the Council of State debated the draft Mass Media Law, "which proposes regulations to guarantee freedom of expression, as well as to defend the interests of the country and its people, who could be affected by an irresponsible use of this freedom."[29] The media law was intended to replace the hodgepodge of laws and decrees affecting the media before the 1984 elections, but the Council of State was unable to reach agreement on provisions, such as registration of journalists, state ownership of television, post hoc sanctions for wrongful publication, and a variety of other media controls. Although the legislation was not finalized, the FSLN proposal was highly significant because it would have institutionalized the continuation of *nongovernment,* albeit closely regulated, channels of public communication and criticism. In contrast, all media in a totalitarian Marxist system are owned and operated by the party and state and such complex regulations are unnecessary.[30]

2. *Economy.* International communication researchers consistently have found close correlations between a nation's level of economic development and the degree of controls on the media. Poor countries have a much more narrow range of public debate and criticism than rich countries.[31] Attempting to recover from a devastating revolutionary war and series of natural disasters and facing a counterrevolutionary war aimed in large part at the country's productive capacity, Nicaragua did not have the economic conditions that historically have fostered a wider range of public debate. In fact, the range of debate that existed during the first five years of the revolution exceeded what would be expected in a country at its level of economic development.

3. *Social Differentiation.* The media are integral threads woven into the fabric of society and reciprocally affect and are affected by social conditions. The media are not autonomous actors but rather reflect the relevant power groupings in society. Consequently, complex social systems in which social power is highly differentiated tend to have media that serve a critical function. In these societies, mostly large, modern industrial states, the media initiate social action and maintain discourse among the diverse power bases that would not be able to solve their conflicts without the channels of mass communication. On the other hand, less complex systems in which social power is monolithic tend to have media that avoid conflict and attempt to build a consensus. Because the relatively few powerholders in these primarily Third World societies can easily resolve their differences through interpersonal communication, conflict-oriented mass media are not necessary for maintaining the social system.[32]

While Nicaragua in 1984 was far less complex than a modern industrial state such as the United States and political power was concentrated in the hands of the Sandinistas, the Nicaraguan power structure was far from monolithic. The Church, the private business sector, and active political opposition groups were also important powerholders. To the extent that these and other groups retained power, Nicaraguan channels of public communication were likely to carry a commensurate degree of criticism of the government. "If we have a mixed economy, we must have a political system that corresponds to that," said Carlos Chamorro, director of the FSLN's *Barricada.* "We want to institutionalize dissent and opposition.[33] In preparation for the 1984 elections, the Nicaraguan Council of State passed two laws accomplishing just that. The Political Parties Law guaranteed the right to establish political parties and to disseminate one's political ideology, and the Electoral Law guaranteed the political parties access to the media during the election campaign period.[34]

Of particular importance was the relationship between *La Prensa* and the Church, a major powerholder in Nicaragua. Following the purge of progressive elements from *La Prensa,* the newspaper markedly increased its coverage of religious matters and consistently advocated the position of the Church in the escalating confrontation between the curia and the government. In turn, Archbishop Miguel Obando y Bravo repeatedly expressed solidarity with *La Prensa* and, in his homilies and pastoral letters, called for an end to censorship of the newspaper. In August 1981, while *La Prensa* was suspended by the government, the archbishop even held a mass in *La Prensa*'s offices to pray for the future publication of the newspaper. *La Prensa* had been suspended for erroneously reporting that a high government official had accused Obando y Bravo of instigating counterrevolution. This symbiosis was crucial to the continued power of both the church hierarchy and *La Prensa* and presented formidable opposition to the government.[35]

Conclusions

Given the prevailing ideology, the level of conflict, and the socioeconomic conditions, the limits of media criticism that existed during the first five years of the Nicaraguan revolution seemed likely to continue for the next five years. A major impediment to a wider debate was *La Prensa*. For decades, the newspaper derived its power from being censored. *La Prensa*'s rhetoric about press freedom notwithstanding, an end to censorship was not in its best interests. Although the Sandinistas might replace censorship with other forms of media control, any overall reduction of control was likely to result in a new round of provocations by *La Prensa* and repression by the government.

All members of the Chamorro family and the Sandinista leadership agreed that censorship had done great harm to the Nicaraguan revolution. The only disagreement was whether the benefits outweighed the debits. Commanders Tomás Borge and Carlos Núñez, the members of the FSLN Directorate primarily responsible for media issues, took the position that censorship was a necessary evil.[36] Perhaps in time they would come to realize that their censorship of *La Prensa* was ultimately a greater threat to the regime than the uncensored content of the newspaper.

The perspective of Carlos Chamorro, both a prominent member of the newspaper family and an avid Sandinista, was a hopeful sign that such an evolution was possible.

> The revolution was not born with a preconceived communication policy, nor does it have for the moment something that we are able to call a model. We are in a process of learning, experimenting and searching, and we believe that our most valuable school has been this permanent confrontation with the bourgeois press inside the framework of Nicaraguan political pluralism.[37]

Notes

1. John D. Stevens, "Freedom of Expression: New Dimensions" in *Mass Media and the National Experience: Essays in Communications History,* edited by Ronald T. Farrar and John D. Stevens (New York: Harper & Row, 1971), pp. 15–17. Frederick S. Siebert, *Freedom of the Press in England 1476–1776* (Urbana: University of Illinois Press, 1965), pp. 9–10; Paul L. Murphy, *The Constitution in Crisis Times 1918–1969* (New York: Harper & Row, 1972); John Spicer Nichols, "The Mass Media: Their Functions in Social Conflict," in *Cuba: Internal and International Affairs,* edited by Jorge I. Domínguez (Beverly Hills, Calif.: Sage Publications, 1982).
2. For more detailed discussion of the history and development of the Nicaraguan media, see John Spicer Nichols, "The News Media in the Revolution," in *Nicaragua in Revolution,* edited by Thomas W. Walker (New York: Praeger, 1982), pp. 181–199; and Nichols.
3. Jerry W. Knudson, "The Inter-American Press Association as Champion of Press Freedom: Reality or Rhetoric?" Unpublished paper presented to the meeting of the International Communication Division, Association for Education in Journalism, Fort Collins, Colorado, August 21, 1973.
4. John A. Booth, *The End and the Beginning: The Nicaraguan Revolution* (Boulder, Colo.: Westview Press, 1982), pp. 157–158; Walker, *Nicaragua in Revolution,* passim.
5. Jonathan Evan Maslow, "Letter from Nicaragua: The Junta and the Press—A Family Affair," *Columbia Journalism Review,* March/April 1981, pp. 46–52 (also see "Footnote to Nicaragua," *Columbia Journalism Review,* November 1981, p. 82); Instituto Histórico Centroamericano, "The State of Emergency: Background, Causes and Implementation," in Rosset and Vandermeer, *The Nicaraguan Reader,* pp. 65–71; Lars Schoultz, "Human Rights in Nicaragua," *LASA* (Latin American Studies Association) *Newsletter* 13 (Fall 1982), pp. 9–13.
6. "Government Establishes Control of Media," Managua Domestic Service, translated and transcribed in *Foreign Broadcast Information Service* (hereafter *FBIS*), March 17, 1982, p. 9.
7. M. L. Stein, "A Lone Free Voice in Nicaragua," *Editor & Publisher,* May 19, 1984, p. 16.
8. "Chamorro Brothers Discuss Freedom of Press," *O Estado de São Paulo* (Brazil), translated and transcribed in *FBIS,* April 17, 1983, p. 74.
9. Nichols, "News Media in the Revolution," p. 188; "La Prensa Journalist Sentenced to 3 Years," Radio Sandino, translated and transcribed in *FBIS,* June 19, 1981, p. 13; Stephen Kinzer, "Nicaraguan Rebels Ask Peace Talks," *New York Times,* December 2, 1983, p. A3; Karl E. Meyer, "The Editorial Notebook: Sticks, Stones and Somocistas," *New York Times,* June 28, 1983, p. A26.
10. Lawrence Wright, "War of Words: Nicaragua's Newspaper Family Tears Itself Apart Over Its Revolutionary Legacy," *Mother Jones,* June 1983, p. 40.
11. Hodding Carter, "Nicaragua: Campaign '84," *Inside Story,* Public Broadcasting Service, April 13, 1984; Charles Burke, "Ideological Bias in Nicaraguan Newspapers," Paper presented to the Association for Education in Journalism, Corvallis, Oregon, August 1983; Nigel Cross, "Revolution and the Press in Nicaragua," *Index on Censorship* 2 (1982), pp. 38–40; David Kunzle, "Nicaragua's *Prensa*—Capitalist Thorn in Socialist Flesh," typewritten manuscript.
12. Katherine Ellison, "The Censor and the Censored: Nicaragua's High-Stakes Cat-and-Mouse Game," *The Quill* (Society of Professional Journalists), November 1982, p. 29.
13. "Chamorro on Censorship, Economy, Military," Radio Cadena YSKL (San Salvador), translated and transcribed in *FBIS,* December 1, 1983, p. 18.
14. Hodding Carter, "Nicaragua: House Divided," *Inside Story,* Public Broadcasting Service, October 13, 1983.
15. The following discussion of U.S. media during World War I is a synthesis of John D. Stevens, *Shaping the First Amendment: The Development of Free Expression* (Beverly Hills, Calif.: Sage Publications, 1982), pp. 44–54.
16. Ibid., p. 48.
17. Ibid., p. 47.
18. Ibid., p. 51–52.
19. "Prepared Text of Reagan Speech on Central American Policy," *New York Times,* May 10, 1984,

p. A16; *Central America: Defending Our Vital Interests* (Address by President Reagan before a joint session of Congress, April 27, 1983), Current Policy No. 482, (Washington: U.S. Department of State, Bureau of Public Affairs, April 1, 1983); "Sandinista Law Ends Freedom of the Press," *IAPA News,* July 1982, pp. 12, 13.

20. Interview with Xavier Chamorro, director of *El Nuevo Diario,* Managua, October 4, 1982; Hedrick Smith, "Nicaragua Elections Likely in '85 Despite New Snag, Diplomats Say," *New York Times,* February 6, 1984, pp. A1, 8; Richard J. Meislin, "Nicaraguan Assails Bishops in Renewed Conflict," *New York Times,* April 26, 1984, p. A10.
21. Interview with Carlos Fernando Chamorro Barrios, director of *Barricada,* Managua, October 4, 1983; Carlos F. Chamorro, "Experiences of the Revolutionary Communication in Nicaragua." Speech to the International Forum of Social Communication on the Twentieth Anniversary of *El Día,* Mexico City, June 25, 1982 (mimeograph in Spanish).
22. Interview with Lieutenant Nelba Blandón, director of Directorate of Communication Media, Ministry of Interior, Managua, October 6, 1983.
23. Interview with Leonel Espinoza, head of communication media, Department of Political Education and Propaganda, Managua, October 5, 1983; Carlos Chamorro, "Experiences of Revolutionary Communication"; "Junta Creates Radio Broadcasting Corporation," Radio Sandino, translated and transcribed in *FBIS,* May 14, 1981, p. 14; "Advances in National Broadcasting Reported," Radio Sandino, translated and transcribed in *FBIS,* July 22, 1982, p. 13.
24. U.S. Information Agency, "Country Data: Nicaragua," January 1, 1983 (mimeograph).
25. Interview with Carlos García Castillo, general director of the New Nicaraguan Agency, Managua, October 5, 1982; and interview with Blandón.
26. Clarence W. Moore, "Censors Mightier Than Pen?" *The Times of the Americas,* September 14, 1983, p. 8.
27. "Commander Borge Speaks at *El Nuevo Diario,"* Managua Domestic Service, translated and transcribed in *FBIS,* May 24, 1982, pp. 16–18; "Ramírez Discusses Press Freedom," Radio Sandino in *FBIS;* Carlos Nuñez Téllez, untitled speech given on the fourth anniversay of *Barricada,* Managua, August 29, 1983 (mimeograph).
28. "Luis Carrión Views on Revolutionary Journalism," Radio Sandino, translated and transcribed in *FBIS,* May 17, 1983, p. 17.
29. "The Mass Media Law," *Weekly Bulletin,* New Nicaraguan Agency, May 19, 1984, pp. 4–5.
30. "Parliament Suspends Media Law Debate," *Weekly Bulletin,* New Nicaraguan Agency, June 16, 1984, pp. 1–2; interview with Manuel Eugarrios, delegate of the Union of Nicaraguan Journalists to the Council of State, Managua, October 5, 1983; interviews with Espinoza and Carlos Chamorro.
31. Stevens in Farrar and Stevens, *Mass Media;* John C. Merrill and Ralph L. Lowenstein, *Media, Messages, and Men: New Perspectives in Communication* (New York: David McKay Co., 1971); Francisco J. Vásquez, "Media Economics in the Third World," in *Comparative Mass Media Systems,* edited by L. John Martin and Anju Grover Chaudhary (New York: Longman, 1983), pp. 265–280.
32. Phillip J. Tichenor, George A. Donohue, and Clarice N. Olien, *Community Conflict and Press* (Beverly Hills, Calif.: Sage Publications, 1980); Nichols, "Mass Media in Social Conflict," in Domínguez, *Cuba;* Vásquez, "Media Economics," in Martin and Chaudhary, *Comparative Mass Media Systems;* Stevens, "Freedom of Expression," in Stevens and Farrar, *Mass Media.*
33. Smith, "Nicaragua Elections," p. 8.
34. "Law of Political Parties: Decree No. 1312," *La Gaceta* (official daily of Nicaraguan government), September 13, 1983, p. 2 (in Spanish); "Nicaragua," *Mesoamerica,* April 1984, pp. 6–7; "Electoral Law Takes Effect," *Weekly Bulletin,* New Nicaragua Agency, March 31, 1984, pp. 4–6.
35. "Archbishop Expresses Solidarity with *La Prensa,"* Radio Corporación translated and transcribed in *FBIS,* August 24, 1981, p. 13; Raymond Bonner, "Humiliation of Priest Fires Nicaragua," *New York Times,* August 21, 1982, p. 2; Meislin, "Nicaraguan Assails Bishops."
36. "Núñez Stresses Importance of Press Censorship," Central American News Agency translated and transcribed in *FBIS,* July 14, 1982, p. 12; "Chamorro Brothers Discuss Freedom of Press"; "Commander Borge Speaks,"; Carter, "House Divided."
37. Carlos Chamorro, "Experiences of Revolutionary Communication," p. 16.

*17. Country Reports on Human Rights Practices for 1984: Nicaragua**

By the U.S. Department of State

During 1984 the government continued to tighten Sandinista control over Nicaraguan society and to intimidate the remaining opposition. The state of emergency declared in 1982 remained in effect throughout 1984, although some provisions were modified. The government continued to use special tribunals established outside the judicial system to try cases of suspected subversives. This denies the accused the better, though still flawed, legal protection provided by the regular courts. The Sandinistas continued to rely on organizations controlled by the Sandinista National Liberation Front, such as the ubiquitous "block committees," to help implement their policies at the local level and to exert control, instill loyalty, and to identify and implement sanctions against suspected opponents. Using both its own powers and intimidation by Sandinista organizations, the government systematically harassed opposition political parties, independent labor confederations, the private sector, the Catholic Church, and the independent media. The government continued prior censorship of the print and electronic media, and cracked down with new vigor in this area after some relaxation during the 1984 campaign period. Sandinista block committees and other organizations frequently disrupted campaign rallies held by opposition political parties, contravening guarantees in the electoral law. The police often did not intervene to prevent such harassment or violence. Through both legal and extralegal means, the government continued to seize private property. The 10,000 Miskito Indians forcibly resettled from their Rio Coco homelands in 1982 continued to be prohibited from returning there. About 2,000 more Miskitos fled en masse to Honduras in April and May. There are continuing credible reports that the security forces have tortured and killed Miskito Indians and have confiscated or destroyed their food supply and property.

Two domestic human rights organizations operate in Nicaragua. The Permanent Human Rights Commission (CPDH) is an independent agency established in 1977. It played a key role in exposing human rights violations committed under the Somoza regime. After the Sandinistas came to power in 1979, the CPDH also publicized human rights abuses committed under the new government. Since 1981, the CPDH has been subject to constant harassment by the Sandinista National Liberation Front, impeding its work but not silencing its voice. The government founded the National Commission for the Promotion and Protection of Human Rights in 1980. The National Commission claims to be independent, but the government appoints its members and funds its budget. It is the only organization permitted by the government to file applications for pardon or to request the review of cases on human rights grounds.

---

*Excerpts from *Country Reports on Human Rights Practices for 1984*, submitted to the Committee on Foreign Relations, U.S. Senate, and Committee on Foreign Affairs, U.S. House of Representatives, 1985.

It is also charged with reporting incidents of human rights abuses to the proper authorities and promoting the observance of human rights within the government.

Respect for Human Rights
Section 1 Respect for the Integrity of the Person, Including Freedom from:

a. Political Killing

There is credible evidence that the military and security forces were responsible for the deaths of a number of detained persons in 1984. The CPDH documented six such cases, and it estimated that many more went unreported. The government responded to these accusations by claiming some were "killed while attempting to escape" or "killed while resisting arrest," while others were allegedly guerrillas killed in combat. The CPDH also reported that military and police officials arbitrarily shot a number of suspected subversives. In one case three officials reportedly shot a mentally handicapped farmer who they claimed was a dangerous suspect, though they had no warrant and did not present any charges to the family. Displaced persons reported that military and security forces operating in remote areas summarily executed local peasants whom they suspected were antigovernment guerrillas or their sympathizers, sometimes after physically mutilating them. In the section on Nicaragua of its 1984 annual report, the Inter-American Human Rights Commission of the Organization of American States stated, "Concerning the right to live, human rights organizations have continued to denounce violations, especially in the forms of forced disappearances and as a result of the abuse of power by members of the security forces. The Commission has been able to verify that a large number of denunciations referred to events that took place in the zones of conflict."

The government claimed that guerrillas killed around 1,000 civilians in 1984. Some civilians have died in the fighting between the government and the guerrillas, although no reliable information is available on their number. Some reportedly died in guerrilla ambushes of government military vehicles carrying civilian passengers. The government has charged the guerrillas with torturing and summarily executing prisoners. The guerrillas have denied that they target civilians and have asserted that the security forces' indiscriminate use of heavy artillery near population centers has caused civilian casualties.

b. Disappearance

The security forces often hold suspected guerrillas and subversives incommunicado indefinitely without notifying family members. In 1984 the CPDH documented sixty cases of disappearances in which security forces were implicated, but in which the government would not acknowledge involvement. In some of those cases, though reported in 1984, the individuals had actually disappeared in earlier years. The government for its part claimed the guerrillas kidnapped many civilians. It is widely believed that many of these alleged kidnappings may have been voluntary desertions to the guerrillas. Anti-Sandinista guerrilla forces took captive three Sandinista Front members, including Sandinista National Assembly candidate Ray Hooker, on September 5. The guerrillas released all three on October 30 in exchange for three prisoners held by the government. During 1984, one guerrilla group turned over fifty-four captured soldiers to the Costa Rican Red Cross.

c. Torture and Cruel, Inhuman, or Degrading Treatment or Punishment

In 1984 the CPDH continued to collect evidence of systematic physical and psychological abuse and torture. Prisoners were reportedly kept in cramped, dark cells and fed meals at irregular intervals in order to disorient them, ordered to use only their prison numbers and not their names, and subjected to physical abuse and to threats against their family. One prisoner claimed that food and medical attention were almost nonexistent, and that whatever supplemental foodstuffs were brought in through relatives were stolen by the guards. Another reported that he was kept naked in a cold cell with a ceiling so low he could not stand upright. Other reports alleged prisoners were suspended from the ceiling by their hands during interrogation. Prisoners also reported being beaten with chains, fists, and gun butts. It was alleged that, as a form of punishment, one prisoner was placed in a cell with several tuberculoid prisoners. Cases of psychological torture were also frequently reported. Prisoners were forced to listen to the screams of those being tortured, then were told by security officials that the screams came from members of their families. One prisoner was told, falsely, that his family had been arrested by security officials, who forced the spouse to don prison garb. She and her husband were then allowed to see each other but not to converse. Reportedly, security officials physically abused and threatened alleged "subversives" and political suspects. Nicaraguans who fled to Costa Rica reported incidents of rape, torture, and murder of children by security and military forces. In the case of Prudencio Baltadano, soldiers tied him to a tree and cut off his ears. Interior Minister Tomás Borge admitted that some cases of physical abuse and killings of detained persons by security forces had occurred, but claimed the government was working to resolve the problem. The National Human Rights Commission also stated that occasional individual abuses of authority had occurred, but insisted that those guilty had been found and punished.

d. Arbitrary Arrest, Detention, or Exile

According to the government, there were approximately 5,000 persons in jail, including about 2,000 ex-national guardsmen or persons accused of cooperation with former President Somoza. The CPDH estimated 900 prisoners had been convicted for "subversive" activities and an additional 500 were being held pending charges.

The 1982 state of emergency suspended those provisions of the Fundamental Statute promulgated by the government in 1979 which granted detained persons the right to be held for no more than seven days without arraignment. Habeas corpus was also suspended in security-related cases. Both of these rights were partially restored on August 6, 1984. As antigovernment activities increased in 1984, the security forces arrested hundreds of suspects under the Law of Maintenance of Order and Public Security. Open expression of dissent on occasion resulted in harassment or detention. Suspected guerrillas and "subversives" continued to be held in special holding facilities with no access to legal counsel or to domestic or international humanitarian organizations. Some were released after the completion of an investigation lasting from three to six months on the average, others were remanded to the special tribunals, and many simply remained in detention. In 1983 the government declared that because of the security situation, some former National Guard members had to remain in custody even though they had completed their sentences and this practice continued in 1984. Others held on security charges also remained incarcerated after they had been exonerated or had served their sentences. Former Minister of Defense Bernardino Larios, charged in 1981 with plotting the assassination of Sandinista leaders, was held for three years until the Supreme Court overturned his conviction and ordered his release. Larios was held an additional forty days before the government finally honored the release order, and after his release, he was refused permission to leave the country and was subjected to other government-inspired harassment. The Inter-American Human Rights Commission's 1984 annual report called attention to "numerous detainees holding release orders issued by a competent judge, but who are kept in prison for prolonged periods, with no reason given for the detention. Situations such as the above represent a violation of the right to personal freedom and to due process, and they must be remedied promptly to lend substance to the Nicaraguan government's statements concerning the independence and authority of the country's judiciary. The Commission repeats, with respect to the right to a trial and to due process, that the remedy of habeas corpus or amparo may not be suspended as it has been in Nicaragua."

e. Denial of a Fair Public Trial

Under the 1979 Fundamental Statute, the judiciary was to be an autonomous branch of government, an independence generally exercised in ordinary criminal cases. In cases where the accused was charged with "counterrevolutionary" or "subversive" activity, however, judges have routinely decided in favor of the prosecution. Nevertheless, some judges have continued to exercise limited independence. For example, the Supreme Court ruled in January that the conviction of former Defense Minister Bernardino Larios was improper, due to an absence of convincing evidence, and ordered that the prisoner be freed.

*18. Human Rights in Nicaragua: Reagan, Rhetoric, and Reality**

By the Americas Watch Committee

Americas Watch is one of a select group of human rights organizations—Amnesty International, Helsinki Watch, the Lawyers Committee for International Human Rights—

*Excerpts from the July 1985 Americas Watch report of the same name.

with international reputations for accuracy in reporting abuses. Americas Watch is the organization that focuses specifically on the Western Hemisphere.

Introduction

> The Nicaraguan people are trapped in a totalitarian dungeon.
>
> President Reagan
> July 18, 1984[1]

> Some would like to ignore the incontrovertible evidence of the Communist religious persecution—of Catholics, Jews, and Fundamentalists; of their campaign of virtual genocide against the Miskito Indians.
>
> President Reagan
> June 6, 1985[2]

> The United States will continue to view human rights as the moral center of our foreign policy.
>
> President Reagan
> to UN General Assembly
> September 24, 1984[3]

The Reagan administration, since its inception, has characterized Nicaragua's revolutionary government as a menace to the Americas and to the Nicaraguan people. Many of its arguments to this effect are derived from human rights "data," which the administration has used in turn to justify its support for the *contra* rebels. The Americas Watch does not take a position on the U.S. geopolitical strategy in Central America. But where human rights are concerned we find the administration's approach to Nicaragua deceptive and harmful.

This report is addressed to the deception and harm done when human rights are manipulated. Allegations of human rights abuse have become a major focus of the administration's campaign to overthrow the Nicaraguan government. Such a concerted campaign to use human rights in justifying military action is without precedent in U.S.–Latin American relations, and its effect is an unprecedented debasement of the human rights cause.

This debasement of human rights contradicts President Reagan's professed commitment to such rights. Far from being the "moral center" of U.S. foreign policy toward Nicaragua, the human rights issue has been utilized in the service of a foreign policy that seeks to advance other interests. Whether or not those interests are legitimate is not the province of the Americas Watch; what is of concern to us is an attempt to proclaim a false symmetry between promoting those interests and promoting human rights.

The administration has disregarded the norms of impartial human rights reporting when it deals with Nicaragua. The administration's accusations against Nicaragua rest upon a core of fact; the Sandinistas have committed serious abuses, especially in 1981 and 1982, including arbitrary arrests and the summary relocation of thousands of Miskito Indians. Around the core of fact, however, U.S. officials have built an edifice of innuendo and exaggeration. The misuse of human rights data has become pervasive in officials' statements to the press, in White House handouts on Nicaragua, in the annual *Country Report* on Nicaraguan human rights prepared by the State Department, and most notably, in the president's own remarks. When inconvenient, findings of the U.S. embassy in Managua have been ignored; the same is true of data gathered by independent sources.

In Nicaragua there is no systematic practice of forced disappearances, extrajudicial killings, or torture—as has been the case with the "friendly" armed forces in El Salvador. While prior censorship has been imposed by emergency legislation, debate on major social and political questions is robust, outspoken, even often strident. The November 1984 elections, though deficient, were a democratic advance over the past five decades of Nicaraguan history and compare favorably with those of El Salvador and Guatemala and do not suffer significantly by comparison with those of Honduras, Mexico, or Panama. The Sandinista Party obtained a popular mandate, while the opposition parties that chose to participate secured some 30 percent of the seats in the Constituent Assembly. Nor has the government practiced elimination of cultural or ethnic groups, as the administration frequently claims; indeed in this respect, as in most others, Nicaragua's record is by no means so bad as that of Guatemala, whose government the administration consistently defends. Moreover, some notable reductions in abuses have occurred in Nicaragua since 1982, despite the pressure caused by escalating external attacks.

The Nicaraguan government must be held to account for the abuses which continue to take place, like restrictions on press freedom and due process. But unless those abuses are fairly described, the debate on Nicaragua ceases to have meaning.

Inflammatory terms, loosely used, are of particular concern. President Reagan has described Nicaragua's elected president, Daniel Ortega, as "a little dictator" and has termed the Nicaraguan government's recent relocations of civilians a "Stalinist" tactic.[4] Such epithets seek to prejudice public debate through distortion. Perhaps most harmful in this respect is the term most frequently used by President Reagan and administration officials to denounce the Nicaraguan government—that is, "totalitarian." This is a misuse of the term and it misrepresents the situation in Nicaragua.

In a totalitarian state, the state—or an institution such as the party or the military that effectively exercises the power of the state—destroys all independent associations and silences all independent voices. Churches, labor unions, newspapers, academic institutions, political parties, business organizations, and professional associations are forced to become organs of the state, or subservient to the state, or they cease to exist. A certain amount of criticism may be tolerated in a totalitarian state, but certainly not criticism that challenges the legitimacy of the state, or its governing bodies, or its leadership. Moreover, such limited scope for dissent as may be tolerated in a totalitarian state tends to disappear entirely when the state considers itself to be threatened.

This description of a totalitarian state bears no resemblance to Nicaragua in 1985. The Catholic Church and several Protestant denominations not only operate independently in Nicaragua but they are outspoken in expressing their views on religious matters and also on every conceivable secular issue; similarly, business and professional associations and labor unions are not only independent but are unhesitatingly critical of the government and its leaders. Political parties representing a wide spectrum of views not only operate, but have elected representatives who debate issues in the Constituent Assembly. The parties that chose to participate in the 1984 national elections—from which no party was banned—were free to be as strident as they chose in attacking the Sandinista Party and its leaders, and frequently exercised this right on television and radio time provided to them without cost to conduct this campaign. An independent human rights commission maintains professionally staffed offices in Managua, prints and distributes—both nationally and internationally—detailed monthly reports on human rights abuses by the government, and does not seem to circumscribe itself in denouncing those abuses. A newer human rights group operates without restraint in seeking redress for Miskito Indians who have been victims of human rights abuses.

Any Nicaraguan and any visitor to Nicaragua can walk into a score or more of offices in the country's capital and encounter the officers and employees of various independent institutions who will not only voice their opinions freely in criticism of the government and its leaders, and even challenge the legitimacy of the state, but will also do so for attribution. Some will hand out literature expressing those opinions. This is inconceivable in any state appropriately described as totalitarian. Moreover, it is inconceivable in many of the countries vigorously supported by the United States. While a visitor to nearby El Salvador, Guatemala, or Haiti for example, may encounter criticism of the government, if it is criticism that is as strong as one regularly encounters in Nicaragua, the speaker will ordinarily request anonymity. Similarly, it is impossible to find independent institutions speaking so freely in more distant allies of the United States such as Turkey, Saudi Arabia, Indonesia, Zaire, Morocco—to name just a few.

To point out that dissent is expressed openly and robustly in Nicaragua is not to deny that many of those expressing dissent have legitimate grievances. We believe that the abuses that led to those grievances should be carefully documented and condemned vigorously. In our previous reports on Nicaragua, and in the body of this report, we discuss such abuses as restrictions on expression and association; denials of due process of law in many cases in which defendants have been accused of security-related crimes; the government's failure to acknowledge detentions promptly and the relationship of that failure to other abuses against detainees; the mistreatment of prisoners; the violent abuses against the Miskito Indian minority that took place in late 1981 and 1982; and the abuses that have accompanied forcible relocation of thousands of Nicaraguans from war zones.

It is, of course, extremely difficult to assess to what degree liberties have been restricted in Nicaragua because of the U.S.-sponsored effort to overthrow its government. The difficulty in assessing what might have been is all the greater because the Reagan administration has argued, at least implicitly, that such openness as prevails in Nicaragua today reflects the effort of the Sandinistas to win international support for their effort to resist the *contras*.

According to this logic, it is because of the *contra* war, rather than in spite of the *contra* war, that Nicaragua maintains some of the characteristics of an open society. (There is, of course, a contradiction between acknowledgment that there is some openness in Nicaragua and the allegation that it is a totalitarian state; this contradiction is occasionally resolved by the suggestion that it is the totalitarian *tendency* of the Sandinistas that is objectionable.)

If it were true that the openness in Nicaragua is a consequence of the *contra* war, this would, of course, contradict everything that is known about the way that nations behave when they are at war. Even the freest nations radically circumscribe liberties under such circumstances.[5] At the very least, such use of human rights arguments to justify military interference should be regarded with skepticism. Given the consequences of the U.S. policy to Nicaraguan civilians, that skepticism may justifiably become concern.

For the past two years the most violent abuses of human rights in Nicaragua have been committed by the *contras*. Here too the administration has substituted rhetoric for a clear look at the facts. After several on-site investigations into *contra* practices, we find that *contra* combatants systematically murder the unarmed, including medical personnel; rarely take prisoners; and force civilians into collaboration. These abuses have become a rallying point inside Nicaragua. Indeed, Sandinista rhetoric on these questions is often almost as heated as the administration's, such that the *contras* are officially referred to as ''beasts,'' ''mercenaries,'' and, even though a number are disillusioned supporters of the revolution, they are invariably labeled as ''Somocistas''; all civilians who leave Nicaragua with the *contras* are considered ''kidnapped,'' although there is evidence that many go voluntarily.

This report attempts to put the rhetoric into perspective. We have selected representative U.S. allegations—and, where we have found them, Nicaraguan official statements on the same subjects—and compared them with the facts we have gathered in four years of monitoring Nicaraguan conditions. We have not attempted to cover every facet of Nicaraguan life in detail, but have taken our guidance from the administration's own chosen themes. These are: the issue of respect for life and personal integrity; Nicaraguan government relations with the opposition press, religious constituencies, and human rights monitors; the Miskito Indians; the November 1984 national elections; number of refugees as an index of repression; and the character and practices of the *contras*.

Americas Watch has published seven previous reports on Nicaragua.[6] We have evaluated administration evidence in each of those reports, but our focus has been on investigating at first hand and on working closely with Nicaraguan human rights investigators. Our purpose here is to offer a guide to the Nicaraguan case, supplemental to our more detailed reports, and to present that case in a manner free of rhetoric. We are convinced that only neutral reporting can encourage improvements by either side in Nicaragua. The Reagan administration, by forsaking neutrality on human rights, has done damage both to the cause of human rights generally and to Nicaraguans in particular.

Summary

A. In examining the Reagan administration's treatment of human rights in Nicaragua, we find that:

1. Far from being "the moral center" of policy toward Nicaragua, human rights has been used to justify a policy of confrontation.
2. To that end, human rights data have been distorted in the annual State Department *Country Reports* on Nicaragua, in White House informational handouts on Nicaragua, in speeches and public statements by senior officials and most notably, in the president's own remarks on Nicaragua.
3. Such misuse of human rights to justify military interference is in U.S.-Latin American relations an unprecedented debasement of the human rights cause.
4. Of particular concern is the administration's constant—and inaccurate—use of the term "totalitarian" to characterize Nicaragua.

B. With respect to actual human rights conditions in Nicaragua, we have examined the administration's claims in the areas where U.S. accusations are most forceful (and have also compared the facts to Nicaraguan government claims, where we have found them), and find that:

1. There is not a policy of torture, political murder, or disappearances in Nicaragua. While such abuses have occurred, principally in 1981 and 1982, the government has acted in some cases to investigate and punish those responsible, although we continue to urge a full accounting of seventy Miskito disappearances from 1982 and 1983 and of the deaths (totally twenty-one to twenty-four) in the Leimus and Walpa Siksa incidents of 1981 and 1982.
2. The administration has misrepresented the denial of press freedom in Nicaragua, attempting to convey the impression that former freedoms were eliminated by the Sandinistas. On the other hand, serious problems of censorship persist and censorship should be ended except to the extent strictly necessary to deal with the national emergency.
3. The issue of religious persecution in Nicaragua is without substance, although it is evident that the political conflict between the Catholic Church and the government has included cases of clear abuses, such as the expulsion of ten foreign priests. There is not a policy of anti-Semitism, nor are Christians—Catholic or Protestant—persecuted for their faith.
4. The Miskitos, who have become this administration's favored symbol of alleged Sandinista cruelty, suffered serious abuses in 1981 and 1982. Since then, the government's record of relations with the Miskitos has improved

dramatically, including an amnesty, efforts at negotiations, and the beginnings of repatriation, while the *contras'* treatment of Miskitos and other Indians has become increasingly more violent.

5. The November 1984 Nicaraguan national elections, though deficient, represented an advance over past Nicaraguan experience and a positive step toward pluralism, resulting in significant representation of opposition parties in the Constituent Assembly. Nicaragua should be prodded to take additional steps to advance a democratic process.
6. There is no evidence to support administration claims that a U.S. failure to interfere in Nicaragua would generate waves of "feet people."
7. To state the above is not to disregard or in any way to diminish the importance of abuses that have taken place in Nicaragua. A newspaper, such as *La Prensa,* openly proclaims its opposition character, but it suffers heavy-handed prior censorship; some leaders of business associations and of labor unions have endured jailings for their peaceful activities; ten foreign priests were expelled from Nicaragua for taking part in a peaceful demonstration that the government considered illegal; except during the 1984 elections, the political parties have not been permitted to conduct outdoor rallies; and there have been a number of occasions when *turbas* (mobs) presumably controlled by the government or by the Sandinista Party have been used to intimidate those expressing opposition views. Perhaps most disturbing of all, since the revolution succeeded in 1979, there has been an interlocking relationship between the Sandinista Party and the state so that, for example, it is the Popular Sandinista Army that defends the state and it is Sandinista-sponsored organizations that choose two of three members of the tribunals that try those accused of a variety of security-related offenses.

C. With respect to the human rights practices of the *contras,* we have examined the administration's claims for the moral character of these insurgents and find, to the contrary, that the *contras* have systematically engaged in the killing of prisoners and the unarmed, including medical and relief personnel; selective attacks on civilians and indiscriminate attacks; torture and other outrages against personal dignity; and the kidnappings and harassment of refugees. We find that the most violent abuses of human rights in Nicaragua today are being committed by the *contras,* and that the Reagan administration's policy of support for the *contras* is, therefore, a policy clearly inimical to human rights.

Notes

1. Quoted in "New Effort to Aid Nicaraguan Rebels," *New York Times,* July 19, 1984.
2. "Remarks of the President to Fundraising Luncheon for Senator Jeremiah Denton," Birmingham, Alabama, June 6, 1985.
3. "Most at UN Commend Talk," *Washington Post,* September 25, 1984.
4. With regard to the latter epithet, it is worth noting that Stalin's forcible relocation of the Crimean

Tartars was so inhumane that half of them died in the process. Any comparison with Nicaraguan relocation practices is entirely specious. The Nicaraguan government has been criticized by Americas Watch for providing inadequate notice in many cases, and the process of relocation has been physically and emotionally difficult for the persons affected; there is no evidence, however, that the government has used relocation as a punishment of any social or ethnic group, nor that evacuees from war zones have been treated inhumanely. We also note that President Reagan has opposed economic sanctions against South Africa—where 3.5 million have been relocated in the past twenty years for reasons having nothing to do with military necessity, and 2 million more are scheduled for forced relocation—but he has applied economic sanctions against Nicaragua citing the relocations as one reason.

5. Consider, for example, the experience of the United States which fought four major wars during the twentieth century—the First World War, the Second World War, the Korean War, and the Vietnam War—but which did not endure invasion or serious threat of being overthrown during any of those wars. The restrictions on liberty during the First World War were the most severe in our history and included some 1,900 federal prosecutions for the peaceful expression of opinion; an untold number of state prosecutions; the closing and banning from the mails of various periodicals; and a wartime hysteria that persisted following the war and that included the summary detention of thousands and summary exile of hundreds in the raids on aliens and suspected leftists led by Attorney General A. Mitchell Palmer and his aide, J. Edgar Hoover. During the Second World War, Americans were almost entirely united in support of the war effort, but the war was nevertheless marked by the forcible evacuation and internment in detention camps of some 112,000 Japanese-Americans; and by the enactment of the Smith Act and by the prosecution of twenty-nine members of the Socialist Workers Party and the imprisonment of eighteen of them for violating its prohibitions against advocacy and conspiracy. The Korean War was marked by the rise of Senator Joseph McCarthy and of the Congressional investigations of associations and beliefs conducted by McCarthy and several others; by the imprisonment of scores who declined to name names; and by loyalty oaths and loyalty-security tests for employment that cost thousands their jobs. The Vietnam War was marked by the imprisonment of thousands for resisting the draft; the jailing of tens of thousands for demonstrating against the draft and the war; and by an enormous escalation in spying on peaceful political activities of Americans by the CIA, the FBI, the army, several other federal agencies, and state and local police departments all over the country; and by such programs as COINTELPRO which were used by government agencies (in this case the FBI) to destroy organizations engaged in peaceful dissent.
6. Our previous reports are:

1. Violations of the Laws of War by Both Sides in Nicaragua—1981–1985—First Supplement (June 1985); 2. Violations of the Laws of War by Both Sides in Nicaragua—1981–1985 (March 1985); 3. Freedom of Expression and Assembly in Nicaragua During the Election Period (December 1984); 4. The Miskitos in Nicaragua 1981–1984—(November 1984); 5. Human Rights in Nicaragua—April 1984. 6. Human Rights in Nicaragua: November 1982 Update; 7. On Human Rights in Nicaragua—May 1982.

*19. Sandinistas Aren't the Worst**

By Raymond Bonner

Raymond Bonner, former Central American correspondent for the New York Times, *is the author of* Weakness and Deceit: U.S. Policy and El Salvador (New York: Times Books, 1984).

*From the *New York Times,* September 14, 1984.

The Reagan administration has spent more than $1 billion to prop up the Salvadoran government and $150 million to overthrow the Sandinistas in Nicaragua. A comparison of the human rights records of both countries raises serious questions about this choice of friends and enemies.

One does not have to—indeed, one should not—defend the anti-democratic practices of the Sandinistas to recognize that there has been more freedom and less brutality in revolutionary Nicaragua than under any recent United States-backed government in El Salvador.

"I don't understand how they call that government Communist, and say that this government is Christian and democratic," a senior Salvadoran bishop once said, comparing Nicaragua with El Salvador. In Nicaragua, he noted, "They don't shoot priests and workers, do they?" A Roman Catholic leader in the United States, the Rev. R. J. Henle, former president of Georgetown University, has also suggested comparing the human rights records of El Salvador, Guatemala, Honduras, and Nicaragua. Do so, he said, and "the record of Nicaragua would stand out as a remarkably clean record."

The Sandinistas have indeed censored the opposition newspaper, *La Prensa*—censorship that cannot be justified solely on the basis of the country's being under attack. But in El Salvador, there is no opposition press to censor. Opposition journalists have been murdered, their newspaper facilities bombed into silence. The editor in chief and a photographer for *La Crónica* were seized mid-day in a downtown coffee shop. Their bodies, hacked by machetes, were found a few days later. *El Independiente* closed after repeated bombings of its offices and assassination attempts on the publisher.

In Nicaragua, the government has harassed some church leaders, including Archbishop Miguel Obando y Bravo, and the Sandinistas recently expelled ten foreign priests on charges of antigovernment activity. Such interference with the Church is pernicious and probably self-defeating. Nevertheless, the fate of clergy who have challenged the Sandinistas has been far better than that of their brethren in El Salvador, where soldiers and death squads have murdered at least sixteen priests and nuns, including Archbishop Oscar Arnulfo Romero.

In Nicaragua, there are no death squads. Mutilated, decapitated bodies do not show up on dusty roads and garbage dumps, as they have in El Salvador. A State Department human rights report has charged the Sandinistas with the deaths of twelve people in 1983. There were also thirty-one disappearances that year, according to Nicaragua's independent human rights commission. By contrast in El Salvador, each month during 1983 an average of one hundred forty people were killed by military or paramilitary units and thirty-nine people disappeared, according to the State Department's figures, which are lower than those of many human rights groups.

In Nicaragua, the activities of political leaders have been restricted. In El Salvador, opposition politicians have been tortured and murdered. A prominent leader of the Nicaraguan opposition, Arturo Cruz, former ambassador to Washington, has returned to Nicaragua and held mass campaign rallies—something that his counterpart in El Salvador, Guillermo Ungo, could never hope to do. United States diplomats in

El Salvador knew it wouldn't be safe for Mr. Ungo or any other opposition politician to return for the elections: the embassy suggested they campaign from abroad using videotapes.

Probably the most deplorable aspect of the Sandinistas' human rights performance has been the treatment of the Miskito Indians. (That treatment has not, however, been nearly as horrendous as the Reagan administration claims, and according to the human rights group Americas Watch, there has been "important improvement" in the Sandinistas' relations with the Miskitos.) The Sandinistas have relocated Miskitos from areas where counterrevolutionary fighters are operating. But in El Salvador, according to Americas Watch, thousands of civilians have been killed in "indiscriminate" bombings, artillery shellings, and ground sweeps as part of a "deliberate policy" to force civilians to leave areas of guerrilla activity.

In Nicaragua, human rights abuses by soldiers have been punished. As the result of one investigation, and the appointment of a special prosecutor, for example, thirteen individuals, including the commander of a security force unit, were sentenced for up to seventeen years for murder, torture, rape, and robbery. That doesn't happen in El Salvador. Some 40,000 civilians have been killed there in the past four years. Women have been raped. Villages have been plundered. Yet not one death squad member, not one officer who has carried out the massacres of peasants, not one soldier—with the exception of the national guardsmen who killed four American churchwomen and a civil defense guard—has been convicted and sentenced for human rights crime.

President Reagan has excoriated Nicaragua as a "totalitarian dungeon." What does that make El Salvador?

*20. We Are Sandinistas**

By Deirdre English

"Every time you see the phenomenon of nationalism in Latin America, and the recovery of a nation's own natural resources, it has provoked confrontations with the United States," said Daniel Ortega, the Sandinista leader who became Nicaragua's president after last year's elections, when I interviewed him in April in a former country club now turned into a government retreat in Managua. "Ronald Reagan is nothing more than heir to the historical relationship of the United States with Nicaragua, except that he uses the Soviet Union as a justification."

It would be absurd to believe that the Sandinistas' 1979 revolt against the dictator Anastasio Somoza was Soviet-inspired, continued Ortega. "Here it was almost like an instinctive struggle. There was resistance to North American occupation. We fought

*Excerpts from *Mother Jones,* August/September, 1985.

for our sovereignty. And so Sandinismo arises as a third force, the force of those Nicaraguans who want the right to self-determination."

Are the Sandinistas committed to human and civil rights and democratic freedoms? Or are they left-wing dictators who will eventually eliminate all dissent, political opposition, and religious freedom? Are the Sandinistas Marxist-Leninists? Is Nicaragua on the way to becoming another Cuba?

To these questions Ortega replies, "You can judge for yourself." This answer is in part, his invitation to the world to come to Nicaragua, to travel without restriction, and to fully investigate the government's behavior. But Ortega's answer also seems to imply that Nicaragua's situation is too complex for easy yes-or-no answers.

Nicaragua's leaders are a group of relatively young, well-educated men and women whose success at working together surpasses their ability to offer precise ideological compass points. They know one another well and seem to value their shared history and a kind of improvisational pragmatism, more than any labels.

I found that the leaders I met in Nicaragua often liked to respond to questions about the political definition of their revolution with a basic restatement, at once evasive and stubborn: "We are *Sandinistas.*" In other words, we do not fit your preconceptions. We are building something new.

What, then, *is* "Sandinismo"? Americans, whose government treats it as an enemy ideology, should know how Nicaragua's leaders describe it in their own words. To find out, a number of visiting Americans conversed at length with Bayardo Arce, coordinator of party affairs for the Sandinista National Liberation Front (FSLN):

"If you find a political project such as ours where 70 percent of the economy is in private hands, where you have twelve legally existing political parties, where all religion is freely operating, where you have radios and newspapers that freely operate pro and con; but simultaneously has still been able to diminish illiteracy, multiply by two our student population, and distribute land among the *campesinos,*" said Arce—"that is Sandinismo, and that type of project certainly does not attract communists! Not in Cuba or the Soviet Union will you find twelve political parties, will you find private property, will you find opposition papers."

"During the time of Somoza it was only we who were courageous enough to call ourselves Sandinistas," said Arce, "and to say you were a Sandinista was to put your life in jeopardy, . . . and we fought. But then, after the revolution triumphed, everybody wanted to call themselves a Sandinista and we couldn't stop that. . . . But for us, to be a Sandinista means that you are able to renounce everything for social justice, and that means you are also willing to give your life."

The North American visitors, who had arrived on one of the last Aeronica flights the Reagan administration allowed to depart from U.S. soil, had come motivated by concern over United States policy toward Nicaragua. Yet they seemed equally anxious not to fall into an uncritical enthusiasm for the Sandinistas, which might fade in the harsh light of reality. Their two hours with Bayardo Arce was therefore spent peppering him with skeptical questions, which he answered with apparent candor, wit, and detail.

"What is Sandinismo today? It is a synthesis of all of this here in Nicaragua. So I guess you could say that Sandinismo is Marxist-Leninism applied in Nicaragua. But I would also say that Sandinismo is Christianity applied in Nicaragua. And I can also tell you that it is liberalism applied in Nicaragua. . . . Reagan says we are Marxist-Leninists because with that he means to scare everybody. I have asked people who are afraid of that if they know what Marxist-Leninism is. And I have come to realize that usually they don't know. All that they know is that it must be something quite awful, something you would not want on your skin. It is a little bit difficult to explain to people who don't even know what Marxist-Leninism is anyway.

"So I ask them, do you think we're going to be like the Soviets? . . . We will not be. . . . We aren't going to be like the Cubans or the Czechoslovakians or the Vietnamese. Nor like the U.S. citizens or the French or the Spanish. Nor even the Mexicans. We are going to be what we are, learning from everything. For example, I would like to include the methods of the U.S. electoral system the next time we have elections. It's a good system."

The Nicaraguan revolution raises the question of whether it is possible for a successful national liberation movement to overthrow a despot like Somoza, and then take a democratic and egalitarian stand that borrows the best from Western democracy and tolerance along with the best from the greater distributive justice of a country like, say, Cuba. Cuba accomplished miracles in economic development, but at the price of many individual liberties. The United States has those liberties, and great wealth as well, yet a fifth of its children are raised in poverty, often of the most decadent kind. Why should this be the order of things? Why cannot economic justice be established in an atmosphere of democratic freedom?

The Sandinistas have declared their intention to show the world a third path, and because they have promised "the best of both worlds," they have invited close inspection. How well does their practice match their propaganda? They ask to be judged by standards not lived up to anywhere else in the developed or underdeveloped world. If they can achieve that ideal they *will* become a prototype for a new society, one undoubtedly far more inspiring to the rest of the Third World than Vietnam or Cuba, on the one hand, or countries such as the Philippines, Taiwan, or South Korea, on the other.

This is the primary reason, Arce has concluded, why the U.S. government is determined to crush the Sandinistas: not because they are communists, but because they are establishing an alternative model for the Third World. Their very innovativeness poses a far greater threat to U.S. interests by virtue of its attractiveness. Arce puts it bluntly: "Nicaragua is a bad example."

Speaking to us the week before Reagan's trade embargo, Arce seemed to know it was coming. He explained how Nicaragua's independence could serve as a model for breaking Latin America's dependency on U.S. trade: "This attracts the attention of all your neighbors. It interests businessmen because, for example, when the U.S. cuts off our sugar quota we are immediately able to get markets in Algeria, East Germany, and Iran. And we find out that if they cut our meat quota we already have

Canada and Mexico guaranteed. When Standard Fruit withdrew from Nicaragua, we could still sell our bananas in the U.S. to other private business; if they close off that market we may go to Bulgaria and France.

"But no other Central American nations can do that. In the first place they don't have relations with Algeria, Bulgaria, or Iran because the United States has told them they shouldn't. And so you find that our political decision to have trade relations with anyone who's interested in them benefits the businessman. And what does that show? It shows that we poor little countries can breathe without our only lungs in the United States because there are answers in Europe. There are answers in the Arab nations and in the communist nations. So we are a bad example."

In the week following Arce's forecasts several things occurred. The U.S. Congress voted to deny Reagan's request for $14 million in aid for the *contras*. Within a few days, President Ortega left for a twenty-day tour of the Soviet Union and numerous Eastern and Western countries. Almost at once Reagan cut off all U.S. trade with Nicaragua. Ortega returned from his trip with guarantees of substantial trade or aid from all the countries he had visited—especially the Soviet Union, but also France, Finland, Spain, and Italy. And the Sandinistas revealed that an imminent oil crisis of vast proportions was averted by the USSR-Nicaragua agreement. The Nicaraguan commercial office stationed in Florida was transferred to Canada, and expanded trade relations between Nicaragua and Canada were announced, to the displeasure of the United States.

On hearing about Ortega's trip, many Democrats in the U.S. House of Representatives acted as if they had been shot in the back and voted to send $27 million in aid to the *contras*.

Arce had said: "Although there are a number of Democrats who are good friends of ours, still they are unable to totally comprehend us. . . . Even the Democrats tell us to cut off all ties with the Soviet Union and Cuba. But for us that friendship meant $400 million worth of cooperation last year—and we're going to end it?"

And Daniel Ortega asked me, "Should the United States be the only country allowed to have trade relations with the Soviet Union?"

Part Two

HISTORICAL SETTING

Editors' Introduction

This section gives a broad historical framework to the current crisis. Recent Nicaraguan history has been dominated by two themes: the penetration of the United States and the countervailing influence of Sandinista revolutionaries. It was as true when the Marines landed in 1926 as it is today. The tenets of the Monroe Doctrine and Manifest Destiny summarize one side of the argument, the battle cry "*Patria Libre o Morir*" (free homeland or death) the other. When the United States regards hegemony as not only its right but its moral duty, and Nicaraguans prefer death to that hegemony, a situation of conflict will obviously arise. Part Two explores this fundamental conflict between the two nations which has existed for over a century.

Chapter I:

Nicaragua and the United States: A Pattern Develops

Editors' Introduction

From the Monroe Doctrine, Manifest Destiny, Roosevelt's "big stick" and its replacement by Taft's "dollar diplomacy," through three invasions and two major occupations by U.S. Marines, FDR's "good neighbor" policy, and finally, to the cold war, the United States has perhaps played *the* key role in the history of Nicaragua and the Caribbean region.

The reading by Ilene O'Malley focuses on the critical period of the 1920s and 1930s where the modern roots of *Sandinismo* and *Somocismo* may be found. During this period, "containing Mexican Bolshevism" was as important as "protecting American lives" in the official justifications for U.S. intervention. The real reasons were more complicated, having to do with protecting U.S. capital, and securing the U.S. position of power in the world. President Reagan's admonition that

> The national security of all the Americas is at stake in Central America. If we cannot defend ourselves there, we cannot expect to prevail elsewhere*

is interesting in light of the events of the 1920s and 1930s.

The final article in this chapter picks up the story with the assassination of Sandino in 1934, and covers the rise of the Somoza family dictatorship and its operations.

---

*Address to Joint Sessions of Congress, April 27, 1983.

21. The Nicaraguan Background*

By Henri Weber

Nicaragua, like all the other provinces of Central America, was conquered by Cortés's lieutenants about the year 1523. In fact, the invaders only really subjugated the plains of the Pacific coast, the richest and most highly populated region inhabited by Chorotec Indians of the Aztec family. The jungle-covered mountains of the North West, the dense forests of the East, and the whole Atlantic region, or Miskitu Coast, inhabited by Carib Indians, resisted the Spaniards stubbornly and never fell completely under their control. In these hard-to-reach areas, Indian communities lived until the late nineteenth century in a state of semiautonomy based on their traditional mode of social organization. On the Atlantic Coast, moreover, they enjoyed British political and military support throughout and beyond the period of Spanish occupation, for Britain was anxious to acquire an operational base for its rivalry with Spain and France, and later with the North Americans. Indeed, in the eighteenth century Moskitia became a *de facto* British protectorate, which has left its mark in a number of cultural traits, most notably the speaking of "coastal English." It was only in 1894, under the presidency of General Zelaya, that the region was truly integrated into the country.

Bartolomé de las Casas, a bishop who took up the Indian cause, left the following indignant account of the hell on earth to which the peoples of the Pacific plains were subjected: "In 1522 or 1523, this tyrant [the governor of the mainland] went off to subjugate the perfectly happy province of Nicaragua, and made a most wretched entry into the region. Who can speak too highly of the cheerfulness, good health, friendliness, and prosperity of the numerous people? It was truly wondrous to see that there were so many villages, spread over the length of three or four leagues and full of wondrous orchards owing to the great number of inhabitants. The land was flat and smooth, so that the population dared not foresake it save with great trouble and difficulty. Hence, they suffered as much as possible the tyranny and bondage which the Christians imposed upon them. For they were by nature very mild and peaceable. This tyrant and his companions, all the other tyrants who had helped him to destroy the other kingdom [Panama], subjected this people to so much evil, butchery, cruelty, bondage, and injustice that no human tongue would be able to describe it. . . . Today [1542], there must be four or five thousand persons in the whole of Nicaragua. The Spaniards kill more every day through the services they exact and the daily, personal oppression they exercise. And this, as we have said, used to be one of the most highly populated provinces in the world."

*Reprinted from *Nicaragua: The Sandinist Revolution* (London, Verso Editions and NLB, 1981).

The Burden of Spanish Colonization

Placed under the authority of the Viceroy of New Granada, the Nicaraguan province suffered the common fate of Spanish colonies for a period of three centuries.

It exported slaves to Panama, Santo Domingo, Peru, Ecuador, and Chile; wood, dried meat, tallow, leather, cocoa, and coloring to other colonies and to the mother country. Manufactured goods were legally imported from Spain and smuggled from Britain and France. But such trade was a surface phenomenon, and the colony of Nicaragua remained an essentially subsistence economy. Spanish aristocrats in their haciendas, Indian communities on their collective lands, mestizos and "ladinos" on their *chacras* or small family plots—these all lived in a condition of virtual autarky. Besides, war and piracy often interrupted trade with Europe for long intervals.

Spanish domination brought the introduction of Catholicism and aristocratic structure from the metropolis. At the apex of the social hierarchy, royal functionaries levied tribute and ensured that the colony respected the sovereign's decrees. At a lower level, the provincial aristocracy ruled over huge landed estates, fiercely exploiting an Indian and mestizo work force held in bondage or subjected to forced labor. The *Señor* in his hacienda had more or less the same powers as the feudal nobleman in his fiefdom.

This social system survived the coming of independence in 1821. Slavery was abolished in 1824, and forced Indian labor gradually became a thing of the past. But in one form or another, servile labor persisted until the last quarter of the nineteenth century, profoundly marking social relations in the country.

In this context of extreme social and economic backwardness, political conflicts took the form of unrelenting struggle among regionally based clans. Throughout the nineteenth century and part of the twentieth, endemic warfare pitted the Léon "liberals" against the Granada "conservatives": the former being, in principle, modernist, masonic admirers of the American and French Revolutions, the latter traditionalist bigots attached to aristocratic values. As in the rest of Central America, however, this did not involve a European-style opposition between pro-conservative landowners on the one side and an industrial bourgeoisie plus a feeble, craft-based petty-bourgeoisie on the other. The Nicaraguan "liberals" were champions of free trade more than civil rights and freedoms, and the personal dictatorships they established were not a whit less severe than those of the conservatives. In both camps, moreover, the troops were essentially peasants pressed into service under the command of landowners. The civil wars, very much like wars between clans of rival nobles, plunged the country into a chronic state of instability, all the deeper in that both sides unhesitatingly sought rescue from foreign powers.

The Walker Episode

Ever since its discovery in the sixteenth century, Nicaragua has always been of interest to the great powers. The British were ever present in the field, contending with the Spanish in the period before independence and with the North Americans until the Clayton-Bulwer Treaty of 1850. This country, at the heart of the isthmus between the two Americas, was strategically placed to inflame covetous desires. Its west-facing coastline made it a key point for control of the Caribbean, while its topography and the size of its lakes marked it out as one of the best possible sites for an Atlantic-Pacific canal.

The Central American Federation, of which Nicaragua formed part after independence, broke up into autonomous provinces in 1843. In Nicaragua itself, the struggle between "liberals" and "conservatives" for control of the new state degenerated into civil war. But when the "liberal" Francisco Castellán suffered defeat in the field, he looked for outside support against the "conservative" troops of Frutos Chamorro. William Walker, a journalist with ambitious ideas, responded to the appeal. With the financial backing of the new Accessory Transit Company directors, who were eager to strengthen their hold on the interocean route, he raised an American "phalanx," which took the conservative capital of Granada in October 1855.

It was not long before Walker turned against his liberal bedfellows and seized power in his own right. A Southerner and ardent supporter of slavery, Walker dreamt of shepherding the five isthmus states into a single white republic. This was the period just before the Civil War, and Walker hoped that the construction of a model slave society in Central America would bolster the Southern side against the abolitionists of the North. On June 10, 1858, he duly had himself "elected" president of Nicaragua. His government was at once recognized by the president of the United States, Franklin Pierce. English was declared the official language, and the property of "enemies of the Republic" was handed over to "naturalized Nicaraguans." Slavery was reintroduced.

If Nicaragua's independence was saved, it was because the other Central American states grew alarmed at the ambitions of a pro-slavery privateer whose flag bore the motto: "Five or None!" Financed by the Accessory Transit Company and the British government (concerned at Walker's designs on Moskitia), Central American troops entered Nicaragua and scored a first victory in May 1857 at the port of Rivas. Walker found shelter on an American ship and made a triumphant landing in New York. Four years later, he was back in Central America to recover his presidency, managing to seize the Honduran town of Trujillo. Captured by the British Navy, however, he was delivered to the Honduran authorities and shot on September 12, 1861. This first contact with the United States did not bode well for the future of the region.

The Coffee Era

Once "the American phalanx" had been repelled, the two factions in Nicaragua made their peace. The conservatives would now rule the country for some thirty years.

In the second half of the nineteenth century, coffee rapidly became the major export commodity, far outstripping other products. Twenty years after Guatemala, El Salvador, and Costa Rica, Nicaragua in turn discovered the "green gold" and was swept into the world capitalist market. Coffee represented 50 percent of the value of Nicaraguan exports until the cotton boom of the 1950s and 1960s. The *cafeteleros* were hungry for good land and a "free" labor force with which to exploit it. The colonial legacy of a subsistence economy vaguely tied to the market could no longer satisfy them. Nor could the rudimentary state that corresponded to it.

The U.S.-inspired liberal constitution of 1826, and even the conservative constitution of 1858, emancipated the peasants from obligatory labor. As a result, the Indians returned to their community lands, and small family plots sprang up again. As long as the landed gentry concentrated on extensive animal-rearing and subsistence agriculture, they could accommodate themselves to this development. But when the coffee boom broke, it became necessary to recover land and labor ready for exploitation.

During its thirty-year rule, the conservative aristocracy attempted to realize this goal by creating the legal basis for expropriation and forced labor.* The most reactionary law, promulgated in 1877 by the Pedro Chamorro government, unleashed an uprising of Indian communities in 1881 that was drowned in blood.

A Nicaraguan Bismarck

In 1893 the new plantation bourgeoisie brought to power the strongly nationalist head of the Liberal Party, General José Santos Zelaya. The sixteen-year-long Zelaya dictatorship embarked upon an authoritarian modernization of the country, only to be cut short by the U.S. Marines. After a fashion, Zelaya tried to assemble and guarantee "the general external conditions of capitalist production."

A whole battery of laws considerably strengthened the process of expropriation-appropriation of the soil and proletarianization of the labor force. Farmers had to justify their occupation of land by reference to a newly created register of civil property; so that when, unbeknown to the small peasants and Indian communities, a chain of legislation demarcated national lands and identified irregular smallholdings, the legal basis for expropriations existed. In very many cases, moreover, illegal methods were hastily adopted (intimidation, terror), or usurious interest rates of 30–60 percent resulted in the short-term alienation of land and revival of forced labor. As part of the same process, land belonging to the Church and the Indian communities became legally alienable. The effective incorporation of the Atlantic coastal region, now given the name Zelaya, at last created a unified national territory. As a genuine labor market was coming into existence, the economic infrastructure (transport, electricity, communications) and the state infrastructure (public education, administrative apparatus) underwent considerable development. The growing of coffee was officially encouraged through a government bonus of 5 centavos per tree for those who already owned more than 5,000 square feet. In order to finance public investment and expenditure, Zelaya had recourse to international loans (not always on favorable terms) and to the printing of money.

*Jaime Wheelock, *Imperalismo y Dictadura,* Mexico City, 1979.

This small country was not, however, able to contain the ambitions of a liberal dictator who dreamt of commanding a new Central American Federation. In 1906 a war that pitted Nicaragua against Guatemala, Honduras, and El Salvador led to the intervention of the United States and Mexico. The various states of Central America then signed the 1907 Washington Convention, undertaking not to interfere in one another's internal affairs and to submit their differences to an international court of arbitration.

Scorning the Monroe Doctrine, then still very much in force, Zelaya carried his craze for independence so far that he shunned the New York financiers and contracted a major loan with a British banking syndicate. Relations between Washington and Managua, which had at first been excellent, now continually deteriorated as Zelaya's nationalism collided with the growing power of North American imperialism.

The U.S. decision to dig the Panama Canal set the tinder alight. General Zelaya had been counting on an interocean water route for the country's economic development, and he opened negotiations with Germany and Japan for the construction of a rival canal. This was more than Uncle Sam could stand.

22. *The Eagle Rises**

By Jenny Pearce

"Fate Has Written Our Policy . . ."

In 1823 President Monroe of the United States declared that interference by any European power in newly emerging Latin American republics would be considered an unfriendly act towards the United States itself. This became known as the Monroe Doctrine. It established the right of the United States to "protect" Latin America and it was based on the assumption that the two regions shared common interests which the northern power had the right to interpret.

During the nineteenth century an aggressive expansionism was added to the defensive paternalism of the Monroe Doctrine. It was rationalized at the time by the phrase "manifest destiny." The United States came to believe that it had been singled out for a special mission: to carry its particular brand of economic, social and political organization initially westwards within North America and later throughout the Western Hemisphere. Westward expansion was completed by the end of the nineteenth century at the expense of the Indian population, which was decimated, and neighboring Mexico, which lost nearly half of its territory (Texas, New Mexico, and California) in a war deliberately provoked by the United States.

*Reprinted from *Under the Eagle: U.S. Intervention in Central America and the Caribbean* (Boston: South End Press, 1982).

In the mid-nineteenth century the United States gave a foretaste of its future role in Central America and the Caribbean when it began to challenge British power in the region. At this time British naval superiority and commercial dominance were considerable, and, in addition to its West Indian colonies, Britain controlled part of the Atlantic coast of the Central American isthmus including Belize and the eastern part of Nicaragua.

As the United States pushed westwards and became a Pacific as well as an Atlantic power, its desire for a cheap route linking the two oceans came into conflict with Britain's own wish to control such a route, for which Nicaragua was a favored location. In 1850 the United States signed the Clayton-Bulwer Treaty with Britain. By this agreement neither power was to hold exclusive control over the Nicaraguan route, but this only temporarily resolved Anglo-American rivalry. Tensions between the two nations mounted in the 1850s and 1860s, particularly after the United States had recognized the short-lived "conquest" of Nicaragua by an American adventurer, William Walker. In 1867 the United States violated the 1850 treaty it had signed with Britain and made an agreement with Nicaragua granting it exclusive rights of transit across the country.

By 1890 United States westward expansion was almost complete and "manifest destiny" came to include wider dreams of empire. It was a period of great change in the United States. By 1870 more people were working in the cities than on farms, half a million immigrants a year came to the United States between 1880 and 1893 till its population (almost 70 million by 1890) overtook that of any single European country. In the 1890s the United States began to outpace Europe in the production of steel, coal, and iron and giant monopoly firms emerged with surplus capital for export and in need of raw materials and markets. The strong links between United States big business and the country's foreign policy were forged in these years.

In 1890, following the publication of an influential book which suggested that sea power was the key to greatness, the United States built its first battleship. Expansion overseas seemed the logical next step and Senator Albert Jeremiah Beveridge reflected the mood of the times when he stated in 1898 that

> [American factories] are making more than the American people can use. . . . Fate has written our policy. . . . the trade of the world must and can be ours. And we shall get it, as our Mother England has told us how. . . . We will cover the ocean with our merchant marine. We will build a navy to the measure of our greatness. Great colonies, governing themselves, flying our flag, and trading with us, will grow about our ports of trade. Our institutions will follow. . . . And American law, American order, American civilization and the American flag will plant themselves on shores hitherto bloody and benighted by those agents of God henceforth made beautiful and bright.

The nearest shores, and those most likely to be granted the privileges offered by Senator Beveridge were in Central America and the Caribbean—the "backyard."

"The Great American Archipelago"

The first target was Cuba, which, since the 1840s, had been considered a prime objective of the United States' southward expansion. Unfortunately it was still a Spanish colony and the Spanish refused to agree to United States proposals to purchase and annex the island.

By the 1880s United States capital was heavily involved in the Cuban economy, particularly the sugar industry: "It makes the water come to my mouth when I think of the State of Cuba as one in our family" wrote an American financier in 1895.

In 1898 the Americans decided they would rescue Cuba from Spanish despotism and they went to war with Spain in support of Cuban independence. The contribution of the Cuban population to the country's war of independence, which had been going on for some time before the United States entered it, was subsequently written out of history and the United States declared it had "liberated" Cuba. The United States then took responsibility for Spain's other colonies. It invaded Puerto Rico and purchased the Philippines for $20 million. Guam and Puerto Rico were later ceded to the United States by Spain as "spoils of war."

One of the most important results of the Spanish-American War was to turn the United States into a world power with strategic frontiers in the Caribbean and interests across the Pacific Ocean. The scene was set for the American eagle to spread its wings still further. José Martí had foreseen the danger as early as 1895. Although he was at the time engaged in a struggle against Spain he saw his duty also "to prevent the United States with the independence of Cuba extending itself through the West Indies and falling with added weight upon our lands of America." Early in the twentieth century the Nicaraguan poet, Rubén Darío, speculated on what "that Cuban [José Martí] would say today in seeing that under cover of aid to the grief-stricken pearl of the West Indies, the 'monster' gobbles it up, oyster and all."

The Big Stick

Theodore Roosevelt had been the United States' hero of the Spanish-American War; it made his political career and in 1901 he became President.

Roosevelt's particularly truculent use of power in Central America and the Caribbean—invasions, threats and treaties made at gunpoint characterized his presidency though they were not exclusive to it—has associated his period in office with the use of the "big stick."

Roosevelt stressed the strategic importance of the region to United States interests and frequently expressed his impatience with the unstable governments which threatened them. Behind his impatience was a thinly disguised racism which maintained that the Anglo-Saxon was duty bound to help backward races who were incapable of governing themselves. Such views clearly lie behind Roosevelt's famous 1904 addition to the Monroe Doctrine known as the Roosevelt Corollary:

> Chronic wrongdoing or an impotence which results in a general loosening of the ties of civilized society, may in America, as elsewhere, ultimately require inter-

> vention by some civilized nation, and in the Western Hemisphere the adherence of the United States to the Monroe Doctrine may force the United States, however reluctantly, in flagrant cases of such wrongdoing or impotence, to the exercise of an international police power.

Once again the pursuit of national self-interest was disguised by appeals to moral obligations and United States destiny.

The Panama Canal was completed in 1914 and became an important symbol of growing United States power in the Western Hemisphere. But the United States was not the only imperial power in the Caribbean. Rivalry between the United States and the European powers for control of the Caribbean was intense in these years. Great Britain, France, the Netherlands, and even Denmark, until it sold the Virgin Islands to the United States in 1917, all had colonies in the region, and in these years America had to assert its right to defend its "backyard." It would often portray its interventions as well-intentioned acts to prevent more sinister European incursions and in this way tried to conceal its own imperial objectives.

Most of the intervention at this time involved the collection of debt by gunboat. Many countries of the region had borrowed heavily from European and United States creditors in order to build railroads and ports, pledging their customs duties as security. When a country defaulted on interest repayments and the creditors were unable to collect the customs duties they would call on their own governments to help. Thus in 1904 the government of the Dominican Republic defaulted on its payments to a United States financial company. The United States took over the collection of customs duties before any European government who was owed money could do likewise and then distributed the proceeds amongst foreign creditors. At the same time it imposed the United States dollar as the national currency, thus opening the door to American business interests. In 1912 the U.S. National Bank was established in the country.

In 1909 the Liberal government of José Santos Zelaya in Nicaragua defied the United States by negotiating a loan with a London syndicate and opening negotiations with the Japanese over a canal through its territory. The United States backed an insurrection against his regime and once it was overthrown appointed its own representative to collect and retain customs revenues, while U.S. bankers Brown Brothers and Seligman negotiated new loans. The Americans were particularly anxious to secure control over river canal routes in the region.

Sugar Satellites and Banana Republics

Coffee and bananas were to Central America what sugar was to the Caribbean. As European and North American demand for coffee grew towards the end of the nineteenth century changes took place within the region which would lock it into a system of dependency on the export of one or two crops. The needs of the indigenous population suffered total neglect as the local landowning elites—often referred to as oligarchies, for indeed they were—were encouraged to produce solely for the consumption of European and North American markets.

The so-called Liberal reforms of this period paved the way for the expansion of coffee production by permitting the further concentration of land ownership, mostly at the expense of communally-owned Indian lands, and by creating a labor force. As Indians lost their land they were forced to work on the coffee plantations in conditions of semislavery. In El Salvador, Honduras, and Nicaragua the land itself remained mostly in the hands of the local elite though the processing and marketing of production was in foreign hands. In Guatemala German immigrants as well as the local oligarchy came to own land, and by 1914 nearly 50 percent of Guatemala's coffee production was grown on German-owned lands. In Costa Rica the large rural estates or *latifundios,* characteristic of the other countries in the region, did not emerge, mostly due to Spanish lack of interest in the country during the colonial period as it lacked both Indians and mineral resources. However, the opportunities offered by the coffee export trade enabled the wealthiest agricultural producers to enrich themselves and this elite consolidated both its political and economic power in this period.

The early twentieth century thus saw on the one hand the emergence of the United States as an imperial power in Central America and the Caribbean, prepared to back up its authority and protect its interests with brute force. On the other, it saw the beginnings of the penetration of United States capital into economies which were already weak, export-oriented, and dependent. The effect on political and social developments in the region was as profound as the economic impact.

Dollar Diplomacy

William Howard Taft, who followed Roosevelt as U.S. president, is said by one historian to have replaced bullets with dollars in his policy towards the region, although use of military force was never, in fact, totally abandoned. The basic objectives remained the same, however, as Taft himself made clear in 1912: "The day is not far distant when three Stars and Stripes at three equidistant points will mark our territory: one at the North Pole, another at the Panama Canal, and the third at the South Pole. The whole hemisphere will be ours in fact as, by virtue of our superiority of race, it already is ours morally."

Taft's policy of safeguarding United States financial interests and promoting United States investments, partly to counteract European penetration of the region, was reinforced with even greater vigor by Woodrow Wilson. The United States was now seriously challenging British capital within the hemisphere. In 1914 the United States held 17 percent of all investments in Latin America; by 1929 the figure was 40 percent. Between 1914 and 1929 United States investment in Central America and the Caribbean tripled, though the majority was still concentrated in Mexico and Cuba. On the Central American mainland United States investment was greatest in Guatemala and least in Nicaragua.

The growing United States economic stake in the region received United States government protection. In the 1920s the Evart Doctrine developed under President Coolidge justified intervention in the internal affairs of Latin American countries to protect the foreign holdings of United States nationals.

The marines were sent into Cuba in 1917 and they stayed until 1923 putting down strikes and protecting United States property. A United States governor virtually managed the finances of the Cuban government and representatives of American sugar interests became leading political figures. The United States was thus able to ensure that the Cuban government pursued policies such as free trade, which suited its own needs for markets for its manufactured goods and cheap sugar imports, at the expense of Cuban national development.

Using the pretext of a civil war, the United States occupied the Dominican Republic in 1916 and stayed until 1924. It claimed it was responsible for maintaining order in the country and it established martial law and a United States military government. Shortly afterwards two American companies set up business in the country: the Central Romana Sugar Refinery and the Grenada Fruit Company; and in 1917 the International Banking Company of New York arrived.

Haiti had assumed considerable strategic importance to the United States after the building of the Panama Canal; the sixty-mile stretch of water between Haiti and Cuba, known as the Windward Passage, was part of the only direct water link between the eastern coast of the United States and the Panama Canal. Political instability, economic bankruptcy, and increasing French and German involvement in the country convinced the United States of the need to take direct action to defend its interests. In December 1914 a contingent of marines arrived to occupy the country; they took over the customs houses and established martial law. They were mostly from the Deep South and they exacerbated racial and social divisions between the negroes and mulattos on the island and reinforced the rigid social structure. When they finally withdrew in 1934 their only contribution to the country was a few roads and sewers and a pro-United States local militia; the American presence in these years has been described as "socially and politically sterile."

United States Marines occupied Nicaragua from 1912 until 1925 and returned again in 1926 after a civil war had broken out, provoked by the results of a United States-supervised election. This second intervention was "to protect American lives and property" and maintain United States supremacy in the region, which the secretary of state at the time claimed was threatened by "Mexican fostered Bolshevik hegemony between the United States and the Panama Canal." At the time the Mexican government was supporting the Liberals in Nicaragua while the United States backed the Conservatives. This time, however, the United States did face a serious challenge. Augusto César Sandino refused to accept a United States-imposed political solution to Nicaragua's civil war. He was a nationalist, opposed to foreign intervention and to the concentration of land in the hands of a tiny oligarchy, and he drew the Americans into the first antiguerrilla war they had to face in Latin America. Four thousand United States Marines were sent to the country and the techniques used against Sandino's forces included aerial bombing.

However, the involvement of U.S. troops in the struggle brought strong criticism at home and no outright victory in Nicaragua. In 1931 the United States began a gradual withdrawal but not before it had solved the problem of maintaining order in the country. The Americans created a local Nicaraguan military force—the National Guard—trained, equipped, and advised by the United States, and when they finally withdrew in 1933 they crowned their legacy to the country by selecting the National Guard's commander: Anastasio Somoza. Somoza, who subsequently became president, as did his two sons after him, gave the first indication of the perfidy which characterized his dynasty's forty-three year rule in Nicaragua. Sandino had been persuaded to accept a gradual disarmament and in 1934, in good faith, he came to Managua to negotiate with the government, where he was murdered on Somoza's orders.

General Smedley D. Butler, who headed many of the American interventions in the region in the early part of the twentieth century gives a frank account of his achievements in his writings in 1935:

> I spent thirty-three years and four months in active service as a member of our country's most agile military force—the Marine Corps. I served in all commissioned ranks from a second lieutenant to major-general. And during that period I spent most of my time being a high-class muscle man for Big Business, for Wall Street, and for the bankers. In short, I was a racketeer for capitalism. . . . Thus I helped make Mexico and especially Tampico safe for American oil interests in 1914. I helped make Haiti and Cuba a decent place for the National City Bank to collect revenues in. . . . I helped purify Nicaragua for the international banking house of Brown Brothers in 1909–1912. I brought light to the Dominican Republic for American sugar interests in 1916. I helped make Honduras "right" for American fruit companies in 1903.

The Dictators

As the 1920s progressed there was a growing feeling in United States government circles that the frequent use of the services of General Smedley D. Butler and Co. were becoming too costly. The Nicaraguan experience reinforced this doubt; over one hundred marines were killed in that escapade. The United States sought means of avoiding direct intervention while safeguarding their interests.

The "Somoza" solution seemed ideal and had already been successfully tried out in the Dominican Republic. Before their final withdrawal from that country, the United States had created a National Guard and placed at its head a man called Rafael Trujillo. In 1930, backed by American companies, Trujillo ousted the incumbent president and began a tyrannical rule which was to last thirty-one years. A United States-trained army and a friendly dictator became the established and favored means of maintaining order in the region and protecting American interests. It was only a minor embarrassment that these dictators shared basic characteristics of extreme cruelty, corruption, and megalomania, and that their rule reinforced the already grinding poverty in which the majority of the people lived.

Even when the United States was not directly responsible for the installation of dictatorial regimes, the desire to protect American interests led to tacit support when such regimes appeared all over Central America in the early 1930s. These were years of the Great Depression. The world economic crisis affected the vulnerable Central American economies with particular severity due to their dependence on external markets and United States investment, both of which contracted with the crisis.

Coffee and banana prices plummeted as demand slumped. Peasants, unable to pay their debts, were evicted from their land, while workers were thrown out of their jobs or had their wages slashed. The result was a wave of social unrest in city and countryside throughout the region. Strikes broke out on the American-owned plantations and, as in Costa Rica in 1934, were ruthlessly suppressed by the local armed forces. The oligarchies, alarmed by the course of events, looked to the military as the only way to suppress the social conflicts and maintain their domination. In this way the workers and peasants were forced to bear the brunt of the depression.

A series of strongmen emerged to dominate the political scene throughout the depression: Jorge Ubico in Guatemala (1931–44), Tiburcio Carías Andino in Honduras (1931–48), and Maximiliano Hernández Martínez in El Salvador (1931–44). Although the latter did not enjoy immediate support from the United States—the banana companies had not established themselves in El Salvador and the country had not yet come as directly into the American orbit as the other countries—the United States sent a cruiser and two destroyers to stand by during the peasant rebellion of 1932 (two Canadian destroyers were also sent at the behest of the British). Though the revolt was eventually crushed without their help and with the massacre of some 30,000 peasants, the Americans had shown themselves to be "good neighbors."

Good Neighbor Policy

President Franklin D. Roosevelt declared in his inaugural address in March 1933 that United States foreign policy towards Latin America would henceforth follow the policies of the "good neighbor" and that it was opposed to armed intervention.

In practice this policy meant the temporary abandonment of direct intervention at a time when the depression preoccupied the government at home. United States investment in the region also declined in these years as there was little surplus capital. Investment did not begin to rise again until the 1940s, by which time the relative importance of Central America to American business had declined as it turned increasingly to South American oil and to manufacturing industry.

The new policy did not mean that the United States entirely gave up interference in the affairs of its backyard, nor did it abandon the threat of force. In September 1933 United States warships were stationed in every harbor of Cuba as a hint that events there did not please Uncle Sam.

The War Years

The United States military presence in the Caribbean increased considerably during the Second World War when it expanded its installations in Panama, Puerto Rico, and the Virgin Islands. In Puerto Rico, for instance, $200 million were spent on military building projects. Roosevelt Roads, a huge naval complex, and Ramsey Air Force Base were built in these years.

But the United States now began to assert a claim to the Caribbean basin as a whole, much of which was still under British, Dutch, and French colonial rule. The immediate aim was to defend the area from the German menace. In return for fifty obsolete destroyers, Britain allowed the United States to set up bases in Trinidad, Barbados, St. Lucia, and British Guiana. As Gordon Lewis, author of *The Growth of the Modern West Indies,* has written: "The kaleidoscope fortunes of the islands have been made and unmade by the treaty arrangements of European congresses or, more latterly as with the 1940 Anglo-American bases-destroyers deal, of British prime ministers and American presidents." The American presence was to have a profound impact on the countries concerned, particularly Trinidad. American culture penetrated the country through the occupying troops, and U.S. dollars amassed by local operators servicing the Americans' needs helped create the financial basis for local politics.

Roosevelt also made clear to the British in these years that the Americans would no longer accept their colonial presence in the region. The Commonwealth Caribbean was not only strategically part of the American "sphere of influence," it was also of growing economic importance. Large United States corporations had begun to penetrate the West Indies: United Fruit, W. R. Grace, Standard Oil and Texaco, the Chase Manhattan and First National City banks, and, of particular importance, the bauxite companies. Alcoa and its sister company, Alcan, had secured an almost complete monopoly over bauxite deposits in the British and Dutch Guianas between 1912 and 1925, mostly through double-dealing and trickery. The companies did not process the low-value ore in the Guianas, however, but shipped it back to North America to be smelted into aluminum, so that the Guianas never reaped the benefit of locally produced, high-value aluminum. Aluminum is used in the aircraft and arms industry and Guianese bauxite made a substantial contribution to the Anglo-American victory in the Second World War. There was no reward for the impoverished Guianese people, however. When Arthur Vining Davis of Alcan Aluminum died in 1962 he left a fortune of $400 million, most of which he gave to a foundation on condition that its funds could not be used to benefit the citizens of the Caribbean bauxite-producing countries or any country other than the United States and its possessions.

During the war an Anglo-American Caribbean Commission was set up with headquarters in Trinidad. Its purpose was to maintain "stability" in the region during the war but also to consolidate the growing United States influence in the area. The results of British and American collaboration in these years was the emergence of a joint strategy for the post-colonial Commonwealth Caribbean which rested on the establishment of a West Indian Federation. The Federation, which was set up in 1958, was virtually imposed by the British and took almost no account of the real needs and interests of the people of the region: it collapsed in 1961. Instead of the Federation becoming independent as a unit as planned, the individual countries became independent on their own. The United States was forced to think again.

This increasing American involvement in the Commonwealth Caribbean reflected the gradual emergence throughout the war years of United States economic and political supremacy over Europe as a whole. In Central America the United States pressured governments to confiscate German investments and property and as European markets were closed the countries of the region came to depend on the single market of the United States. Between 1930 and 1934 Central America sold 20 percent of its total coffee harvest to the United States and 75 percent to Europe; between 1940 and 1944 the United States share increased to 87 percent. As coffee represented 70–80 percent of the region's total exports, its dependence on the United States was consolidated still further.

The Postwar World

Throughout the war the United States was planning and preparing for its future role in the postwar world. The United States was in a unique position to impose its world view; it emerged from the war unrivalled economically and militarily. The new order it would help shape would center around its need for large export markets and unrestricted access to key raw materials. United States planners identified three separate areas—the Western Hemisphere, the Far East, and the British Empire—which had to be economically integrated and militarily defended in order to safeguard America's interests.

The United States therefore planned for a cooperative and stable worldwide economic system based on the elimination of trade restrictions, the creation of international financial bodies to stabilize currencies, the establishment of international banking institutions to aid investment, and the development of backward areas. In the words of Cordell Hull, Roosevelt's secretary of state:

> Through international investment, capital must be made available for the sound development of latent natural resources and productive capacity in relatively undeveloped areas. . . . Leadership towards a new system of international relationships in trade and other economic affairs will devolve largely on the United States because of our great economic strength. We should assume this leadership and the responsibility which goes with it, primarily for reasons of pure national self-interest.

Short Chronology of U.S. Activities in Central America and the Caribbean

1823	Monroe Doctrine pronounced
1850	Clayton-Bulwer Treaty
1898	Spanish-American War
1898–1902	U.S. troops occupy Cuba
1901	U.S. acquires Puerto Rico
1903	Panama becomes independent from Colombia
1905	U.S. Marines land at Puerto Cortes, Honduras

1906–1909	U.S. troops occupy Cuba
1908	U.S. troops sent to Panama
1909	U.S.-backed overthrow of Zelaya in Nicaragua
1910	U.S. troops land in Honduras
1912	U.S. troops sent to Panama
1912	U.S. troops occupy Cuba
1912	U.S. troops briefly occupy Puerto Cortes, Honduras
1912–25	U.S. Marines occupy Nicaragua
1914	Panama Canal is completed
1914–34	U.S. Marines occupy Haiti
1916–24	U.S. Marines occupy Dominican Republic
1917–23	U.S. Marines occupy Cuba
1918	U.S. troops sent to Panama
1919	U.S. Marines occupy Honduras' ports
1926–33	U.S. Marines occupy Nicaragua and set up national guard under Somoza. Sandino defeated and assassinated
1924	U.S. Marines land in Honduras
1932	U.S. warships stand by during El Salvador *matanza*
1933	Franklin Roosevelt declares "good neighbor" policy
1944	Bretton Woods conference sets up World Bank and International Monetary Fund
1947	The Truman Doctrine signals the beginning of the cold war
1948	Organization of American States is founded
1954	CIA-backed invasion of Guatemala
1959	Cuban Revolution
1961	Abortive CIA-backed Bay of Pigs invasion of Cuba
1962	Cuban missile crisis

The institutional bases of the new order were elaborated by the Bretton Woods conference in 1944 which was followed by the establishment of the World Bank and the International Monetary Fund. The overseas expansion of United States capital which took place subsequently was unprecedented and centered around the emergence on a grand scale of giant companies with interests in all parts of the globe. These multinational corporations came to dominate the United States economy and that of many regions of the world.

The United States was thus instrumental in establishing an integrated international economic system which for many years it was able to dominate and which it was committed to defending. The emergence of the socialist bloc and the cold war provided the rationale for United States economic aggression. United States capital was in the vanguard of a crusade: to stem the tide of international Communist subversion; "manifest destiny" re-emerged in a new form and to meet new needs. American capital would bring development to backward regions and Latin American elites came to see it as the key to progress. The years following the Second World War saw a huge inflow of United States capital into Latin America. Direct investment grew from

$3 billion in 1946 to $8 billion in 1961. In Central America direct investment increased from $173 million in 1943 to $389 million in 1959 (see table). The economic importance of Central America to the United States was slight, but the region's dependence on virtually one source of foreign investment consolidated the United States' hold over its economic development.

U.S. Direct Investment in Central America 1936–1959
(in millions of dollars)

Country	1936	1940	1943	1950	1959
Costa Rica	13.0	24.0	30.0	60.0	73.2
El Salvador	17.0	11.0	15.0	17.0	43.9
Guatemala	50.0	68.0	87.0	106.0	137.6
Honduras	36.0	38.0	37.0	62.0	115.5
Nicaragua	5.0	8.0	4.0	9.0	18.9
Total	121.0	149.0	173.0	254.0	389.1

SOURCE: *Donald Castillo Rivas,* Acumulación de Capital y Empresas Transnacionales en Centroamérica, *Siglo XXI, Mexico, 1980.*

The United States encouraged the belief that there was an identity of interests between the two regions, an inter-American system based on mutually compatible objectives. In 1948 the ninth Pan-American conference set up the Organization of American States (OAS); one of its aims was "to provide facilities for United States investors wishing to exploit the resources of Latin America." It was also to be used by the United States as a means of isolating regimes which tried to withdraw from the inter-American fraternity or to challenge its ideological basis. In 1954 a resolution passed by the OAS "updating" the Monroe Doctrine became known as the Caracas Declaration:

> The domination or control of the political institutions of any American state by the international Communist movement, extending to this hemisphere the political system of an extracontinental power, would constitute a threat to the sovereignty and political independence of the American states, endangering the peace of America, and would call for a meeting of consultation to consider the adoption of appropriate action in accordance with existing treaties.

The cold war had reached Latin America.

23. Play It Again, Ron*

By Ilene O'Malley

Ilene O'Malley received her Ph.D. in Latin American History from the University of Michigan.

In his address to Congress, the President of the United States warned of the threat of communism:

> I have the most conclusive evidence that arms and munitions in large quantities . . . have been shipped to the revolutionists. . . . The United States cannot fail to view with deep concern any serious threat to stability and constitutional government . . . tending toward anarchy and jeopardizing American interests, especially if such a state of affairs is contributed to or brought about by outside influence or by a foreign power.[1]

Are these the words of Ronald Reagan speaking about the USSR in El Salvador? No. The country referred to is Nicaragua, but the year is not 1980 or 1981. The year is 1927, and the president is Calvin Coolidge. Many of us are shaken to find the United States seemingly headed for "another Vietnam," but we should contemplate the response that the Mexican novelist Carlos Fuentes gave to the question of whether El Salvador would be another Vietnam: "No," he said, "it's another Latin America."[2]

Although we are loath to remember, Latin Americans cannot afford to forget the long history of U.S. intervention in their affairs. One of the most instructive examples of this long history is the six-year war (1927–1933) the United States waged to stamp out the guerrilla movement led by Augusto Sandino, a man impudent enough to think that Nicaraguans should run their own country. To understand that war, as well as current affairs in Central America, we must begin with the roots of U.S. interventionist policy: the Monroe Doctrine formulated some 160 years ago.

Grade school history aside, the Monroe Doctrine was not a brotherly act to protect the fledgling nations of the newly independent Spanish-American colonies. It was a move to procure for our own enrichment the resources and markets formerly monopolized by Spain, and to scare off our competitors, especially Britain, who already had a foot in the door in the Caribbean. The Monroe Doctrine declared our intention to dominate the hemisphere.

Mexico was the first to fall victim to the expansionism we called our "manifest destiny." In 1847 we invaded Mexico City—later memorialized in the Marine Corps hymn, "From the Halls of Montezuma"—with the result that Mexico was forced to "sell" one half of its territory to the United States: what is now Texas, New Mexico,

---

*Reprinted from *The Alternative Review of Literature and Politics*, September 1981.

Arizona, California, Nevada, and part of Colorado. These events were to have great repercussions on the fate of Nicaragua.

When the great gold rush of the 1850s occurred in the newly acquired but rather inaccessible California, the United States cast entrepreneurial eyes upon Nicaragua, the easiest place to traverse the Central American isthmus before the Panama Canal was built. The Golden West promised fortunes to merchants as well as prospectors, *if* they could get there. U.S. shipping magnate Cornelius Vanderbilt constructed a ferry system across Nicaragua, stepping on the toes of the British, who had a protectorate along the Atlantic coast. "Firm" U.S. policy eventually supplanted the British, and throughout the rest of the 1800s Yankee business interests dominated the strategic and lucrative interoceanic transportation system as well as the banana, coffee, mahogany, and gold industries.

By 1909 the nationalist dictator Zelaya decided to break up some of the U.S. control. Although weak and small, Nicaragua could acquire more autonomy by diversifying its foreign creditors. Zelaya negotiated a loan with the British, and considered granting canal rights to Japan, whose imperialist ventures on its side of the Pacific made the United States anxious about its intentions on this side. Secretary of State Philander Knox began denouncing Zelaya as a tyrant, and the United States may have promoted the Conservative revolt, led by the hitherto unknown Adolfo Díaz, which broke out against Zelaya. Rafael de Nogales writes:

> Zelaya had committed the indiscretion of trying to cancel the concession of the La Luz and Los Angeles Mining Company, in which . . . Knox was the principal stockholder, while a nephew of his was the manager of the company . . . and was, therefore, also the "boss" of Adolfo Díaz . . . a minor clerk at a salary of twenty or twenty-five dollars a week. . . .[3]

When the revolt broke out, Díaz suddenly had $600,000 to contribute to the cause.[4] The revolt was on the verge of defeat when the U.S. Marines landed on the Atlantic coast to save it. Conservative general Estrada became president of a government which, according to the U.S. commander in Nicaragua was

> . . . not in power by the will of the people; the elections were in their greater part fraudulent . . . [T]he present government . . . is in power because of the United States troops. . . .[5]

When Estrada proved to be too independent-minded, he was pressured by the United States to resign. He was succeeded by his vice-president, Adolfo Díaz. The United States then moved to secure the financial interests which Zelaya had jeopardized. The Nicaraguan canal zone was sold to the United States for $3 million but the money could be used by Nicaragua only with U.S. consent. That sale was ratified by the Nicaraguan Congress while it was surrounded by U.S. Marines and the terms of the sale were read to the congressmen in English.[6] Nicaragua was forced to replace its British loans with loans from U.S. banks, which took half the national railroad, full control of customs duties, and the currency system as "security."[7] A legation guard of 100 marines remained in Nicaragua to assure that peace would prevail.

After World War I, the United States no longer had to worry about Japanese or British competition in Central America; Nicaragua was paying off its loans to Wall Street.[8] The United States began to think about withdrawing from Nicaragua, but not before setting up a national guard which was to be manned with U.S. troops until they trained Nicaraguan personnel to take over. In 1925 the United States supervised an election which made a Conservative, Solárzano, president, and a Liberal, Sacasa, vice-president.

Within weeks Solárzano was ousted by a right-wing coup and replaced by Emiliano Chamorro, who purged the Liberals from the government. The Liberals resisted the coup in the name of Sacasa, the legal successor to Solárzano. Civil war ensued, and the U.S. Marines returned to Nicaragua. The United States "settled" the war by replacing both contenders with a third, "neutral" president, the old quisling Adolfo Díaz. The Liberals, the traditionally more nationalistic party, nevertheless continued to fight against the imposition of Díaz. More marines were sent in to quell the growing opposition.

In the 1920s the State Department feared not that communism would spread from Nicaragua north, but from Mexico south to Nicaragua. After a decade of revolution, Mexico had a government which took a turn to the left in 1924, threatening to expropriate the large U.S. oil companies there.

There was strong sentiment in the United States for invading our southern neighbor, and relations between the two countries were extremely tense. Thus, when the United States discovered that war matériel was being shipped from Mexico to the Liberals in Nicaragua, the reaction was hysterical. Mexican ships were blown up in a Nicaraguan harbor by the United States, and Sacasa was branded an agent of Mexico "bolshevikism," which had to be stopped before it tainted the rest of Central America red. When Calvin Coolidge warned about "outside influence" in Nicaragua, he was speaking of Mexico.

By July 1927, military and diplomatic pressure laced with offers of wealth and position, reconciled the Liberal generals to the new "supervised" government—with one exception. While Anastasio Somoza hastened to ingratiate himself with the U.S. supervisors, Augusto Sandino, a liberal officer, decided to fight to rid Nicaragua of the U.S. presence once and for all. He took to the hills with 400 followers, and defied the Yankees to come and get him. The war with Sandino was on.

The United States, as well as Nicaraguan leaders, tried to pass Sandino off as a bandit and to deny his political stance. The campaign to defame his character was as futile as the campaign to catch him. As one marine officer remembered:

> By . . . 1929 it was becoming more and more evident that the marines . . . had been called upon to perform an almost impossible task. . . . Neither the people nor their [local] officials stood behind the marines in their attempt to put down

> lawlessness. . . . So long as the people would not assist the marines, the bandits could continue to operate . . . and carry on their depredations in spite of everything the marines could do.[9]

The heart of the U.S. problem was that the common people did not suffer from Sandinista depredations and lawlessness, and the only ones in need of protection were the marines themselves and collaborators. The presence of so many soldiers (about 1 for every 100 Nicaraguans) inflamed anti-Yankee sentiment, and many Nicaraguans who might otherwise have never supported Sandino did so in reaction against the often brutal behavior of the Yankee soldiers. One lieutenant was photographed holding a human head. A marine historian claimed that the officer had not personally performed the decapitation, yet admitted that U.S. soldiers shot and abused prisoners, used the ''water torture,'' and mutilated the bodies of their victims.[10] U.S. troops abused Nicaraguan women, a practice cavalierly dismissed by the same marine historian as the ''natural concomitants of military occupation.''[11]

In contrast, it is generally agreed that the Sandinistas avoided victimizing the people.[12] Sandino prided himself on the discipline of his men, instinctively following the principles of a conscientious and sincere guerrilla. ''Do you think,'' asked Sandino,

> that we could have existed . . . half a year with all the might of the United States against us, if we had been merely bandits? If we were bandits, every man's hand would be against us; every man would be a secret enemy. Instead, every home harbors a friend.[13]
>
> We have taken up arms from the love of our country because all other leaders have betrayed it and sold themselves out to the foreigner. . . . What right have foreign troops to call us outlaws and bandits and to say we are the aggressors? . . . We declare we will never live in cowardly peace under a government installed by a foreign power.[14]
>
> . . . We are no more bandits that was [George] Washington. If the American public had not become calloused to justice and to the elemental rights of mankind, it would not so easily forget its own past. . . . If their consciences had not become dulled by their scramble for wealth, Americans would not so easily forget the lesson that, sooner or later, every nation, however weak, achieves freedom, and that every abuse of power hastens the destruction of the one who wields it.[15]

Sandino promised to lay down his arms if and only if the United States withdrew completely from Nicaragua.

Opposition to U.S. policy ran high abroad and at home. One paper denounced it as ''murder''; the United States, it said, ''. . . created the anarchy she is now trying to suppress. . . . American marines are doing police work for a government which would collapse in sixty seconds'' if they withdrew.[16] The news filled up with stories and photos of U.S. atrocities, civilian populations bombed by U.S. planes, refugees fleeing not only the guerrillas, but the Yankees. As official explanations wore thin, *The Nation* complained that throughout the course of the war, the government had "deliberately and persistently lied to the North American people."[17]

Montana Senator Burton K. Wheeler summed up U.S. intervention with these words:

> Reduced to the simplest terms, the . . . Coolidge policy has led to armed intervention . . . in behalf of an American-made puppet president foisted upon the people against their own will for the simple reason that he is ready, at whatever cost . . . , to serve the New York bankers who are, and for seventeen years have been, mercilessly exploiting Nicaragua under the aegis of the State Department.[18]

Government criticism of such opposition to its policies provoked more popular outrage. The *St. Louis Post Dispatch* wrote:

> Apparently, the American people have made a great mistake in believing that the protests of conscience have any place in the council of the Coolidge administration. The story of Nicaragua belies it. We may think ourselves better or more merciful than that, but in truth we are not. These are the transports, the warships, the marines, the cannons, the troop trains, the airplanes and the Stars and Stripes—all testifying to the terror of the Empire.[19]

The *New Leader* warned:

> The American government cannot be a despot abroad without becoming a despot at home. Despotism cannot stand criticism. It always commands obedience. . . . All that remains is federal legislation to square with the reality of the American mailed fist in the Caribbean and Central America. Once having made us all intellectual conscripts of American imperialism the bureaucracy will have an excellent machine to hurl at trade unions and their struggles, to fill the nation with peacetime spies and informers, to penalize all who dissent. . . .[20]

Nevertheless, the United States forged ahead with the war. But it was a war we were not winning, and by 1930 Washington began looking for a way out. A plan—which would be seen again in Vietnam—was devised for replacing the U.S. soldiers who comprised the Nicaraguan national guard with natives, and to expand the guard so that it and not Yankees, could kill Sandinistas. The plan took pressure off the United States without jeopardizing U.S. interests, for the guard was under the command of the pro-Yankee enthusiast Anastasio Somoza. Officers were selected through political appointments, distributed as favors to the upper classes of the nation, thereby assuring that the guard function not as a "neutral" policing agent, but the military arm of the elite. The guard's distance from the common people was soon recognized. Somoza jailed the man who wrote:

> The Yankee marines taught the Nicaraguan soldier to be cruel. . . . They gave him lessons so he could break the holy law of brotherhood, killing compatriots. They taught the guardsmen to behave like mercenaries in their own land.[21]

As the "Nicaraguaization" went ahead, the United States prepared for its exit, permitting an election in late 1932. Sacasa became president. In early 1933, the last marine left and Sandino, true to his word, ceased hostilities. He was given a grandiose hero's welcome in Managua and then retired with his men to farm in the countryside.

Somoza, who had wanted to destroy Sandino, was displeased with Sacasa's conciliatory attitude toward him. Rumors began to circulate that Somoza was planning a coup. Sacasa therefore had to depend all the more on Sandino's support in order to shore up his government, which increased tension with Somoza. Somoza, however, did not have a coup in mind.

On February 21, 1934, Somoza's men picked Sandino up as he left a dinner at the National Palace. He was machine-gunned to death in a field not far away. The guard crushed Sandinista resistance throughout the country. Although Sacasa finished the rest of term in office, Somoza was thenceforth the real power in Nicaragua. He enjoyed full U.S. support. As Franklin Roosevelt said, "He's a sonofabitch, but he's ours."[22]

Notes

1. Quoted in Belden Bell, *Nicaragua: An Ally under Siege* (Council on American Affairs, 1978), p. 17.
2. "Murder by Proxies," *Nation,* April 15, 1981, p. 481.
3. Rafael de Nogales, *The Looting of Nicaragua* (Robert McBride & Co., 1928), pp. 7–8.
4. Ibid.
5. Quoted by Senator Elihu Root in Nogales, p. 10.
6. Nogales, p. 11.
7. Mary Helms, *Middle America: A Culture History of the Heartlands and Frontiers* (New York: Prentice-Hall, 1975), p. 256.
8. Bell, p. 16.
9. Neil Macauley, *The Sandino Affair* (New York: Quadrangle Books, 1967), p. 135.
10. Macauley, pp. 228–229.
11. Macauley, p. 45.
12. Carleton Beals, "With Sandino in Nicaragua, V: 'Send the Bill to Mr. Coolidge,' " *Nation,* March 21, 1928, p. 317.
13. Beals, *Nation,* March 21, 1928, p. 316.
14. Beals, "With Sandino in Nicaragua, IV: 'Sandino Himself,' " *Nation,* March 14, 1928, p. 289.
15. Beals, "With Sandino in Nicaragua, VI: 'Sandino—Bandit or Patriot?' " *Nation,* March 28, 1928, p. 341.
16. *Nation,* July 27, 1927, p. 75.
17. *Nation,* November 2, 1927.

18. Speech by Senator Wheeler given in Boston on March 6, 1927. Quoted in Nogales, p. 57.
19. *St. Louis Post Dispatch,* March 15, 1927.
20. Nogales, p. 126.
21. Santos López, quoted in Gregorio Selser, *Sandino: General de Hombres Libres,* vol. 1 (Editorial Triángulo, 1959), p. 313. My translation.
22. *Time,* November 15, 1948, p. 43.

*24. A Dictatorship "Made in the USA"**

By Edmundo Jarquin C. and Pablo Emilio Barreto

With the assassination of General Sandino in 1934 and the subsequent coup d'etat against President Sacasa in 1936, Somoza García initiated the longest, most corrupt dictatorship in Latin American history, a dictatorship continually supplied and supported by the United States.

Sustained by his family's monopolistic control of the economy and by the military power of the National Guard, the Somoza dictatorship passed through several stages. Until the mid-1940s, the dictator held relative legitimacy among those sectors of the society who, in their own self-interest, cloaked their leader with an image of "pacifier" and "innovator." By the mid-1940s, Somoza's intentions to establish himself in perpetuity became clear, thus betraying the nationalist recovery goals of the Liberal Party, which Somoza now dominated. Furthermore, because of the democratic surge developing in Central America (emerging from the struggle against fascism during World War II), Somoza entered a period of total isolation. The dictatorship lost its legitimacy and maintained its control only through the coercion and power of the National Guard. By this time large numbers of liberals abandoned Somoza and formed the Independent Liberal Party, which together with the Conservative Party, subsequently constituted a solid bloc of opposition against the dictatorship.

Once the crisis of the second half of the 1940s had passed, a new stage developed. Worldwide economic recovery in the postwar period and technological developments in the area of agricultural chemicals facilitated the development of cotton cultivation. The rapid expansion of cotton production gave Nicaragua a primarily agrarian export economy. The resulting profits had a major impact on the overall economy, extending and diversifying the productive potential of the country.

Based primarily on cotton production and secondarily on the expansion of coffee and beef exports, significant economic growth led to the rapid modernization of the economy. Capital accumulation, mainly agrarian based, was transferred to other economic sectors such as industry, finance, and commerce. This new wealth was dominated by the Somoza family, which had become synonomous with "the State." With

---

*Reprinted from *Nicaragua: A People's Revolution* (Washington, D.C., EPICA Task Force, 1980).

this control over the expansion and diversification process, Somoza greatly increased his impact upon the social life of the country.

As a result of these economic changes, new social sectors emerged while others rapidly deteriorated. Cotton cultivation, developed primarily in the departments of Managua, Masaya, and along the west coast, accelerated a process of concentrating vast agrarian properties into a few hands. This same process converted large numbers of small farmers into plantation peasants and produced a significant migration of other *campesinos* off the land. These migrants converged particularly on the cities of the Pacific coast (Léon and Chinandega) and on Managua, the capital, overloaded the urban employment market, and put a tremendous strain on the weak social service structures (housing, schools, hospitals). This created those sociological imbalances commonly called "marginalization."

At the same time, because of the expansion of employment in the industrial, financial, and state bureaucracy sectors, a new salaried middle class emerged. Social and economic success came to this middle class so rapidly that it failed to question the roots of its development. This created, intentionally or not, a new social stratum which legitimized the dictatorship. This stratum, together with the emerging capitalist class—the cotton producers, who also were completely dependent on the financial and technical assistance apparatus of the state—further strengthened Somoza's political control.

Despite the growing political legitimation by these new and ascending sectors, the vitality of the traditional liberal-conservative conflict was sustained during the 1950s. The conservative oligarchy maintained its economic independence from the state with the production and sale of coffee and beef inside and outside the country. This translated into their political autonomy from the Somoza regime.

In 1956 the founder of the dynasty was killed by a young poet and patriot, Rigoberto López Pérez. Following Somoza García's death a conflict developed between the traditional opposition and Somoza's sons during the election campaign to select his successor. At that moment United States Ambassador Whelan came to the rescue of the dynasty by giving total support to the succession of the dynasty through Luis Somoza Debayle, Anastasio's eldest son.

The creation of the Central American Common Market in the early 1960s stimulated the process of industrialization and thus accelerated the pace of modernization. However, this industrial expansion did not lead to any independence from Somoza. The state bureaucracy and the agrarian-export market, which developed at a parallel pace with industry, kept the Somoza interests in control of this expansion. The exploitative agrarian structure remained untouched, however, and this weakened the potential for industrial expansion.

> The seed of Sandino's blood
> lashes the murderous rooftops;
> multiplied, in torrents
> it will cover exposed rooftops;
> and will insure, inevitable apocalypse.

It will exterminate all of the murderers,
and each and every one
of the murderers' seed.

Their treacherous embrace of Sandino
is pregnant with biblical premonitions
like the crime of Cain
like the kiss of Judas.

And then peace will reign . . .
and Nicaragua will fill with olive branches and voices
that loft to the heavens
an everlasting psalm of love.

Rigoberto López Pérez
patriot and executioner of Anastasio I

At the same time, the portion of Nicaraguan capital in the Conservative Party was finally forced into dependency upon the state apparatus (i.e., upon Somoza) because all industry in Nicaragua functioned under the control of the state through its fiscal, credit, and commercial concessions and privileges. The conservative faction, unable to gain control over this apparatus through election, rebellion or coup d'etat, could only obtain services from the state apparatus through coming to an *understanding* with Somoza. This ended the independence of the conservatives and thus the vitality of the old liberal-conservative conflict. This *understanding* was formalized in a pact between the conservative leader, Fernando Aguero and President Anastasio Somoza Debayle (Tacho), who inherited the dynasty following the death of his brother Luis in 1967. The pact was the product of the increasing concentration of control by those few economic groups in the parasitic bureaucracy linked to Somoza.

The decade of the 1960s was, without doubt, the period of Somoza's greatest power and social legitimation. The expanding state apparatus and the growing economy gave Somoza an unprecedented degree of influence among the upper-class sectors—through coercion, blackmail, and fraud. His secure position was guaranteed by the accumulation of family assets, multiple links with North American capital, and close associations with the Central American bourgeoisie, a factor that consolidated his borders. And, when none of these factors was able to resolve any domestic controversy, there was always the National Guard.

History Will Never Forgive You

But history creates its own contradictions. The Somoza model of growth during the two previous decades, while producing wealth, modernization, and political consolidation, also produced incredible social injustices and inequalities. As both the old and new social elites enriched themselves and prospered under Somoza, broad sections of the population became ever poorer and were swallowed up by the most brutal misery.

Urban development was incapable of absorbing the growing unemployed work force that emerged from natural population growth as well as from the enormous migration of people expelled from the land. Within the poor rural population, a third of the *campesinos* were landless while another third subsisted on tiny farm plots located on marginally productive land. Administrative corruption—induced and encouraged by the dictatorship—prevented an adequate or planned expansion of social services, despite a growing economy and increased foreign investment.

This increasingly unequal distribution of wealth placed a brake on the expansion potential of the internal market and in turn on the growth of the entire economy. Despite agrarian and industrial diversification, Nicaragua's economy continued to depend largely on exported agricultural products, which suffered from constantly fluctuating world prices.

In summary, these inequalities represented a profound and growing social contradiction on top of an extremely fragile model of growth. These two factors ultimately precipitated the irreversible crisis of the Somoza dictatorship.

The Struggle against the Dictatorship

Despite the expanding control of the dictatorship, a prodemocratic spirit persisted in the country—holding fast to its goals of justice and freedom.

This spirit was present in all the rebellions, resistance, protests, and martyrdoms of young people from 1959 onward, including the struggle of the Sandinista Front for National Liberation (FSLN).

The weakening of the liberal-conservative conflict which became obvious during the second half of the 1960s created a political vacuum that was not immediately filled by the FSLN. While the FSLN was accumulating experience, the Sandinistas remained politically and strategically isolated. But the reformist tendencies also lacked a social base from which to fill this vacuum. The middle class, where such reforms traditionally arise, did not recognize the crisis because it was caught up in the process of social and economic self-improvement.

Gradually, the contradictions in the model of economic and social growth created the conditions for a final crisis of the dynasty. The struggle for freedom and justice merged out of new organizational molds, with new content and perspectives, and with a greater intensity than ever seen before in Nicaragua. These forms began to appear after 1972.

The Crisis on the March

The crisis in the Central American Common Market—precipitated by the armed conflict between Honduras and El Salvador in 1969—coincided with a decline in international prices for primary agricultural and beef products. Together, these two factors induced a market deceleration in the level of economic growth and a decline in the level of private investment.

Somoza was unable to adjust to the economic crisis. He tried to compensate for this decline through increased public spending, but his methods only increased unemployment while decreasing real income, especially of the popular sectors. This led to economic stagnation in general.

Then, in December 1972, an earthquake destroyed a large part of Managua. But, despite its tragic human consequences—10,000 died and over 100,000 were dislocated—the quake actually stimulated the economy. The destruction of housing, buildings, roads, furniture, and inventories created new opportunities for investment and production to replace the items lost. In addition, a huge influx of international and public and private funds for reconstruction and insurance created the financing needed for the new investments. When this influx of funds was followed by favorable prices for sugar and beef in 1974–1975 and for coffee in 1975, a significant reactivation of the Nicaraguan economy occurred.

However, the earthquake and its consequences led to a profound conflict between the bureaucratic bourgeoisie (Somoza and his friends) and the traditional bourgeoisie. The Somoza bloc, sustained by state power, exacerbated the existing administrative corruption by excluding other sectors of the bourgeoisie from the opportunities for investment created by the earthquake. Somoza enriched himself personally in the process by organizing his own bank, insurance company, finance and construction firms. Overstepping the traditional ethical bounds of capitalist competition, Somoza took over the most dynamic areas of capital accumulation.

At the same time, the government's failure to respond to the critical needs of the people following the earthquake precipitated a crisis of support among the middle class and especially among the masses of suffering poor. The exaggerated administrative corruption had led to an alarming decline in the level of public administration. The government's inability to adequately administer the reconstruction process increased the already sharp social inequalities. In turn, Somoza's failure to act, coupled by his selfish exploitation of the quake, led to a widespread political radicalization of the people.

Given this fraud, and in order to finance some postquake reconstruction, Somoza borrowed large sums of money, leading to a sharp increase in foreign indebtedness. This practice, in time, further reduced the dictator's space for political and economic maneuvering. Incurring debts, by itself, might not be questionable if the new funds are destined to finance productive investments which will generate income to repay the loans. But such borrowing is dubious when it is done at such an accelerated rate (from $200 million at the beginning of 1973 to $800 million by the end of 1977) and on the basis of repayment terms that are incompatible with the development project supposedly being financed. Above all, such borrowing is suspect when the institutions that are to administer the foreign debt (such as Somoza's *Banco de Vivienda* and *Instituto de Fomento Nacional*) are inefficient, dishonest, and already without capital assets as a result of corruption.

But to fully understand the depth of Somoza's crisis one must also look at the other significant developments in the postquake period. First, as a result of Vatican Council II, and the Latin American Episcopal Conference in Medellín in 1968, the Catholic Church had been redefining its goals and reorganizing its hierarchy. This was particularly true of the Church in Nicaragua. This process led to a gradual divorce of the Church from the dictatorship, especially as Somoza lost public support. Initially, the Church only reduced its official support of Somoza, but later it began to take overt actions challenging the regime.

Second, in the strictly political arena, organizational and ideological opposition to the dictatorship arose from the nontraditional parties. In December 1974, the Democratic Union of Liberation (UDEL) was created, led by Pedro Joaquín Chamorro. UDEL represented a broadly pluralistic convergence of political forces, including conservatives, liberal democrats, Christian and social democrats, and even the Nicaraguan Socialist Party. These forces united around a platform calling for the recovery of democratic rights and a social and economic transformation of the society.

In addition, the Sandinista Front was becoming more closely associated with the struggle for democratic renewal, and especially with the immediate problems and demands of the masses. Toward this end, the FSLN established bases among the people which in time helped the organization overcome its political and strategic isolation.

Finally, with the ascendancy of the Carter administration, the dimension of human rights appeared as a new strategy in North American politics. Whether or not this strategy implied any fundamental change towards Latin American problems, the overwhelming proof and continued denunciations of human rights violations in Nicaragua weakened the support of Somoza by the U.S. government—the creator and patron of the dictatorship during its entire existence. Thus, the United States' relationship passed from one of unconditional support for Somoza to one that took on an ambiguous stance.

Chapter II:

Building the Revolution

Editors' Introduction

This chapter covers the Sandinista revolution. "Nicaragua: Zero Hour," written in 1969 by FSLN cofounder Carlos Fonseca Amador, was the first major analysis put forth by the FSLN. In it Fonseca analyzed the Nicaraguan situation as it was in those years, and examined previous FSLN efforts in a critical light. The future strategy of the FSLN was to a large extent based on this important work. This is followed by the "Historic Program of the FSLN," in which the framework for a revolutionary government was first articulated. One can see in this 1969 document the theoretical roots of the policy being implemented by the present government of Nicaragua.

Description of the final buildup and triumph of the revolutionary forces begins with an excerpt by George Black about the ever deepening crisis of the Somoza dictatorship following the 1972 earthquake. Henri Weber then describes the final struggle for power, including the organization and unification of the major tendencies or factions of the FSLN and the critical differences among them. Finally, a short statement on revolutionary justice by Tomás Borge, the last surviving original member of the FSLN and current minister of the interior, reflects the moral tone of those who led the overthrow of Somoza.

25. Nicaragua: Zero Hour*

By Carlos Fonseca Amador

Carlos Fonseca Amador was the central leader of the FSLN from the time he helped found it in July 1961 until his death at the hands of Somoza's National Guard on November 7, 1976. Today an eternal flame burns for him at the Plaza de la Revolución *in Managua, where in November 1979, 100,000 people gathered to mark the anniversary of his death. The following article first appeared in the Spanish language edition of* Tricontinental, *No. 14, 1969. This translation is by Michael Taber and Will Reissner, and is based on a 1979 reprint in Managua.*

The Economic Situation

The people of Nicaragua have been suffering under the yoke of a reactionary clique imposed by Yankee imperialism virtually since 1932, the year in which Anastasio Somoza G. was named commander in chief of the so-called National Guard (GN), a post that had previously been filled by Yankee officials. This clique has reduced Nicaragua to the status of a neocolony—exploited by the Yankee monopolies and the local capitalist class.

At the present time, the economic crisis that the country has been suffering has gotten worse. In the years immediately preceding 1966, the national economy grew at an annual rate of 8 percent. By contrast, in the years 1966 and 1967 the growth rate declined to 3.1 and 4.6 percent respectively.

The production of cotton, which has been increasing since 1950, will increase only slightly in the future. This is due, on the one hand, to a saturation of the foreign capitalist market supplied by national production. And in addition, it is due to the growing competition from synthetic fibers. There has, in fact, been a major drop in the prices offered by the foreign capitalist market for the harvest from the 1968 planting. This last fact has persuaded the country's government to establish commercial relations with some socialist countries, which will take part of the cotton harvest. This crop amounts to 26 percent of the cultivated land in Nicaragua.

Regarding coffee, which is the second largest export product, there is already overproduction, which cannot be sold on the capitalist market. Regarding sugar production, official sources state that it is unlikely that the pace of growth can be maintained in the immediate future.

The exploitation of minerals such as gold and copper, which is directly in the hands of foreign investors, pays ridiculously small sums to the national treasury through taxes. Parallel with this, the handing over of the national riches to the Yankee monopolies has continued to increase. In 1967, for example, a law went into effect that

*Reprinted from a pamphlet published by Pathfinder Press, New York, 1982.

gave Magnavox, a company specializing in the exploitation of forest, absolute ownership of a million hectares of national territory.

At the same time, the ruling clique handles the funds of the state banks as if they were personal funds, while fraud and smuggling reach staggering dimensions. The Somoza family, which had very limited economic resources when it took power, has obtained a vast fiefdom, whose domains go beyond Nicaragua's borders and extend into the other countries of Central America.

In Nicaragua, moreover, there is an unjust distribution of land. Statistical reports for the year 1952 show that a few proprietors control 55 percent of the total area of privately owned farms.

Nicaragua offers exceptional conditions for the development of cattle raising. Nevertheless, the consumption of products derived from cattle has declined and the increase in exports has largely been due to foreign sales of cows that would have contributed to an increase in the quantity of animals.

The advantages provided to producers of products for foreign markets—in this case for growing cotton—has led to a situation where food products are grown on the worst lands, which also means that imports are needed to satisfy this important sector.

Nicaragua is among the countries that have been hurt by the so-called Central American economic integration. It is well known that this integration has been simply a plan to increase the economic hold of the Yankee monopolies over Central America. This scandalous fact has reached such a magnitude that even spokesmen of the Nicaraguan regime itself have been put in the situation of publicly stating that the industries established as a result of this integration do not enhance national economic development.

As with the other countries of Central America, there is no oil production in Nicaragua. It has been stated, however, that if there were possibilities for oil exploitation in Central America, the Yankee monopolies would have an interest in hiding it, in order to maintain it as a reserve in case revolutionary governments were established in the countries that currently produce oil.

Although the governmental capitalist sector represents the dominant segment of the country's capitalist class, it must be pointed out that the sector of capitalists who call themselves "oppositionists" are also involved in exploiting the Nicaraguan people. Many times, the governing and "opposition" groups jointly exploit important sectors of the national economy, as is the case regarding sugar, milk, the press, banking, liquor distilleries, etc.

The economic system described above turns the other classes making up Nicaragua's population into victims of exploitation and oppression. The poor diet of the working classes has caused numerous deaths through hunger. It's known that in 1964 hundreds of peasants died of hunger in the Tempisque area, in the department of Matagalpa. In various regions in the north, the incidence of goiters is very high. In the Malacaguas area, there have been cases of collective dementia provoked by poor diet; night blindness resulting from Vitamin A and protein deficiencies has occurred in areas around the town of Darío.

A few years ago, some tests carried out in a school in Jinotepe, a region located near the country's capital, indicated that every one of the 200 students suffered from tuberculosis.

Only 1.1 percent of the Nicaraguan population has completed primary school. Fifty percent of the population has had no schooling whatever. The proportion of students that leave school in the first grade or repeat grades is extremely high (73 percent). Only 21 percent of the student population comes from the sector of society with income levels at or below the country's average. Out of 200,000 young people from fourteen to nineteen years of age, barely 20,000 are enrolled in high school or commercial, vocational, or agricultural education.

Infant mortality reaches dreadful levels in Nicaragua. More than 50 percent of the deaths in the country occur among persons under fourteen years of age. Out of every thousand children born, 102 die. Six out of every ten deaths are caused by infectious—meaning curable—diseases. In recent investigations 9.28 percent of the population had a positive reaction in tests for malaria, while in Costa Rica it is 0.96 percent, and in Panama, 4.98 percent.

A Tradition of Rebellion

A notable feature of Nicaraguan history, particularly during the stage that began with independence from Spanish rule in 1821, is the use of violence by different political forces within the exploiting classes, fighting over control of the government. Peaceful changes between different factions of the ruling classes, which have been rather frequent in other Latin American countries, have not taken place in Nicaragua. This traditional experience predisposed the Nicaraguan people against electoral farces and in favor of armed struggle. There is no doubt, then, that the Nicaraguan people have a rich tradition of rebellion.

It is a fact that the Nicaraguan people have taken up arms to fight specific forms of oppression many times through movements headed by individuals, movements that in no sense could lead to progressive revolutionary change. This represents another characteristic of the Nicaraguan people throughout their history. This characteristic relates to the lack of a deepgoing revolutionary consciousness.

The ideological obscurantism inherited from the colonial epoch has continued to weigh heavily in preventing the people from marching with full consciousness toward struggle for social change. It is indisputable that throughout their history the Nicaraguan people have endured numerous battles in which they have demonstrated their courage. But they have marched to these struggles more by instinct than through consciousness. Perhaps it is useful to repeat in the case of Nicaragua the words that Marx wrote in relation to Spain. Marx pointed out that the Spanish people had traditionally been a rebel people, but not a revolutionary people.

The national and international conditions that currently prevail make it possible for at least a sector of the Nicaraguan people to initiate armed struggle, conscious that they are trying not simply to achieve a change of men in power, but a change of the system—the overthrow of the exploiting classes and the victory of the exploited classes.

Origin and Prolongation of the Present Regime

It is not possible to analyze the conditions that have permitted the ruling clique to remain in power for more than three decades without stopping to study the country's situation at the time this regime was installed, as well as the situation that has been developing for more than thirty years.

From 1926 to 1936 the Nicaraguan people went through one of the most intense periods in their history. The armed struggle, through which the people sought change, produced more than 20,000 deaths. The struggle began as a fight against a conservative government imposed by the North Americans, went through the Sandinista resistance, and concluded with Anastasio Somoza's military coup against Juan B. Sacasa.

The struggle was carried out without an industrial proletariat existing. The incipient bourgeoisie betrayed the Nicaraguan people and sold out to the Yankee intervention. The bourgeoisie could not be immediately replaced as the vanguard of the people's struggle by a revolutionary proletariat. The Sandinista resistance, which became the heroic vanguard of the people, had an almost totally peasant composition, and therein lies the glory and the tragedy of that revolutionary movement.

It was a glory for the Nicaraguan people that the most humble class responded to the stains against the honor of the homeland, and at the same time a tragedy because it involved a peasantry lacking any political level whatsoever. Moreover, there were leaders of important guerrilla columns who were totally illiterate. As a result, once Sandino was assassinated his movement could not maintain its continuity.

The prolonged armed struggle, which ended in betrayal and frustration, exhausted the people's strength. The sector headed by Anastasio Somoza won hegemony over the traditional Liberal Party, while the opposition to Somoza's government came to be dominated by the traditional Conservative Party, a reactionary political force profoundly weakened because in the 1930s this party's sell-out to the Yankee interventionists was fresh in the people's memory.

An important factor that also seriously contributed to the interruption of the anti-imperialist struggle was the situation arising from the outbreak of the Second World War, which concentrated the focus of the world's reactionaries on Europe and Asia. Yankee imperialism, the traditional enemy of the Nicaraguan people, became an ally of the world antifascist front. The lack of a revolutionary leadership in Nicaragua prevented this reality from being interpreted correctly, and Somoza took advantage of the situation to consolidate the rule of his clique.

The Rise of the Old Marxist Sector

For many years, the influence of the Marxist sector in the opposition was almost completely under the control of the conservative sector, the political force representing the interests of one sector of the capitalist class. One of the factors that contributed to the weakness of the Marxist sector originated in the conditions in which the Nicaraguan Socialist Party (the traditional Communist organization in Nicaragua) was formed. That organization was formed in June 1944, when the Second World War was still not over, and in a period when the views of Earl Browder were in full force. Browder, the general secretary of the Communist Party of the United States, proposed conciliation with the capitalist class and with North American imperialism in Latin America.

In those years, the Nicaraguan workers' movement was basically made up of artisans, and this provided a base for anti-working-class deviations. In addition, the leadership of the Socialist Party was also of artisan origin, and not of proletarian roots as the Nicaraguan Socialist Party demagogically asserts. It was a leadership that suffered from an extremely low ideological level.

For many years, the revolutionary intellectual was a rare exception in Nicaragua. The radical and free-thinking intellectuals of the years of the U.S. armed intervention, who as a class represented a bourgeoisie that ended up capitulating, could not be replaced by intellectuals identified with the working class, for the reasons previously explained. As a result, the intellectual movement in Nicaragua came to be the monopoly of a Catholic element, who for a period even began to openly identify with fascism. In this way, the door of thought remained shut to the revolutionary movement.

The Nicaraguan Socialist Party was organized in a meeting whose objective was to proclaim support to Somoza's government. This took place on July 3, 1944, in the Managua gymnasium. To be rigorously objective, it's necessary to explain that this very grave error was not the result of simple bad faith by the leaders. We must look at the factors that brought it about.

The Marxist leadership did not possess the necessary clarity in the face of the conservative sector's control over the anti-Somozist opposition. It could not distinguish between the justice of the anti-Somozist opposition and the manuevers of the conservative sector.

Once Somoza had used the pseudo-Marxist sector for his own benefit, he unleashed repression against the workers' movement, which, due to the comfortable conditions in which it was born, did not know how to defend itself with the necessary revolutionary firmness.

Parallel to this, the capitalist sector of the opposition (Conservative Party, Liberal opposition grouping) carried out all kinds of compromises with the Somoza regime.

Role of the Cuban People's Struggle and Revolutionary Victories

The principal characteristic of the period from the assassination of Sandino in 1934 until the triumph of the Cuban revolution in 1959 was the interruption of the traditional armed struggle as a systematic tactic to fight the ruling regime. Another main characteristic was the almost total domination that the conservative sector exerted over the anti-Somozist opposition. That was the situation, lasting for twenty-five years, that preceded the new stage, which began with the armed struggle of the Cuban people and their victorious revolution.

There were a few exceptions to that long pacifistic period. But these were almost always insignificant actions by the conservative sector, behind the backs of and against the people. In April 1954, an armed coup was foiled, which although under conservative hegemony, involved elements that had revolutionary inclinations. The attitude of these revolutionary elements, along with the action of the patriot Rigoberto López Pérez, who gave his life in bringing Anastasio Somoza G. to justice on September 21, 1956, must be viewed as precursory events to the insurrectional stage that developed several years later.

The Cuban people's rebellion had an influence even before its victorious outcome. Thus, in October 1958, there was the guerrilla action in which the leader, the veteran Sandinista Ramón Raudales, was killed. There were a whole series of armed actions against the reactionary government of Nicaragua, including the following: Ramón Raudales, in the mountains of Jalapa, in October 1958; El Chaparral in June 1959; Manuel Díaz Sotelo, in Estelí, in August 1959; Carlos Haslam, in the mountains of Matagalpa, in the second half of 1959; Heriberto Reyes, in Yumale, in December 1959; Las Trojes and El Dorado, in early 1960; Orosí, on the southern border, in the second half of 1959; Luis Morales, on the San Juan River on the southern border, in January 1960; Poteca River on the northern border, January 1961; Bijao River, November 1962; the Coco River and Bocay River, in 1963; clash between peasants and local authorities in 1965 in the Uluse region of Matagalpa; economic actions against banks in 1966; actions in Managua, January 22, 1967; incursions in Panacasán in 1966 and 1967; economic bank action in Managua and certain revolutionary executions in some areas of the countryside in 1963; battle with the National Guard in Oaosca, Matagalpa, February 1969.

In some encounters, especially in the first months of the new stage, elements linked to the traditional capitalist parties were influential in the leadership of these actions. But in general, these efforts increasingly revealed the determination of the revolutionary sector to take up arms to win the country's liberation.

The period of gestation of the current revolutionary armed struggle has lasted almost ten years and this length of time is clearly a result of the characteristics of the revolutionary movement that have been explained.

The Rise of the Revolutionary Armed Organization

Especially in the first years of the new stage, the revolutionary leadership was obliged to take up arms with leaders who often lacked the political conviction needed to lead the struggle for national liberation. As the process has developed, these leaders have been replaced by comrades who possess a profound conviction and an unbreakable determination to defend the people, arms in hand.

Another very prominent aspect of the first period of the new stage was the lack of an adequate revolutionary organization linked to the broad masses of the people, and especially to the peasants. It should be noted that the composition of what could be called the revolutionary groups was primarily made up of artisans and workers with a very low political and ideological level. At that time, revolutionary militants with a university student background were an exception. Students fell in different actions, but each group as such lacked the numbers needed to enable it to play a very important part in assimilating the experiences that the individual students were acquiring. The revolutionary groups lacked cadres who had the ability to solve the difficult problems that the situation posed.

One aspect that is worth looking at regarding the work that has been done over the last decade is that no one knew how to combine underground activity with work among the popular masses. In general, importance has been given only to underground activity, although after the defeat at the Bocay River in 1963 and the Coco River between 1964 and 1966 the error was committed of interrupting insurrectional work in order to pay attention to work among the masses.

It must be pointed out that for a period of time, more precisely up to 1962, each individual armed action came from a different group. That is, they reflected the total anarchy that the insurrectional revolutionary sector suffered from. The Sandinista National Liberation Front (FSLN) marked the overcoming of that problem, providing this sector with its political and military instrument.

Between 1959 and 1962, some of the components of the FSLN retained the illusion that it was possible to accomplish a change in the pacifistic line of the leadership of the Nicaraguan Socialist Party. In the year 1962 this illusion was dissolved in practice with the establishment of the Sandinista Front as an independent grouping, although for some time to come the idea was maintained that it was possible to arrive at specific unity with the Socialist Party, something which reality has refuted.

The movement that culminated at the Coco River and the Bocay River was the first action prepared by a more or less homogeneous revolutionary group. This first attempt was like a dry run for the revolutionary sector.

This first defeat led to a position marked with a reformist streak. It is true that armed struggle was not renounced and the conviction remained that this form of struggle would decide the unfolding of the Nicaraguan revolution. But the reality was that for some time the practical work of continuing the preparations for armed struggle was interrupted. It is also true that after the 1963 defeat our movement was seriously splintered, but we did not know how to adequately overcome the internal crisis that developed.

One factor that undoubtedly influenced the deviation was that our armed defeat coincided with a downturn in the anti-Somoza movement in Nicaragua. In 1963, the political ascent initiated by the struggle and victory of the Cuban people was interrupted. The basis for the downturn was that in February 1963 the Somozist clique successfully carried out the maneuver of holding an electoral farce to impose the puppet René Schick.

In any case, although this downturn in the general situation took place, the FSLN leadership did not fully understand this to be no more than a partial phenomenon, inasmuch as the direction of the revolutionary movement was fundamentally toward progress and in transition toward maturity.

It was correct in that period to pass over to rebuilding the insurrectional organization and accumulating new forces with which to relaunch the armed struggle, but this goal naturally demanded an uninterrupted maintenance of a series of insurrectional-type tasks: accumulating material resources, training combatants, carrying out certain armed actions appropriate to the strategic defensive stage, etc.

This deviation in tactics was also expressed in the ideology that the Sandinista Front adopted. Although it raised the banner of anti-imperialism and the emancipation of the exploited classes, the Front vacillated in putting forward a clearly Marxist-Leninist ideology. The attitude that the traditional Marxist-Leninist sector had maintained in the Nicaraguan people's struggle contributed to this vacillation. As has been stated, this sector in practice has openly played the game of the Somozist clique. This factor, together with the ideological backwardness prevailing in the revolutionary sector of the country, led to vacillation in adopting an ideology that on the national level was rooted in compromise. It can be said that at that time there was a lack of clear understanding that it was only a question of time before the youth and people of Nicaragua would begin to distinguish between the false Marxists and the true Marxists.

Consequently, in the years 1964 and 1965, practically all the emphasis was put on open work, which included legal work among the masses. Clandestine tasks were carried out, above all in the countryside, but the main emphasis of the work during that time was legal. Reality showed that legal work carried out in that manner did not serve to accumulate forces and that the progress achieved was minimal. Neither can it be overlooked that the legal work through the now-disappeared Republican Mobilization group, the student movement, and peasant movement suffered from lack of discipline, audacity, and organization.

One must also conclude that revolutionary work (whether it be public, legal, or clandestine), cannot be advanced in an accelerated way if the armed revolutionary force is lacking. It was the lack of such a force that determined the extreme limitations of the legal work carried out in the years 1964–65.

Our experience shows that the armed revolutionary force (urban and rural) is the motor force of the revolutionary movement in Nicaragua. The armed struggle is the only thing that can inspire the revolutionary combatant in Nicaragua to carry out the tasks decided on by the revolutionary leadership, whether they be armed or of any other revolutionary character.

Parenthetically, during the years 1964 and 1965 important contact with the peasant sector was developed. Comrades of urban extraction permanently established themselves in areas situated on both ends of the northern region of the country, and made trips to learn the peasants' problems firsthand and organize the revolutionary struggle in the countryside.

It must be said, however, that full advantage was not taken of the broad contact that was established with the peasants. In the countryside, some mass peasant meetings were held, some peasant delegations were sent to the city to expose the problems of the countryside, and the peasants occupied some lands, challenging the violence of the big landlords. However, an accelerated pace of peasant mobilization was not maintained. Contact was preserved at specific points and was not extended to other places where the peasants suffered terrible living and working conditions. In addition, if the few peasant marches to the city had been organized with more audacious methods, a much larger number of peasants would have participated, and at the same time a greater number of areas would have gone into action.

In various places, individual contact with certain peasants was prolonged for too long a time without proceeding to the mobilization of the peasant masses. Land invasions by the peasants who had been dispossessed were hardly ever carried out.

The lack of both adequately developed leading cadres and the necessary determination to organize the struggle of the popular masses played a decisive role in the fact that we did not fully utilize the possibilities that were presented. Lacking guerrilla camps, it was impossible to train cadres to organize the struggle of the diverse sectors of the Nicaraguan people.

The Armed Movement of Pancasán

In the course of 1966, practical steps were taken to relaunch armed actions. That year the Sandinista Front became conscious of the deviation that had occurred as a result of the blows of 1963 and it proceeded to prepare the Pancasán guerrilla base. Although this preparation showed organizational progress compared with the FSLN's armed movement in 1963, it did not represent serious progress in political and military tactics. It was a notable step forward organizationally because it did not follow the usual practice of preparing the armed movement in a neighboring country, which had provided distance from the enemy's observation; rather it was preparation of an armed movement in mountains situated in the very center of the country.

An extremely important factor that hindered the success of the Pancasán movement was the mistaken method used to get the peasants to participate in the struggle. The form used was to recruit a number of peasants to become part of the regular column. This means that these peasants were completely mixed in with the working-class and student fighters, i.e., combatants with an urban background.

The militants who came from urban areas generally possessed a higher revolutionary consciousness than the peasants as a whole, who became demoralized when faced with the first difficulties that we ran up against: scarcity of supplies, certain slow marches, and the first rumors of the presence of enemy soldiers on nearby roads. This obligated the leadership to send back the majority of the peasants, although there were honorable exceptions of peasants who firmly refused to be let go and who are an example of the combative possibility of this sector.

In addition, in the first stage of the revolutionary war that was beginning, we did not find a way to incorporate the peasants in those areas some days distant, with whom contact had previously been established through organizing them in the struggle for land and for other demands. Some of the peasants who temporarily joined the guerrillas had been moved from their areas to the encampments.

When the breakup of the Pancasán guerrilla movement had already taken place, it became known that once some of the peasants who had deserted the guerrillas arrived back in their own areas, they took part in armed assaults on local government posts or rural commercial establishments, as well as executions of known informers. This indicates that to a large extent some of the peasants who had become demoralized went through that crisis because they were not organized in the most appropriate manner. It means that they probably should have been irregular rather than regular guerrillas. This experience leads us to think about the possibility of organizing irregular guerrillas parallel to the regulars. We should not fail to point out that we can now evaluate the importance of work among the peasants much better, thanks to our own experience. We don't only base ourselves on the experiences of other Latin American guerrilla movements.

Another aspect that must be highlighted was the insufficient number of cadres to handle all tasks that the preparation of the work demanded, not only in the city and the countryside, but even outside of the country. For too long the leadership of the Sandinista Front tolerated sectarianism, which stood in the way of promoting a sufficient quantity of new cadres coming from politically advanced working-class backgrounds and from the university sector. Feverish attempts were made to achieve excessively big goals instead of always making progress in carrying out suitable, everyday tasks.

The insurrectionary work was not related to the general people's struggle—especially the peasant, student, working-class struggles. It was good that the Front put its principal emphasis on insurrectionary work, but it was an error to abandon other revolutionary forms of struggle. Sectarian tactics weighed heavily and these determined the course of activity in the preparation for the movement in the mountains.

The individualistic bad habits that leadership comrades often displayed was the factor that helped hold back the initiatives that could have resolved many problems; on different occasions individual problems were mixed with political problems. This may have decisively contributed to depriving certain initiatives of the seriousness that was due them.

In regard to placing cadres in charge of various tasks, it was a mistake to be confident that comrades who had not experienced the privations of guerrilla life would be able to work among the masses—for example, among the student masses. For some years now, our organization has been conscious of the ballast that the Nicaraguan revolutionary movement carries as a result of the stance of the capitalist parties, which for many years usurped the leadership of the anti-Somozist opposition. However, at the time when the guerrilla base was established in the mountains, there was insufficient thought given to the fact that due to the prevailing conditions the tasks required by the work in the cities could not be attended to by militants who did not possess the necessary firmness and discipline. In view of this, the comrades in the forefront of urban resistance work could count on the practical collaboration of a very reduced number of militants. The situation of the urban resistance became more acute due to the sectarian attitude of those charged with responsibility.

Organized mass work (student, peasant, worker) was paralyzed. On the one hand, there were not enough cadres to handle this work, and on the other, there was an underestimation of the importance this activity could play in the development of the armed struggle. This weakness led to the situation where when the death of comrades in the mountains and in the cities was recorded, there was not consistent solidarity on the part of all the members of the Front.

In the cities, only violent actions of an individual nature were planned. And there was no attempt to develop a policy of using violence involving the participation of the popular masses in the cities—something that is possible mainly in Managua, the country's capital, which has a population of more than 300,000.

Under Nicaraguan conditions, as well as in most countries of Latin America, the center of action of the revolutionary war has to be the countryside. However, the cities must also play a role of particular importance, given that in the first stage of the war the city has to supply the countryside with the most developed cadres to lead the political and military detachment. In general, the revolutionary elements from the cities have a greater ability to develop themselves in the first stage. These elements are composed of the revolutionary sector of workers, students, and a certain layer of the petty bourgeoisie.

One must take into account the habits that the capitalist parties and their faithful servants have imposed on the popular masses through their electoral policy. These parties have conditioned broad sectors of the people to participate in the hustle and bustle of electoral rigamarole. This circumstance must be taken into account to fully understand why many sectors of the population, despite their sympathy with the revolutionary armed struggle, cannot demonstrate that sympathy through action. This forces us to consider the need to fully train a broad number of persons from among the population to have the material capacity to support the armed struggle. To seek out the people is not sufficient; they have to be trained to participate in the revolutionary war.

Some Current Tasks

Several months ago, work in the countryside was reestablished. The FSLN is simultaneously developing political and military work, with the objective of reorganizing the guerrilla struggle.

In the countryside a study of the peasants' problems is already under way, and this investigation has required militants to stay in the rural zones for several weeks. Militants with an urban background (workers and students) are participating in this political work. It has been said that the mountain (the guerrilla base) proletarianizes, and we agree with this statement. By as our experience has shown, it can be added that the countryside—political contact with the peasants—also proletarianizes. The urban militant, in contact with the countryside, including the zones where a guerrilla base is not organized, lives the abject poverty that the peasants suffer and feels their desire to struggle.

A phenomenon that has been seen in this country since the Pancasán movement is the growth of the Sandinista National Liberation Front's political authority over the broad sectors of the popular masses. Today the Sandinista Front can claim, and has obtained, a much greater degree of cooperation from the population than in the past. It must also be said that if we do not get greater cooperation than we actually are receiving, it is because we lack cadres who are competent in asking for this type of help, and also because the cadres now active are not functioning systematically enough.

Simultaneously, new methods are being found so that we can gain the practical collaboration of new sectors of the population in the clandestine conditions under which we function (a small country with small cities). This has led us to not depend exclusively on the old militants and collaborators (a large proportion of whom are "jaded").

Furthermore, we have reestablished squads that are prepared to act in the cities, and they have carried out some actions.

We now have plans to undertake actions in harmony with the period of reestablishment we are now going through.

The Sandinista National Liberation Front believes that at the present time and for a certain period to come, Nicaragua will be going through a stage in which a radical political force will be developing its specific characteristics. Consequently, at the current time it is necessary for us to strongly emphasize that our major objective is the socialist revolution, a revolution that aims to defeat Yankee imperialism and its local agents, false oppositionists, and false revolutionaries. This propaganda, with the firm backing of armed action, will permit the Front to win the support of a sector of the popular masses that is conscious of the profound nature of the struggle we are carrying out.

In order to outline a strategy for the revolutionary movement, it is necessary to take into account the strength that the capitalist parties represent, due to the influence they still wield within the opposition. One must be alert to the danger that the reactionary force in the opposition to the Somoza regime could climb on the back of the revolutionary insurrection. The revolutionary movement has a dual goal. On the one hand, to overthrow the criminal and traitorous clique that has usurped the power for so many years; and on the other hand, to prevent the capitalist opposition—of proven submission to Yankee imperialism—from taking advantage of the situation which the guerrilla struggle has unleashed, and grabbing power. In the task of barring the way to the traitorous capitalist forces, a revolutionary political and military force rooted in the broad sectors of the people has a unique role to play. Sinking these roots is dependent on the organization's ability to drive out the liberal and conservative influences from this broad sector.

The policy we follow later on regarding the old parties that now have a capitalist leadership will be determined by the attitude that the people as a whole have toward these parties.

Relating to the situation of the Nicaraguan Socialist Party, it can be stated that the changes that have taken place in that political organization's leadership are purely changes in form. The old leadership builds illusions regarding the conservative sector, and calls for building a political front in which these stubborn agents of imperialism participate. The so-called new leadership currently justifies having participated in the electoral farce of 1967, supporting the pseudo-oppositional candidacy of the conservative politician Fernando Aguero. Like the old leadership, the so-called new leadership keeps talking about the armed struggle, while in practice it concentrates its energies on petty legal work.

The above statements do not contradict the possibility of developing a certain unity with the anti-Somozist sector in general. But this is unity at the base, with the most honest sectors of the various anti-Somozist tendencies. This is all the more possible due to the increase in the prestige of the Sandinista National Liberation Front and the discrediting and splintering of the leadership of the capitalist parties and the like.

The Sandinista National Liberation Front understands how hard the guerrilla road is. But it is not prepared to retreat. We know that we are confronting a bloody, reactionary armed force like the National Guard, the ferocious GN, which maintains intact the practices of cruelty that were inculcated in it by its creator, the U.S. Marines. Bombardment of villages, cutting of children's throats, violation of women, burning huts with peasants inside of them, mutilation as a torture—these were the study courses that the U.S. professors of civilization taught the GN during the period of the guerrilla resistance (1927–1932) led by Augusto César Sandino.

The frustration that followed the period of the Sandinista resistance does not have to be repeated today. Now the times are different. The current days are not like those in which Sandino and his guerrilla brothers battled alone against the Yankee empire. Today revolutionaries of all the subjugated countries are rising up or preparing to go into the battle against the empire of the dollar. At the apex of this battle is indomitable Vietnam, which with its example of heroism, is repulsing the aggression of the blond beasts.

The combative example of our fallen brothers carries us forward. It is the example of Casimiro Sotelo, Danilo Rosales, Jorge Navarro, Francisco Buitrago, Silvio Mayorga, Otto Casco, Modesto Duarte, Robert Amaya, Edmundo Pérez, Hugo Medina, René Carríon, Rigoberto Cruz (Pablo Ubeda), Fermín Díaz, Selín, Shible, Ernesto Fernandez, Oscar Florez, Felipe Gaitán, Fausto García, Elías Moncada, Francisco Moreno, Carlos Reyna, David Tejada, Carlos Tinoco, Francisco Córdoba, Faustino Ruíz, Boanerges Santamaría, Iván Sanchez.

We will faithfully fulfill our oath: "Before the image of Augusto César Sandino and Ernesto Che Guevara; before the memory of the heroes and martyrs of Nicaragua, Latin America, and humanity as a whole; before history: I place my hand on the black and red flag that signifies 'Free Homeland or Death,' and I swear to defend the national honor with arms in hand and to fight for the redemption of the oppressed and exploited in Nicaragua and the world. If I fulfill this oath, the freedom of Nicaragua and all the peoples will be the reward; if I betray this oath, death in disgrace and dishonor will be my punishment."

26. The Historic Program of the FSLN*

By the Sandinista National Liberation Front (FSLN)

This document was first presented to the Nicaraguan people in 1969. It was reprinted by the FSLN in June 1981. This translation from that edition is by Will Reissner.

The Sandinista National Liberation Front (FSLN) arose out of the Nicaraguan people's need to have a "vanguard organization" capable of taking political power through direct struggle against its enemies and establishing a social system that wipes out the exploitation and poverty that our people have been subjected to in past history.

The FSLN is a politico-military organization, whose strategic objective is to take political power by destroying the military and bureaucratic apparatus of the dictatorship and to establish a revolutionary government based on the worker-peasant alliance and the convergence of all the patriotic anti-imperialist and anti-oligarchic forces in the country.

The people of Nicaragua suffer under subjugation to a reactionary and fascist clique imposed by Yankee imperialism in 1932, the year Anastasio Somoza García was named commander in chief of the so-called National Guard (GN).

The Somozist clique has reduced Nicaragua to the status of a neocolony exploited by the Yankee monopolies and the country's oligarchic groups.

The present regime is politically unpopular and juridically illegal. The recognition and aid it gets from the North Americans is irrefutable proof of foreign interference in the affairs of Nicaragua.

The FSLN has seriously and with great responsibility analyzed the national reality and has resolved to confront the dictatorship with arms in hand. We have concluded that the triumph of the Sandinista people's revolution and the overthrow of the regime that is an enemy of the people will take place through the development of a hard-fought and prolonged people's war.

Whatever maneuvers and resources Yankee imperialism deploys, the Somozist dictatorship is condemned to total failure in the face of the rapid advance and development of the people's forces, headed by the Sandinista National Liberation Front.

Given this historic conjuncture the FSLN has worked out this political program with an eye to strengthening and developing our organization, inspiring and stimulating the people of Nicaragua to march forward with the resolve to fight until the dictatorship is overthrown and to resist the intervention of Yankee imperialism, in order to forge a free, prosperous, and revolutionary homeland.

---

*Reprinted from *Sandinistas Speak* (New York: Pathfinder Press, 1982).

I. A Revolutionary Government

The Sandinista people's revolution will establish a revolutionary government that will eliminate the reactionary structure that arose from rigged elections and military coups, and the people's power will create a Nicaragua that is free of exploitation, oppression, backwardness; a free, progressive, and independent country.

The revolutionary government will apply the following measures of a political character:

A. It will endow revolutionary power with a structure that allows the full participation of the entire people, on the national level as well as the local level (departmental, municipal, neighborhood).

B. It will guarantee that all citizens can fully exercise all individual freedoms and it will respect human rights.

C. It will guarantee the free exchange of ideas, which above all leads to vigorously broadening the people's rights and national rights.

D. It will guarantee freedom for the worker-union movement to organize in the city and countryside; and freedom to organize peasant, youth, student, women's, cultural, sporting, and similar groups.

E. It will guarantee the right of emigrant and exiled Nicaraguans to return to their native soil.

F. It will guarantee the right to asylum for citizens of other countries who are persecuted for participation in the revolutionary struggle.

G. It will severely punish the gangsters who are guilty of persecuting, informing on, abusing, torturing, or murdering revolutionaries and the people.

H. Those individuals who occupy high political posts as a result of rigged elections and military coups will be stripped of their political rights.

The revolutionary government will apply the following measures of an economic character:

A. It will expropriate the landed estates, factories, companies, buildings, means of transportation, and other wealth usurped by the Somoza family and accumulated through the misappropriation and plunder of the nation's wealth.

B. It will expropriate the landed estates, factories, companies, means of transportation, and other wealth usurped by the politicians and military officers, and all other accomplices, who have taken advantage of the present regime's administrative corruption.

C. It will nationalize the wealth of all the foreign companies that exploit the mineral, forest, maritime, and other kinds of resources.

D. It will establish workers' control over the administrative management of the factories and other wealth that are expropriated and nationalized.

E. It will centralize the mass transit service.

F. It will nationalize the banking system, which will be placed at the exclusive service of the country's economic development.

G. It will establish an independent currency.

H. It will refuse to honor the loans imposed on the country by the Yankee monopolies or those of any other power.

I. It will establish commercial relations with all countries, whatever their system, to benefit the country's economic development.

J. It will establish a suitable taxation policy, which will be applied with strict justice.

K. It will prohibit usury. This prohibition will apply to Nicaraguan nationals as well as foreigners.

L. It will protect the small and medium-size owners (producers, merchants) while restricting the excesses that lead to the exploitation of the workers.

M. It will establish state control over foreign trade, with an eye to diversifying it and making it independent.

N. It will rigorously restrict the importation of luxury items.

O. It will plan the national economy, putting an end to the anarchy characteristic of the capitalist system of production. An important part of this planning will focus on the industrialization and electrification of the country.

II. The Agrarian Revolution

The Sandinista people's revolution will work out an agrarian policy that achieves an authentic agrarian reform; a reform that will, in the immediate term, carry out massive distribution of the land, eliminating the land grabs by the large landlords in favor of the workers (small producers) who labor on the land.

A. It will expropriate and eliminate the capitalist and feudal estates.

B. It will turn over the land to the peasants, free of charge, in accordance with the principle that the land should belong to those who work it.

C. It will carry out a development plan for livestock raising aimed at diversifying and increasing the productivity of that sector.

D. It will guarantee the peasants the following rights:

1. Timely and adequate agricultural credit.
2. Marketability (a guaranteed market for their production).
3. Technical assistance.

E. It will protect the patriotic landowners who collaborate with the guerrilla struggle, by paying them for their landholdings that exceed the limit established by the revolutionary government.

F. It will stimulate and encourage the peasants to organize themselves in cooperatives, so they can take their destiny into their own hands and directly participate in the development of the country.

G. It will abolish the debts the peasantry incurred to the landlord and any type of usurer.

H. It will eliminate the forced idleness that exists for most of the year in the countryside, and it will be attentive to creating sources of jobs for the peasant population.

III. Revolution in Culture and Education

The Sandinista people's revolution will establish the bases for the development of the national culture, the people's education, and university reform.

A. It will push forward a massive campaign to immediately wipe out "illiteracy."

B. It will develop the national culture and will root out the neocolonial penetration in our culture.

C. It will rescue the progressive intellectuals, and their works that have arisen throughout our history, from the neglect in which they have been maintained by the anti-people's regimes.

D. It will give attention to the development and progress of education at the various levels (primary, intermediate, technical, university, etc.), and education will be free at all levels and obligatory at some.

E. It will grant scholarships at various levels of education to students who have limited economic resources. The scholarships will include housing, food, clothing, books, and transportation.

F. It will train more and better teachers who have the scientific knowledge that the present era requires, to satisfy the needs of our entire student population.

G. It will nationalize the centers of private education that have been immorally turned into industries by merchants who hypocritically invoke religious principles.

H. It will adapt the teaching programs to the needs of the country; it will apply teaching methods to the scientific and research needs of the country.

I. It will carry out a university reform that will include, among other things, the following measures:

1. It will rescue the university from the domination of the exploiting classes, so it can serve the real creators and shapers of our culture: the people. University instruction must be oriented around man, around the people. The university must stop being a breeding ground for bureaucratic egotists.

2. Eliminate the discrimination in access to university classes suffered by youth from the working class and peasantry.

3. Increase the state budget for the university so there are the economic resources to solve the various problems confronting it.

4. Majority student representation on the boards of departments, keeping in mind that the student body is the main segment of the university population.

5. Eliminate the neocolonial penetration of the university, especially the penetration by the North American monopolies through the charity donations of the pseudophilanthropic foundations.

6. Promotion of free, experimental, scientific investigation that must contribute to dealing with national and universal questions.

7. Strengthen the unity of the students, faculty, and investigators with the whole people, by perpetuating the selfless example of the students and intellectuals who have offered their lives for the sake of the patriotic ideal.

IV. Labor Legislation and Social Security

The Sandinista people's revolution will eliminate the injustice of the living and working conditions suffered by the working class under the brutal exploitation, and will institute labor legislation and social assistance.

A. It will enact a labor code that will regulate, among other things, the following rights:

1. It will adopt the principle that "those who don't work don't eat," of course making exceptions for those who are unable to participate in the process of production due to age (children, old people), medical condition, or other reasons beyond their control.

2. Strict enforcement of the eight-hour work day.

3. The income of the workers (wages and other benefits) must be sufficient to satisfy their daily needs.

4. Respect for the dignity of the worker, prohibiting and punishing unjust treatment of workers in the course of their labor.

5. Abolition of unjustified firings.

6. Obligation to pay wages in the period required by law.

7. Right of all workers to periodic vacations.

B. It will eliminate the scourge of unemployment.

C. It will extend the scope of the social security system to all the workers and public employees in the country. The scope will include coverage for illness, physical incapacity, and retirement.

D. It will provide free medical assistance to the entire population. It will set up clinics and hospitals throughout the national territory.

E. It will undertake massive campaigns to eradicate endemic illnesses and prevent epidemics.

F. It will carry out urban reform, which will provide each family with adequate shelter. It will put an end to profiteering speculation in urban land (subdivisions, urban construction, rental housing) that exploits the need that working families in the cities have for an adequate roof over their heads in order to live.

G. It will initiate and expand the construction of adequate housing for the peasant population.

H. It will reduce the charges for water, light, sewers, urban beautification; it will apply programs to extend all these services to the entire urban and rural population.

I. It will encourage participation in sports of all types and categories.

J. It will eliminate the humiliation of begging by putting the above mentioned practices into practice.

V. Administrative Honesty

The Sandinista people's revolution will root out administrative governmental corruption, and will establish strict administrative honesty.

A. It will abolish the criminal vice industry (prostitution, gambling, drug use, etc.), which the privileged sector of the National Guard and the foreign parasites exploit.

B. It will establish strict control over the collection of taxes to prevent government functionaries from profiting, putting an end to the normal practice of the present regime's official agencies.

C. It will end the arbitrary actions of the members of the GN, who plunder the population through the subterfuge of local taxes.

D. It will put an end to the situation wherein military commanders appropriate the budget that is supposed to go to take care of common prisoners, and it will establish centers designed to rehabilitate these wrongdoers.

E. It will abolish the smuggling that is practiced on a large scale by the gang of politicians, officers, and foreigners who are the regime's accomplices.

F. It will severely punish persons who engage in crimes against administrative honesty (embezzlement, smuggling, trafficking in vices, etc.), using greatest severity when it involves elements active in the revolutionary movement.

VI. Reincorporation of the Atlantic Coast

The Sandinista people's revolution will put into practice a special plan for the Atlantic Coast, which has been abandoned to total neglect, in order to incorporate this area into the nation's life.

A. It will end the unjust exploitation the Atlantic Coast has suffered throughout history by the foreign monopolies, especially Yankee imperialism.

B. It will prepare suitable lands in the zone for the development of agriculture and ranching.

C. It will establish conditions that encourage the development of the fishing and forest industries.

D. It will encourage the flourishing of this region's local cultural values, which flow from the specific aspects of its historic tradition.

E. It will wipe out the odious discrimination to which the indigenous Miskitos, Sumos, Ramas, and Blacks of this region are subjected.

VII. Emancipation of Women

The Sandinista people's revolution will abolish the odious discrimination that women have been subjected to compared to men; it will establish economic, political, and cultural equality between woman and man.

A. It will pay special attention to the mother and child.

B. It will eliminate prostitution and other social vices, through which the dignity of women will be raised.

C. It will put an end to the system of servitude that women suffer, which is reflected in the tragedy of the abandoned working mother.

D. It will establish for children born out of wedlock the right to equal protection by the revolutionary institutions.

E. It will establish day-care centers for the care and attention of the children of working women.

F. It will establish a two-month maternity leave before and after birth for women who work.

G. It will raise women's political, cultural, and vocational levels through their participation in the revolutionary process.

VIII. Respect for Religious Beliefs

The Sandinista people's revolution will guarantee the population of believers the freedom to profess any religion.

A. It will respect the right of citizens to profess and practice any religious belief.

B. It will support the work of priests and other religious figures who defend the working people.

IX. Independent Foreign Policy

The Sandinista people's revolution will eliminate the foreign policy of submission to Yankee imperialism, and will establish a patriotic foreign policy of absolute national independence and one that is for authentic universal peace.

A. It will put an end to the Yankee interference in the internal problems of Nicaragua and will practice a policy of mutual respect with other countries and fraternal collaboration between peoples.

B. It will expel the Yankee military mission, the so-called Peace Corps (spies in the guise of technicians), and military and similar political elements who constitute a bare-faced intervention in the country.

C. It will accept economic and technical aid from any country, but always and only when this does not involve political compromises.

D. Together with other peoples of the world it will promote a campaign in favor of authentic universal peace.

E. It will abrogate all treaties, signed with any foreign power, that damage national sovereignty.

X. Central American People's Unity

The Sandinista people's revolution is for the true union of the Central American peoples in a single country.

A. It will support authentic unity with the fraternal peoples of Central America. This unity will lead the way to coordinating the efforts to achieve national liberation and establish a new system without imperialist domination or national betrayal.

B. It will eliminate the so-called integration, whose aim is to increase Central

America's submission to the North American monopolies and the local reactionary forces.

XI. Solidarity among Peoples

The Sandinista people's revolution will put an end to the use of the national territory as a base for Yankee aggression against other fraternal peoples and will put into practice militant solidarity with fraternal peoples fighting for their liberation.

A. It will actively support the struggle of the peoples of Asia, Africa, and Latin America against the new and old colonialism and against the common enemy: Yankee imperialism.

B. It will support the struggle of the Black people and all the people of the United States for an authentic democracy and equal rights.

C. It will support the struggle of all peoples against the establishment of Yankee military bases in foreign countries.

XII. People's Patriotic Army

The Sandinista people's revolution will abolish the armed force called the National Guard, which is an enemy of the people, and will create a patriotic, revolutionary, and people's army.

A. It will abolish the National Guard, a force that is an enemy of the people, created by the North American occupation forces in 1927 to pursue, torture, and murder the Sandinista patriots.

B. In the new people's army, professional soldiers who are members of the old army will be able to play a role providing they have observed the following conduct:

1. They have supported the guerrilla struggle.

2. They have not participated in murder, plunder, torture, and persecution of the people and the revolutionary activists.

3. They have rebelled against the despotic and dynastic regime of the Somozas.

C. It will strengthen the new people's army, raising its fighting ability and its tactical and technical level.

D. It will inculcate in the consciousness of the members of the people's army the principle of basing themselves on their own forces in the fulfillment of their duties and the development of all their creative activity.

E. It will deepen the revolutionary ideals of the members of the people's army with an eye toward strengthening their patriotic spirit and their firm conviction to fight until victory is achieved, overcoming obstacles and correcting errors.

F. It will forge a conscious discipline in the ranks of the people's army and will encourage the close ties that must exist between the combatants and the people.

G. It will establish obligatory military service and will arm the students, workers, and farmers, who—organized in people's militias—will defend the rights won against the inevitable attack by the reactionary forces of the country and Yankee imperialism.

XIII. Veneration of Our Martyrs

The Sandinista people's revolution will maintain eternal gratitude to and veneration of our homeland's martyrs and will continue the shining example of heroism and selflessness they have bequeathed to us.

A. It will educate the new generations in eternal gratitude and veneration toward those who have fallen in the struggle to make Nicaragua a free homeland.

B. It will establish a secondary school to educate the children of our people's martyrs.

C. It will inculcate in the entire people the imperishable example of our martyrs, defending the revolutionary ideal: Ever onward to victory!

27. The 1972 Earthquake and after: Somocismo *in Crisis**

By George Black

George Black is a writer and researcher specializing in Central American affairs. He is on the staff of the North American Congress on Latin America where he is editor of NACLA's Report on the Americas. *He is a frequent contributor to* The Guardian *(London),* United Nations Development Forum, Latin America Weekly Report, Latin America Regional Report *(London), among other journals.*

A little after midnight on December 23, 1972, the center of Managua was torn apart by a massive earthquake. Up to 20,000 died, 75 percent of the city's housing and 90 percent of its commercial capacity was destroyed beyond repair, and damage was conservatively estimated by the United Nations at $772 million. Every contradiction of the Somoza regime was immediately heightened. Overnight, patterns of economic control and Somoza's relationship with the bourgeoisie were transformed. A boom in the construction industry brought new opportunities for speculation as well as an explosion in the size and militancy of the urban working class. In the aftermath of the earthquake, National Guard corruption was seen at its ugliest. The importance of the earthquake as a pivotal moment in the disintegration of *Somocismo* can hardly be overstated.

The true nature of the *Guardia* stood exposed. Officers led their men in systematic looting of the ruined capital and a complete breakdown of discipline meant that Somoza was unable to guarantee public order without the prompt arrival of 600 U.S.

*Reprinted from *Triumph of the People: The Sandinista Revolution in Nicaragua* (London: Zed Press, 1981), pp. 58–62.

soldiers and other Central American troops. Any remaining public respect for the military evaporated. Until the *Guardia* recovered its discipline, Managua residents described the city as under virtual American occupation, leaving an indelible impression of U.S. troops storming through the devastated streets, shouting orders in English to a bewildered population and incinerating corpses with flamethrowers. In its rush to get rich, the *Guardia* forgot all about guerrillas. A thriving black market sprang up, filled with stolen property and medical and food aid from overseas. One observer described the sale of goods donated by Catholic relief agencies and foreign governments in hastily opened shops staffed by the National Guard: "Tinned food, clothing . . . you can even buy anything from a small electric generator to a water purifier, electric torches, pickaxes and spades, complete factory-sealed blood transfusion equipment. There are also shops selling goods from looted warehouses: in Chichigalpa, for example, where the military commander's wife looks after marketing goods stolen from the *Casa Mantica* in Managua. *Guardia* demolition crews directed by Anastasio Somoza Portocarrero made off with anything they could shift: toilet fittings, furniture, street lights, electric wiring. And unemployed rural laborers of Carazo and the north were press-ganged to help in the so-called Civil Reconstruction Corps."

Somoza described the earthquake as a "revolution of possibilities," and certainly for members of the ruling elite the phrase was accurate enough. Paradoxically, the earthquake was a means of pulling the country out of its stagnation and inducing immediate economic growth, but at the cost of new economic distortion and an insoluble political crisis which went to the heart of bourgeois rule. The loans contracted for reconstruction projects brought an escalating foreign debt, and Somoza's increased tendency to stave off economic disaster by resorting to foreign loans was reflected in an external debt which shot up from $255 million in 1972 to more than $1 billion by 1978, half of it at interest rates above 8 percent.

Somoza himself cornered the reconstruction of Managua. His company ESPESA took charge of demolition work; *Inmuebles SA* of real estate speculation; a host of other companies, generally with a monopoly, took on contracts for concrete, building materials, metal structures, roofing, asbestos, and plastics. Fifty new construction companies mushroomed, the most prominent controlled by the Somoza clan, and speculative property corporations threw together cheap housing (11,132 temporary homes in 1973 and 4,033 permanent ones), which they resold at four or five times their original value. The streets were no longer paved with the traditional asphalt but with paving stones *(adoquines)* from a Somoza factory using Somoza-produced cement. The quality of new housing was scarcely better than what had gone before. "Our climate lends itself to good living without our needing to make massive investments in housing," Somoza was later to tell *Le Monde* in a cynical 1978 interview.

Politicians like Alfonso Love Cordero of the ruling triumvirate* were awarded

*The "triumvirate" was composed of the Conservative leader Fernando Aguero plus two Somoza appointees. It was part of a deal in which a Constituent Assembly was to reform the Constitution yet again and pave the way for Somoza's reelection in 1974. It ruled from May 1972 to December 1974.

building contracts even when lower tenders were submitted, and speculation with prime housing land became a national scandal. In one incident, Cornelio Hueck—president of the Constituent Assembly—bought up empty land earmarked for temporary housing for the homeless. Having paid $17,000, he resold the land two days later to the state housing bank for $1.2 million—the funds having been received from the U.S. AID. But whatever private doubts the United States may have had, it was no time for niceties. Above all, the strong man had to be pulled out of the chaos. Although some of the aid which arrived was disinterested—like a Cuban hospital in Managua—the purpose of the vast American aid effort was clear; to shore up the dictatorship; and there was evidence that a large part of ostensibly humanitarian funds was placed at the disposal of the Pentagon. Even AID money not expressly designed to prop up the dictatorship ended up in Somoza's pockets because of the monopoly control he exercised over the reconstruction projects which that money paid for. The sums were large: $78 million from AID ($12.7 million in emergency grant assistance and a further $65.3 million in reconstruction loans) plus $54 million from the Inter-American Development Bank (IDB)—a striking contrast to the United States's later meager initial response to the devastation of the 1979 war.

The earthquake accelerated the class struggle in Nicaragua. It came in the middle of a two-year drought which wrecked the production of staple food crops, bringing hunger to the countryside and a wave of peasant migration to the capital. The rapid growth in construction and related industries absorbed many of Managua's unemployed, causing a dramatic rise in numbers of the urban proletariat. Rampant government corruption, coupled with longer working hours, lower wages, a generalized attack on working-class living standards, and the agitational work of the FSLN, all brought a corresponding rise in class consciousness. Organized working-class activity was on the increase, highlighted by *campesino* land invasions in the north and the big 1973 construction workers' strike led by the CGT, the trade union federation of the Socialist Party. The aftermath of the earthquake also introduced a new phrase into the vocabulary of the bourgeois opposition: *competencia desleal,* unfair or disloyal competition. The rules of the capitalist game, and with it the fragile consensus which held the dictatoral state together, had been broken.

A new phase of absolute power opened. The triumvirate survived in name but Somoza ruled by decree from the newly invented position of president of the National Emergency Committee. To comply with the new constitution ruling that no serving military officer could stand for the presidency, Somoza gave up the title of *Jefe Director* of the National Guard and instead took the title of *Jefe Supremo* of the armed forces. The September 1974 election, which Somoza won with the traditional overwhelming majority over the traditional hand-picked Conservative opponent, was boycotted by a number of dissident bourgeois politicians including Pedro Joaquín Chamorro, who by now had organized an opposition coalition, UDEL. For their pains, twenty-seven leaders of the boycott were arrested and deprived of their political rights until March the following year. But they did not give up. They filed charges with the Supreme Electoral Tribunal, a body composed of one representative of Somoza's Supreme Court, two of the Liberal Party and the guaranteed 40 percent minority of two Conservatives. The charge of fraud, bribery, and coercion was dismissed out of hand, but the Tribunal's replies to the two charges of constitutional violation were remarkable for their candor. The accusation that Somoza's rule had been continuous, thereby infringing the constitution, was quashed by citing the two-year rule of the figurehead triumvirate, and the Tribunal ruled that Somoza's new post as *Jefe Supremo* of the *Guardia* was purely administrative, and did not disqualify him from the presidency on the grounds of active military service. The Tribunal even admitted that the Junta's February decree creating the post of *Jefe Supremo* had been specifically designed to allow Somoza's candidacy in September. It was a bizarre attempt to provide a legal fiction for a wholly discredited regime.

The Frente Sandinista had other more impressive ways of registering its disgust with *Somocismo*. On December 27, 1974, it launched a spectacular commando raid in Managua. This was the catalyst for a new chapter of institutionalized repression. Within hours, Somoza decreed a state of siege, martial law, permanent military courts, and press censorship, just as much to smash trade union militancy as to drive the FSLN into clandestinity and prevent the raid from having its desired impact on class consciousness and perhaps fusing two hitherto unconnected facets of the popular struggle—the guerrilla war and the open trade-union work of the PSN. The new repressive legislation might also allow all Nicaraguan capitalists to increase their profits by permitting superexploitation of the work force, a calculated move by Somoza to woo back some of the bourgeois support forfeited after the earthquake.

The emergency press laws were Draconian. All newspaper copy had to be submitted to the National Guard before publication, and was sent back with all offending articles blocked out in red ink. An offending article was any which made reference to trade unions, labor disputes, allegations of defective public services, including transport, roads, and housing conditions, precisely the issues which the mass movement was beginning to mobilize around in the *barrios*. The Church, whose acceptance of Somoza was fast waning, protested vigorously about the peasant massacres which were taking place under the blanket of press censorship: Somoza's only response was to extend censorship to include Church publications and radio broadcasts. Even U.S. Ambassador Theberge acknowledged the scale of human rights violations, and with the election of Jimmy Carter in November 1976 and the ensuing human rights policy of the U.S. government, Somoza's attempts to dismember the popular opposition led to grave doubts in Washington about the future viability of the dictatorship.

Somoza's repression of the mass movement was designed in part to restore favorable conditions for the capitalist class as a whole, but the result was the opposite. Within the bourgeoisie, contradictions merely deepened, and institutionalized terror frightened off every bourgeois group which preferred government by consensus. At the same time, the reign of terror of the mid-1970s failed to root out the popular movement led by the FSLN, and the basis for mass radicalization grew. New possibilities for economic growth, by contrast, contracted. By the end of 1977, the combination of these three factors threw *Somocismo* into its acute final crisis.

28. The Struggle for Power*

By Henri Weber

> The truth is that we always thought of the masses, seeing them, however, as a prop for the guerrilla campaign that would enable it to deal some blows at the National Guard. Reality was quite different: guerrilla activity served as a prop for the masses, who crushed the enemy by means of insurrection.
>
> Comandante Humberto Ortega

In the early 1970s, all the contradictions of Nicaraguan society took a turn for the worse, and the economy began to suffer the harsh effects of the world crisis. According to official statistics, which generally softened the reality, the rate of inflation increased from an annual average of 1.7 percent before 1970 to 9.7 percent between 1971 and 1975, remaining high at 9.4 percent in 1976 and 11 percent in 1977. Industry was hard hit by the wave of factory closures and layoffs, the crisis being especially severe in construction. Sharply contested strikes broke out in the building, health, and education sectors. The state debt rose to a record level. Savage repression struck on a mass scale.

Exasperated by the way the Somozist regime profited from the Managua earthquake, the bourgeois oppositions began to assert themselves and sought to unify their efforts. In late 1970, when Conservative Party leader Fernando Aguero announced his intention to sign a pact with Somoza, a wing headed by *La Prensa* director Pedro Joaquín Chamorro split to form the Conservative National Action (ANC). In Somoza's Nationalist Liberal Party, another split produced the Constitutionalist Movement (MC) under Ramiro Sacasa. And in 1973, the newly formed National Mobilization and National Salvation movements sought to relaunch an opposition based on leading personalities. On July 8, 1974, twenty-seven notables, representing seven political movements and two trade unions, called for a boycott of the elections. Somoza was, of course, reelected in September with the help of the *Magnifica* and the National Guard. But the rate of abstention reached an all-time high.

On December 15, 1974, a Democratic Liberation Union (UDEL) was officially formed by the groups that had supported a boycott: the Christian Social Party, Independent Liberal Party, Socialist Party of Nicaragua, Conservative National Action, Constitutionalist Movement, National Mobilization, National Salvation, General Confederation of Labor, and National Workers Federation. It was a Popular Front alliance against the dictatorship, bringing together on a moderate democratic program both liberal bourgeois formations and organizations representing the workers' movement. Bourgeois hegemony was evident in the Union's program, methods of struggle, and leadership. But it was nevertheless not appreciated by broad sections of the

*Reprinted from *Nicaragua: The Sandinist Revolution* (London: Verso Editions and NLB, 1981).

employers, including the giant BANIC and BANAMERICA groups, who saw the UDEL notables as sorcerers' apprentices.

The UDEL constitution, which called for respect for political and trade-union freedoms, marked a further stage in the anti-Somoza radicalization of a portion of the ruling class, and hence a narrowing of the dictatorship's social base.[1] On December 27, 1974, less than two weeks after the UDEL was proclaimed, the FSLN recommended military operations, kidnapping two high figures in the regime, later exchanged for the release of a number of political prisoners and the publication in the press of long communiqués denouncing official corruption.

Somoza saw a growing risk that the apparently sectoralized and unrelated movements of protest and opposition might converge politically, especially since UDEL and its president, enjoying solid support in the United States, now represented a liberal alternative to the dictatorship.

His reply was a good example of the tactics he would adopt throughout the revolutionary crisis, though they contributed to his own downfall. Far from trying to splinter his opponents by reaching an agreement with the least determined of them, he simply tried to terrorize them all into silence. Thus, in winter 1975, on the pretext that the FSLN had revived its activity, a state of emergency was declared, martial law and press censorship imposed. UDEL was paralyzed. The strikes and student movement were brutally suppressed. And an annihilation campaign, Operation *Aguila Sexta,* was launched against the FSLN.

By September 1977, Anastasio Somoza Debayle seemed to have won: "social peace" had been restored on the basis of a cut in real wages; the FSLN, bled white in the military campaign, was split into three factions; and UDEL had given proof of its lack of consistency. Believing he had achieved his objectives, the dictator now agreed to comply with Washington's injunctions. But no sooner had he lifted the state of emergency in exchange for U.S. military credits, than the opposition movements resurfaced with even greater vigor.

In October 1977, a month after the state of emergency was lifted, the *Tercerista* tendency of the FSLN launched a series of assaults on National Guard barracks in the northern town of Ocotal, in Masaya, and in San Carlos near the Costa Rican border. The operation was a military failure, but it had a resounding political echo. By showing that repression had solved nothing, it acted as a spur to the popular opposition.

In November *La Prensa* published a full-page appeal in which twelve well-known figures from economic, cultural, and religious life called for a democratic alternative to the regime. Significantly, this was the first declaration of its kind to include the FSLN among the suggested participants in such an alternative. Somoza refused to make any concessions to this renewal of oppositional activity. On the contrary, he raised the stakes still higher, and on January 10, 1978, Pedro Joaquín Chamorro, *La Prensa* director and UDEL leader, was assassinated in Managua. By eliminating the very man who embodied the liberal solution, Somoza attempted to place the Nicaraguan bourgeoisie and the Carter administration before a dire choice: "Either Somoza or the Sandino-Communists.'' Once again, he had deliberately opted for catastrophist politics.

The Revolutionary Crisis: January 1978 to July 1979

The assassination of Chamorro was the spark that lit the prairie fire. The resulting outrage coalesced all opposition to the regime into a single movement. Henceforth there would be a continual succession of mass demonstrations, general strikes, and partial insurrections, gradually leading to a situation of dual power. The oppositional bourgeoisie, working first through UDEL and later the *Frente Amplio de Oposición* (FAO), managed to stay at the head of the movement until January 1979. But as the masses grew increasingly radical, the leadership gradually slipped away to the FSLN.

On January 13, 1978, some 120,000 demonstrators attended the funeral procession of the liberal leader. The COSEP employers' federation, speaking for medium capital if not for the BANIC and BANAMERICA groups, called for a ''civil stoppage'' to demand punishment of the assassins and the resignation of Somoza. The mass strike, virtually total by January 24, was punctuated by huge demonstrations and bloody clashes with the National Guard.

The FSLN took advantage of this formidable popular mobilization to step up its level of activity, attacking the garrison at Rivas and Granada on February 1 and 2. ''It was the first great blow we had struck since the outbreak of the crisis,'' stated Humberto Ortega, the strategist of victory. ''These large-scale operations encouraged the masses and strengthened their determination to fight against Somozism. This time, the people saw that the vanguard was more solid, capable of fighting, capable of hitting the enemy, capable of seizing towns. . . . The February actions had an impact that reached its highest expression in the insurrection of Monimbo Indians.''[2] Afraid that they were being outflanked, UDEL and COSEP appealed for a return to work on February 6. And although the labor federations tried to continue the strike, the call was generally observed.

Strictly in terms of its immediate objectives, the *paro cívico,* or civil stoppage, was a failure. Yet this first massive mobilization of the urban population, lasting for a considerable period, had an enormous impact upon the political maturation of the movement. It was crucial, too, that petty-bourgeois layers in the commercial and service sectors stood shoulder to shoulder with industrial workers and subproletarians.

The toiling population became aware of its own strength, learning to confront the ever active police collectively at a time when divisions within the ruling class were nearing the breaking point. The FSLN grew in prestige and authority, while its project of a definitive, armed overthrow of the regime gained much greater credibility. The popular movement now took a decisive step towards political autonomy of the bourgeoisie.

Characteristically for a period of revolutionary upsurge, partial defeats and even savage repression did not cause demoralization or demobilization. On the contrary, the population increasingly met the *Guardia*'s actions with forms of mass violence, spontaneously seeking the road of armed resistance. Thus, on February 20, 1978, the local inhabitants of Monimbo, in Masaya, broke out in open rebellion. For nearly a week, they held their own against the National Guard, backed by artillery and aerial bombing. On the 26th, however, the uprising was drowned in blood.

The Broad Opposition Front (FAO)

Deeply affected by the scope and determination of the movement, Somoza finally decided to make some concessions: a one-month annual bonus and a rise in the minimum wage for the industrial workers; social security provisions for the agricultural laborers; and a "national dialogue" for the oppositional bourgeoisie.

But it was too late. The people now called for the ouster of "the little Nero." In any case, after the extremely costly general strike of January-February, the dictator no longer had the wherewithal to grant social concessions. The civil-war climate was hardly propitious for a business recovery, and capital was fleeing to more clement skies. Official sources placed the outflow of foreign currency in 1979 at $315 million, or 75 percent of the total value of exports. GDP fell by 25 percent, while inflation soared past 75 percent and unemployment hit 42 percent of the work force.[3]

In a spiral characteristic of revolutionary situations, political agitation fueled the economic crisis, while economic decline maintained and extended political agitation.

It was a sign of the times when the Nicaraguan Democratic Movement (MDN), based on the cotton growers of the northwest, was formed within the bourgeois opposition. Led by millionaire industrialist Alfonso Robelo, former president of the Nicaraguan Chamber of Industry (1972 to 1975), the Nicaraguan Development Institute, and COSEP (1975 to 1978), this new movement brought together a number of young company directors who had stood in the forefront of the employers' strike of January-February. The MDN called for the immediate dismissal of Somoza, the involvement of the FSLN in a future government, and the enactment of a number of democratic reforms.

In order to impose a political solution that would still afford it control, the anti-Somoza bourgeoisie finally agreed to establish a broad alliance of all forces hostile to the dictatorship, even including the FSLN *Terceristas* by way of "the Group of Twelve." The Frente Amplio de Oposición (FAO), enjoying Church support that counted for a great deal in this intensely Catholic country, was accordingly proclaimed in July 1978. Prominent among its sixteen demands was a call for the withdrawal of Somoza—a point publicly endorsed on August 3 by Monsignor Miguel Obando y Bravo, archbishop of Managua.

The oppositional bourgeoisie had devised a clear strategy: it would exploit the mass mobilization and the Carter administration's support so as to force a negotiated compromise on Somoza, removing him from power in accordance with the constitution. There was to be no question of nationalizing the clan's property or of dissolving the National Guard.

The phase of bourgeois hegemony over the movement, lasting from the creation of UDEL in July 1974 to the disintegration of the FAO in January-February 1979, was marked by moderate goals and methods of struggle. The goal was to end the usurpation of power by a narrow *camarilla* that had systematically abused office—not, however, by force of arms, but by intensifying the converging pressures that would eventually force the dictator to yield.

For its part, the FSLN was far from inactive during this period. The "proletarian tendency" and the advocates of "protracted people's war" carried out wide-ranging agitation and political organization in the *barrios*, the factories, and the plantations. Work stoppages, street demonstrations, and riots succeeded one another in an unbroken chain: the strike of municipal and health workers in June-July 1978; the student strike to win the reopening of *Mi Preferida* radio station; the huge demonstrations celebrating the return of "the twelve" to Managua; the protest general strike against the murder of eight students by the National Guard in Jinotepe and San Marcos on July 19, 1978; another, FAO-sponsored general strike on August 27.

At the same time, the FSLN *Terceristas* stepped up their acts of war. On July 20, they fired rockets from the upper floors of the Hotel Intercontinental at National Guard headquarters and Somoza's famous "bunker." On August 22, guerrilla *comandante* Edén Pastora took over the National Palace and imprisoned more than 500 leading figures of the regime, including sixty deputies, several ministers, and Somoza's own cousin. All these lights of high society were eventually exchanged for $5 million, the publication of a press communiqué, and the release of Tomás Borge and eighty-two other FSLN prisoners. On August 24, the commando group and the Sandinist prisoners left for Panama to popular acclaim.

The Limits of Peaceful Forms of Struggle

Despite the broad strikes and mass demonstrations, the daring guerrilla activity, and the pressures exerted by the bourgeoisie, the dictator still refused to yield. Apparently convinced that no one could oust him so long as the National Guard was under his control, Somoza set out to drown the popular movement in blood and to persuade the liberal bourgeoisie to come to terms. Once they tired of the chaos, they would eventually accept his orders. Time seemed to be on Somoza's side, provided he maintained a ruthless attitude and kept careful watch over the loyalty of his praetorians. With this in mind, he relieved thirty National Guard officers of their functions and on August 27 ordered the arrest on conspiracy charges of a number of army officers, whose "brain" was Lieutenant-Colonel Bernardino Larios.

Somoza's obstinacy exposed the limitations of FAO strategy. A general strike and street demonstrations, however massive, could not alone oust an opponent who clung to power through naked violence and did not flinch even from bombing his own towns. An enemy bent upon civil war could be vanquished only by the methods of civil war, and only an armed movement could overcome the National Guard. Unless it culminated in an insurrection, any general strike would inevitably be defeated.

The strategic superiority of the FSLN, which enabled it to wrest the leadership of the popular movement from the bourgeois opposition in less than a year, lay in its clear understanding of these necessities. Far from counterposing mass struggle to armed combat, the FSLN asserted and organized their convergence. Strikes and demonstrations would pave the way for armed insurrection as the climax of the general strike.

The Regime's Last Chance

By early September, two other features typical of a revolutionary situation were in evidence in Nicaragua. First, there was an *uneven development* of popular radicalization: in some sectors and regions, the mass of workers were urging an immediate insurrection, while in others they still had confidence in the FAO. Second, the combativity of the most radicalized sectors had outstripped the preparedness of the revolutionary forces. Unless the latter could effectively assume their political-military functions, however, any mass insurrection would be doomed to end in a bloodbath.

Sensing that the traditionally radical northwest was approaching an inevitable conflagration, the FSLN *Terceristas* decided to press ahead. They hoped in this way at least to restrict the damage and to retain the leadership of the armed struggle.

On September 9, 1978, FSLN columns attacked León, Estelí, Chinandega, Masaya, and several other towns, unleashing a general uprising of the local populations. The National Guard replied by bombing the insurgent towns and intensifying its ferocious repression in the rest of the country.

On September 20, when the Sandinists were compelled to withdraw, imposing columns of civilians fled in their wake to escape the savage reprisals that followed. Somoza set out to make an example of León and Estelí. The National Guard tortured and executed anyone "suspected of sympathy with the Sandino-Communists," concentrating especially on teenagers. The September insurrection cost a total of 6,000 lives.

When Humberto Ortega was later asked if the action had been a mistake, he answered:

> We could not say no to the insurrection. The mass movement had grown to such a size that the vanguard was incapable of leading it. We could not oppose this torrentlike movement; all we could do was stand at its head, so as to lead it as much as possible and give it some direction. In this sense the vanguard, aware of its limitations, bowed to the general decision of the masses and took up a position at their head. Their decision and resolve stemmed from the example of Monimbo. . . .
>
> If we had not given form to this mass movement, it would have lapsed into general anarchy. In other words, the vanguard's decision to call for the September insurrection made it possible to channel the torrent, giving form to the insurrection so that victory could subsequently be achieved.

> I would like to repeat that we threw ourselves into the insurrection because of the prevailing political situation. Our aim was not to abandon the people to a massacre, for, as in Monimbo, the people are already plunging into action.[4]

That this fresh defeat was not a serious blow to the popular movement revealed the depth of the accumulated potential for revolt.

Somoza seemed jubiliant, convinced that he had won a decisive victory. But the bourgeois opposition, too, thought that its hour had come. The defeat of the September insurrection would surely force the FSLN to retreat, weakening the revolutionary wing of the movement, and would also demonstrate its dangerous potential in a situation of prolonged polarization. The Carter administration, aware of this peril, would be bound to step up its pressure on Somoza to abdicate.

Both pro- and anti-Somoza sections of the bourgeoisie, then, believed their own position stronger and therefore agreed to negotiate under an international "commission of mediation" composed of representatives of the United States, Guatemala, and the Dominican Republic.

The talks dragged on for several months. The idea was to force the dictator to accept "Somozism without Somoza": a conservative government, from which the FSLN would be excluded; maintenance of the National Guard; guarantees for Somoza property.

The FSLN—the national leadership, or *Tercerista* tendency which had gone furthest in a policy of alliance with the bourgeoisie—could not agree to such a compromise. Too much blood had flowed for the people to be content with a mere refurbishing of the system.

The FAO program now lagged behind the state of mind of the masses, including the petty bourgeoisie, which wanted an end to the regime and the root-and-branch destruction of Somozism. Evidence of this new awareness could be seen in their growing combativity against extremely fierce repression. The FSLN slogans—expropriation of the Somozists, dissolution of the National Guard—gave accurate expression to the people's aspirations at this point.

Overtaken by the new course of the class struggle, the FAO lost its political authority and suffered progressive dislocation. In November 1978 the "Group of Twelve," a cover for the FSLN *Terceristas,* announced its break from the FAO in protest against direct U.S. interference in the talks. Other organizations followed suit.

On January 10, 1979, a gigantic demonstration took place in Managua to mark the first anniversary of the assassination of Pedro Joaquín Chamorro. Dozens of people were killed, and five days later health workers began a hunger strike. But the coup de grâce came on January 19, when Somoza rejected the proposals of the "commission of mediation," reaffirming that he would remain in power until his mandate expired in 1981. The FAO, with American support, continued to advocate "moderate" solutions to the crisis, but it met with growing indifference and frustration on the part of the population.

Toward the "Final Offensive"

The breakup of the FAO opened a new and deeper phase of the revolution. It removed a major obstacle to the unification of the FSLN, since *Tercerista* participation in a bourgeois-dominated front striving for a bourgeois solution of the crisis had been one of the main points of contention with the other two tendencies. On December 9, 1978, all three set up a unified command structure, and organizational fusion followed on March 26, 1979.

Most crucially, the course of the FAO compelled the Sandinists to promote a new alliance policy, one independent of the bourgeoisie and in line with the FSLN's own revolutionary goals.

Greater effort was now put into the United People's Movement (MPU), an umbrella structure of twenty-two popular organizations that had been formed in mid-July 1978. Neighborhood committees, trade unions, women's and youth associations were strengthened and reorganized. The aim of the FSLN was to augment the capacity for initiative and organization in all sectors of the mass movement and to fortify their independence of the FAO bourgeois opposition, now more concerned with keeping the revolutionaries out of power than with sealing the fate of the dictatorship. On February 1, 1979, a new structure, the National Patriotic Front (FPN), brought together the MPU, the Twelve, the trade unions, and a few minor bourgeois formations. It was an alliance under Sandinist hegemony that was to assume the task of organizing a general strike. The leadership of the mass movement had now changed hands. The bourgeoisie and imperialists had lost the initiative.

On February 8, the United States suspended military and economic aid to Somoza in retaliation for his rejection of the mediating commission's proposals. But the pro-Somoza lobby remained a powerful force in Washington, and money withdrawn with one hand was restored with the other. Thus, on May 14, the International Monetary Fund, whose sensitivity to American behests needs no elaboration, granted the Nicaraguan government a $65 million loan. Among those voting in favor was the representative of the United States. Somoza retained the support of many Latin American dictatorships, and continued to receive arms from Argentina and Israel. However, Costa Rica, Panama, Mexico, and Venezuela grew increasingly hostile in their public statements and their attitude within international bodies, thereby contributing to the dictator's isolation. On May 20 Mexico broke diplomatic relations with Managua. On May 28 the heads of state of the five Andean Pact countries condemned the Somoza government at a meeting in Colombia, and on June 16 they recognized the Sandinists' status as "belligerent." On June 24, the Organization of American States rejected Cyrus Vance's proposal to send a "peacekeeping force" to Nicaragua, demanding the resignation of Somoza instead. All these measures, in varying degree, lent real aid to the FSLN.

On April 6, 1979, a 42 percent devaluation of the córdoba relative to the dollar, the first since 1932, confirmed the regime's economic catastrophe. Galloping inflation deepened popular discontent, while hitherto neutral sections of the bourgeoisie and petty bourgeoisie joined the ranks of the opposition. Entirely divested of its social base, the Somoza dictatorship was reduced to its quintessence: the National Guard.

Dual Power: March to July 1979

The FSLN resumed its military offensive in March 1979, occupying the town of Estelí between the 8th and the 14th. But the "final offensive" really began on May 21 in Jinotega and elsewhere. Unlike the Batista forces in Cuba, however, the National Guard continued to mount determined resistance.

Drawing inspiration from the Vietnamese experience, the FSLN sought to compensate for its military inferiority by forcing the *Guardia* to spread itself thinly. Its tactic was to create an indefinite number of operational zones through combinations of strike movements, local uprisings, and the activity of its own military units. The 15,000-strong repressive forces, only half of them seasoned national guardsmen, would be unable to control a country of 132,000 square kilometers and 2,300,000 inhabitants. If they tried to do so, they would suffer dispersion, thus losing strategic superiority at many points that could then be attacked by the guerrillas. But if they set themselves a more limited objective, concentrating their forces at a few strong points, the FSLN could use the surrendered territory to prepare a fresh assault. This is how Humberto Ortega later described the development of FSLN thinking:

> We realized that our principal strength lay in our capacity to maintain total mobilization at the social, economic, and political levels, thereby dispersing the enemy's technico-military capacity. . . . We saw that if we were to win, we had not only to move our own guerrilla contingents into combat, but also ensure through our actions that the masses would take an active part in the struggle. . . .
>
> The truth is that we always thought of the masses, seeing them, however, as a prop for the guerrilla campaign that would enable it to deal some blows at the National Guard. Reality was quite different: guerrilla activity served as a prop for the masses, who crushed the enemy by means of insurrection. . . .
>
> After the September events, we saw the need to combine, at the same time and in the same strategic space, a nationwide mass uprising, a frontal offensive by our military forces, and a general strike which the employers actively supported or approved. . . .
>
> Had we not combined these three factors in a single time and space, victory would not have been possible. Several calls for a national strike had already been issued, but without being linked to a mass offensive. The masses had already risen up, but their action had not been combined with a strike and had taken place at a time when the vanguard's military capacity was too weak. Finally, the vanguard had already inflicted blows on the enemy, but at a time when the other two factors were not present.[5]

This strategy determined the specific character of dual power in Nicaragua. Despite the great heterogeneity of forms and situations, the basic units of people's counterpower were civil defense committees (CDS) in the localities and joint union committees in the factories. Where the Somozists still controlled a town, these committees carried out the task of preparing an insurrection and giving logistic support. In the liberated towns, they came together in a central committee of civil defense committees (Estelí) or a junta of reconstruction (Matagalpa), assuming all the civil functions connected with public safety, health, material supplies, distribution, and so on.[6]

In the north and center of the country, similar bodies administered a kind of "war communism." And sometimes when they did not function satisfactorily, additional bodies like the Fabio Martínez Labor Unit in Matagalpa were created alongside them.

But the real center of revolutionary power, recognized as such by the population, was the local FSLN headquarters. It appointed members of the central committees or municipal juntas, and it embodied the new legitimacy and the new political authority.

In the conditions of dual power in Nicaragua, then, which were embryonic and sectoralized after January 1978 but became fully fledged after the May 1979 FSLN offensive, the Somozist state apparatus, essentially reduced to the National Guard, stood opposed to the Sandinist Front resting on a dense network of mass organizations.

The Insurrectional General Strike

Three fronts were opened between May and June: to the north in El Jicaro, Estelí and later Jinotega; to the south in El Naranjo, Peñas Blanca, and Sapoa; to the west in Masaya, Granada, and Carazo. The southern front, reinforced by many internationalist fighters from the whole of Latin America, tied down one of the regime's two elite units, the EEBI.

At every level, women were involved in the struggle to an exceptionally high degree. They made up 25 percent of the ranks of guerrilla columns. There were a number of women commanders: Mónica Blateono and Leticia Herrera, to name but two. And Dora Téllez, "Comandante No. 29," directed operations on the Rigoberto López western front, one of the most important in the war.

On June 4, the FSLN issued a call for an "insurrectional general strike," and the next day the country was totally paralyzed. One after another, the main towns received their insurrection orders. On June 10, the people of Managua rose up spontaneously, well before the date scheduled by the Sandinists. Elite troops had to move back to the capital urgently, thereby relieving the other fronts.

On June 12, Mexico and Venezuela informed the U.S. government that they would not tolerate a "hot pursuit" incursion by Somozist troops into Costa Rica. Four days later, a provisional government was actually formed in the Costa Rican town of San José. It included Sergio Ramírez from the Group of Twelve; Alfonso Robelo, leader of the MDN; Violetta Chamorro, widow of the murdered liberal-conservative leader; Moisés Hassan from the MPU; and Daniel Ortega from the FSLN. Despite appearances, the FSLN had a majority in virtue of the support it enjoyed from the Group of Twelve and MPU representatives.

One hundred and thirty U.S. congressmen now demanded the restoration of military aid to Somoza. At the Assembly of the Organization of American States, called by the United States on June 22, Cyrus Vance formally proposed that a "peacekeeping force" be sent to Nicaragua. But only Argentina supported the idea. Almost unanimously, the OAS firmly opposed any North American interference in the Nicaraguan civil war.

As James Petras has pointed out, this virtual unanimity was the fruit of a curious combination of opposites. The military dictatorships, incensed by Carter's human rights doctrine, wanted no truck with a precedent that might later be used against them. For although an OAS military intervention might have blocked the FSLN, it would also have brought down a regime with many analogs to the south. By contrast, the hostile regimes held that the OAS should not compromise itself alongside Somoza, and should refrain from interfering in a purely internal affair of the Republic of Nicaragua. Somoza's dictatorship had been condemned by the Andean Pact countries, several of which were openly aiding its enemies. It had been abandoned by the OAS, deprived of direct intervention by U.S. Marines, and confronted with a general insurrection. Somoza now saw that the game was up.

Paradoxically, even the unbelievable savagery of repression began to tell against him. For in this atrocious war, people had greater chances of survival fighting in the FSLN than remaining at home at the mercy of a *Guardia* raid. Most of the 50,000 dead—two percent of the population—were civilians who fell under the machine-gun fire of hate-crazed guardsmen. Whenever the FSLN had to abandon a position, thousands of young men and women would follow in its train. On June 27, for example, a convoy of 6,000 civilians left Managua.

By July 16, the major towns in Nicaragua (León, Estelí, Matagalpa, Masaya, Diriamba) were in FSLN hands. On the 17th, Anastasio Somoza Debayle fled the country, leaving to Francisco Urcuyo, after agreement with Washington, the task of negotiating a provisional government take-over. In the U.S. government view, a cease-fire should have come into force, freezing each side in its positions and allowing as much as possible to be salvaged from the Somozist state apparatus. A fusion of "healthy" *Guardia* elements with the Sandinist columns would then have constituted the armed power of the new regime. Above all, the relationship of forces between liberal bourgeoisie and the Sandinist revolutionaries would have become less unfavorable.

Unfortunately for the authors of this scheme, the National Guard began to disintegrate as soon as news of Somoza's flight had been confirmed. This praetorian militia, which unlike the usual national army had not fractured under the impact of crisis and class struggle, could not survive the downfall of its boss. And the crowning piece of ill luck was that even Urcuyo, no doubt secretly advised by Somoza, declined to respect Washington's scenario. Instead he renounced the agreement with the government junta and resolved to stay in office until expiration of the presidential mandate in 1981. The FSLN could scarcely have hoped for such a volte-face, but it immediately responded by calling the final assault.

On July 19, then, the Sandinist columns triumphantly entered Managua. The

National Guard evaporated, 7,000 men being taken prisoner and the rest trying to reach Honduras. Any prominent person or official with good reason to fear the people's vengeance packed his bags and left.

The FSLN had won a total victory, but it had cost 50,000 lives and incalculable destruction. To punish the oppositional bourgeoisie, Somoza had systematically bombed its factories. In the industrial zone of Managua, all along the north motorway, their burnt-out shells pointed accusing fingers to the heavens. Only the clan factories remained intact. On July 20, they were all nationalized.

The FSLN: Three Unite into One

When Somoza's *Aguila VI* operation came to an end in 1976, the FSLN was reduced to a few dozen militants. Carlos Fonseca Amador had fallen in November in the Zelaya region. Tomás Borge, the only surviving founding leader, was in prison. Strategic differences, latent since the 1967 Pancasán defeat and fueled by the repression that followed the Juan José Quezada commando raid of December 27, 1974 were dividing the movement into three hostile factions.

The protracted people's war (GPP) tendency, as we have seen, was inspired by Maoist and Vietnamese conceptions, not a contradiction at the time. According to its strategy, centered on rural guerrilla activity, the creation of liberated zones in the mountains of the north would provide support bases from which to harry the towns and develop urban guerrilla warfare. The establishment of such zones was thus the strategic objective to which all else had to be subordinated. Mass work in the union and student movements was seen mainly as a means by which to recruit forces for rural guerrilla operations. Moreover, since it was overwhelmingly likely that U.S. imperialism would intervene against a successful revolution, any strategy of armed struggle that did not entail the creation of such bases would be built on sand.

The proletarian tendency, by contrast, laid claim to the classic Marxist tradition, locating itself among the urban working class, subproletariat, and youth as the driving forces of the revolution. In its view, the GPP strategy would lead to isolation in half-deserted regions, far from the active masses and nerve centers of the country. Holding that a powerful and independent mass movement was a precondition of victory, the proletarian tendency opposed not only military adventures, that would substitute the violence of revolutionaries for mass violence as part of a private war against the dictatorship, but also alliances in which revolutionaries were subordinated to the anti-Somoza wing of the bourgeoisie. In 1978, it began talks with *Frente Obrero,* another revolutionary splinter from the FSLN deeply involved in mass organizing work in the towns.

The *Tercerista* insurrectional or national leadership tendency developed as a reaction to both the GPP and the proletarian tendency. It accused them both of upholding strategies based on "passive accumulation of forces": the idea that there is an interruption between preparation for combat and the combat itself, that it is possible coolly to accumulate militants, arms, and experience without systematically intervening in both the political and military arenas.

According to their alternative conception, defined as "active accumulation of forces," the contradictions of the regime were such that even a numerically weak revolutionary group, if it knew how to seize the initiative, could have a powerful impact on the depth of the crisis.

The *Tercerista* strategy combined the ideas of an FSLN-led armed offensive with a broad alliance policy that sought to exploit divisions within the bourgeoisie, to isolate the dictatorship, and to advance a credible government alternative.

Its military audacity, which earned it the label "insurrectional," was rooted in a conviction that the U.S. Army was not capable of direct intervention in Nicaragua. Its openness to a united course rested upon a closely argued analysis of divisions within the ruling class[7] and upon a belief that, so long as freedom of political and military action was preserved, revolutionaries had nothing to lose and everything to gain from an alliance with the bourgeois opposition. The *Terceristas* therefore joined the FAO, at a time when they were already stepping up their attacks on *Guardia* barracks. Internationally, they managed to win political and material support from Social Democracy, and even from certain liberal forces. But it would require a peculiar blindness to accept James Petras' characterization of them as a Social Democratic tendency.[8] A strange Social Democracy indeed that engages in revolutionary war and an insurrectional general strike!

If we have to give the *Terceristas* an internationally known label, "Castroist" would seem to suit them much better.

Taken together, all three Sandinist tendencies numbered barely 200 in 1977, and no more than 500 when they entered Managua on July 19, 1979. Being a political-military organization, the FSLN was forced to exercise great selectiveness in its choice of recruits. But thousands of sympathizers were active in its mass organizations. And tens of thousands of people who fought against the dictatorship spontaneously recognized the political authority of the Sandinists.

The Question of Alliances

The *Tercerista* policy of alliance was denounced as opportunist and capitulationist by various far-left currents in Nicaragua and elsewhere. Some saw it as a relic of Stalinist popular frontism, involving the sacrifice of proletarian unity and class independence within a subordinate alliance with the national bourgeoisie, the natural leadership of the democratic stage of the revolution. These critics opposed the idea of an antifascist front against the dictatorship, putting forward the workers' united front for socialism as an alternative.

Now, it does seem that at least some of the *Terceristas* had illusions in the anti-imperialist potential of the Nicaraguan bourgeoisie.[8] These illusions were quickly destroyed in winter 1978, under the combined impact of the radicalization of the masses and the bourgeoisie's support for the commission of mediation. But in any case, the *Terceristas* never subordinated the development of their own strategy—armed confrontation with the regime—to their activity within the FAO. It would be quite wrong to identify their alliance policy with Stalinist-type popular or antifascist fronts.

From the point of view of class alliances, the Nicaraguan proletariat could triumph only on three conditions: if it was itself united around a revolutionary program and strategy; if its political alternative polarized the middle layers; and if the ruling class was deeply and lastingly divided.

Only an alliance strategy that related to all three conditions could enable an absolutely dominated class, weaker than its enemy in every respect, to gain the upper hand over not only the dictatorship but the whole of the ruling class as well. It was, to be sure, a complex strategy, for the three conditions contradict one another in part.

Whereas supporters of a popular or antifascist front sacrifice the first to the two other conditions, advocates of a class-against-class policy do exactly the opposite. They pay no heed to the tasks of exploiting contradictions within the ruling class and winning the broadest sectors of the petty bourgeoisie to the side of the proletariat. They thus deny themselves any prospect of victory, as surely as if they deliberately placed themselves in the tow of the bourgeoisie.

The anti-imperialist front policy the FSLN applied immediately after its break with the FAO met all three conditions. As Adolfo Gilly has correctly argued: "If the FSLN had counterposed a socialist workers' front to the anti-imperialist front, treating the latter as an instrument of the bourgeoisie or as equivalent to a popular front . . . they would have taken a narrowly sectarian position which, on the false pretext of defending principles, would have been doomed to failure and would have forsaken any mobilization of the real mass movement as it first appeared under the dictatorship."[9]

The March 1979 Fusion

If the split in the FSLN had occurred during an ebb in the mass movement, it would doubtless have had disastrous consequences. But occurring as it did in a period of rising popular combativity and deepening crisis of the regime, it never had time to harden into an intractable rift. Indeed, within the context of a fruitful strategic debate, a kind of functional division of labor developed among the three groups. The *Terceristas* assumed responsibility for military initiatives and the policy of alliances, while the GPP and proletarian tendencies conducted mass organizational work in the *barrios,* the university, the factories, and the plantations.

This effectively complementary activity gave a certain perspective to tendency differences. Above all, the concrete evolution of the revolutionary process, much more varied and complex than any of them had envisaged, swept away the old lines of division and gave each one a share of truth and a share of error.

GPP supporters admitted that they have underestimated the insurrectional character of the situation in the urban Pacific coast centers, and that on crucial days their columns had consequently been rather a long way from the theater of operations. At the same time, they correctly maintained that rural guerrilla activity had provided the

FSLN with its most experienced cadres and established its moral authority among the population.

The proletarians also drew a self-critical balance sheet, but emphasized the key role of the urban mass organizations in preparing and accomplishing the insurrection.

The *Terceristas* naturally emerged the strongest from the comparison, since the course of events had essentially confirmed their analysis and strategy. But they readily agreed that, as mass insurrection was playing a decisive role in the struggle, the patient organizational work that alone made it effective had been as crucial as their military offensive and alliance policy.

Each tendency thus had reason for both pride and humility. Spurred by the enthusiasm of the offensive, the three leaderships first set up a joint command and then, in March 1979, smoothly effected an organizational fusion on the basis of equality. The new National Directorate comprised three representatives from each tendency: Daniel Ortega, Humberto Ortega, and Victor Tirado *(Terceristas);* Tomás Borge, Henry Ruíz, and Bayardo Arce (GPP); Jaime Wheelock, Luís Carríon, and Carlos Núñez (Proletarian Tendency). Still, some did appear to be more equal than others, for as Comandante Luís Carríon explained: "We have all made mistakes throughout our struggle, but in varying degrees. Hence some cadres are better prepared, having had the fullest experience of the process of war and revolution. This has undeniably played a role in the constitution of the army and the organization of its command structure."[10]

Notes

1. See María Esperanza Valle Buitrago, "Unión democrática de Liberación: la expresión política de una alianza de clase en Nicaragua, 1974–78," *Estudios sociales centroamericanos* (Sept.–Dec., 1979).
2. H. Ortega, "Interview with Martha Harnecker," *Granma,* French-language edition (January 27, 1978). Reprinted as *Nicaragua: du rêve à la réalité.*
3. Oscar Rene Vargas, "La Crisis del Somocismo y el movimiento obrero nicaraguense," *Estudios sociales Centroamericanos* (April 1978).
4. "Interview with Martha Harnecker," p. 31.
5. "Interview with Martha Harnecker," pp. 28, 35.
6. See Pisani's report on the situation in Estelí and Matagalpa, *Los Muchachos,* pp. 133–39 and 189–91. See also, for the whole period under consideration here, Charles Andre Udry, "Nicaragua: la revolution en marche," *Inprecor* (September 1979).
7. See the series of articles in *Pensamiento Crítico,* many of which are reproduced in López, Nuñez, Chamorro, and Serres, *La caída del somocismo y la lucha sandinista* (Managua, 1980).
8. See the programmatic document of March 1979, in which the newly unified leadership made a critique of the FAO, *Cuadernos Politicos,* no. 20 (Mexico City, April–June 1979).
9. Adolfo Gilly, *La Nueva Nicaragua: anti-imperialismo y lucha de clase* (Mexico, 1980).
10. See the interview in Pisani, p. 253.

29. *Our Vengeance toward Our Enemies Will Be the Pardon**

By Tomás Borge

Comandante Tomás Borge, the most charismatic and popular Nicaraguan leader, is currently minister of the interior and a member of the nine-person National Directorate of the FSLN. He is the only surviving original member of the FSLN, which he founded in 1961 with Carlos Fonseca Amador and Silvio Mayorga. Originally members of the Nicaraguan Socialist Party (PSN), they broke away from its traditional Latin American Communist party dogmatism. When the FSLN split into factions, Borge and Henry Ruíz stayed "in the mountains" leading the Prolonged People's War (GPP) tendency. He spent many years in Somoza's prisons, reportedly suffering brutal torture.

What are we doing in the prisons?

"We are not interested in destroying the sinners, but rather in eliminating the sin," I said.

And what are we doing with these assassins [ex-national guardsmen]? We are trying to convert them into something they have never been: true human beings. I believe that it is our moral obligation to raise them from their condition like beasts to the condition of human beings.

This then is the philosophy of our revolution, but clearly, they do not understand. When I was a prisoner I spoke with them. I told them that someday we would help them. They didn't believe me then, and they still doubt it.

A few days ago my wife's murderer was captured. When he saw me coming—that woman had been savagely tortured, she had been raped, her fingernails had been pulled out—he thought I was going to kill him, or at least hit him. He was totally terrified when we arrived, but we treated him like a human being. He did not understand then, nor can he understand now. I think he may never understand.

We once said, "Our vengeance toward our enemies will be the pardon, it is the best of all the vengeances."

---

*Excerpts from *No pedimos que elogien la revolución, sino que digan y divulgen la verdad,* 1981. Translated by Peter Rosset.

Chapter III:

Since the Sandinistas: Historical Developments since 1979

30. U.S.-Nicaraguan Relations since 1979

By Judy Butler

Judy Butler was editor of NACLA Report on the Americas *until August 1983, when she took a leave of absence to work for the* Centro de Investigaciones y Documentacion de la Costa Atlantica *(CIDCA) in Nicaragua. She also works with the Jesuit-based* Instituto Histórico Centroamericano, *which publishes* Envío *from Managua.*

If the Committee of Sante Fe's 1980 document, *A New Inter-American Policy for the Eighties,* has indeed become a blueprint for the Reagan administration's overall Latin America policy, the Heritage Foundation's backgrounder called *U.S. Policy and the Marxist Threat to Central America* is the detail sheet for that conflictive region.

"In the near future," counseled Heritage Foundation document author Cleto Di Giovanni, an ex-CIA officer for Latin America, "the U.S. must revert to a more traditional view of Central America if the spread of Marxism is to be contained. . . . As long as it exists in any great strength in any one of [the Central American countries], the others will be in danger. Thus, although the Marxist government in Nicaragua might fall eventually of its own failures, the security of El Salvador requires the acceleration of the *removal of the government in Managua*" [editors' emphasis].[1]

That the new administration has set about to do just that was not publicly acknowledged until early 1985, when President Reagan finally admitted that he wanted "to remove" the "present structure" of the Nicaraguan government, and Secretary of State George Shultz elaborated that one way of accomplishing this would be "through the collapse of the Sandinista regime."[2] An examination of the administration's propagandistic, economic, diplomatic, and paramilitary initiatives over these five years, however, shows an uncommonly straight line in that direction. That these initiatives, both overt and covert, have not achieved their objective has much to do with the astute countermoves of the Nicaraguan government, both within Nicaragua itself and in important international circles. The administration, on the other hand, has succeeded in isolating itself dangerously from world opinion as it moves ever closer to direct U.S. military intervention.

Reversion to a More Traditional View

The firmly held view of the U.S. Right to which Reagan is responsive is that the United States is now paying for two decades of Democratic Party "neglect, shortsightedness, and self-deception" in its foreign policy toward the Soviet Union, exemplified by what it terms President Carter's "accommodation process" toward "pro-Soviet socialist models of political and economic development" in Latin America. "Even the Caribbean, America's maritime crossroad and petroleum refining center," warns the Committee of Sante Fe, "is becoming a Marxist-Leninist lake."[3]

"U.S. global power projection," Di Giovanni wrote, "rests upon a cooperative Caribbean and a supportive South America."[4] But this "traditional" view predates even the existence of the Soviet Union. It is the tradition of the Monroe Doctrine and Manifest Destiny, of banana republics and the Caribbean as the "backyard" of the United States. Revolutionary Nicaragua, the Right was convinced, with its belligerent new sense of sovereignty, would not be sufficiently cooperative.

Even worse, as Di Giovanni implied, Nicaragua could be expected to favor a revolutionary change in the status quo in other countries of the region; and might even provide an alternative model that would inspire oppressed populations throughout the then military-dominated continent. In the administration's "perception management" vernacular, this is termed "exporting revolution," despite the fact that revolution is no more exportable to areas lacking the internal conditions than is U.S.-style democracy.

Right-wing criticism of Carter's accommodationism begs the question, "Compared to what?" His administration did everything it believed possible in the last months of the insurrection to at least maintain the structures of *Somocismo* in Nicaragua, once it was clear that Somoza himself was on the way out. Carter also buckled under the pressure by the growing Right to take a harder line on Nicaragua in the last years of his presidency and, according to the recent revelations of Edgar Chamorro, a disillusioned *contra* leader, members of his group were getting CIA money to make contact with former Somoza national guardsmen as early as late 1980.[5]

It was indeed Reagan, however, who made the strategic shift from cooptation to coercion, and from respect for international opinion to blatant U.S. hegemonism in decision-making. Within three months of taking office, he had cut the undisbursed balance of a $75 million loan to Nicaragua, together with wheat shipments sold to that country under the PL-480 Food Assistance Program. Even before that, he had given the green light for future *contras* to conduct their paramilitary training on U.S. soil, the first of what would become many violations of international law.

Five years into the Reagan presidency, military options are in place and most of the key players have taken their positions. What has been accomplished, and how? What has not, and why? What are the scenarios under consideration?

Step One: Managing Perceptions

> The whole issue of running the presidency is control of the agenda. We deal with what ought to be the buildup of things six to nine months out. It's a process question.
>
> Richard S. Beal, survey research expert for Reagan's political management team.[6]

The Sandinista revolution came into power on July 19, 1979, amid cheers from many quarters. Inside Nicaragua, the unbridled avarice of the last Somoza (Anastasio) had won him the wrath of even the acquiescent opposition business sector. The political as well as military acumen of the Sandinista National Liberation Front (FSLN) netted it support that cut across class lines, and meant that at least for a time after the overthrow of the Somoza regime it could count on a measure of national unity under its leadership.

Internationally, governments and a broad spectrum of political parties offered support, thanks in part to the diplomatic work of "the twelve," a group formed in 1977 of Nicaraguan religious, business, and intellectual figures who lent their prestige to the Sandinista cause. At a popular level as well, the romantic antidictatorial struggle of the Sandinistas, their creative pragmatism once in power, and the Christian component of their ideology has engendered an unusually high level of international solidarity for a small, underdeveloped country few had ever heard of before.

This legitimacy would have to be undermined—in the United States, in Nicaragua, and internationally—before the removal of the new Nicaraguan government would become politically or militarily feasible. Pentagon leaders have made clear the lessons they take from the Vietnam experience: don't go in unless we intend to win, and don't begin until domestic public support is assured or the means of silencing opposition is legalized.

The chief means of delegitimization within the United States has been the propaganda war. This war has two major and complementary tactics: "control of the agenda" (what will be discussed) and "perception management" (how it will be discussed). Since the beginning, the Reagan administration team has been highly successful in its control of the agenda on Nicaragua in both the foreign policy debate and in the media; only recently has it conquered the battlefield of perception management. In its content and ferocity, this propaganda war has often reverberated to the rhythm of the insurgent struggle in El Salvador, although in recent years it has achieved an accelerated momentum of its own.

On January 10, 1981, just as President Carter was preparing to cede the Oval Office to his successor, the Farabundo Marti Forces of National Liberation (FMLN) launched a major offensive in El Salvador. Within five days there were reports in the U.S. press of a 100-strong guerrilla force, reputedly Nicaraguan, which had landed by boat on a Salvadoran beach. A week later, on the eve of Carter's departure, U.S. aid to Nicaragua was suspended in order to review evidence that the Sandinista government had been supplying the Salvadoran guerrilla force with arms.

Within months, the two-year-old revolution was being described as "a forward base of operations for Cuba," in turn a "puppet of the expansionist Soviet Union" which is carrying out a "strategy to turn all of Central America into a Marxist enclave." The Reagan administration used the theme as a rationale to cut off aid definitively in April 1981, even though the boat story itself was eventually exposed as a hoax. The administration's hastily concocted 1981 *White Paper on Communist Interference in El Salvador* was also discredited by both the *Washington Post* and the *Wall Street Journal*.

In fact, the administration has been repeatedly embarrassed in its efforts to fabricate evidence of continuing Nicaraguan military support to the FMLN, but undaunted, it gave this as the pretext for assistance to the counterrevolutionaries for the next four years. The *contras* themselves quickly made it clear that if arms interdiction was Reagan's goal, theirs was to overthrow the Sandinista government. Despite sophisticated surveillance equipment the administration said it was using for the purpose, no arms transfers were ever interdicted.

By late 1981, a new, complementary message was being hyped: Nicaragua was a Marxist-Leninist dictatorship. Reagan strategists had clearly concluded that the East-West campaign would fly better if the ideological component were brought more into play. If people were not warming to the idea of a Central American war in the name of stopping Soviet expansionism, they would surely be motivated to defend the region's great democratic traditions against totalitarianism.

On November 12, 1981, speaking before the House Foreign Affairs Committee, General Alexander Haig, then secretary of state, warned that policymakers would exclude no options to deal with "mounting evidence in Nicaragua of the totalitarian character of the Sandinista regime." *New York Times* and *Washington Post* editorials unabashedly took up the term as well.

A measure of the success of the administration's perception management technique is that, of the still relatively small portion of the U.S. population that can remember from one day to the next where Nicaragua is, many assume it is a Communist regime. A measure of its failure is that the percentage of those who therefore agree with Reagan's Central America policy is much smaller. And the polls barely change. An April 1984 *New York Times*/CBS news poll showed that only 19 percent knew that the United States supported "rebels" in Nicaragua; of those, 9 percent opposed helping them and 8 percent were in favor. By June 1985, those who knew which side the United States backed had increased to 26 percent, with 11 percent opposing help to the U.S. allies and 13 percent favoring it. (Of the others polled, 27 percent favored help in 1984 and 32 percent in June 1985. In the latter poll, 45 percent said they were more worried about a war in Central America than about a "Communist takeover" in that area and 43 percent had the opposite worry.)[7]

While these themes have continued, the administration has thrashed around for pithier material. Taking advantage of historic conflicts between the peoples of Nicaragua's Atlantic Coast and the country's central government, Reagan has accused the Sandinistas of committing "genocide" against the Miskitos, "slaughtering thousands or herding them into concentration camps."[8] In early 1985 it came out with murky photographs purportedly showing an aide to a top Sandinista leader loading contraband drugs onto a plane bound for the United States. Unsubstantiated links were drawn between Cuba's Fidel Castro, the Sandinistas, and the Colombian drug traffickers.

Unhappy with the small support for its policy and an equally small but growing opposition, the administration hit upon what seemed like a winner in July 1985. In the midst of a worldwide rash of terrorist activities of differing ideological stripes, six Americans—four of them U.S. Marines—were killed in a San Salvador restaurant by a FMLN commando team. Reagan, speaking before the American Bar Association, linked Nicaragua with what he called a confederation of terrorist nations. Two days before the sixth anniversary of Nicaragua's revolution, the U.S. ambassador in Managua delivered a "diplomatic note" threatening Nicaragua with direct reprisals for any future "terrorist acts against U.S. citizens in Honduras . . . in other countries of Central America, or elsewhere."[9] A "surgical bombing" of an abandoned militia camp in northeast Nicaragua, alleged to be an FMLN guerrilla training camp, was publicly considered and discarded for the time being.

Although this constant campaign has not reaped the desired public support for administration policy, it has made opposition much more difficult, and in Congress the neutralization effort has taken its toll. In December 1982, concerned that the CIA was using its funds for purposes more nefarious than just interdicting arms or harassing the Sandinistas, Congress passed an amendment offered by Representative Edward P. Boland, chairman of the House Intelligence Committee. The amendment banned financial support for "military equipment, military training or advice, or other support for military activities . . . for the purpose of overthrowing the government of Nicaragua or provoking a military exchange between Nicaragua and Honduras."

The importance of that amendment today is not, as it was then, that it was a successful effort to block the more forthright Harkin amendment, which would have cut *all* funding for military activities "in or against Nicaragua." It is not even that in the ensuing two-and-a-half years, Congress ignored all evidence that the Boland Amendment itself had been blatantly violated. It is rather that by early June 1985, on top of voting $27 million in "humanitarian" aid to forces that had been amply demonstrated to be conducting a terrorist war against the population of Nicaragua, an amendment to extend the expiring Boland Amendment was roundly defeated.

The event which cowed congresspeople who in April had denied military aid to the *contras* was a presidential visit by Daniel Ortega to the Socialist-bloc countries in search of oil contracts. But many analysts say the swing voters in April were very soft, and would have found any pretext to avoid risking Reagan's wrath twice.

Step Two: Divide and Conquer

Painting a picture of Nicaragua as an "authoritarian regime of the left," as Senator Ted Kennedy called it as early as the debate of fiscal 1982 foreign aid allocations, requires canvas and models. The 1980 Heritage Foundation document suggested a "well-orchestrated program targeted against the Marxist Sandinista government" as the canvas, and identified allies within Nicaragua to be the models.

"The Catholic Church is influential," notes the document. "There are many political parties . . . united in their opposition to the Sandinistas. There is one free newspaper in Nicaragua, *La Prensa*. . . . Free labor unions are competing successfully for the loyalty of workers. The private sector is united under an umbrella organization, COSEP, which speaks authoritatively for it. . . . Finally, among the free democratic forces in Nicaragua is the Permanent Commission on Human Rights, headed by José Esteban González."[10]

As *Newsweek* pointed out*, Washington's covert involvement in Nicaragua began even before Somoza fled the country, when in 1978 President Carter authorized covert CIA support for "democratic elements" in Nicaraguan society, such as the press and labor unions. Since then, support has extended to other sectors targeted by the Heritage Foundation and has come from private right-wing sources in the United States as well as from U.S. government agencies such as AID and the CIA.

AID grants, dispersed directly by the U.S. embassy in Managua, totalled $5 million in 1980 and $7.5 million in 1981—even after all other aid had been cut. Recipients included the hard-line business umbrella organization COSEP, as well as two of its member organizations, FUNDE and the Chamber of Industry. In 1980 the Moravian Church's Social Action Committee (CASIM) on the Atlantic Coast of Nicaragua was allotted $300,000 from this fund. CASIM was restructured and renamed after a clergyman, arrested in 1982 for aiding some Miskitos in insurgent activities, testified that he had obtained money for arms and supplies from this allotment.[11]

It is undeniable that some sectors, particularly those in business who felt they were supposed to be the national heirs of government following Somoza's defeat, are unhappy with a government that favors the poor and marginalized. But as one FSLN leader said in November 1981, "Were it not for imperialism, we could talk to the business sector, establish rates of profit based on their productive experience and say to them, this is the new situation of Nicaragua."[12] People who had complained little during the Carter period saw in the election of Ronald Reagan a shift in their balance of power. They quickly learned that any time they could provoke an overreaction on the part of the young and skittery government they could count on full coverage in the U.S. media that had never responded to abuses by the Somoza regime. They

*November 8, 1982.

soon developed contacts with newly strengthened right-wing organizations in the United States* who saw to it that their cause was backed up in proper forums.

Not a month after the U.S. elections, the U.S. press reported the arrest and conviction of eight Nicaraguans, most of them business leaders in COSEP. Virtually unreported was the fact that in a press conference they admitted conspiring to overthrow the Nicaraguan junta.[13] One testified that Jorge Salazar, a vice-president of COSEP, had provided $50,000 to buy arms for the counterrevolutionary movement. The plan had been aborted a few days earlier with the killing of Salazar in a gun battle between his driver and Sandinista security police when they tried to stop his pickup truck, reportedly full of weapons.

By November 1982, Salazar's widow Lucia and four prominent Nicaraguan businessmen in exile were among seven people named by the CIA to front as the civilian directorate of the *contra* group called Nicaraguan Democratic Front (FDN) that the CIA had been forging out of disparate bands and individual malcontents for the previous two years.[14]

The opposition political parties may be united against the Sandinistas, but in little else; their fragmentation and weakness became abundantly clear in the 1984 electoral process. Four small parties, grouped together in the *Coordinadora Democratica,*† permitted COSEP to push them into a U.S.-prompted abstentionist position that cost them their juridical legitimacy under the Political Parties Law. Provoked by COSEP leader Enrique Bolaños, who advocated abstention as early as December 1983, the four parties had vacillated all spring about whether to run. Two days before the closing of candidate registration in July, Nicaraguan banker Arturo Cruz suddenly arrived in Managua to be the unified candidate of the *Coordinadora*. But before the parties could register, Cruz was just as suddenly gone again, saying conditions did not exist for free elections.

If anything about the elections deserved Reagan's characterization "sham," it was the game the *Coordinadora* played out for the next three months. While Archbishop Obando voiced Cruz's criticism that "conditions did not exist," and *La Prensa* refused to even carry the list of voter registration and polling sites, the *Coordinadora* demanded from the government, and received, three postponements of the final date for registering their candidate. The fourth and last negotiation took place in Brazil between Arturo Cruz and Sandinista negotiator Bayardo Arce, in the presence of Socialist International leaders. In this meeting, held in the last days of October, it was agreed that the government would postpone the election date itself, scheduled

---

*Among such counterparts that count are the following: for pressure on the liberal and progressive religious community, the Institute on Religion and Democracy; on the purveyors of news, Accuracy in Media; on human rights groups, Freedom House; on indigenous and indigenous rights groups, Indian Law Resource Center; paramilitary recruiting (in addition to the CIA, of course), *Soldier of Fortune* and Civilian Military Assistance.

†The *Coordinadora* also includes two small "free" trade unions (one of which gets AID funding and is affiliated to the AFL-CIO); the "free" newspaper *La Prensa;* and COSEP, together with the tacit support of the Church hierarchy and the assistance of José González's Permanent Commission on Human Rights. It is, in short, the institutionalized embodiment of Heritage Foundation's cast of characters.

for November 4, if the *Coordinadora* would ask the *contra* groups for a cease-fire. But when Cruz called Managua, COSEP refused the deal, and the elections were held as scheduled, without the *Coordinadora* parties. The three other parties to the right of the FSLN that did run, one of which included in its platform every *Coordinadora* position, received a total of 30 percent of the valid votes. The FSLN took 67 percent, and the three parties to the left of it garnered about 1 percent each.

If the parties, the trade unions, and COSEP have a higher profile in the exterior than they do in Nicaragua, that does not mean that the U.S. ideological line has no voice there. To the educated middle classes it comes from *La Prensa* and to the masses it comes from the Catholic Church hierarchy, particularly the recently cardinated Obando y Bravo.

Apart from opposition to the Sandinistas, another element unifies these sectors. They are necessarily on the tour agenda of visiting press, congressional fact-finding missions, and delegations such as the Kissinger Commission which met with all of them in its six-hour visit to Nicaragua on which the writing of its policy recommendations was partly based. These are virtually the only voices of Nicaraguan public opinion made available in the U.S. media.

Step Three: Relegate Nicaragua to the Diplomatic Isolation Ward

The administration has played diplomatic hardball in what appears to be an effort to self-fulfill its prophecy that Nicaragua would move into a tight and narrow alliance with the Socialist-bloc countries. Yet from the European and Canadian wheat shipments that flooded in after the U.S. cutoff in 1981, to the estimated $200 million in credit assistance from the same countries that followed Reagan's embargo announcement in April, the international response to U.S. pressures has not been what the Reagan administration would have liked.

European countries, now strong enough economically to prevent Nicaragua from being isolated as Cuba was two decades ago, have maintained trade relations with Nicaragua despite U.S. pressure. Nicaragua, which from the beginning has said it wants to ''diversify its dependence'' rather than rely on *any* one country or bloc, has worked hard to keep such economic channels open. As late as 1984 26 percent of Nicaragua's imports came from the Socialist bloc (including Cuba), 25 percent from Central and South America, 21 percent from Western Europe, and 20 percent from the United States. The largest portion of its exports went to Europe (37 percent), followed by Japan (25 percent) and the United States (12 percent). Only 6 percent went to the Socialist-bloc countries. Loans and lines of credit contracted between 1979 and 1984 break down as follows: Latin America, 30.3 percent; multilateral organizations, 25.3 percent; Socialist countries, 24.2 percent; Western Europe, 11.3 percent; Africa and Asia, 5.6 percent; United States and Canada, 3.3 percent.[15]

Nicaragua has not diversified its military purchases as successfully. In 1980, the United States denied military assistance to the new Nicaraguan government, but other Third World countries such as Algeria offered their old weapons as a donation. In early 1982, France sold Nicaragua $16 million worth of what it termed defensive military equipment, but the United States promptly forced it to delay shipment and agree to make no additional sales. When pressure on other European countries closed off all possibility of military acquisitions, Nicaragua turned to the Soviet Union. It is still not as well equipped as its hostile neighbors, and particularly lacks fighter aircraft capable of defending against air attacks, which could come from Honduras, Panama, or aircraft carriers off the two shores.

France is the only European country to have involved itself openly in peace initiatives, but it was quickly quieted by the United States. Mexico, which had coparticipated in the French effort, continued seeking support, and in September 1982, following major *contra* attacks on Nicaragua from base camps in Honduras, Mexico and Venezuela sent a joint letter to Reagan proposing measures to reduce the border tensions. Congress was supportive of the initiative, but Reagan ignored it.

In January 1983, these two countries joined with Panama and Colombia to create what is called the Contadora Group. By September, after meetings with the foreign ministers of all the Central American countries, Contadora had reached agreement on twenty-one objectives in the areas of security, economic cooperation, and politics.

The most conflictive category has been that of security. In mid-1984 Nicaragua announced that it was prepared to sign the Contadora peace proposal, which included a prohibition on foreign military bases and troops, a reduction of foreign military advisors, a halt to a regional military buildup, and an end to external support for insurgencies. The United States, caught by surprise, quickly rallied and, through Costa Rica, El Salvador, and Honduras, demanded changes in the proposal.

The administration has given lip service to Contadora, and characterized all of Nicaragua's bilateral diplomatic initiatives toward the United States as an effort to subvert that forum, despite the fact that Nicaragua remains the only country willing to sign its accords. Yet when in July 1985 Contadora itself appealed to the United States to resume bilateral talks begun a year earlier in Manzanillo, Mexico, Secretary of State Shultz refused to do so until Nicaragua agreed to dialogue with the *contras* themselves. Both the United States and the *contras* have proposed Cardinal Obando as mediator of such a dialogue, and Obando himself is promoting the idea within Nicaragua. (Asked by a journalist if Nicaragua's government refused to dialogue with the *contras* because they were terrorists, President Ortega responded that if that were the reason, they would not be able to talk with the United States itself. Rather, he said, it was because the United States provides the money and makes the decisions, not the *contras*.)

Over the last five years the United States has found itself increasingly without a forum. Nicaragua, which against the wishes of the United States was voted onto the United Nations Security Council in 1982, has brought complaints about U.S. aggressions to that body on several occasions. By the last time, in October of 1983, not one single Security Council member voted with the United States. The Reagan administration response has been that the Organization of American States (OAS), not the United Nations, is the appropriate body to deal with the Central American problem.

But other Latin American countries, historically subservient to U.S. diplomacy, have begun to recoil from the repeated arrogance of the Reagan administration. It started with the U.S. support for Great Britain in the conflict with Argentina over the Falklands (Malvinas) Islands, grew after the U.S. military invasion of Grenada in October 1983, and chafed when Reagan likened the *contra* struggle to that of Simon Bolivar. On July 19, 1985, the sixth anniversary of Nicaragua's revolution, the OAS itself, in what was considered a significant gesture, voted Nicaragua's OAS ambassador, Edgard Parrales, to head a special commission. The following month four other OAS members—Peru, Brazil, Uruguay, and Argentina—formed a support commission to Contadora, which, it can be assumed, will further strengthen it.

The United States, in an ultimate defiance of international law, also walked out of the World Court in January 1985, when the court began to hear a suit brought against it by Nicaragua. The court began its final hearing in September, despite the United States' withdrawal of its membership.

Step Four: Turn the Economic Screws

"The economic embargo has been a blessing in disguise," said Nicaraguan Foreign Minister Father Miguel d'Escoto, referring to the April 1985 announcement by President Reagan that he was cutting off all commercial trade between the two countries. D'Escoto was talking about the $400 million in assistance that President Ortega received from his tour through Eastern and Western Europe just following the announcement. But it had another benefit as well, which was that it brought into the open something that had been a disguised reality for years—a U.S. economic blockade.

Once again, it was all previewed, albeit subtly and overoptimistically, in the 1980 Heritage Foundation report: "There are some indications of growing broadly based support to take to arms to overthrow the Sandinista government, and this support could increase as further economic problems develop." It even predicted that "economic shortcomings might provoke at least limited civil unrest by the end of the current harvest season (May–June 1981)." Reagan's cancellation of the $75 million loan and halting of credits for wheat purchases in April created civil unrest all right, but it was aimed mostly at him.

The Reagan administration has counted from the beginning on massive support within Nicaragua for its strategy to destroy the revolution. The thinking, as is shown above, is that liberation followed by austerity will frustrate rising expectations and produce an uprising such as the one that toppled Somoza. Not only would the troublesome Sandinista revolution be out of the way, but its failed example would discourage other such struggles. To that end, both administration actions and counterrevolutionary attacks have aimed in good measure at the fragile economy.

Structurally deformed, as is all Third World dependent capitalism, and weakened by the economic crisis which has wracked underdeveloped countries for the past decade, Nicaragua's economy was also devastated by the insurrectionary war. It has experienced as well a short-term instability due to the effort to redistribute wealth, reorganize production, and replace Somocista managers with insufficiently skilled new people.

The cutoff of bilateral aid in 1981 carried with it the automatic end to credits from the Export-Import Bank and investment insurance from the Overseas Private Investment Corporation, both U.S. government agencies. This meant that from the outset Nicaragua would have to put up cash in advance even to buy spare parts for its U.S.-made tractors.

To make sure there would be little cash, administration representatives next went after private banks and multilateral lending agencies. The banks have felt the pressure since 1981, but in early 1983 the U.S. government's Inter-Agency Exposure Review Committee rated Nicaragua's creditworthiness as ''doubtful,'' despite the fact that Nicaragua was still repaying its massive inherited debt on schedule at that time. Although no private banks have lent money to the Nicaraguan government, the difference between their interests and Reagan's were shown in June 1985, when they agreed to renegotiate their portion of the outstanding debt under terms exceedingly favorable to Nicaragua.

State Department spokesperson Sue Pitmann confirmed in January 1982 that the Reagan administration would oppose any Nicaraguan credit or aid request to any international lending institution. The World Bank, where the United States has fewer votes than in the Inter-American Development Bank (IDB), did, however, approve a $16 million loan for the improvement of Managua slums in 1982. The IDB, which had provided $179 million to Nicaragua in 1979, finally approved a $30 million loan for Nicaragua's fishing industry in late 1983, after several years of stalling tactics by the United States, then turned down a $58 million agricultural loan in 1985. Ironically, the delay in providing the money for the fishing industry meant that U.S. firms interested in the boat-building contracts have been penalized out of the bidding by the total commercial embargo the Reagan administration imposed in April 1985.

Hints of a direct trade embargo began as early as 1982, when the United States threatened to stop buying Nicaraguan beef (75 percent of which went to the United States) if Nicaragua did not cancel its planned purchase of high-grade, low-cost breeding bulls from Cuba. In May of 1983 the United States canceled its long-standing quota of Nicaraguan sugar purchases at protected prices. Nicaragua, which exported 83 percent of its sugar to the United States, quickly found new markets in Algeria, Iran, and East Germany, although at suppressed world-market prices, which meant a loss of desperately needed foreign exchange. Other countries also rallied when Standard Fruit, which had pulled out its production activities in 1982, dropped its distribution contract in early 1984. Belgium quickly picked it up, and now markets Nicaraguan bananas throughout Europe.

A more dramatic facet of economic warfare is direct sabotage. At one end is the withdrawal of productive capital through any number of difficult-to-detect means. At the other lies such activities as the bombing of a Nicaraguan state-owned passenger jet in Mexico City in December 1981 or the June 1985 fire-bombing of the Nicaraguan embassy in Washington. Somewhere in the middle of this continuum are the daily acts of sabotage suggested in an illustrated manual designed by the CIA that was discovered in early 1984, a few months before the CIA-designed psychological warfare manual for the *contras*.

Such scattered actions, however, make little economic dent compared to the systematic destruction of economic activities—much of them private or cooperative enterprises—carried out by the U.S.-financed and -directed counterrevolutionaries. According to figures prepared by the Nicaraguan government's Secretariat of Planning and Budget in May 1985 for its World Court case, direct material loss or damage from the *contra* war went from $1.4 million in 1980 to $184 million in 1984, a total of $379.6 million over the five-year period. The calculated effect on Nicaragua's balance of payments caused by the military aggression and the financial blockade totals an additional $521.3 million for the same period—an estimated 56 percent of export earnings for 1984 alone.[16] These figures undoubtedly include the direct damage and the loss of trade that resulted from the blowing up of oil storage tanks in October 1983, and the mining of Nicaragua's harbors in February 1984, both done by the CIA itself.

Step Five: Get Others to Fight Your War

In November 1981, Reagan signed a "scope paper," authorizing in its first stage $19.9 million to create a U.S.-trained, 500-man paramilitary force. Argentina, then under a five-year-old-military dictatorship, would train an additional 1,000. Nowhere do the documents talk about overthrowing the Nicaraguan government, said a senior official involved in the planning, "but there are secondary and tertiary consequences which you can't control."[17]

Ex-national guardsmen and other exiles had already been contacted with the help of several small bands already operating along the border. As those who were trained in Miami, California, and private ranches in various parts of Central America were ready, they were sent off to Honduras. The size of the CIA station in Honduras doubled the following year to about fifty operatives, with orders to train the Honduran security forces in intelligence gathering and interrogation, provide logistical support for raids into Nicaragua, aid the Honduran coast guard, and help the Argentines and other non-Nicaraguans train anti-Sandinista Nicaraguans in sabotage operations using small arms supplied by the Americans.

By October 1983, attacks on oil storage facilities on Nicaragua's Pacific and Atlantic coasts were being carried out in fancy speedboats, refueled by U.S. mother ships lying offshore. At least three U.S. helicopters have been shot down over Nicaragua, on missions to drop supplies to *contras* who had infiltrated inland; several Americans have been killed in these crashes. The *contras* now even have surface-to-air missiles, which has reportedly somewhat unnerved the Hondurans.

By 1984, the *contras,* by then unified into two groups, FDN and ARDE, totaled some 13,000, and had received up to $100 million from the U.S. government, mostly through the CIA's yearly "Classified Schedule of Authorizations." This figure does not include private funding from wealthy Nicaraguan exiles and right-wing Americans, or assistance that has come from other governments and political parties. (Argentina was a significant supporter until the Falklands war, and Israel is a current supplier of arms to the *contras*.) An unknown portion of this other funding has also gone to two armed Miskito groups—Misura, allied with the FDN, and Misurasata, allied with Edén Pastora's group, ARDE.

The *contras* have also received significant transfers of older weaponry from the Honduran army, which has been significantly reoutfitted, both through the U.S. military assistance the country has received in the past four years (which went from $3.9 million in fiscal year 1980 to $78.5 million in 1984), and through the tons of equipment and weaponry left behind in the joint U.S.-Honduran military maneuvers that have taken place since 1981.

Honduras has been turned into a U.S. military annex: eleven strategic airstrips and numerous roads have been built with U.S. funds in the last three years, and since the beginning of continuous, large-scale military maneuvers in early 1983, often including heavy naval support, there has been a constant presence of from 1,500 to 6,500 U.S. troops, training in all aspects of what could end up being a regional war.

Costa Rica, too, is being transformed through Reagan's determination to save Central America at any cost. Costa Rica's neutrality, ratified in 1983, is violated by the presence of *contra* bases on its soil, and its peacefulness, ratified in 1948 when the army was abolished, is being destroyed by U.S. supplies of heavy military equipment to the civil and rural guards, who are now also being trained by Green Berets. President Monge's slavish pro-U.S. positions (for example, his unwillingness to even discuss a demilitarized common border zone with Nicaragua) have cost him international prestige in the last year.

In July 1985, news was leaked about recommendations Vice-President George Bush had requested from the CIA, the National Security Council, and the Defense Intelligence Agency. The recommendations included attacks by air or by commandos against rebel bastions in El Salvador or training camps in Nicaragua, permission for U.S. agencies to "eliminate" terrorists or anti-U.S. foreign leaders such as the Sandinistas or the Salvadoran guerrillas, additional U.S. advisers to train Salvadoran military forces, greater military assistance to Honduras and Costa Rica for antiterrorist training, supplementary military exercises in Honduras and off Nicaragua's coasts, additional funds from Congress to increase the Nicaraguan rebel force from 17,000 to 30,000, and new sanctions against Nicaragua which could include breaking diplomatic relations.

Perspectives

During the first year of the Reagan administration, there appeared to be a debate within administration circles about whether the goal was to force the Sandinistas to negotiate or to simply destroy them. One could speculate that the debate was between those who saw U.S. national security issues as definable and negotiable, and those who included the revolution's internal development itself as such an issue and knew the Sandinistas would not bargain it away. Today that debate has been silenced, replaced with one about how to eliminate the revolution—whether by continuing the long, slow war of attrition (''low-intensity war,'' as it is being called today) or by direct U.S. invasion. The former is the preferred option of those in the Pentagon who do not want to trigger unmanageable opposition to overall U.S. militarization plans such as the MX missile program, Star Wars, etc., and by those in Congress who prefer to let others fight their war. The latter is being pushed by ideological hawks who believe that the Nicaraguan population has been softened up and would stand out of the way to ''let [American troops] take care of the Sandinistas,'' making an invasion ''as easy as falling off a log.''[18]

There are several misconceptions in that belief. First, it sorely underestimates the importance of Nicaraguan national sovereignty and the sense of dignity awakened by the revolution; second, it thus wrongly assumes that any disenchantment with the Sandinistas' ability to fulfill their promises will accrue to the ''Yankees''; and third, it ignores the 2-300,000 Nicaraguans, military and civilian alike, who not only support the revolution but are armed and ready to defend it.

It is hard to contemplate winners in the Reagan administration's game. Surely they will not be the Nicaraguan people; but then the people of Central America have never before been the noticeable beneficiaries of any government's policy. But it cannot benefit legitimate U.S. interests either. As one pundit put it, what happens after we fall off the log?

The longer the United States pursues its low-intensity war strategy while flagrantly ignoring Nicaragua's search for a negotiated settlement with dignity, the more isolated the United States becomes, and the more willing to help Nicaragua other countries become. Alternatively, the ''surgical'' bombing of Nicaragua's few strategic facilities, such as the Esso refinery, would be insufficient in and of itself to either bring the country to its knees or remove the Sandinistas from power, given the country's increasing decentralization. There are no plans to cede Managua without a tremendous house-to-house fight, which means that the population centers would have to be bombed as well.

No scenario is imaginable in which U.S. occupational forces would not be required, and they could expect to suffer high casualty figures, unacceptable to an American population that has made clear its opposition to this war. Reagan would have to be prepared to send in ever more troops, or have on his hands a country effectively ungovernable for an indeterminate period—all in the name of democracy and stability in the region.

Nicaragua has acknowledged U.S. security concerns in the region, and more than a year ago expressed its willingness to sign the Contadora peace accords which would protect those interests. Yet in late June 1985, Congress gave Reagan the pretexts necessary to justify direct military intervention without prior congressional approval.[19] It remains to be seen whether Reagan can continue to ignore international law and growing political opposition worldwide in his determination to stamp out a new model of Third World revolution, or will be forced to learn to live with it. Nicaragua, meanwhile, is forced to live with this unrelenting threat, unable to turn its full attention to the aspirations of a people who have already paid dearly to get out from under U.S. domination.

Notes

1. Cleto Di Giovanni, Jr., *U.S. Policy and the Marxist Threat to Central America, Heritage Foundation Backgrounder,* No. 128, October 15, 1980.
2. *New York Times,* February 23, 1985.
3. The Committee of Santa Fe, *A New Inter-American Policy for the Eighties,* (Council for Inter-American Security, Inc.), p. 2.
4. Ibid., p. 4.
5. Edgar Chamorro, ''Confessions of a 'Contra',''*The New Republic,* August 5, 1985.
6. Sidney Blumenthal, ''Marketing the President,'' *New York Times Magazine,* September 13, 1981.
7. *New York Times,* June 5, 1985.
8. Public speech by President Reagan on Central America, May 4, 1984.
9. Translated from Spanish version reprinted in *Barricada,* July 18, 1985.
10. Di Giovanni, *U.S. Policy and the Marxist Threat,* pp. 4–5.
11. Jeff McConnell, ''Counterrevolution in Nicaragua: The U.S. Connection, in *The Nicaragua Reader,* eds. Peter Rosset and John Vandermeer, 1st rev. ed. (N.Y.: Grove Press, 1983), p. 179.
12. Interview with Bayardo Arce, Managua, November 1981.
13. *Miami Herald,* November 23, 1980.
14. Chamorro, ''Confessions of a 'Contra'.''
15. Nicaraguan Central Bank figures, taken from chart in ''Sandinista Foreign Policy—Strategies for Survival,'' *NACLA Report on the Americas,* vol. 19, no. 3 (May/June 1985), p.49.
16. Data prepared as evidence to International Court of Justice by Nicaraguan Secretariat of Planning and Budget.
17. *Newsweek,* November 8, 1982.
18. *New York Times,* June 4 and 5, 1985.
19. On June 26, 1985, the House passed the Foley Amendment which prohibits the use of U.S. troops in Nicaragua *unless* Nicaragua receives advanced combat aircraft, is involved in a ''terrorist'' act against the United States or its allies, threatens the U.S. embassy in Managua, or poses a ''clear and present danger'' to U.S. citizens or allies in Central America (*Envío,* July 1985).

Part Three

THE WAR

Editors' Introduction

As late as 1983, the *contra* war against Nicaragua was referred to as ''America's secret war.'' Even though major exposés had appeared in *Newsweek,* the *New York Times* and elsewhere, the Reagan administration had yet to announce the extent of United States involvement. Today, the Reagan administration not only admits that the United States has armed, financed, advised, and at times directed the *contras* in their war against the Nicaraguan government, but it repeatedly calls for support from Congress and the American people in what it portrays as a just cause.

As documented in part one of this book, the administration's justification has shifted over the years. From its claim that support for the *contras* was simply a means to interdict alleged arms shipments from Nicaragua to El Salvador, the administration changed to a rationale of ''applying pressure'' on the Sandinistas, and finally, in early 1985, to a call to alter the ''present structure'' of the Nicaraguan government. Whatever the justification, however, the war remains a fact.

The documents in part three present the various components of the war being waged against the Nicaraguan government. Chapter 1 covers the *contra* war itself, beginning with a history of the Central Intelligence Agency's involvement with the *contras,* and continuing with descriptions of the makeup of the *contra* forces, their financing, and the human and material costs of the war.

The second chapter treats what might be the most worrisome prospect for the future: a potential U.S. invasion of Nicaragua. While such an invasion is not inevitable it remains, nevertheless, a strong possibility. Recent U.S. military maneuvers in Honduras, and the general militarization of both Honduras and Costa Rica, highlight this chapter because of the strategic role that they could play in plans for a U.S. invasion of Nicaragua.

Chapter 3 covers the less obvious aspects of the U.S. war against Nicaragua: issues of international law, economic sanctions, and the attempt to marshal U.S. public opinion in support of the war. This chapter also reports on what is called the "solidarity movement" in the United States: organized internal U.S. opposition to the Reagan administration's Nicaragua policy.

Chapter I:

The *Contra* War

Editors' Introduction

> These freedom fighters are our brothers, and we owe them our help. . . . They are the moral equivalent of our Founding Fathers and the brave men and women of the French Resistance. We cannot turn away from them.
>
> President Reagan
> March 1, 1985

> General Washington and his men, on an expedition in Tory territory, came upon a wedding party. "Fire when ready," Washington ordered, "and be sure not to miss the bride."
>
> The Life of George Washington,
> as revised by Ronald Reagan.[1]

> The day after Christmas 1984, those freedom fighters attacked a wedding party that was on its way home from church. . . . They killed six people, including the bride. Why did they do that? . . . Their strategy is to terrorize the population.
>
> Anthony Lewis, *New York Times*[2]

It is on the issue of the U.S.-backed counterrevolutionaries, or *contras,* that statements by the Reagan administration and its critics differ the most. President Reagan refutes the charge that the *contras* are responsible for widespread atrocities committed against the civilian population of Nicaragua (see reading 32). Yet numerous independent press accounts[3] and human rights organizations such as Amnesty International and Americas Watch maintain that, in the words of Americas Watch, "the FDN [a *contra* group] has routinely attacked civilian populations. Their forces kidnap, torture, and murder health workers, teachers, and other government employees."[4] Included in this chapter is an article by the *New Yorker* staff on the subject of *contra* atrocities and the Reagan administration's way of handling them.

A major change has taken place in the last several years in the Reagan administration's public stance with respect to the *contras*. The war against the Nicaraguan people is no longer "America's secret war." As the opening quote demonstrates, the president now publicly addresses the need for continued support for the proxy war against the Sandinistas. The first article in this chapter, taken from the *Wall Street Journal,* is a history of support for the *contras*. Following this is an analysis of the composition of the *contras* by the congressional Arms Control and Foreign Policy Caucus, which focuses on the role of Somoza's former National Guard.

Also included is an excerpt from the infamous CIA manual prepared for *contra* distribution inside Nicaragua, an analysis of private U.S. funding sources for the war, and a summary of the toll that the war has taken inside of Nicaragua. Finally McGeorge Bundy, who helped plan the Bay of Pigs invasion of Cuba during the Kennedy administration, offers his words of caution against repeating the errors of the past.

Notes

1. Anthony Lewis, "When Reason Flees," *New York Times* March 10, 1985.
2. Ibid.
3. For example, the *Manchester Guardian Weekly,* November 25, 1984; the *Christian Science Monitor,* January 25, 1985; the *New York Times,* October 8, 1984; etc.
4. Cynthia Brown, ed. *With Friends Like These: The Americas Watch Report on Human Rights and U.S. Policy in Latin America* (New York: Pantheon Books, 1985).

31. Aiding the Contras*

By David Ignatius and David Rogers

José Francisco Cardenal still has the dog-eared index card that the Central Intelligence Agency man in Miami gave him before Mr. Cardenal's first meeting in July 1982 with "John," his CIA contact in Tegucigalpa, Honduras.

The card instructed the Nicaraguan exile leader to arrive at 7 P.M. at the Hotel La Ronda in Tegucigalpa and take the stairs—not the elevator—to room 303. He should knock on the door and say, "I am early." The CIA man would respond,

*Excerpts from the *Wall Street Journal,* March 5, 1985.

"No. You are exactly on time." The rendezvous went like clockwork, and it opened a direct channel between the then-leader of the *contras* and the CIA station in Tegucigalpa.

The CIA's secret war against the Marxist Sandinista government in Nicaragua has rarely worked so smoothly. From its start in 1981, the agency's *contra* program has been plagued by mishaps and political misjudgments. The troubled history of the program shows that, however adept the CIA may be at arranging secret meetings abroad, it has considerable difficulty trying to run a covert war from an open society like the United States.

Gains and Losses

- American goals in the *contra* program were confused. The Reagan administration originally sold the program to Congress as a way to harass Nicaragua and to halt arms shipments to El Salvador, even though some U.S. officials and most *contra* leaders from the beginning held the broader goal of removing the Marxist government in Managua. The official CIA position was a catch-22: The secret war didn't violate a 1982 congressional ban against overthrowing the Sandinistas because the *contras* weren't strong enough to win.
- The program got off to a bad start when the CIA turned to a surrogate, the right-wing military dictatorship in Argentina, to organize and train the *contras*. The Argentines already had a small training program for the *contras* in Honduras, and by working with them the United States shielded its own involvement. But the heavy-handed Argentine approach tainted the movement in the eyes of many Nicaraguans. The United States had few alternatives, since the CIA at the time didn't have any reliable paramilitary capability of its own.
- CIA planners, eager to show results once they began running the program directly, used aggressive military tactics that sometimes backfired politically. In addition to training the *contras,* the agency used a separate and secret paramilitary force composed of what were called UCLA—unilaterally controlled Latin assets—to mine harbors and raid targets in Nicaragua. A U.S. official who helped run the program concedes that tactics were sometimes "overzealous."

A secret CIA document lists nineteen such operations in early 1984, and the intensity of the attacks and the level of U.S. involvement are larger than previously reported. Americans flew—and fired from—a helicopter launched from a CIA "mother ship." A fixed-wing U.S. plane provided sophisticated radar guidance for the nighttime attacks. In the turmoil following one attack, Nicaragua shot down one of its own C-47 planes, according to the CIA summary.

"The Priest of Death"

The CIA officers involved in the *contra* program were enthusiastic and sometimes eccentric. One, a retired Army major who wrote a controversial CIA manual on psychological warfare, liked to dress entirely in black and called himself "the Priest of Death"; the *contras* used a less pretentious name for him: "the Umpire." Duane "Dewey" Clarridge, the senior CIA official who ran the program, sported safari suits in the field and at home decorated his jeep with a post-Grenada bumper sticker that read: "Nicaragua Next."

From its first days in office, the Reagan administration viewed Central America as a test of U.S. ability to contain communism. The situation there seemed to be deteriorating fast in early 1981, as Nicaragua rushed weapons into El Salvador by the truckload. To the new administration the question wasn't whether to use American power against Nicaragua and its patron Cuba, but how—overtly or covertly.

An internal debate raged in early 1981 about what strategy the United States should adopt. Alexander Haig, then the secretary of state, argued that the United States should "go to the source" by pressuring Cuba directly. After Mr. Haig outlined a set of tough military options against Cuba at a National Security Council meeting in mid-1981, one NSC member turned to another and whispered: "Did you hear what I heard? This guy will get us into a war."

Instead of going to the source, the Reagan administration decided to go to the CIA. Officials viewed covert action as a sensible middle course between doing nothing and declaring war. But the precise strategy wasn't well formulated. The CIA, says one U.S. official, became "a substitute for a policy."

The crisis nature of the program put pressure on the CIA to find a quick fix. The administration's immediate worry was to cut down arms shipments to leftist Salvadorans, and this put a priority on military action—rather than politics—in building the *contras* as an insurgent movement. And although the administration talked repeatedly about developing a broad economic and political strategy in Central America, in practice the emphasis was on military pressure.

President Reagan approved the basic elements of the program: In early 1981, he agreed to begin rebuilding the CIA's covert-action capability; a March 1981 decision authorized the agency to develop a broad political-action effort in Latin America; a November 1981 directive committed the United States to "assist" in developing an anti-Sandinista guerrilla army.

The political decision to conduct a covert war in Central America revived an old problem for the CIA. Agency officials don't like running secret armies because the programs usually don't stay secret and because U.S. political leadership often gets cold feet. From the outset, the *contra* program carried these same risks and worried many career CIA officials.

Bad Track Record

The U.S. track record hasn't been very good: In Cuba, Indonesia, Laos, and Kurdistan, the CIA has recruited guerrilla armies and then, when the political winds changed back home, abandoned them. One CIA paramilitary veteran, bemoaning the cutoff of funds to the *contras,* says ruefully: "We leave them hanging every time."

A more immediate problem for the CIA was the lack of paramilitary skills at the agency. During the 1970s, the CIA training camps and bases had been closed and the agency's paramilitary experts, derided by the brass as "knuckle-draggers," had been purged. A special covert-action unit, known as the International Activists Division, was little more than a shell, staffed by wary survivors of the 1970s.

"When we started up the program, you couldn't find five guys who knew what they were doing in terms of organizing a resistance operation," says a U.S. official who helped manage the program. To gain expertise quickly, the agency tried to lure back the old-timers, the "hairy-neck paramilitary types," offering them one-year contracts. The agency also began acquiring the assets—boats, airplanes, helicopters and Third World nationals—for the secret strike force that would later be used to mine Nicaraguan harbors.

La Tripartita

The structure of the program was known as *La Tripartita.* The idea was to combine American money, Argentine trainers, and Honduran territory to create a guerrilla army known as the *Fuerza Democratica Nicaraguense,* or FDN. Later, the U.S. financed other guerilla groups operating from Costa Rica.

The FDN embodied the political tensions that have plagued the *contras* from the beginning: Founded in August 1981, the group combined a rightist military leadership, directed mostly by people who had been loyal to deposed Nicaraguan dictator Anastasio Somoza, with a moderate political leadership. It wasn't a comfortable marriage.

The head of the Argentine training mission in Honduras was Col. Osvaldo Ribeiro, known as *Ballita,* or the Little Bullet. He became a prominent figure in Tegucigalpa, living in a large house, distributing American money, and dispensing what CIA officials viewed as unsound military advice. For example, since his own experience was in urban rather than rural combat, he advised the *contras* to mount a program of urban terrorism. The CIA wanted to cultivate a popular insurgency in the countryside.

The Argentines also apparently tolerated a practice of killing prisoners. A former *contra* official describes the informal rule for dealing with captives: If a prisoner has ammunition when captured, let him live, since he hasn't fought to the last bullet; if a prisoner hasn't any ammunition, kill him. (To stop the killing, CIA officials ordered in mid-1982 that all prisoners be brought back to base for interrogation.)

The CIA's goal was for the *contras* to coordinate with insurgents inside Nicaragua, but that proved difficult. One U.S. official recalls: "The moderate opposition was in flight. We would make contact with people in Managua and ask them to help us and they would say, 'Can you get me a green card?' " [to live in the United States].

To supervise the expanding American effort, the director of central intelligence, William Casey, named Mr. Clarridge head of the Latin American division of the agency's directorate of operations. The *contra* program to some extent had been thrust on the CIA, but Mr. Casey who helped run covert operations during World War II, was determined to make it work. He seemed to have found a soulmate in Dewey Clarridge, an ambitious, hard-charging intelligence officer.

Mr. Clarridge impressed the CIA director as an activist in an agency that had become cautious and demoralized during the 1970s. He had served most recently in Rome, where he had won points by giving an elegant late-night supper for Mr. Casey in 1981. He had little background in Latin America but much enthusiasm.

"Dewey is more responsible than anyone for what success there was," says one U.S. official. "But Dewey cut corners and rammed things through. He crossed the line from being a professional intelligence officer to being an advocate."

The program was managed in Washington by a "restricted interagency group," or RIG. The group was headed by the assistant secretary of state for Latin America, initially Thomas Enders and later Langhorne "Tony" Motley. Other members were U.S. Army Gen. Paul Gorman, representing the Joint Chiefs of Staff, who was later replaced by Navy Vice Adm. Arthur Moreau; Lt. Col. Oliver North, a Marine officer with extensive paramilitary experience who served on the NSC staff; and the CIA's Mr. Clarridge. All were, by temperament and background, aggressive risk-takers.

Mixed Assessments

Within the CIA there were mixed assessments about the *contras'* prospects. An internal planning memo prepared in 1982 had set out a timetable leading to the fall of Managua by Christmas 1983. Later CIA officers encouraged the *contras* to attack the Rama Road, a route for arms shipments from the port of El Bluff to Managua, and there were even dreams of splitting the country in two and establishing a *contra* shadow government.

But the optimism faded, at least officially. An internal report by the CIA inspector general in early 1983 concluded that the insurgency couldn't succeed at its current levels. A June 30 National Intelligence Estimate, representing the collective judgment of the intelligence community, was even blunter. It said the *contras* would have difficulty holding large population centers, let alone toppling the Sandinistas.

Conservatives were angered by the intelligence estimate, but it also served Mr. Casey's purposes by giving him a shield against criticism that he was trying to overthrow the government. CIA officials recognized that they were running out of time and might soon lose congressional support for any paramilitary effort. So they began planning, in mid-1983, what would prove the decisive operation of the secret war: the mining of Nicaraguan harbors.

Armed speedboats and a helicopter launched from a Central Intelligence Agency "mother ship" attacked Nicaragua's Pacific port, Puerto Sandino, on a moonless New Year's night in 1984.

A week later the speedboats returned to mine the oil terminal. Over the next three months, they laid more than thirty mines in Puerto Sandino and also in harbors at Corinto and El Bluff. In air and sea raids on coastal positions, Americans flew—and fired from—an armed helicopter that accompanied the U.S.-financed Latino force, while a CIA plane provided sophisticated reconnaissance guidance for the nighttime attacks.

The operation, outlined in a classified CIA document, marked the peak of U.S. involvement in the four-year guerrilla war in Nicaragua. More than any other single event, it solidified congressional opposition to the covert war.

32. *World Court Affidavit**

By Edgar Chamorro

Edgar Chamorro is a former member of the civilian directorate of the FDN, the largest contra *organization. The following piece is his sworn affidavit presented to the International Court of Justice (World Court) during the case brought by Nicaragua against the United States.*

I, EDGAR CHAMORRO, being first duly sworn, depose and say the following:

1. I am a citizen of Nicaragua. I was born in Granada, Nicaragua on July 23, 1931. I presently reside in the United States of America with my wife and two children, at 640 Allendale Road, Key Biscayne, Florida. I have applied to the government of the United States for permanent resident status so that I can live permanently in the United States. I am currently awaiting final action on my application. I have been advised by my attorneys that I should not travel outside the United States until my application for permanent resident status is formally approved; travel outside the United States at the present time, according to my attorneys, could prejudice my application and result in my being permanently excluded from the United States. Since I am unable to appear in person before the International Court of Justice, I am submitting my testimony to the Court in written form.

2. I will begin by describing my background. I was raised in Nicaragua. At the age of 19, I joined the Jesuit order of the Roman Catholic Church, and subsequently became a Roman Catholic priest. I studied at the following Jesuit-affiliated institutions: Catholic University in Quito, Ecuador; St. Louis University in St. Louis, Missouri; and Marquette University in Milwaukee, Wisconsin. I later served as full professor and dean of the School of Humanities at the University of Central America, a Jesuit-affiliated institution in Managua, Nicaragua. I left the priesthood in 1969, but continued my career in education. In 1972, I received a master's degree in education from Harvard University, Cambridge, Massachusetts.

3. I returned to live in Managua, and went into private business. I worked for an advertising agency called Creative Publicity. I developed an expertise in advertising, public relations, and mass communications. In 1977, I was appointed by the

*Deposition of Edgar Chamorro before the International Court of Justice, September 5, 1985.

Nicaraguan government to be a member of the mission of Nicaragua to the United Nations in New York. I served in that capacity for one year, after which I returned to Nicaragua. In June 1979, I took up residence with my family in Miami, Florida. At that time, there was a full-fledged insurrection against the government, and the *Guardia Nacional* (National Guard), the Nicaraguan armed forces loyal to the president, General Anastasio Somoza, were bombing residential neighborhoods and shooting innocent civilians in the streets. I did not wish to remain in Nicaragua under such conditions.

4. On July 19, 1979, the insurrection succeeded in overthrowing the Somoza government and a new government of national reconstruction was established in its place. The new government was led by the *Frente Sandinista de Liberación Nacional* (Sandinista National Liberation Front) or FSLN, which favored broad social and economic change in Nicaragua. I traveled back to Nicaragua in September 1979 to learn about the new government first-hand, and to decide whether to move back to Nicaragua with my family. Although I, too, favored social and economic changes in Nicaragua, I felt then—and still feel—that the policies and programs of the FSLN were and are too radical, and that I could not lend my support to a government dominated by that political party. I decided to remain in Miami.

5. Toward the end of 1979 I began to work with a group of Nicaraguan exiles living in Miami who, like me, opposed the policies of the new government. In 1980 we constituted ourselves as the *Union Democratica Nicaraguense* (Nicaraguan Democratic Union), or UDN. Our principal activity was to write letters to members of the United States Congress urging them to vote against financial assistance for the Nicaraguan government. We also held political meetings and rallies with other like-minded Nicaraguan exiles in Miami, and we set up regional committees in other cities of the United States where substantial numbers of Nicaraguans were residing. The leader of our organization, with whom I worked closely, was José Francisco Cardenal. Cardenal had served briefly as vice-president of the Council of State, the legislature of the new Nicaraguan government, but had resigned his post and left Nicaragua because of his disagreements with the new government's policies.

6. In 1981, the UDN underwent a transformation. During the first half of the year, Cardenal was contacted by representatives of the United States Central Intelligence Agency, and he began to have frequent meetings with them in Washington and in Miami. He also began to receive monetary payments from these people. He was told that the United States government was prepared to help us remove the FSLN from power in Nicaragua, but that, as a condition for receiving this help, we had to join forces with the ex-national guardsmen who had fled to Honduras when the Somoza government fell and had been conducting sporadic raids on Nicaraguan border positions ever since. Cardenal was taken to Honduras by his CIA contacts on several occasions to meet with these guardsmen. The UDN, including Cardenal, initially opposed any linkage with the guardsmen. The CIA, and high-ranking United States government officials, insisted that we merge with the guardsmen. Lt. General Vernon Walters, then a special assistant to the U.S. secretary of state (and formerly deputy director of the CIA) met with Cardenal to encourage him to accept the CIA's pro-

posal. We were well aware of the crimes the guardsmen had committed against the Nicaraguan people while in the service of President Somoza, and we wanted nothing to do with them. However, we recognized that without help from the United States government we had no chance of removing the Sandinistas from power, so we eventually acceded to the CIA's, and General Walters's, insistence that we join forces with the guardsmen. Some UDN members resigned because they would not associate themselves with the National Guard under any circumstances, but Cardenal and I and others believed the CIA's assurances that we, the civilians, would control the guardsmen in the new organization that was to be created.

7. At that time, the ex-national guardsmen were divided into several small bands operating along the Nicaragua-Honduras border. The largest of the bands, headed by Enrique Bermúdez, a former colonel, was called the 15th of September Legion. The bands were poorly armed and equipped, and thoroughly disorganized. They were not an effective military force and represented no more than a minor irritant to the Nicaraguan government. Prior to the UDN's merger with these people, General Walters himself arranged for all the bands to be incorporated within the 15th of September Legion, and for the military government of Argentina to send several army officers to serve as advisers and trainers. The merger of the UDN with the 15th of September Legion was accomplished in August 1981 at a meeting in Guatemala City, Guatemala, where formal documents were signed. The meeting was arranged and the documents were prepared by the CIA. The new organization was called the *Fuerza Democratica Nicaraguense* (Nicaraguan Democratic Force) or, by its Spanish acronym, FDN. It was to be headed by a political junta, consisting of Cardenal, Aristides Sanchez (a politician loyal to General Somoza and closely associated with Bermúdez), and Mariano Mendoza, formerly a labor leader in Nicaragua; the political junta soon established itself in Tegucigalpa, Honduras, taking up residence in a house rented for it by the CIA. Bermúdez was assigned to head the military general staff, and it, too, was based in Honduras. The name of the organization, the members of the political junta, and the members of the general staff were all chosen or approved by the CIA.

8. Soon after the merger, the FDN began to receive a substantial and steady flow of financial, military, and other assistance from the CIA. Former national guardsmen who had sought exile in El Salvador, Guatemala, and the United States after the fall of the Somoza government were recruited to enlarge the military component of the organization. They were offered regular salaries, the funds for which were supplied by the CIA. Training was provided by Argentinian military officers, two of whom—Col. Oswaldo Ribeiro and Col. Santiago Villejas—I got to know quite well; the Argentinians were also paid by the CIA. A special unit was created for sabotage, especially demolitions; it was trained directly by CIA personnel at Lepaterique, near Tegucigalpa. Arms, ammunition, equipment, and food were supplied by the CIA. Our first combat units were sent into Nicaraguan territory in December 1981, principally to conduct hit-and-run raids. The first military successes of the organization came in March 1982, when CIA-trained saboteurs blew up two vital bridges in northern Nicaragua—at Rio Negro and Ocotal.

9. 1982 was a year of transition for the FDN. From a collection of small, disorganized, and ineffectual bands of ex-national guardsmen, the FDN grew into a well-organized, well-armed, well-equipped, and well-trained fighting force of approximately 4,000 men capable of inflicting great harm on Nicaragua. This was due entirely to the CIA, which organized, armed, equipped, trained, and supplied us. After the initial recruitment of ex-guardsmen from throughout the region (to serve as officers or commanders of military units), efforts were made to recruit ''foot soldiers'' for the force from inside Nicaragua. Some Nicaraguans joined the force voluntarily, either because of dissatisfaction with the Nicaraguan government, family ties with leaders of the force, promises of food, clothing, boots, and weapons, or a combination of these reasons. Many other members of the force were recruited forcibly. FDN units would arrive at an undefended village, assemble all the residents in the town square and then proceed to kill—in full view of the others—all persons suspected of working for the Nicaraguan government or the FSLN, including police, local militia members, party members, health workers, teachers, and farmers from government-sponsored cooperatives. In this atmosphere, it was not difficult to persuade those able-bodied men left alive to return with the FDN units to their base camps in Honduras and enlist in the force. This was, unfortunately, a widespread practice that accounted for many recruits. The FDN received all of its weapons from the CIA. In 1982, the CIA provided FAL rifles to all FDN combatants. These were acquired used from the Honduran army, which found these rifles expendable after the United States government reequipped the Honduran army with American-made M-16 rifles, thus enabling the CIA to purchase the FALs for the FDN. (Later, in 1983, the CIA acquired AK-47 assault rifles for the FDN.)

Training continued under the direction of Argentinian military officers, although gradually the Argentinians were replaced and CIA personnel performed all military training themselves. By the end of 1982, we were ready to launch our first major military offensive designed to take and hold Nicaraguan territory, which the CIA was urging us to do. Our principal objective was the town of Jalapa, in northern Nicaragua. More than 1,000 of our fighters were involved, and we used light artillery (mortars, supplied by the CIA) in combat for the first time. Although we inflicted casualties on the Sandinistas and caused substantial destruction in Jalapa and other neighboring towns, our offensive was repulsed and we were forced to retreat to Honduras and regroup without having accomplished our objective.

10. My specific job during the first year after the creation of the FDN was to serve as staff person to the political junta. I was based in Miami, where I did political propaganda work, wrote letters, organized rallies, set up committees in various parts of the United States and generally worked at building support for our cause within the United States. During this period Cardenal grew increasingly unhappy over his lack of influence within the FDN. He had frequent conflicts with the CIA personnel who were supervising and directing the FDN's political and military activities and found that he had no control over Bermúdez or the other members of the FDN general staff, who answered only to the CIA. Eventually he quit the organization, returned to Miami, and entered the insurance business.

11. In November 1982 I was approached by a CIA agent using the name "Steve Davis" and asked to become a member of the "political directorate" of the FDN, which the CIA had decided to create as a substitute for the "political junta." (I am able to refer to "Davis" by name because I know that it is a pseudonym; United States law makes it a criminal offense to reveal the real name of any undercover CIA operative.) I had lunch with "Davis" at a restaurant near my home in Florida. "Davis" told me he was speaking in the name of the president of the United States, who wanted "to get rid of the Sandinistas." "Davis" explained to me that the FDN had a bad image in the United States, and particularly among members of the Congress, because it was perceived as an organization of ex-national guardsmen. He told me that in order to maintain the support of the Congress for the CIA's activities it was necessary to replace the political junta with a group of prominent Nicaraguan civilians who had no ties with the National Guard or the Somoza government. "Davis" left without asking me to make a commitment. He told me I would be contacted again in the near future.

12. Later that month, "Davis" telephoned me and asked me to have dinner with him in his hotel suite at the Holiday Inn in Miami. When I arrived, "Davis" introduced me to another CIA man, who used the name "Tony Feldman." "Feldman" was introduced as "Davis" 's superior from Washington, and he acted as though "Davis" worked for him. "Feldman" told me that the CIA had decided on a seven-member political directorate for the FDN, because any larger group would be unmanageable. He said that I had been selected as one of the seven, and he asked me to accept. He told me that the United States government was prepared to give its full backing to the FDN so that, by the end of 1983, we would be marching into Managua to take over the Nicaraguan government. I was glad to see that the United States government was committed enough to our cause to be taking such an active role, and I agreed to join the directorate they were creating. Over the next several days "Feldman" took control of the operation and moved the headquarters to the Four Ambassadors Hotel, also in Miami, where we met constantly. "Feldman" and his assistants discussed with me possible candidates for the directorate, but it was obvious that they had already decided who they wanted. The most important thing, "Feldman" emphasized, was that the directorate be formed immediately. He told me that the CIA was worried that the Congress might enact legislation to prohibit the use of United States funds for the purpose of overthrowing the Nicaraguan government, and that the creation of a political directorate composed of prominent, respectable civilians might persuade the Congress not to enact such legislation.

13. The press conference was held the next day, December 8, 1982 at the Hilton Conference Center in Fort Lauderdale, Florida. We filed in and introduced ourselves as the directorate of the Nicaraguan Democratic Force (FDN), and then I read our statement of principles and goals. A CIA officer named "George" had rewritten our original version of the statement, and I had to read his words. In January 1983, at the instruction of CIA agent "Thomas Castillo," we put out a twelve-point "peace initiative" drafted by the CIA, which essentially demanded the surrender of the Sandinista government. I thought this was premature, but "Castillo" insisted that it be

done to get the FDN favorable publicity. Also at this time, another Nicaraguan civilian—Adolfo Calero—who had just left Nicaragua, was added to the directorate. Calero had been working for the CIA in Nicaragua for a long time. He served as, among other things, a conduit of funds from the United States embassy to various student and labor organizations. "Feldman" had told me that the CIA was bringing him out of Nicaragua, where he had run the local Coca-Cola distributorship, to serve on the FDN's political directorate. Despite these public-relations efforts, the United States Congress enacted a prohibition on CIA efforts to overthrow the Nicaraguan government, although it appropriated millions of dollars to the CIA for clandestine military and paramilitary activities against the Nicaraguan government. Before this prohibition was enacted, the CIA agents we worked with spoke openly and confidently about replacing the government in Managua. Thereafter, the CIA instructed us that, if asked, we should say that our objective was to interdict arms supposedly being smuggled from Nicaragua to El Salvador. If any of us ever said anything publicly about overthrowing the Nicaraguan government, we would be visited immediately by a CIA official who would say, "That's not the language we want you to use." But our goal, and that of the CIA as well (as we were repeatedly assured in private), was to overthrow the government of Nicaragua, and to replace the Sandinistas as a government. It was never our objective to stop the supposed flow of arms, of which we never saw any evidence in the first place. The public statements by United States government officials about the arms flow, we were told by the CIA agents with whom we worked, were necessary to maintain the support of the Congress and should not be taken seriously by us.

14. From January 1983 through June 1984, I worked for the FDN full time and remained a member of the political directorate until November 1984. The CIA paid me a salary of $2,000 a month to support myself and my family, plus expenses. Similar arrangements were made with the other FDN "directors." I was put in charge of public relations for the FDN. We wanted to set up highly visible headquarters in a shopping center or office building, but the CIA did not like the idea. They said it would become a target for demonstrations or violence. They insisted that we take an elegant suite at the David Williams Hotel in Coral Gables, Florida, which the CIA paid for.

15. At the end of January 1983, I was instructed to relocate to Tegucigalpa, Honduras, to establish and manage the FDN's communications office. The CIA station in Tegucigalpa, which at that time included about twenty agents working directly with the FDN, gave me money, in cash, to hire several writers, reporters, and technicians to prepare a monthly bulletin called *Comandos,* to run a clandestine radio station, and to write press releases. I was also given money by the CIA to rent a house, office space, and automobiles, and to obtain office supplies and communications equipment. I also received money from the CIA to bribe Honduran journalists and broadcasters to write and speak favorably about the FDN and to attack the government of Nicaragua and call for its overthrow.

Approximately fifteen Honduran journalists and broadcasters were on the CIA's payroll, and our influence was thereby extended to every major Honduran newspaper and radio and television station. (I learned from my CIA colleagues that the same tactic was employed in Costa Rica in an effort to turn the newspapers and radio and television stations of that country against the Nicaraguan government.) I worked very closely in all of these matters with several CIA agents based in Tegucigalpa, but most closely with one of the deputy station chiefs, named "George," who had drafted the FDN's first press statement in Miami and was then transferred to Tegucigalpa to continue working with us. Together with "George," and subject to his approval, I planned all the activities of my communications office and prepared a budget. The budget was reviewed by the CIA station in Tegucigalpa and, if approved, sent to Washington to obtain the necessary funds, which were always provided to me in cash.

16. I was not the only member of the directorate to prepare a budget in this fashion. Indalecio Rodriguez, who was put in charge of "civilian affairs," which meant assistance for Nicaraguan refugees in Honduras or family members of our combatants, worked with his CIA "adviser" in the same manner in which I worked with "George." Adolfo Calero and Enrique Bermúdez worked on the military and logistics budget. This budget was not as large as one might suppose. The FDN never received money to purchase arms, ammunition, or military equipment. These were acquired for us and delivered directly to us by the CIA. One of the senior agents at the CIA's Tegucigalpa station, known to us as "the Colonel," was an expert in these matters, and he, together with his assistants, determined what we needed and obtained it for us, including arms, ammunition, uniforms, boots, radio equipment, etc. As long as I was in Honduras (until June 1984), the FDN never acquired its own arms, ammunition, or other military equipment. We were just the end receivers. The main items in the military and logistics budget that Calero and Bermúdez worked on were things that could be acquired locally, such as food for our men, for which money had to be obtained from the CIA. Calero and Bermúdez were our main links with the CIA. They met constantly with the CIA station chief (whose name I cannot reveal here because I am uncertain whether it is his real name or a pseudonym) and his principal deputies.

17. Most of the CIA operatives who worked with us in Honduras were military trainers and advisers. Our troops were trained in guerrilla warfare, sabotage, demolitions, and in the use of a variety of weapons, including assault rifles, machine guns, mortars, grenade launchers, and explosives, such as Claymore mines. We were also trained in field communications, and the CIA taught us how to use certain sophisticated codes that the Nicaraguan government forces would not be able to decipher. This was critical to our military operations because it enabled various units, or task forces, to communicate with each other, and to coordinate their activities, without being detected by the Sandinistas. Without this communications capacity, our forces inside Nicaragua would not have been able to coordinate their activities with one another and they would have been unable to launch effective strikes at the designated targets. Even more critical to our military activities was the intelligence that the CIA provided to us. The CIA, working with United States military personnel, operated various electronic interception stations in Honduras for the purpose of intercepting

radio and telephonic communications among Nicaraguan government military units. By means of these interception activities, and by breaking the Nicaraguan government codes, the CIA was able to determine—and to advise us of—the precise locations of all Nicaraguan government military units. The information obtained by the CIA in this manner was ordinarily corroborated by overflights of Nicaraguan territory by United States satellites and sophisticated surveillance aircraft. With this information, our own forces knew the areas in which they could safely operate free of government troops. If our units were instructed to do battle with the government troops, they knew where to set up ambushes, because the CIA informed them of the precise routes the government troops would take. This type of intelligence was invaluable to us. Without it, our forces would not have been able to operate with any degree of effectiveness inside Nicaragua. The United States government also made it possible for us to resupply our troops inside Nicaragua, thus permitting them to remain longer inside the country. Under cover of military maneuvers in Honduras during 1983, United States armed forces personnel constructed airstrips, including the one at Aguacate, that, after the CIA provided us with airplanes, were instrumental in resupplying our troops.

18. The CIA was also directly involved in our military tactics. The agency repeatedly ordered us to move our troops inside Nicaragua and to keep them there as long as possible. After our offensive at the end of 1982 was turned back, almost all of our troops were in Honduras and our own officers believed that they needed more training and more time before they would be ready to return to Nicaragua. The FDN officers were overruled by the CIA, however. The agency told us that we had to move our men back into Nicaragua and keep fighting. We had no choice but to obey. In 1983, the CIA instructed us not to destroy farms or crops because that would be politically counterproductive. In 1984, however, we were instructed to destroy export crops (especially coffee and tobacco), and to attack farms and cooperatives. Accordingly, we changed our tactics in 1984.

19. In July 1983, we were visited in Tegucigalpa by Duane Clarridge, the CIA official, based in Washington, who was in charge of the agency's military and paramilitary activities against Nicaragua. At that time we were introduced to Clarridge as "Maroni." (I am free to state his real name because his identity has already been publicly disclosed in the United States.) During a meeting with the political directorate, Clarridge told us that the CIA had decided that something must be done to cut off Nicaragua's oil supplies, because without oil the Nicaraguan military would be immobilized and its capacity to resist our forces would be drastically reduced. Clarridge spoke of various alternatives. He said the agency was considering a plan "to sink ships" bringing oil to Nicaragua, but that one problem with this plan was that if a ship belonging to the Soviet Union were sunk it could trigger a serious international incident. Clarridge said that the CIA was also considering an attack on Nicaragua's sole oil refinery, located near Managua. According to Clarridge, however, the refinery was located in a densely populated area, and the civilian casualties resulting from such an attack would be politically counterproductive. Finally, Clarridge

said that the agency had decided on a plan to attack the oil pipeline at Puerto Sandino, on Nicaragua's Pacific coast, where the oil tankers delivering oil to Nicaragua discharge their cargo.

20. In September 1983, the CIA blew up the pipeline at Puerto Sandino, just as Clarridge had advised us it would. The actual operatives were agency employees of Hispanic descent, referred to within the agency as "Unilaterally Controlled Latino Assets" or UCLAs. These UCLAs, specially trained underwater demolitions experts, were despatched from a CIA "mother ship" that took them to within striking distance of their target. Although the FDN had nothing whatsoever to do with this operation, we were instructed by the CIA to publicly claim responsibility in order to cover the CIA's involvement. We did. In October, CIA UCLAs attacked Nicaragua's oil storage tanks at Corinto, also on the Pacific coast. This was a combined sea and air attack involving the use of rockets. It was a complete success; all of the tanks were destroyed and enormous quantities of oil were consumed by fire. Again, the CIA instructed us to publicly claim responsibility, and we did. Later in October, there was another UCLA attack on Puerto Sandino, which again resulted in the demolition of the oil pipeline. We again claimed responsibility per instructions from the CIA. Subsequently, the UCLAs attacked Nicaraguan government military facilities at Potosí and radio antennas at Las Casitas. We again were told to claim responsibility and we did.

21. We had a second visit from Clarridge in October 1983. Clarridge told us that the agency had decided that the FDN needed a single spokesman in order to more effectively persuade the Congress to continue supporting the CIA's activities against Nicaragua, and that Calero should be the one. He asked us to make Calero the head of the political directorate and we did so without objection. Clarridge also told us that the agency wanted us to launch another major offensive with the objective of seizing and holding Nicaraguan territory, no matter how small. He said that as soon as our hold on that territory was secured, we should establish a provisional government, which the United States and its Central American allies would promptly recognize as the legitimate government of Nicaragua.

22. The offensive was launched at the end of 1983, after the Congress had appropriated—openly for the first time—$24,000,000 to the CIA for military and paramilitary activities in and against Nicaragua. While our forces inflicted greater casualties on the government's troops and on civilians, and destroyed more property than in previous attacks, we nevertheless failed to take or hold any Nicaraguan territory and the majority of our troops were forced to return to their bases in Honduras.

23. On January 5, 1984, at 2:00 A.M., the CIA deputy station chief of Tegucigalpa, the agent I knew as "George," woke me up at my house in Tegucigalpa and handed me a press release in excellent Spanish. I was surprised to read that we—the FDN—were taking credit for having mined several Nicaraguan harbors. "George" told me to rush to our clandestine radio station and read this announcement before the Sandinistas broke the news. The truth is that we played no role in the mining of the harbors. But we did as instructed and broadcast the communiqué about the min-

ing of the harbors. Ironically, approximately two months later, after a Soviet ship struck one of the mines, the same agent instructed us to deny that one of ''our'' mines had damaged the ship to avoid an international incident.

24. In May 1984 the United States Congress voted not to provide more assistance to the CIA for military and paramilitary activities against Nicaragua. Many of us became worried about receiving continued support from the United States government and we expressed these concerns to our CIA colleagues in Tegucigalpa. We were repeatedly assured by the station chief and his deputies, in the strongest possible terms, that we would not be abandoned and that the United States government would find a way to continue its support. At around this time we were visited by Ronald F. Lehman II, a special assistant to the president of the United States who was serving then on the National Security Council. Mr. Lehman assured us that President Reagan remained committed to removing the Sandinistas from power. He told us that President Reagan was unable at that time to publicly express the full extent of his commitment to us because of the upcoming presidential elections in the United States. But, Mr. Lehman told us, as soon as the elections were over, President Reagan would publicly endorse our effort to remove the Sandinistas from power and see to it that we received all the support that was necessary for that purpose. We received a similar assurance of continued United States government support, notwithstanding the refusal of the Congress to appropriate more funds, from Lt. Col. Oliver North, another official of the National Security Council.

25. It was still important to these officials, and to the CIA, to obtain additional appropriations of funds from the Congress, and they had not abandoned hope that the Congress could be persuaded to resume funding our activities. Our CIA colleagues enlisted us in an effort to ''lobby'' the Congress to resume these appropriations. I attended meetings at which CIA officials told us that we could change the votes of many members of the Congress if we knew how to ''sell'' our case and place them in a position of ''looking soft on communism.'' They told us exactly what to say and which members of the Congress to say it to. They also instructed us to contact certain prominent individuals in the home districts of various members of Congress as a means of bringing pressure on these members to change their votes. At various times Calero, Callejas, Zeledon, Salazar, Rodriguez, and I participated in these ''lobbying'' activities.

26. A major part of my job as communications officer was to work to improve the image of the FDN forces. This was challenging, because it was standard FDN practice to kill prisoners and suspected Sandinista collaborators. In talking with officers in the FDN camps along the Honduran border, I frequently heard offhand remarks like, ''Oh, I cut his throat.'' The CIA did not discourage such tactics. To the contrary, the agency severely criticized me when I admitted to the press that the FDN had regularly kidnapped and executed agrarian reform workers and civilians. We were told that the only way to defeat the Sandinistas was to use the tactics the agency attributed to ''Communist'' insurgencies elsewhere: kill, kidnap, rob, and torture.

27. These tactics were reflected in an operations manual prepared for our forces

by a CIA agent who used the name "John Kirkpatrick." I assisted "Kirkpatrick" in translating certain parts of the manual, and the manuscript was typed by my secretary. The manual was entitled: *Psychological Operations in Guerrilla Warfare.* It advocated "explicit and implicit terror" against the civilian population, including assassination of government employees and sympathizers. Before the manual was distributed, I attempted to excise two passages that I thought were immoral and dangerous, at pages 70 and 71. One recommended hiring professional criminals. The other advocated killing some of our own colleagues to create martyrs for the cause. I did not particularly want to be "martyred" by the CIA. So I locked up all the copies of the manual and hired two youths to cut out the offending pages and glue in expurgated pages. About 2,000 copies of the manual, with only those two passages changed, were then distributed to FDN troops. Upon reflection, I found many of the tactics advocated in the manual to be offensive, and I complained to the CIA station chief in Tegucigalpa. The station chief defended "Kirkpatrick" and the manual, and no action was ever taken in response to my complaints. In fact, the practices advocated in the manual were employed by FDN troops. Many civilians were killed in cold blood. Many others were tortured, mutilated, raped, robbed, or otherwise abused.

28. As time went on, I became more and more troubled by the frequent reports I received of atrocities committed by our troops against civilians and against Sandinista prisoners. Calero and Bermúdez refused to discuss the subject with me, so I went straight to our unit commanders as they returned from combat missions inside Nicaragua and asked them about their activities. I was saddened by what I was told. The atrocities I had heard about were not isolated incidents, but reflected a consistent pattern of behavior by our troops. There were unit commanders who openly bragged about their murders, mutilations, etc. When I questioned them about the propriety or wisdom of doing those things they told me it was the only way to win this war, that the best way to win the loyalty of the civilian population was to intimidate it and make it fearful of us. I complained to Calero and Bermúdez, and to the CIA station chief, about these activities, but nothing was done to stop them. In June 1984, Clarridge visited us again. Although he was well aware of the terrorist tactics the FDN troops were employing, he spoke warmly to Bermúdez: "Well done, Colonel," I remember him saying, "Keep it up. Your boys are doing fine." It was the last time I saw him. Shortly thereafter, I acknowledged to a newspaper reporter that our troops had killed some civilians and executed some prisoners, though I tried to explain these practices as best I could. Calero told me I could no longer work in Honduras and I was reassigned to the local FDN committee in Miami. I was given nothing to do and I no longer had much interest in working for the FDN, or to be more accurate, for the CIA.

29. When I agreed to join the FDN in 1981, I had hoped that it would be an organization of Nicaraguans, controlled by Nicaraguans, and dedicated to our own objectives which we ourselves would determine. I joined on the understanding that the United States government would supply us the means necessary to defeat the Sandinistas and replace them as a government, but I believed that we would be our

own masters. I turned out to be mistaken. The FDN turned out to be an instrument of the United States government and, specifically, of the CIA. It was created by the CIA, it was supplied, equipped, armed, and trained by the CIA and its activities—both political and military—were directed and controlled by the CIA. Those Nicaraguans who were chosen (by the CIA) for leadership positions within the organization—namely, Calero and Bermúdez—were those who best demonstrated their willingness to unquestioningly follow the instructions of the CIA. They, like the organization itself, became nothing more than executioners of the CIA's orders. The organization became so thoroughly dependent on the United States government and its continued support that if that support were terminated, the organization would not only be incapable of conducting any military or paramilitary activities against Nicaragua, but it would immediately begin to disintegrate. It could not exist without the support and direction of the United States government.

30. I became more and more distanced from the FDN in the second half of 1984. I had, for all intents and purposes, ceased to be a part of the organization. Finally, on November 20, 1984, I received a letter stating that the political directorate had decided to relieve me of my duties. I made no protest.

31. My opposition to the Nicaraguan government continues. I oppose its policies and programs and I would like to see it removed or replaced. This should be accomplished, however, by the Nicaraguan people themselves, and not by the United States government or by its instruments, including the FDN, which follow its dictates and serve its interests instead of those of the Nicaraguan people. My presentation of this testimony to the International Court of Justice is not an expression of support or sympathy for the present Nicaraguan government or its case against the United States. It is a result of my commitment to tell the truth, to all interested parties, about my personal experiences in the FDN. Since I left the organization at the end of 1984, I have spoken publicly in the United States about my experiences and I have made myself available to journalists whenever they have requested interviews. When Nicaragua's attorneys approached me and asked if I would present testimony about my experiences to the International Court of Justice, I decided to do so. This decision is consistent with my practice of speaking openly and honestly about my experiences before any interested body or forum. Whatever the best solution for the Nicaraguan people may be, I am convinced that it can only come about on the basis of truth, and that those of us with relevant personal experience are under a moral obligation to make the truth known.

(Signed) Edgar Chamorro
September 5, 1985
[notarized]

33. Who Are the Contras?*

by the Arms Control and Foreign Policy Caucus

The Arms Control and Foreign Policy Caucus is a bipartisan joint House and Senate body chaired by Representative Jim Leach, Republican from Iowa.

The United States has been supporting armed opposition to the Nicaraguan government since 1981. Over $20 million reportedly has been spent to build and maintain a force of from 10,000 to 15,000 *contras*.

Information published by the Nicaraguan government has not been used in this report. Instead, the report is based primarily on extensive interviews with former high-ranking officials of the primary *contra* force (the FDN), literature published by the FDN, and interviews with representatives of organizations that aid the *contras*. While we recognize there are limitations in this approach, the executive branch has thus far failed to respond to our requests for specific information on the structure and leaders of the FDN military command. We hope that publication of this report will focus closer attention on the significant questions it seeks to address.

Summary

In summary, the conclusions of the report are as follows:

While the "foot soldiers" of the FDN army are largely peasants, the army is organized and commanded by former national guardsmen. In the first publicly available organizational chart of the high command of the FDN military force, the report finds that forty-six of the forty-eight positions in the FDN's command structure are held by former guardsmen.

While the FDN's civilian directorate has been cleansed to minimize the role of former guardsmen and Somoza associates, the military leadership has not been. As a result, the key military strategist positions, including the strategic commander, are held by ex-national guardsmen, as are all of the general staff, four out of five of the central commanders, six out of seven of the regional commanders, and probably all thirty task force commanders.

Up to twenty private groups in the United States have provided the *contras* with substantial financial and material aid (apparently some $5 million) in the past year. Most of these groups are not traditional relief organizations or other established groups recognized as providing humanitarian aid, but rather are ultraconservative or paramilitary groups on the fringe of American political opinion.

These groups are largely operated by a small group of about half a dozen men, mostly with military or paramilitary backgrounds, whose close association often means that the groups work in tandem.

A major "relief" effort for the Miskito Indians living on the Honduran-Nicara-

*Excerpts from the *Congressional Record,* April 23, 1985.

guan border has had the effect of maintaining the Misura *contra* army. One of the groups contributing to this effort is funded in large part by Rev. Moon's Unification Church.

Section 1: Who Are the Contras?

AN ANALYSIS OF THE MILITARY LEADERSHIP OF THE FDN

Contrasting claims have been made about the background of the *contras* by the United States and Nicaraguan governments. Nicaragua states that they are "basically former Somoza national guardsmen who are engaged in terrorism against the Nicaraguan people," while the United States maintains that in the "democratic resistance . . . nearly all the opposition leaders opposed Somoza." Our research indicates that the truth is somewhere in between.

This section attempts to resolve the differences between these two extreme positions by describing for Congress—to the best of our knowledge, for the first time in unclassified form—the military makeup of the Nicaraguan Democratic Force (FDN).

This section concludes that:

FDN and U.S. government claims that the FDN is largely a "peasant army" of Nicaraguans disaffected with their government are accurate.

In contrast to FDN claims about the military leadership of the *contras* (which the State Department has given credence by publishing), forty-six of the forty-eight positions in the FDN military leadership are held by ex-national guardsmen. These include the strategic commander, the regional command coordinator, all five members of the general staff, four out of five central commanders, five out of six regional commanders, and all thirty task force commanders.

While the core of the general and central command staff is admittedly fluid, with personnel changing titles and duties over time, regional and task force commanders acquire personal control over their forces, and change infrequently. In any event, the overall structure detailed here has existed for the past sixteen months, and the personnel and duties listed were verified less than two weeks ago.

Certain individuals in the leadership, including especially controversial ones such as Ricardo Lau (an ex-National Guard official reputed to have engaged in numerous atrocities both in the guard and in the FDN), have taken a less "visible" role in recent months in order to make the nature of the *contra* army more acceptable to Congress. Our interviews with former FDN officials, as well as the recent refusal of ARDE commander Edén Pastora to ally his forces with the FDN because of the involvement of Lau and other ex-guardsmen, indicate that these individuals nonetheless retain significant power in the FDN.

Blanket FDN denials of the military structure and individuals and their guard background described in this section appear to lack credibility. The FDN representative in Washington, for example, claims that ex-guard officers Armando "the Policeman" Lopez and Walter "Tono" Calderon Lopez, identified by three independent sources and numerous on-site news reports as two of the top three independent

FDN commanders, serve in the minor ancillary roles of "warehouse keeper" and "supply assistant for a base camp." Further, the FDN representative denies that Col. Enrique Bermúdez is the strategic commander who runs the military effort (this task is attributed to the civilian president of the FDN directorate), or even that a conventional military command structure exists in the FDN. These denials directly contradict literature published by the FDN in Honduras, which displays a military command structure, and places Bermúdez at its head.

While the executive branch will likely dispute some of the findings in this report at a later date, it has thus far failed to respond to a written request for specific information on the military leadership by Caucus Chairman McHugh, or to numerous telephone inquiries. At this point, the only information the administration has made public about the FDN military command appears to concede that FDN claims may not be verifiable: Rather than submit to Congress its own analysis of FDN leadership, the State Department attributes virtually all of its information to "FDN reports."

This section focuses on the FDN because it would receive the great majority (if not all) of U.S. funds approved for expenditure, and because the FDN is the only significant *contra* military force at present. Leadership struggles and lack of funds have combined to virtually bring to a halt major military activities by ARDE's roughly 1,000 fighters in the south and the Miskito Indians' roughly 1,500 fighters in the north.

This section analyzes the military rather than the political leadership of the FDN for three reasons: (a) because it is the military leaders who make the key decisions on military strategy and on the direction of the war. For instance, it is the military and not the political leaders who decide on military operations, on tactics, and on the disciplining of commanders and troops for human rights abuses; (b) because it remains an open question whether the civilian leaders, who have little if any decision-making power now, would be able to wrest power from the military leaders should the rebel forces gain victory; and (c) because very little information has heretofore been made available on the military leadership of the FDN—in contrast to the wealth of material the administration has provided on the "new" civilian leadership. Critics call this leadership "repackaged": Prior to a reorganization in 1982 nearly the entire directorate was drawn from the 15th of September Legion, formed by ex-guard officers and associates of President Somoza shortly after his ouster in 1979. For example, a recent State Department publication provides biographical information on twenty-seven "top leaders" of the *contras,* only one of whom—Bermúdez—is in the FDN military apparatus.

The conclusions in this section are based on extensive interviews with two former high-ranking FDN officials, and with one of the foremost American experts on the Nicaraguan National Guard. News reports, including those in the Central American press and those based on the on-site interviews, formed the basis for the interviews. Information published by the Nicaraguan government, which was found to be dated and of questionable accuracy, was not used.

The two ex-FDN officials, Edgar Chamorro Coronel and Salvador Icaza, served respectively as a member of the FDN civilian directorate and the FDN's communications liaison from 1983 to 1984. Both spent substantial time at the FDN's central base and other bases in Honduras, assisted in the investigation of regional commanders for alleged human rights abuses, and left the FDN largely because it failed to purge itself of high personnel with connections to President Somoza or the National Guard. In the course of the interviews, Chamorro checked with sources still in the FDN and brought this material up to date.

The academic expert interviewed was Professor Richard Millett of Southern Illinois University, a frequent congressional witness who is widely respected as one of the most knowledgeable Americans on politics and power within Somoza's National Guard.

The following chart displays the current structure and leadership of the military command of the FDN. Most leaders are identified by their noms de guerre, as they are in the FDN. Of the forty-eight positions in the command structure, our two sources who were formerly in the FDN claim that forty-six are filled by former national guardsmen.

FDN MILITARY COMMAND STRUCTURE

Strategic Commander: Enrique Bermúdez *(el Comandante Estrategico)*, supreme commander and chief of staff. Coordinator, Regional Commands: Walter "Tono" Calderon Lopez; coordinates from 8,000 to 12,000 combatants.

General Staff
G–1, Personnel: "The Deer"
G–2, Intelligence: "The Bull"
G–3, Operations: "Mike Lima"
G–4, Logistics: Armando "the Policeman" Lopez
G–5, Psychological Warfare: "Invisible"

Central Commanders
Air Operations: Juan Gomez
Counterintelligence: Ricardo Lau
MISURA Liaison: Justiciano Perez
Special Forces: "Little Bird"
Infantry Training School: ?

Regional Commanders (direct from 500 to 2,000 combatants)
Nicarao: Comandante "Mack"
Segovia; Comandante Dr. "Aureliano"
Jorge Salazar: Comandante "Quiche"
Rafaela Herrera: Comandante "Little Tiger"
Diriangen: Comandante "Dimas"
San Jacinto: Comandante "Renato"

Task Force Commanders
Two to eight task force commanders serve under a regional command; each directs some 250 combatants.

General Description
In this command structure, the strategic commander is the director of military strategy and operations. He is assisted in planning and implementing strategy by his general staff and central commanders. All but one of the twelve top central staff were formerly in the guard. Overall control of the primary combat units is given to the second-ranking officer, the coordinator of regional commands.

Each of the six regional commanders (five of whom were in the guard) has a number of task force commanders operating under his control. The regional and task force commanders are referred to as *comandante* and command the personal loyalty of their troops. These are the key military field leaders. Our sources claim that most and probably all of the thirty task force commanders are former guards. These commanders in turn break their 250-combatant commands into three groups of 70 (with the remaining personnel performing central command duties for the task force).

Roughly 80 percent of the group leaders have no prior service in the National Guard; this ratio is the reverse of what existed two years ago, before the expansion of the FDN. The groups are then broken down into three detachments of twenty combatants each (again, with the remainder performing central command duties for the group). Nearly all the detachment leaders have no prior guard service.

FDN combatants are estimated at between 8,000 and 12,000, rather than the 15,000 claimed by the FDN. The lower figure was provided by Chamorro, who states that when he was responsible for public relations for the FDN, he was under instructions to routinely double the actual size of the FDN. Whatever the true figure, FDN combatants are largely peasants who are disaffected with Sandinista policies. In sum, the FDN is a peasant army with ex-guard leadership.

IDENTIFICATION AND DESCRIPTION OF MILITARY LEADERS

Strategic Commander: Enrique Bermúdez
Mr. Bermudez is a former colonel in the National Guard. Along with Aristides Sanchez (general secretary of the FDN's civilian directorate; formerly a wealthy landowner and close associate of the late General Somoza) and Adolfo Calero (head of the civilian directorate, and a leader of the business opposition to Somoza) Bermúdez is part of the informal triumvirate that decides strategy for the civilian directorate. Bermúdez controls military operations.

Bermúdez, who led the Nicaraguan contingent in the OAS occupation of the Dominican Republic in 1965, was Nicaragua's military attaché in Washington for the last three years of Somoza's rule. Following Somoza's ouster, he helped found the 15th of September Legion with some sixty former guard officers, which was the nucleus of the FDN at its founding in 1981.

Bermúdez increased his operational control over the FDN when he dismissed his chief of staff, former guard officer Emilio Echevarry, and a number of his assistants in 1983 following a CIA-assisted investigation into Echevarry's handling of FDN funds. Bermúdez did not replace Echevarry, and instead has assumed many of his functions.

Bermúdez is assisted, in addition to the military described below, by a number of former Somoza supporters and National Guard officers who arrange for the procurement of weapons and supplies, and carry out a variety of special missions in surveillance, communications, and special military tasks. These individuals are not part of the formal structure of the FDN, but are an important operations component. They include Enrique "Cuco" (The Cuckoo) Sanchez, a former landowner and deputy for Somoza's party in the Nicaraguan parliament and brother of General Secretary Aristides Sanchez; the Teffel brothers, José and Jaime, associates of Somoza; and two brothers, former guard officers, the "Shermans."

Bermúdez's presence in the FDN has been cited by some *contra* leaders, such as Edén Pastora and Brooklyn Rivera, as a primary reason why they refuse to join in a coalition with the FDN. Chamorro and Icaza left the FDN in large part because Bermúdez would not remove his associates from the 15th of September Legion from the FDN command structure.

Coordinator, Regional Commander: Walter "Tono" Calderon Lopez
"Tono," a former guard officer who was once a regional commander in the FDN, occupies this second most powerful military position—the equivalent of what is known in Western military parlance as a theater operations commander. He directs the six regional commanders, and he can call on the general staff and central commanders to assist them. Tono is identified in a February 1984 publication of the FDN in Honduras as commander of tactical operations, which appears to be the same functional role as regional coordinator.

General Staff, Personnel (G–1): "El Venado" (the Deer)
"El Venado," a former guard officer, was a task force *comandante* for the FDN. When he was badly wounded in an attack on the town of Ocotal, in the northernmost Nicaraguan province of Nueva Segovia, he moved to the general staff. G–1 is responsible for the recordkeeping and advises the strategic commander on personnel placement.

General Staff, Intelligence (G–2): "El Toro" (the Bull)
"El Toro" was a colonel in the National Guard. G–2 is responsible for ascertaining the whereabouts and abilities of Nicaraguan military units. "El Toro" replaced Edgard Hernandez, a former guard officer dismissed with chief of staff Emilio Echevarry in 1983.

General Staff, Operations (G–3): "Mike Lima"
"Mike Lima," or "M.L.," was the most widely renowned of the FDN's regional commanders prior to moving to the general staff. A former guard officer, he led the Diriangen regional command, with up to 2,000 fighters. This was the most militarily

active of the commands. While a regional commander, he was badly wounded in a mortar explosion and lost an arm. G–3's responsibilities include planning overall requirements and strategy for operations, in consultation with the coordinator of regional commands.

General Staff, Logistics (G–4): Armando ''El Policia'' (the Policeman) Lopez
Armando Lopez, a former captain in the National Guard, was one of the founders of the 15th of September Legion. He is extremely close to Bermúdez, and has been seen by some as his second-in-command at times. He has dismissed the possibility of negotiations with the Nicaraguan government, although this is a stated goal of the FDN's civilian directorate: ''He who speaks of dialogue with the Communists speaks of wasting his time.'' G–4's responsibilities focus on supplying the regional commands and task forces.

General Staff, Psychological Warfare (G–5): ''El Invisible''
''El Invisible,'' a former guard officer, is responsible for planning activities that weaken the control of the Nicaraguan government over its armed forces and the civilian population. Such activities can include distributing leaflets that offer rewards for desertion, or broadcasting information that discredits the Sandinistas. ''El Invisible'' replaced Manuel Caceres, a former guard officer now living in the Dominican Republic. This staff position has rotated more frequently than others, and ''El Invisible'' may return to task force command.

Central Command, Head of Air Operations: Juan Gomez
Gomez was a guard officer who served as Somoza's personal pilot. He now performs the same function for Bermúdez, as well as overseeing the operation of the small number of reconnaissance, cargo, and rotary aircraft that form the FDN's air force. Gomez was in the 15th of September Legion, as well as the original FDN directorate.

Central Command, Head of Counterintelligence: Ricardo Lau
Lau is a former guard officer whose service in the FDN has been cited by *contra* leaders Edén Pastora and Brooklyn Rivera as a primary reason for their refusal to participate in a coalition with the FDN. Lau has recently been accused (by a former Salvadoran army colonel) of procuring former guards to assassinate Salvadoran Archbishop Oscar Romero in 1980—a new accusation which comes on top of longstanding charges that he has engaged in numerous atrocities, both as a guardsman and in the FDN.

Lau was in the 15th of September Legion as well as the original FDN directorate. In 1983, the FDN announced that Lau had been removed from the formal post of head of counterintelligence, apparently to encourage the formation of a broad coalition of *contra* groups. Nonetheless, our sources contend that Lau continues to function as he had before, albeit with a lower public profile, and retains responsibility for preventing infiltration of the FDN by agents of the Nicaraguan government and for enforcing discipline for Bermúdez. Lau's extremely close alliance with Bermúdez leads our former FDN sources to believe that as long as Bermúdez is strategic commander, Lau will play an important role in the FDN—''forever.'' Lau is assisted in counterintelligence by Armando Lopez's son, known as "El Policito" (the Little Policeman) and "El Bestia" (the Beast).

Central Command, Misura Liaison: Justiciano Perez
Perez, a former guard officer, has also been cited by other *contra* leaders as an unacceptable member of any military or political coalition. Perez commanded Somoza's infantry training school, and was personally close to Somoza. He too was formally removed from the FDN leadership in 1983, but continues in a key role as Bermúdez's liaison with the Misura military force, which operates in northeastern Nicaragua under the command of Miskito Indian leader Steadman Fagoth.

Central Command, Special Forces: "El Pajarito" (Little Bird)
"El Pajarito" leads small groups (of up to seventy-five fighters) into Nicaragua to perform sabotage and other special missions requiring rapid movement. He is a young man, and although his father was a guard officer, he was a medical student in Mexico during the revolution and never served in the guard.

Central Command, Infantry Training School: name unknown.
A former guard officer commands the infantry training school at Las Vegas, which is currently diminishing in size. This officer replaced Hugh Villagra, a former guard officer whom Bermúdez allegedly ousted as a rival in 1984. Assisting the head of the training school in the recent past was a third Sanchez, Victor, whose two other brothers, Aristides and Enrique "Cuco" have been discussed above.

Regional Command, Nicarao: Comandante "Mack"
The Nicarao (a popular contraction of "Nicaragua") command is led by Comandante "Mack," a former guardsman. His four task forces are all commanded by former guardsmen, known as "El Cascavel" (the Rattlesnake), "03," "Ersi," and "Ocran." FDN publications in Honduras confirm Mack's identity as head of this command.

Regional Command, Rafaela Herrera: Comandante "Tigrillo" (Little Tiger)
The Rafaela Herrera command, named after a legendary Nicaraguan heroine, is commanded by Comandante "Tigrillo," the only regional commander (in fact, the only one of the top forty-eight military leaders in the FDN besides "El Pajarito," head of the special forces) who is not a former national guardsman. Tigrillo participated in the revolution, although he may not have been a Sandinista. His task force commanders are all former guards. Two of them are identified by their nicknames, "Atila" (Attila the Hun) and "Tiro Al Blanco" (Target-Shooter). FDN publications in Honduras confirm the identities of Tigrillo, Atila, and Tiro Al Blanco in these roles.

Regional Command, Diriangen: Comandante "Dimas"
The Diriangen command, named after a legendary Indian chief, is commanded by Comandante "Dimas." Dimas, a former guardsman, had been a task force commander in Diriangen. He replaced "Mike Lima" when Lima was wounded and became G–3. All of Dimas's task forces are commanded by former guards. FDN publications in Honduras confirm Dimas's prior role of task force commander.

Regional Command, Segovia: Comandante Dr. "Aureliano"
The Segovia command, named after the province of heaviest FDN activity, the mountainous border province of Nueva Segovia, is commanded by a former guardsman who also has studied medicine. All of Aureliano's task forces are commanded by former guardsmen. FDN publications in Honduras confirm Aureliano's role in this regional command.

Regional Command, Jorge Salazar: Comandante "Quiche"
The Jorge Salazar command, named after a leader of the business coalition COSEP who was killed by Nicaraguan police in 1980 (and whose widow serves on the FDN's civilian directorate), is commanded by a former guardsman. Comandante "Quiche" has adopted an Indian name, although he is not himself an Indian. He was a task force commander under Walter "Tono" Calderon Lopez, who left this regional command to become coordinator of the regional commands. All of Quiche's task forces are commanded by former guards. One task force is led by "Franklin."

Regional Command, San Jacinto: Comandante "Renato"
The San Jacinto command, named after a famous battle in Nicaraguan history, is commanded by a former guardsman. Comandante "Renato" presides over this smallest of the regional commands (probably some 500 fighters). His task forces are all commanded by former national guards. Renato has been identified in this role in FDN publications in Honduras.

34. Major Contra *Groups*

By the Editors

FDN (Nicaraguan Democratic Forces)

This is by far the largest *contra* organization, variously estimated as having between 3,000 and 15,000 troops. Most of these troops are based in Honduras, although the FDN has opened a southern front from Costa Rica. The FDN has been the major recipient of U.S. funding, and was forced by the CIA to accept a "civilian" directorate, composed of various right-wing intellectuals and businessmen who were not directly linked with Somoza. Its military command, however, is almost exclusively former National Guard, while there are several not necessarily exclusive theories as to who exactly makes up the bulk of its troops:

- other former national guardsmen,
- disaffected Nicaraguan peasants,
- Nicaraguan peasants forced to particpate because their kidnapped families are held hostage in "refugee" camps in Honduras,
- and/or poor Honduran, Costa Rican, and Nicaraguan peasants recruited as mer-

cenaries with the promise of quick earnings equal to many times their annual income.

ARDE (Democratic Revolutionary Alliance)

This Costa Rican-based organization was originally formed as an alliance of different groups loyal to businessman and former opposition member of the junta, Alfonso Robelo; right-wing *contra* ''el Negro'' Chamorro-Rappaciolo; Miskito leader Brooklyn Rivera; and former revolutionary hero Edén Pastora.* Never a very large organization, ARDE has recently fractured, with those troops loyal to Robelo forming an alliance with the FDN.

Misura

A right-wing Miskito organization led by former Somoza security agent Steadman Fagoth, MISURA has an estimated 1,500–3,000 troops operating out of Honduras in coordination with the FDN.

Misurasata

This Costa Rica-based Miskito group claims to be fighting only for Atlantic Coast autonomy, rather than against the revolution itself. Its leader, Brooklyn Rivera, has in the past entered into negotiations with the Nicaraguan government, at one point agreeing to a short-lived cease-fire.

UNO (Nicaraguan Opposition Union)

UNO was formed in August 1985, at the insistence of the Reagan administration, to receive the $27 million in ''humanitarian aid'' approved by Congress. It is composed of FDN director Adolfo Calero, Alfonso Robelo of ARDE, and international banker and former opposition member of the junta, Arturo Cruz. Although UNO will apparently control the purse strings for the *contras,* it remains to be seen exactly what its role will be.

---

*For more on Pastora, see earlier editions of this book.

35. *Combatant's Manual for Liberty**

By the Central Intelligence Agency

1. PLACE AN UNLIGHTED CIGARETTE BETWEEN TWO ROWS OF MATCHES. UNITE THEM TOGETHER BY TYING THEM FIRMLY WITH A STRING.
2. WRAP THE MATCHES IN DRY PAPER OR ANY OTHER INFLAMMABLE SUBSTANCE. PLACE THE DEVICE

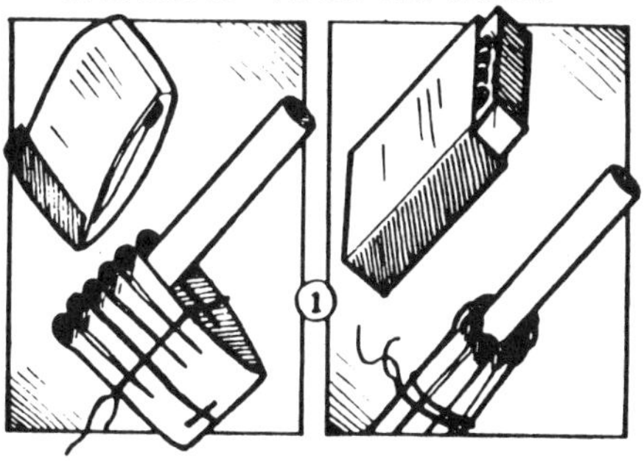

1. COLOCAR UN CIGARRILLO NO ENCENDIDO ENTRE AMBAS HILERAS DE FÓSFOROS. UNIRLOS FIRMEMENTE ATÁNDOLOS CON UNA CUERDA.
2. ENVOLVER LOS FÓSFOROS EN PAPEL SECO O CUALQUIER OTRA SUSTANCIA INFLAMABLE. COLOQUE EL DISPOSITIVO ENTRE CAJAS VACÍAS DE CARTÓN O MADERA.
3. ENCENDER EL CIGARRILLO POR SU EXTREMO LIBRE. LOS FÓSFOROS SE ENCENDERÁN EN 5 O 10 MINUTOS.

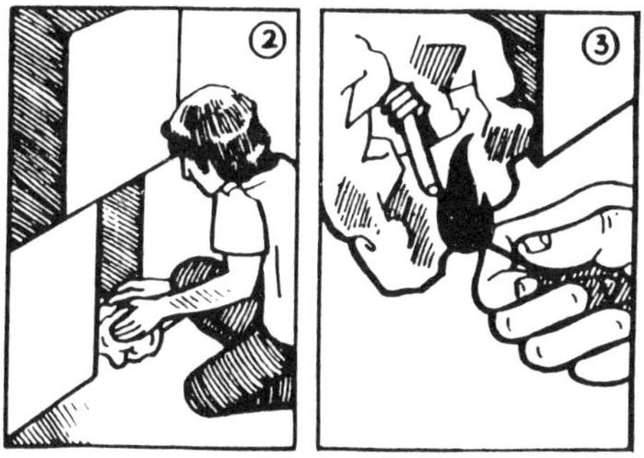

BETWEEN EMPTY WOODEN OR CARTON BOXES.

3. LIGHT THE CIGARETTE AT THE FREE END. THE MATCHES WILL LIGHT IN 5 OR 10 MINUTES.

INCENDIARY BOMB ("MOLOTOV COCKTAIL")

1. FILL A NARROW-NECKED BOTTLE WITH GASOLINE, KEROSENE, OR BURNABLE DIESEL; BETTER STILL, IF SHREDDED SOAP OR SAWDUST ADDED.
2. INSERT A RAG IN THE BOTTLE UNTIL ONE END TOUCHES THE LIQUID AND THE OTHER EXTENDS NO MORE THAN 20cm FROM THE RIM OF THE BOTTLE. SEAL THE BOTTLE TIGHTLY WITH A STRING OR TAPE.

BOMBA INCENDIARIA ("COCTEL MOLOTOF")

1. LLENAR DE GASOLINA, LUZ BRILLANTE (KEROSÉN) O COMBUSTIBLE DIESEL UNA BOTELLA DE CUELLO ESTRECHO; MEJOR AÚN SI SE LE AÑADE ASSERRÍN DE MADERA O JABÓN RAYADO.

2. INTRODUCIR UN TRAPO EN LA BOTELLA HASTA QUE UN EXTREMO ROCE EL LÍQUIDO Y EL OTRO SE EXTIENDA NO MENOS DE 20 CMS DE LA BOCA DE LA BOTELLA. SELLAR FIRMEMENTE LA BOTELLA CON UNA CINTA O VENDA.

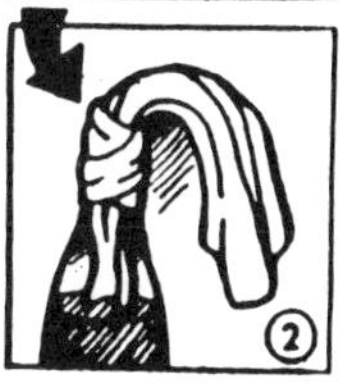

3. PARA ACTIVAR EL DISPOSITIVO:
   A) SOSTENER LA BOTELLA EN UNA MANO EXTENDIENDO BIEN EL BRAZO.
   B) ENCENDER CON LA OTRA MANO EL TRAPO.
   C) LANZAR INMEDIATAMENTE LA BOTELLA ENCENDIDA CONTRA EL OBJETIVO, CON FUERZA SUFICIENTE PARA QUE SE ROMPA AL HACER IMPACTO.

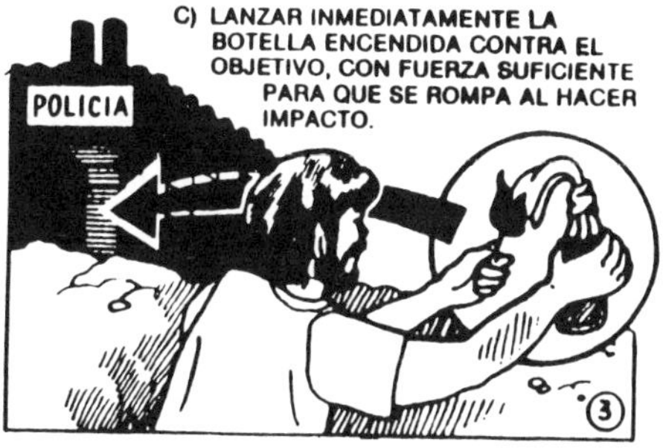

3. TO ACTIVATE THE DEVICE:
   A) HOLD THE BOTTLE IN ONE HAND WITH YOUR ARM EXTENDED.
   B) LIGHT THE RAG WITH YOUR OTHER HAND.
   C) IMMEDIATELY THROW THE LIGHTED BOTTLE AT YOUR OBJECTIVE WITH SUFFICIENT FORCE THAT IT BREAKS ON IMPACT.

*Excerpts from a "comic book" of the same name, written by the CIA and distributed in Nicaragua.

36. U.S. Found to Skirt Ban on Aid to Contras*

By Alfonso Chardy, *Miami Herald* staff writer

The Reagan administration helped organize and still supports efforts to provide private aid for Nicaraguan insurgents despite a congressional prohibition against assisting them, according to government sources, legislative aides, and a former rebel.

A three-week examination of the rebels' supply sources revealed a definite, albeit blurred, link between the administration and a supposedly spontaneous effort to raise military and humanitarian assistance for the rebels totaling more than $10 million over the last year.

Former rebel leader Edgar Chamorro, ousted November 24 from the largest *contra* army, known as the Nicaraguan Democratic Force (FDN), said the administration apparently began organizing the effort when Congress balked at providing aid last year.

Central Intelligence Agency spokeswoman Patti Volz said the CIA . . . declined to respond to questions about whether the CIA provided money for ads or if one of its officers traveled to Honduras to reassure the *contras*.

Circumstantial evidence also suggests the administration contacted conservative allies to enlist their help as well as private groups that already were involved in aiding Nicaraguan refugees. They receive logistical support from the Pentagon and the State Department's Agency for International Development.

Coors, Grace

Also involved in the anti-Sandinista effort are several of Reagan's millionaire friends including beer tycoon Joseph Coors and industrialist J. Peter Grace.

Their names appeared on invitations by the Nicaraguan Refugee Fund for a $250-a-plate dinner April 15 where Reagan launched his latest campaign to restore official funding.

Adolph Coors Company spokesman Don Shug said the beer company is not aiding the *contras* but indicated it was possible that individual executives may have helped them.

Grace spokesman Fred Bona said his boss "may have" asked the Central American chapters of the 900-year-old Knights of Malta order to help distribute privately collected humanitarian aid among Nicaraguan refugees. Grace heads the group's U.S. chapter.

Former Treasury secretary William Simon and CIA Director William Casey also belong to the Knights of Malta. Simon and Grace declined comment on whether they had ever discussed with Casey alternate ways to help the *contras*.

---

*Excerpts from the *Miami Herald,* June 24, 1985.

Simon heads the Nicaraguan Freedom Fund, a private aid group initially launched by the Unification Church-owned newspaper the *Washington Times* which received a letter from President Reagan dated May 30, 1985, expressing "wholehearted" support for its activity on behalf of the *contras*.

Singlaub's Role

While the *contras* get humanitarian aid from these groups, they rely mainly on retired Army Maj. Gen. John Singlaub and his World Anti-Communist League for private military aid.

Singlaub said in a telephone conversation from his Phoenix, Arizona, office that he has advised "administration contacts" about his efforts.

Singlaub said he helps the *contras* through foreign corporations and governments that deposit money in a secret overseas bank account from which the *contras* draw cash to purchase military equipment.

In this way, said Singlaub, he and the *contras* avoid violating the 187-year-old Neutrality Act that prohibits arming expeditions from U.S. soil against a country with which the United States is not at war.

Singlaub declined to identify the location of the account or the firms and governments involved. Congressional aides said they believe that the account is in Panama or Switzerland and that the governments are those of Taiwan, South Korea, and Saudi Arabia.

In 1977, Singlaub, then the third-ranking U.S. Army commander in South Korea, was fired from that post by President Carter for publicly criticizing Carter's plans to withdraw U.S. ground troops from the Asian nation.

Administration officials, meanwhile, acknowledged a role in refugee-related programs but denied involvement in a private fund-raising effort. However, when asked about specific activities, they declined comment.

U.S. Assurances

Chamorro said the officials assured the *contras* the administration never would abandon them.

"Afterwards," he added, "it was discussed among ourselves that the CIA soon would let us know who to contact for aid."

Shortly afterward, an informal network of Republican Party members, wealthy businessmen, conservative activists, and former military and intelligence officers emerged to raise funds for rebels and refugees.

Chamorro indicated that their activities were coordinated through an NSC "*contra* planning committee." The NSC declined comment. But the Associated Press, quoting an administration source, reported that the NSC staff handled contacts with private groups.

Administration sources familiar with the subject said officials had contacted conservative allies, including businessmen and retired government officials, to aid the *contras*. The sources said the White House did not direct the private-aid campaign but told private groups—presumably Simon's and Singlaub's—it would support their efforts.

Chamorro said that in June 1984, . . . FDN leader Adolfo Calero called him from Washington "with orders from the CIA" to place ads in several U.S. newspapers appealing for private funds for Nicaraguan refugees. The *Herald* published such an ad July 2, 1984. Among other papers the ad appeared in were the *Washington Times* and the New Orleans *Times-Picayune*. Chamorro said the total cost for the ads was about $5,000.

Chamorro said that three Nicaraguan businessmen in Miami—David Raskosky, Enrique Pereira and Octavio Sacasa—used the Panama-based Human Development Foundation as a front to collect aid, but that funds for the ads came from the CIA.

Sacasa, however, said the ad funds "came from private donors who do not want their names published" and Calero said Chamorro's claim that the CIA provided the money for the ads was a "lie."

The *contras* raised only $700, along with several protest letters including one accompanied by dead cockroaches, Chamorro said.

Sacasa's wife, Marta, an informal FDN spokeswoman in Miami, said between $2,000 and $3,000 was collected by the time the group halted its activities because Florida authorities warned it was not registered to solicit funds.

37. *Notes and Comment on the Moral Equivalent of Our Founding Fathers**

By the *New Yorker*

Several commentators in recent years have been struck by the extraordinary convergence of talent, grace, genius, and wisdom in the current generation contesting for legitimacy in Poland. How is it possible, these observers wonder, for a single generation in a relatively small, relatively isolated country in the middle of Eastern Europe to have produced such a host of great-souled men and women—Lech Walesa, Adam Michnik, Jacek Kuron, Karol Modzelewski, Karol Wojtyla, Jerzy Popieluszko, Anna Walentynowicz, Alina Pienkowska, Andrzej Wajda, Krzysztof Zanussi, Czeslaw Milosz, Andrzej Gwiazda, Zbigniew Bujak, and on and on? At something of a conceptual loss before this historical mystery, the commentators occasionally have recourse to analogy, and one that frequently recurs in their writings is to the remarkable generation that arose in the British colonies in North America during the seventeen-sixties, seventies, and eighties. There historians have long been confronted with that wondrous fluke, the manna descending, the sudden, unexplain-

*From the "Talk of the Town" section of the *New Yorker,* March 25, 1985.

able upwelling of greatness—Benjamin Franklin, Thomas Jefferson, Samuel Adams, Thomas Paine, George Washington, John Adams, Alexander Hamilton, James Madison, and on and on, all acting at the same moment in the same place. It is a useful analogy, and an appropriate one: it does honor to both sides of the equation. On the Polish side, we Americans are afforded a sense of what history must have felt like as it was unfolding for our own Founding Fathers; of what it must have been like to wake up each morning faced with impossible odds and hopeless choices and yet somehow summon the resolve to act and the composure to act sagely; of what the declaration of independence must have felt like before it became the Declaration of Independence, when the spirit was building but had yet to find expression, when expression had yet to coalesce into inevitability. Through the analogy to our Founding Fathers, Poles, for their part, can draw a lesson concerning the future consequences of present acts—how a noble project honestly conceived and earnestly carried through becomes a source, a wellspring, refreshing and sustaining generation after generation to come. These corollaries suggest what is at stake in historical analogy, and the sense of care and responsibility with which we must exercise our propensity for it. Not only must the two sides of the equation be worthy of each other but we must be worthy of them.

A few weeks ago, President Reagan, as part of his current siege of Congress on behalf of his administration's Central America policy, tried his hand at historical analogy. He declared that the *contras,* the fighting forces currently attempting to undermine the Sandinista regime in Nicaragua, "are the moral equal of our Founding Fathers." The analogy is a strange one: our Founding Fathers accomplished a revolution, whereas the *contras* are by definition *contrarevolucionarios*—counterrevolutionaries. The revolution they so vigorously oppose is one that overthrew a tyrant, Anastasio Somoza, who made George III seem positively small-time. Of course, President Reagan claims that the *contras* were initially supporters of that revolution who subsequently found themselves co-opted by their onetime Sandinista allies, but the historical record offers precious little to sustain that characterization. (The commander of the principal *contra* force, the man who set about organizing it immediately after Somoza's downfall and still commands it, is Enrique Bermúdez, who was Somoza's military attaché in Washington; one of the few *contra* leaders who might truly fit Reagan's definition of a disenchanted onetime revolutionary, Edén Pastora, will have nothing to do with most of the other *contra* military groups, precisely because so many of their leaders were former officers in Somoza's National Guard, and as a result of this hesitancy Pastora's group was being frozen out of most American covert funding even when Congress was allowing the practice.) And even if Reagan's version of a co-opted revolution were historically accurate the analogy that might be drawn would be to the French Revolution, or the Russian—certainly not the American.

The problem, however, isn't just that the Founding Father analogy is specious; it's also pernicious. Within days of the President's statement, two reports were issued evaluating the behavior of *contra* forces in the field. Americas Watch released a comparative study, *Violations of the Laws of War by Both Sides in Nicaragua, 1981–*

1985, that documented the behavior of both the *contra* and the Sandinista forces. The report was careful and precise in tone; if anything, it was understated. Its authors concluded that whereas the Sandinista forces had committed ''major abuses,'' particularly against the Miskito Indians on Nicaragua's Atlantic coast, during the first few years after the Revolution, ''the evidence that we have gathered shows a sharp decline in violations of the laws of war by the Nicaraguan government following 1982.'' By contrast, Americas Watch reported, ''The *contra* forces have systematically violated the applicable laws of war throughout the conflict. They have attacked civilians indiscriminately; they have tortured and mutilated prisoners; they have murdered those placed *hors de combat* by their wounds; they have taken hostages; and they have committed outrages against personal dignity.''

In the past, State Department and White House spokesmen confronted with charges like these have dismissed them as being based on idiosyncratic cases, or else on hearsay. Partly in response to that type of defense, lawyers affiliated with the Washington Office on Latin America and the International Human Rights Law Group two weeks ago released the results of a series of studies undertaken during the past six months. To begin with, one lawyer went down to Nicaragua and compiled evidence relating to twenty-eight incidents of *contra* violence aimed at civilians—''reliable evidence of a kind that would be legally sufficient in a court of law,'' his report specified. That is to say, he took sworn affidavits, based almost exclusively on eyewitness testimony, from over a hundred and forty persons; he challenged the witnesses with questions designed to confirm their personal knowledge of the events related (''Did you actually see that?'' ''What color were their uniforms?''). This testimony was transcribed; the transcripts were read back to the witnesses; and the witnesses signified their approval by signing them with their full names, their place of residence, and, in most cases, the names of their parents. Wherever possible, corroboration was sought. WOLA and the I.H.R.L.G. subsequently sent two other lawyers down to verify the accuracy of the affidavits. Following the report's release, several independent journalists in Nicaragua further confirmed the reliability of several of the accounts. The affidavits make for chilling reading.

Item: Noel Benavides Herradora, a coffee-picker, telling of his abduction by the *contras* from a farm near the Honduran border, along with a married couple, prominent church leaders, in December, 1982: ''Mr. Felipe Barreda and his wife were already there. He was bleeding heavily. He was being beaten and had blood all over him. [His wife] was also being beaten. They tied them. I was walking ahead, he was tied behind me, and she was tied further behind. He could hardly walk. He kept slipping and falling. And every time he fell they struck him and threatened to get rid of him right there so that he would stop being a burden. Then he would kneel and ask to be allowed to pray to Our Father. But they just beat him, kicked him, slapped him in the face, and cursed him.'' The Barredas were later tortured and killed.

Item: Doroteo Tinoco Valdivia, testifying about a large *contra* attack in April, 1984, on his farming coöperative, near Yalí, Jinotega: ''They had already destroyed all that was the cooperative: a coffee-drying machine, the two dormitories for the coffee cutters, the electricity generators, seven cows, the plant, the food warehouse.

There was one boy about fifteen years old, who was retarded and suffered from epilepsy. We had left him in the bomb shelter. When we returned . . . we saw . . . that they had cut his throat, then they cut open his stomach and left his intestines hanging out on the ground like a string."

Item: Inocente Peralta, a lay pastor who went out looking for victims of another attack on a Jinotega coöperative: "We found one of them, Juan Perez, assassinated in the mountains. They had tied his hands behind his back. They hung him on a wire fence. They opened up his throat and took out his tongue. Another bayonet had gone in through his stomach and come out his back. Finally, they cut off his testicles. It was horrible to see."

Item: Orlando Wayland, a Miskito teacher who was kidnapped by the *contras* in December, 1983, and force-marched into Honduras, where he was tortured along with eight others: "In the evening they tied me up in the water from seven p.m. until one a.m. The next day, at seven a.m., they began to make me collect garbage in the creek in my underwear, with the cold. I was in the creek for four hours. . . . Then they threw me on the anthill. Tied up, they put me chest down on the anthill. The [red] ants bit my body. I squirmed to try to get them off my body, but there were too many. I was on the anthill ten minutes each day. . . . They would beat me from head to heels. . . . They would give me an injection to calm me a little. Then they would beat me again."

Item: Myrna Cunningham, a Miskito Indian doctor, describing what happened to her and to a nurse following their kidnapping by the *contras,* in December, 1981: "During those hours we were raped for the first time. While they were raping us, they were chanting slogans like 'Christ yesterday, Christ today, Christ tomorrow. . . .' And although we would cry or shout, they would hit us, and put a knife or a gun to our head. This went on for almost two hours."

And so forth, for over 140 affidavits.

No one is claiming that every *contra* soldier has behaved in this manner, but both of these recent reports have documented a pattern of activity—countenance for which, in the case of the assassination of civilians, was, in fact, spelled out in the belatedly disowned CIA instruction manual.

And this brings us back to the President's analogy. Jefferson? Washington? Madison? How are the *contras* the moral equal of our Founding Fathers? History is real; analogies have weight; statements have consequences. In days to come, when we find ourselves thinking of those men, the framers of our democracy, might we now find ourselves free-associating to images of torture and indiscriminate murder? It's as if the president had carelessly dumped toxic waste in the very wellspring of our nation's heritage. Already the poison is leaching into the stream, irretrievably contaminating the very waters that we need to drink every day.

38. *Nicaragua 1984: Human and Material Costs of the War**

By the Central American Historical Institute

The Central American Historical Institute is an independent research organization based in Washington, D.C. It is affiliated with the Instituto Histórico Centroamericano in Managua.

In 1984, antigovernment forces continued to inflict significant human and economic losses, which have directly affected not only Nicaragua's armed forces and government, but the civilian population as well (see appendix).

In early 1984 Nicaragua's ports were increasingly targeted, and the focus of the war shifted to economic sabotage. Aerial attacks, some with direct U.S. participation, occurred at the northwest port of Potosí in early January and February, and at the fishing port of San Juan del Sur in March. CIA mining of Nicaragua's three main ports—Corinto, San Juan del Sur, and El Bluff—was carried out in January and February, raising a major U.S. domestic controversy in March and April.

Nicaragua turned to the International Court of Justice at the Hague in search of a legal ruling to back up its call for an end to U.S. intervention. In May the Court, in a preliminary ruling, called on the United States to halt all support for military actions that jeopardize Nicaragua's "sovereignty and political independence." (*New York Times,* 5/11/84). In November the Court refused to accept the U.S. argument that the matter was not in the Court's jurisdiction, and two months later the Reagan administration pulled out of the case.

In early 1984, the Nicaraguan Democratic Force (FDN), based in Honduras, regrouped in the wake of its abortive attempt in late 1983 to seize a part of Nicaraguan territory near Jalapa. The FDN also began to operate for the first time in southern Nicaragua, where the Costa Rican-based Democratic Revolutionary Alliance (ARDE) has been the predominant anti-Sandinista force. Attempts to unite the FDN and ARDE literally blew up in ARDE commander Edén Pastora's face in late May. Since then Alfonso Robelo, who in late 1984 announced he was abandoning the military arena, has entered into an alliance with the FDN and Steadman Fagoth's Honduran-based MISURA. The alliance, known as UNIR (Unity for National Reconciliation), however, has yielded little more than formal declarations. Robelo continues to sign as the leader of ARDE.

Pastora, however, appears to have the loyalty of the ARDE fighting force. He has resisted U.S. pressure to unite with the FDN, saying its leadership is *Somocista.* Pastora's major 1984 action was the two-day seizure last April of the isolated Caribbean port of San Juan del Norte.

In late 1984 ARDE was further weakened by the apparent withdrawal of Miskito

*From *UPDATE,* vol. 4, no. 1. (January 29, 1985).

leader Brooklyn Rivera and MISURASATA. Rivera traveled to Managua, where he met with government leaders, and entered into a negotiation process. In January 1985, however, the negotiation broke down, and their future course is uncertain.

The counterrevolutionary forces set out in mid-1984 to disrupt the July 19 celebration of the overthrow of Somoza, late-July voter registration, and the November elections. Eight electoral officials were killed by rebel forces during the entire electoral process, and sixteen polling places were unable to open or function normally on election day due to *contra* harassment.

Economic sabotage and indiscriminate killing of civilians were the main methods employed. The June 1 attack in which FDN forces entered Ocotal for several hours was indicative of the economic sabotage strategy. The sawmill, radio station, electric power company offices, and grain silos were all destroyed or seriously damaged with losses totaling almost $7 million, according to an independent report by Maryknoll Sisters in Nicaragua.

The participation of U.S. mercenaries fanned the flames of controversy over U.S. policy when two members of the Civilian Military Assistance—one of them an Alabama national guardsman—were killed in a *contra* attack on the northern town of Santa Clara in early September.

While the elections proceeded without major disruptions, FDN attacks in late 1984 took a significant toll on the coffee harvest. Such attacks resulted in material destruction as well as the deaths of many civilians, including road workers, coffee pickers, or members of farm cooperatives.

The fall 1984 revelation that the CIA had prepared the *Psychological Warfare Manual* for the counterrevolutionary forces was a political blow to the Reagan Administration, as the manual suggests killing government officials and sympathizers of the Sandinistas.

As 1984 drew to a close, both the Nicaraguan government and U.S.-backed antigovernment forces presented figures describing the year's balance, as well as prospects for 1985.

Military Balance

The Nicaraguan government reported that the *contra* forces suffered 4,000 casualties of which 3,000 were deaths, while Nicaragua's armed forces lost 1,000 soldiers in combat. In addition 600 civilians—including 100 children under twelve—were killed by the counterrevolutionaries, and 2,400 Nicaraguans (both civilians and military) were wounded or kidnapped by the antigovernment forces in the course of the year.

The FDN, the largest anti-Sandinista group, increased its capacity to operate on a mobile basis in the mountainous northcentral region, including significant areas of the departments of Jinotega, Nueva Segovia, and Estelí in 1984. The FDN recently claimed to have a force of 14,000 fighting in Nicaragua (*Washington Post,* 11/21/84). The Nicaraguan government estimates that most of the FDN forces are in Honduras, with several thousand at a time crossing into northern Nicaragua. FDN units in Nicaragua are resupplied by planes which, in the words of one FDN member, "fly very quietly at night." (Sister Nancy Donovan, press statement, 1/11/85).

The Democratic Revolutionary Alliance (ARDE), which claims to have a force of 7,000, reported 250 dead in 1984. ARDE claims to control an area of sparsely populated southeastern Nicaragua totaling 9,500 square kilometers (Voice of Sandino, 1/1/85, in *Foreign Broadcast Information Service (FBIS),* 1/2/85; and Voice of Sandino, 12/31/84, in *FBIS,* 1/4/85).

The FDN's ability to temporarily control limited areas in the north has resulted in increased civilian deaths, a deterioration of social services, and greater economic difficulties. Most recently, in a January 8 attack in the municipality of San Juan de Limay, department of Estelí, the FDN killed fourteen civilians: nine workers from the Ministry of Construction, two workers from the Ministry of Natural Resources, two young coffee pickers, and a tractor driver. Maryknoll sister Nancy Donovan, currently living in Limay, was kidnapped by the FDN forces that same day, and released eight hours later. According to Sister Donovan, "Just in Limay, almost forty civilians have been killed in the past month. The attacks have been made on civilian, not military, targets and they are increasing." The forty deaths in San Juan de Limay represent 1 percent of the township's total population.

Americas Watch reported in April 1984 that "the FDN has engaged repeatedly in kidnappings, torture, and murder of unarmed civilians, mostly in villages and farm cooperatives." FDN activity in Limay and other attacks reported in recent months (see appendix) indicates that this trend continues.

The January 3 attack on a jeep resulting in the deaths of two young schoolteachers, nineteen and twenty-two years old, who were returning to their schools near the Honduran border (*New York Times,* 1/15/85) suggests that *contra* roadside ambushes will continue in the north and that teachers will continue to be hard hit. The Nicaraguan government reported that in the last six months of 1984 121 people were killed in roadside ambushes.

Minister of Education Fernando Cardenal reported that in 1984 98 adult education teachers were killed and 171 kidnapped; 15 primary school teachers were killed and 16 kidnapped; 14 schools were destroyed; 840 adult education centers were shut down; 354 schools did not operate; and material losses totaled 20 million córdobas for the first nine months of the year (Radio Sandino, 12/22/84; in *FBIS,* 12/28/84).

Economic Difficulties Compounded by War

The war has had several negative effects on Nicaragua's economic growth: On the one hand, material damages resulting from actions in 1984 totaled $254.9 million, equivalent to 70 percent of Nicaragua's annual export revenues. On the other hand, defense allocations have accounted for a rising share of the national budget. According to official figures, 40 percent of the 1985 28 billion córdoba budget will go to defense (including, in addition to armaments, military construction and food and clothing for the armed forces).

The other top priorities for the 1985 budget are health and provision of social services to persons displaced by the war. As of November 1984 the Nicaraguan Social Security Institute reported that some 143,000 persons have had to abandon their homes because of counterrevolutionary attacks.

In late 1984 the FDN set out to disrupt the coffee harvest, which got underway in November. Most of the coffee, Nicaragua's major export earner, is grown in the mountains of Jinotega and Matagalpa.

In early December an agricultural official reported that of a total of eighty-nine *contra* attacks on cooperatives and state farms in Matagalpa and Jinotega since 1982, twenty-two such attacks have taken place since September 1984. While some coffee is physically destroyed in such attacks, more is lost due to actions directed against those who pick the beans. On December 4 a truckload of coffee pickers was attacked north of Estelí. Twenty-two people were killed and six wounded; the truck was set ablaze while at least three people were still inside (*Washington Post,* 12/6/84). By late November the Agricultural Ministry was estimating a $25 million loss in coffee revenues due to such actions.

In a year-end speech, Head of State Daniel Ortega described the principal economic problems as: 1) a drop in supply; 2) deterioration of the transportation and communication infrastructure; 3) inflation; 4) growing speculation; 5) the fiscal deficit; 6) lack of uniformity in prices; and 7) a precipitous fall in agricultural productivity.

1985: War Economy Announced as Heavy Fighting Predicted by Both Sides

In the most sweeping policy statement on the economy since the October 1983 speech outlining nine "war economy" points, Ortega announced several "urgent" economic measures for 1985. These include:

- A freeze on the extension of services such as water and electricity, housing, and supply networks for basic goods in urban areas, and a greater emphasis on extending such activities in rural areas. This will affect Managua which, with a population of 800,000, is overpopulated, and may slow down the steady migration from the countryside to the capital.
- Readjustment of salaries for workers involved in production, and a redistribution of income so as to favor production. This measure is aimed at stimulating production and will hit the large tertiary (commerce and services) sector, some 40 percent of the economically active population.
- Rationalization of the subsidy policy, even with regard to basic goods, so as to overcome supply and demand imbalances. Government subsidies on basic goods will be eliminated, or maintained at diminished levels for lower income groups.

The government summarized its goals for 1985 in the watchword, "For peace, all against the agression." The major emphasis will be fighting the war in an attempt to prevent the antigovernment forces from operating within Nicaraguan territory.

The FDN, however, has other plans. In a January 3 "15th of September" radio broadcast, FDN Directorate member Indalecio Rodríguez described 1985 as "the year of freedom's triumph and Nicaragua's new independence'' (Agence France Press, 1/4/85; in *FBIS,* 1/9/85). Rodríguez stated, ''We have recruited up to 1,000 men in a week, and in the next few months we will have between 35,000 and 40,000 fighters. With that number we will defeat the Sandinistas militarily'' (Ibid.). Former National Guard Col. Enrique Bermúdez, commander in chief of FDN operations, stated that the FDN will soon open a new war front in León. (*Rumbo Centroamericano,* San Jose, November 22–28, 1984; in *FBIS* 11/28/84).

In contrast to the FDN, ARDE stressed the political aspect of its 1985 plans. According to ARDE's New Year's communiqué, ''In 1985, the Revolutionary Directorate and all ARDE's political cadres will undertake a political-diplomatic offensive in Latin America, the United States, and Europe.'' The communiqué, in reference to the November election and subsequent inauguration of Daniel Ortega as president, indicated that ''in 1985 the struggle is going to be harder because the dictatorship is trying to legalize itself'' (Voice of Sandino, 1/1/85; in *FBIS* 1/3/85).

The FDN saw the election as a sign of Sandinista intransigence. Said Commander Bermúdez, ''After the electoral farce a dialogue is useless, since the Sandinistas have shown that they have no intention of reaching an agreement.'' Bermúdez feels the dialogue should be between the ''FDN's FALs and the Sandinistas' AK–47s,'' a reference to the Belgian and Soviet-made machine guns (*Rumbo Centroamericano,* San Jose, November 22–28, 1984; in *FBIS,* 11/28/84).

The Reagan administration in a similar vein announced earlier this month its intention to pull out of the U.S.-Nicaraguan talks which since June 1984 have unfolded in Manzanillo, Mexico, and its refusal to participate in the World Court suit brought by Nicaragua to challenge the legality of U.S. actions aimed at Nicaragua. U.S. plans to block the Contadora regional negotiations were made public in November (*Washington Post,* 11/6/84). Thus, the prospects for a negotiated solution to differences between the United States and Nicaragua and the armed conflicts in Central America in 1985 appear dim.

I. Military/Summary Figures

Deaths from War
(1982–June 1984)

	Wounded	Kidnapped	Murdered	Total Victims
Government employees				
Workers	102	655	226	983
Technicians	38	68	78	184
Professionals	8	11	25	44
Subtotal	148	739	329	1,211

	Wounded	Kidnapped	Murdered	Total Victims
Teachers (adult education)	—	118	89	207
Peasants in cooperatives, Christian Delegates of the Word, and Miskitos	5	2,179	436	2,620
Total civilian victims	153	3,031	854	4,038
Total military casualties				3,353
Grand Total				7,391

(Embassy of Nicaragua, "In Brief")

Since 1982 134 children under 12 have been killed by the *contras* and 37 maimed. 6,239 children have lost one or both parents.

—Daniel Ortega, speech at Fourth National Children's Festival, August 1984

1984 Summary	
Armed encounters	1,500
Contra casualties	4,000
Contra deaths	3,000
Nicaraguan army deaths	1,000
Nicaraguan civilian deaths	600
Nicaraguan wounded or abducted (civilian and military, excluding *contras*)	2,400

An average of 4.3 Nicaraguans have been killed per day as a result of the war.

—Speech by Humberto Ortega, December 26, 1984

II. Social Sector: Education and Health

Since 1981, eighteen doctors and nurses, including two Europeans, have been killed, according to the Ministry of Health.

153 teachers have been killed since 1982.

—New Statesman, *August 31, 1984*

In 1984:

98 adult education teachers killed by *contras*
171 adult education teachers kidnapped by *contras*
15 primary teachers killed; 16 kidnapped by *contras*
14 schools destroyed
840 adult education centers shut down

354 schools did not function
(Córdobas) $20m losses in education from January to September 1984

—*Fernando Cardenal as quoted on Radio Sandino December 12, 1984; in* FBIS *December 28, 1984*

III. Economy

Contra attacks on Nicaragua's port, the burning of granaries, warehouses, farms, factories, and fields, the mining of harbors, the destruction of hospitals and schools, have caused an estimated $200 million worth of damage (in 1984).

—New Statesman, *August 21, 1984*

U.S. actions since Reagan became president, including the freeze on bilateral aid, blocking international loans, and the cut in sugar quotas, have cost Nicaragua $550 million.

—*Cesar Arostegui, deputy director of the International Fund for Reconstruction as quoted in the* New York Times, *October 22, 1984*

Nicaragua will lose more than $25 million in coffee revenue in the 1984–85 harvest due to the counterrevolutionary actions. Approximately 100,000 quintales [1 quintal = 100 lbs.] of coffee planted near the border with Honduras can not be picked this year.

—*Ministry of Agriculture quoted on Radio Sandino November 28, 1984; in* FBIS *November 29, 1984*

An average of ten cooperatives per month are being destroyed by the anti-Sandinista rebels.

—*Ministry of Agriculture Jaime Wheelock, September 25, 1984*

N.B.: These figures have been garnered from a variety of sources. Nonetheless, due to the nature of the situation, most of the data originate from Nicaraguan government sources. This list does not attempt to be complete.

39. *Beware of Aiding the* Contras*

By McGeorge Bundy

McGeorge Bundy served as national security advisor to Presidents John F. Kennedy and Lyndon B. Johnson.

The president has won the Senate's support for a renewal of "nonmilitary" aid, through the Central Intelligence Agency, to the Nicaraguan *contras*. No one

*From the *New York Times,* June 10, 1985.

should be deceived by the word "nonmilitary." If the House should agree, this money will be used to pay for everything short of weapons and bullets, and the rest of the needed funds will be sought in other places it would be embarrassing to explore. The Senate has voted for continued war by the CIA against the Nicaraguan government. The House should reverse this vote, on the simple and fundamental ground that this "covert" operation will not work.

I speak as someone with direct exposure to the ineffectiveness of covert operations. For five years in the Kennedy and Johnson administrations, I was chairman of the committee of the executive branch charged with approving or disapproving them. In 1961, I listened with a beginner's credulity to the arguments of the eager operatives who promoted what became the Bay of Pigs, and I did not know enough to ask the other side of the CIA—the estimators—for their judgment. Through the next two years and more, I watched with increasing skepticism as the Kennedy administration kept the pressure on the CIA for more and better—if smaller—covert operations.

I think that eventually I played a small part—his own learning from experience was much more important—in President Kennedy's growing recognition that covert action simply did not work and caused more trouble than it was worth. It is just plain wrong for President Reagan to suggest, as he has repeatedly, that President Kennedy's opposition to Cuban adventurism, which was indeed strong, would translate today into support for covert operations.

The dismal historical record of covert military and paramilitary operations over the last twenty-five years is entirely clear. Characteristically, the exiles who are willing to accept money and direction from the CIA are not as a group the most dedicated democrats. Characteristically, agency recruiters prefer military professionals to enthusiastic amateurs, but such professionals, especially the graduates of repressive armies, do not ordinarily have great skill in guerrilla operations. Characteristically, CIA officials under pressure for results are driven to increasingly harebrained schemes, and not all of them are honestly and fully explained to superiors or to Congress.

Characteristically, moreover, revolutionary governments under this kind of attack give the highest priority to defeating it. The existence of antigovernment forces becomes a powerful incentive to increased militarization and domestic repression. Particularly in the Caribbean area, where fear and suspicion of the Yankee colossus have deep historical roots, the knowledge that an operation is bought and paid for by the CIA strongly reinforces the very government whose overthrow is sought.

My judgment about the *contras* is entirely independent of any certain conclusion, one way or the other, about whether the Nicaraguan regime is or is not irrevocably committed to the establishment of a totalitarian Marxist-Leninist regime and the export of violent revolution. I do not know how to make a firm prediction on that important question. What I do know is that covert action, without more, makes the worst result more, not less, likely. The very existence of the *contras* plays into the hands of the hardest of the hard-liners in a government about which we have good reason to be wary.

There is one other lesson from history. Repeatedly, covert operations have been the consequence of a belief that no better instrument is available. I believe that this way of thinking is deeply wrong and arises from too timid an estimate of what can be justified when a good case is made.

Let us consider the two basic possibilities that lie ahead for the Nicaraguan government. It may well be that this government, if it remains in power, will inexorably persist in an increasingly Marxist-Leninist course, with increasing reliance on Soviet and Cuban aid and an increasing commitment to the export of violent revolution. I do not know that this will be the result, but I do know that if that is the chosen course, the United States will indeed have a deep national interest in taking fully effective means to reverse it.

In my view, the most effective means, for the Caribbean area, was defined by our experience in the Cuban missile crisis. It is our control of the seas that can defeat and reverse any such Nicaraguan choice. What we would require for the use of our sea power is regional support, which would in turn require a clarity of expression and purpose that, to put it mildly, we have not yet had from this administration.

President Reagan seeks to frighten Americans with the specter of 100 million enslaved by Moscow and of refugees assaulting our borders by the tens of millions. If the situation were in fact this dangerous, surely we would be more likely to prevent it with naval forces than with a group of fighters open to purchase by the CIA.

Now let us consider the other possibility: that there is no inevitability in the future course of the Nicaraguan government, that it may come to accept pluralism in its own country and respect the rights of its neighbors, that it can become a party to a live-and-let-live arrangement and back away from the slippery slope of increasing dependence on Havana and Moscow. Let us suppose also that Nicaragua's neighbors, in the region and the Contadora group, and indeed in Latin America as a whole, can exert their own substantial influence in this direction. Is there not advantage in leaving this road open, rather than building roadblocks across it by implacable insistence on covert war?

I do not have a crystal ball to tell me which way the Sandinistas will move. We must be prepared to make continuing judgments on their course, and we will be helped and not hindered if in that process we make a much more serious use of diplomacy than any we have chosen so far.

This covert enterprise, by itself, is doomed to failure. It will not bring the Sandinistas to President Reagan's feet, and it will not overthrow them. It will confirm and not undermine their Marxist-Leninist leanings. It will not fulfill the hopes of the democrats among the *contras*. It will shed blood on all sides, and it will intensify the existing polarization among Nicaraguans. It will bring discredit on our government among millions of our own citizens and more millions of our friends abroad. It will make constructive change in Nicaragua less likely, and regional support for any necessary stronger course much harder to obtain. It will do great harm along the way, and it simply will not work.

Chapter II:

The Escalation

The problem, of course, is that a future protracted U.S. intervention seems likely to come much closer to the mold of Vietnam than to that of Korea. Indeed, the next protracted limited war the United States attempts to wage may make Vietnam appear, in retrospect, the way Vietnam made the Korean war seem.[6]

Editors' Introduction

Members of the Reagan administration have always responded with a firm negative when confronted with the question of U.S. plans to invade Nicaragua. This changed in 1985 when the administration openly broached the possibility. Secretary of State George Schultz, for example, warned members of Congress that if they did not approve aid for the *contras,* they would be "hastening the day when the threat will grow, and we will be faced with an agonizing choice about the use of U.S. combat troops."[1] In May, President Reagan sent a classified report to Congress which said the use of American military force "must realistically be recognized as an eventual option in the region, if other policy alternatives fail."[2]

These comments can, of course, be viewed as mere hyperbole designed to convince a reluctant Congress to approve aid to the *contras;* yet history has taught us never to dismiss completely the possibility of direct U.S. intervention. Given President Reagan's stated unwillingness to live with the "current structure" of the Nicaraguan government, we must wonder what policy option he will choose if it ever becomes apparent that the *contras* cannot force a change in that structure.

The same questions arise in assessing the significance of the U.S. military maneuvers in Honduras. Are they designed simply to intimidate Nicaragua, or are they, in the words of Col. Charles Pearcy who commands the U.S. task force in Honduras, supposed to "provide us with a significantly improved capability to operate in the region"?[3] The consensus is that the maneuvers, described in the first article in this chapter, probably serve both functions.

Is the militarization of Honduras, as documented by the *Dallas Times Herald* in the second article in this chapter, designed to guard against possible Sandinista aggression? Or will Honduras be used as a U.S. proxy in an eventual regionalization of the Central American conflict? A recent article in *Military Review,* the journal of the U.S. Army Command and General Staff College, outlines "general guidelines" to be followed in future U.S. military interventions in what are called "counterrevolutionary wars." "One is that collective action, involving some relevant regional powers as well as the United States, is a political precondition for success. Unilateral U.S. action is most precarious in terms of domestic U.S. public opinion and should be avoided at all costs."[4] The nations of the Caribbean community (CARICOM) provided such a collective role, for instance, in the U.S. action in Grenada, just as, two decades earlier, the signatories to the Southeast Asia Treaty Organization (SEATO) had provided moral and material support to the United States in its intervention in Vietnam.

There have been a number of invasion scenarios put forth, based on studies supposedly conducted by the Pentagon.[5] The final article in this chapter is such a scenario, presented by Rear Admiral Gene R. La Roque and Lt. Col. John H. Buchanan, both retired.

Perhaps it is fitting to conclude with another excerpt from the *Military Review* discussion of counterrevolutionary war:

> In comparison with the clean-cut, all-out struggle of World War II, Korea was indeed a nasty, protracted, frustrating, dirty little war. Now, in comparison with Vietnam, Korea looks like a neat, conventional, sensible sort of war. . . .
>
> The problem, of course, is that a future protracted U.S. intervention seems likely to come much closer to the mold of Vietnam than to that of Korea. Indeed, the next protracted limited war the United States attempts to wage may make Vietnam appear, in retrospect, the way Vietnam made the Korean war seem.[6]

Notes

1. *New York Times,* June 4, 1985.
2. *New York Times,* June 5, 1985.
3. *New York Times,* June 4, 1985.
4. Col. William O. Staudenmaier and Alan N. Sabrosky, "A Strategy of Counterrevolutionary War," *Military Review,* Vol. LXV(2):2–15, February, 1985.
5. For example, Theodore Moran, "The Cost of Alternative U.S. Policies Toward El Salvador 1984–1989," in *Central America: Anatomy of a Conflict,* ed. Robert S. Leiken (New York: Pergamon Press, 1984).
6. Staudenmaier and Sabrosky.

*40. Readying the Troops**

By NARMIC

National Action Research on the Military Industrial Complex (NARMIC) is a research and publications project of the American Friends Service Committee.

The United States has conducted almost continuous military maneuvers in Central America and in the Caribbean Sea since August 1983. Land exercises are based primarily in Honduras, but in 1985 land exercises lasting longer than several weeks are being carried out in Panama, too. U.S. troops based in Panama and the United States and members of the U.S. and Puerto Rican National Guards participate in the exercises. The land exercises usually involve troops from the host country as well as U.S. troops, and sometimes troops from neighboring countries. Naval maneuvers are frequently multinational, involving NATO or other Latin American countries. SOUTHCOM directs land exercises, and the U.S. Forces Caribbean directs naval maneuvers. On several occasions major naval maneuvers have overlapped with land exercises, bringing 33,000 U.S. troops to the region in May 1984, with the coincidence of Ocean Venture '84 in the Caribbean and Grenadero I in Honduras. In April 1985, two exercises, Big Pine III and Universal Trek '85, brought a total of 9,000 troops to Honduras.

The military exercises are part and parcel of the Reagan administration's commitment to expand U.S. military might worldwide and to maximize capabilities for intervention. Officially, the purpose of the exercises is to improve the capabilities of local militaries to resist attack and insurgency and to train U.S. troops. In reality, they serve several other purposes as well: to acquaint U.S. troops with local conditions and local troops; and to provide opportunities to develop, test, and evaluate a number of military options. In Honduras they are a cover for constructing the facilities needed for deployment of U.S. combat troops; in Central America and the Caribbean they are a means for threatening Nicaragua and the guerrilla forces in El Salvador. In March 1984, at the time of the Salvadoran presidential elections, U.S. military exercises in Honduras doubled the number of U.S. troops there to 1,700 as a "warning" to the guerrillas; at the same time, as well as sporadically throughout the year, U.S. aircraft carriers, battleships, frigates, and hovercraft were deployed to the coastal waters surrounding Central America in show-the-flag missions. On numerous occasions the U.S. military has flown high-ranking officials from Honduras, El Salvador, Guatemala, Costa Rica, and Panama out for shipboard visits, providing opportunities for them to confer with one another and with their U.S. counterparts, and for exhibitions of U.S. military might. The U.S. naval presence and U.S. military exercises were kept in low profile only during the fall 1984 months of the U.S. presidential campaign.

The exercises in Honduras differ from U.S. military maneuvers in other parts of

---

*Excerpts from *Invasion: A Guide to the U.S. Military Presence in Central America*, 1985 (NARMIC/AFSC).

the world in that they have been continuous; they have been announced only a few days prior to their beginning; they involve construction which has permanently improved Honduran military facilities; and they have left huge quantities of military equipment behind. The military maneuvers provide training to tens of thousands of U.S. troops, including practice in paratroop drops, mock air assaults, construction, evacuation, mining waters, and amphibious landings. They have paralleled the growth of the CIA-sponsored covert war against the Sandinistas in Nicaragua; some of the U.S.-built facilities and U.S. equipment have been used for the covert war. For many U.S. troops the Honduran exercises are their first Third World experience. Since summer 1983, the number of U.S. troops in Honduras has not dropped below 700–800 and has often been as high as several thousand.

Puerto Rico plays an increasingly important role in the exercises in Central America and in the Caribbean Sea. Commodore Diego Hernandez, commander in 1983 of U.S. naval forces in the Caribbean headquartered at Roosevelt Roads Naval Station, Puerto Rico, described Roosevelt Roads as where "the orchestra rehearses together just before playing for the public. . . ." Vieques, an offshore island of Puerto Rico, long a weapons testing site for the U.S. military and practice ground for maneuvers in the Caribbean Sea, is the location of repeated practice of invasion, mining, evacuation, and weapons testing. Ocean Venture '81 featured a simulated invasion of an eastern Caribbean island designated "Amber in the Amberdines" on Vieques; the exercise rehearsed an invasion and the rescue of hostages, followed by the setting up of a pro-U.S. government. This exercise forecast the invasion of Grenada two years later.

MILITARY MANEUVERS IN THE CARIBBEAN SEA AND CENTRAL AMERICA BEGINNING SUMMER 1983

Big Pine II—August 6, 1983, to February 5, 1984
The longest military exercise held in Honduras, Big Pine II brought a total of 10,000 U.S. troops—as many as 5,000 U.S. troops at one time—to Honduras. The exercise included military training in interdiction and counterinsurgency techniques, airlifts, an amphibious landing similar to the invasion of Grenada, and vast construction projects.

Small Scale Emergency Readiness Exercises—late March 1984
These "no notice" exercises involved U.S. and Honduran troops. U.S. Special Forces from Panama trained with Honduran soldiers. The exercise involved troops picking up weapons and moving to the field to test their ability to respond in a crisis.

Kilo Punch—March 24, 1984
Starting with a paratroop drop from C-130s by a unit from the 82nd Airborne Division near Palmerola Air Base, Honduras, 350 U.S. and 130 Honduran troops proceeded to San Lorenzo Air Base for combined airborne and air assault practice.

Fuerzas Unidas—April 1984
National Guard units from Louisiana, Florida, and Puerto Rico, along with personnel from the 193rd Infantry Brigade and the Panama Defense Force, joined in Panama for a road-building exercise.

Grenadero I—April 1–June 30, 1984
This exercise took place in Honduras, mostly at Cucuyagua near the Salvadoran border and Jamastran near the Nicaraguan border. In the first phase U.S. Army engineers constructed C-130-capable airstrips at Cucuyagua and Jamastran; the second phase included joint practice of airborne and helicopter assault operations. Panamanian, Guatemalan, and Salvadoran armed forces were invited to join U.S. and Honduran troops; only the Salvadorans accepted.

Lightning II—April 13, 1984
This paratroop drop near Aquacate, Honduras, involved 170 Honduran special forces and 120 U.S. Army troops; its purpose was "to secure an operations base from which to stage an assault on an airfield."

Ocean Venture '84—April 20–May 6, 1984
Involving 30,000 personnel from all branches of the U.S. military and costing $25 million, this naval exercise took place in the Caribbean Sea, Straits of Florida, Gulf of Mexico, and the Atlantic Ocean. Taking part were the aircraft carrier *America* and 350 support ships, including a frigate, a guided missile destroyer, and an oil tanker. The exercise included the evacuation of 300 people from the U.S. naval base at Guantanamo Bay, Cuba, live-fire training on the island of Vieques, and mock bombing runs and aerial dogfight exercises in the Gulf of Mexico off Tampa.

King's Guard—April 26–May 7, 1984
This coastal surveillance exercise in the Gulf of Fonseca involved 500 U.S., 75 Honduran, and 100 Salvadoran personnel, two U.S. destroyers, and patrol boats, officially for practice in interdiction techniques.

Unitas XXV—June 15–November, 1984
Involving military units from the United States, Brazil, Chile, Colombia, Ecuador, Paraguay, Peru, Uruguay, and Venezuela, these exercises were held in the Caribbean Sea, the western Atlantic and eastern Pacific oceans. Officially they were to "promote hemispheric solidarity and foster good will and military professionalism among participating countries." Unitas XXV included six U.S. Navy ships, the newly recommissioned battleship U.S.S. *Iowa,* a destroyer, a guided missile frigate, an amphibious tank-landing ship, two submarines, and airplanes and helicopters from SOUTHCOM and from bases in the United States. Port visits were made to ten South American nations and Caribbean islands, during which the task group engaged in bilateral and multilateral operations with the navies and air forces of the coastal nations.

Operation Lempira—Phase 1, July 23–August 6, 1984
This counterinsurgency exercise based in west central Honduras involved a small team of U.S. Army Green Berets and troops from the Honduran army's 10th infantry battalion. The official purpose of the exercise was to "improve the skills of U.S. and Honduran personnel to deploy and operate in realistic conditions, usually on very short notice." It included a parachute jump near Palmerola Air Base and a mock helicopter attack at Marcala.

Operation Lempira—Phase 2, August 20–31, 1984
This counterinsurgency exercise based in the mountainous areas west and southwest of Comayagua, Honduras, involved nearly 200 U.S. Green Berets and three battalions of the Honduran army, and included a parachute drop near Palmerola Air Base. Its official purpose was to give counterinsurgency forces experience in rapid deployment tactics "under combined operating conditions."

Crown Dragonfly—September 22–27, 1984
Four U.S. A-37 planes and eight from the Honduran air force practiced bombing runs using dummy noise bombs near San Pedro Sula and Palmerola Air Base.

Army Preventive Medicine Exercise—September 1984–end of 1984
Army medical teams of about two dozen soldiers each were deployed for two-week tours to the hospital at Palmerola Air Base, Honduras.

Air Force Exercise—October 28–November 17, 1984
A-37 attack planes from the Pennsylvania Air National Guard and observation planes from Howard Air Force Base, Panama, participated in exercises in Honduras at Palmerola Air Base, La Mesa, near the Guatemalan border, and San Lorenzo, near the Nicaraguan border.

High Altitude Training—November 1–15, 1984
Four U.S. helicopters and crew from Howard Air Force Base, Panama, trained in Costa Rica; the helicopters were used to assist the Costa Rican National Park Service and in a joint "nation-building" activity with the Costa Rican Civil Guard.

Composite Training Unit Exercise 1-85—November 1–19, 1984
These maneuvers in the Caribbean Sea and western Atlantic Ocean involved twenty-five U.S. Navy warships including the battleship U.S.S. *Iowa,* several cruisers, destroyers, frigates, minesweepers, auxiliary vessels, an ammunition ship, and two attack submarines. In addition to the U.S. fleet, two ships from the Netherlands and one each from West Germany, Canada, and Britain practiced antiair, antisubmarine, and antisurface maneuvers, including live firing.

Naval Exercise—November 6, 1984
Led by the U.S. guided missile destroyer, *MacDonough,* this exercise involved U.S. Navy units and the coast guards of Barbados, Antigua, St. Lucia, Dominica, and St. Vincent.

Medical Exercise—November 7–20, 1984
A medical clearing company from Fort Stewart, Georgia, which would conduct triage in wartime, trained at Palmerola Air Base, Honduras.

Engineering Exercise—November 7–20, 1984
About 120 engineers from Fort Bragg, North Carolina, built roads at Palmerola Air Base, Honduras, and built and resurfaced dirt airstrips.

Patrolling Exercises—November 7–20, 1984
A company of 150 to 180 infantry troops from Fort Hood, Texas, conducted patrolling exercises near Palmerola.

King's Guard—November 8–19, 1984
This exercise in the Gulf of Fonseca involved a U.S. ship and several hundred U.S., Honduran, and Salvadoran troops. According to the Pentagon, a small contingent of U.S. military personnel were to be deployed to El Salvador for "command and control" purposes. The exercise was officially designed to practice interdiction techniques.

Minute Man II—January–May 1985
Members of the Panama Defense Forces, 193rd Infantry Brigade, and units of the U.S. National Guard from Puerto Rico, Louisiana, Missouri, Alabama, Florida, Texas, New Jersey, and other states joined to construct about twenty-seven kilometers of roadway on the Azuero Peninsula, Panama. Up to 1,600 National Guard personnel were involved at any one time. Special units provided command, logistical, military police, communications, and medical support. U.S. participation was funded from money earmarked for U.S. Army National Guard training exercises, while the Panama Defense Forces paid for fuel and materials.

Kindle Liberty '85—February 4–13, 1985
An annually held, joint SOUTHCOM-Panama Defense Forces exercise series, Kindle Liberty '85, was conducted outside the immediate Panama Canal area in order to add "realism to the guerrilla insurgency scenario." There was ground, air, and sea activity; U.S. troops from SOUTHCOM were augmented by units of the U.S. Readiness Command and the Atlantic Command. A total of 4,000 U.S. and Panamanian military personnel took part.

Universal Trek '85—April 12–27, 1985
On the northeastern coast of Honduras 3,000 U.S. troops practiced an amphibious landing with support from attack helicopters and a guided missile ship, destroyer, and frigate. A total of 7,000 troops participated in the exercise.

Big Pine III—February 11–May 3, 1985
Eleven weeks of joint U.S.-Honduran military maneuvers involving 2,200 U.S. troops, including units of the U.S. National Guard. The exercises included construction and improvement of runways and aprons at Cucuyagua, near the Salvadoran border, and

at San Lorenzo, near the Nicaraguan border, extending tank obstacles in the border region between Honduras and Nicaragua, counter-insurgency training in Yoro province, and antitank maneuvers near San Lorenzo. M60A3 tanks and M113 armored personnel carriers were flown to Honduras for the antitank maneuvers.

Two members of the Pennsylvania National Guard were killed when their plane crashed while on a training flight during Big Pine III.

During one week in April Universal Trek '85 and Big Pine III overlapped, bringing a total of 5,300 U.S. troops to Honduras at one time.

*41. Honduras Changed into a U.S. Fortress**

By Richard Beene

Nowhere in Honduras is the U.S. military presence more apparent than at Palmerola Air Force Base, nerve center for the Reagan administration's strategy to contain communism in Central America by projecting U.S. military power.

Nestled in a fertile farming valley forty-two miles northwest of the Honduran capital of Tegucigalpa, Palmerola is home to American intelligence units and U.S. reconnaissance planes that routinely fly missions over El Salvador in search of leftist guerrillas fighting the U.S.-backed government.

From here, U.S. officials keep an eye on the tense Nicaraguan frontier and coordinate joint war games designed to convert the long neglected Honduran armed forces into a fighting machine capable of fending off possible aggression from the Sandinista government in Managua.

If U.S. combat troops were to fight in the jungles of Central America, their actions would be coordinated from here, headquarters for Joint Task Force Bravo, the U.S. high command in Honduras.

"Clearly this is not Vietnam," says Col. Charles Pearcy, head of the task force. "All you have to do is look on a map and see that. We are here to demonstrate U.S. resolve in this region that is clearly important to U.S. national security interests and to demonstrate support for our friends and allies."

In name, Palmerola remains a Honduran air force facility. But the vast majority of troops are U.S., and the C-130 transport planes and helicopters parked on the 8,000-foot-long airstrip bear the markings of the U.S. Air Force and Air National Guard.

As part of the Reagan administration's plan to convert Honduras into a fortress against Communist inroads in Central America, the U.S. Congress has allocated about

*From the *Dallas Times Herald,* November 26, 1984.

$13 million to lengthen Palmerola's runway, improve access roads, and build storage facilities.

Palmerola is just one of a series of U.S. military bases in Honduras that extend from the Gulf of Fonseca in the south to a Green Beret training center for Honduran troops near the northern Pacific coastal town of Trujillo.

The bases have been built and steadily improved since the United States began a series of almost continuous military maneuvers with Honduran forces two years ago.

The largest of the war games, called Big Pine II, ran for six months and involved about 6,000 U.S. troops at a cost of $75 million. Small maneuvers followed, and Pentagon planners are gearing up for Big Pine III next spring.

The exercises have pumped millions of dollars of U.S. military aid into Honduras, creating an impressive network of bases: Palmerola—Base for a 300-member military intelligence unit from Hunter Army Airfield near Savannah, Georgia, as well as a field hospital equipped to handle almost any kind of war injury. La Ceiba—On the northern Pacific coast the United States is spending $8 million to build taxiways and ramp space at Goloson air base.

Trujillo: Congress last year authorized funds to build a regional military training center staffed by U.S. Special Forces to train Honduran and Salvadoran troops. Critics charge the Pentagon is using the training center to circumvent the 55-person limit on U.S. military advisers to El Salvador.

U.S. troops maintain two radar facilities in Honduras, one near Tegucigalpa at Cerro la Mole and the other on Tiger Island in the Gulf of Fonseca, the body of water where the southern borders of Honduras, Nicaragua, and El Salvador converge. The radar stations are used to electronically monitor East-bloc arms shipments to Nicaragua and the movement of Salvadoran guerrillas.

U.S. funds have been used to build and repair a number of airstrips, including one at Aguacate, base of Central Intelligence Agency operations in support of the Nicaraguan *contra* guerrillas. A 3,000-foot-long dirt runway capable of accommodating C-130 cargo planes was built at San Lorenzo and another dirt airstrip was constructed at Jamastran, another *contra* staging area.

The Pentagon earlier proposed spending $160 million to build a port and airfield at Puerto Castilla on the northern coast. The proposal was withdrawn under heavy congressional criticism, but may be reintroduced next year. A large U.S. base at Puerto Castilla could become a candidate for the next headquarters of the U.S. Southern Command, currently based in Panama.

Critics charge the U.S. buildup threatens to drag the United States and Honduras into direct conflict with either Nicaragua or the leftist Salvadoran guerrillas forty-five miles to the south.

And critics say the U.S. role is reminiscent of the gradual American buildup in Thailand in the 1960s that eventually led to the commitment of 500,000 U.S. troops in Vietnam.

U.S. officials reject the parallels to Southeast Asia and insist their role is limited to helping Honduras build an adequate deterrent force to possible aggression from neighboring Nicaragua.

Sensitive to the comparisons to Vietnam, the Pentagon has taken steps to make sure U.S. forces in Honduras keep a low profile.

U.S. facilities have been constructed in the remote Honduran countryside, and weekend passes into Tegucigalpa are rare for most of the 1,500 U.S. soldiers stationed in Honduras, although some do end up at the Hotel Honduras Maya and other establishments in the capital. And U.S. troops are told not to wear combat fatigues when on leave in urban centers.

''We have had the foresight to put our troops in isolated areas,'' said one official who asked to remain anonymous. ''They lecture them ad nauseam to behave themselves. So far we have had only one incident of trouble.''

That came earlier this year when two GIs driving a rental car accidentally hit a student at a busy crosswalk near the National University in Tegucigalpa, seriously injuring him. A group of students overturned and burned the car after the soldiers were rescued by Honduran police.

The university has now been declared off-limits to U.S. troops on leave in the Honduran capital.

While the Pentagon does not consider any of the U.S. facilities in Honduras ''permanent,'' critics charge it is only a matter of time before the Reagan administration proposes permanently stationing U.S. soldiers in Honduras.

There also have been charges that U.S. construction projects have been conducted without congressional approval.

The General Accounting Office charged in June that some Pentagon funding projects had violated federal law because they were carried out without congressional oversight.

In a recent interview with *Common Cause* magazine, Rep. Lee Hamilton (D., Ind.) charged the U.S. buildup was a result of ''a group within the administration that wants to win a military victory in Central America . . . and is going to push the law to its limits to get the support and resources down there that they think they need.''

Among Honduran businessmen profiting from the influx of U.S. dollars, there is a feeling that the U.S. buildup has just begun, that it will soon ''take off'' now that President Reagan has been reelected.

In the small farming town of Comayagua a short drive from the Palmerola base, business is booming at ''The Rose,'' a favorite brothel for U.S. troops.

On a typical night, dozens of U.S. soldiers at Palmerola make their way into Comayagua for a date ''with the ladies'' at a cost of 40 lempiras—roughly $20.

''I don't know hardly anyone from the base who hasn't been here,'' said one Army recruit. ''We hardly ever get passes into Tegucigalpa, so this is where we hang out.''

To prevent the spread of venereal disease among the troops, the U.S. medical facility at Palmerola performs weekly checkups on the prostitutes at ''The Rose.'' The women are issued passportlike books that bear the dates of their last examination.

"All you do is look in their book to make sure they are clean," said one Marine. "It's a good system, as safe as you can get."

For John, a Canadian who owns "The Rose," the future has never been brighter.

"With the Big Pine III maneuvers coming up, things are really going to take off," he said. "Before you know it, there will be one-year tours of duty down here."

*42. The Road from Switzerland to Honduras: The Militarization of Costa Rica**

By Alan Hruska

"Costa Rica, the Switzerland of Central America," proudly proclaims the inviting tourist poster at the airport in San José. Based on their shared attributes of mountainous beauty, political stability, and lack of an army, the parallel has fit for a long time. But recent events in Costa Rica are rapidly souring the cheerful comparison. Costa Rica's physical beauty remains, but the country is beginning to feel less like Switzerland, and more like Honduras, which has become a garrison for U.S. military strength in Central America. The rapid militarization of Costa Rica threatens to drag the historically pacifist country deeper into war with its northern neighbor Nicaragua and endangers the country's internal political stability.

Costa Rica has been without an army since 1949 when the armed forces were dismantled and the constitution prohibited their reestablishment. The absence of an army has been the centerpiece of Costa Rica's tradition of pacifist democracy, of which many Costa Ricans are proud.

The U.S. government has long provided security assistance to Costa Rica and has periodically urged it to create an army. Although Costa Rica has usually accepted aid to train police, it has, until recently, declined military aid.

The United States provided police training for Costa Ricans throughout the 1960s, both at the International Police Academy in Washington, D.C., where 122 police officers received training, and at the U.S. Army School of the Americas in Panama, where 1,639 Costa Ricans received training in counterinsurgency.

In 1963, in the wake of the Cuban revolution, the United States helped to establish CONDECA, the Central American Defense Council *(Consejo de Defensa Centroamericano)*. The council brought together the armies of El Salvador, Honduras, Guatemala, and Nicaragua to coordinate activities, share information, and to centralize military command for the region, with a strong U.S. role. Despite not having an army, Costa Rica was persuaded to join CONDECA in 1966 and participated in

---

*An unpublished manuscript based on information from CRISIS (Costa Rican Information Service in Solidarity) bulletin.

planning meetings and joint military exercises with its police. Public reaction, however, quickly put a brake on this attempt to militarize Costa Rica. Public opinion was strongly opposed to Costa Rica's participation in CONDECA and especially objected to becoming partners with Nicaragua's dictator, Somoza, who was feared and hated by most Costa Ricans. Due to the public outcry, Costa Rica withdrew from CONDECA in 1967, but maintained its status as an "observer."

After U.S. fears of Latin American revolutions subsided in the late 1960s, the pressure to increase military aid to Costa Rica quieted. Security assistance from the United States to Costa Rica ended in 1967 and did not resume during the 1970s. In July 1975, the Foreign Assistance Act of 1961 was amended to prohibit the use of aid to train or advise foreign public security forces, killing any chances to renew security assistance to Costa Rica.

The July 1979 victory of the Sandinistas in Nicaragua and subsequent U.S. talk of communism in the region once again fueled the heat on Costa Rica to militarize. Initially the administration of Costa Rican President Monge resisted the pressure to accept military aid: He turned down the U.S. ambassador's offer to train Civil Guard members at the Regional Military Training Center (CREM) in Honduras, denied the U.S. Navy permission to conduct maneuvers in Salinas Bay on the Costa Rican-Nicaraguan Pacific border, and declined invitations to participate in CONDECA "war games" and to visit the U.S. aircraft carrier *Ranger*. But he did accept $30,000 in 1981, and $50,000 in 1982, in security assistance from the United States, through the International Military and Education Program, resuming U.S. military assistance to Costa Rica for the first time in thirteen years.

U.S. pressure on Costa Rica intensified throughout the early 1980s. At one point, U.S. Ambassador to the United Nations Jeane Kirkpatrick, exasperated with Costa Rica's lack of cooperation, suggested that the United States cut off all aid to Costa Rica until the country established an army. But while U.S. pressure mounted, it appeared that the Costa Rican resolve would hold. In November 1983, President Monge made an official declaration of Costa Rican neutrality, and 50,000 citizens turned out to support him.

But forces within Costa Rica began a campaign of their own to overcome Monge's antimilitarization position. In early 1984, a smear campaign was launched against the minister of public security, Angel Solano, an outspoken proponent of neutrality and dialogue with Nicaragua. In July 1984, a group of right-wing groups issued a statement giving President Monge thirty days to fire Minister Solano, break diplomatic relations with Nicaragua, and get tough with internal social movements. In less than a month every member of Monge's cabinet was asked to resign, including Minister Solano. Appointed in his place was Benjamin Piza Escalante, founder of the fascist Free Costa Rica Movement *(Movimiento Costa Rica Libre)*.

In 1984 Costa Rica became more receptive to U.S. overtures, and U.S. military assistance to Costa Rica skyrocketed. From zero in 1980, U.S. military aid to Costa Rica went to $18.35 million for the years 1984–1985. In March 1985, the Foreign Aid Authorization Bill for 1986 included a waiver specifically for Costa Rica from the ban on U.S. assistance for training police.

A large part of the $18.35 million has been spent on uniforms, personnel carriers, boats, helicopters, ammunition, and arms, including M-16 rifles, 40mm grenade launchers, machine guns, and mortars, described as the "first lethal aid provided by the United States since its Costa Rican security assistance program began in 1981."

These arms and the establishment in May 1985 of a military training camp run by U.S. Green Berets just ten miles from the Nicaraguan border are bringing into serious question the validity of Costa Rica's claim of "perpetual unarmed neutrality." The camp, set up on a huge ranch that was a vacation property of the former Nicaraguan dictator Somoza is staffed by twenty-four Green Beret special forces instructors who will train a 750-man Costa Rican "rapid reaction" unit. The unit is officially described as a "paramilitary police force to face the threat of a spillover from Central American conflicts." President Monge strenuously denied accusations that Costa Rica had departed from its thirty-seven-year-old policy as a nation without an army, after a Spanish-language broadcast from the Voice of America had described the counterinsurgency training program in May 1985 as the formation of "the first military unit in Costa Rica since it dismantled its army in 1949."

The establishment and secrecy of the training camp drew sharp protest from some members of the Legislative Assembly. One deputy, Alvaro Montero, charged that the presence of U.S. military personnel in Costa Rica violates the nation's constitution. When CBS and ABC television crews went to film the arrival of the Green Berets, they were permitted to film the arrival on the condition that the videos "not be shown on Costa Rican TV, because it might upset the public."

There are signs that the increased military support for Costa Rica may lead not only to deeper conflict with Nicaragua, but to repression of domestic protest as well. In April 1985, 300 demonstrators blocked streets in Guadalupe to protest the fact that they had been without water for over a month. The protest was met by hundreds of well-equiped riot squads, who used tear gas to disperse the demonstrators, then pursued them into a Catholic church where they were dragged out and arrested for obstructing public roads.

Costa Rica's claim of "unarmed neutrality" is seriously questioned by the open use of Costa Rican territory for training and refuge for *contras* attacking Nicaragua. In April 1985, fifteen *contras,* including one French, two American, and two British mercenaries were arrested in Costa Rica after they had drifted into cattle rustling. One of the arrested, British mercenary Peter Glibbery, said that the group had seen the Rural Guard come to the *contra* camp, but weren't worried, because some of them had often visited the camp before. "They were telling us what base to attack and where everything was. They gave us all our information," he said of the guard. Responding to questions about the incident, Minister of Public Security Benjamin Piza said, "I cannot guarantee that a couple of our men might not have been involved with the *contras* without our knowledge."

In April 1985, Holland withdrew $750,000 that it had budgeted for refugee projects in Costa Rica, citing statements made to a Dutch journalist by an armed Nicaraguan in a northern Costa Rican refugee camp. The Nicaraguan swore his support for the *contras* and vowed to return to the fight as soon as possible.

Finally, Costa Rican President Monge flew to Washington in April 1985 and met with President Reagan. During his visit, Monge pledged his support for Reagan's plan to fund the *contras,* as long as the aid was not spent on military supplies, explaining that this "would be contrary to Costa Rica's neutrality."

Asked how President Monge's support for the *contras* fit with the claim of "unarmed neutrality," Communications Minister Armando Vargas said, "Neutrality is a military concept. But ideologically, morally, and politically, we are not neutral."

43. Blueprint for Disaster*

By Rear Admiral Gene R. LaRocque, U.S. Navy (Ret.) and Lieutenant Colonel John H. Buchanan, U.S. Marine Corps (Ret.)

Rear Admiral Gene R. La Roque, U.S. Navy (Ret.), is the director of the Center for Defense Information in Washington, D.C. Lieutenant Colonel John H. Buchanan, U.S. Marine Corps (Ret.), is a senior analyst at the center.

July 4, 1985. 3:45 A.M.

After weeks of stepped-up *contra* activity, Nicaraguan government forces accidentally cross the border into Honduras in "hot pursuit" of the anti-Sandinista raiders. The Honduran government, briefed in advance by U.S. intelligence, requests military assistance from Washington. Under the guise of conducting the latest Big Pine (Ahaus Tara) exercise, U.S. troops are already in position. Two hours before dawn, naval gunfire from an eleven-ship carrier battle group and a battleship-led surface action group begins to pound the beaches along Nicaragua's Pacific coast. At the same time, another carrier battle group opens fire on the Caribbean beaches along the country's east coast. Operation Founding Fathers—the U.S. invasion of Nicaragua—has begun.

During the last few days, SR-71 Blackbird reconaissance planes have gathered high- and low-level photographic and infrared data on Nicaragua's meager antiaircraft defenses—mostly 57mm and 37mm guns. When the invasion itself begins, shortly before dawn, fighter and attack aircraft from the carriers take these guns out almost immediately, paving the way for an air attack on Nicaraguan military facilities. Though a Pentagon spokesman has described a potential U.S. invasion as "mostly air strikes against major facilities," Nicaragua is too poor to have more than a handful, and this portion of the invasion is soon over.

Also using SR-71 data to guide them, U.S. Air Force A-10 Thunderbolts begin firing Coke-bottle-sized armor-piercing bullets at a rate of 4,200 shots per minute, systematically destroying Nicaraguan tanks and antipersonnel carriers. The Thunder-

*From the *Village Voice,* June 25, 1985.

bolts concentrate much of their fire on the Punta Huete airfield. (Punta Huete is the new 10,000-foot concrete runway that the Nicaraguans and Cubans constructed twenty miles northeast of Managua; it can handle the largest bombers and transport aircraft.) After the field has been "softened up," 1,600 Rangers of the 75th Infantry, airlifted from Fort Benning, Georgia, parachute in, followed closely by the Division-Ready Brigade of the 82nd Airborne Division (4,000 combat-ready soldiers with their essential assault equipment), which has been airlifted from Pope Air Force Base in North Carolina.

Due to the efforts of carrier-based EA 6B electronic jamming aircraft, Nicaraguan radar has been rendered useless. Radio and television links with the outside world have also been severed, though a select "pool" of Pentagon reporters accompanies two marine amphibious units (about 4,500 marines with 60 helicopters, 10 M-60 tanks, and 24 amphibious landing craft) as they seize the seaport of El Bluff and the airport of Bluefields on the east coast of Nicaragua. Their counterparts on the Pacific coast (16,500 marines, 120 helicopters, 20 M-60 tanks, and 45 amphibious landing craft) meet much stiffer resistance. But after sustaining heavy losses, the marine amphibious brigade succeeds in taking the airfield at Montelimar and the seaport of Puerto Sandino.

The 3,500 soldiers, 48 M-60 tanks, and 60 infantry fighting vehicles of the 24th Mechanized Division smash their way south, cutting off the Sandinistas' access to the Pan American Highway, while 12,000 to 15,000 *contras* sweep down from Honduras. The tiny Nicaraguan air force, caught in a surprise attack on Sandino International Airport, is helpless to stop either the *contras* or the 6,000 soldiers and 200 helicopters of the U.S. 101st Air Assault Division, who slice down the center of the country from the north.

Following a policy of letting Nicaraguans kill Nicaraguans whenever possible, U.S. forces stay out of Managua. The only exception is the 1st Special Forces Operational Detachment Delta (best known for its disastrous attempt to rescue U.S. hostages in Iran in 1980), which slipped into the capital the night before the invasion to kill or capture as many high-ranking Sandinistas as possible.

After the first two weeks Nicaragua's airports, seaports, and riverports are under U.S. control. Water and air transport are blocked. Managua's single water pipeline is in U.S. hands; the city's food supply has been cut off. All forms of communication—radio, telegraph, telephone, television, and newspapers—are strictly censored by U.S. authorities.

Because Nicaragua (unlike Vietnam) is so close to U.S. medical facilities, only 1,500 Americans are killed during the first two weeks (7,560 are wounded). The figures for the more poorly armed Sandinistas are much higher: 6,300 dead and 37,800 wounded.

In the second two-week period U.S. forces establish their presence throughout the country and combat a relatively high level of insurgency and sabotage. Once the main military objectives are secured, there is little the surviving Sandinistas can do to mount effective counterattacks. They begin to exhaust their existing stock of munitions and have no way to replace them. Nicaragua has no equivalent of Vietnam's Ho Chi Minh Trail, which can be used to deliver significant amounts of arms and ammunition to the Sandinistas. Owing to its peculiar geographical position, with oceans on two sides and U.S. allies on the other two, Nicaragua is relatively easy for American forces to police.

Estimates of U.S. casualties for the second two-week period are 380 killed in action, 2,270 wounded, and 75 nonbattle fatalities (from road accidents and weapons mishaps). Nicaragua has 1,890 killed and 9,450 wounded.

During the following three months U.S. forces continue to expand their presence throughout Nicaragua as the Sandinistas continue to exhaust their resources—men and women combatants, weapons, munitions, and supplies. In this period U.S. forces face continuous low-level sabotage and insurgency.

The United States also begins to withdraw its assault forces (marines, airborne, and air assault) and establish an occupation army with elements of the light infantry division (motorized) and the light divisions. These soldiers fight the guerrillas mostly on foot—individually and in small teams—in cities, towns, and countryside. Some armored, mechanized, artillery, and helicopter elements remain with them to provide support as needed.

U.S. casualties for this three-month period are 430 killed and 2,160 wounded. Nicaragua suffers 1,800 killed and 10,800 wounded.

In the succeeding three and half to four years the United States tries to establish and legitimize a Nicaraguan government more to its liking. U.S. Army Special Forces (Green Berets) will become deeply involved in training a "new" Nicaraguan army. But the Sandinistas continue guerrilla operations in Nicaragua and neighboring countries for many years, forcing 8,000 to 10,000 Americans to keep fighting a low-grade, festering guerilla campaign. Another 1,580 Americans die in the Nicaraguan war; another 7,920 are wounded. The Sandinistas lose 6,600 guerillas and supporters killed and 39,600 wounded, but the fighting continues.

By July 4, 1989, the war has cost Americans about $2 billion for munitions and supplies and another $2 billion to replace the jets, helicopters, tanks, and other equipment, for a total of about $4 billion. Restoring Nicaragua's economy, which has been totally destroyed by the war, costs another $6 billion, bringing the cost of Operation Founding Fathers to about $10 billion. It has also cost over 20,000 Nicaraguan and American lives. And the fighting continues.

Chapter III:

Legal, Diplomatic, and Economic Facets of the War

Editors' Introduction

Like all wars, the one being waged by the United States against Nicaragua is more than just military. Earlier chapters in this part dealt with the military situation; this chapter focuses on the U.S. strategies designed to complement the *contra* war.

The first reading is the May 10, 1984 ruling by the International Court of Justice (World Court) ordering the United States to "cease and refrain" from a variety of actions taken against the Republic of Nicaragua. The next article, by Dr. Richard Ullman, professor of international affairs at Princeton University, examines the Reagan administration's decision to deny the World Court's jurisdiction over any disputes involving the United States and the nations of Central America. Also included is a tabulation of instances of possible violations of law by the Reagan administration.

The next three readings focus on the economic dimension of U.S. policy toward Nicaragua. Professor Michael Conroy reviews political and economic policies designed to disrupt or injure the economy of Nicaragua. Foremost among those policies, in terms of public awareness, is the economic embargo imposed by President Reagan on May 1, 1985. The president pleaded that "the policies and actions of the government of Nicaragua constitute an unusual and extraordinary threat to the national security and foreign policy of the United States," and declared a state of national emergency to respond to that threat. On that basis, he was able to impose the embargo without submitting it to Congress as proposed legislation. Included is the text of his executive order and message to Congress declaring the embargo and state of emergency. This is followed by an article by the *Financial Times* of London arguing that the embargo's impact, less than anticipated, was more symbolic than economic. John B. Oakes then compares this policy to the Brezhnev Doctrine of 1968.

The Reagan administration, of course, needs public and congressional support in order to carry out its policies. To that end, the administration has had to undertake a public relations campaign to marshal public opinion. On November 14, 1984, for instance, shortly after the "MiG scare" proved to be unfounded, the *New York Times* reported that:

> Administration officials said today that presenting Nicaragua as a potential base for the projection of Soviet power in the hemisphere was part of an effort to persuade Congress and the public that the United States should resume support to Nicaraguan rebels and apply diplomatic and military pressure on Nicaragua to change its behavior.[1]

The article by Robert Borosage and Peter Kornbluh of the Washington-based Institute for Policy Studies describes what they call "Reagan's propaganda blitz."

The major diplomatic initiative for peace in the Central American region is known by the name of the island where representatives from Mexico, Venezuela, Colombia, and Panama first met to organize it—Contadora. The reading by Phillip Berryman describes the Contadora process, for which the U.S. State Department has publicly expressed great support (see reading 12). Yet, the National Security Council document that follows, leaked to the *Washington Post,* reveals that the Reagan administration has secretly sought to undermine Contadora.

The Reagan administration has not succeeded entirely in marshaling public support for its Nicaragua policy: public opinion polls have consistently shown that more than 50 percent of the American people oppose administration policy. The final reading, "The War at Home," describes the organized opposition to that policy in the United States.

Notes

1. Philip Taubman, "U.S. Seeks to Sway Opinion on Nicaragua Policy," *New York Times,* November 14, 1984.

44. *The Decision of the World Court*

By the International Court of Justice

The court,

A. Unanimously,

Rejects the request made by the United States of America that the proceedings on the application filed by the Republic of Nicaragua on 9 April 1984, and on the request filed the same day by the Republic of Nicaragua for the indication of provisional measures, be terminated by the removal of the case from the list.

B. Indicates, pending its final decision in the proceedings instituted on 9 April 1984 by the Republic of Nicaragua against the United States of America, the following provisional measures:

1. Unanimously,

The United States of America should immediately cease and refrain from any action restricting, blocking or endangering access to or from Nicaraguan ports, and, in particular, the laying of mines.

2. By fourteen votes to one,

The right to sovereignty and to political independence possessed by the Republic of Nicaragua, like any other state of the region or of the world, should be fully respected and should not in any way be jeopardized by any military and paramilitary activities which are prohibited by principles of international law, in particular the principle that states should refrain in their international relations from the threat or use of force against the territorial integrity or the political independence of any state, and the principle concerning the duty not to intervene in matters within the domestic jurisdiction of a state, principlcs cmbodied in the United Nations Charter and the Charter of the Organization of American States.

In Favor: President Elias, Vice-President Sette-Camara, Judges Lachs, Morozov, Nagendra Singh, Ruda, Mosler, Oda, Ago, El Khani, Sir Robert Jennings, de Lacharriere, Mbaye, Bedjaoui.

Against: Judge Schwebel.

3. Unanimously,

The governments of the United States of America and the Republic of Nicaragua should each of them ensure that no action of any kind is taken which might aggravate or extend the dispute submitted to the court.

4. Unanimously,

The governments of the United States of America and the Republic of Nicaragua should each of them ensure that no action is taken which might prejudice the rights of the other party in respect of the carrying out of whatever decision the court may render in the case.

C. Unanimously,

Decides further that, until the court delivers its final judgment in the present case, it will keep the matters covered by this order continuously under review.

D. Unanimously,

Decides that the written proceedings shall first be addressed to the question of jurisdiction of the court to entertain the dispute and of the admissibility of the application,

And reserves the fixing of the time limits for the said written proceedings, and the subsequent procedure, for further decision.

Done in English and French, the English text being authoritative, at the Peace Palace, The Hague, this 10th day of May, 1984, in four copies, one of which will be placed in the archives of the court, and the others transmitted respectively to the government of the United States of America, the government of the Republic of Nicaragua, and the Secretary-General of the United Nations for transmission to the Security Council.

(Signed) T.O. Elias, President

(Signed) Santiago Torres Bernardez, Registrar

*45. World Court Evasion**

By Richard H. Ullman

Dr. Richard H. Ullman is professor of international affairs at Princeton University.

Like the American officer who ordered a Vietnamese village destroyed in order to save it, the Reagan administration is boycotting the World Court to prevent it from being "misused" by Nicaragua. That was the administration's justification for its abrupt declaration last weekend that its 1946 pledge to accept the court's jurisdiction "temporarily" no longer applies to disputes involving the United States and any of the countries of Central America.

The administration acted in what it hoped was the nick of time. Nicaragua was only hours away from going to the court with its contention that by mounting a scarcely covert war against Nicaragua—including, as officials concede the Central Intelligence Agency is now doing, laying mines in its harbors—the United States is violating international law.

For Nicaragua to ask the court to stop these operations would be, the State Department says, "to divert attention from the real issues in the region and to disrupt the on-going regional peace process by a protracted litigation of claims and counterclaims." Hauling the United States into court "would allow the Sandinistas to focus attention away from their own actions in El Salvador and in their own country."

George Orwell would not have been surprised at such language, nor at the State Department's explanation that refusing to go before the international tribunal "is a

*From the *New York Times,* April 11, 1984.

tactical litigation move, not a sign of disrespect for the court.'' So much for notions like the rule of law to which, in previous complaints against the Sandinistas and others of whom it disapproves, the Reagan administration has given such emphasis.

For Washington, the ''real issues'' are Managua's support of the insurgents in El Salvador and restrictions on civil liberties within Nicaragua itself. Not surprisingly, the Sandinistas see the issues differently. Whatever aid they may have given the 5,000 or so Salvadoran guerrillas pales by comparison with the C.I.A.-run mining and air strikes against Nicaragua and the 15,000-man army the agency has recruited, armed, and trained in Honduras to fight the Sandinistas across the border. The administration is now pressing Congress for another $21 million to keep the supposedly covert operations on track. Its bill to provide those funds bears a doublespeak label that would have choked even Orwell's dictators—the Central America Democracy, Peace and Development Initiative.

Nicaragua's lawyers argue that the administration cannot escape judgment because its move to deny the court jurisdiction requires six months' notice. If the court agrees, the way would be clear for the test of claims and counterclaims the administration hopes to avoid.

Given its contention that Nicaragua is violating international law by aiding the Salvadoran revolutionaries, the administration should not shun such a test—unless it fears that its case against the Sandinistas may not appear persuasive. (It has consistently refused to make public the evidence it says it has that large quantities of weapons from Nicaragua are somehow escaping intensive American, Salvadoran, and Honduran surveillance and reaching the rebels.)

The most cynical part of the administration's effort to remove itself from the reach of the court is its claim that litigation would ''disrupt the on-going regional peace process.'' One would never know from any of its recent statements that Nicaragua has joined the other Central American States and the four Contadora powers—Mexico, Panama, Colombia, and Venezuela—in agreeing to a framework of verifiable measures to assure that no state in the region would harbor or support groups that are destabilizing any of the others.

Rather than dismiss Managua's participation in the Contadora process as ''not serious,'' Washington should encourage Nicaragua—and the other countries of the region—to press ahead to develop the detailed procedures that would give reality to the framework.

Doing so, however, would risk having the process succeed. That would leave the administration face to face with the facts—that the insurgents in El Salvador (unlike the government) no longer depend upon outside support, and that only by forging a new relationship with the population can the Salvadoran security forces hope to forestall defeat. It would also deprive President Reagan and his associates of their *idée fixe* that tiny Nicaragua, with 100th the population of the United States, poses a major threat to the hemisphere's security.

The administration seems committed to bringing down the Sandinistas by force of arms. How inconvenient for international law to stand in the way.

46. *Possible Violations of Law**

By the Institute for Policy Studies

The following U.S. and international laws appear to have been violated by the Reagan administration's policies vis-à-vis Central America. This is by no means a comprehensive list. The laws compiled here represent those which

a) have been possibly violated by the direct conduct of U.S. policy inside Central America, and which simultaneously
b) have been misrepresented, circumvented, or ignored by administration officials during testimony before Congress.

Boland Amendment

Prohibits funding which would be used for the overthrow of the Nicaraguan government.

"None of the funds provided in this act may be used by the Central Intelligence Agency or the Department of Defense to furnish military equipment, military training or advice, or other support for military activities for the purpose of overthrowing the government of Nicaragua or provoking a military exchange between Nicaragua and Honduras."

The Defense Appropriations Act of 1984

Limits FY84 funding for military or paramilitary operations against Nicaragua to $24 million.

Section 775

"During fiscal year 1984, not more than $24 million of the funds available to the CIA, the Department of Defense, or any other agency or entity of the United States involved in intelligence activities may be obligated or expended for the purpose of which could have the effect of supporting, directly or indirectly, military or paramilitary operations in Nicaragua by any nation, group, organization, movement or individuals."

Suspension of Aid to Contras

Prohibits aid for operations against Nicaragua in fiscal year 1985. This ban could be lifted only if both houses of Congress vote after February 1985 to authorize resumption of such aid.

"During FY 1985, no funds available to the Central Intelligence Agency, the Department of Defense, or any other agency or entity of the United States involved in

*Excerpts from *In Contempt of Congress* (Washington, D.C.: Institute for Policy Studies, 1985).

intelligence activities may be obligated or expended for the purpose of which would have the effect of supporting, directly or indirectly, military or paramilitary operations in Nicaragua by any nation, group, organization, movement or individual.''

Intelligence Oversight Act

Requires that Congress be currently informed of intelligence activities.

Reporting Full and Current Information

''The Director of Central Intelligence . . . shall (1) keep the Select Committee on Intelligence of the Senate and the Permanent Select Committee on Intelligence of the House of Representatives fully and currently informed of all intelligence activities which are the responsibility of, are engaged in by or are carried out for or on behalf of any department, agency or entity of the United States, including any significant anticipated intelligence activity. . . .''

Executive Order 112333

Prohibits involvement of U.S. government in assassinations.

''No person employed by or acting in behalf of the United States government shall engage in or conspire to engage in assassination. . . . No agency of the intelligence community shall participate in or request another person to undertake activities forbidden by this order.''

Charter of the United Nations: Commitment to Nonaggression

Prohibits U.N. members from using force against other nations, except in individual or collective self-defense.

Article 2 (3): ''All Members shall settle their international disputes by peaceful means in such a manner that international peace and security, and justice, are not endangered.''

Article 2 (4): ''All Members shall refrain in their international relations from the threat or use of force against the territorial integrity or political independence of any state, or in any manner inconsistent with the purpose of the United Nations.''

Charter of the Organization of American States: Commitment to Nonaggression

Prohibits OAS members from using military force as an instrument of foreign policy except in individual or collective self-defense.

Article 18: ''No State or group of States has the right to intervene, directly or indirectly, for any reason whatever, in the internal or external affairs of any other States. The foregoing principle prohibits not only armed force but also any other form of interference or attempted interference. . . .''

Article 20: ''The territory of a State is inviolable; it may not be the object, even temporarily, of military occupation or of other measures of force taken by another State, directly or indirectly, on any grounds whatever.''

War Powers Resolution

Requires the president to submit to Congress within forty-eight hours after U.S. forces have been introduced into hostilities.
Section 4 (a) "In the absence of a declaration of war, in any case in which the United States Armed Forces are introduced (1) into hostilities or into a situation where imminent involvement in hostilities is clearly indicated by the circumstances; (2) into the territory, airspace, or waters of a foreign nation, while equipped for combat . . . the President shall submit within forty-eight hours to the Speaker of the House of Representatives. . . ."

Foreign Assistance Act of 1961

Human rights conditions on security assistance.
Section 502B(a) (2)
"Except under circumstances specified in this section, no security assistance may be provided to any country the government of which engages in a consistent pattern of gross violations of internationally recognized human rights."

Violations are defined in this section as "torture or cruel, inhuman or degrading treatment or punishment, or prolonged detention without charges or trial, causing the disappearance of persons by the abduction and clandestine detention of those persons, and other flagrant denial of the right to life, liberty, or the security of the person."

1949 Geneva Conventions

Articles on the protection of civilians obligates the United States to insure respect of the conventions by other governments which the United States exercises influence upon.
Common Article 1: "The High Contracting Parties undertake to insure respect for the present Convention in all circumstances."

Military Construction Codification Act

Limits on construction with military exercise funds.
10 USC 2802(b): "A military construction project includes all military construction work, or any contribution authorized by this chapter, necessary to produce a complete and usable facility or a complete and usable improvement to an existing facility."
10 USC 2805(c): "Only funds authorized for minor construction projects may be used to accomplish unspecified minor construction projects, except that the Secretary concerned may spend from appropriations available for operation and maintenance amounts necessary to carry out unspecified military construction projects costing not more than ($200,000)."

Military Construction Appropriations Act of 1984

Mandatory filing of a regional construction plan.

". . . None of the funds made available for airfield improvements in Honduras may be obligated until the Committees on Appropriations have been notified as to the complete U.S. construction plan for the region."

Export Administration Act

Human rights stipulation on military sales.

Applications to export crime control and detection equipment will generally be granted "unless there is evidence that the government of the importing country may have violated internationally recognized human rights and that the judicious use of export controls would be helpful in deterring the development of a consistent pattern of such violations or in distancing the United States from such violations."

International Financial Institutions Act

Human rights conditions on loans.

Section 701(f) "The United States Executive Directors . . . are authorized and instructed to oppose any loan, any extension of financial assistance or any technical assistance to any country described in subsection (a) (1) or (2), unless such assistance is directed specifically to programs which serve the basic human needs of the citizens of such country."

(The subsection referred to refers to "countries . . . whose governments engage in a pattern of gross violations of internationally recognized human rights, such as torture or cruel, inhumane or degrading treatment or punishment, prolonged detention without charges, or other flagrant denial of life, liberty, and the security of person.")

*47. U.S. Economic Policies as Economic Aggression**

By Michael E. Conroy

Dr. Michael E. Conroy is associate professor of economics at the University of Texas at Austin, and is codirector of the Central American Resource Center.

Economic aggression is not a term found in the glossaries of most U.S. economics texts. It is not a theoretical concept that has been well defined, analyzed,

*Excerpts from *Latin American Perspectives,* 1985.

characterized, or typified. There is a rather strong tendency among U.S. academic economists to dismiss the term as the reflection of concepts or approaches that are in the realm of political science but certainly are not part of the domain to which economists' traditional analytical tools may be applied legitimately. This rather ingenuous approach reflects, I believe, both an act of faith in the nature of market economies and a deeply held moral belief that the U.S. government does not engage in such practices. In the case of Nicaragua, however, that naiveté may have met its overdue end.

One of the best analytical treatments of the notion of economic aggression has been provided by Pedro Vuskovic in a little-known essay first published by *Le Monde Diplomatique* and reproduced in *El Nuevo Diario* (June 4, 1981). Vuskovic was himself a victim of the U.S. destabilization policies against Chile while he served as minister of the economy under Allende. He wrote the essay in early 1981, at a time when the Reagan administration had begun to announce its opposition to aid for Nicaragua but when the magnitude and full characteristics of its anti-Sandinista economic policies were not yet apparent. His analyses were prescient.

Vuskovic discussed the nature and the objectives of U.S. programs of economic destabilization with reference to a relatively wide variety of nations and national experiences, not just to the experience of Chile. Economic aggression, he noted, has ranged from simple warnings and notices that policies might be enacted to the open implementation of deliberate policies designed to have a direct effect on particularly vulnerable areas of an economy. The objectives have ranged from "dissuading" a government from a planned or proposed policy to "delegitimizing" whole governments by using less visible, more "conventional" means. Under conditions where elections are about to occur, for example, Vuskovic showed that the United States attempted to create a perceptible worsening in the social and economic conditions of a country in order to lessen the likelihood that the ruling government would be retained in power. He cites not only the overt attempts to depose Fidel Castro through the U.S. economic embargo, but also U.S. economic policy toward the Goulart government of Brazil just prior to its overthrow in 1964, the measures taken by the Nixon administration to limit and restrain economic policies of the Velasquez government in Peru, the pressures that led to the overthrow of the Torres government in Bolivia in 1971, the deliberate destabilization attempts made against Allende in Chile, the policy changes that hurt the Peronist government of Argentina from 1973 to 1976, and comparable but lesser destabilization efforts directed at General Torrijos of Panama, Prime Minister Manley of Jamaica, and the Echeverria regime in Mexico.

All of these experiences share a set of common characteristics, Vuskovic noted, that are useful for understanding the coherence behind the policies that were then beginning to be enacted against Nicaragua:

1. The economic aggression is articulated through policies that link the interests of international institutions, such as the IMF, with the economic interests of

local elites, who attempt to claim representation of broader social groups, such as small businesspersons or the salaried professional class.

2. The destabilization programs are developed gradually and at first discretely, beginning with actions that may create an adequate response and then escalating both the nature and the public defense of the policies with deliberately misleading demagoguery to justify increasingly open economic aggression.
3. The initial phases are accompanied by a campaign of delegitimization—claims of "inefficiency," charges that the government is violating nationalist commitments, and demands for change that are as great as possible (effectively eliminating any possibility that they will be met)—while the opposition is linked to "private enterprise."
4. At intermediate stages, repeated in most of the cases cited above, conditions based on campaigns of fear about the future are created that encourage destructive behavior on the part of businesspeople in the country: liquidation of assets, capital flight, reduction of inventories, postponement of maintenance, and the gradual increase in shortages created simply by hoarding. As the inflationary pressures are brought to bear and domestic production suffers from the climate of fear and uncertainty, international finance is increasingly blocked or delayed and demands for protection of private enterprise are escalated.
5. In its most ferocious stages, the coordinated policies become open, public, international economic aggression: sources of international finance are deliberately blocked; concerted efforts are made to deny access to international markets for essential products; and conditions are created that cause the entrepreneurial class in the country to refrain from rational economic activity, producing as little as possible, hoarding, and in general, disrupting normal production and commerce.

If we define economic aggression as the introduction of political and economic policies that are designed to disrupt or injure the economy of another country, including the deliberate withdrawal of economic assistance with an intent to injure, there is little doubt that U.S. policies toward Nicaragua have constituted blatant aggression. The list of the specific elements of those policies is too long to reproduce completely at this point, but they have been outlined extensively elsewhere (Sholk, 1983; Morrell and Biddle, 1983; Cavanaugh and Hackel, 1984).

The United States began its economic pressure immediately after Ronald Reagan was inaugurated. Disbursement of the last $15 million in committed economic assistance was halted and a much-needed shipment of wheat was stopped. By late 1981 the United States was publicly organizing in the Inter-American Development Bank to block one loan after another, especially in the Fund for Special Operations—the concessional loan facility over which the United States has unusually great influence (Sholk, 1983: 9). An October 1980 World Bank mission, named by outgoing World Bank President Robert McNamara, provided a fundamentally supportive analysis of the Nicaraguan situation and the need for substantial and immediate assistance. This report, completed in February 1981 and circulated for eight months before being published in October of that year, unintentionally provided, it now seems, the blueprint for the Reagan administration's aggression against Nicaragua (World Bank, 1981).

The Bank's October 1980 mission reported that the damaging economic consequences of the insurrection were real and persistent. "Per capita income levels of 1977 will not be attained, in the best of circumstances," it noted, "until the late 1980s." It envisaged high probabilities of debt-servicing and financing problems, but it noted that "if Nicaragua can obtain substantial financing in the near term, a considerable improvement in its creditworthiness three to four years hence [could] be foreseen" (p. 57). And the report urged that "it would be highly desirable for the country to receive external assistance at concessional terms and in excess of the foreign exchange component." The consequences of withholding financial support were also clear:

> Any untoward event could lead to a financial trauma, since the country would not be able to obtain commercial financing as a buffer. Moreover, it would be very difficult indeed to restrain consumption for such a long period (World Bank, 1981: 57).

Shortly after that World Bank team returned from Nicaragua, Robert McNamara retired and was replaced by William Claussen, previously president of the Bank of America. Ronald Reagan was inaugurated, the presidential transition team expressed much concern about World Bank lending to socialist countries, a new team was sent to Nicaragua, and a radically different report was written on Nicaragua. The report was labeled "confidential" and was intended for use within the bank alone (World Bank, 1982).

This new report admitted that the bank had taken on the role of negotiating for the private sector in Nicaragua, insisting on new "clear and consistent rules of the game for the private sector" acceptable to the bank, as a precondition for any further bank lending. The new report found Nicaragua only "marginally creditworthy," a condition blamed primarily on problems in the growth rate of export earnings that left Nicaragua with foreign exchange shortages as its "overwhelming medium-term problem." It then argued against funding most of the projects that the Nicaraguan government had requested (p. 12). Noting that Nicaragua "is likely to be a very controversial client" (p. 17), the new report recommended ending all lending for water supply projects, road building, or education programs and offering only limited financial assistance for agricultural credit programs "directed to the private sector." The report then called for slowing the processing of the requests for even those funds, awaiting the Sandinista government's responses to its demands with respect to the private sector (p. 16).

The International Development Association (IDA) is the "soft-loan" or concessional branch of the World Bank; it was founded and functions similarly to the Fund for Special Operations of the Inter-American Development Bank. The United States had made considerable donations to this fund and exercises effective veto control. The application of that veto has never been publicly announced, but Nicaragua has not received any funds from the IDA since 1980. The February 1982 bank report also includes a tacit admission that the United States had, by that date, blocked all loans and grants to Nicaragua from IDA.[1]

The United States has attempted to undercut Nicaragua's export earnings in more direct ways as well. In 1983 the United States unilaterally reduced Nicaragua's quota of sugar for U.S. markets by 90 percent, an act designed to cost Nicaragua more than $23 million in differential sugar prices. The United States was a founding member of the General Agreement on Tariffs and Trade (GATT), which is the international organization charged with policing fairness in trading relations. In recent years the United States has depended heavily on GATT to condemn "unfair" dumping and subsidizing of Japanese and Third World products being sent to U.S. markets. The Nicaraguans complained to GATT that the arbitrary reduction of the sugar quota constituted an "unfair practice." GATT has ruled that it was, indeed, a violation of binding agreements; but the United States has decided to ignore this decision (*New York Times,* April 16, 1984).

The U.S. government has used a plethora of harassment techniques to slow, delay, or deter Nicaraguan trade with the United States. According to officials interviewed at the Ministry of Foreign Commerce, they range from restrictions on exports of chemical feedstocks to Nicaragua because of their alleged use in products traded with Cuba, inconsistently scrupulous and exaggerated agricultural inspections, the closing of the Nicaraguan consulates to lessen the ability of U.S. producers to meet Nicaraguan import technicalities, and pressure on U.S. firms to avoid dealings with Nicaragua. The mining of all Nicaraguan harbors and undeveloped anchorages in January and February 1984 represented the most direct form used by the United States to inhibit trade with Nicaragua. The consequences have been far greater than just the well-publicized damage to some vessels. Representatives of the Ministry of Planning indicate that during the first two months after the mining, shippers with contracts to deliver goods to Nicaragua off-loaded much of them in Costa Rica and shipped them overland to Nicaragua, often with delays of many weeks. Several shipping lines declined future shipments until it could be demonstrated that the mines had been cleared, shipping insurance costs were increased, and the already precarious foreign supply of goods was further disrupted. Although the U.S. government agreed to cease the placement of new mines in March 1984, the mines were not removed. They continued exploding through the summer of 1984.

The most important deterrent to Nicaraguan trade, however, has been the collapse of private credit links for both imports and exports. These are simple "transactions credits"[2] rather than the borrowing more commonly recorded under public borrowing, and there is no international system for recording them or evaluating their magnitude. The pervasiveness of international credit in the financing of even the simplest transactions between the United States and many Third World nations represents a form of "hidden dependency" that has cost Nicaragua dearly. Much of this dependence is never manifested in international statistics for it is based on links to the importing or exporting firms themselves.

It is often the U.S. firm, for example, that arranges for the credit needed to consummate an international transaction with Third World importers and exporters. The U.S. firm uses its domestic lines of credit with U.S. banks to finance shipments or receipts of goods rather than requiring that the Third World country that is party to the transaction obtain a loan that would produce a recorded international transaction. Prior to the revolution, for example, a Nicaraguan importer of fertilizer could often obtain six-month credit terms directly from the manufacturer; the manufacturer would obtain the financing in its name from a local bank. The distributor then extends comparable credit to the farmer until the crop is harvested. Once the crop is in, the distributor is paid by the farmer, the manufacturer by the distributor, and the bank in the United States is repaid. A similar process was often used for Nicaraguan exports: U.S. importers would obtain loans from U.S. banks to provide advances to Nicaraguan producers; the advance would be deducted from payment due for the crop itself, and the bank would be repaid without a recorded international credit transaction. There is not necessarily any fear of the recorded credit transaction; the point is, however, that international statistics understate the extent of this "hidden dependence."

When the Ministry of Foreign Trade was organized in 1979 to control all imports and exports (specifically to avoid the capital flight that occurs surreptitiously through "overinvoicing" procedures), the first great problem that it encountered was the complete breakdown of that suppliers' credit system. There is no way to know precisely how much of Nicaragua's imports and exports prior to the revolution were financed with this kind of short-term credit. The ministry has estimated, conservatively, that if 50 percent received such financing the loss in credit amounted to more than $500 million. For a nation to lose all such credit almost instantaneously is devastating; it forces the nation to operate totally on cash, causing dramatic contractions in spending until the needed cash can be accumulated.

In theory Nicaragua should have then been able to turn directly to the banking community for loans to replace the suppliers' credits and importers' credits that had been lost. Whereas credit had previously been extended to myriad small businesses in Nicaragua on a strictly private basis, the state was now willing to offer formal state guarantees for short-term import and export credits. Nicaragua should have been viewed as an especially good credit risk for most banks, for the new government had taken the unusual step of officially accepting responsibility for the $1.6 billion Somoza-era debts and had succeeded in restructuring and refinancing the vast majority of its debts.[3]

The restructuring set important precedents. Nicaragua was given until 1986 to resume principal payments, and the interest payments on most loans were lowered to 7 percent for that period with the difference between that rate and the actual rate on the loan capitalized into the principal (IMF, 1983). In fact, the World Bank reported that Nicaragua had brought itself up to date on all international debt payments by early 1980 (World Bank, 1982); and it was reported in the North American press that Nicaragua was "one of the few countries in Latin America that continues to pay its debts on time" (*The Washington Post,* December 18, 1982).

The pattern of economic aggression, however, has included State Department efforts to discourage bank-lending to Nicaragua. These activities appear to have been very widespread, and they are epitomized by the history of a loan that was organized by the Bank of America and announced in December 1982. The loan amounted to approximately $30 million for 90 days, and it was guaranteed by an effective mortgage on a share of the nation's cotton crop. It would have been "the first significant bank loan to Nicaragua since 1979" (*New York Times,* December 14, 1982). The loan was sought to meet interest payments due on foreign debt, but the Nicaraguans committed themselves to making those payments whether or not the loan was finalized. The loan was stopped. Later reports have indicated that the State Department took an active role in discouraging the loan, calling Bank of America loan officers and threatening to call members of the bank's board of directors. The official State Department response was that it had not formally blocked the loan, but that it had made certain that the bank's officers knew what the administration's feelings were about such loans (*New York Times,* February 21, 1984).

Under normal circumstances the process of restructuring existing debt is undertaken so that a nation is once again considered credit worthy for additional short-term and medium-term borrowing. Revolutionary Nicaragua, however, has encountered an almost total withdrawal of short-term financing, precisely the form of financing on which the Somoza regime had become so totally dependent. In December 1978, 73.3 percent of all the bank debt owed by Nicaraguans to U.S. banks was short-term debt, debt that had to be renegotiated or repaid in one year or less. That short-term share was 15 percent of the regionwide average of 62.8 percent, and it was one of the highest encountered in Central America for the entire period for which data are available (FFIEC, various dates).

As the medium-term loans of the Somoza era came due, the proportion increased to 75.5 percent by mid-1980. Since that time the total absence of short-term lending by U.S. banks is reflected in the plummeting of the share of Nicaragua's debt that was short term. From June 1980 to June 1983 the share fell to 10.5 percent, a condition that was totally inconsistent with relative economic indicators, totally inconsistent with the banks' lending policies in the rest of Central America, and totally inconsistent with the expressed preferences of the Nicaraguan government. Despite the almost total collapse of the economy of El Salvador, the refusal of the Costa Rican government to agree to an International Monetary Fund (IMF) adjustment program and the burgeoning there of the highest debt in Central America, and massive capital flight from Honduras, the banks have continued to make short-term loans to each of these countries in relatively constant shares of total borrowing.

The treatment by U.S. banks of El Salvador is particularly noteworthy. U.S. banks reduced their lending to El Salvador from roughly $200 million at the time of the coup that brought the Salvadoran junta to power in November 1979 to $100 million six months later. But El Salvador has continued to receive a constant flow of U.S. bank financing at that level, despite the fact that the Salvadoran banking system was also nationalized by the government just a few months after the Nicaraguan government took over its own banks.

In July 1983, a Reagan administration spokesman, James Conrow, the Treasury official responsible for U.S. votes in the Multilateral Banks, announced that the United States would vote against all loans for Nicaragua "unless the revolutionary Sandinista government takes steps to revitalize the private sector" and "improve the efficiency of the public sector" (*The Washington Post,* July 1, 1983). These are, of course, precisely the policies that the Nicaraguan government has been pursuing most vigorously, even amid criticism from the Left (cf. Conroy, 1984). The same news report that announced the policy also noted its inconsistency. The United States regularly votes in the World Bank for loans to countries with predominantly socialist economies, such as Yugoslavia; and it supports policies in El Salvador that it criticizes in Nicaragua, such as the nationalization of the banking system. There is virtually no explanation for depriving Nicaragua of its access to credit from the United States—whether supplier's credits or bank credit—other than a conscious policy of economic aggression.

External Financial Assistance to Nicaragua

The inherited financial dependency of Nicaragua in 1979, the country's deteriorated export earnings, and the wide range of measures aimed at undermining the economy financially have increased the urgency with which Nicaragua has sought international financial assistance. Data on total assistance to Nicaragua are difficult to accumulate; many forms of assistance, such as commercial loans and other trade concessions from Third World nations, are not monitored and published in any consistent fashion. The Organization for Economic Cooperation and Development (OECD), however, publishes annually the most comprehensive survey of the geographic distribution of financial flows from its member countries (and selected other countries) to all the nations of the Third World.

The OECD data relevant to Nicaragua are shown in Table 1 for the period from 1976 to 1982, as well as data on IMF flows not covered by the OECD.[4] It is important to understand the nature of the data in this table. They constitute, first of all, net disbursements of assistance. That is, they are actual payments made to, or on behalf of, the Nicaraguan government; and they are adjusted for any repayments that the government may have made. The payment of an outstanding loan and the issuance of another loan of the same amount would appear here as a zero net flow. So these funds constitute real increases in assistance each year. Disbursements must be distinguished from commitments or contracts, for the announcement that a loan has been granted seldom means that the funds flow immediately. The actual disbursement of the funds is normally dependent on the fulfillment of an often complex series of conditions, including purchasing materials in a specific country, providing progress reports, monitoring the project, and so on. As political conditions change commitments may never be disbursed, as with the case of U.S. aid committed to Nicaragua but never disbursed.[5]

The data in Table 1 do not include financial flows from the Latin American and other Third World sources that have also assisted Nicaragua. There is no organization that gathers and publishes systematic data of that sort, but fragments of information are available to indicate the extent to which the OECD data include most of Nicaragua's economic assistance.

From July 1979 to March 1982, Nicaragua received a total of $1.2 billion in commitments, of which only $677 million had been disbursed. The distribution of those disbursements across all sources suggests that the OECD data include approximately 81 percent of all flows (*Latin America Weekly Report,* November 12, 1982). Data on the distribution of commitments (provided in Table 2) demonstrate the relative levels of aid promised by all major groups of countries, but they do not indicate what Nicaragua actually received.

For the period prior to the insurrection, 1976 to 1978, average net financial flows to Nicaragua from the sources covered by the OECD amounted to slightly more than $200 million, an average of $67 million per year. The U.S. government and U.S.-controlled agencies provided the majority of the official development assistance for Somoza during those last years before his downfall. In the first two years of that period, aid from the U.S. and the U.S.-dominated multilateral agencies (the World Bank and the Inter-American Development Bank) amounted to an average of 52 percent of the financial assistance received by the Somoza government. During 1978 that share rose to 71 percent of all assistance. Throughout the period the direct and indirect assistance from the United States increased while aid from the rest of the world was decreasing.

Data for 1979 are confounded by the fact that there is no separation between financial assistance received prior to the July 19 triumph of the revolution and that disbursed after that date. The IMF credit amounted to 32 percent of total financial assistance for 1979, but it was extended to the Somoza government during the spring of that year. Net disbursement of financial aid from 1980 through 1982, however, clearly reflects the postrevolutionary response of the international community to the new government.

Nicaragua received a total of $809 million in net financial flows from 1980 to 1982 from the sources covered by the OECD data. Nearly 83 percent of that came from non-CMEA countries—in other words, those outside of the Socialist bloc. Only 17.5 percent came from the Socialist-bloc countries, a total of $141.6 million; and 99 percent of that aid was received in 1981 and 1982, after the U.S. government had announced its intentions of suspending all assistance to Nicaragua. The United States provided only 12 percent of the economic assistance received by Nicaragua from 1980 to 1982; the United States and its closely controlled agencies provided 35 percent. Western Europe, Japan, and Canada provided Nicaragua with $154 million in aid during that period, 19 percent of total aid. The remainder of the aid totaled here came from countries in the Organization of Petroleum Exporting Countries (OPEC), other regional multilateral agencies, and the principal relief and assistance agencies of the United Nations.

Table 1 also shows that the IMF generated negative aid flows. The IMF is the

Table 1

Net Financial Flows to Nicaragua from the Industrialized Countries, Multilateral Agencies, the IMF, and OPEC: 1976–1982

(millions of $)

	1976	**1977**	**1978**	**1979**	**1980**	**1981**	**1982**	**1980–1982**
Total estimated flows[a]	73.8	69.9	57.9	177.2	235.8	367.4	205.8	809
	1	2	3	4	5	6	7	
Net from non-CMEA[b]	73.8	69.9	57.9	177.2	235.2	287.4	148.8	671.4
(Percentage from non-CMEA)	100.00	100.00	100.00	100.00	99.75	78.23	72.30	82.99
Net ODA from DAC[c]	18.5	24.9	29.6	73.8	116.6	59.9	76.9	252.7
(Percentage of ODA from DAC)	25.07	33.62	51.12	41.65	49.45	16.11	37.37	31.24
Net ODA from U.S.	14	14	24	29	79	14	6	99
(Percentage of ODA from U.S.)	18.97	20.03	41.45	16.37	33.50	3.81	2.92	12.24
Net from OPEC[d]	0	0	0	1	0	100	0	100
(Percentage from OPEC)	0.00	0.00	0.00	0.56	0.00	27.22	0.00	12.36
Net IMF Credit[e]	0	2	.013	55.9	−4.9	−20.4	−4.02	−29.32
(Percentage from IMF)	0.00	2.86	0.02	31.55	−2.08	− 5.55	−1.95	−3.62
Net multilateral[f]	20.6	31.2	18.9	42.3	111.1	111.3	54.2	276.6
(Percentage of Multilateral)	27.91	44.64	32.64	23.87	47.12	30.29	26.34	34.19

IBRD/IDA	5.8	14.5	5.9	5.5	26.5	36.5	13.9	76.9
IDB	12.5	14.6	11.3	29.3	34.2	49.3	22	105.5
sum + U.S.	32.3	43.1	41.2	63.8	139.7	99.8	41.9	281.4
(Percentage of IBRD/IDA and IDB)	24.80	41.63	29.71	19.64	25.74	23.35	17.44	22.55
Net CMEA countries	0	0	0	1.6	.6	80	61	141.6
(Percentage of CMEA)	0	0	0	.9	.2	21.9	32.1	17.50
Net private sector[g]	n.a.	.2	1.1	3.6	5.3	33.2	15.1	53.6
Net export credits	n.a.	10.8	−5.9	−5.9	−8.6	31.7	13.4	36.5

SOURCES: OECD, *Geographical Distribution of Financial Flows to Developing Countries* (various issues); IMF (1984).

a. From DAC, OPEC, and CMEA countries and the IMF; totals in this line equal "Total Receipts Net" in the OECD tables, plus net IMF credits, plus gross CMEA credit.

b. Includes Official Development Assistance, as defined in note c below; other non-ODA official flows from DAC countries; ODA and non-ODA financing from multilateral agencies listed in note f below; and other private financial flows.

c. ODA (Official Development Assistance) is defined here as grants and loans to developing countries provided primarily for development objectives and containing a "grant element" of 25 percent or more. The DAC (Development Assistance Committee) of OECD consists of 17 countries: Australia, Austria, Belgium, Canada, Denmark, Finland, France, West Germany, Italy, Japan, the Netherlands, New Zealand, Norway, Sweden, Switzerland, the United Kingdom, and the United States.

d. Here effectively Libya; does not include petroleum credits from Venezuela or Mexico.

e. Calculated from changes in "Use of Fund Credit," converted from SDRs to U.S. dollars.

f. The multilateral agencies include the World Bank (IBRD), the International Finance Corporation, the International Development Association (IDA), the Inter-American Development Bank (IDB), ten other regional and OPEC-financed institutions, and the principal relief and economic assistance agencies of the United Nations.

g. Includes primarily direct and portfolio investments and private export credits.

Table 2

Total New Commitments of Multilateral and Bilateral Assistance to Nicaragua, by Major Country Grouping: 1979–1983 (millions of $)

		1979	1980	1981	1982	1983	1979–1983
Multilateral	($)	213	170.9	86.2	93.6	65.1	628.8
organizations	(%)	78	32	13	17	15	26
World scale	($)	22	67	33.7	37	0	159.7
	(%)	8	13	5	7	0	7
Regional	($)	191	103.9	52.5	56.6	65.1	469.1
	(%)	70	20	8	10	15	19
Official bilateral	($)	58.7	356.7	600.9	448.1	35	1499.4
	(%)	22	68	87	83	8	61
Capitalist	($)	58.7	254.7	495.7	195.2	204	1208.3
countries	(%)	22	48	72	36	48	49
Western	($)	14.6	63.2	60.2	38.7	86.7	263.4
Europe	(%)	5	12	9	7	20	11
North America	($)	0	72.6	0	0	0	72.6
	(%)	0	14	0	0	0	3
Latin America	($)	44.1	118.9	332.5	153.5	83.5	732.5
	(%)	16	23	48	28	20	30
Africa and Asia	($)	0	0	103	3	33.8	139.8
	(%)	0	0	15	1	8	6
Socialist	($)	0	102	105.2	252.9	146	606.1
countries	(%)	0	19	15	47	34	25
Total	($)	271.7	527.6	687.1	541.1	425.1	2452.6
	(%)	100	100	100	100	100	100

SOURCE: Fondo Internacional para la Reconstrucción (FIR), Managua.

only international organization that forced Nicaragua to pay back prerevolutionary loans during the period immediately following the insurrection. The IMF had extended an exceedingly controversial credit facility to Somoza for $66 million during the waning months of his regime. Pressure from the United States had overcome the opposition of European and Latin American representatives at the IMF, and Somoza drew down $55.9 million of the credit facility before he was overthrown. When the Sandinista government revealed to the IMF that the credits had been used inappropriately by Somoza, the IMF invoked a seldom-used clause in its agreements and demanded immediate repayment from the new government, exercising total indifference to the disastrous financial conditions that Somoza had left behind. Nicaragua responded by excluding the IMF from the debts that it renegotiated and restructured in 1980 and 1981. The distance that it now maintains from the IMF leaves it effectively barred from receiving further IMF credits until that loan is completely repaid; and IMF data indicate that all but $10 million has been repaid (cf. Sholk, 1983; Morrell and Biddle, 1983; IMF, 1984).

Total commitments to the Sandinista government from 1979 to 1983 reflect a fundamental pattern. Nicaragua continues to receive offers of assistance from a wider and more diversified set of nations than it did before the revolution. The total magnitude of the commitments continues to provide considerable assistance—beyond the assistance that is available to virtually any other Central American nation. The commitments from the socialist-bloc countries have fluctuated; but they remain, on average, only 25 percent of the total economic aid offered to Nicaragua. The U.S.-affiliated multilateral agencies provided relatively large shares of aid during the first years of the period, but the policies of the U.S. administration are clearly reflected in the reduction in their commitments since 1981.

It is important, once again, to reflect carefully on the meaning of the data presented in Table 2. These data on commitments represent signings of loan packages, many of which will be disbursed over many years. They also represent some promises of aid that will never materialize. They do not include the value of outright grants, such as emergency relief after the May 1982 floods or the many millions of dollars in direct donations by private, nongovernmental organizations in the United States and Western Europe.

It is most important, furthermore, to recognize that these are indications of future *gross* flows of aid. Each commitment has its own schedule of payout. The differences between commitments from the Socialist-bloc countries in 1980 to 1982 ($460 million) and the actual disbursements that occurred, according to OECD data ($141.6 million), is illustrative. A trade credit extended for a year and then rolled over annually is counted as a new commitment every time that it is rolled over. Approximately $200 million per year is being used just to amortize older credits, leaving much smaller quantities of net financial flows. That is, the data in Table 2 cannot be compared directly with those of Table 1. The total commitments of $425.1 million shown for 1983, for example, do not mean net flows of that amount; they mean, rather, that commitments of that magnitude were offered both to pay off (or roll over) old loans and to finance new projects.

Nicaragua has received offers of $2.5 billion in economic assistance during the first four and one-half years of the revolutionary period. Fully 49 percent of that has come as official bilateral assistance from nonsocialist countries of Western Europe, North America, Latin America, Africa, and Asia. Another 26 percent has been provided by multilateral organizations in the nonsocialist countries. The share of commitments from the Socialist-bloc countries amounted to 25 percent, a total of $606 million.

Total aid offered by the major multilateral agencies has followed a pattern of rapid decline from peaks in 1981 to very low levels in 1983. This trend can be juxtaposed with the increase in commitments from the Socialist-bloc countries. The peak year for commitments from the Socialist countries was 1982, and the increase from 1981 to 1982 was almost exactly the amount by which U.S. and multilateral aid fell between 1980 and 1981. Total aid offered to Nicaragua peaked in 1981, thanks largely to a single loan of $100 million from Libya provided in direct and defiant response to the announcement of the cancellation of bilateral U.S. assistance and the announcement by the United States that it would use its influence to block further loans from the World Bank and the Inter-American Development Bank.

Commitments from nonsocialist countries and organizations have been greater than those offered by the socialist countries in every year except 1982. Economic assistance from the Third World (Latin America, Africa, and Asia) has amounted to 36 percent of the total received by Nicaragua since 1979. That aid peaked in 1981 with a total of $438 million, 63 percent of the total. It has run at slightly under 30 percent for the last two years of the period under study, 1982 and 1983. Western European economic assistance has fluctuated between 5 percent and 20 percent of the total, reaching its highest level in 1983.

These data reflect Nicaragua's continuing need to seek substantial external financial assistance, whether in the form of trade credits or direct long-term loans for development projects. The pattern across countries and across time reflects a strong and effective response to the attempts by the United States to isolate and delegitimize the Nicaraguan revolution. They illustrate the considerable success that Nicaragua has had in obtaining external support to replace that which the United States has successfully blocked and to replace the export earnings that have been hurt by U.S. economic policies designed to harm Nicaragua.

Conclusion

Nicaragua is at present the object of U.S. economic aggression. It is aimed at depriving Nicaragua of many forms of international assistance to which that nation has as much right as any other nation. The Reagan administration has put pressure on the private sector in the United States to deprive Nicaragua of credit, imported products, and markets for its exports, even though normal economic criteria would dictate that conditions for trade and finance are better in Nicaragua than in much of Central America. Moreover, the U.S. government has increasingly resorted to military measures designed to overthrow Nicaragua's revolutionary government, knowing that the minimal consequences of such activities will be very destructive for the economy. The overall pattern of so-called covert aid to the counterrevolutionaries has profound economic implications, for it provides the critical basis for creating terror within the country, disrupting investment, and delaying acceptance of the new social order by many private-sector entrepreneurs who are being invited to participate in the reconstruction of Nicaragua.

The vulnerability of Nicaragua to this economic aggression has been determined largely by the previous economic dependence of Nicaragua upon trade with the United

States, by extensive short-term U.S. financing of Nicaragua's chronic external imbalance prior to 1979, and by concessional assistance from the United States for development programs. The nature of that dependence is typical of the present situation in much of the Third World. What is being repeated in Nicaragua is the willingness of a U.S. administration to use all the economic and political leverage that it can muster to do damage to another economy by exploiting the very essence of the inherited dependence.

What is new in Nicaragua is the extent to which international financial assistance from around the world is now assisting in the process of counteracting that economic aggression. The Socialist-bloc countries came to the assistance of Cuba in the 1960s when explicit economic aggression on such a broad front was last seen; few Third World nations or Western European nations were willing then to provide support of the magnitude that Nicaragua continues to receive. Nicaragua sought assistance first from both the public sector and the private sector in the United States at the same time that it was seeking and receiving new levels of assistance from Western Europe and parts of the Third World. Nicaragua has now responded to the deliberate withholding of aid by the United States and by U.S. dominated multilateral agencies by replacing it with growing commitments from Western Europe, the Socialist-bloc countries, and the Third World.

If there is a lesson apparent in this experience, it is that nations such as Nicaragua that attempt to escape from the system of economic dependence that conditions the very nature of the social order can only expect economic aggression as a response from those who have perennially benefitted from that dependence. It is also clear that solidarity among capitalist Third World countries for efforts to escape that dependence can also assist such a transformation, even if it is unable to lessen the virulence of the aggression.

Notes

1. While discussing loans for educational projects, frequently covered by IDA, the report notes on page 14 that "no IDA resources can be allocated to Nicaragua." There is no basis other than a U.S. veto for denying access of any country to IDA funds.
2. I am indebted to Linda Hudgins for suggesting this apt distinction.
3. The decision to accept responsibility for Somoza's debt remains controversial in Nicaragua. The decision was made deliberately to maintain contacts with the international financial community upon which Sandinista leaders knew Nicaragua would have to depend for many years into the future. As the costs of that commitment have come due under conditions of considerable financial isolation, the wisdom of the initial decision continues to be questioned.
4. More recent data covering 1983 was published by the OECD in March 1985.
5. The financial flows in Table 2 labeled "ODA" (official development assistance) are grants and loans whose terms are generally concessional. Loans at current market rates of interest from banks or other lenders are not included; the specific technical criterion used by the OECD for ODA is that the loan must have at least a 25 percent grant element. Financial assistance from the Socialist-bloc countries, the CMEA, is given by OECD as gross flows, but they are treated here as net flows.

References

Cavanaugh, John, and Joy Hackel. "U.S. Economic War against Nicaragua." *Counterspy* (March–May 1984): 12–17.

Conroy, Michael E. "False Polarization? Differing Perspectives on the Economic Strategies of Postrevolutionary Nicaragua." *Third World Quarterly* 6, 4 (October 1984): 993–1032.

FFIEC (Federal Financial Institutions Examination Council). "Country Exposure Lending Survey, June 1979." Statistical release, issued semiannually in June and December. Washington, DC: Board of Governors of the Federal Reserve System, 1979.

IDB (Inter-American Development Bank). *Social and Economic Progress in Latin America* (separate issues for 1975, 1976, 1977, 1978, and 1982). Washington, DC: Inter-American Development Bank.

IMF (International Monetary Fund). *Recent Multilateral Debt Restructurings with Official and Bank Creditors.* Occasional Paper 24, December, 1983. Washington, D.C.: International Monetary Fund.

———. *International Financial Statistics, 1984 (April).* Washington, D.C.: International Monetary Fund.

Morrell, Jim, and William Jesse Biddle. "Central America: The Financial War." *International Policy Report* (March 1983): 7–11.

OECD (Organization for Economic Cooperation and Development). *Geographical Distribution of Financial Flows to Developing Countries* (April 1984). Paris: Organization for Economic Cooperation and Development.

Sholk, Richard. "U.S. Economic Aggression against Nicaragua." Paper presented jointly with Sylvia Maxfield at the Eleventh International Congress of the Latin American Studies Association, Mexico City, October 1, 1983.

World Bank. *Nicaragua: The Challenge of Reconstruction.* Report 3523-NI, October 9, 1981. Washington, D.C.: International Bank for Reconstruction and Development.

———. "Country Program Paper: Nicaragua." February 16, 1982.

———. *World Debt Tables, 1982 Edition.* Washington, D.C.: International Bank for Reconstruction and Development, 1983.

*48. Executive Order and Message to Congress**

By Ronald Reagan

Executive Order

By the authority vested in me as President by the Constitution and laws of the United States of America, including the International Emergency Economic Powers Act (50 U.S.C. 1701 et seq.), the National Emergencies Act (50 U.S.C. 1601 et seq.), Chapter 12 of Title 50 of the United States Code (50 U.S.C. 191 et seq.), and Section 301 of Title 3 of the United States Code,

I, Ronald Reagan, President of the United States of America, find that the policies and actions of the government of Nicaragua constitute an unusual and extraor-

*Executive Order of May 1, 1985.

dinary threat to the national security and foreign policy of the United States and hereby declare a national emergency to deal with that threat.

I hereby prohibit all imports into the United States of goods and services of Nicaraguan origin; all exports from the United States of goods to or destined for Nicaragua, except those destined for the organized democratic resistance, and transactions relating thereto.

I hereby prohibit Nicaraguan air carriers from engaging in air transportation to or from points in the United States, and transactions relating thereto.

In addition, I hereby prohibit vessels of Nicaraguan registry from entering into United States ports, and transactions relating thereto.

The Secretary of the Treasury is delegated and authorized to employ all powers granted to me by the International Emergency Economic Powers Act to carry out the purposes of this order.

The prohibitions set forth in this order shall be effective as of 12:01 A.M., Eastern daylight time, May 7, 1985, and shall be transmitted to the Congress and published in the Federal Register.

Message to Congress

Pursuant to section 204(b) of the International Emergency Economic Powers Act (50 U.S.C. 1703), I hereby report to the Congress that I have exercised my statutory authority to declare a national emergency and to prohibit: (1) all imports into the United States of goods and services of Nicaraguan origin; (2) all exports from the United States of goods to or destined for Nicaragua except those destined for the organized democratic resistance; (3) Nicaraguan air carriers from engaging in air transportation to or from points in the United States; (4) vessels of Nicaraguan registry from entering into United States ports.

These prohibitions will become effective as of 12:01 A.M., Eastern daylight time, May 7, 1985.

I am enclosing a copy of the executive order that I have issued making this declaration and exercising these authorities.

1. I have authorized these steps in response to the emergency situation created by the Nicaraguan government's aggressive activities in Central America. Nicaragua's continuing efforts to subvert its neighbors, its rapid and destabilizing military buildup, its close military and security ties to Cuba and the Soviet Union, and its imposition of Communist totalitarian internal rule have been described fully in the past several weeks. The current visit by Nicaraguan President Ortega to Moscow underscores this disturbing trend. The recent rejection by Nicaragua of my peace initiative, viewed in the light of the constantly rising pressure that Nicaragua's military buildup places on the democratic nations of the region, makes clear the urgent threat that Nicaragua's activities represent to the security of the region and, therefore, to the security and foreign policy of the United States. The activities of Nicaragua, supported by the Soviet Union and its allies, are incompatible with normal commercial relations.

2. In taking these steps, I note that during this month's debate on U.S. policy toward Nicaragua, many members of Congress, both supporters and opponents of my proposals, called for the early application of economic sanctions.

3. I have long made clear that changes in Sandinista behavior must occur if peace is to be achieved in Central America. At this time, I again call on the government of Nicaragua:

- To halt its export of armed insurrection, terrorism, and subversion in neighboring countries;
- To end its extensive military relationship with Cuba and the Soviet bloc and remove their military and security personnel;
- To stop its massive arms buildup and help restore the regional military balance; and
- To respect, in law and in practice, democratic pluralism and observance of full political and human rights in Nicaragua.

4. U.S. application of these sanctions should be seen by the government of Nicaragua, and by those who abet it, as unmistakable evidence that we take seriously the obligation to protect our security interests and those of our friends. I ask the government of Nicaragua to address seriously the concerns of its neighbors and its own opposition and to honor its solemn commitments to noninterference, nonalignment, respect for democracy, and peace. Failure to do so will only diminish the prospects for a peaceful settlement in Central America.

*49. Nicaragua Eases into New Export Markets**

By Tim Coone

As the U.S. trade embargo against Nicaragua begins to bite this week, the Nicaraguan government has begun to devote the same resourcefulness to the problem as it did when the U.S. closed its doors to most of Nicaragua's sugar exports in 1983.

Then, Nicaragua quickly found new markets in the Middle East and North Africa at preferential prices. Two years later, the Nicaraguan export products most seriously affected by the trade embargo are bananas and shellfish, worth some $15 million each in the U.S. market.

According to Mr. Orlando Solorzano, the Nicaraguan deputy foreign trade min-

*From the *Financial Times* of London, May 8, 1985.

ister, however, "We have already found new markets in Europe for our bananas and we are in the process of finding more."

Until the embargo, Nicaragua exported some 4 million boxes of bananas annually to the United States. According to Mr. Alfredo Alaniz, the Nicaraguan fisheries minister, the first major shipment of shrimps and lobsters to Europe are also to be sent on the same refrigerated ships that will take to Belgium the Nicaraguan bananas that were formerly sold in California.

Nicaragua will be able to take advantage of temporary shortfalls in deliveries of bananas to Europe as a result of droughts in Colombia and shipping difficulties in other Central American countries, according to British banana traders.

But the long-term prospects for a small exporter obliged to trade outside the channels controlled by U.S. companies such as United Brands—which includes the British Fyffes operation—are not encouraging, they add.

It appears that U.S. business will suffer as much if not more than the Nicaraguan government as a result of the embargo, bearing the main costs of the Reagan administration's hard-line stance against the Sandinista government in Managua.

Four U.S. shipping companies which carry the bulk of Nicaraguan trade with North America now stand to lose between $15 million and $20 million in freight charges a year. According to Mr. Alaniz, four U.S. shipyards which topped the list to win a $38 million tender to construct fifty new fishing vessels will now lose out through the embargo.

Other U.S. manufacturers stand to lose an annual market of $10 million in exports of animal and vegetable fats, between $20 million and $25 million in crop protection chemicals and fertilizers, and an equivalent amount in electrical machinery, pumps, transport, and scientific equipment. Latin American suppliers will most likely fill the gap in raw material supplies, while Western and Eastern European manufacturers stand to become the principal suppliers of advanced technology and machinery.

So for the Nicaraguans the immediate effects of the embargo will be irritating rather than devastating. According to Mr. Marvin Norguera, director of the state importing agency Enimport which handles some 20 percent of Nicaragua's annual import bill of $800 million, many spare parts for U.S.-made machinery can be obtained through U.S. subsidiaries overseas, such as the Esso oil refinery in Managua. Where that is not possible, sections of plants will gradually be replaced by machinery from countries that have a more reliable trading relationship with Nicaragua.

"The embargo will be serious," he said, "but the country will not grind to a halt."

The immediate sectors to be hit by the embargo will be in agriculture and health, says Mr. Norguera. Crop protection chemicals come primarily from the United States and new sources of supply will have to be found rapidly to avoid pest damage to the important export and basic grain crops.

However, practically all Nicaraguan purchases from the United States are on cash terms only, and so can be relatively easily substituted by other foreign suppliers, according to Mr. Norguera.

The principal economic cost will be in increased shipping costs and delays in delivery, he said. Shipping charges to Europe are around 20 percent higher than to the United States.

So it seems that if the trade embargo is to really bite against Nicaragua it will have to embrace U.S. subsidiaries overseas and include pressures against other major trading partners with Nicaragua, both of which will entail heavy political battles for the Reagan administration.

The Nicaraguan government, by refusing to make any political concessions to the United States, has thrown the ball back into the White House's court. If the Reagan administration now balks at pursuing the embargo to its ultimate consequences, the final word may rest with Mr. Xabier Gorostiaga, head of an economic research institute based in Managua who said on Monday night, "The embargo will in the medium- to long-term be beneficial to Nicaragua, in that it will produce better trading relationships with Europe, Latin America, the Socialist bloc and the rest of the world; but in the short term it will be painful to readjust."

*50. Reagan's Brezhnev Doctrine**

By John B. Oakes

John B. Oakes is the former senior editor of the New York Times.

If Ronald Reagan were a paid agent of the Soviets, he couldn't do any better for them than he is doing in Central America. He has managed to blur the distinction between the foreign policy goals of the United States in the Americas and those of the Soviet Union everywhere else. This is an achievement for which Leonid I. Brezhnev's successors should be truly grateful.

The Reagan doctrine of 1985 is, continent for continent, virtually indistinguishable from the Brezhnev Doctrine of 1968. The essence of the Brezhnev Doctrine, according to so dispassionate a source as the *Encyclopedia Britannica,* is that "the USSR and the community of Socialist nations had the right to intervene if, in their judgment, one of their number was pursuing policies that threaten the essential common interests of the others."

The essence of the Reagan doctrine, as his message to Congress of May 1 justifying the Nicaraguan embargo makes clear, is of even broader scope. It is that the United States has the right to intervene if any nation in the region pursues policies—or has a form of government—that the United States alone deems to be threatening to the common interest.

Only his closest allies accepted Mr. Brezhnev's justification for his brutal overthrow of the Czechoslovak government in 1968. None of his closest allies accepts

*From the *New York Times,* May 20, 1985.

Mr. Reagan's justification for his attempted overthrow of the Sandinista government in 1985.

The irony in all this is that Mr. Reagan claims—and possibly even believes—that he is upholding American democratic values. In reality, he is eroding those values.

To pile futility on top of irony, his policy is grotesquely counterproductive. It is driving Nicaragua steadily closer to dependency on Moscow as a similar embargo did to Cuba a quarter-century ago.

Most if not all of the world's major democracies will ignore the United States' embargo on trade with Nicaragua—as several have already stated—thus rendering it ineffective, except in one respect; it will weaken the core of anti-Sandinista business leadership inside Nicaragua. "The Reagan people behave as if they have written us off," said a major dealer in pesticides, the United States' principal export to Nicaragua last year.

Some 60 percent of Nicaragua's economy is still in private hands, mostly agricultural. However, Mr. Reagan's unremitting and illegal economic warfare seems almost deliberately to have been designed to destroy the private sector. The Russians could hardly have done better.

The Reagan policy in Central America reflects a consistent pattern of ignoring both national and international law, evading it, or breaking it:

- The embargo itself, declaring a nonexistent "national emergency," is based on a "fraudulent' interpretation of the International Emergency Economic Powers Act of 1977, as one of its principal authors, former Representative Bingham of New York, has publicly stated.
- The Boland Amendment of 1982 forbids the use of United States funds—even indirectly—for the military overthrow of the Sandinistas.
- The Neutrality Act forbids United States-organized paramilitary expeditions—for example, Mr. Reagan's "freedom fighters"—against countries with which the United States is at peace.
- The Foreign Assistance Act prohibits military aid to governments violating human rights. The president, through his secretary of state, falsely certified in 1982 and 1983 to Congress that El Salvador qualified for such aid; the 1984 State Department report on human rights continues the tradition of deceiving Congress and the public on human rights issues, especially in Central America.
- The Charter of the Organization of American States forbids intervention "in the internal or external affairs of any other state." Mr. Reagan's Nicaragua policy violates its letter, and, in his continued sabotage of the Contadora peace efforts, its spirit as well.
- The United States walkout from the International Court of Justice last winter gave conclusive evidence of Mr. Reagan's contempt for international law when it interferes with his administration's policy.

Serious as it is, what Mr. Reagan is doing to Central America is not nearly so serious as what he is doing to the United States. He is not merely violating domestic law; he is turning the United States into an international law breaker. He is depriving us of our strongest weapon: adherence to the rule of law and to the rule of reason.

*51. Behind Reagan's Propaganda Blitz**

By Robert Borosage and Peter Kornbluh

Robert Borosage is the director of the Institute for Policy Studies in Washington, D.C. Peter Kornbluh is a fellow at the institute, and is the author of a forthcoming book, Nicaragua: The Price of Intervention.

On February 16 Ronald Reagan launched a massive propaganda offensive in behalf of U.S. aid to the rebels fighting to overthrow the Nicaraguan government. Reporters who were camped outside the president's Rancho del Cielo in Santa Barbara were told that his radio address to the nation, in which he hailed the *contras* as ''our brothers'' and compared assisting them to French support for the American Revolution, was the beginning of an ''educational drive'' to win public support for $14 million to renew Central Intelligence Agency operations in Nicaragua.

Since then, the administration's propaganda machine has shifted into high gear. Its latest production, a glossy multicolored ''white paper'' titled *The Soviet-Cuban Connection,* depicts Nicaragua as a military threat to its neighbors and is intended to lend credibility to the administration's diatribe against what Secretary of State George Shultz calls the Sandinistas' ''bad-news government.'' Almost daily, Shultz and other administration mudslingers have hurled insults at the Sandinistas. Meanwhile the president has canonized the *contras* as the ''moral equal of our Founding Fathers.'' In recent weeks, *contra* leaders from the Nicaraguan Democratic Force and ARDE have trooped through Washington, trying to convince members of Congress that they are not the terrorists guilty of systematic atrocities against civilians, as reported recently by prominent human rights organizations, but rather democratic freedom fighters, deserving of U.S. financial support.

But the administration is playing for higher stakes than petty cash for the *contras*. For U.S. policymakers, Nicaragua has become the test case of a strategy to seize the offensive against the Soviet Union by sponsoring insurgencies in the Third World. The so-called covert war, which ironically has received lavish publicity, is but one component of a broader policy of ''low-intensity warfare'' against Nicaragua: protracted paramilitary, economic, and psychological pressures designed to erode the Sandinistas' popular base until the regime collapses from within, becomes an easy mark for external invasion or, in the president's words, learns to ''say uncle.'' To salvage this war against the Sandinistas, Reagan has escalated his four-year campaign of distortion and disinformation against the U.S. public.

---

*From *The Nation,* April 13, 1985.

The Reagan administration's propaganda war actually predates CIA involvement with the *contras.* On February 23, 1981, two weeks before the president signed his initial authorization for the agency's campaign against the Sandinistas, the Reagan State Department released its first white paper on the region, *Communist Interference in El Salvador.* The report, received with great fanfare by the press, subsequently became a major public relations embarrassment for the administration (see James Petras, "White Paper on the White Paper," *The Nation,* March 28, 1981). Claims that "200 tons" of weapons had been delivered to the Salvadoran guerrillas, "mostly through Cuba and Nicaragua," were not substantiated by the captured documents that allegedly had served as the basis for the report. Even the white paper's author, Jon Glassman, admitted to the *Wall Street Journal* that the statistics on the arms flow were based on extrapolation and that parts of the report were "misleading" and "overembellished."

The use of propaganda became more important to the White House in March 1982, after the CIA's operations were exposed in the press. To counter the negative public reaction, the administration began a frenetic campaign "to convince skeptics," according to *Time,* "that the struggles in Central America are not simply indigenous revolts but rather are crucial battlegrounds in a broad East-West confrontation."

That effort also backfired. On March 12 the State Department held a press conference for Orlando José Tardencillas, a Nicaraguan who had been captured by Salvadoran security forces and who, the administration hoped, would present irrefutable evidence that the Sandinistas were exporting revolution. But instead of repeating what he had told his captors—that he had been trained in Cuba and Ethiopia and had been sent to command Salvadoran guerrillas—Tardencillas told the assembled reporters that he had been tortured and "forced to say many things about the connection between Nicaragua and El Salvador." In El Salvador, Tardencillas said, he had been offered a choice: "I could come here or face certain death." As State Department officials squirmed, Tardencillas added that he had "obviously been presented for purposes of propaganda."

Concern about the administration's inability to build public support for its hard-line policies in Central America was expressed during an April 1982 meeting of the National Security Planning Group, which includes the vice-president, the director of central intelligence, the president's national security adviser, the U.S. ambassador to the United Nations, and top White House aides. An internal summary of the meeting noted, "We continue to have serious difficulties with U.S. public and congressional opinion, which jeopardizes our ability to stay the course." To address "the public affairs dimension of the Central American problem," the group recommended that "under the auspices of the White House, the public information effort be augmented and targeted on improving communications with the Congress and with opinion leaders."

Subsequently the administration has waged what National Security Council documents call a "public diplomacy" campaign to win the hearts and minds of the American people and manipulate the debate on U.S. involvement in Central America. The effort reflects the Hollywood style of the Reagan presidency. The Great

Communicator has given two nationally televised speeches on Central America, one to a rare joint session of Congress, on April 27, 1983, and one from his pulpit in the Oval Office a year later, in which he repeated the litany of official accusations against the Sandinistas. The creation of the Kissinger Commission on Central America was another attempt to promote policy via a media spectacle. Supposedly formed to provide the president with bipartisan advice, the commission was, NSC documents show, part of the administration's "invigorated strategy" to "help build support for our long-term regional policy."

To market U.S. intervention in Nicaragua, the president has set up a veritable propaganda ministry in the executive branch. The Outreach Working Group on Central America, established in the spring of 1983 with the primary purpose of rallying domestic constituencies, operates out of the White House. Directed until recently by Faith Ryan Whittlesey, assistant public liaison for the president, the group has published a series of "White House Digests" which depict Nicaragua as a "terrorist" nation; it also hosts a forum every Wednesday for interested parties at the old Executive Office Building. The speakers addressing those meetings make up a Who's Who on the right. Arnaud de Borchgrave, co-author of *The Spike* and now editor of the Moonie newspaper *The Washington Times,* has vented his views there no less than three times. When Lynn Bouchey, formerly a flack for the Pinochet dictatorship and currently president of the Council for Inter-American Security, spoke there last December, bumper stickers made by his organization proclaiming, "I support the Nicaraguan Freedom Fighters" were disseminated—although White House officials say that was done without authorization. Last April, the evangelists who filled the room to hear a panel discussion of religious persecution in Nicaragua called out "Amen!" after every anti-Sandinista pronouncement.

There is less of a circus atmosphere at the State Department's Office of Public Diplomacy on Latin America and the Caribbean, which participated in the effort, according to its director, Otto Reich, "to convince the American people of the correctness of our policy." Like the White House outreach group, the Office of Public Diplomacy publishes and distributes anti-Sandinista tracts. Titles include "Broken Promises: Sandinista Repression of Human Rights in Nicaragua," "Misconceptions About U.S. Policy Toward Nicaragua" and "The Contadora Process." The State Department office also serves as a distribution center for reports by such anti-Communist groups as the Cuban American National Foundation and the Gulf and Caribbean Foundation.

This public relations bureaucracy played a major role in the administration's efforts to discredit Nicaragua's elections of last November 4. "Our handling of the Nicaragua elections issue," an October 30, 1984, NSC background paper states, has "shifted opinion against the sham elections." According to the document, the State Department prepared a "public diplomacy guidance" on the elections for use by government officials and distributed a pamphlet titled *Resource Book: Sandinista Elections in Nicaragua* [See reading 14—eds.] to selected journalists and members of Congress. The administration also sought to manipulate media coverage of the elections by encouraging nongovernment foreign policy experts "to make public statements, prepare articles, and appear on media programs, especially immediately prior to and following the November 4 elections, e.g., the morning TV shows on November 5."

The NSC background paper also shows that the Reagan administration made a major effort to delegitimize the Nicaraguan elections in the eyes of the world. The NSC document details "Plans to Provide the Facts to the International Community." These include requesting journalists in Europe and Latin America to "write editorials questioning the validity of the elections" and asking U.S. labor leaders to solicit critical statements from their international counterparts. The memorandum states:

> We will approach significant and knowledgeable national leaders, in and out of government, to encourage public statements condemning the Nicaraguan elections as they are now set up. Useful statements should come from government officials, political party leaders (including international parties, such as SI [Socialist International] . . .), intellectuals, church and labor leaders.

Thus Washington has trained its guns on the citizens of its Western allies. "International opinion, particularly in Europe and Mexico, continues to work against our policies," the National Security Planning Group observed in April 1982. In a strategy paper dated July 6, 1983, the NSC noted, "The need is to build domestic and bipartisan support; then to turn that support into international understanding and support for our objectives." A subsection of this document, titled "Action Plan," calls on the Secretary of State to:

> Increase communication/public diplomacy efforts in Western Europe, Mexico, and other Contadora countries to highlite [*sic*] U.S. support for democracy. . . .
>
> In Europe, systematically emphasize the military nature of Soviet/Cuban/Nicaraguan policies and actions.
>
> In Latin America, and with European Socialists, emphasize the Sandinista betrayal of the original anti-Somoza revolution. Undertake major effort to have Christian Democrats condemn Cuban/Nicaraguan intervention.

To convince allies that the United States supports a peaceful solution to the crisis but that Nicaragua, as President Reagan stated in April 1983, "has rejected our repeated peace efforts," the administration has engaged in what might be called showcase diplomacy. Washington paid lip service to the Contadora peace process only because it was supported by major U.S. allies in Latin America and Europe. In practice, however, it has consistently subverted the Contadora process, most recently last September, after Nicaragua agreed to sign the treaty worked out by Mexico, Venezuela, Colombia, and Panama. "We have trumped the latest Nicaraguan/Mexican efforts to rush signature of an unsatisfactory Contadora agreement," an internal NSC assessment stated, adding that "the situation remains fluid and requires careful management."

While the State Department has gone through the motions of negotiating with the Sandinistas, Washington's terms for an agreement require the Nicaraguan government's virtual capitulation. Diplomacy's only role in U.S. policy is as a weapon in the war. The July 6, 1983, strategy paper, for example, directs George Shultz to "develop and monitor a comprehensive diplomatic strategy of Central America with specific attention to the isolation of Nicaragua."

Despite this highly popular president's use of his bully pulpit, the four-year propaganda war has failed to sway public opinion at home or abroad. While President Reagan dismisses the Nicagaruan elections as a "Soviet-style sham," European leaders of all political stripes view the Sandinistas as the duly elected government of Nicaragua. In the United States, as the administration's rhetoric escalates, so does public opposition. A recent ABC/*Washington Post* poll showed that 70 percent of the respondents opposed the administration's effort to overthrow the Sandinistas, and only 18 percent supported that effort. (And 59 percent knew that this is the president's goal.)

Nevertheless, the administration's pitch has had an effect where it counts—in Congress. Although a majority of legislators object to aiding the *contras,* even liberal Democrats have come to believe that the Sandinistas are an affront to the United States and that they deserve some form of punishment. During the MiG scare, Senator Christopher Dodd lined up to voice his support for "taking out" Soviet aircraft if Nicaragua obtained them. Liberal Representative Michael Barnes, chair of the subcommittee on Western hemisphere affairs, stated recently, "I continue to struggle with trying to find a compromise that could achieve the ends the administration wants to achieve while getting us out of this *contra* program." As Representative David Obey, chair of the subcommittee on foreign relations, put it, "There is something to be said for keeping the Sandinistas under pressure or in doubt as to our intentions . . . but our involvement with the *contras* tends to make the gringos the point at issue, rather than the shortcomings of the Sandinistas."

Thus, the debate between Capitol Hill and the executive branch over aid to the *contras* threatens to turn into a squabble over means rather than ends. The administration may lose the vote on aid to the *contras* but nonetheless gain congressional sanction for continuing, indeed even intensifying, its economic and military pressure on the Sandinistas.

Already the administration has stepped up its economic war. On January 30 Secretary of State Shultz personally intervened with the president of the Inter-American Development Bank to block a $58 million agricultural loan to Nicaragua. The Pentagon has announced that Universal Trek-85, the largest military maneuvers in the region to date, will be held in Honduras later this month. And efforts are being made to find alternative sources of aid to fund the *contras*. Even if Congress votes against further aid for CIA operations, the war will not end.

This bodes ill not only for Nicaragua but for the rest of us. If the major casualties of the Reagan administration's intervention are Nicaraguan civilians, the principal victims of its propaganda campaign are the citizens of the United States. Nicaragua now stands not only as a test of a strategy of low-level warfare abroad but as a test of the viability of the "big lie" technique at home. It remains to be seen whether Congress will pass the test.

52. *The Contadora Initiative**

By Phillip Berryman

Phillip Berryman, once a pastoral worker in Panama, has been Central America representative for the American Friends Service Committee.

If any countries could claim that Central America was in their backyard, it would be those adjacent: Mexico, Panama, Colombia, and Venezuela—the so-called Contadora group. Yet it is these nations that have made sustained efforts to find negotiated solutions since early 1983.

None of these governments are left-wing: they have become involved for pragmatic, not ideological, reasons. Instability threatens them, and they recognize that all parties will lose in the regional war entailed in U.S. policies that treat Central America solely as an arena of East-West confrontation in which the West must prevail.

Their Latin American identity may be another motivating factor for the Contadora governments. Latin Americans of all stripes, from leftists to conservatives, bear a memory of U.S. heavy-handedness in their region. They view the Monroe Doctrine, for example, not as an altruistic offer of protection against outside aggression but as a unilateral U.S. declaration of a right to intervene.

In this light, we may view Contadora as an assertion by Latin American governments that they are mature and capable of carrying out a diplomacy that might save the United States from the disastrous consequences inherent in its present policies. Latin Americans feel they are able to understand the crisis in Central America. They insist that the conflicts are primarily internal and should not be defined as problems of East-West confrontation. Brazil, Argentina, Bolivia, and Ecuador have expressed their support for the Contadora initiatives, as have Canada and most European governments.

Procedurally, the Contadora Group began by seeking to mediate border disputes, especially those between Honduras and Nicaragua, and thereby reduce the danger of war. The group has since sought to move from general principles, subscribed to by the five Central American countries, toward verifiable and binding treaties.

In September 1983, the Contadora countries drew up Twenty-One Points, principles that could provide a basis for settling conflicts. Aside from those dealing with trade, aid, and development, and others on "democratization" (the result of lobbying

*Excerpts from Phillip Berryman, *Inside Central America* (New York: Pantheon Books, 1985).

by El Salvador, Costa Rica, and Honduras to draw attention to the fact that Nicaragua had not held elections), the main planks expressed the intentions of the region's governments to:

- Halt the arms race in all its manifestations and initiate negotiations on the subject of control and reduction of the current arms inventory and actual number of arms.
- Forbid the establishment in the region of foreign military bases or any other form of foreign military interference.
- Concert agreements to reduce, and eventually eliminate, the presence of foreign military advisers and other forms of foreign military and security actions.
- Establish international mechanisms of control for the prevention of the traffic of arms from the territory of one country to the region of another.
- Eliminate the traffic of arms, within the region or from abroad, forwarded to persons, organizations, or groups attempting to undermine Central American governments.
- Prevent the use of their own territory for, and neither to lend nor allow, military or logistic support to persons, organizations, or groups attempting to destabilize Central American governments.
- Abstain from promoting or supporting acts of terrorism, subversion, or sabotage in the countries of the area.
- Create mechanisms and coordinate systems of direct communication aimed to prevent or, if necessary, to resolve incidents among states of the region.

These were simply guidelines that the Contadora Group intended to translate into verifiable and binding treaties.

Such principles, if accepted and adhered to, would satisfy U.S. requirements regarding its own security. Soviet or Cuban military bases would be excluded, military advisors and other forms of foreign presence in Nicaragua would be reduced and then eliminated, and any arms traffic from the Sandinistas to the Salvadoran insurgents would be ended.

However, the Contadora principles would apply equally to U.S. bases in Honduras, U.S. advisors and military aid to El Salvador, and the U.S. support for the *contras*. It is because of the requirements of this reciprocity that the United States has consistently refused to support the Contadora process, and has largely thwarted it.

Applied across the board, the Contadora proposals would frustrate U.S. policy objectives. If the *contras* were deprived of their sanctuaries in Costa Rica and Honduras, their supplies from the U.S. and Honduran armies, and their CIA funding, they would cease to be a serious threat to the Sandinista government. The Salvadoran insurgency's main strength, on the other hand, is internal. It is the government and army that are propped up by the United States. Even a curtailing of U.S. aid and hints that the army might not be able to count on the United States as its ultimate backup might induce panic—or force the Salvadoran government to agree to negotiations.

In this light, it is not surprising that despite its verbal support, the Reagan administration has in fact undermined the Contadora process. During the first half of 1983, it largely ignored the group's initial diplomatic efforts. In July, whether by design or by coincidence, at the very moment that the Contadora countries were making proposals and the Sandinistas were for the first time accepting the principle of multilateral negotiations, President Reagan sent U.S. warships to patrol both coasts of Nicaragua and announced extensive U.S. military maneuvers in Honduras—actions that were taken as direct threats by the Sandinistas. In September 1983, as the five Central American governments were accepting the Twenty-One Points, the United States was reconstituting the Central American Defense Council (CONDECA) with Honduras, El Salvador, and Guatemala as members. The result was the creation of a potential regional army that could attack Nicaragua or fight the Salvadoran insurgents.

Despite the Reagan administration's efforts to thwart the Contadora effort, the negotiating teams patiently worked to put the Twenty-One Points into treaty form. At one point, over one hundred technical advisors and diplomats were involved. Finally on September 7, 1984, the four Contadora countries agreed on a compromise version and submitted it to the Central American governments, which had been consulted extensively during its preparation.

If implemented, the proposed treaty would reverse the present thrust toward militarization in several ways. The countries of the region would agree to submit inventories of their present arms, suspend new arms acquisitions, and establish limits on certain types of equipment, particularly offensive weapons. Next they would establish limits on personnel. A Commission of Verification and Control, made up of four other Latin American countries, would assure compliance. Moreover, the governments would agree to not authorize foreign military bases, and to eliminate existing ones within six months of signing the treaty. International military maneuvers would be forbidden. Other provisions dealt with foreign military advisors, and with support for insurgencies or terrorism in other countries. Following recommendations by the United States and its allies, there were also provisions on electoral processes.

Nicaragua agreed to the draft version on September 21. Although it had frequently voiced its verbal support, the Reagan administration was caught off guard. Administration spokespersons called the treaty proposals unfair, citing for example the fact that foreign military advisors engaged in training and operations (such as U.S. personnel in El Salvador) would have to leave while those involved in maintenance (such as the Cubans and Soviets in Nicaragua) would not. They further stated that it was one-sided to end U.S. military exercises and close U.S. military bases without exacting anything from Nicaragua. However, that objection only underscores the onesidedness of U.S. military involvement: no other foreign power was constructing bases or holding maneuvers. The Reagan administration also feared that Nicaragua would be allowed to retain large military forces. Stated another way, this was simply a recognition that a neutral commission might well accept Nicaragua's argument that it needed a large military force to deter a U.S. invasion.

By October 19 the U.S. allies, Honduras, El Salvador and Costa Rica, had come back with a counterproposal, eliminating or attenuating some of the Contadora proposals and adding the Central American nations themselves to the verification commission. That proposal would make it much less likely that the commission itself could be truly neutral, especially regarding Nicaragua.

Neither Mexico nor Venezuela regarded the September 7 treaty as unfair. It remained to be seen whether Contadora had been destroyed, or whether it could yet prove to be a vehicle for a diplomatic solution.

The U.S. rejection of the Contadora initiatives reflects a characteristic American attitude that goes beyond the Reagan administration. The United States objects to foreign intervention in Central America but seems blind to the fact that in Central America the United States itself is a "foreign" power—arguably more so than Cuba. This blind spot is especially obvious in the Kissinger Commission report.

U.S. intervention in Central America not only is foreign but is on a scale far exceeding that of any other foreign actor. In both 1983 and 1984, U.S. expenditures in the region exceeded $700 million, not including the cost of extensive military maneuvers, which came from the Pentagon budget and cost many more millions.

President Miguel de la Madrid of Mexico presented many of these themes in an address to the U.S. Congress in May 1984. He stressed that Central America should not become a theater for East-West confrontation and reforms should not be regarded as threatening security: "We therefore reject, without exception, all military plans that would seriously endanger the security and development of the region. . . . For our countries, it is obvious that reason and understanding are superior to the illusion of the effectiveness of force."

*53. Document Describes How U.S. "Blocked" a Contadora Treaty**

By Alma Guillermoprieto and David Hoffman

The Reagan administration believes it has "effectively blocked" what it views as an "unsatisfactory" regional peace settlement in Central America, according to a secret background paper prepared for a National Security Council meeting last Tuesday that the president attended.

The paper also outlines a wide-ranging plan to convince Americans and the rest of the world that Sunday's Nicaraguan elections were a "sham," promoting this view through U.S. embassies, politicians, labor organizations, nongovernment experts, and public reports.

The briefing paper, marked "secret/sensitive," was obtained by the *Washington Post* from governmental sources. It provides a detailed look at the administration's

*From the *Washington Post,* November 6, 1984.

approach to the Sandinista government just days before elections in Nicaragua and the United States.

It is not known whether all the items in the briefing paper were discussed. Secretary of State George P. Shultz and Assistant Secretary for Inter-American Affairs Langhorne A. Motley also attended what was described by officials yesterday as a "briefing."

The paper discussed the administration's approach to the draft version of the Contadora peace treaty that was completed September 7. It was negotiated by the foreign ministers of Mexico, Panama, Colombia, and Venezuela, who first met for the purpose in 1982 on the small Panamanian island of Contadora.

The treaty's principal thrust is to reduce foreign military influence, establish mechanisms for arms control, and prevent the Central American countries from making or sponsoring war on each other.

On September 21, Nicaragua unexpectedly announced it would sign the fifty-five-page draft treaty. The Reagan administration had not publicly criticized it up to that point.

Since the Sandinistas announced their willingness to sign it, three countries—Honduras, El Salvador, and Costa Rica—reversed their previous position of support for the treaty and, along with the United States, sought extensive modifications in the draft to improve verification and execution mechanisms.

The paper declares: "We have effectively blocked Contadora Group efforts to impose a second draft of a revised Contadora Act. Following intensive U.S. consultations with El Salvador, Honduras, and Costa Rica, the Central American [sic] submitted a counterdraft to the Contadora states on October 20, 1984 . . . [that] shifts concern within Contadora to a document broadly consistent with U.S. interests."

The United States repeatedly has portrayed the decision by Central American countries not to approve the initial draft treaty as one made independently by those countries, despite consultations.

The briefing paper expresses concern that a fourth Central American country, Guatemala, has been reluctant to back its three neighbors in seeking changes in the treaty. "We will continue to exert strong pressure on Guatemala to support the basic Core Four position," the paper says. The "uncertain support" of Guatemala is "a continuing problem," it adds. "Core Four" refers to Guatemala, Honduras, El Salvador, and Costa Rica.

Mexico has been the most insistent promoter of signing the September 7 version of the Contadora treaty. The briefing paper notes that Guatemala, because of its problems with guerrilla insurgency along the Mexican border, is seeking closer ties to Mexico, providing a "strong incentive" for Guatemala to lean toward the Mexican view.

But the paper concludes in a summary: "We have trumped the latest Nicaraguan/Mexican efforts to rush signature of an unsatisfactory Contadora agreement, and the initiative is now with the Core Four, although the situation remains fluid and requires careful management."

The paper notes that the administration recently has had "mixed" success in dealing with Nicaragua. "Congressional failure to fund the armed opposition is a serious loss, but our handling of the Nicaraguan election issue and Sandinista mistakes have shifted opinion against the sham elections," it says.

This was the administration line before and after the election. But the paper outlines ways in which this view should be promoted throughout the world.

It calls for encouraging "sympathetic American intellectuals and academics," "U.S. labor" and "selected U.S. political figures" to lobby their counterparts in Europe and Latin America, seeking critical statements about the election.

Another proposal was for the United States to use "selected embassies" in Europe and the Western hemisphere to promote administration views.

"Embassy Bonn will approach [West German ex-chancellor] Willy Brandt to determine if he plans to make any public statements" on the election following the withdrawal of a key opposition party.

That withdrawal "has now left the Sandinistas holding a near worthless hand," the paper says.

The document also refers to the bilateral U.S.-Nicaraguan talks hosted by Mexico. At the sixth round, held in September, the U.S. side "tabled" a comprehensive statement by Nicaragua, the background paper says, adding that the Sandinistas have adopted the September 7 version of the Contadora treaty as their negotiating position vis-à-vis the United States as well.

54. The War at Home

By Debra Reuben

Debra Reuben was a professor of English at the National Autonomous University of Nicaragua from 1982 to 1983. She currently is the national coordinator of the Nicaragua Network.

As Central America has increasingly become a focal point of world attention during the past six years, a dramatic rise in activity by U.S. citizens concerned about our government's role in the region has also occurred.

Part of this widespread concern is due to the large numbers of Americans who have visited the region themselves, have met Central Americans in the United States, or have otherwise had direct contact with the effects of U.S. foreign policy. The strong religious component of social change in Central America coupled with the experience of U.S. religious workers in the region has been a factor of particular importance in this unusual abundance of personal contact with a key international issue.

Nowhere has this been more true than in regard to Nicaragua. Literally tens of thousands of U.S. citizens, eager to see for themselves a society and a social experiment they have heard so much about, have traveled to that country, for the most part since 1982.

Many of these visitors, and other Americans who have met Nicaraguans in the United States, have come away from their experience greatly concerned about the impact of U.S. policy and with a desire to play a role in keeping the channels of communication and friendship open and healthy between our peoples. These desires have taken shape in concrete projects and organizations in the United States. Among them, on the national level, the Nicaragua Network, Witness for Peace, the Pledge of Resistance, and coordinated national humanitarian aid efforts for Nicaragua have figured prominently.

In February 1979, a conference was called by the Washington Office on Latin America, an organization made up of a number of prominent individuals and various committees in the United States concerned with the situation of the Nicaraguan people and with traditional U.S. support for dictator Anastasio Somoza. Out of this conference was born the Nicaragua Network (formerly, National Network in Solidarity with the Nicaraguan People).

The Nicaragua Network was initially composed of about twenty–thirty committees. Its work focused on organizing tours of Nicaraguans to the United States (particularly of Nicaraguan religious workers and Nicaraguans from the Atlantic Coast area) and organizing delegations of U.S. citizens to Nicaragua. In 1980 the Nicaragua Network launched a material aid drive to purchase materials for Nicaragua's National Literacy Crusade and continued its humanitarian aid work through the devastating floods of 1982 and projects to aid Miskito Indians on Nicaragua's Atlantic Coast.

During 1980, expectations of an imminent victory for the revolutionary forces in El Salvador began to mount. U.S. public awareness of conditions in El Salvador grew as well, with the brutal murder of the four U.S. churchwomen and the assassination of Archbishop Oscar Romero. Many individuals and committees active around Nicaragua eagerly extended their concern to El Salvador and the Nicaragua Network supported this development.

By mid-1983, however, this trend meant a lessened visibility of Nicaragua work as well as a weakened understanding of issues and facts regarding Nicaragua. At the same time, serious efforts by the Reagan administration to embark on an all-out negative publicity campaign against Nicaragua were just getting underway.

Individuals from various religious communities, concerned about escalating tensions in the region, decided to form a nonviolent border watch along the Nicaragua-Honduras border. One hundred and fifty religious leaders and individuals from a wide range of denominations arrived in Nicaragua for the initial border vigil in July 1983.

Out of the July vigil came Witness for Peace, an ongoing program that sends short-term teams of faith-based individuals into zones of conflict as nonviolent witnesses to the war. After two-week stints in Nicaragua, Witness for Peace participants often speak of their experience in their local communities.

Long-term Witness for Peace volunteers have gone to other sites of *contra* attacks for purposes of documentation. Witness for Peace also maintains a hotline with reports from its volunteers in Nicaragua.* Over 1,300 Witness for Peace volunteers have visited Nicaragua in the past two years.

In August 1985, twenty-nine volunteers and fourteen journalists on the first Witness for Peace boat down the Rio San Juan, the river that acts as the Nicaragua-Costa Rica border, were held captive by *contras* who identified themselves as members of Edén Pastora's *contra* group ARDE. Witness for Peace responded to the mining of Nicaragua's harbors by sending boats into Corinto, and will probably begin a Witness trip down the Rio Escondido on the Atlantic Coast.

At the end of 1983, the Nicaragua Network organized the first Volunteer Work Brigades to Nicaragua. Over 650 Americans spontaneously responded to Nicaragua's urgent call for volunteer help with its coffee and cotton harvest; 120 people have participated in volunteer reforestation projects; and over 600 more have gone on subsequent harvest and construction brigades. The wide range of ages, seventeen to eighty, and professions—school bus drivers to computer programmers to stockbrokers to students—indicates that *brigadistas* have participated both out of a desire to learn firsthand about Nicaragua and to express their concern about U.S. policy. They, too, have returned to speak in their communities and, with the exception of significant ''pacifist-baiting'' during the August 1985 boat incident, media coverage of both the Brigades and Witness for Peace has been by and large positive.

After the U.S. invasion of Grenada, fears of similar action against Nicaragua rose sharply. A group of religious peace leaders met to discuss an organized response mechanism should the United States attempt to invade Nicaragua.

This plan evolved into the Pledge of Resistance, and by the summer of 1984 major peace organizations such as the Nuclear Freeze, AFSC, SANE, the Nicaragua Network, the Committee in Solidarity with the People of El Salvador (CISPES), the Network in Solidarity with the People of Guatemala (NISGUA), and Mobilization for Survival had signed on and the Pledge of Resistance was sweeping like wildfire across the country.

The Pledge itself consists of a commitment to engage in peaceful civil disobedience in the event of serious escalation of the U.S. war in Central America or to demonstrate legally in support of those committing civil disobedience. Its numbers have grown rapidly from less than 20,000 to over 70,000.

The Pledge of Resistance has regional, state, and local coordination throughout the country. ''Signals'' for Pledge activity are issued through the Signal Group, composed of experts, analysts, and constituency group leaders with direct access to information regarding U.S. policy moves in the region and through the Executive Committee, composed of national organizations committed to the development of the Pledge of Resistance.

The Pledge of Resistance mobilized during the spring of 1985 in response to congressional moves to aid the *contras* and U.S. trade sanctions against Nicaragua. The number of participants and press coverage have increased with each mobilization.

---

*(202) 332-9230.

Mention should also be made of coordinated efforts against aid to the *contras,* which resulted in congressional votes in 1983, 1984, and spring of 1985 to restrict, then eliminate, funds designated to support the *contras*. These efforts peaked in a whirlwind of activity during April 1985, when the majority voted against *contra* aid. Unfortunately, congressional strength of conviction behind these votes was outstandingly weak and in a June reversal, aid to the *contras* was re-instated.

Mobilizing around Central America has periodically taken the form of national demonstrations or nationally coordinated regional and local actions. A national demonstration in Washington during November 1983 brought out around 25,000 people. The national April Action for Peace, Jobs, and Justice brought out over 100,000 people around the country in April 1985. Concern about aid to the *contras* and U.S. intervention in Central America, as well as opposition to apartheid in South Africa, were paramount in demonstrators' minds.

Another significant manifestation of accelerating pro-Nicaragua activity in the United States has been the mushrooming of humanitarian aid projects on a local and national level.

Aid projects before 1979 were largely generated by church-related earthquake relief and development projects, such as the efforts of the Mennonite Central Committee, Church World Service, and Catholic Relief Services.

In 1979–1980 the Nicaragua Network initiated its humanitarian aid efforts (see above) together with the AFSC. This represented the first national project to aid the people of Nicaragua as they developed new social programs and rebuilt the destruction left by the 1978–1979 war.

Since that time, many humanitarian aid efforts have sprung up as a result of U.S. citizens visiting Nicaragua and a number of national projects have come into being. These national efforts include: OXFAM-America's Tools for Peace Campaign, which has sent tools to Nicaragua for two years; MADRE, a women-to-women project that has sent powdered milk to Nicaragua, provides "twinning" programs between U.S. and Nicaraguan child-care centers, and is currently raising $1 million for the Bertha Calderon Women's Hospital in Managua; the National Central America Health Rights Network, which collects medical aid through committees across the United States; the Quixote Center, which has sent more than $5 million worth of medical aid to Nicaragua; ongoing shipments from the American Friends Service Committee (AFSC), Church World Services, and the Mennonite Central Committee that total several million dollars apiece; HAP-NICA, a program to send badly needed agricultural assistance to Nicaragua; TecNica, which provides technical assistance and computer expertise to Nicaragua; Bikes Not Bombs, dedicated to helping Nicaragua relieve some of its transportation pressures through the use and production of bicycles; the Sister Cities and Friendship groups throughout the United States, now formed into their own Nicaragua-U.S. Friendship Cities Association; and the Nicaragua Network's own Let Nicaragua Live campaign, designed to meet the priority needs of persons displaced due to the U.S. war against Nicaragua, with monies sent through the Humanitarian Aid for Nicaraguan Democracy (HAND) fund, co-coordinator of the campaign.

Tens of thousands of U.S. citizens are clearly concerned about the situation in Central America and the negative impact of our government's role there. This level of concern is expressed in national polls indicating a steady 70 percent opposition to a U.S. invasion of Nicaragua and an ever increasing percentage of individuals who can identify which side the United States is on in the conflict.

The breadth of those concerned is also impressive. Business leaders, church leaders and members, elected officials, recognized artists, small, medium and large farmers, medical professionals, and thousands of conscientious, deeply patriotic U.S. citizens all count themselves as friends of Nicaragua.

The challenge before us is to take the extraordinary quantity of *motion* that exists around the country and convert that into a *movement*. Through mobilizing, through coordinated projects, and through expanding our abilities to reach new constituencies and help them become active around Central America, we can build a powerful and united movement, capable of stopping U.S. intervention in Central America and of developing the kinds of relationships with the peoples of that region that both we and they so richly deserve.

Organizations Active in Aiding and Disseminating Information about Nicaragua

American Friends Service Committee
1501 Cherry Street
Philadelphia, PA 19102
(215) 241-7000

Bikes Not Bombs
P.O. Box 5595
Friendship Station
Washington, D.C. 20016
(202) 965-2786

Catholic Relief Services
1011 First Avenue
New York, N.Y. 10022
(212) 838-4700

Church World Service
475 Riverside Drive #656
New York, N.Y. 10115

CISPES
(Committee in Solidarity with the People of El Salvador)
P.O. Box 50139
Washington, D.C. 20004
(202) 887-5010

HAP-NICA/Guild House
(Humanitarian Assistance Project for Independent Agricultural Development in Nicaragua)
802 Monroe
Ann Arbor, MI 48104
(313) 761-7960

MADRE
853 Broadway, Rm. 905
New York, N.Y. 10003
(212) 777-6470

Mennonite Central Committee
21 South 12th Street
Akron, PA 17501

Mobilization For Survival
853 Broadway #418
New York, N.Y. 10003
(212) 533-0008

National Central America Health Rights Network
600 Minnieford
Bronx, N.Y. 10464

Nicaragua: Through Our Eyes
Newsletter of the Committee of U.S. Citizens Living in Nicaragua, monthly.
P.O. Box 4403–159
Austin, TX 78765

Nicaragua Network
2125 I Street NW #1117
Washington, D.C. 20006
(202) 223-2328

NISGUA
(Network in Solidarity with the People of Guatemala)
930 F Street NW #720
Washington, D.C. 20004

Oxfam-America
115 Broadway
Boston, Mass. 02116
(617) 482-1211

Pledge of Resistance
c/o Sojourners
P.O. Box 29272
Washington, D.C. 20017
(202) 636-3637

Quixote Center
3311 Chauncey Place #301
Mt. Rainier, Md. 20712
(301) 699-0042

SANE
(Committee for a Sane Nuclear Policy)
711 G Street SE
Washington, D.C.

TecNica
110 Brookside Drive
Berkeley, CA 94705
(415) 654-7768

Washington Office on Latin America (WOLA)
110 Maryland Avenue NE
Washington, D.C. 20002
(202) 544-8045

Witness for Peace
P.O. Box 29241
Washington, D.C. 20017
(202) 636-3642

Nicaragua-U.S. Friendship Cities Association
P.O. Box 7452
Boulder, CO 80306

Part Four

NICARAGUA TODAY

Editors' Introduction

While Nicaragua remains in the spotlight of world attention, the focus of that spotlight carries quite an anti-Nicaraguan bias. Most people in the world know more about what the U.S. State Department *thinks* about Nicaragua's internal policies than about what is in fact developing inside that country. A great deal of copy has been generated from State Department publications about Nicaragua's international policies and alignments, while reports of successful domestic programs and innovative future plans receive scant public attention. And despite the unprecedented number of political diatribes, either damning or praising the failures or successes of the revolution, few constructive critiques have appeared.

Addressing these problems, this section presents material on the internal events in Nicaragua. First discussed is the question of Nicaragua's developing political system, a subject frequently clouded by the needs of international propaganda. Following this are analyses of universally recognized successes of the revolution, successes rarely emphasized in the mass media. The last section deals with the very difficult questions of the failure of the revolution to deliver on some of its basic promises.

Chapter I:

Political Power in Contemporary Nicaragua

Editors' Introduction

Nicaragua's political processes have been subjected to more scrutiny than those of most Third World countries. Both supporters and detractors have provided extensive analysis of Nicaragua's internal political procedures. Much of this literature has been polemical, advocating or attacking with passion and urgency. Detractors have played on the theme of Nicaragua as a repressive totalitarian state. Supporters have argued, somewhat defensively, that what might appear as totalitarian is only a result of the U.S.-backed war. Missing in much of this debate is an honest presentation of the evolving political structure of Nicaragua.

To gain a reasonably accurate picture, we must see beyond our own basic political assumptions. Setting the Nicaraguan situation in the framework of the mortal battle between "freedom" and "communism" will not only prove inaccurate but hopelessly confusing as well. Nicaragua's electoral system looks Western and democratic, its emphasis on the political power of labor unions and mass organizations appears socialist in orientation, and its guarantees to small businesses and free enterprise reflect old-fashioned Jeffersonian Democracy. Concentrating on only one or the other of these tendencies permits the political pundit ample grist for the propaganda mill, but it does not provide an accurate picture of Nicaragua's developing internal polity.

The first and overriding concern has to do with democracy. Nicaraguans at all levels of society express a commitment to democratic principles. They have, for instance, shown strong support for the idea of elections. The vast majority of them (84 percent of the registered voters) participated in the elections of 1984. Yet it is important to keep in mind that while elections at all levels in society (in organizations, workplaces, neighborhoods, towns and cities, regions and nations) are crucial components of democracy, they are only part of its workings—their presence alone guarantees nothing. To provide easy examples: Hitler, Mussolini, and Somoza were "elected," but few would emulate their "democracies."

Nicaraguans are attempting to construct a broader framework for their democracy. Going beyond what we know in the United States as the direct and indirect election of policymakers responsive to the needs of their constituencies, their system aims to guarantee each individual's active participation in the formulation of policy at the local and national levels. The question for them, then, is how best to effect this broad degree of participation.

The first three articles in this section address this basic question. Andrew Reding's provides an overview of the developing political system. *The Central America Bulletin* then analyzes the structure of mass organizations, perhaps the most important domestic political force within the country. This is followed by a discussion of the new constitution presently being elaborated.

Presented in a previous chapter was an analysis of the procedures involved in Nicaragua's 1984 national elections. The selection below explores the structure of the national electoral system as it is evolving as part of the new Nicaraguan polity.

One controversial aspect of the internal political scene is that of the role of trade unions. While few would deny that trade unions are important in Nicaraguan society, there is considerable difference of opinion concerning their independence and freedom to operate. The two articles in this section explore opposite sides of this issue.

Finally, the question of the role and share of political power to be accorded the private sector is particularly troublesome. Alive and vital in Nicaragua, the private sector comprises, among others, thousands of street vendors, shopowners, farmers, owners of small factory-like operations, as well as several multimillionaires engaged in bigger businesses. Despite the range in activity and income levels, however, many Nicaraguans view the entire private sector as "the rich people." Many of Nicaragua's critics, on the other hand, believe the private sector is harassed, repressed, or nonexistent. Both misconceptions are borne out by stories of such people as Alfonso Robelo, a businessman who left Nicaragua to join the *contras,* and whose personal net worth was estimated at $21 million. He, for one, garnered much publicity with his allegations that the Nicaraguan government was denying the private sector its share of political power. This section closes with a sober analysis of this issue by Nicaraguan economist Xabier Gorostiaga.

55. *Under Construction: Nicaragua's New Polity**

By Andrew Reding

Last fall, after observing the political campaign and national elections in Nicaragua, I was able to report in these pages that "for the first time in history, a Marxist-Leninist 'vanguard' party that came to power through armed struggle has submitted itself to an open electoral test against a wide range of opposition parties." At that point, however, no one could predict whether the Sandinistas and the other parties that took part would be willing and able, as they promised one another before the election, to continue the "democratic institutionalization of our revolutionary process." In mid-April I returned to Managua for a month's visit aimed at testing the performance to date.

In the interim a new government had been inaugurated. On January 10, with Bishop Pablo Antonio Vega giving the invocation in his role as president of the Nicaraguan Conference of Bishops, Daniel Ortega Saavedra was sworn in as president of the republic, followed by Sergio Ramírez Mercado taking the oath as vice-president. Two days later the National Constituent Assembly held its inaugural session, electing Carlos Núñez Tellez its first president. In those moments the Junta of National Reconstruction and the Council of State passed into history.

The change represented no major shift in the country's top leadership: Ortega and Ramírez had been the two most important members of the junta, and Carlos Núñez had been president of the Council of State. What did change was the structure of government. The junta, a three-member revolutionary committee, was the creation of the *Frente Sandinista de Liberacion Nacional.* The Council of State was an essentially consultative (or "colegislative") body made up of delegates from organizations chosen by the Frente to represent business, professional, political, ethnic, and other sectoral interests. The transition of January 10 gave the country an elected presidency and a Western-style elected parliament, all of whose members represent independent political parties. There may be an echo here of our own history, in that no significant change in political leadership accompanied the shift from the Articles of Confederation to the new Constitution. There's a secondary echo as well: In the London of the late 1780s the new U.S. governmental structure was ridiculed as widely as were the Nicaraguan elections of 1984 in Washington.

What is going on now is not so much ridiculed as ignored. A rhetorical battle is being waged in the United States over whether the Nicaraguan revolution is keeping or betraying its promises, but without the ammunition of facts. During the days I observed the National Assembly at work, no other foreign correspondent was on hand, with the exception of reporters who were representatives of the (U.S.) Socialist Workers party. I have seen no coverage in mainstream media since my return, even

*From *Christianity and Crisis,* July 22, 1985.

though yards of space have been given to Nicaragua-related stories emanating from the White House and Capitol Hill. It's because of the vacuum of reportage that this account will provide an unusual amount of detail.

A Set of Goals

The Assembly is in fact functioning, working both on current legislation and on drafting the new constitution it is required to complete by January 1, 1987. In agreements reached last October, before the elections, the seven political parties now represented in the Assembly committed themselves, on paper, to a set of basic constitutional principles, including: periodic national elections; freedom of the press and free dissemination of ideas; freedom to organize; freedom of movement; free and democratic labor unions; guarantees for personal, private, cooperative, and state property rights; democratic election of municipal governments immediately following enactment of the new constitution. The FSLN insisted on a commitment to national defense, including a military draft; it agreed to a depoliticization of the armed forces, conditioned on the willingness of non-Frente members to serve.

However admirable the goals, it won't be possible to reach final judgment on the integrity of the process until the constitution is in place and its provisions tested in practice. Meantime, however, a reporter wanting to learn how seriously the Assembly members take the process—and whether the FSLN, with its nearly two-thirds majority, is turning the legislature into a rubber stamp for the Sandinista-dominated executive branch—can pick up evidence in plenty. I was able to interview the leaders and other members of all four major parties. I was also able to sit in on the floor debates in the Assembly. Some were tediously long, but the discussion was free and far-ranging. (It's permissible even to voice open support for the counterrevolution, and not only in the Assembly, but also in the streets and in the pages of *La Prensa,* the fiercely anti-Sandinista paper.) And sometimes the debate is lively indeed; once I saw a fist fight in which both participants suffered some damage before they were separated.

In my interviews with members of the Assembly, by far the most negative judgments came from Virgilio Godoy, nominal leader of the Independent Liberal party (PLI). Godoy is a brilliant pessimist, as skeptical of U.S. intentions as he is about the Frente. He described the Assembly as "an institution that was practically stillborn." In its first legislative act, he said, it had enfeebled itself by transferring broad powers to the presidency, including the right to suspend the Assembly by declaring a state of emergency, to exercise legislative powers during the three months of the year the Assembly is not in session, to control the budget, and to veto acts of the Assembly.

Godoy gave other criticisms in an article in *La Prensa* (March 22) quoting his views. The rules of the Assembly, he wrote, give unfair advantage to the Sandinistas by granting the presiding officer unilateral power to close off debate when in his judgment the topic at hand has been sufficiently discussed. The rule that requires a minimum of five sponsors before a bill can be brought up for deliberation is "clearly discriminatory and antidemocratic,'' since it deprives the three smaller (all Marxist-Leninist) parties, with only two delegates apiece, from initiating legislation on behalf of their constituents. Godoy's most sensational (or oddest) accusation accounted for *La Prensa's* banner headline: ''35 Sandinistas Will Be Able to Approve the Constitution.'' It rested on legislative arithmetic. Under Assembly rules, 60 percent of the ninety-six members (or fifty-eight) constitute a quorum; final approval of the constitution will require a 60 percent majority of the quorum, or a minimum of thirty-five votes. (The arithmetic is accurate, but the parliamentary rules are hardly bizarre; it is not the rules but the election results that put the FSLN in a commanding position. Further, Godoy's argument assumes the absence of a large number of opposition delegates from the Assembly's most critical vote.)

I asked Godoy what he thought about the fate of the pre-election accords pledging all the parties that signed to creation of a democratic system. ''There isn't any evidence that the FSLN intends to respect the signature it placed on those accords,'' he said. ''The first accord of the summit meetings [among the parties] was to reestablish freedom of the press, and that accord was violated the same day it was signed,'' when *La Prensa* chose to suspend publication after government censorship of its lead story for that day (October 21).

Because he was a supporter of the revolution for a considerable period, because he is *La Prensa*'s principal source on Assembly actions, and because he is sometimes described in the U.S. media as ''the'' leading opposition figure, Godoy's opinions have to be included in an article for readers in this country. In other interviews, however, I found few members of opposition parties (including his own) who echoed his views or followed his leadership, and a number who disagreed violently.

I talked, for instance, with Clemente Guido, a medical doctor who is a vice-president of the Assembly and leader of the Democratic Conservative party (PCD), the Assembly's second largest. Guido, a commandingly tall man who speaks with animated confidence, said Godoy's criticisms were half-truths, ''and half-truths are worse than lies.'' Yes, he said, the president of the republic can veto acts of the Assembly, but the Assembly can override a veto with a 60 percent majority (in the United States a two-thirds majority of both Houses is required). Again, Assembly actions that gave power to the presidency did not rise solely from the FSLN: Guido's own party had been advocating such provisions since well before the Frente was founded. Members of the three small parties can introduce legislation by joining together or seeking cosponsors from other parties. Other provisions attacked by Godoy, said Guido, are provisional, subject to revision in the drafting of the new constitution. (As for the charge that the ''excessive'' power of the Assembly's presiding officer favors the FSLN, I observed later that when Guido himself presided he was far quicker to use his authority than the Sandinista president, Carlos Núñez.)

An Internal Struggle

From other sources I learned that Godoy's account of the censorship incident was less than candid: He failed to mention that the censored article was a story reporting his own decision to pull the PLI out of the elections, or that he had been able to announce that decision to the nation in a televised address on the government station, delivered on the evening of the same day *La Prensa* failed to appear.

Without defending the censorship, a fellow member of Godoy's party shed further light on the incident. He was Constantino Pereira, Godoy's vice-presidential running mate on the PLI ticket in the November elections. Pereira is a coffee grower (two plantations) and a cosmopolite who speaks fluent English and French and once lived in exile in Switzerland and France. Last fall, after Godoy's announcement, Pereira made a dramatic televised appeal asking PLI members to ignore their party chief and cast their ballots. His largely successful plea rescued the PLI from political oblivion and helped restore credibility to the elections themselves.

It was the PLI, Pereira reminded me, that originally convened the summit meetings, inviting first the other opposition parties and then the FSLN to participate. By his account, the basic provisions the PLI and other opposition parties had demanded as preconditions for taking part in the election had been incorporated in the agreements. Apart from the constitutional principles already mentioned, he said, they provided for "a democratization of the army, and likewise of the famous CDSs." The FSLN also agreed to free some political prisoners, to review some land confiscations, to provide all the parties with continued access to state-controlled media, and to observe the right of habeas corpus—so that "all conditions were in place for us and the other parties to participate in the elections." Thus, in Pereira's version—confirmed by all other signatories except Godoy—the first violation of the accords was Godoy's still unexplained decision, concurrent with his signing of the agreements, to pull the PLI out.

The ironies run deep. Though Godoy didn't vote in the elections, and though, according to other delegates, he had vowed never to set foot in the National Assembly, it is he and not Pereira who today is seated in the legislature. When I asked him about that, he explained his reluctant participation as providing "evidence of protest." It may be more to the point that if Godoy were to resign or fail to appear, by law his place would be taken by his alternate: Pereira. And in fact, when Godoy absented himself from the first session, Pereira did replace him and was immediately elected to the Assembly's governing council. That was evidently too much for Godoy, who promptly reclaimed his seat, though his performance, as I observed it, has been perfunctory.

The secondary agreements included in the accords of last October provide a checklist to help measure the sincerity of the FSLN's commitment. The promised release of prisoners was accomplished in part during the election period, when a couple of hundred were set free. Some 108 more were released during my visit, and I was present as Clemente Guido hosted a reception for them at party headquarters (most were PCD members) late in the evening of May 3. Confiscations of land taken from purported former allies of Somoza or active collaborators with the counterrevolution have also come under review, in some instances concluding with the return of tracts to their original owners. Though negotiations took several months, the provision for access to state-controlled radio and television is in process of being implemented.

The outcome has been an agreement to structure the programs around the debates in the National Assembly, affording every party the opportunity to present its point of view on each issue of substance. The programs began airing in early May. It was unclear to me how far the FSLN has gone in "democratizing" the CDSs. I did hear two top Sandinistas lashing out at abuses before an assembly of local CDS leaders but when I asked one of them, Interior Minister Tomás Borge, whether there was a connection between his speech that day and the Sandinistas' pre-election promises, he denied it emphatically. Other Sandinista leaders I talked with similarly insisted that the basic democratic and pluralist ideas embodied in the accords were elements of their own program, not "concessions" reluctantly given to legitimate the elections.

A Growth of Trust

Apart from Godoy, opposition party leaders appeared increasingly willing to trust the Frente's democratic professions, some guardedly, some with enthusiasm. The progress made on the secondary agreements (release of prisoners, access to state media, review of land confiscations, etc.) accounted for some of this: It gives greater confidence that the constitution will in fact institutionalize political freedoms that will enhance the opposition parties' chances of growing in strength.

There are other reasons for the emerging level of trust. One is the makeup of the Assembly itself. Thanks to provisions of the electoral law put in place by the provisional government, minority currents representing as little as 1 percent of the voters are represented. In all other countries with proportional representation systems, the threshold percentage is higher: 2 percent in Denmark, 4 percent in Sweden, 5 percent in West Germany. The Nicaraguan electoral system ensures a forum for political viewpoints ranging from Trotskyite to Christian, from traditional conservative to social democrat to Leninist.

Together the opposition parties hold over a third of the seats, enough to create considerable leverage. Clemente Guido told me that if the FSLN were to use its absolute majority to overwhelm the opposition and, in effect, create a one-party system, "I'm sure my party will withdraw from the Assembly," creating a crisis of credibility for the Frente. So far, he said, it isn't happening: the FSLN has shown "flexibility," and opposition parties have been successful in some of their efforts. One major success, in Guido's view: "The General Statute of the National Assembly that we have approved is profoundly Western in nature."

Guido regarded his own election and that of Mauricio Diaz of the Popular Social Christians (PPSC) as vice-presidents of the Assembly as further proof of "flexibility." (Largely thanks to Diaz, an extraordinarily bright, creative, and driven man, the PPSC is the only party that has drawn up a complete draft of a proposed constitution.) Another sign was the inclusion on the FSLN's electoral slate last fall of a dozen nonparty members, nearly 20 percent of the party's representation in the Assembly. One is Ray Hooker, a prominent black educator from the Bluefields region. Another is Sixto Ulloa Dona, a Baptist/evangelical leader. Ulloa, a broad-faced, stocky man who can be jovial or tough as the occasion demands, has a sense of mission; he wants to see the principles of liberation theology incorporated into political life, and particularly to have them accepted as pillars of the Sandinista movement. From my talks with Hooker and Ulloa, it was clear that neither would have run on the FSLN slate if they thought the party might renege on its democratic promises.

Apart from the actual working of the Assembly, to be reported below, perhaps the best test of Sandinista intentions is the makeup of the Constitutional Commission, which has been given the primary role in carrying out the Assembly's most important assignment. The commission has twenty-one members, of whom eleven represent the Frente; the other ten include representatives of all six other parties. Thus the opposition has been accorded a substantially greater weight on the commission (almost half) than it achieved in the elections (about a third). Further, four members of the FSLN delegation, more than a third, are not members of the Frente. One of these is lawyer Danilo Aguirre, assistant editor of *El Nuevo Diario* (of the three Managua dailies, it provides the fullest and least ideologically flavored coverage of the Assembly). The other three are liberationist Christians: cattle-raiser Juan Tijerino; appellate judge Humberto Solis, who is active in the Christian Base communities; and Sixto Ulloa. According to Mauricio Diaz, one of two PPSC commissioners, the presence of these nonparty FSLN delegates greatly facilitates the search for consensus between government and opposition parties. Predictably, Assembly President Carlos Núñez is an FSLN commissioner and Clemente Guido is one of the three PCD delegates; but Virgilio Godoy, though officially the PLI leader, is not one of its two members. Lawyers are the single largest group, but medicine, the Church, labor, the *campesinos,* and business are also represented.

If the best indication that the commission will respect pluralism is its own pluralistic makeup, the course it has adopted offers confirmation. Its first task will be to conduct the "Great Consultation" with Catholic and Protestant religious bodies, women's groups, labor unions, business and farming organizations, and any other groups or persons who want to be heard—including, if possible, the three parties that opted out of the elections last November and that together form the umbrella group *Coordinadora Sacasa,* fronted by Arturo Cruz.

Meantime, the commissioners will be looking for ideas elsewhere, following the model used in framing the Electoral Law. Its members, Sixto Ulloa told me on the day of his appointment, will read "the constitutions of other Central American countries, the European countries, even the constitution of the United States and of other countries, socialist and nonsocialist." The product, he predicted, will reflect the process. He was echoed by Carlos Tunnermann, Nicaragua's ambassador to the United States, an FSLN delegate in the Assembly, and a militant Christian, when I interviewed him in Washington. Nicaragua's commitment to democracy, he said, "needs to be understood here in the United States where everything is reduced to either Western democracy or Soviet socialism. It isn't understood that there can be something different, an original revolution that selects the good there may be in one or the other."

Democracy, Si; Socialism, Si

As examples of good Western ideas, Tunnermann cited the electoral system and pluralism. From socialism, he said, Nicaragua will accept "the idea that wealth shouldn't be concentrated in privileged minorities but should rather be spread out a little more." In Managua, Rafael Solis of the FSLN, a secretary of the Assembly and a member of the commission, carried the point further. Despite the openness of the constitutional process, not everything is up for grabs:

> There are, of course, some points that we consider essential elements of the constitution. We [the Sandinistas] believe it must not dismember the accomplishments of the past five, six years: the agrarian reform and the nationalization of the banks and mines, for instance. As achievements of the revolution, these programs have already attained a constitutional character. . . . They are irreversible. The constitution must reflect the revolutionary change that has occurred in Nicaragua.

And there's the rub. In Washington, institutionalization of any socialist revolution, particularly in the Americas, is frightening because of its potential, strong appeal in other countries. The situation becomes still more frightening if the revolution is made permanent through a democratic, self-determining, and pluralistic process.

At least some members of the U.S. public would take a different view of the process if they knew more about it. It's for that reason I was sorry to be the sole *periodista* from outside Nicaragua present on April 29 when the Assembly opened its sixth session since January. It began conventionally: Assembly President Núñez pronounced the session open, everyone stood for the national anthem, a roll call was taken, and Assembly Secretary Solis sped through the minutes of the preceding session at the pace of a racetrack announcer.

The first item on the agenda was a proposed amnesty for all Miskitos, Sumos, Ramas, and Creoles (English-speaking blacks of the Caribbean Coast). The bill was a direct outcome of the negotiations between the government and the indigenous peoples' organization Misurasata, held in Mexico City April 20-22, and sought to extend a previously announced amnesty so as to encompass members of Misura as well as Misurasata. Misurasata, led by Brooklyn Rivera, is an armed movement that is fighting for autonomy—not independence—for the peoples of the Caribbean Coast; Misura is a competing armed movement of indigenous peoples whose leadership—most notably Steadman Fagoth—is allied with the counterrevolutionary *Fuerza Democratica Nicaraguense* (FDN) and the CIA. Why then the concession to Misura? Rivera had asked for it in order to strengthen his hand as he seeks to unite his people around a goal (autonomy), a posture (nonalignment with the FDN), and a policy (negotiation) that the FSLN wants to encourage.

With the floor open for debate, the opposition went on the offensive. Clemente Guido said he thought the proposal was wonderful, but pointedly asked why it was that "one day we propose something like this to no effect, and the next day the

FSLN proposes it?'' PPSC leader Mauricio Diaz suggested that if amnesty could be extended to one set of *contras* it should be extended to all. Carlos Cuadra, a sharp young delegate in blue jeans and wire-rimmed glasses from the ''antirevisionist'' Marxist-Leninist Movement of Popular Action (MAP-ML), then objected that ''we don't know what has transpired in the accords with Misurasata, yet we are asked to deal with such matters from one moment to the next.'' He was echoed by Allan Zambrana of the Moscow-line Nicaraguan Communist party, who insisted that the ''fruits of the Misurasata accords should be known to the Assembly.'' The full text of the agreements had already been published in *El Nuevo Diario;* Zambrana and Cuadra were apparently demanding an ''inside'' account of the negotiations themselves. Humberto Solis (FSLN) responded that ''there are negotiations that by their nature have to be secret, as with those at Manzanillo'' [with the United States].

Domingo Sanchez, of the Nicaraguan Socialist party (PSN, likewise Moscow-affiliated), asked—rhetorically—how many prisoners were being held without due process, then went on to propose a general amnesty to clean out the prisons, asserting that most prisoners are peasants and that many of their families are suffering economic hardship. Solis replied: ''I think a lot of the *compañeros* are out of order, that they're being demogogic and irresponsible. The Assembly has a Human Rights Commission. If the other parties keep wanting to harp on these accusations [of unjustly held prisoners], we should examine the charges in detail. . . . You just can't go and release all the former National Guard members.'' Isidro Tellez (MAP-ML) supported Solis, asking: ''When you let the National Guard free, where will it all end?'' He reminded the Assembly that these people had been mass murderers, whereas the Miskitos ''have been taken advantage of by the *contras* and improperly treated by the FSLN.''

Virgilio Godoy (PLI) angrily attacked the bill as illegal ''because it discriminates by race.'' He called for a general amnesty encompassing all Nicaraguans. Danilo Aguirre (FSLN) countered that the path to peace needs to be a responsible one, that delegates shouldn't be carrying on like this in the National Assembly while Nicaraguans are dying in war. He emphasized ''that Misurasata has never denied the legitimacy of the revolutionary government.''

Before calling for a vote, Carlos Núñez pointed out that, ''as you can read in the newspapers, no actual accords have yet been reached with Misurasata, only a preliminary agreement to prepare conditions for serious talks.'' With regard to calls for extending amnesty to the *contras,* he asked the delegates to ''remember that there are some who don't so much as hesitate before knifing a *campesino.*'' It was an allusion to the graphic series of photographs published in *Newsweek* showing the execution of an alleged spy by a *contra* band. Núñez cautioned against ''naïveté and foolishness.''

The bill was approved with only seven abstentions, among them those of Godoy and of the right wing of the PCD. Interestingly, a majority of every party voted affirmatively. Embarrassingly, Godoy, though nominally party leader, was the only PLI member I saw abstain. He immediately walked out of the Assembly, not to return for the remainder of the session. The bill then advanced to consideration of particulars, and the debate reopened. Carlos Núñez soon had to leave, and with Leticia Herrera likewise absent, PCD leader Clemente Guido assumed the presidency.

Communist delegate Allan Zambrana opened by saying that Article 1 set a bad precedent as it discriminated by race. Dorothea Wilson (FSLN), representing the Creole population of the Caribbean Coast, countered by inviting the other delegates to visit the region so that they could appreciate the uniqueness of its circumstances. She was seconded by Sumo alternate Ronas Dolores (FSLN), filling in for Miskito delegate Hazel Lau, who reiterated that Sumos and Miskitos were now prisoners only because they had been manipulated by the FDN. And so it went for just about three hours, all on this one topic. (I was grateful when coffee and sweet rolls were served at 6:20 P.M.) Despite the tedium, it was useful to contrast the reality with Godoy's claim that debate is prematurely terminated.

The session resumed early the next day, with Clemente Guido again presiding for the better part of the day. His demonstration of the president's authority to cut short debate came on a proposal to grant incorporated status to an association of cattle ranchers. MAP-ML delegate Carlos Cuadra argued against approval on the basis of the organization's "bourgeois" nature, saying it was "likely to join up with COSEP," the counterrevolutionary High Council of Private Enterprise. Rafael Solis responded for the FSLN by insisting that "the mixed economy is a principle of this revolution." Then, when Isidro Tellez, the other MAP-ML delegate, sought recognition from the chair, Guido abruptly declared the subject to have been sufficiently discussed, and proceeded to a vote. Tellez and Cuadra broke out laughing. Their two votes were the only nays.

Next there was a long debate over a bill to regulate the sale and rental of housing in foreign money. The bill, which eventually passed after heated debate but without substantial opposition, was designed to funnel scarce foreign exchange away from the black market and into the government banking system.

Finally the Assembly took up President Ortega's request that pardons be granted to one hundred eight prisoners, suspensions of sentences to six others, and reductions in sentences to another two. The Rev. José Maria Ruiz, Baptist minister and FSLN delegate, described the approval of the pardons as a "fiesta for all the delegates." But two PCD delegates, while happy with the pardons, used the debate period to vent their anger at fellow-PCD delegate Felix Pedro Espinoza, for failing to attend four of seven preparatory meetings in which pardons for PCD members were considered case by case. Conservative delegate Eduardo Molina then accused the ultra-right-wing Espinoza of publicly insulting his family on the CIA-sponsored *Radio Impacto,* based in Costa Rica, and before long the two came to blows on the Assembly floor. Espinoza ended up with a battered face and Molina with broken eyeglasses. All this as their own party leader presided. The photographs of the event were the sensation of Managua in the morning papers.

It had been a very revealing session. The forcefulness and range of the debate underscored PCD leader Guido's remark to me: "You can see there is a wide range of ideologies within the Assembly [he might have said the same for his party]. There are wide differences, for example, between ourselves and the MAP-ML, or between the PPSC and the FSLN. So that there is simply no truth in the propagandists' assertions that we of the opposition parties are no more than disguised Sandinistas.'' In fact, some of the delegates, including the PCD's Espinoza and his colleague Enrique Sotelo Borgen, openly sympathize with the counterrevolutionaries.

I noted that about eighty-five of the ninety-six delegates were on the floor at any given time. Most were attentive to the proceedings, and many joined in the debate, some repeatedly. Critics like Godoy contend that, given the FSLN's overwhelming majority, all this deliberation is only a meaningless show. But the numbers don't tell the whole story, as is evident elsewhere: Margaret Thatcher's Conservatives enjoy a similar margin over the opposition in the British Parliament, and François Mitterand's Socialists likewise hold an absolute majority. Watching the actual workings of the Assembly gave reason to accept the accuracy of Clemente Guido's judgment, already quoted, on the ''flexibility'' of the FSLN and its preference for negotiation over confrontation.

Indeed, it is hard to accuse the Sandinistas of taking unfair advantage of their near two-thirds majority when two of the three vice-presidents are from parties of the opposition, and when Guido is presiding over a good portion of the sessions. Or when debate on a given bill is stretched out over hours, and at least half the speakers are from opposition parties. Or—most significantly—when not once in the session I witnessed did any vote split along party lines, with the FSLN forcing its will upon the other parties.

*56. Building Democracy through Mass Organizations**

By the *Central America Bulletin*

An extremely important aspect of the FSLN-led revolution is the formation of organizations which attempt to incorporate the majority of the population in the socio-economic transformation taking place in Nicaragua. This process of involving the majority in the determination of the course of the revolution is a broad and deep democratization that complements the holding of fair national elections. Prior to the revolution, neither of these avenues to participation in the political process were available.

The creation and strengthening of what the Nicaraguans call mass organizations is one of the most important manifestations of this developing participatory democ-

*From *Central America Bulletin,* November 1984.

racy.* The worker, peasant, student, women's, professional, and neighborhood organizations involve approximately one million citizens at 40 percent of the total population. The significance of their role in the democratization process is seen in the participation of representatives of the mass organizations in the Council of State beginning in May 1980.

Nature of the Mass Organizations

One of the goals of the mass organizations is to serve as "schools for popular democracy" through which people participate in the political, economic, and social decision-making process. Over the last five years, changes and reorganizations based on day-to-day experiences have deepened their internal democracy. In their meetings, members assess the actions of their executive officers. Through their electoral process, all the mass organizations can ratify or reject their leadership in assemblies held at the base, zonal, regional, and national levels.

The relationship between the Sandinista National Liberation Front (FSLN) and the mass organizations is a mutual one, with the mass organizations developing a significant autonomy from the FSLN. In the view of the FSLN, the mass organizations must not become mere appendages of the party, set up to carry out the work of a top-down revolution. The Sandinistas are committed to preserving the autonomy of the mass organizations as the "architects of history" in the new Nicaragua. According to one regional political secretary of the FSLN:

> The FSLN has the conception that the role of the masses in the revolutionary process is something fundamental: it is not an accessory nor something secondary. The masses themselves have demonstrated that they themselves are the principal agent in revolutionary transformations: they are the active and conscious agents of the revolution. As a political organization we relate ourselves to them.

The way the FSLN relates itself to the mass organizations is in terms of its self-conception as the vanguard. This conception is inseparable from its relationship to the masses. Comandante Carlos Núñez, a member of the nine-man directorate of the FSLN says that:

> The FSLN came to be and is the vanguard of the Nicaraguan people not only for having defined the correct way of struggle, but also for having clearly defined that the masses were the forces capable of moving the wheel of history. If yesterday, oriented and directed by their vanguard, they were the motor of the overthrow of the dictatorship, then today, directed by that vanguard, they are the motor of the revolution.

---

*In this article, unions are considered to be mass organizations.

While this perceived role entails carrying out a leadership function, this does not mean that the FSLN regards the relationship between it and the mass organizations as a monolithic one. "In Nicaragua the people weren't isolated from the vanguard or vice versa," points out Ricardo Wheelock of the FSLN. "There's intercommunication between the two of them."

The intercommunication between the FSLN and the mass organizations has been institutionalized. Zonal and regional officials of the mass organizations regularly send written reports to the zonal and regional offices of the FSLN. These reports include details concerning both the achievements and problems of the mass organizations. In turn, the FSLN sends "orientations" to each leadership body of the mass organizations calling on them to help carry out some task of the revolution.

Leaders of the mass organizations also have frequent face-to-face meetings with FSLN party leaders. These meetings may be of an ad hoc nature to discuss the special concerns of a mass organization, or may be regularly scheduled encounters where an interchange of concerns takes place. Mass organization leaders emphasize that the FSLN does not interfere with the mass organizations' prioritization of tasks or work methods. An official of one regional Sandinist Defense Committee (CDS) remarked that "if the Frente has a task for us we talk with them and decide whether we can do it or not. We negotiate with them to see whether it's possible. We are an autonomous organization. We don't have a vertical relation with them."

The relationship between the FSLN and the mass organizations is not tension-free. For example, in early 1980 the Association of Farm Workers (ATC) mobilized its membership in support of legalizing land seizures that had taken place in the months following the triumph of the revolution. The FSLN, concerned with maintaining the support of the national bourgeoisie and ensuring the survival of the revolution, tended to oppose postvictory land takeovers. For the ATC, however, any return of land to private owners symbolizes a reversal of the process of agrarian reform at a time when thousands of workers and peasants expected its continued advance. In the end, the FSLN backed down from its previous position and decided to support the demands of the ATC.

In 1983 AMNLAE voted against the FSLN in the Council of State on the issue of women's participation in the military draft. The FSLN's original proposal was to make military service obligatory only for men. Women in AMNLAE vigorously opposed this position and eventually won the right for women to volunteer for the Patriotic Military Service.

The Sandinista Defense Committees

The most important of the mass organizations is the CDS. With 60,000 members—almost 25 percent of the total population—organized at the base in 15,000 block organizations, it is the largest mass organization.

The origin of the CDS is in the grass-roots organization that multiplied rapidly following a devastating earthquake in 1972. Little by little, these groups took on insurrectional tasks. One of the major limitations in *barrio*-level fighting against the Somoza regime was need for organized provision of food, water, medical care, and civil defense to the civilian population. To counter this weakness, the FSLN pushed the organization of Civil Defense Committees (CDC), the predecessors to the CDSs. The CDC were organized block by block. They provided the necessary infrastructure to support the population during the insurrections. From the outset, their membership was open to all "honest Nicaraguans"—those who were willing to participate in the resistance against Somoza. Membership or political unity with the FSLN was not a requirement, except on the issue of opposition to Somoza. The overwhelming majority of the CDS membership is not in the FSLN.

The leadership of the CDCs was chosen by the people in the neighborhoods rather than by the FSLN. On occasions, landlords or businessmen were chosen to head committees because of their high standing in the community.

The CDCs reflected the character of the mass organizations in general. They were organized at the initiative of the FSLN in response to a concrete need of the revolution. The FSLN also gave them overall direction and insisted on a democratic internal structure. Nevertheless, the leadership and the day-to-day direction came from the people who actually set up the committees.

On July 19, 1979, the FSLN inherited a country in which there was a certain vacuum of power. There was an immediate need to organize distribution of essential services and maintain order in a situation of near anarchy. The CDCs—now renamed the CDSs—were a principal element in establishing and maintaining order and organizing the delivery of essential services in the absence of any governmental agencies capable of exercising those functions. The FSLN issued a call for the organization of CDSs in every neighborhood, and CDSs were formed throughout the country.

The basic element of the CDS is the block committee. Each committee elects its own leadership. They discuss and work on neighborhood problems and also study national political questions. Decisions are made by majority rule.

The next level of the CDS is the *barrio* committee, which typically has severa thousand people under its jurisdiction. It is at the *barrio* level that campaigns ar organized and tasks are undertaken. The *barrios* elect their leadership to the nex level which is the zone. After the zone is the district.

It is only at the zonal level and above that the staffs are professional. At thos levels, the leadership is limited to dealing with larger policy issues. Day-to-day or ganization and tasks are left to the *barrio* and block committees, which are compose of all volunteers. Despite the FSLN stress on organization through the workplace, i the CDS structure it is quite common for the head of a block committee to be retired man or woman or a housewife, since they are almost always at home. Th result of this structure is a considerable level of autonomy on the local level. Th block and *barrio* committees are forced to resolve their problems with minimal inp from above other than the broad policy guidelines of the national organization.

In the beginning, the CDS carried out many para-statal functions. For exampl there are no national identification cards, and the CDSs were used to identify peop based on personal acquaintance of people in the neighborhood. They also organized the distribution of food and services.

The CDSs assumed these para-statal functions primarily because of the lack of a state apparatus capable of carrying them out. Nicaragua is extremely poor and has limited resources for the establishment of a bureaucracy. CDS members are all volunteers who carry out their tasks after work and on the weekends. In addition, the services that the CDSs initially undertook were needed immediately and the already existing CDC structure allowed them to be organized in a matter of days or weeks, rather than the months that the organization of a bureaucratic structure would have entailed.

Even today, the CDSs are relied on to perform many tasks the state is economically and organizationally unable to carry out. They carry out the health campaigns, such as the massive vaccinations for polio and measles. They have taken steps to control malaria by removing standing water and mosquito-breeding areas throughout the country. Once a year they vaccinate all dogs against rabies. They organize neighborhood cleanup and weed and trash control. They organize janitorial services for all schools on a daily basis. The CDSs find volunteer teachers and donated classrooms for the adult education programs. Before each rainy season, CDS members climb into the sewer system to remove trash and debris to prevent flooding.

The most controversial task of the CDS is the "revolutionary vigilance." Members of the CDS serve one or more four-hour shifts per week at night patroling the neighborhood. Originally, the vigilance was organized to monitor and defend against counterrevolutionary activity. It still fulfills this function along the borders where *contra* activity is high. The vigilance is similar in many ways to neighborhood watch programs in the United States. Because the state does not have the economic resources to patrol the neighborhoods, it formally relies on the CDS to assume this function. Except in areas of high *contra* activity, the CDSs are unarmed and rely on shouts for assistance in case of emergency.

One striking result of the vigilance is an enormous drop in the crime rate. Prior to 1979, few people ventured out after dark because of the presence of criminals and the National Guard. Now, thanks to the destruction of the National Guard, and the formation of the vigilance, people stay in the streets until late.

The CDS role in the distribution of rationed foodstuffs is also very important. Many basic products such as rice, beans, corn, eggs, milk, toilet paper, and cooking oil are rationed because they are in tight supply. The CDS has been assigned this task due to the lack of any other bureaucracy that could take it on.

Finally, the CDSs are active in mobilizing people for political events as well as civil defense. They also encourage people to participate in the militias and army to fight the *contras*.

Critics of the CDS focus on the last three activities. They argue that the CDS is both a para-statal and party structure that allows the FSLN to perpetuate and expand its control over society—and influence elections—by blurring the distinction between the state and the party. In support of their argument they point to incidents of CDS members harassing opposition party supporters, tearing down their posters, painting over their graffiti, and disrupting their rallies. There is a dispute about how widespread these abuses were, but the FSLN admits that they have occurred.

The Development of Internal Democracy

The following example provides insight into the internal workings of the CDS. In 1983, the CDSs underwent a round of restructuring at the zonal and regional levels throughout the country to correspond with the decentralization process of the government. A regional secretary in Las Segovias explained how the executive committee in his region was chosen:

> At the zonal and regional levels we are approved or rejected in public assemblies. Our record of struggle against Somoza is taken into account, as well as our level of acceptance by the people. All block, *barrio, comarco* [rural district], and community leaders participate. So in this zone, 400 CDSs and 200 people can participate. In October 1983, the regional assembly met and chose the regional secretaries. Each zone put forth two or three candidates that were chosen at the base level. Seven people were elected and we then decided among ourselves who should be responsible for each position.

The FSLN takes an interest in the process of democratization in the CDSs. The CDSs are quite autonomous, and despite the influence that the FSLN has on them, abuses result from the spontaneous response of the membership. Recognizing some of the problems in the functioning of the CDSs, Comandante Bayardo Arce wrote a letter to them in October 1982. The letter expresses the strong belief "that the CDS leadership and members should express qualities that can be measured by . . . their willingness to be the best servants of the people, avoiding and combating opportunism, bureaucracy, favoritism, and bossism." It goes on to describe "arbitrary attitudes and actions that exert influences which are contrary to Sandinista principles."

In addition to the fact that this letter constitutes a frank admission by the FSLN of some of their critics' charges, the timing of it and the use to which it was put indicate that FSLN policy is to respond to those problems. Between the middle of October and November 7, 1982, there was a reorganization of the CDS throughout Nicaragua, prompting a reevaluation of the leadership which was either reratified or replaced at that time. On November 1, an election assembly for CDS leaders took place in Ciudad Sandino, a poor *barrio* on the outskirts of Managua. After reading Arce's letter, one woman asserted: "We should make copies of that letter and give it to everyone. Here our rights are underlined. And we ought to show it to our leaders often so that they fulfill it faithfully."

Despite measures such as these, however, abuses do exist. Part of it is explained by the reality that for five years, CDS members have donated millions of hours of free labor in the projects of the CDSs and resent criticism from those who do not participate yet who benefit from the safer neighborhoods and healthier lives.

Another reason for abuses is the very autonomous structure of the CDS. CDS members by-and-large strongly support the revolution and take steps on their own initiative to protect it even when those actions go against the wishes of the FSLN. The FSLN itself asserts that the abuses are the result of a minority of the CDSs. Finally the FSLN points out that Nicaragua is undergoing a "rigorous class struggle" and that a certain amount of tension is natural as the new sectors gain access to political power in Nicaragua and the old power holders attempt to protect their position to the extent that they can under the new conditions.

Domingo Banchez, the leader of the Socialist party, and its presidential candidate, criticizes the FSLN for giving the CDS too much authority.

Other Mass Organizations Represent Farmers, Workers, Women, Youth

The National Union of Farmers and Cattlemen (UNAG) with over 100,000 members now brings significant weight to bear on agricultural policy toward the small and medium peasant sector. The areas in which UNAG most effectively represents its constituency are those of production and commercialization. UNAG helps peasants gain access to land through its representatives on the national and regional councils of agrarian reform. UNAG also participates in the process of allocating credits to small and medium farmers and ranchers via its seats in credit committees at the zonal, regional, and national levels. The peasant's union also helps set prices for basic grains and exercises power in the realm of gaining services and technical assistance for its membership.

The Sandinista Trade Union Federation (CST) now groups together over 100,000 industrial workers. It was created after July 19, 1979, as a result of the merger of all trade unions with ties to the FSLN. It is by far the strongest industrial federation in the country. It has played a key role in the reactivation plans of the economy, in securing the demands of its membership, and taking the first steps toward worker participation in the production process. The CST helped elaborate the new salary scheme in the country, is working to upgrade the working conditions in its members' workplaces, and backs important training programs designed to increase the technical knowledge of industrial workers. The CST is also promoting a pilot project to increase the level of worker participation in the decision-making process in eight state enterprises.

The Association of Farmworkers (ATC) with its 45,000 full-time and 80,000 part-time agricultural workers, has managed to make its organized power felt in three areas crucial to a membership historically marginalized in Nicaragua. It has managed to gain significant wage increases for its members, has pushed for more health and housing improvements and for additional government stores selling basic goods at low fixed prices in the countryside, and has raised the level of worker input in reviewing and approving production plans as well as raising their ability to understand the technical and financial aspects of the production process.

The Association of Nicaraguan Women (AMNLAE), with its membership of approximately 60,000, has had the most influence on policy regarding education, health, child care, family law, employment for women, and the image of women in Nicaraguan society. AMNLAE sat on the Council of State where it introduced, and submitted for discussion to its base, legal proposals that are contributing to the struggle against sexist attitudes and practices in Nicaragua. Its law concerning relations between parents and children has been especially effective in requiring men who abandon their children to pay child support. AMNLAE has worked with government ministries to establish day-care centers in both the city and the countryside. It has also campaigned to increase the number of women members in agricultural cooperatives, the number of women in the professions, and women's participation in health care, education, and defense.

The Sandinista "19th of July" Youth Organization has over 30,000 members organized in 880 base assemblies, constituting 16 percent of the students between the ages of fourteen and twenty-eight. Many of their members were mobilized in production brigades, participated in the literacy campaign, and have joined the civil defense and the reserve battalions of the Popular Sandinista Army.

Mass Organizations: Successes and Challenges

The mass organizations, after more than five years of existence, have exercised a considerable degree of autonomy and have challenged both the FSLN and the state in order to meet the demands of the sectors they represent. At the same time, the FSLN has demonstrated a disposition to encourage the autonomous development of these organizations.

The mass organizations have made significant advances in democratizing their internal structure and have demonstrated their power to the extent that they have been able to win some of the demands of their membership and influence certain revolutionary policies.

Their rapid growth in the last five years is all the more remarkable in face of objective difficulties. The limited development of the productive forces in an underdeveloped country such as Nicaragua acts as a brake on the development of social organizations. The mass organizations are working with very meager resources of capital, technology, skilled personnel, and means of transportation and communication. The tremendous growth in membership and the influence of these organizations is one of the most important aspects (if not the most important aspect) of the quality, nature, and depth of the development of democracy in Nicaragua.

57. *Toward a New Constitution**

By the Instituto Histórico Centroamericano

The Greatest Challenge in Constructing the Juridical Structure

The process of elaborating the constitution is part of a juridical effort to institutionalize the revolution that began in the very first days after July 19, 1979. The commitment has been to use law as an aid to social transformation in a revolutionary way. Among its major efforts are the following: the Fundamental Statute of the Republic, the Statute of Rights and Guarantees, the Law of the Army, the Agrarian Reform Law, the Political Parties Law, the Electoral Law, and the Patriotic Military Service Law.

Through this effort to construct a new body of law, the juridical disorder inevitable in any revolution has been maintained at a low level. The disorder that has existed is more a result of deficiencies in the organization of the judicial system—caused in part by budget limitations—and to the judiciary's historic lack of independence from the power of the executive. The resulting deeply rooted habits have not yet been totally eradicated.

The political will to resolve the conflict of ethnic diversities on the Atlantic Coast through an autonomy statute is a challenging example of the decision to mobilize the symbolic efficacy of law in the service of revolutionary change. Further proof of Nicaragua's commitment to this process is its submission to the juridical findings of the International Court at The Hague in an effort to resolve the conflict with the U.S. government. The most important challenge of this commitment, however, is the framing of Nicaragua's new constitution.

For the past six years, the new Fundamental Statute of the Republic and the Statute of Rights and Guarantees of Nicaraguans has served in place of a constitution. The previous constitution and the complementary constitutional laws were repealed by Article 3 of the Fundamental Statute, instituted one day after the overthrow of the Somoza dictatorship.

In the first quarter of 1985, the National Assembly, elected the previous November 4, fully debated its own General Statute, which would provide the norms for the functioning of the new legislative body. That debate itself brought up a profoundly polemical point: Could the Assembly appoint itself the highest state power simply by virtue of having the popular mandate to elaborate the constitution? The parties that proposed this hoped thus to subordinate the executive power to the constituent assembly, using the argument, common in Latin American politics, that prior to the existence of a constitution, the constituent assembly itself is the maximum authority. The fundamental issue was whether the Assembly was starting from zero in the preparation of the constitution.

---

*From *Envío*, vol. 4, no. 53 (November 1985).

The Sandinista position that opposed it was based on the recognition of a historic act, the revolution, and on the reality that the population had elected a president with a well-known program, oriented toward the consolidation of that revolution. Having elected this program with their votes, the majority of the Nicaraguan people ratified what, to use the popular Nicaraguan phrase, "they had already voted for with their lives." By defending a revolutionary articulation of state powers and not a subordination of the executive to the legislature, or a system of "checks and balances," the FSLN was reaffirming in the Statute of the Assembly that the revolutionary project was continuing on its course, now within a constitutional framework.

When the debates and voting had ended, it was clear that the National Assembly would be able to pursue legislative functions even before the constitution was written, and that the executive would retain powers enabling it to continue developing the revolutionary project. For example, the president has the power to write and approve the national budget, establish taxes, decree a state of emergency (submitted to the ratification of the Assembly), etc. In its fifth session, on April 29, 1985, the National Assembly initiated the process of preparing the new constitution.

Structures and Functions in the Constitutional Process

In accordance with Article 44 of the National Assembly's General Statutes, Assembly president Carlos Núñez appointed a Special Constitutional Commission, in charge of drafting the constitution. This process, plus the subsequent debate and revision, can take no more than two years. The current schedule is to present the draft to the floor of the National Assembly for debate in March 1986. At the end of this process the Special Commission will be dissolved.

The commission is made up of twenty-two members: twelve from the FSLN, three from the Conservative Democratic Party (PCD), two each from the Liberal Independent Party (PLI) and the Popular Social-Christian Party (PPSC), and one each from the Nicaraguan Socialist Party (PSN), the Nicaraguan Communist Party (PC de N) and the Marxist-Leninist Popular Action Movement (MAP-ML). This composition is roughly proportional to the number of seats held by each of the seven parties in the Assembly, although the FSLN is underrepresented. The commission's executive board is made up of three FSLN representatives plus one each from the PCD, PSN, and PPSC. Both the commission and its board are chaired by Carlos Núñez, also a member of the FSLN National Directorate.

To streamline its work, the Special Commission divided into three subcommissions. Similar to a commission of the earlier Council of State which helped draft the Electoral Law, the Subcommission on the Exterior is in charge of organizing delegations to countries with a wide range of political systems, to study each country's constitution and the historical circumstances that gave birth to it. "We cannot disregard the abundant history of political and juridical thought left to us by the great political thinkers. . .through their contributions to the theory of the State and of constitutional law," commented Núñez, when he inaugurated the legislative Assembly on January 9, 1985.

The Subcommission on National Consultation is hearing the constitutional proposals made by parliamentary and extraparliamentary political parties, unions, and religious, cultural, professional, and popular organizations and associations. Once hearings are held with all organized sectors wishing to contribute, the first phase of the national consultation will be finished. During this phase, still ongoing, a preliminary first draft is being written, incorporating these proposals and the findings of the Commission on the Exterior. This draft will be presented to the public during the second phase of the national consultation, through a series of open forums around the country.

Finally, there is the Subcommission on Constitutional Affairs, which works in conjunction with the other two commissions, processing and ordering their results. It is this commission which will draw up the general lines of content and character of the constitution and will write the finished draft to be presented for debate in the Assembly. To facilitate this, the commission members are systematically studying theories on constitutional law, Nicaraguan laws written over the last six years, and the country's previous constitutions, all with the assistance of the National Assembly's judicial advisers.

What Has Been Done

The Subcommission on the Exterior has almost concluded its visits to other countries. In July, it visited various Socialist countries, including the Soviet Union, Bulgaria, Poland, Czechoslovakia, and East Germany. In August, the commission visited Argentina, Colombia, Peru, Venezuela, Costa Rica, and Cuba. It was scheduled to visit Mexico as well, but had to cancel due to the devastating earthquake there. In October the commission visited Western Europe, including Sweden, West Germany, France, England, and Spain. A trip to the United States is planned for December, during which the commission will attend various national seminars on constitutional law scheduled for that month.

The Subcommission on National Consultation has already heard the constitutional proposals of the seven political parties represented in the Assembly. Of the extraparliamentary parties, only two have accepted the Assembly's invitation to present their proposals: the Revolutionary Workers Party (PRT) and the Party to Reunite Central America (PUCA). Meetings have also been held with the Sandinista Workers Confederation (CST), the Agricultural Workers Association (ATC), the National Association of Teachers (ANDEN), the National Union of Farmers and Ranchers (UNAG), the Women's Association (AMNLAE), the prorevolution branch of the association of professionals (CONAPRO Héroes y Mártires), and the Evangelical Development Support Committee (CEPAD). Still to come are meetings with the Federation of High School Students (FES), the University Students Union (UNEN), the Sandinista Defense Committee (CDS), the Communist Workers' Central (CAUS), among others. The various constitutional proposals are being published or broadcast through all media.

The Nicaraguan Workers' Central, a Social Christian-based union, requested a hearing with the commission, but canceled at the last moment. The *Coordinadora* parties (which abstained from the November elections), the AFL-CIO-affiliated Confederation of Trade Union Unity (CUS), the Supreme Council of Private Enterprise (COSEP), and the Catholic Church all noticeably refrained from contributing to the National Consultation.

On October 26, during its eighth plenary session, the Special Commission approved its schedule for the months of November, December, and January. Most important on the agenda is the second phase of the National Consultation. The open forums, to be held all over the country, will begin in December and continue through January. The many foreign observers who have asked to attend the sessions will be invited.

In his evaluation of the process to date, Carlos Núñez remarked during this session that the proposals of the mass organizations emphasized more than did those of the political parties the need to give constitutional rank to "the rights for which the people struggled against Somoza." At the next meeting of the Special Commission the parties will discuss the differences and similarities in their criteria regarding the constitution.

Concurrent with this entire process, the peoples of the Atlantic Coast are being consulted extensively in preparation for the drafting of an autonomy statute by a separate eighty-member commission of coastal peoples. The autonomy statute will also be ratified by the National Assembly and incorporated into the constitution.

Similarities and Differences between the Political Parties

The following summary [of the positions of the various parties is] intended only to highlight significant positions within the spectrum of views and, when possible, where the bulk of opinion tends to fall. It does not attempt a detailed interpretation of the phraseology used by the parties, nor does it necessarily distinguish those parties who have expressed no views at all on a given topic.

Fundamental Principles

As mentioned earlier, the [parties basically agree] on nonalignment, a mixed economy, and political pluralism. The MAP-ML is the only party to oppose these three fundamental principles, on the grounds that they would represent the institutionalization of a bourgeois-capitalist policy.

Organization of the State

The PSN, PD de N, PPSC, PLI, and PCD proposed a democratic, unitary, and representative state of law that would be organized into executive, legislative, judicial, and electoral branches. The PLI additionally emphasized the need for a conceptual, real, and effective separation between political parties, the armed forces, and the Church. The FSLN's main criterion was participatory democracy. It proposed the institutionalization of its unique 1979 program and maintained that the state must be free, sovereign, and independent. The MAP-ML explicitly rejected the division of the state into separate powers, representative democracy, and a presidential form of government. Instead, it proposed fundamental principles designed to defend the interests of the proletariat and to establish the rule of the masses.

Economic and Agrarian Policy

All the parties except the MAP-ML supported the principle of a mixed economy. The PPSC and the PSN proposed the creation of a body to plan and control the national economy. The Conservatives and the Socialists agreed on the need for the implementation of an import substitution policy. The Liberals and the Sandinistas backed the nationalization of exports. Only the FSLN proposed formalizing the "eradication of the exploitation of man by man" in constitutional language. The four parties that presented positions on agrarian reform—the PSN, PCD, MAP-ML and FSLN—agreed that it should be institutionalized. The Conservatives added that when the productivity of state lands proved deficient, they should be turned over to the private sector.

Labor Policy

With the exception of the PCD, which expressed no position on the issue, all the parties proposed that every Nicaraguan has the right to a job, to form free trade unions, and to strike. As to the manner in which workers would participate in production, the PSN proposed "workers' control of production and of enterprises," and the PLI called for a "law on comanagement, especially with respect to state enterprises."

Responsibilities of the State

All parties except the PCD and the PC de N agreed that the state is responsible for providing assistance to the population in the areas of health, education, housing, and welfare. The FSLN added food provision to the list. The PPSC and the PLI, respectively, proposed that education be free of "official ideology" and "apolitical." The MAP-ML expressed that religious education should be "extracurricular and voluntary."

Atlantic Coast

Under a category titled "Territory," the PSN, the MAP-ML, and the FSLN supported concepts of autonomy for the Atlantic Coast. The PC de N opposed the inclusion of an autonomy statute in the constitution, fearing it would jeopardize territorial integrity, and the PLI proposed greater autonomy "of the territories" without specifying the Atlantic Coast.

Foreign Policy

All the parties, again excepting the MAP-ML, supported the principle of nonalignment. The MAP-ML, the PLI, the PSN, and the FSLN were the only parties to explicitly support the principle of self-determination; the latter two also included anti-imperialism as a principle. These same two, together with the Conservatives, proposed a policy of "interamericanism," while the FSLN also postulated Central American integration and international solidarity.

Domestic Political Policy

The seven parties concurred on a domestic policy of political pluralism and subscribed to an electoral process open to the entire population, governed by an electoral law. The PCD, PPSC, and the PC de N stated their support for the present electoral law, although the PCD proposed that it be revised. The PLI specifically called for the institutionalization of the Supreme Electoral Council.

Nonparty Organizations

How will the civic organizations and the armed forces fit into this framework of political pluralism? For the Socialists, Liberals, and Conservatives, all civic organizations should be apolitical and nonpartisan. The Conservatives also suggest[ed] that existing organizations suspend their activities until a law is drafted regulating their formation and function. The PPSC proposes that organizations be democratic, pluralistic, voluntary, and autonomous from the state. The Communists simply endorsed the agreement reached on civic organizations at the top-level meeting of political parties held in October 1984. The FSLN was the only party to postulate unrestricted organization, whereas the MAP-ML proposed the formation of a "worker's council" to oversee organizations. With the exception of the PPSC, which took no position, all parties agreed that the function of the armed forces is national defense and that military service to that end is obligatory. The PCD and the PLI stated that the armed forces should be apolitical and nonpartisan.

The Constitution

The PSN, the PCD, and the PLI sustained that the constitution should be revised when necessary, while the PPSC proposed that it not be subject to any reform for a period of ten years. The PCD listed sixteen laws it would like to see receive constitutional status. While all seven parties agreed on the need for a body to control the enforcement of the constitution, they did not agree on what this body should be. The Socialists proposed a court of constitutional guarantees, the Conservatives and Communists some form of constitutional tribunal. For the PPSC, the enforcing body should be the National Assembly itself, and for the Liberals, the existing Supreme Court of Justice. The FSLN stated that the workers themselves should see to the enforcement of the constitution, and the MAP-ML more specifically proposed its idea of a workers' council.

The Debate on Hegemony: An Important Educational Process

Speaking to the First Congress of Anti-Imperialist Thought, Comandante Bayardo Arce of the FSLN National Directorate defined the Sandinista project as consisting of "a mixed economy, political pluralism, genuine nonalignment, and participatory democracy." Normally, only the first three principles have been emphasized. The fourth, participatory democracy, expresses in political terms the very nucleus of the new sources of legitimacy in Nicaraguan society. The principle that most clearly parallels it in international terms is nonalignment—the expression of the paramount value of national dignity in foreign policy. This is the meaning of statements such as this by Nicaragua's president: "We would like to be able to be received in Washington with the same respect that we are received in Moscow."

A mixed economy and political pluralism, on the other hand, constitute the creative efforts by which a state, oriented primarily towards workers' interests, tries to bring other social classes into a pact of national unity. This unity permits development projects to be as effective as possible and political organization projects to be carried out with a minimum of conflict.

It has escaped no one's attention, however, that participatory democracy, when combined with the new economic orientation of the state, will lead over time to a logical shift of managers of private capital into administrators of public enterprises, and to a more social orientation of the profits from production. Similarly, participatory democracy, together with the state power authenticated in the elections, will lead to the logical adaptation of political pluralism to the reversal of prerevolutionary power relations.

The elaboration of the constitution, particularly the consultations with the parties and organizations and the open meetings with all sectors of the population, is in fact a social debate on the juridical ordering of the new hegemony. The more open and less sectarian this debate, the greater the possibility that the rules of the game will express flexible agreements between interests, a greater degree of consensus, and less coercive use of political power in the future. If this massive consultation manages to involve a majority of the population, it could be another important lesson for Nicaraguans on how to work together, as well as how to confront each other during the long process of constructing the new Nicaragua. In other words, it could have a transcendence similar to that of the electoral process, the literacy campaign, or the insurrection itself, all recent examples of Nicaraguans' capacity to undertake a challenge of this caliber.

The inexperienced National Assembly, for its part, still carries the mortgage of historic political practice in Nicaragua. A temptation to drown debate in the heavy-handed use of power, for example, has not been completely shaken. Submission to arbitrary rule and the devaluation of political rights to which Nicaraguans had grown accustomed during the long decades of dictatorship still remain, hindering many sectors of the population from feeling genuinely called upon to participate in the constitutional process. Similar impediments existed at the beginning of the literacy campaign and the electoral process. In response, creative learning techniques and mechanisms for participation using a collective teaching methodology were developed with positive results. The consultation on autonomy for the Atlantic Coast is also attempting to awaken similar participatory energy.

There is still a long way to go before the outlines of the Nicaraguan constitution become clear. The political parties offer few guidelines for the juridical forms that could give institutional structure to participatory democracy. Will some type of popular assembly arise, a council of workers, a parliament of mass organizations and guilds? And if such an initiative flourishes, can it be effectively articulated with the National Assembly, the pole of representative democracy? Will the interpretation of the constitution be in the hands of the electoral power, the Supreme Court, or the National Assembly? Or will a new autonomous state body be created to act as a constitutional tribunal? Above all, will the result be a constitution which stabilizes fundamental values while maintaining the capacity for change in a society that wants to continue critically examining its own institutions in order to adapt them to a changing reality? The answers to these questions will determine if Nicaragua will continue to be "a new point of reference in the realization of the social change that the Third World needs," as Bayardo Arce affirmed in the aforementioned speech.

The constitutional process is laboring not only under the harsh weight imposed by the survival economy and the war, but also the continued abstention of the Catholic hierarchy and the parties and unions that boycotted the electoral process. Does their silence presage a rejection of the product that will emerge from this process? If so, it would only increase the level of conflict during the construction of the new social order.

It is not by chance that the Reagan administration is reinforcing the pretensions of the counterrevolution, itself inspired by the U.S. government, and places as a condition for the renewal of bilateral talks the dissolution of the present National Assembly. Nothing could better symbolize its refusal to recognize the new hegemony emerging in Nicaragua. In sum, nothing shows more clearly what has been and continues to be at risk—Nicaragua's claim to sovereign dignity.

58. *The Structure of the Electoral System**

By the Latin American Studies Association

Negotiating the Structure

One of the most notable characteristics of the electoral process in Nicaragua this year was its "open-endedness," based on a continuous process of negotiation between the politically dominant FSLN and opposition parties and civic organizations. There are strong indications that this process of formal and informal bargaining will continue in the postelection period, both within the newly elected, ninety-six seat National Assembly and through the formal "National Dialogue" that was convoked in early October by the seven political parties participating at that time in the elections. By election time, the National Dialogue had evolved into a much broader negotiation involving all thirty-three major political groupings in the country, including all political parties (whether participating in the election or boycotting it), all trade union federations, all church groups, and all the private sector organizations.

At earlier stages of the movement toward elections, the FSLN also demonstrated its openness to pragmatic compromise with opposition groups. FSLN proposals for the Political Parties Law (passed in final form by the Council of State in August 1983) and the Electoral Law (finalized in March 1984) were altered in many ways through a long process of discussion and debate with opposition groups. The Electoral Law, which went through multiple drafts between initial discussions in 1981 and final enactment in 1984, was further modified at several points during the precampaign period, in response to new demands by opposition parties. Among the concessions to opposition groups that resulted from this bargaining process are the following:

- A definition of political parties that characterizes them as contenders for power, not just participants in public administration or political discussions. The object of a political party, according to the final version of the parties law, is to achieve political power.
- The expansion of the Supreme Electoral Council (CSE) from three members, appointed by the Nicaraguan Supreme Court, to five members, including two nominated by the National Council of Political Parties, in which all opposition parties participating in the elections were represented. The expansion was sought by the opposition parties because they questioned the independence of the three initial CSE appointees from the FSLN government.
- The allocation of a seat in the National Assembly elected on November 4 to any losing presidential candidate who receives the "electoral quotient" (effectively, 1/90 of the total votes cast nationally in the election). This provision has

*Excerpts from *The Electoral Process in Nicaragua: Domestic and International Influences. The Report of the Latin American Studies Association Delegation to Observe the Nicaraguan General Election of November 4, 1984*. (Published November 19, 1984.)

the effect of increasing opposition party representation in the Assembly, beyond the number of seats that they won through the proportional representation system established by the Electoral Law.

- A significant increase in the amount of free campaigning time on state-run radio and television stations provided to all parties that had registered candidates for the November 4 election.
- Extension of the closing date for campaign activities from October 31 to November 2.
- Multiple extensions of the deadline for registration of candidates, from July 25, to August 4, to October 1. None of the opposition parties (i.e., those affiliated with the *Coordinadora*) which had declined to register their candidates by the original deadline took advantage of the extension periods.
- A guarantee that all political parties participating in the November 4 elections will maintain their legal status, regardless of the number of votes they received in the 1984 elections.
- A review by the FSLN government of the cases of all opposition party militants who were in jail ostensibly for violations of criminal laws. As a result of this review, the Council of State released 40 out of approximately 300 such "political prisoners" prior to the elections.
- A procedure whereby all voter registration cards presented on election day would be retained by election officials, to eliminate any possibility that in the future the failure to vote (as evidenced by the lack of a validated voter credential) could be used as the basis for government reprisals or denial of public services. (Our delegation observed on election day that some voters were reluctant to surrender their voter registration card, which they had expected to retain.)

On a few points, the FSLN refused to accommodate opposition party proposals. The Sandinistas insisted that the minimum voting age remain sixteen years, because of the extensive participation of this age group in the national literacy campaign, defense, and agricultural production. There was also a powerful demographic rationale: The median age in Nicaragua is about sixteen (as compared with thirty years in the United States). The FSLN also insisted that members of the armed forces have the right to vote (the opposition wished to exclude them from the electorate). The FSLN rejected an opposition party proposal to require representatives (poll-watchers) from *all* of the parties participating in the November 4 election to sign the final vote tally for each precinct before the votes from that precinct would be considered valid. Since most of the opposition parties were unable to supply poll-watchers for more than a minority of the 3,892 polling places, the practical effect of the proposed requirement would have been to throw more than half of the total number of ballots cast into a "contested" category, which would have provided further ammunition for abstentionist groups and external forces seeking to discredit the elections. Most importantly, in its negotiations with Arturo Cruz and the *Coordinadora,* the FSLN refused to accede to the demand for direct talks between the government and the *contras* prior to the November 4 elections.

Reviewing the history of the negotiations between the FSLN and the opposition parties since 1981, and especially during the current election year, Stephen Kinzer, the Managua-based correspondent of the *New York Times,* told our delegation: "The FSLN gave in on almost all of the opposition parties' demands concerning how the electoral process would be run. Their stance seemed to be, 'If any clause of the Election Law causes serious controversy, we'll modify it.' Most of the opposition's complaints about the process had nothing to do with the mechanics of the elections, but rather were more general criticisms of the political system. . . . What some of these groups want is a complete change in the political system: to abolish the CDSs (Sandinista Defense Committees), get the Sandinistas out of the army, prohibit [incumbent] government officials from running for office, and so forth. In short, they want Nicaragua to become a parliamentary democracy first, before they will participate. But this isn't Switzerland!"

At least one of the opposition parties—the Popular Social Christian Party (PPSC)—apparently shares this assessment. As the PPSC's vice-presidential candidate told our delegation, in his view, *"El Frente Sandinista negocia todo—menos el poder."* ("The FSLN Front negotiates everything—except political power.") Other opposition party representatives whom we interviewed were less generous in their views toward the FSLN's negotiating posture, but most indicated that the Sandinistas had given important ground on one or more points of major concern to their party. These acknowledgments, as well as the record of changes actually made in electoral laws and procedures, led our delegation to conclude that the FSLN had shown considerable flexibility and a disposition to compromise in its dealings with opposition groups during the pre-election period. This evidence contrasts markedly with the image of FSLN intransigence and rigidity emphasized in most U.S. media coverage and official U.S. government statements about the Nicaraguan electoral process.

The Electoral Law

The electoral system established by Nicaragua's 1984 Electoral Law (as modified) is rooted in the classical liberal-democratic concepts of territorial representation and "one citizen, one vote." The law provides for presidential government and separation of powers between executive and legislative authorities and functions. The electorate is defined as all citizens sixteen years of age or older, who would cast one ballot for the offices of president and vice-president and one ballot for a predetermined, party-specific list of candidates for the Assembly.

In the short term, the key institution will be the National Assembly, since it will function first as a constituent assembly empowered to define and promulgate the basic constitution of a new political system. At the outset, the National Assembly will be a unicameral body with ninety-six members (ninety regular members plus the defeated presidential candidates of the six opposition parties, who are entitled by law to hold a seat in the Assembly) who will serve six-year terms.

As presently stipulated, the Assembly will function first for up to two years as a constituent assembly, then become a legislature unless the Assembly itself, acting in its constituent role, modifies its own term, powers, and functions. Under the law, the Assembly could dissolve itself and call new elections as soon as the constitution has been drafted and promulgated. As mentioned above, this course of action has been specifically advocated by the Popular Social Christian Party (PPSC), among others. For the moment, the FSLN government is downplaying any possibility of new elections in the near future (i.e., before the six-year term of the Assembly members just elected expires).

The election of the Assembly was based on a standard model of proportional representation. The country was divided into nine territorial districts with a varying number of members per district, apportioned by population. The members elected to the Assembly were chosen from ordered lists of candidates stipulated by each legally inscribed party; the number elected from each party depended upon the fraction of the vote won in each district by each party. The choice of this kind of proportional representation system is significant because it tilts the National Assembly toward political pluralism, by assuring the representation of a wider range of interest and opinions within the electorate than would be achieved under a U.S.-style single-member district system. Proportional representation should also encourage the institutionalization of a multiparty opposition in the legislature. Without it, the smallest opposition parties would have had virtually no chance of winning seats in the National Assembly. Also, the system of legislative election based on a single ballot with candidates rank-ordered by the parties themselves is likely to strengthen internal control and discipline within all the existing political parties.

Election of the president under the 1984 Electoral Law is by simple plurality. The future functions, powers, and term of the executive branch are all subject to modification by the newly elected Assembly, acting in its role as a constitutional convention. The powers of the National Assembly itself remain to be determined, as part of the constitution-making process. A key question is whether the Assembly will have the power to approve or reject proposals for the national budget. The constituent assembly will also define the basic terms of the future relationship between the state and the private sector.

The Supreme Electoral Council

The 1984 Electoral Law created the Supreme Electoral Council (CSE), which immediately assumed responsibility for the electoral apparatus. Following the pattern of Costa Rica and several other Latin American republics, the CSE was given the status of a fourth, fully autonomous branch of government. It was given the authority, at least in theory, to make decisions independently of the Junta de Gobierno, the Council of State, and the National Directorate of the FSLN.

The CSE was required by law to consult with the National Council of Political Parties on such matters as the electoral calendar and voter registration procedures. The National Council of Political Parties is comprised of one representative from each of the legally recognized political parties. Actions taken by the CSE during the 1984 campaign indicate that it did, in fact, exercise considerable independence.

Nevertheless, as noted above, the Electoral Law was modified several times during the pre-election period in response to pressure from opposition parties seeking even stronger guarantees of CSE impartiality.

In addition to managing the registration of voters, parties, and specific candidates, the CSE was charged with supervising the use of campaign propaganda, distributing paper donated by several foreign countries to the participating parties, providing them with substantial portions of their campaign funding, responding to complaints of campaign law violations or abuses, training local and regional election officials, distributing ballots and other voting equipment, and counting and reporting the vote.

Two advisers from the Swedish Electoral College assisted the CSE in technical design of electoral procedures and in training matters. For example, the decision to print dark colored stripes across the back of the white ballot so that one's vote could not be seen by holding the folded ballot up to the light was one result of the Swedish technical assistance.[1]

Voter Registration: Procedures and Results

The Electoral Law called for a mandatory nationwide registration process that was carried out over a four-day period from July 27–31, 1984. Registering to vote (but not the act of voting itself, which remained voluntary) was required by law because the information generated through this process was to serve as a basis for the first official, nationwide census to be carried out since 1971. Although it was illegal not to register, there have been no reported cases in which penalties were imposed for nonregistration.

The registration procedure was technically straightforward and occasioned very few complaints, either formal or informal. The CSE organized and paid for a national education campaign using radio, television, newspapers, local governments, and the various mass organizations (labor unions, CDSs, etc.) to inform people of the requirement to register and of the procedure to be followed. Residents of each precinct registered either by presenting positive identification (birth certificate, driver's license, social security card) or by the testimony of two registered witnesses from the same precinct. Each registrant received a registration card *(libreta civica)* bearing the person's name, date of birth, place of habitual residence, sex, type of identification presented, signature, and thumbprint. The *libreta civica* also identified the location of the precinct and the volume, page, and line number of the registration catalogue that includes the entry for the registrant. At the end of each of the four registration days, lists of the new registrants were posted for a ten-day period. Both individual citizens and political parties were invited to inspect the lists and to file complaints about persons who had registered improperly or who did not live within the precinct.

The results of the registration process were remarkable. In just four days, a total of 1,560,580 persons registered, representing 93.7 percent of the estimated voting-age population.[2] The proportion of eligible voters registered ranged from a low of 58.5 percent in one war-troubled Atlantic Coast region to nearly 100 percent in other regions. The overall results surprised even Sandinista government leaders, who had expected only about 1.2 million persons to register.[3] The Swedish electoral technicians who had advised the government expressed pleasure at the outcome. A spokesman remarked that "To carry out a voter registration like the one that has been done in Nicaragua is quite difficult, above all when there are inexact data on the total population of the country. If we add together all the difficulties that the Supreme Electoral Council has had in carrying out registrations [under wartime conditions], we consider them to be a total success."[4]

No political party or other group in Nicaragua—including those that boycotted the November 4 elections—will now admit that they opposed voter registration. Even the Church hierarchy publicly supported the registration effort. However, the parties affiliated with the *Coordinadora* did not advocate registration until just before the process began, and their organ, *La Prensa,* refused to accept paid promotional advertising for the registration effort from the Supreme Electoral Council.[5]

Guarantees and Protections in the Electoral Process

Electoral laws are only as good as the means they establish to assure fair access, procedural honesty, and an accurate count. The Nicaraguan Electoral Law of 1984 provided a broad array of protections and guarantees.

As noted above, the law created a system of open scrutiny of all electoral proceedings (registration, campaigning, voting, vote tabulation) by party-nominated observers, at each level of electoral organization. Systems for receiving complaints and appeals for each step in the process were also established, as well as mechanisms for evaluation of complaints, reports to the interested parties, and correction of abuses or violations of the law. The Supreme Electoral Council had ultimate appellate authority over disputes and complaints that were not resolved at local or regional levels. The electoral councils at local and regional levels as well as the precinct-level voting boards were endowed with legal authority to require cooperation from all other governmental agencies in order to carry out their functions. The precinct boards were also provided with electoral police (trained volunteers from the regular police force and private citizen volunteers) under the control of the precinct board, to guarantee public order and compliance with legal procedures for voting and registration (e.g., the prohibition on electioneering, placement of party propaganda, or bearing of arms near polling places).

The Electoral Law provided for equity in financial resources among the competing parties, through public financing of the campaign in the amount of 9 million córdobas ($900,000) for each party. This amount probably covered only a fraction of the costs for a full national propaganda and organizing effort for the larger parties. But the law also permitted parties to receive additional funding from both domestic and foreign sources. The CSE also sought, received, and distributed substantial donations of materials (paper, ink, etc.), which it provided to the parties in equal amounts. The total government outlay for the elections was 400 million córdobas ($40 million), including the costs of the registration drive and government contributions to the participating parties for their campaign expenses.[6]

The actual voting process on November 4 was meticulously designed to minimize the potential for abuses. The citizen arriving at a polling place presented his or her registration card, which was then verified against the precinct's registration lists. When approved for voting, the citizen received his or her two ballots (one for the presidential race, one for the National Assembly), and a check mark was placed next to the voter's name in the voter registration catalogue to indicate that that person had voted. (This also provided an independent basis for determining the total number of votes cast in each precinct.) The voter's registration card was stamped in a box indicating that it had been used. In response to a request by opposition parties, all voter registration cards were retained by election judges so that there would be no possibility of their being used as an *ex post facto* way of checking on whether a person had voted (as allegedly happened in connection with the 1984 elections in El Salvador).

Each voter was then shown to a heavily curtained booth in which he marked the ballots, using an indelible marker, with a simple X beneath the party name and symbol of his choice. Ballots were designed for simplicity, and all party emblems were printed in full color. Once marked, each ballot was then folded, brought out of the booth, and deposited in one of two ballot boxes color-coded to match the dark colored stripes on the back of each ballot (gray for the Assembly ballot; blue for the presidential–vice-presidential ballot). The voter then placed his right thumb or forefinger in a dish of indelible red ink, covering the nail, as a final means of preventing multiple voting.

In order to assure that the voting occurred in secret and free of coercion, only one voter at a time was allowed into the room containing the election officials and voting booth. (At some of the larger polling places, which had two lines of voters, two sets of election officers, and two voting booths, it was possible for two voters to be in the room simultaneously.) This procedure clearly slowed the pace of voting, but guaranteed maximum secrecy. In addition, polling places were required to be free of all party propaganda, last-minute electioneering activity, and all firearms other than the sidearm of the electoral police officer at each precinct. No persons other than the precinct voting board members, official (CSE-certified) international election observers, and accredited poll-watchers were allowed in the room where voting occurred.

Prior to opening each polling place, ballot boxes were opened, certified to be empty by all the precinct voting board members and party poll-watchers, and then sealed. The voting period lasted from 7:00 A.M. until either 100 percent of the precinct's registered voters had cast ballots, or until 7:00 P.M. (The average precinct had approximately 400 registered voters.) Anyone still in line at 7:00 P.M. was also allowed to vote.

Once the poll was closed, precinct election officials counted the check marks beside the names of those who had voted, recorded the count on an official form in the registration book, and signed the report. Poll-watchers were also permitted to sign the report if they wished. The ballot boxes were then opened, and votes were tallied in the presence of poll-watchers.

After the votes were counted at each precinct, the totals were recorded in official reports and signed by all members of the precinct electoral board and by any poll-watchers who wished to sign. One copy of the results was sent by courier to the CSE in Managua, and a telegram reporting the results was also sent to the CSE. The registration books, ballots (including any unused ones, which had to be carefully accounted for), and the precinct voting report were taken to the regional Electoral Council office, where the tally of ballots was repeated and another telegram reporting the results was sent to the CSE in Managua. Poll-watchers from the participating parties were present at the regional Electoral Councils and at the CSE, and copies of the telegrams from precinct-level officials were made available to each poll-watcher.

Notes

1. The ballots were also printed on heavy, opaque white paper. The contrast with Somoza-era elections is striking: The Somozas used translucent ballots, so virtually everyone assumed that their vote was not secret. The same problem occurred in the 1984 elections in El Salvador, where thin-paper ballots were deposited in transparent ballot boxes. The vote in Nicaragua in 1984 was truly a *secret* ballot.
2. The base population of eligible voters was estimated using population projections prepared by the United Nations' Latin American Center of Demography, CELADE (fascículo F-NIC, November 1, 1983) and by the Nicaraguan Institute of Statistics and Census, INEC. The country's total population in 1983 was estimated at 3,057,979, with the capital city of Managua accounting for 27.3 percent of the national total (833,298 inhabitants). Breakdowns of the estimated 1983 population by geographic region *(departamento)* and age group can be found in: Instituto Nacional de Estadísticas y Censos, *Nicaragua en cifras, 1983* (Managua: INEC, July, 1984), Tables 1–6 and 1–7.
3. Interview with Comandante Jaime Wheelock, Managua, November 3, 1984.
4. Consejo Supremo Electoral, *Boletín Informativo,* no. 5 (September, 1984), p. 2.
5. "Los partidos políticos de Nicaragua en dos meses de campaña electoral," *Envío* (Instituto Histórico Centroamericano, Managua), vol. 4, no. 40 (October, 1984), p. 2B
6. Data supplied to our delegation by the Supreme Electoral Council.

*59. "Fraud" in Nicaragua**

By John B. Oakes

John B. Oakes is the former senior editor of the New York Times. *He traveled to Central America shortly before writing this article.*

The most fraudulent thing about the Nicaraguan election was the part the Reagan administration played in it.

By their own admission, United States embassy officials in Managua pressured

*From the *New York Times,* November 15, 1984.

opposition politicians to withdraw from the ballot in order to isolate the Sandinistas and to discredit the regime.

"It was really very light pressure," said one diplomat dryly. Some politicians affected did not see it quite that way. One conservative leader who refused to withdraw commented with some bitterness: "Two weeks before the election, a U.S. embassy official visited my campaign manager and promised to help him with money to succeed me as party leader if he withdrew from my campaign. He did."

Yet the results demonstrate that while the election was flawed by intimidation, some human rights violations, and some violence, it was not a fraud nor was it carried out Soviet-style, as the Reagan administration regularly charged. Exercising the coercive powers of an entrenched Marxist ruling party, the Sandinistas were still able to collect only 67 percent of the total vote. This was not so very much better than President Reagan himself did with 59 percent in his American-style election.

Eighty-four percent of the registered voters in Nicaragua went to the polls, where they were free to choose by secret ballot among seven parties. More than 30 percent of them chose to vote against the Sandinistas.

Nicaragua is neither an American-style democracy nor a totalitarian dictatorship. It is a revolutionary socialist state only five years removed from the violent overthrow of the infamous Somoza regime, which no Nicaraguan can forget was originally installed and long supported by the United States. Even today in Managua there stand the skeletons of factory buildings destroyed by the last Somoza in his vain attempt to bomb the revolution and the revolutionaries out of existence. Even today over the National Palace there flies not the Nicaraguan flag but the red and black standard of the Sandinistas, still celebrating their revolutionary triumph.

Hardly over its revolution, the country is still at war. It is at war with the Miskito Indians, whose remarkable leader Brooklyn Rivera was in Managua recently under safe conduct to begin the first feelers toward peace. It is at war with the counterrevolutionaries, whose army of some 12,000 is fighting, killing, and sometimes pillaging, largely inside Nicaragua's northern border. It is at war, above all, with the United States, whose planes fly out from Honduran airfields and daily menace Managua with their sonic booms, whose ships invade Nicaraguan waters, and whose money, arms, and advice sustain the rebels.

Under such circumstances, most revolutionary governments wouldn't hold an election at all, and they would certainly be adding to their arms—as the Nicaraguans are doing—wherever they could find them.

"November 4, 1984," said a State Department spokesman referring to Nicaragua's election day, "was a lost opportunity for Nicaragua." True enough, but not quite in the way he meant.

Those anti-Sandinista politicians and parties that refused to take part in the election—some at Washington's behest—lost the opportunity to add their strength to the thirty opposition members who have just been elected to the ninety-seat National Assembly. Its first job when it meets in January will be to write a new constitution.

November 4 was a lost opportunity for the United States as well. Instead of encouraging the democratic opposition to fight within the system, the Reagan administration did just the opposite. It tried to torpedo the election, thus helping to lose for its clients the considerable influence they otherwise would have had.

As it turned out, the mixed voices of a divided Nicaraguan people were heard through the ballot box. It is still not clear whether they will be heeded. But one thing is certain: the present American policy of military "diplomacy" in the name of anticommunism has not helped the cause of democracy in Nicaragua. On the contrary, it is much more likely to bury it for another generation.

*60. Nicaraguan Repression of Labor Unions**

By the White House Office of Media Relations and Planning

In Communist countries throughout the world, trade unions serve not to advance the interests of the workers, but to serve the political interests of the rulers. They serve not to organize strikes but to forbid them; not to improve wages and benefits but to restrain them; not to bargain collectively on behalf of the workers but to organize the collective submission of the workers to their employer—the state.

This same path is being pursued by the Communist leaders of Nicaragua. The primary purpose of labor unions in today's Nicaragua is to assist in the forced transformation of society along the lines determined by the Sandinista leadership.[1] Existing independent trade unions are being harassed, their members blacklisted, threatened, and sometimes jailed. Most of the unions and most of the union members in the country have been pressed into Sandinista labor confederations subservient to the government. These confederations have surrendered hard-won contract concessions and have forced lower pay and inferior working conditions on their members. Strikes have been forbidden; collective bargaining has become a farce.[2]

Edgard Macias, Sandinista vice-minister of labor before he was forced to seek asylum for criticizing the regime, has summed up the situation well:

> Thus the Nicaraguan workers have been reduced to being objects . . . the workers cannot choose, free of fears, either their labor union, or their central labor organization, their ideological option, [or] their political party.[3]

Immediately after the revolution, the Sandinistas formed two large labor confederations—the Sandinista Workers Central (CST) for nonagricultural workers, and the Rural Workers Association (ATC)—to replace the *Somocista* labor organizations and to compete with the two leading democratic labor confederations, the Nicaraguan Workers Central (CTN) and the Confederation for Labor Unification (CUS), both of which opposed the Somoza dictatorship.

---

*Excerpts from the *White House Digest,* August 24, 1983.

At first, the CST, the Sandinista nonfarmworkers confederation, worked for traditional labor goals—better wages, better working conditions.

But by late 1980 it had shifted its emphasis toward organizing political support for the government and enforcing government economic policies. It endorsed Sandinista policies blocking wage increases and forbidding strikes. The Sandinista Ministry of Labor participates in all collective bargaining negotiations and must approve all final agreements.[4] The CST cooperates with the Ministry's policy of revising labor agreements to deny workers wage and benefit increases previously secured—even when the employers are willing to maintain the original, costlier contracts. It pressures members into taking an active role in "defending the revolution" and into joining the Sandinista militia.[5] The ATC similarly adheres to Sandinista labor policies.[6]

In 1981 the CST joined the Moscow-led World Federation of Trade Unions, and since has signed friendship and cooperation agreements with the Soviet Central Council of Trade Unions. It receives technical and training assistance from the Soviet Union and Eastern Europe.

In spite of their refusal to pursue their members' interests, the Sandinista confederations are overwhelmingly the largest in the country. Workers who refuse to join and labor leaders who refuse to affiliate with Sandinista labor organizations are subjected to punishments ranging from harassment, unemployment, threats, and official denunciations all the way to arrest, destruction of personal property, and beatings. In Macias's words:

> The [Sandinista front] and its central organizations unleashed a war against all other central organizations, using all of their resources including the Ministry of Labor, the army, the militias, and the manipulation of the right to a job . . . against the CTN and . . . the CUS.[7]

Government favoritism toward Sandinista labor organizations is the simplest method of persuasion.

The Sandinista unions have access to official government communications outlets, which are used to promote the Sandinista unions as well as to attack the independents. Also the Sandinista unions have the use of government buildings, meeting places, and offices free of charge.[8]

The Ministry of Labor has, in effect, a veto over the workers' choice of unions. It expedites agreements between workers and Sandinista unions while interfering with those between independent unions and workers.[9] In some cases it has even forcibly removed members of legitimately elected unions from their workplaces. In other cases it has created dummy pro-Sandinista unions, enrolled a few workers in them, and arbitrarily designated the dummy unions as the bargaining agents for enterprises at which a majority of the workers belong to independent unions.[10]

Workers have been denied social benefits or jobs[11]—especially in nationalized enterprises[12]—for not belonging to a Sandinista labor organization. And, as mentioned, when an independent union does reach a favorable settlement for its workers, the Ministry of Labor can void the agreement, thus severely punishing the workers for their choice of unions.

Leaders of the independents have repeatedly been denied the right to carry on the normal activities of a free trade union. They have been forbidden to hold normal meetings, to collect dues, to bargain without government intervention, to hold seminars, to organize, or to leave the country without the explicit approval of the Council of State.[13]

To quote Macias again:

> There are two different labor worlds in Nicaragua: on one side the workers who are protected and privileged by the FSLN, and on the other side those who . . . belong to the "second class" labor unions and for whom life is much harsher.[14]

But, short of real terror, perhaps the Sandinistas' most potent weapon is political intimidation. In a totalitarian society, expressions of disapproval from the government transmit fears that we as free people find it difficult to comprehend. Since coming to power, the Sandinistas have loudly and consistently labeled the independent unions "counterrevolutionary," "destabilizing," and "conspiratory."[15]

The charges are false—the independent trade unions were in the vanguard of the opposition to Somoza. But the charges mark the independent unions as enemies of the ruling clique, which is sufficient to frighten many workers away.

Even so, outright terror and repression of the independents have been common all along. From the start of the CST organizing drive, CST representatives—in reality Sandinista activists with little or no trade union experience—would arrive at union meetings accompanied by armed militiamen, whose very presence intimidated the workers into favoring the CST in affiliation votes.

Notes

1. Annual Labor Report, "Labor Trends in Nicaragua," p. 1.
2. The Permanent Committee for Nicaraguan Human Rights, "A Union Report On Nicaragua." (This committee is one of the few remaining bodies in Nicaragua with the right to criticize the government.)
3. Edgard Macias (former Sandinista vice-minister of labor) statement of February 11, 1983: "Labor Relations in the Sandinista Regime," p. 14.
4. "Labor Trends," p. 15.
5. Ibid, p. 6.
6. Ibid, p. 8.
7. Macias, p. 13.
8. "A Union Report"
9. "Labor Trends," p. 16
10. Macias, p. 6.
11. Verbal report from Latin American area advisor, Bureau of International Labor Affairs, U.S. Department of Labor.
12. Petition of the Leaders of the United Confederation of Workers to Sandinista Comandante Bayardo Arce Castano, p. 2.

13. Unclassified attachment to March 1, 1983, AFL-CIO letter to Bureau of International Labor Affairs, U.S. Department of Labor.
14. Macias, p. 10.
15. Petition, p. 5.

*61. Labor, Democracy, and the Struggle for Peace**

By the West Coast Trade Union Delegation

The West Coast Trade Union Delegation comprises the Oregon Federation of Teachers, Screen Actors Guild, AFSCME, SEIU, ILWU, ACTWU, and other unions.

In 1944 Somoza signed a new labor law which for the first time gave legal status to trade union organizations. On paper things looked rosy, but in actuality, labor organizing was severely repressed.

This was especially true in the countryside, where agricultural workers were condemned to a life of servitude. Agriculture has always been the base of the Nicaraguan economy. Coffee, cotton, sugar, and tobacco account for nearly 75 percent of Nicaragua's exports. And 60 percent of Nicaragua's workers are employed in agricultural production (with many of the rest working in related industries). During Somoza's time, much of this labor force worked the land held by Somoza and a few other wealthy landholders. Farmworker unions, or other organizations that threatened profits, were crushed unmercifully by Somoza's National Guard.

Under Somoza, the industrial sector of Nicaragua's economy was very small and underdeveloped, even in comparison to other Central American countries. During the 1960s there was an influx of U.S. capital, which led to the emergence of a small urban industrial work force, predominantly in Managua. A few "company" unions closely tied to the Somoza regime, for example, the Confederation of Trade Union Unity (CGT) and General Confederation of Labor-Independent (CUS), were formed during this period, as well as several other more independent unions. But the great bulk of the urban work force remained unorganized.

During the 1970s, there was very little open union activity. Six thousand construction workers struck for twenty-six days during the building boom following the 1972 earthquake that leveled Managua. Health, textile, and sugar refinery workers also conducted strikes, but Somoza responded by arresting union leaders and breaking their unions.

Sebastian Castro of the Sandinista Workers Confederation (CST) told our delegation that the government immediately declared these strikes illegal, even when every prerequisite required by law was fulfilled. Once the strike was declared illegal,

*Excerpts from *Nicaragua: Labor, Democracy, and the Struggle for Peace*. Report of the West Coast Trade Union Delegation to Nicaragua. (Labor Network on Central America, November 1984).

Article 119 of the National Labor Act was invoked. This stated that abandoning one's workplace represented just cause for firing. So management would fire all the workers. The workers then would go and picket the company's front gates, and when they blocked the strikebreakers, the National Guard would throw the union leadership in jail. That was the end of the strike.

"Large numbers of people went to jail," explained Castro. "They were accused of being Communists and subversives who wanted to destroy public order. That's why the trade union movement couldn't grow. Somoza made sure that every trade unionist who was not in agreement with his government or with his boss was branded a Communist subversive and thrown in jail. I can't remember a single union leader," continued Castro, "who didn't go to jail at least once for having participated in a strike."

As a result, most union activity was forced underground. The struggle for workers' rights and improved conditions took the form of the popular uprising against Somoza. Clandestine workers' committees led extended strikes throughout 1978 and 1979 as part of the general insurrection.

The Labor Movement Today

In July 1979, the Ministry of Labor recorded some 133 unions representing 27,000 workers, about 6 percent of the work force. Today there are an estimated 1,100 unions comprising 260,000 workers, about 55 percent of the work force. In only five years the number of organized workers has increased nearly tenfold.

(In Nicaragua 80 percent of the unions are organized by workplace rather than trade or industry. Under Somoza's 1944 Labor Code, industrial unions were forbidden. In recent years, efforts have been made to build new industrywide organizations.)

Nicaragua's large number of local unions are organized into a broad diversity of trade union confederations and associations (journalists, teachers, health workers, etc.). All of the major trade union organizations are represented in the Council of State, but are otherwise independent of the government. They reflect, in fact, a broad range of political philosophies. Each of the confederations, for example, is allied with a political party of corresponding political outlook. (This is a common feature of trade union confederations in most of the world, similar to the AFL-CIO's link to the Democratic Party.)

On the local level, individual union members have the right to affiliate with any confederation they choose—they are not restricted to the affiliation chosen by the local. For example, many members of the dockworkers union in Corinto, including three members of the executive board, are affiliated to the CUS, while the union as a whole is affiliated to the CST.

In November 1980, the CST called a conference of all of Nicaragua's unions and confederations to discuss united trade union action. Out of that conference came the Nicaragua Trade Union Coordinating Council (CSN).

The CSN plays an important role today in developing a common trade union response to the important issues of concern to Nicaraguan workers: defense of the country, maintenance of production levels, distribution of consumer goods, equitable salaries, improved working conditions, resolution of labor disputes, economic planning, labor legislation, health and safety, worker education, etc.

Edgardo Garcia, general secretary of the ATC and coordinator of the CSN, told our delegation that all the major trade union confederations and organizations in Nicaragua are members of the CSN. Only the CTN and the CUS—which together represent less than 2 percent of the organized workers—have not joined. Garcia said that the CTN boycotted the November 1980 meeting. The CUS was originally a founding member of the CSN, but withdrew one month later.

The CUS and the CTN (Huembes faction) are affiliated instead to the Ramiro Sacasa Coordinating Committee. The Sacasa Committee is composed of these two unions, the Private Enterprise Council (COSEP), and three rightist parties (PSD, PSC, and PLC), all of which oppose the Sandinista government. Many unionists we met believe the Sacasa Coordinating Committee works closely with the CIA and the U.S.-backed *contras* to try to overthrow the Sandinista government.

According to the Ministry of Labor, over 1,000 collective bargaining agreements have been signed since 1979, compared to only 160 during the entire forty-three years of the Somoza regime.

Every union has its own collective bargaining agreement, and the terms vary somewhat depending on whether the enterprise is state-owned, privately owned, or mixed, and on the profitability of the enterprise. Nevertheless, most contracts have very similar features.

We were frankly surprised by some of the provisions that are normal in Nicaraguan collective bargaining agreements. They are ahead of contracts in the United States in several respects. Typical contract provisions include full health and maternity coverage; subsidies for lunch, transportation, and consumer goods; and educational leaves and subsidies.

In almost all instances unions also have access to the company's books, enabling them to review the finances and estimate the margins of profit. Imagine the thought of having contract rights to the complete financial records of General Motors, J.P. Stevens, AT&T, or Continental Airlines!

Aside from these contract benefits, workers also benefit directly from several government programs. These include free medical services provided by the Ministry of Health (MINSA), pensions and pay subsidies provided by the Ministry of Social Security (INSSBI), and extensive occupational health and safety programs and technical training administered by the Ministry of Labor (MINTRAB).

In a number of workplaces our delegation visited, especially state-owned enterprises, the role of the trade union has taken on a new dimension.

At Timal, the new sugar cane processing complex, the union, the engineering staff, and the plant administration jointly participate in the planning process. "In this plant," explained Raul Baca, engineer, "We're trying to form the new kinds of production relationships which push forward our revolution: That is, to get rid of the traditional antagonisms between the professional and the workers. Because today our interests are one. In our revolution, the main objectives are to resolve the profound social and economic problems of our people: food, housing, health, and education."

In a similar vein, at the Texnicsa textile plant, Bayardo Enriquez of the union executive board told us that the factory is comanaged by the union and the plant administration. We asked how this is done.

He explained that there are two mechanisms. The first is a committee that meets monthly to survey the production of the previous month and set new production goals. The production committee has representatives of the administration (the managers of production and of human resources) and of the union (the secretary of production and the secretaries from all the different sections of the plant).

Long-term planning, however, is carried out by a larger committee, again composed of representatives of both the union and the administration. This factory committee reviews the different fabrication processes, the state of the machinery, and all economic considerations in order to set long-term goals.

In addition, the union executive board meets weekly with workers in all the sections of the plant. The union then takes any problems to the administration, to be mutually resolved.

The Issue of Strikes

Just three weeks before our delegation's arrival in Nicaragua, workers at the Victoria Brewery in Managua conducted a five-day strike. The strike received a lot of press in Nicaragua (and in the United States as well), and was widely discussed within the trade union movement.

Our delegation spent several hours at the Victoria Brewery, speaking to workers on the shop floor and to members of the union negotiating committee.

On August 20, 1984, workers at Victoria stopped work and occupied the plant, after an impasse was reached in negotiations between the union's fifty-two-member negotiating committee (representing all the departments in the brewery), the plant administrator, and the Ministry of Labor. The workers were demanding raises of 50–100 percent and the state administrator (the plant is 80 percent state-owned and 20 percent private) was seeking to implement the salary levels consistent with SNOTS.*

Victoria is the oldest brewery in Nicaragua (and the best, so we were told). Somoza held majority interest until 1979 when the brewery was confiscated by the revolutionary government. Later that same year, the workers at Victoria affiliated to the CST and received what was considered to be one of the better contracts around. However, wages at the plant have remained fixed over the last few years, and workers there told us it became increasingly difficult to support their families.

The strike ended on August 24 when the Minister of Labor promised to review the SNOTS classifications of jobs at the brewery. A commission including the negotiating committee, the union's executive board, and a representative of the CST national board then commenced negotiations with the Ministry of Labor. As a result

*Maximum salaries allowed under current wage and price controls.

many jobs were upgraded in classification. In the production department, for example, this resulted in a 35 percent increase in salary levels. In the warehouse it meant an increase from 1,658 córdobas per month to 2,270 córdobas per month. We were told by the union that negotiations were going well, and our delegation later got news that an agreement had been reached.

The Victoria strike was interesting to us because it illustrated the kind of struggle taking place within Nicaragua's unions. On the one hand, we talked to many long-time workers in the brewery whose reaction to the economic pinch imposed by the war was simply to make increased demands on the government. They were not concerned about what broader impact increased wages might have on the economy or on national defense under the present circumstances. They were focused on their own personal problems, not the war, the economic blockade, or other causes of the country's economic difficulties. For the most part they blamed their problems on the Sandinistas.

On the other hand, we met many workers who told us about the importance, to them, of defending the revolution. These workers thought that the priority now should be to increase production and strengthen military defense, and that a strike would divert from this. They also felt that the equalization of wages under SNOTS—in particular improvements for lower-paid workers—is far more important in the long run for Nicaraguan workers than the immediate wage gains of a few.

Juan José Solis, secretary of conflicts for the union, explained why it was difficult to meet all the workers' demands: "We have a critical economic situation. It's a problem of the internal economic structure which the dictator left us, which had as its focus the exploitation and dividing of the workers' movement. It's a problem of our being attacked militarily. And it's a problem of our dependent economy being hit by a boycott from the international monetary institutions. . . . We're like a poor family living in debt, being robbed, being beaten up, and still trying to feed our children."

The Victoria strike was the first to take place in Nicaragua since the strike ban and other state of emergency measures were lifted for the electoral campaign. (They had been imposed in March 1982 due to increased aggression.) Even during the strike ban, however, a number of strikes took place: construction workers in León, workers at the San Antonio Sugar Refinery, and workers reconstructing the National Stadium. While technically against the law, none of these strikes was suppressed by the government. There were no court injunctions against picketing, no arrests, no police, no fines or penalties, and no union busting. In every case, negotiations continued until the matter was resolved, and the workers went back to work.*

*Sebastian Castro, a leader of the CST and a representative to the Council of State, explained that the no-strike clause—which his union supported—was never intended to suppress legitimate economic demands. Rather, he said, it was enacted to prevent any organized attempt to cripple and bring down the government through strikes. Castro pointed out, as did other unionists, that the CIA had instigated several right-wing strikes in Chile as part of the U.S.-backed overthrow of the Allende regime, and Nicaraguan workers were determined to prevent the same thing from happening in Nicaragua. "A revolution which doesn't defend itself doesn't deserve to be called a revolution," he said.

It has not been because of the emergency decree or government suppression that there have been so few strikes in the recent past. The reason is that most trade unions themselves have voluntarily suspended the use of strikes as a method of resolving labor conflicts.

Lily Soto, general secretary of the journalist union (UPN), explained it this way: "The right to strike is for us a great achievement of the workers of the world, and also our own great gain. But for us the problem is that we are in circumstances of counterrevolutionary aggression and war, when we need to produce to support the front. The workers who are most advanced say, 'No Strike.' It's not a right the government has taken away. The workers themselves have decided to say, 'No Strikes,' because obviously it would provoke an economic destabilization greater than what has been provoked by the aggression."

This was not hard to understand. We only had to remember the "No Strike" pledge of U.S. unions during World War II.

The "Opposition" Unions

As we mentioned earlier in this report, only two small union confederations (together representing less than 2 percent of organized workers) oppose the Sandinista government. They also do not participate with the nine other Nicaraguan labor organizations in the CSN. Were it not for the fact that the AFL-CIO regards the CUS and CTN as the only legitimate labor organizations in Nicaragua and maintains close relations with them, they would hardly be worth more than a passing note.

Within Nicaragua itself the CTN and CUS are well known by trade unionists despite their very small following. This is due to their affiliation with the Ramiro Sacasa Coordinating Committee (which includes the Private Enterprise Council and three rightist parties) and their long-established reputation of being directly connected with counterrevolutionary and CIA intrigue.

Our delegation met with the CUS and one of two factions of the CTN.

The CTN

Antonio Jarquin is general secretary of the CTN faction that bears his name. He reported to us that in September 1982 a sharp struggle took place at the Fifth Extraordinary Congress of the CTN. A majority of the leadership, those who received the backing of the Sacasa Coordinating Committee, were expelled by the delegates representing 80 percent of the union's base. The reason for the expulsions, according to Jarquin, was that under the leadership of Carlo Huembes, "the CTN was conducted in a way that was really counterrevolutionary."

Since 1982, Huembes and his followers have attempted to usurp the name of the organization, according to Jarquin. Both groups claim legitimate title to the CTN.

For his part, Jarquin recognized the impressive advances that have been made by Nicaraguan workers in the past five years, pointing out that "the growth of the workers organizations has been fabulous." However, he qualified most everything he said with a criticism of the FSLN, claiming that the Sandinistas were restricting freedom and democracy. In particular he charged that workers in the CTN had been victims of beatings, firings, defamation, and imprisonment. He was also careful to add, however, that, ''We're not going to deny that in some cases some workers have been engaging in counterrevolutionary activities.''

With respect to the aggression against Nicaragua, Jarquin was eloquent: ''We have made clear, and have demanded of the U.S. government that the $19 million that they sent to the *contras* they should send to build roads, hospitals, pay for teachers; and instead of sending U.S. soldiers to die in Nicaragua, they should send doctors to save Nicaraguan lives. We are completely against the policies of the U.S. government.''

Jarquin bemoaned the fact that ''the U.S. embassy has given support to Huembes [the other faction].'' When asked about the AFL-CIO, he stated: ''The group of people recognized by the AFL-CIO are those who are being supported by the small opposition groups in the national private sector and the counterrevolutionary groups. In this we could say there is a mistake being made by the AFL-CIO.''

The CUS

Our delegation met with Alvin Guthrie, the general secretary, José Espinoza, the political secretary, and several other leaders of the CUS.

We asked their opinion about gains made by Nicaraguan workers over the past five years: They were hard pressed to think of any. We asked about U.S. policies, the mining of the ports, and the other *contra* attacks: They responded by talking about Soviet intervention in Afghanistan. We asked about their participation in Nicaragua's electoral process: They defended having walked out of the debate on the Electoral Law in the Council of State.

The CUS takes pains to point out the large ''CIA'' painted on the outside of the office. It's part of their story of how the CUS is being harassed, how free and independent trade unionism (which is what they call themselves) is being repressed by the Sandinista government.

Our delegation discovered little to substantiate this charge.

We found the CUS conducting its union business openly and publicly. Like any other union it has been free to carry out organizing campaigns anywhere in the country, in any sector; in fact, Guthrie cited a 50 percent increase in CUS membership over the past five years. The CUS is free to hold seminars and assemblies every several months to denounce the Sandinista government and the lack of trade union freedom, and they do. They are free to publish a fancy multicolored, twenty-page bimonthly magazine which is full of their charges about the lack of trade union rights in Nicaragua. And they are free to travel all around the world, to Mexico City, Brussels, Panama, (even to Miami to meet with the Kissinger Commission), to international trade union meetings everywhere in order to file charges and give speeches vilifying the Sandinista government for violating free trade union rights. All this they do, and often.

Based on our delegation's investigation, we would characterize the CUS as an anti-Sandinista propaganda organization, with a vanishing trade union base, plenty of money, and close political ties to all the traditional enemies of Nicaragua's workers.

*62. Nicaraguan Trade Unions and Confederations**

By the West Coast Trade Union Delegation

Membership**

CST: Sandinista Workers Confederation *(Central Sandinista de Trabajadores)*
The strongest union confederation in Nicaragua, the CST was formed in 1979 as a result of the merger of all the pro-Sandinista unions that emerged after the Triumph. Has been the fastest growing confederation with a broad base that includes manufacturing, transport, communications, construction, commerce. It describes itself as Sandinista, supports the Sandinista government, has close ties with FSLN, and is affiliated internationally with the World Federation of Trade Unions (WFTU).

112,700

ATC: Association of Farm Workers *(Asociación de los Trabajadores del Campo)*
One of the most important confederations in Nicaragua, the ATC grows out of a long history of farmworker organizing. Officially formed in 1979. Based exclusively in the agricultural work force, organizing laborers on private haciendas and state farms. It describes itself as Sandinista, supports the Sandinista government, and has close ties with the FSLN.

43,000***

CGT: General Confederation of Labor-Independent *(Confederación General del Trabajo)*
Formed in 1963 as a split from the Somoza-dominated CGT. Led

*From *Nicaragua: Labor, Democracy, and the Struggle for Peace*. Report of the West Coast Trade Union Delegation to Nicaragua (Labor Network on Central America, November 1984).

**SOURCE: Data for the CST, ATC, FETSALUD, UNE was supplied by organizations themselves and coincided fundamentally with that of the Ministry of Labor (MINTRAB). Center for Labor Studies (CETRA-MINTRAB) supplied others, updated to June 1984. Figures for independent unions are an approximation based on above sources and interviews.

***NOTE: Membership of ATC swells to 200,000 during the harvest season.

militant strikes of construction workers in early 1970s. Includes the major construction union, SCAAS, and also has base in manufacturing, transport, and communications. It describes itself as Marxist-Leninist, supports the Sandinista government, has ties to the Nicaraguan Socialist Party (PSN), and is affiliated internationally with the WFTU. **17,200**

CAUS: Confederation for Action and Trade Union Unity
(Central de Acción y Unidad Sindical)
Formed in the mid-1970s with a small base in manufacturing and agriculture. It describes itself as Marxist-Leninist, critically supports the Sandinista government, and has ties to the Communist Party of Nicaragua (PCN). **2,000**

FETSALUD: Nicaraguan Health Workers Federation
(Federación de Trabajadores de la Salud)
Formed in 1975 and led many militant struggles in the health sector. Represents health workers of all kinds. Originally affiliated with the CTN, it now describes itself as independent, supports the Sandinista government, and has bilateral ties with unions in many countries. **19,000**

UNE: National Union of Public Employees *(Unión Nacional de Empleados)*
Formed clandestinely in 1978 and became official after the Triumph. Base is in employees of state ministries: banking, communications, energy, water, etc. It describes itself as independent, supports the Sandinista government. **45,000**

CTN: Nicaraguan Workers Confederation *(Confederación de los Trabajadores Nicaragüenses)*
Formed in 1972 and has small base in manufacturing, agriculture, and commerce. In 1982, the CTN split into two factions. Both describe themselves as Social Christian and both oppose the Sandinista government. One faction (Huembes) has ties to the Social Christian Party (PSC) and the other (Jarquin) to the Popular Social Christian Party. Both factions claim to be the legitimate CTN with international links to the World Confederation of Labor. **2,700**

CUS: Confederation of Trade Union Unity *(Confederación de Unidad Sindical)*
Formed in 1962 and organized in many Somoza-owned businesses: ports, airlines, services, and hotels. Its base has dwindled significantly since 1979. It describes itself as Social Democratic, opposes the Sandinista government, and has close

ties with the Social Democratic Party (PSD—a right-wing party which was denied membership in the Socialist International), and is affiliated internationally with the International Confederation of Free Trade Unions, with especially close ties to the AFL-CIO and the American Institute for Free Labor Development (AIFLD). **1,700**

Other Unions:

ANDEN National Association of Nicaraguan Teachers *(Asociación Nacional de Educadores Nicaragüenses)* **16,700**
UPN: Union of Nicaraguan Journalists *(Unión de Periodistas Nicaragüenses)*
FO: Workers Front *(Frente Obrero)*

Total Membership: 260,000

*63. The Private Sector and the Mixed Economy**

By Xabier Gorostiaga

Xabier Gorostiaga is a Jesuit economist and is the director of the independent Regional Center for Economic and Social Research (CRIES) in Managua.

How can the basic needs of the great majority of the population be satisfied, at the same time that a mixed economy is being maintained? How can this mixed economy, which is principally in private hands, be made to respond to the logic of the majority rather than to the logic of profit for capital?

This is a basic issue in the Sandinist revolution. When private enterprise complains about the ''poor business climate,'' it does so exclusively from the perspective of returns to capital. The people complain, on the other hand, about the poor climate in relation to private enterprise, which does not satisfy the needs of the great majority of them. This dilemma, then, springs from two different logics: a logic of the majority, based on the population-at-large; and another logic serving the interests of the owners of capital. How to satisfy these two needs that appear to be contradictory? This is a grave problem for the revolution, and it has no easy solution. The fact that the Sandinist revolution has maintained a largely privately owned economy for three years is an example of the enormous effort the revolution is making to sustain this economic pluralism. The latest report of CEPAL on Nicaragua (July 2, 1982), ap-

*Excerpts from ''Dilemmas of the Nicaraguan Revolution,'' in R. R. Fagen and O. Pellicer, eds., *The Future of Central America: Policy Choices for the U.S. and Mexico* (Stanford University Press, 1983).

praising the tremendous flood damage at $356 million, noted that the state controlled 24 percent of the agricultural sector, 22 percent of industry, and 40 percent of commerce. The Sandinist revolution has made it clear that the logic of the majority prevails in this mixed economy, organized to benefit the people who won the victory against Somoza and the oppressive political-economic system that has historically dominated the country.

A "juxtaposed economy" describes a mixed economy where the public sector and the private sector coexist side by side. Both sectors maintain their own dynamic, and socially the public sector subsidizes the interests of the private sector. In the Sandinist model, there is a tendency toward the creation of a planned mixed economy (a mixed economy planned, at present, without a computer or technological and institutional resources). This planned mixed economy is subject to the logic of the majority, in which the private sector has meaning and purpose, and possibly a long-term strategic position as long as it accepts the logic of the majority and serves the basic needs of the people.

Economists speak of the "trickle-down effect" by which growth and goods are produced and then descend toward the lower sectors. The Sandinist revolution searches for a contrary dynamic, a "trickle-up effect," from the bottom up, which first satisfies basic needs and then raises the goods of the economy upward toward the middle sectors, eventually arriving at nonessential consumption and private accumulation, once the basic needs of the majority have been satisfied. These two concepts respond to different logics: the logic of private accumulation and the logic of the satisfaction of the needs of the majority, with the subsequent initiation of social accumulation and the development of the productive forces that would overcome underdevelopment. The task in Nicaragua today is to overcome the juxtaposition of the two economic sectors, in order to create a planned and integrated economy, programmed according to the logic of the majority. Obviously, this model creates tensions, but is there any other way to overcome the dilemma?

It should be recognized that there are social forces in Nicaragua, and international forces as well, that want to eliminate the very dilemma itself. The supporters of the radical thesis consider a mixed economy to be unmanageable and push for a sudden leap toward a socialist economy. On the other side, there is a reformist position seeking to maintain a juxtaposed mixed economy that would not permit the achievement of the profound social changes for which the people have fought, changes that involve transforming social relations and the economic system.

The leaders of the Sandinist revolution have repeatedly insisted that socialism is not constructed by decree and acts of force. The popular clamor for a socialist society, which prevails in Nicaraguan worker and peasant organizations, has been met with the pragmatism, flexibility, and political originality of *Sandinismo*. Sandinismo attempts to determine the type of socialism that would be both desirable and feasible, given the internal constraints generated by profound underdevelopment and within the regional and international contexts of the Nicaraguan revolution. On the other hand, Sandinismo reaffirms the need to maintain and increasingly to develop a mixed economy consistent with the logic of the majority.

It is important to remember that the mixed economy in Nicaragua appeared not as the product of ideological formulas, but rather as an historical consequence of the special characteristics of the Popular Sandinist Revolution, which knew how to bind together a wide spectrum of society behind a project dominated by workers and peasants. On the other hand, it is also the fruit of realism, achieved after the disasters of an economy destroyed by Somocist corruption, the war, and the 1972 earthquake. The integration of Nicaragua into the Central American Common Market has supported the maintenance at the regional level of those links that favor the economic reconstruction of the country.

The mixed economy is made necessary by an additional set of factors such as the maintenance of political pluralism; national unity; maximum utilization of scarce technical and financial resources; minimization of the social costs of reconstruction; reduction of the risks of a possible international boycott; diversification of the structural dependency of the country; and the creation of a nonaligned economy in support of a policy of international nonalignment.

The accumulated experience of other revolutionary processes demonstrates the risks of a mixed economy as well as its positive aspects. In Nicaragua there is an awareness of the ambiguity of this solution, but the consensus is that a sufficiently stable balance can be achieved, in the long as well as the short term, through control of the financial system, by nationalizing foreign trade, and by gaining the support of labor organizations. This original solution seems to be possible in terms of the constellation of internal forces, but the situation is made more difficult when external economic and political forces try to use the internal tensions of the Sandinist model to destabilize the revolution. The dilemma, therefore, remains in force after three years of the revolutionary process; if it should some day disappear, history will judge which factors facilitated the originality of the Sandinist experience.

Chapter II

Accomplishments of the Revolution

Editors' Introduction

Rumor has it that the Hon. Anthony Quainton, President Reagan's first ambassador to Nicaragua, was dismissed for being "soft on the Sandinistas." His crime, according to the stories, was to have included a list of the "gains of the revolution" in his classified 1983 year-end summary of events in Nicaragua. While he and the State Department have vehemently denied these allegations, many people who met him report that he openly acknowledged that the revolution had achieved significant successes in the areas of land reform, health care, and education. The fact is that the Sandinistas *do* have some feathers to put in their caps that are almost universally recognized except by the Reagan administration.

This chapter reviews Nicaragua's most successful programs since 1979. Agricultural economist David Kaimowitz and environmentalists Karliner, Faber and Rice outline the government's agrarian reform and efforts to reduce environmental problems, respectively. Nicaragua's poet laureate and minister of culture, Father Ernesto Cardenal, then gives a moving account of the post-1979 resurgence of traditional Nicaraguan culture. This is followed by two articles and a statistical summary of the growth in education that has been promoted by the Sandinista-led state. The last reading is a summary of the wide-ranging transformations in health care delivery.

These successes are often pointed to as the basis of the real popularity that the Sandinistas enjoy among the rural poor. It has likewise been suggested by many observers that it is precisely because these successful programs are popular that the *contras* seek to interrupt them by targeting their attacks on health care and educational facilities and agricultural cooperatives. That is a sobering thought to introduce this chapter.

*64. Nicaragua's Agrarian Reform: Six Years Later**

By David Kaimowitz

David Kaimowitz is a doctoral candidate in agricultural economics at the University of Wisconsin. He spent four years studying the agrarian reform in Nicaragua.

Six years after the triumph of the Nicaraguan revolution in 1979, the agrarian reform process shows no signs of running out of steam. Faced with increased demands for land on the part of landless peasants, the Nicaraguan government responded in mid-1985 with a renewed commitment to land redistribution and, for the first time, a demonstrated willingness to redistribute significant amounts of land to small individual farmers.

Responding to pressure by thousands of landless peasants in the region of Masaya, one of Nicaragua's poorest and a traditional base of support for the Sandinistas, in June 1985 the Nicaraguan government declared parts of the region an "agrarian reform zone" and turned over 14,652 acres to 1,300 small individual farmers who had been demanding it.

Days later the government announced that it would increase from 392 to 3,616 the number of individual farmers programmed to receive land from the agrarian reform in 1985. In addition to the peasants of Masaya, farmers displaced by the war were also offered the option of receiving new individual plots in areas where they are being relocated. The total number of families programmed to benefit from the agrarian reform in 1985, including those who receive lands as members of a cooperative or indigenous community, or who receive titles for lands they already work, was raised from 15,066 to 23,526.

The decision to redistribute land to individual farmers represents a radical reversal of the agrarian reform policies of the first years of the Sandinista revolution. Following the overthrow of the Somoza dictatorship, the immense holdings of Somoza and his associates (about 20 percent of the country's arable lands) were taken and turned into state farms. This formed the basis for the creation of the Area of People's Property (APP) which continues to control some one-fifth of the country's agricultural land.

Between 1979 and 1982 little land was given out to small farmers and landless workers. Rather, the government concentrated on helping the rural poor through increased employment in the state sector, better working conditions, and greater access to credit, marketing facilities, health, and education.

This changed somewhat with the passage of the Agrarian Reform Law in 1981. Under this law, the private property rights of all those who use their properties efficiently are guaranteed. However, properties abandoned or underexploited, or used

*Original manuscript, August 1985.

for sharecropping, were subject to expropriation. In addition, as in the case of Masaya, if the government has pressing need for an area for agrarian reform purposes it can declare an area an "agrarian reform zone" and purchase lands from their owners.

In this context, large private farms continue to exist. Many of them have even received favorable treatment in agricultural prices and credit from the government. This is particularly true for sugar, rice, sorghum, and cotton producers. Nevertheless, as a result of the expropriation of Somoza's lands and the subsequent enforcement of the Agrarian Reform Law, the percentage of lands in private farms larger than 850 acres declined from 36 percent in 1978 to 11 percent in 1985.

Once expropriated or purchased, land can be turned over to agricultural production cooperatives (CAS), state farms, or small private farmers. Until recently, most lands had been turned over to agricultural production cooperatives (CAS). At the beginning of 1984 there were 890 of these production cooperatives with over 18,000 members. While they controlled less than 2 percent of the land in 1982, over 9 percent of all farmland was in the hands of production cooperatives by 1985. Most of the CASs are groups of ten to thirty farmers who come together to farm collectively and request land for that purpose from the government. The government gives "agrarian reform" land titles making them owners of the land. Land obtained through this process can be inherited. It cannot, however, be sold.

In 1984 significant numbers of farmers living on Nicaragua's "agricultural frontier" began to receive titles to their lands for the first time. These farmers are homesteaders who had gone into previously uninhabited areas in the interior of Nicaragua and laid claim to lands without obtaining title.

Trying to play on the insecurity of these farmers who have no clear title to their lands, counterrevolutionary soldiers began spreading rumors that the government

Changes in Agrarian Structure
1978–1985

	1978		**1983**		**1985**	
Farm size	**Area***	**%**	**Area**	**%**	**Area**	**%**
Individual farms	13,725	100	10,264	74	9,841	72
Farms greater than 850 acres	4,964	36	1,926	14	1,503	11
340–850 acres	2,229	16	1,736	13	1,736	13
85–340 acres	4,133	30	4,197	31	4,197	31
17–85 acres	2,110	16	1,659	12	1,659	12
Less than 17 acres	289	2	746	5	746	5
Production co-ops	—	—	644	5	1,251	9
State farms	—	—	2,817	21	2,633	19
Total	13,725	100	13,725	101	13,725	100

*Thousands of acres

SOURCE: Nicaraguan General Department of Agrarian Reform (DGRA), 1985.

would use the lack of titles as an excuse to take their lands away. In response the Nicaraguan government began a massive program of land titling designed to guarantee permanent property security to farmers without titles. By January 1985, 56,189 such farmers had received title to their lands.

While the titling of land is not the same as redistributing land to individual farmers, it did set an important precedent by reaffirming the importance the Sandinistas place on the role of small individual farmers in the Nicaraguan revolution. It paved the way for the present increase in redistribution of lands on an individual basis.

Critics have accused the Nicaraguan government of titling and redistributing land only as a tactic to maintain peasant support for Nicaragua's war against U.S.-sponsored counterrevolutionaries. The truth is more complex.

During the first years of the revolution, the government felt it necessary to operate directly the farms confiscated from Somoza and his supporters in order to avoid the fall in agricultural production and marketed surplus that had occurred with the parcelization of land in other Latin American land reform programs. But over the last few years, the state farm sector has begun to consolidate itself. Presently, it plays a leading role in the production of sugar, rice, tobacco, and bananas, as well as being the center of a number of large agroindustrial investment projects in dairy, sugar, corn, tobacco, and oil crop production.

In the process of consolidating themselves, the state farms have become increasingly specialized and capital intensive. Their managers have preferred to concentrate their efforts on relatively small areas of land and turn unused lands over to cooperatives and small farmers.

Cooperative development has been outstanding over the last few years and the Nicaraguan government continues to prefer cooperative production over production by small individual farmers. There are, however, a significant number of farmers who want land but are not yet ready to take the step of joining a production cooperative. Faced with this reality the Nicaraguan government has been pragmatic and has sought out innovative and nondogmatic solutions.

Due to the consequences of the war and the worsening economic conditions in the country, it is increasingly difficult to improve these farmers' standard of living through increased services and better prices. Land redistribution and titling has become one of the few viable ways the government can demonstrate its commitment to the rural poor.

In all the Nicaraguan government claims that by the end of 1985 over 120,000 Nicaraguan families will benefit from the agrarian reform, half receiving new lands to which they previously had no access and half receiving titles to lands they are already working. This represents the majority of all rural families in the country, making Nicaragua's agrarian reform one of the most far-reaching in Latin American history.

No one knows for sure what course the Nicaraguan agrarian reform will take in the future. As we have seen over the years, the emphasis has shifted from state farms to cooperatives. More recently, increased attention has been paid to the problems of individual small- and medium-sized farmers. One aspect has been constant: the com-

Number of Families and Area Covered by the Agrarian Reform 1979–1985

Form of tenure	Area*	Number of families
Cooperatives	1,857,037	49,514
Individuals	221,358	4,985
Indigenous communities	251,464	7,928
Land titles	4,634,259	65,233
Total	6,712,654	127,660

*In acres

SOURCE: General Department of Agrarian Reform (DGRA), 1985 (this includes government projections through the end of 1985).

mitment on the part of the Sandinista government to seek out solutions to the basic problems of its rural poor. This commitment, expressed in policies such as those described above, is the fundamental reason that, in spite of tremendous economic and military difficulties, the Sandinista government continues to be popular today, six years after the revolution.

*65. An Environmental Perspective**

By Joshua Karliner, Daniel Faber, and Robert Rice

Not only humans desired liberation.
The entire ecology cried for it. The revolution
Is also for lakes, rivers, trees, and animals.

Ernesto Cardenal,
Minister of Culture

From the air, Nicaragua, largest of the Central American nations, seems a tropical paradise. On the Pacific coast, smoking volcanoes slope down to fertile checkerboard plains. Two giant pools of blue water, the largest freshwater lakes in Central America, sit nestled in a rolling green landscape. To the east, pine-covered mountains descend into Central America's largest pristine rain forests, which are sliced by steaming rivers headed for the Caribbean. From the ground, however, the stark reality of environmental devastation is shocking. Pesticide pollution, deforestation, and industrial contamination all besiege this economically impoverished nation's natural resources.

*Reprinted from Environmental Project on Central America (EPOCA), *Nicaragua: An Environmental Perspective*, Green Paper no. 1.[1] (San Francisco, Ca.).

In 1979 the Nicaraguan government initiated a bold new experiment in environmental policy to combat decades of ecological destruction. A country the size of Pennsylvania with a population of only three million, Nicaragua is developing a series of projects that could serve as models for ecologically sound development throughout Central America. Ambitious pesticide policies, rain forest and wildlife conservation measures, and alternative energy programs all illustrate a governmental commitment to environmental protection rarely seen anywhere in the world.

The greatest environmental problem in Nicaragua today, however, is war. The U.S.-backed *contras* directly attack environmentalists and their projects in the field, forcing the Nicaraguan government to divert its scarce economic resources from environmental protection to military defense. Moreover, natural resources earmarked for protection are increasingly being exploited to support the war-torn economy. Escalating U.S. military and economic pressure on Nicaragua promises not only to destroy that government's environmental programs, but also threatens to explode into a high-intensity war that would jeopardize the ecological stability of the entire Central American region.

Historical Lessons

Nicaragua's environmental problems are deeply rooted in the pillage of natural resources by local elites and foreign corporations. In the early twentieth century U.S. timber, banana, and mining companies began to invest in Nicaragua. Nicaraguan attempts during that time to control corporate exploitation of the environment encountered stiff U.S. opposition. In 1909, when Nicaraguan President José Santos Zelaya tried to regulate foreign access to natural resources, the U.S. corporations paid $1 million to have him overthrown.[2] Four hundred U.S. Marines also landed to "protect American lives and property."[3]

The marines occupied Nicaragua from 1912 to 1933, installing Anastasio Somoza García as dictator in 1934. The Somoza family ruled the country until 1979 when a popular uprising overthrew the dictatorship. The Sandinista National Liberation Front (FSLN) came into power on July 19, 1979, facing the monumental task of rebuilding and transforming a crippled and impoverished society. Over 50,000 people died in the civil war against the U.S. backed Somoza regime. The United Nations estimated material damage from the revolutionary war to be $480 million, a huge sum for a small, underdeveloped country.[4] Malnutrition, disease, and illiteracy were rampant.

A LEGACY OF ENVIRONMENTAL DESTRUCTION

The Sandinistas also found an environmental crisis of massive proportions. Most of Nicaragua's Pacific coastal plain suffered serious pesticide contamination. The country held the dubious distinction of being a world leader in pesticide poisonings; nearly 400 pesticide-related deaths were reported annually.[5] Pesticide runoff from agriculture, toxic chemical pollution from lakeside industries, and untreated sewage dumped from the capital city had virtually killed Lake Managua; a body of water equivalent in size to California's Lake Tahoe had become the "Lake Erie" of Central America.

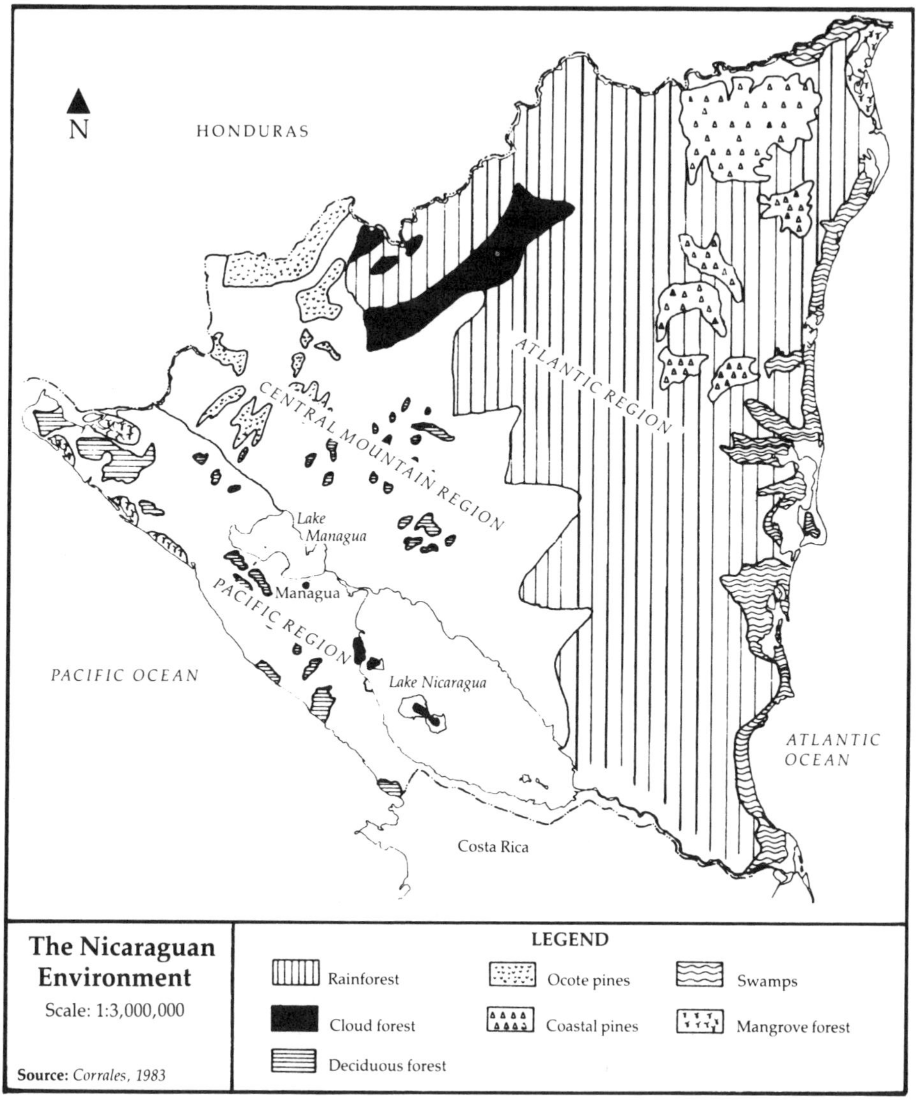

The Nicaraguan Environment
Scale: 1:3,000,000

Source: *Corrales, 1983*

Deforestation had caused widespread soil erosion, dust storms, and flash floods. In 1968 the World Health Organization found that polluted water led to 17 percent of all Nicaraguan deaths.[6] In the eastern half of the country, cattle ranching was eating into Nicaragua's extensive tropical rain forests, 30 percent of which disappeared in the 1970s.[7] Many species of wildlife teetered on the brink of extinction, the result of habitat destruction and unregulated sale in local and world markets. These environmental problems merged with poverty and the lack of social services to give the Nicaraguan people the lowest life expectancy in all of Central America.

A LEGACY OF POVERTY

Poverty and environmental destruction in Nicaragua are both products of a particular political and economic system which, since the colonial period, has placed natural resources in the hands of a small local elite and a few powerful foreign interests. By the time of the insurrection in 1979, large landholders representing a mere 1 percent of the population controlled half the land in Nicaragua. Somoza himself owned 20 percent of the nation's prime farmland. Cash crops for export—cotton, coffee, sugar, and cattle—dominated the agricultural landscape. Over 60 percent of rural people were deprived of the land they needed to feed themselves.[8] Over half of Nicaragua's children were undernourished under Somoza.[9] Landless Nicaraguan peasants working on the large plantations during the short harvest season received wages as low as a dollar a day. In desperation, many of these poor laborers migrated east, seeking their own land at the rain forest's edge.

CONTROL OF NATURAL RESOURCES

Other patterns of resource ownership mirrored those of land tenure. Profits derived from the exploitation of nature were not used to serve the majority of the population by building schools or hospitals, but rather flowed north into the elite's bank accounts or were reinvested to expand corporate activity. Both foreign and domestic companies had access to the country's resources, as long as they paid the necessary "concessions" to the government and to Somoza himself. For example, the U.S.-owned Nicaraguan Long Leaf Pine Company (NIPCO) directly paid the Somoza family a percentage of the company's multimillion dollar timber business from 1945–1960 in exchange for favorable terms of trade, such as not having to reforest clear-cut areas. Thus, by 1961, NIPCO had cut all of the commercially valuable coastal pines *(Pinus caribea)* in northeast Nicaragua, leaving over 3,000 km^2 denuded.[10]

Although there were a few United Nations-sponsored environmental projects in Nicaragua, most attempts by environmentalists, trade unions, and other citizen organizations seeking a more equitable distribution and rational management of the country's resources were seen as a threat to the "stability" of the system.

In 1976 a group of Nicaraguan environmentalists proposed that the government create a ministry of natural resources. Somoza quickly rejected their proposal and threatened the group with harsh reprisals if they met again. The social and environmental crisis had reached the point where more and more people recognized the need for change. Environmentalists saw that only a fundamental transformation in the country's power structure could open the door to ecologically sound and socially beneficial development policies. Some even took to the hills and joined the Sandinista guerrillas who were waging war against the Somoza regime. As limnologist Salvador Montenegro, one of the proponents of the ministry of natural resources told us, "Revolutionary struggle and environmentalism became one."

An Environmental Ethic Emerges

Although many of the Sandinista government's land reform, literacy, and vaccination programs have received wide international recognition, their efforts to improve environmental quality have gone largely unnoticed. Three days after the Sandinistas came to power, the same group of environmentalists that proposed a ministry of natural resources to Somoza brought a similar proposal to the new government. The Sandinistas had already prohibited natural resource extraction by foreign companies by nationalizing Nicaragua's forest, mineral, and aquatic resources. Sandinista leader Sergio Ramírez, today Nicaragua's vice-president, commented that nationalization gave Nicaraguans the ability to protect their natural resources and "to develop them and exploit them in accordance with our own needs and our own vision of the future."[11] The new government responded to the environmentalists' proposal by creating the Nicaraguan Institute of Natural Resources and the Environment (IRENA).

The Sandinistas put IRENA in charge of environmental protection, as well as the study, inventory, planning, and rational management of all the country's newly nationalized natural resources. IRENA quickly initiated programs in reforestation, watershed management, pollution control, wildlife conservation, national parks, environmental education, and the conservation of genetic diversity. Other government agencies began working on pesticide control and regulation, energy conservation, and appropriate technology.

Why did a strong environmental policy suddenly emerge in Nicaragua when none had previously existed? The new Sandinista government recognized that implementing sound environmental measures was central to the revolution's goal to improve the quality of life for all citizens. The Sandinistas also fostered the idea that nature belonged to all Nicaraguans and that the diverse Nicaraguan environment is a part of a heritage that should be a source of great national pride. As Nicaragua's National Parks Director Lorenzo Cardenal told us, "Our revolution is recovering the link between people and nature. Rational use of our natural resources is a fundamental part of our new society: We have to leave our children a country in better condition than we received in 1979."

ENVIRONMENTAL ECONOMICS

The government recognized that any long-term development plans which would serve the majority of Nicaraguans needed to be based on ecologically sustainable forms of production. Building a new society which served "the logic of the majority" meant that natural resource use could no longer benefit a privileged few at the expense of the larger population.

However, such a grand vision of environmental harmony in an egalitarian society is not easily achieved. For although the Sandinistas are vigorously pursuing environmental and social reforms, they are still locked into a global system in which Nicaragua's role is to produce natural resources and agricultural products for export to industrialized nations. Saddled with a growing debt, Nicaragua's short-term economic survival depends on its ability to continue exploiting its natural resources.

Faced with this dilemma of *production* vs. *conservation,* the Sandinistas understand that the solution rests in being able to exploit their resources in a rational, environmentally sound fashion, while slowly rebuilding their society around a more ecologically sustainable economy.

CONSERVATION MODELS

In its attempt to implement one of the most comprehensive environmental programs of any country in the Third World, Nicaragua has drawn on many models and forms of assistance from across the globe. Environmentalists from north and south, east and west come together to confront the ecological crisis afflicting this Central American nation. IRENA, for example, receives environmental aid from Sweden, Norway, Denmark, the Soviet Union, France, Holland, Cuba, and Mexico, as well as from organizations such as the United Nations' Environment Programme, the International Union for the Conservation of Nature and Natural Resources, and the Organization of American States. U.S. citizens affiliated with private organizations also lend assistance.

Nicaraguan environmentalists, encouraged by their own government, have founded an independent organization whose 450 members work in various government ministries, universities, and private consulting groups. The Nicaraguan Association of Biologists and Ecologists (ABEN), dedicated to promoting an "ecological approach to natural resources and the environment," is a rapidly growing force with increasing organizational ability. ABEN has gained influence in governmental decision-making processes, making its voice heard in the halls of ministries and its impact felt in the field. The independent organization promises to act as a watchdog for Nicaragua's environmental health and to serve as a spokesperson abroad for the country's environmental concerns.

Although the Sandinista government has demonstrated a strong will to create an ecologically sound society, its stated policy must translate into environmental action. How effective has their policy really been?

In Defense of Nature

TROPICAL FOREST MANAGEMENT[12]

Nicaragua's forests may disappear by the year 2025. Although foreign timber companies are no longer allowed to clear-cut the country's pine barrens in the north-central and northeast regions, tree-cutting for firewood, slash and burn agriculture, development projects, and forest fires all contribute to deforestation that continues at an annual rate of 1,000 km^2. Such massive destruction has resulted in soil erosion, flash floods, and shortages of firewood.

To address critical conditions caused by deforestation, IRENA is directing four major projects around the country. To prevent high winds from blowing away valuable topsoil, the Western Erosion Control Project in the Pacific region of León, planted some 3,000 trees a day over a two-year period to build 1,200 kilometers of windbreaks in cotton-growing areas. In the watersheds surrounding both León and Managua, IRENA is building minidams for erosion control, reforesting, and promoting permanent crop cultivation in order to stop mudslides that continue to damage low-lying areas. In the north-central Estelí region IRENA has replanted over 3,000 acres in an effort to restore the ocote pines *(Pinus oocarpa)* which were decimated by transnational companies in the 1970s. The Northeast Forestry Project is doing the same for the coastal pines that were clear-cut by the U.S. company NIPCO in the 1950s. Nurseries throughout the country now grow 2 million trees annually for use in reforestation projects.

Unfortunately, IRENA's reforestation projects have become targets in a U.S.-sponsored war. The *contras* have attacked forestry and reforestation projects, kidnapping and assassinating environmental workers. In one such attack in 1983 *contras* destroyed 400 km^2 of reforested coastal pine at the Northeast Forestry Project. Such attacks have forced the government to put plans for a sustained-yield forestry industry on hold while concentrating forestry activity almost exclusively on the highly populated, environmentally degraded Pacific coast. It is already difficult for IRENA's reforestation projects to meet Nicaragua's projected needs. The war makes these tasks impossible. U.S. economic pressure has also limited reforestation work. Nicaragua was the leader in a regional wood fuel reforestation project designed to promote ecological stability in Central America. Nevertheless, the Reagan administration recently ordered the project's sponsor, the U.S. Agency for International Development, to cut all funding for Nicaragua.

RAIN FORESTS AND LAND REFORM

In the past three decades, Nicaragua's tropical rain forests, the largest in Central America, have suffered from extensive exploitation. Rain forest destruction has its roots in increasingly unequal land distribution. Expansion of cotton cultivation in the 1950s, and cattle raising in the 1960s, forced peasant families from the fertile Pacific plains they had farmed for decades. Some displaced peasants escaped their landless condition by joining government "colonization projects" in the rain forest. Others were forcibly relocated to such projects by Somoza's National Guard. Still other displaced families moved east into the hills, where they cleared the forests and planted crops. These hills, however, are ill-suited for agriculture; the destruction of the forest canopy soon caused soil erosion, forcing families to move farther east, where they repeated the process. The eastward migration of this "agricultural frontier" quickly reached the rain forests.

On the edge of the frontier, peasants cleared trees to grow crops that soon exhausted the nutrient-poor rain forest soils. A stampede of cattle ranchers quickly claimed the land. This pattern was repeated time and again. With peasants moving deeper into the rain forest, they were, in effect, clearing the forest for cattle ranchers "free of charge." Beef exports jumped from almost nothing in 1958 to $6.7 million in 1965 and then to $26.6 million in 1970. Within a decade, Nicaragua had the largest cattle herd in all of Central America and had become the United States' number one Latin American beef supplier.

As Nicaraguan and other Central American rain forests receded, the links between tropical deforestation and U.S. consumers surfaced. The region's beef exports were fueling fast-food chains and pet food industries across Northern America. The rapid expansion of Nicaragua's cattle industry to meet the demands of this "hamburger/cat food connection" soon distinguished Nicaragua as the only country in Central America with more head of cattle than people. Six Miami meat-packing plants and the largest slaughterhouse in Central America, all owned by Somoza, were key ingredients in this recipe for rain forest destruction.[13]

The most important step the Sandinistas have taken to stem the tide of rain forest destruction involves Nicaragua's comprehensive agrarian reform. By July 1984, the government had given more than 45,000 families titles to over one-fifth of the nation's farmland.[14] By redistributing land to peasant families so that they can grow their own food, the Ministry of Agriculture (MIDINRA) has halted migrations from the Pacific coast to the agricultural frontier on the Atlantic side. By 1983 the government had halted all colonization projects. And while MIDINRA initially continued to encourage peasants still living on the frontier to clear the rain forest for food production, the ministry soon came under fire from IRENA for implementing policies "against the principles of conservation."[15] MIDINRA responded in 1983 by limiting food production to subsistence farming and promoting ecologically sustainable permanent crops such as African palm, coconut, cocoa, and plantains.

NATIONAL PARKS

Land reform, combined with IRENA's plans for a national parks system, could serve as a global model for rain forest conservation. IRENA's National Parks Service is run by Jaime Incer, who is not a Sandinista, and Lorenzo Cardenal, who is. Incer, the grandfather of the environmental movement in Nicaragua, founded the only national park created during Somoza's reign—the Masaya Volcano national park.

In 1983, IRENA targeted 18 percent of Nicaragua's territory for national park lands. The plan, if implemented, would give Nicaragua one of the highest percentages of park lands in the world. Many of these parks would protect fragile rainforested areas. The *contra* war however, has militarized the wilderness, allowing IRENA to protect only three areas comprising .01 percent of Nicaragua's territory. All of these areas are located on the safer and less pristine Pacific Coast. Protection of the few remaining pockets of wilderness on Nicaragua's Pacific side is especially crucial now that the war has forced other industries, such as forestry, to operate exclusively in this ecologically degraded region. However, IRENA currently lacks the trained personnel and economic resources necessary to manage the proposed Pacific parklands.

Undoubtedly, one of Nicaragua's most pressing problems in wilderness conservation is the polarizing tension that emerged between national park plans and indigenous land rights. In 1980 for example, IRENA declared Bosawas, the Western Hemisphere's largest tropical rain forest north of the Amazon Basin, a national reserve and began to make plans for national parks, wildlife refuges, biological reserves, and sustained-yield forestry within Bosawas' 11,000 km-boundaries.[16] The Bosawas reserve, according to Native Americans John Mohawk and Denis Shelton, was established with "the intent of benefiting indigenous communities and protecting the environment." Yet Miskito and Sumo Indians living there saw IRENA's park plans as an attempt to "nationalize" their lands.[17] The clashes that have ensued continued to foreclose opportunities presented by Sandinista environmental policy for conserving Indian land and culture.

WILDLIFE CONSERVATION

Under Somoza, Nicaragua was a Central American leader in the export of rare and endangered species. Spotted and other rare cat pelts brought high prices in rural markets. The international market devoured thousands of skins and birds annually. White-lipped peccary, white-tailed deer, hawksbill turtles, crocodiles, caimans, freshwater otters, jaguars, ocelots, margays, and lobster were all extensively depleted or exterminated throughout Nicaragua.

The green turtle *(Chelonia mydas)* suffered perhaps the most. In 1969, representatives from Costa Rica, Nicaragua, and Panama agreed to prohibit exploitation and sale of green turtles and their eggs for three years. However, within a year Nicaragua opened two new turtle processing plants, one in Puerto Cabezas and the other in Bluefields. Somoza and his associates owned Tortugas SA of Puerto Cabezas, while a foreign company owned Frescamar of Bluefields. Somoza's investment in turtle-meat factories seriously threatened the already endangered green turtle and delivered a blow to the international movement to save this rare species. Between 1969 and 1975, the turtle industry produced roughly 225 metric tons of turtle meat for export.[18] Finally, in 1976, Somoza bowed to international pressure and closed the factories.

Since 1979 the Sandinista government has moved vigorously to protect Nicaragua's diverse fauna population which includes 750 bird species, 600 reptile and amphibian species, 200 mammal species, and 100 species of freshwater fish. When the Sandinistas nationalized the import/export banks, IRENA was able to ban the export of endangered species. By 1982 the environmental agency had established seasonal hunting bans for twenty-six endangered species of mammals, nineteen bird species, and four reptile species.[19] To make wildlife protection effective, IRENA launched extensive educational campaigns and initiated a system of marketplace and roadside inspection. As Nicaragua's Minister of Culture Ernesto Cardenal wrote: "The armadillos are very happy with this revolution." However, Nicaragua's economic crisis, exacerbated by U.S. pressure on the Sandinistas, caused IRENA in 1985 to lift some bans and resume wildlife export.

Most exemplary of IRENA's wildlife initiatives is the Sea Turtle Conservation Campaign. While government bans have halted all green turtle exploitation on the Atlantic Coast, except for subsistence hunting by Miskito Indians, IRENA has initiated an elaborate program to save the Pacific Coast's olive riddley *(Lepidochelys olivacea)*. The effort to conserve this sea turtle, which nests on Nicaragua's beaches by the thousands, revolves around a broad-based environmental education campaign. IRENA stresses that its efforts to save Nicaragua's five species of sea turtles are not esoteric conservation programs, but rather an attempt to ensure the availability of turtles and turtle eggs for the general population. The environmental agency teaches peasants who harvest the riddley's eggs, wholesalers and market vendors who sell the eggs as a delicacy, and the general public which consumes the eggs, that they must observe seasonal bans in order to preserve the species. Harsh fines for anyone who is caught breaking the law complement this highly successful educational work.

ENERGY AND APPROPRIATE TECHNOLOGY

In many developing countries energy and forest conservation issues are intimately connected. Deforestation for firewood is decimating global forest reserves at an unprecedented rate. Nicaragua is no exception. Currently wood accounts for one-half of Nicaragua's energy. Over 90 percent of all fuel used in households and 25 percent of industrial fuel is wood.[20]

The Nicaraguan Energy Ministry (INE) is developing an ambitious program in renewable energy resources that promises to slow deforestation and promote habitat preservation. Innovative policies designed around Nicaragua's own natural resources would not only curtail expensive oil imports, but would also provide low-cost energy to Nicaraguans who currently depend on firewood for fuel. In order to make Nicaragua energy self-sufficient by the year 2000, INE is developing geothermal and small to medium hydroelectric power projects. Decentralized rural energy such as biogass, wind and solar power, and the combustion of agricultural residues are designed to harness Nicaragua's abundant natural resources and propel the nation along an ecologically sound development path[21].

WATER QUALITY AND LAKE MANAGUA

Poor water quality poses an enormous environmental and health problem in Nicaragua. A nationwide IRENA study in 1981 found that 50 percent of the water sources sampled were seriously polluted by sewage, 75 percent by agricultural residues, and 25 percent by highly toxic industrial contaminants.[22] The most highly developed and densely populated region of the country, Lake Managua's southern watershed, is also the most polluted.

Lake Managua currently receives over 70,000 pounds of raw sewage from the capital daily. Soil erosion from surrounding hillsides has also contributed to pollution and sedimentation in Lake Managua. Thirty-seven industrial plants located on the lakeshore have freely dumped their waste there for years. The worst polluter is the U.S. corporation Penwalt, which dumped an estimated 40 tons of mercury into the lake between 1968 and 1981[23]. When Penwalt established operations in Nicaragua, it was able to escape environmental regulations in the United States. This evasion of U.S. environmental law, however, has laden sparkling blue Lake Managua with deadly poison. Contaminated water from Lake Managua has begun to seep into neighboring Asososca Lagoon, the reservoir for the capital city. Fearing mercury poisoning, the government has resorted to a rationing plan where water is shut off in Managua two days per week. In 1980 the government also persuaded Penwalt to reduce its effluents by two-thirds.

In 1983 the United Nations Environment Programme (UNEP) chose Lake Managua as one of three special priority lakes worldwide. UNEP has earmarked $1 million to study Lake Managua and to modernize IRENA's water-analysis capabilities. The French government has also invested $400,000 in the watershed restoration program for Lake Managua's basin. Although the Sandinistas have made building sewage treatment plants a priority, the country's economic crisis so far has prevented the government from moving ahead with this multimillion dollar project.

PESTICIDES[24]

Pesticide abuse probably represents the most serious environmental problem that the Sandinista government inherited from the Somoza dictatorship. In the 1950s, after pushing peasants off the fertile Pacific plain, growers planted cotton, one of Central America's most important cash crops, and began bombarding it with lethal insecticides. Somoza's suppression of workers' rights and environmental regulations also encouraged chemical companies and large growers to begin experimenting indiscriminately with pesticides. Nicaragua quickly became a deadly playground where chemical companies peddled their wares.

The German multinational Bayer began testing methyl parathion, a chemical lethal even in extremely small doses, in the cotton-growing area of León. In 1951 Bayer applied over twelve million pounds of this deadly chemical, causing dozens of deaths and hundreds of illnesses among field workers and their families. The following year, the Ministry of Agriculture banned methyl parathion, only to have Somoza reverse its decision in 1954.

From that time on pesticide use expanded exponentially in Nicaragua and throughout the rest of Central America. In the 1960s and 1970s, 40 percent of all U.S. pesticide exports went to Central America. In the 1970s, Nicaragua consistently led the region in the sheer volume of pesticides applied. By the mid-1970s, Nicaragua was one of the world's leading users of DDT. Nicaragua and its neighbors also widely used other U.S.-banned or restricted compounds, such as endrin, dieldrin, and lindane. Large growers, hooked on pesticides, paid the price for their abuses. As insect resistance increased, the number of sprayings rose, reaching to thirty per season by the late 1960s. Chemical costs began to eat into profits.

By the 1970s pesticides drenched virtually the entire area along the fertile Pacific Coast, entering the densely populated region's water table and food chain. A 1977 study revealed that mothers living in the city of León had forty-five times more DDT in their breast milk than the World Health Organization deems "safe." Western Nicaragua had also become a living example of Rachel Carson's *Silent Spring*. Even today it is rare to hear birds singing in Nicaraguan cotton fields.

The Nicaraguan people and environment were not the only ones being poisoned by the Somoza dictatorship's pesticide policies. DDT came back around to U.S. citizens in the vicious "circle of poison." Despite U.S. environmentalists' success in banning dangerous pesticides such as DDT more than fifteen years ago, chemical factories in the United States continue to manufacture and export these pesticides to the Third World in return for billions of dollars in profits. U.S. citizens complete the "circle of poison" when we eat imported Central American agricultural products contaminated by pesticide residues. In 1967 U.S. Food and Drug Administration inspectors rejected shipments of over 300,000 pounds of beef from Nicaragua when they found excess levels of DDT during port-of-entry tests. In fact, the U.S. Department of Agriculture has repeatedly rejected contaminated beef from Nicaragua and other Central American countries.

Since pesticide poisoning does not restrict itself to national borders, the health and well-being of U.S. citizens depends upon protective policies not only in our country, but in other countries as well. The regulatory policies that the Sandinista government has adopted since 1979 are exemplary for any nation.

By nationalizing the banking and export/import systems, the government found itself with an effective means to regulate pesticides entering the country. Between 1979 and 1981 the Sandinista government banned DDT, BHC, endrin, dieldrin, Phosvel, and DBCP, replacing these extremely dangerous chemicals with more expensive, but less harmful synthetic pyrethroids.

In addition to instituting measures that protect workers from pesticide hazards, the government also created the National Pesticide Commission (CNP). Composed of members from the public and private sectors the CNP has developed an innovative set of pesticide regulations to oversee imports and guard workers' health. The commission has developed a new system that, for the first time in Nicaragua's history, will label pesticide products in Spanish and color-code them for those who still cannot read.

In addition to pesticide regulations, the government implemented a plan to reduce the number of insecticide sprayings per season. In 1980 the Ministry of Agriculture (MIDINRA) resumed and strengthened what was formerly a United Nations' test program in Integrated Pest Management (IPM). The philosophy behind IPM rests on the use of naturally occurring predators and other biological control agents.

Under the Sandinista government, the IPM program has been a huge success. During two years of testing in pilot projects, IPM reduced insecticide use to a record low of sixteen to seventeen applications per year, saving $2.92 million in 1982–83. In 1983 MIDINRA expanded the IPM program to make it the largest such endeavor in all of Central America and quite possibly Latin America. Grower participation in the program is mandatory, but the government subsidizes 30 percent of the costs and insures growers against any financial loss.

IPM's success in 1981–82 has combined with government pesticide regulations to lower the volume of pesticide imports by 45 percent, lessening the environmental impact of insecticide use, while simultaneously bolstering the economic value of the country's cotton crop. Thus, an effort to safeguard environmental and human health has also increased economic productivity, making the Sandinista government's pesticide policy a model for "productive conservation" in the Third World.

Contra War against the Environment

Despite impressive social and environmental gains in the last six years, the Nicaraguan government is under severe economic and military pressure. For the last four years, the Reagan administration has steadily escalated its involvement in Central

America, injecting billions of dollars in military aid into the region. Nowhere have the effects of this intervention been more keenly felt than in Nicaragua, where a U.S.-financed and directed counterrevolutionary war designed to overthrow the government has taken a toll of more than 11,000 lives, 5,000 wounded, 5,000 kidnapped, 250,000 families displaced and has caused more than $1.5 billion in direct and indirect losses.[25]

On April 15, 1985, President Reagan referred to the Sandinista government as "a Communist clique" that sought to "spread poison" through the hemisphere. The President's metaphor is misleading. In fact, Mr. Reagan is mistaken. The Sandinistas are not spreading poison, but rather are committed to stemming the poisonous tide of environmental destruction sweeping through Central America. As responsible citizens we must ask ourselves: Who is really spreading poison in the hemisphere?

Environmentalism in Nicaragua is under direct fire from the U.S.-sponsored war against the Sandinista government. The *contras* have attacked both environmental projects and environmentalists themselves. They have killed more than thirty employees of IRENA and the State Forestry Corporation and kidnapped scores more. To be an environmentalist in Nicaragua today is to be a target of the *contras*. The most notable environmental victim is Marvin José Lopez, formerly in charge of IRENA's projects in the northern city of Ocotal. Lopez was killed during a large-scale *contra* raid on June 1, 1984. He was ambushed as he left town at dawn to visit a reforestation project. In that same raid the *contras* attacked the Energy Ministry's offices, a lumber mill, a hospital, and destroyed six grain silos.[26]

The *contra* war has damaged the government's pesticide programs as well. In 1983, a CIA-coordinated attack on the port at Corinto destroyed $7 million of methyl parathion that had just been unloaded on the docks. The attack occurred during a critical moment in the pest cycle, forcing the government to remove impounded insecticides from warehouses, and dealing Nicaraguan pesticide programs a serious setback. The war has also sapped human resources from environmental projects. Technicians and inspectors trained for environmental programs are constantly being mobilized for the military. Spare parts and machinery are also in critically short supply. Environmentalists often have no means of getting out into the field.[27]

U.S. economic and military aggression has effectively narrowed Nicaragua's room to innovate and experiment. The Reagan administration's economic embargo and actions to block Nicaraguan access to international loans and lines of credit have exacerbated the country's economic crisis and have forced the Sandinistas to revise their development priorities by emphasizing increased short-term production over environmentally sound development models. In 1985, for example, IRENA's budget was slashed by 40 percent. The government is cutting an additional 10 percent in 1986. All of these war-induced problems put Nicaragua's budding environmental policy in serious jeopardy.

Our president continues to claim that Nicaragua is merely a surrogate for the Soviet Union, which hopes to convert the country into a base of "subversion" in Central America and action against the United States. A simple examination of the facts does not support these claims. As President Kennedy's former National Security

Advisor McGeorge Bundy recently stated: ''No one is going to make war on us from Central America. There is something genuinely zany in thinking about the area in those terms.'' As we have seen, social and environmental turmoil in the region is a product of poverty and injustice, not ''outside interference'' by the Soviet Union.

What, then, are the real motives of the Reagan administration and those in Congress who back the president's Central America policies, for intervening in Nicaragua? It is likely that U.S. policymakers see Nicaragua as a ''bad example'' for all of Latin America and the entire Third World. Nicaragua's pesticide policy, for example, if adopted by Latin America, would seriously cut into the chemical corporations' billion dollar operations.

The Reagan administration continues to devote millions of dollars in military aid to our Central American ''allies,'' while cutting back on environmental and social spending at home. Ironically, this policy forces the Sandinistas to play Reagan's game; they are increasingly diverting their economic resources from social and environmental programs to military defense.

Central America is quickly becoming militarized. U.S. armed forces are conducting maneuvers and building bases in the region. As the U.S. military buildup continues, the threat of a full-scale war increases. Such a war would cause massive environmental destruction, similar to that which occurred in Vietnam, where continuous bombing and the use of napalm, agent orange, and other defoliants not only killed millions of Vietnamese, but has also rendered 39 percent of Vietnam's land unsuitable for forestry or agriculture.[28] Historically, a principal goal of U.S. foreign policy in Central America has been regional stability. Current policy, however, not only darkens the political landscape, but also threatens to disrupt and have long-lasting effects on the region's ecological stability.

A ROLE FOR U.S. ENVIRONMENTALISTS: ''ECOLOGY WITHOUT FRONTIERS''

Nicaragua is attempting to implement a comprehensive program to protect its environment and raise the quality of life for its people. The Sandinistas are, in fact, promoting ecological stability in Central America. Yet, the United States government is attempting to end this unique experiment in the name of ''national security.'' The U.S. environmental movement must redefine the concept of ''national security,'' not according to the narrow interests of economic elites, but rather in terms of a better quality of life for all Americans—North, South, and Central Americans. As discussed in *An Environmental Agenda For the Future,* published by leaders of ten major U.S. environmental organizations, ''the United States is vulnerable to disruptions in life-support systems elsewhere in the world. These problems can only be addressed in cooperation with other nations.''[29] It is time for cooperation with, and not aggression against, the country of Nicaragua.

Nicaragua's National Park Service has proposed that the rain-forested regions Nicaragua shares with Costa Rica on its southern border and with Honduras to the north be declared demilitarized biosphere reserves.[30] This attempt to forge a peaceful solution to the region's problems by creating parklands is an exciting stroke of environmental diplomacy. ''Peace through Parks'' deserves support from environmentalists around the globe. As Nicaragua's Parks chief Lorenzo Cardenal notes: "Ecology has no frontiers."

Faced with a legacy of ecological destruction, the Sandinistas have gone beyond responsible environmental protection and created models for ecologically sound development. The challenge is clear. Our responsibility, as U.S. citizens and as environmentalists, is to stop our government's military and economic war against the sovereign nation of Nicaragua.

Notes

1. This Green Paper is a product of a three-year research project, initially sponsored by the Environmental Field Program of the University of California at Santa Cruz. Much of the information contained within was obtained or corroborated through more than fifty personal interviews with Nicaraguan environmentalists, government officials, opposition leaders, United Nations officials, peasants, and workers.
2. *New York Times,* September 9, 1912.
3. For details, see Gregorio Selser, *Sandino* (New York: Monthly Review, 1981), chapter 3.
4. Douglas L. Murray, "Pesticides, Politics and the Nicaraguan Revolution," *Policy Studies Review,* November 1984.
5. Food and Agriculture Organization of the United Nations (FAO), "The Development of Integrated Pest Control in Agriculture: Formulation of a Cooperative Global Programme; Report on Ad Hoc Session," October 15–25, 1974, Appendix B. (Rome 1975).
6. IRENA, *Planificacion de Cuencas Hidrograficas, Plan de Ordenamiento y Manejo,* vol. 3 (Managua: IRENA, 1983), p. 170.
7. Denis Corrales Rodriguez, *Impacto Ecologico Sobre los Recursos Naturales Renovables de Centroamerica (caso particular de Nicaragua)* (Managua: IRENA, 1983), p. 70.
8. Joseph Collins with Frances Moore Lappé, Nick Allen, and Paul Rice, *Nicaragua: What Difference Can A Revolution Make?* 2d ed. (San Francisco: Institute for Food and Development Policy, 1985), chapters 1 and 2.
9. Health PAC Bulletin (special double issue: "Health Care and Revolution"), vol. 13, no. 6, vol. 14, no. 1: p. 9.
10. James D. Nations and Daniel I. Komer, "Tropical Rain Forests in Postrevolution Nicaragua" (Austin: Center for Human Ecology, 1983), p. 8.
11. Sergio Ramírez Mercado, "Discurso Inagural del II Seminario Nacional de Recursos Naturales y del Ambiente," in *Forjando Una Politica Ambiental* (Managua: IRENA, 1984), p. 36.
12. Much information in this section is based on a publication by the Inter-American Development Bank, "Nicaragua: Informe Presentado por la Delegacion del Pais," in *The Forest Sector: Country Reports, Financiamiento del Desarrollo Forestal en America Latina,* (Washington D.C.: June 1982).
13. Nations and Komer, p. 8–13.
14. Collins et al., p. 4.
15. IRENA, *Ill Seminario Nacional de Recursos Naturales y del Ambiente,* (Managua: IRENA, 1982), p. 20.
16. Inter-American Development Bank, p. 13.
17. John Mohawk and Denis Shelton, "Revolutionary Contradictions: Miskitos and Sandinistas in Nicaragua," in *Native Peoples in Struggle* (Ottawa: Anthropology Resource Center, ERIN, 1982), p. 30.
18. Bernard Nietschmann, *Between Land and Water: The Subsistence Ecology of the Miskito Indians in Eastern Nicaragua* (New York: Seminar, 1973), p. 177–199.
19. Corrales, p. 42, 120.
20. Ariane Van Buren, "End of Project Summary, Wood Fuel Commercialization Project." Report to

Funders (Swedish International Development Authority, Agriculture Division, Environment Fund, October 1984), p. 2.
21. For details, see Tim Kuhn, "On the Road to Energy Self-Sufficiency," in *Science for the People* (November–December 1983), p. 25; and Andy Feeney, "Revolutionary Sandinistas Back Wide Range of Renewables," in *Renewable Energy News* (March 1984), p. 1.
22. Corrales, p. 90.
23. IRENA *Planificacion de Cuencas,* p. 159–72.
24. Information in this section comes from Sean L. Swezey, Douglas L. Murray, and Rainer G. Daxyl, "Nicaragua's Revolution in Pesticide Policy," *Environment Magazine* (January–February 1985).
25. Daniel Ortega, "Agenda Item 21. The Situation in Central America: Threats to International Peace and Security, and Peace Initiatives" (United Nations General Assembly, Security Council, November 15, 1985).
26. Reed Brody, Contra *Terror in Nicaragua.* (South End, Boston, 1985), p. 55–58.
27. Swezey et al.
28. Elizabeth Kemt, " 'Ecocide' in Vietnam," *World Wildlife Fund News,* no. 34 (March–April 1985), p. 1.
29. *An Environmental Agenda for the Future* (Washington D.C.: Agenda Press, 1985), p. 140.
30. "Setting Free the Forests," *The Guardian* (London), October 23, 1985.

*66. Toward a New Democracy of Culture**

By Ernesto Cardenal

Ernesto Cardenal is a priest, famous poet, and minister of culture in Nicaragua. Most North Americans probably remember the picture of the pope shaking his finger at him, reportedly admonishing him for remaining in his governmental position.

The community of Miskitu Indians, a very poor community situated on the banks of the river, had been brought together so that I would speak to them. While the interpreter was translating my words, I observed in their faces disinterest, indifference, and boredom. I told them I was the minister of culture who had come to visit them (which I noted also was of no interest to them). Then I began to explain that the Ministry was new and that it had been created by the revolution for the dances (there I noticed a sudden interest), for the songs, the traditions of the ancestors (and the interest became more obvious), the different languages that we speak, such as their language, which we must preserve and defend, and for the folk arts. This, I had explained, consisted of making beautiful things as well as useful items with the hands. I showed as an example some very primitive drawings that they had carved in some maracas and I showed a *tuno* which they had just given to me, a cloth that

*Excerpts from the statement of Ernesto Cardenal before UNESCO, Paris, on April 23, 1982. Reprinted from *La Democratización de la Cultura,* Colección Popular de Literatura Nicaragüense, no. 2 (Ministerio de Cultura, Managua, Nicaragua, 1982). Translated by Rebecca Cohn.

they make from the bark of a tree, and I explained to them how they could paint on this cloth.

What is the importance of all this? For me its importance is that there I saw how these people were just becoming aware that the Ministry of Culture was especially a Ministry for them, for those who had been exploited for various centuries and now had nothing left but their culture and their language (and that, too, they were on the verge of losing). But at the same time, I, as minister of culture, was becoming aware that my ministry was for them and for all those segregated as they were. And that the ministry existed especially to oppose cultural ethnocide.

In other countries in America they try to suppress their cultures and their languages. Also they kill them. They hunt them in the plains like deer and send them donations of sugar with arsenic, and clothes with the virus of cholera. But we have taught them to read in their native language. We believe that they enrich our cultural identity. We want them to progress within their culture, without stagnating, but also without losing it. A language that is lost is an irreparable loss for humanity, a particular view of the world which has been lost.

I founded a small community in Lake Nicaragua in the archipelago of Solentiname, inhabited by poor isolated peasants. There we developed primitive painting and poetry. Their folk arts and crafts were appreciated by other countries and sold in Paris, Switzerland, Germany, and New York. Later the community became involved in the struggle of the Sandinista Liberation Front. Consequently Somoza's National Guard destroyed all the community's installations. They destroyed the big library we had with archeological pieces, records, paintings, ceramic and enamel kilns, everything. Because of us, all the peasants in the whole archipelago were repressed. Since the National Guard had prohibited them from painting, many peasant girls went up into the countryside and painted in hiding. If a national guardsman saw a painting in a hut he broke it with his bayonet.

Why am I telling this? Because I want to show it as an example of the cultural repression in Nicaragua. Literature, theater, and song were suppressed. Books were banned. First it was those books considered more dangerous, and finally it was all books, in that all books were considered subversive. This is why we have a literature which is eminently that of protest, a political song and a popular street theater which was for agitation, although at times clandestine.

At the triumph of the revolution some customs workers gave me a "memorandum" which had a long list of prohibited books (among them were my books) which were burned. Tolstoy was prohibited for being a Russian author. *The Rebellion of the Masses* by Ortega y Gasset was prohibited for its title. On the other hand *The Sacred Family* by Marx was allowed to enter because of its title. That they were burned I can verify because once the person who confiscated my books, when I made a trip to the exterior (the United States), assured me solemnly that they weren't "robbing" the books but rather they were burned every Thursday before a notary public.

When the revolution triumphed there was a great thirst for reading among our people. A vendor who before sold books at a great risk in the street now sold his books on the ground in a pavilion in the Ministry of Culture. Book vendors appeared everywhere. A student exclaimed with enthusiasm, "Definitely we now are free, we can read what we want. Before it was difficult."

The Somoza police who prohibited books were frightening. The people closed their doors and didn't even lift their heads when they passed by. Their green uniform and green helmet symbolized terror and death. Now the police, the soldiers of the army, and members of the State Security and of the Ministry of the Interior are writing poetry—and very good poetry.

A young woman in an infantry battalion wrote this poem:

> It was six in the afternoon on the day of February 17, 1980
> When I fell in love with you, Juan.
> With your camouflage uniform
> and your Galil [machine gun] on the desk
> carrying out your 24 hours of guard post
> I approached you
> and touched your skin, the color of chocolate.

A police officer wrote this poem:

> *Free as the Birds*
> Looking through the window grilles
> that are in front of my room
> I see how the sun comes out
> and its light shines between the leaves of the Guanabana tree,
> On the floor figures are formed
> a zanate poses and sings on the branch of a Jocote tree.
> I think of this bird,
>   in Nicaragua.
> The Salvadorans, the Guatemalans, the Beliceans
>   all of Latinoamerica
> will be free like this bird.

Our armed forces are made up of very young people, many of whom are young women. They are the combatants of our liberation struggle. For that reason our police are very different, our soldiers and our state security people are very different from what those of other countries might think.

Before there also was another army of very young men. Somoza's elite army, the sinister EEBI, was made up of boys from a young age trained to assassinate, those who produced the worst terror, the terror of Somoza's army. The trainer would shout:

"What are you?"

And they'd shout back in chorus, "Tigers."

And, "What do tigers eat?"

"Blood."

"Whose blood?"

"The people's."

And the Office of Security? There torture was carried out—that was where they took hooded prisoners. . . . Best we don't talk of that. There exists a great difference between the horror and the smile, between those who tortured and assassinated and those who now write poetry and love.

Before we had a culture of oppression and now we have liberation. We had oppression in every way—also in culture. You can't have the oppression of a people without cultural oppression. Now we have liberation, in culture and in everything.

Last year the government of the United States abruptly denied us a sale of wheat. Our people were going to be without bread. The Ministry of Culture had the idea of a "Corn Fair" with the slogan "Corn, Our Roots," with the objective of promoting all the national dishes made out of corn. The fair was celebrated locally in all parts of the country and culminated in a national contest in the Indian town of Monimbo, legendary for its heroism in the struggle against Somoza. The 250,000 people attending swelled the plaza and streets of Monimbo. Members of the governing junta, the commanders of the revolution, the ministers, and owners of well-known restaurants of typical food, we were the judges of the best tortillas, tamales (a corn dough wrapped in leaves and eaten with cheese), *Indio Viejo* ("Old Indian," an Indian corn stew with meat and lots of spices and fat), *cosas-de-horno* ("things from the oven," varied sweet biscuits made from corn), *pinol* (our national drink, made from cornflour with water), *cususa* (a strong corn liquor), *chicha* (wine of the Indians made of fermented corn), and innumerable desserts and delicacies made of corn. From some remote regions of the country dishes were presented that even we ourselves didn't know of and only now were discovering.

We named the fair Xilonem after the Indian god of young corn. According to the myth she sacrificed herself for her people and with her blood they produced a great harvest of corn during a drought year. For us this also was a symbol of all the martyrs of the revolution who sacrificed themselves for the happiness of their people. The great corn fair served to reaffirm the national and cultural identity of our people.

It also served to help our own people appreciate our own foods as part of our own dishes. And after the triumph of the revolution, Nicaraguan foods have been appreciated much more along with everything Nicaraguan proceeding from our past—an Indian past, colonial Spanish, and English in our Caribbean coast, and over all our "mestizoness."

These topics of which I have spoken serve as an introduction to the theme I'm going to take up here at UNESCO, the democratization of culture in Nicaragua. Why do I come to present some practical but also theoretical things which make up the cultural task in a small country like Nicaragua, which up until now has been very dependent? Because Nicaragua is one of those countries of Latin America, Africa, and Asia, recently liberated or on the path of liberation, in which today live more than half of the world's population. Countries where powerful social transformations, encompassing all aspects of life, are taking place. The terrible problems of ignorance, disease, hunger, and misery only can be solved by our countries developing their economies in a short historical period and creating new social structures. This is something also eminently cultural, in that our countries are moving forward so rapidly that not only the traditional social structures are changing but also cultural values and cultural necessities. It seems useful that our experience be made known.

The cultural liberation in Nicaragua has been part of the struggle for national liberation. For example, last February in Nicaragua we celebrated the anniversary of the birth of Rubén Dario, our great poet. He was proclaimed a Hero of Cultural Independence and that day was named Cultural Independence Day. The cultural heritage, really anticultural, left by a half-century of dictatorship imposed and maintained by the United States, couldn't have been more catastrophic. When the revolution triumphed on July 19, 1979, more than half of the Nicaraguan people were illiterate. And for the dominant classes the cultural metropolis was Miami.

Our revolution is of the present and over all of the future but it is also of the past. In the first place there was a resurrection of the dead (in the conscience of the people). Our history soon was something else. Our patrimony that before couldn't be seen, made itself present. National traditions flourished. All that was national always was unified with the liberation movement, but liberation has been the condition under which it would be converted into common good.

Folk art had been decaying more and more during the long era of *Somocismo,* and in the end Nicaragua was already a country very poor in folk art. It was thought to be irreversibly lost. The revolution came to rescue it, and in a very short time in many parts of the country there reappeared the ancient lost popular arts and also new art. It is an expression more of our identity as Nicaraguans to be ourselves. For it struggled against foreign domination and we rescued it with the triumph of the Popular Sandinista Revolution.

The hammock is the crib of the Nicaraguan. It has been woven tirelessly in bright colors in the city of Masaya ever since the war ended. It has been said that it is the best hammock in the world. Hammocks have been given to heads of state. Also there are weavings of *heneken* from Masaya and Comoapa, with bright colors and pre-Columbian and modern designs. In San Juan de Oriente, traditionally a potter's village, they are producing replicas of pre-Columbian ceramics or new creations inspired by ancient art. In Matagalpa and Jinotega they make a very delicate black pottery, blackening the clay with pinewood smoke. Only two families were producing it at the time of the triumph. The revolution by means of the Ministry of Culture saved this folk craft from extinction. A delicate work of filigree is the white *jícara* (gourd) that only one old woman knew how to make. This millinery folk art we have saved by giving her students, who have learned to carve this intricate lacework of birds, butterflies, and flowers. In Masatepe and Granada ancient wicker furniture has been revived—cool and well-adapted to our tropical climate with its delicate and resistant weaving. An important cultural change is to *not* prefer the furniture of Miami—rather that of Nicaragua. In the northern part of the country there is a mountain of a soft rock with varying streaks of color that the peasant population of the area converts into birds, fish, and the busts of women. We have sent our best sculptor and sculpting professor of Nicaragua to give them orientation and now San Juan de Limay is a sculptor's town. Much of what they produce isn't folk art but rather modern sculpture. In the Atlantic Coast where we have our gold mines, we have revived the golden filigree, a handicraft that had been lost. Also on the Caribbean coast they make new jewelry of tortoise shell, black coral, shark's vertebrae, and pearls. The Miskitu Indians work precious woods turning them into figures that, like their dances, represent their work, fishing, hunting, and farming. The Sumo Indians have returned to making drawings with the inks of their plants, brown, yellow, and red, as well as *tuno,* which they make from the bark of a tree.

For all this rich and varied and before unknown folk art, the Ministry of Culture has established different stores and the best samples are exhibited in what we call the Gallery of People's Art in Managua, which before was a branch of the bank.

The needs of the artisan are attended to for cultural, political, and economic reasons. To do so, we have found our own way (not the capitalist way), getting rid of intermediaries and giving them state financing. It is a fact that in our countries the penetration of capitalist civilization turns handicrafts into a commodity. They take it out of the marketplace—remove its traditional function and convert it into a product of a boutique. The peasants, deprived of their ceramics, eat off of plastic plates, they stop using *heneken,* and the artisan depends on more and more capital for his production. In Nicaragua we are seeking a completely different path.

Culture for us can't be separated from social development. Also one might say that in Nicaragua it is inconceivable to consider economic development without cultural development. In Solentiname a group of peasants met with me once a week bringing their poems. It was a poetry workshop. Also children came. Once a ten-year-old boy brought this short poem:

> I saw a turtle in the lake
> It was swimming
> And I was going by in a sailboat.

It seems that this illustrates quite well the definition of a culture proposed by UNESCO, that it is all that man adds to nature.

Not long ago in an article in the *Wall Street Journal* it was stated that in the United States works of art and of literature have turned into mere ornaments to be preserved like paper or fiduciary money. The society didn't expect that a secretary of state had more knowledge of history than the chronology taught in the sixth grade, and the article added, "The United States has made a business of its culture, and its culture into a business." In contrast, in Nicaragua we now have a new concept of culture. The writer Sergio Ramírez, who is a member of the governing junta, has said, "If before, culture was a closed circle for a minority, now it is the privilege and right of the masses."

Also we have a new concept of what is intellectual. Colonel Santos López, who fought with Sandino and after was one of the founders of the Sandinista Liberation Front on a jungle river, didn't know how to read. Nevertheless, one of the commanders of our revolution, Víctor Tirado López, has called him an intellectual. It was considered one of his great virtues that he didn't know how to read. As he himself said, that way he kept a clean mind and sensitive heart to be able to understand all that happened in Nicaragua due to North American intervention. Commander Tirado adds: "That he never went to school to learn his first letters was exactly where his great merit lay." This reminds me of Gramsci, who said that culture is the critic of exploitation.

With our democratization of literacy the peasants didn't only learn their letters, but also about their reality and themselves. As Edmundo, a sixteen-year-old literacy teacher said, "They learned quickly because we spoke of their reality, that of the exploitation and the revolution. They weren't just themes in the air."

And for these young literacy teachers it also served as a school of the revolution. Oscar, another sixteen-year-old, said, "For me it was the best school, the best workshop, the best study circle because rather than being told how the *campesinos* lived, we went to see and live in those conditions. We understood that as youth we must try to remedy the errors of past governments. From then I became committed to try to consolidate the revolution."

They had the experience of doing farmwork. Ligia, a seventeen-year-old, said, "It was really nice because I didn't know how to plant." Another girl told about how when she returns she wants to study medicine and she hoped that time would go by quickly because the peasants have such a need here. A young woman of sixteen says, "After the crusade many students became imbued with the collective spirit."

Not only those who always were exploited received literacy training but also the ex-National Guard of Somoza who were in jail for the crimes of the dictatorship (50 percent of them were illiterate). For their ignorance they were manipulated into torturing and killing. The revolution took them out of ignorance. The police in charge of them were their teachers. They didn't use arms while they were teaching literacy. The hand of the Sandinista was placed over the hand of the prisoner in the fraternal gesture of forming the letters. The revolution taught to read and write those whom the dictatorship had taught how to kill. A woman police officer said that she had a very good experience teaching literacy to prisoners in jail in Jinotepe. She had to exercise a lot of patience.

We also had what we call by-products of the literacy crusade. Among other things we collected an oral history of the War of National Liberation, and collected flora and fauna, noting typical foods, medicinal herbs, archeological sites, and mineral deposits, and gathered handicrafts, myths, legends, and popular songs.

By means of its art Nicaragua now reveals artistic participation in social transformations. I would like to give as a concrete example certain primitive religious paintings done by the artists of Solentiname. One artist painted a picture of Christ crucified wearing typical Nicaraguan peasant pants and shirt, which later was repeatedly reproduced in Germany. In the interview, she declared, "I painted Christ like one of us, a man, or you could say another guerrilla who came out of the mountains and was taken by the enemy." *The Killing of the Innocents* appears as a massacre of children and youth by Somoza's National Guard in peasant communities. *The Expul-*

sion of the Traders from the Temple is a Catholic Church of today where Jesus and his peasant disciples get rid of businessmen wearing suits and ties. *The Sermon on the Mount* is Jesus speaking to a group of peasants on Lake Nicaragua. *The Resurrection* is Jesus with the face of Carlos Fonseca Amador, the founder of the Sandinista Liberation Front, rising out of a tomb. Nicaragua is a religious nation. This is part of its popular culture. In this painting the Bible history is the same as the people's history. They are within the history of the Kingdom. Jesus is one of us, a peasant and a guerrilla. The death and resurrection of Jesus are the death and resurrection of the people.

Of course these peasants have had a relationship with theology—the theology of liberation. During the time of Somoza we studied the Gospel and our commentary was published in the book *The Gospel of Solentiname*. There appears a commentary on the resurrection of the dead by a young peasant, Donald, who died in the liberation struggle. He said, "I don't believe that they will be resurrected in a very material form. Rather they will return in the form of consciousness and the love that the person had. That is the form they will return from their tomb—you could say it's not their bones which will rise and go walking around [everyone laughs] rather it will be a changed society." A commentary was made about the parable of the rich Epulon and the poor Lazarus by Elvis, another youth who also died in the struggle. "The message is also that humanity shouldn't continue like this with two classes, one which has a party every day and the other in the doorway covered with sores."

The Poetry Workshops have been created in the popular neighborhoods and Indian communities of Monimbo and Sutiava and in the armed forces. In the workshops, police, soldiers, workers, and peasants learn how to write good poetry. I already spoke about the poetry of our armed forces. In a speech at Harvard, in which I gave the closing words to a congress on peace and disarmament, I said that our army could give technical assistance to other armies on the theme of poetry. The Venezuelan writer Joaquín Marta Sosa has written about these workshops, "We could say that the Sandinista revolution for the first time has socialized the means of production of poetry." He adds, "The people have become masters of poetry in Nicaragua not because they read more cheap editions but because they produce it."

I read last week in *Time* magazine that in the United States "poetry books don't usually pile up by cash registers." In Nicaragua the editions of poetry published by the Ministry of Culture quickly run out. Our magazine *Poesia Libre* that we publish on kraft paper is sold all over on a popular basis. The first editions we have reprinted because the demand continues.

Because of the lack of foreign exchange and the difficulty of importing many articles, we had a fair we called *La Piñata* which has turned into a great national festival for the exposition and sale of Nicaraguan products, handicrafts, and small industry. The people attended by the thousands this great sale of Nicaraguan items: toys, clothes, furniture, books, records, food, and ornamental plants. The children came to break a great number of *piñatas*. Along with the fair was a circus. There was a sale of typical food, music, and song.

La Piñata was organized to create a consciousness in the value of our own products. Before, it was believed that only foreign products were any good. *La Piñata* was not organized to promote a consumer society in the sense of useless consumption and waste. What we do want is good habits of consumption for our people. Our economic-cultural policy has been defined by a person from heroic Monimbo, disabled in the war, who makes toys and who said of the fair, "The question, my friend, is to make better and more durable toys, because a wagon with wheels is something your children can use for years." The great number of sales shows that it was an unprecedented stimulus for handicrafts and cottage industry. Also it was a political response and an alternative to begin to break the dependence on the exterior.

In Nicaragua the bourgeoisie dress from the shops of Miami. The wedding trousseau was bought in Miami (before that in Paris). The revolution has come to resurrect the popular Nicaraguan clothing, not because of its being picturesque but because of its beauty and its being well adapted to our climate. The *cotona* is a white shirt that I wear which has been the traditional shirt of the Nicaraguan peasant. At one time it had practically disappeared while now it is the most popular shirt in Nicaragua. Like the shirt of the peasant it has become a symbol of work, struggle, freedom, and of revolution. The *cotona* was the uniform of the literacy teachers. When thousands of young people came in, triumphant, to Nicaragua they made the commanders of the revolution put on these *cotonas*. The commanders who presided over the great public event were not much older than the young people themselves.

We are also beginning to change our relationship with nature. We've eliminated contraband in wild animals and indiscriminate deforestation. We're coming to learn a new harmony with nature.

Our song has had a social use and an aesthetic value. In Nicaragua the means that UNICEF uses to measure the health of a people (number of doctors, paramedics, etc.) now are no longer enough. As during the literacy crusade, the entire population mobilized to carry out a health campaign to eradicate malaria or vaccinate all the children in the country. And through all, the "song" has been present. During the war, our great composer Carlos Mejía Godoy used the mazurka to put words [to music] teaching how to arm and disarm a Fal, or Galil machine gun. The same happened in popular theater. Without worrying about the crisis in the concepts of action, time, and space which form a big part of contemporary theater, our peasants, workers, and students bring to the stage their daily life in social and psychological conflicts. In film, Nicaragua began with the war, filming on all battle fronts. After, they began presenting all aspects of our new society in the form of documentaries.

Our policy of social communication is to reject all manipulation, to inform rather than "disinform," and to put into practice political discussion. The democracy of information can be seen in the following two programs which I believe only exist in Nicaragua. One is called *Face the People* in which the governing junta weekly goes to a neighborhood in Managua or some other part of the country so that the people can ask them whatever they wish or make any criticism, protest, or petition. And this gets transmitted by television all over the country. The other is called *Direct Line* and is where some leader of the revolution, or minister, or person responsible for a state institution is on a radio program to respond to any question, protest, or criticism made by a telephone caller. This is broadcast live throughout the country. The program is not only made with leaders or functionaries but also with other people who have some relevancy. The ambition of every Latin American journalist is to interview the novelist Gabriel García Márquez. Recently García Márquez was in Nicaragua, and over the air, on *Direct Line,* he was interviewed by the people; for two hours he was responding to telephone questions from all over the country. The restructuring of the new society is a political task of the new culture. This also signifies an encounter with our new identity as a free people. For us this is a cultural democracy and democratic culture.

This is the culture that is now being threatened because our revolution is being threatened. If the *Wall Street Journal* says the United States has made a business of culture and their culture into a business, we could then say that our revolution is a culture and our culture is a revolution. President Reagan is taking food away from the children of the United States to squander on Somoza's ex-National Guard. The most dangerous aspect of it for us and for the whole world including the people of the United States is to confuse the interests of Reagan's personal prestige with national security.

Recently a nineteen-year-old Nicaraguan youth, Orlando Tardencilla, caused a defeat in the U.S. State Department when he was taken as a prisoner from a Salvadoran jail to the United States to repeat forced lies before journalists. On the contrary, he told the truth. He is also a poet and the way he acted before the State Department is a representation of our new culture. From a jail in El Salvador he wrote to his mother, "Now I don't write poetry I write realities." Also he had written these words, which reveal the poet and revolutionary in him, "We were born for all" and also "I feel the song of brotherhood of all peoples so let's join hands as one people."

The greatest advance of our revolution is the brotherhood it has produced, *compañerismo,* the introduction in our new daily language of the new word *compañero*— which means fellow companion and before only existed in guerrilla camps.

I believe that the revolution is a triumph of love. Sandino said, "Our cause will triumph because it is justice and it is love." He also said, "That every man be a brother not a wolf."

Finally in the message I bring from my people I want to say that we want to preserve peace. Our culture is a culture of peace. We made a revolution with weapons so that we could conquer peace. But they don't want to let us live in peace.

The North American writer Margaret Randall said, with respect to Nicaragua, "The little street vendors, and shoeshine boys are beginning to touch their dreams with their fingers." In a big park that the revolution made for children (named after a nine-year-old child leader, killed by Somoza's National Guard) 1,500 children were recently congregated in a demonstration. They said, "We want peace so we can have fun."

Not only has the peace of Nicaragua been threatened, but all of Central America and the Caribbean, and ultimately world peace. Now man is the master of his evolution. We can't allow that there be one less planet in our solar system, converted into nothing more than small asteroids. Or let's say a black ball, not blue or pink as the astronauts have seen in outer space, without color as has been seen in the fields and cities of Vietnam and now in certain parts of Central America.

The earth is round. That means that humanity as it continues to populate it more and more must come closer and closer together in union on the surface of this sphere, until humanity forms a new species, one great planetary organism.

I heard a young Nicaraguan literacy teacher speaking of the happiness of future generations. That was what he was interested in. It made me think how humanity is moving more and more quickly (we see it in the youth) towards unity, towards love. Until we are all one. Then although we are dead we will live. Have I ended up talking like a priest? The Nicaraguan revolution installed a priest as minister of culture.

*67. Education for Change: A Report on the Nicaraguan Literacy Crusade**

By the Council on Interracial Books for Children

The women and men who took up arms against the Somoza regime had as their goal not just the overthrow of a government, but the liberation of a people—and after victory in battle, the next priority was literacy. At the time of Somoza's defeat, half of all Nicaraguans could neither read nor write. In rural areas the illiteracy rate was estimated at 75 to 80 percent, and, for women in many villages, 100 percent.

Plans for a literacy crusade, under the direction of Fernando Cardenal, began five weeks after the new government took control. The Literacy Crusade's goal was to bring functional literacy—reading at the third-grade level—to 50 percent of the population, or as many as could be reached. The crusade organizers conducted an extensive examination of literacy programs in other Third World nations—Cuba, Mozambique, Guinea-Bissau, Cape Verde—and invited the internationally renowned expert Paulo Freire to Managua to consult on methodology.

While method and content were being planned, a village-by-village nationwide census was carried out to determine levels of literacy in each of Nicaragua's sixteen provinces. Efforts were also made to ascertain the availability of volunteer teachers.

Influenced by Freire's methodology, the planners hoped to provide one literacy teacher for every four or five *campesinos* (poor country people). Teachers would be assigned to their own province when possible, but tens of thousands of teachers would have to be transported from the cities to the remote areas in the northern mountains and the Atlantic Coast forest regions where available teachers were scarce.

A serious problem was how to mobilize national resources for such a large-scale campaign without interfering with production. During the revolution, entire sections

*Reprinted from *The Interracial Books for Children Bulletin,* vol. 12, no. 2 (1981).

of Nicaragua's cities had been destroyed by the punitive bombings of the National Guard. Before Somoza fled, he pillaged the national treasury and left massive debts which the new government pledged to honor. Money to pay these debts had to be earned from exports, which meant production of goods had to be increased.

A clever solution was arrived at. Those who volunteered to work in the Literacy Crusade would be divided into two groups. One would consist of young people not yet actively engaged in productive work, who would leave the cities and live with the *campesinos* in the rural areas and mountains for a period of five months. They would give classes in the evenings and by day they would work in the fields, planting crops, harvesting, tending animals, and helping to increase the nation's productive capacity. These volunteers would comprise the Popular Literacy Army (EPA), better known as *brigadistas*. The second group would be factory workers, government workers, housewives, and professionals who would remain at their regular work in the cities and teach in the urban *barrios* during nonworking hours. These were the Popular Literacy Teachers, called ''popular alphabetizers'' (AP).

The volunteers for the *brigadistas* were young people—high school and college students primarily, although some were as young as twelve. Several reasons account for the youthfulness of the *brigadistas*. For one thing, many had fought in the revolution and were committed to its goals. (A striking aspect of the Nicaraguan revolution had been the youth of the liberation fighters—teenagers, or younger.)

In addition, the government made specific efforts to enlist young people in order to raise their consciousness about the realities of the poverty and oppression of the *campesinos* in the rural and mountain areas. (Most of the *brigadistas* were from urban areas, and while illiteracy was high there, it was far, far higher in the country.)

The *brigadistas* were the political descendants of the ''Choir of Angels''—children who had formed part of Augusto César Sandino's guerrilla army during the struggle to oust the occupying U.S. Marines in the 1930s. The Choir worked to ''alphabetize'' the *campesinos* in the mountainous provinces of Matagalpa, Jinotega, and Nueva Segovia, so that they could read Sandino's literature. In the 1960s this same area became the base for the Sandinista forces—nationalists who derived their names and inspiration from Sandino.

Parental Permission Required

Parental permission was a requisite for minors who wished to join the *brigadistas*. The crusade organizers found that they faced opposition from some middle-class parents who were not supportive of the revolution and who, in addition, had traditional parental worries about their children, particularly their daughters. (Working-class parents were not, in general, antagonistic.)

Parent hostility was met by widespread discussions about their concerns. Campaign represenatives held weekly meetings in the schools with parents and students. Posters, newspaper articles, and TV and radio programs addressed the issues. To allay some of the parents' fears, it was decided to organize single-sex brigades, and young girls would be accompanied by their teachers and live in dormitories, farmhouses, public buildings, or schoolrooms. Boys and older girls would live in the homes of the *campesinos*. It is worth noting that children from middle-class homes—who joined the crusade for a variety of reasons—usually became committed to the goals of the new society Nicaragua is trying to build.

Initial preparations lasted six months. The Literacy Crusade first launched a pilot project in the same northern provinces where the Sandinistas had originally made their base. Undertaken by the eighty-member *Patria Libre* brigade, its objective was to test a training design and gain practical experience that would later be transmitted to the other *brigadistas*. The group members also underwent physical training to prepare them for the arduous tasks ahead.

After completing the pilot project, each of the 80 members of the *Patria Libre* conducted workshops and trained 560 more teachers. These, in turn, trained 7,000 teachers. For the final phase, which ended in March 1980, schools and colleges were closed early, releasing thousands of volunteer students for additional training. By the conclusion of the last phase of training, a grand total of 95,000 ''alphabetizers'' were prepared for the campaign. Of these, 60,000 were the young *brigadistas* who would work and teach in the countryside. The other 35,000 were the ''popular alphabetizers,'' adults for the most part, who remained in the cities to work in the *barrios*.

Groups Support Crusade

The Nicaraguan revolution had been successful in large part because of the involvement of the people's organizations that had formed in the years preceding 1978. Some of these were the National Union of Teachers, the Sandinista Trade Union Federation, the Organization of Nicaraguan Women, the block- and street-based Sandinista Defense Committee, and the Association of Rural Workers. The same groups now provided the Literacy Crusade with massive logistical support, transporting 60,000 *brigadistas* from the cities to the countryside, supplying them with food, medical care, textbooks, etc. They also provided protection; security was a major concern, because remnants of Somoza's National Guard, which had fled into the mountains on the Honduras border, threatened that the *brigadistas* would be killed.

On March 24 of last year, truck convoys by the thousands left the cities of Managua, Estelí, León, Granada, and Matagalpa and fanned out to all of Nicaragua's provinces. Because of the terrain, thousands of *brigadistas* had to march by foot. Some traveled by boat, some by helicopter. Each *brigadista* was eventually outfitted with jeans, a gray tunic, a mosquito net, a hammock, a lantern by which to teach at night, and a portable blackboard. On *brigadista* arrival day, a special service was held in every church of every denomination to greet the *brigadistas* and to launch the crusade.

From the end of March until mid-August, the *brigadistas* followed roughly this pattern: by day, work in the fields with the *campesinos* they lived with or chores around the house; by night, two hours of instruction with from five to seven *campesinos* huddled around a gas lamp. On Saturday, there were workshops with other *brigadistas*—usually thirty in number from the same village or a village nearby—to evaluate the week's work, discuss common problems, and plan the week ahead. For those *brigadistas* who could not meet together because of distance, all-day Saturday radio programs informed them of news of the campaign and offered advice and encouragement. In the cities, the popular alphabetizers worked at their regular jobs and, in addition, gave two hours of instruction at night; they also had Saturday workshops. Within this general pattern, there were wide variations.

The campaign took its toll: fifty-six *brigadistas* died during the crusade. Six were murdered by the National Guard, the rest were killed by accidents and illness. Today, the murdered youth are hailed by Nicaraguans as martyred heroes, and their faces are enshrined on posters and paintings hung everywhere.

The campaign itself was extremely successful. At its end, some 500,000 *campesinos* were no longer illiterate, and the rate of illiteracy was down from a national average of 52 percent to just under 13 percent. Confirming the statistics are the documented exams and the simple sentences that all *campesinos* had to write at the end of the five-month learning period. As important as the literacy they gained, however, was their new awareness of themselves and of their significance to the nation. Prior to the revolution, *campesinos* had been considered of little or no consequence; but this campaign, a major indication of positive governmental concern, contributed to a new sense of dignity and self-worth.

The influence of the crusade on the *brigadistas* and other alphabetizers was also dramatic. They gained a new understanding and respect for the rural poor—and often, as noted, a new commitment to the goals of the revolution. Participants also learned a variety of skills—life skills as well as teaching skills. All gained a more profound understanding of their nation—and learned that they could play a role in creating a new society.

68. Pueblo en Marcha*: Adult Education in Nicaragua**

By the National Network in Solidarity with the Nicaraguan People

"I learned to read during the Crusade and now I'm studying at level three as well as working as a zone supervisor for Matagalpa and Compasagua. I supervise six Popular Education Collectives (CEPs)," explained Felipe Alvarado, twenty-four, a worker on a government-run cattle ranch, just before the day's adult education class was to start.

Maritza Dormus is sixteen. She studies second grade in the little town of Muy Muy and in the afternoon teaches sixteen family members in their tiny village. "What inspired you to teach a CEP?" I asked. A tremendous smile suddenly brightened her

*Reprinted from *Nicaragua,* October/November, 1982.

face. "The joy of teaching!" she responded immediately, evidently not needing to give the subject any thought. "Would you like to be a teacher someday?" I asked her. "Oh, yes!" she replied.

People like Felipe and Maritza form the backbone of Nicaragua's Popular Adult Education Program (EPA). They are among 24,000 popular educators who teach 185,000 adults in a two-year program designed "to create a nation of not only literate, but critical revolutionaries." Seventy percent of the popular educators have not yet finished sixth grade—many, in fact, are only one step ahead of their student neighbors. But they teach each night for two hours and on Saturdays they attend workshops to help them evaluate their work, prepare for the next week, and receive technical and political preparation.

The CEPs grew out of the 1980 National Literacy Crusade, which reduced the illiteracy rate from 52 percent to 12 percent. The Education Ministry realized that the literacy level achieved by the new students was minimal and that they could easily backslide and forget what they had learned. They felt that four to six semesters of additional study were needed before the newly literate would be able to enter technical courses. In 1981 the first two levels of the program were taught and this year third and fourth levels are underway. The program has two long-term goals: to encourage participation in mass organizations through a better understanding of Nicaragua's history and current situation and to develop the technical knowledge needed for production, health, and other national needs.

As in the National Literacy Crusade, the method of teaching is based on Brazilian educator Paulo Freire's philosophy that adult education in poor countries must be based on consciousness-raising, not only to make it interesting but, most importantly, for it to be true education. An effort is made to help students understand the causes of problems and what *they* can do to solve them. The idea is that the people are and must be the authors of their own development.

Problems to Overcome

The program has had to face many problems—inexperienced teachers; lack of tables, lights, paper and eyeglasses; the isolation of rural communities; and the tiring nature of agrarian work. Because many rural teachers are newly literate and there is an urgency to complete the exercise books and advance to higher levels of literacy, workshops for popular educators tend to focus more on the use of materials than on pedagogy and participation.

Rural areas often lack adequate facilities for CEPs. Seventy percent of the collectives in Rivas lack sufficient seating, writing surfaces, and blackboards. Three of the seven areas in Estelí are without electricity and many CEPs have not been able to meet because new wicks for Coleman lanterns are not available. Some areas are only reachable by boat and the gasoline supply is often insufficient for supervisors to visit classes and provide materials. It is common for supervisors and popular educators to travel from two to five hours on foot to attend a workshop or meeting.

Special problems exist in agricultural communities. From September to March

1981, 50 percent of the *campesinos* with no land or with small holdings dropped out of the program to migrate north for the harvests. Attempts to hold CEPs in the work camps proved futile bccause of physical exhaustion at the end of the day. The floods in late May meant fields had to be cleaned and entire crops replanted in some areas. Relocation of flood victims and reconstruction of homes broke up many CEPs. In April 1982 increased armed attacks by counterrevolutionaries along the northern border required the mobilization of reserve troops from nearly every community. For these reasons CEPs were postponed for three weeks and the semester extended by a month nationally.

CEPs organized for cooperative farmers and for urban workers have been more successful. In the co-ops, literacy skills are being developed with an eye toward improving production. Information about grain storage was used within the CEPs to significantly improve yield, and construction of grain bins has taken place through the joint effort of CEPs and PROCAMPO, an organization which provides technical assistance.

In many industrial centers all workers are enrolled in CEPs except those awaiting the development of more advanced levels of the program. In the state-run enterprises—and in a few privately owned workplaces—workers spend two hours a day at the CEPs with pay. The advantages of these CEPs extend to the homes of workers as well. "I'm less tired when I get home and since I've already had my class I don't mind taking care of my children while my wife goes," commented one worker.

Counterrevolution Attacks CEPs

The need for critical literacy becomes more important as the counterrevolution escalates its ideological offensive. In isolated rural areas, counterrevolutionaries claiming to be members of evangelical or pentacostal churches denounce the CEPs, militia, and health brigades as "unchristian" and a "tool of Communist indoctrination." In Wiwilí a CEP worker was murdered by a counterrevolutionary band and in Río Blanco CEP study materials were burned. While most people have remained firm, CEP supervisors believe that enrollment is down in some areas due to fear of the counterrevolution.

A Visit to CEPs in Matagalpa

Despite the problems faced by the program and increased counterrevolutionary activities, CEPs are moving forward. During a visit to several CEPs in a poor neighborhood of Matagalpa, we asked students what they wanted to study when they finished all the levels of basic education. There were answers of typing, carpentry, and sewing.

Reyna Mercardo, age seventeen, is interested in learning how to sew so that she can earn something while she continues studying. Right now she has only seasonal work as a coffee sorter. Ethel Ubeda, age thirty-six with five children, already sews but says she needs mathematics, especially division, to make patterns for her clients. She got only as far as second grade as a child and is now in level two.

During a level-two class in the same neighborhood students were discussing what lessons they liked best. Everyone seemed to appreciate the usefulness of math but the favorite lesson had been about the Atlantic Coast region of Nicaragua, a piece of their own country that for centuries was a world apart.

In another classroom a student was asking about shortages of certain food products, and in another students were learning "New Vocabulary Words," which included "decapitalization—when the owners of a company remove machinery and tools from a factory and take the earnings of the company out of the country instead of using them to improve the business or help the development of the country."

Both the trying and promising aspects of the popular adult education program were summed up in the words of a *campesino* woman in Estelí: "Sometimes I just think, why should I be sitting here struggling with these books when I'm so old? But now that I've started reading, even the newspaper, I feel like I've come to a new country and started all over again."

*69. Educational Conditions Pre- and Post-1979**

By the Instituto Histórico Centroamericano

Comparison of Student Enrollment Pre- and Post-1979

	Student Attendance					
	Before the Triumph		After the Triumph			
Educational levels	**1978**	**1979–80**	**1980–81**	**1982**	**1983**	**1984**
Preschool	9,000	18,292	30,524	38,534	50,163	66,850
Primary grades	369,640	431,164	503,497	534,996	564,588	635,637
Secondary grades	98,874	110,726	139,743	139,957	158,215	186,104
Higher education	23,791	29,173	34,710	33,838	39,765	41,237
Special education	355	—	1,430	1,591	1,624	2,800
Adult education	—	—	167,852	148,369	166,208	194,800
Total	501,855	589,855	877,756	897,285	980,563	1,127,428

*From *Envío,* vol. 4, no. 48 (June 1985).

Number of School Teachers Pre- and Post-1979

Educational levels	Before the Triumph 1978	After the Triumph 1980–81	1982	1983	1984
Preschool	—	924	1,212	1,310	1,701
Primary grades	9,986	14,113	14,711	16,382	17,969
Secondary grades	2,720	4,221	4,103	5,027	6,014
Higher education	N.A.	N.A.	N.A.	1,413	1,750
Special education	—	131	123	171	204
Adult education	—	18,449	21,607	21,994	25,760
Total	12,706	37,838	42,167	46,407	53,398

*70. Health Services Reforms in Revolutionary Nicaragua**

By Richard M. Garfield and Eugenio Taboada

Health Personnel

During the 1970s, about 65 percent of the doctors in the country were paid for some public service; for most of them, this constituted only a few hours a day, and many physicians were absent during much of their scheduled work time. A study in one of the main INSS clinics in Managua showed that at the time of the revolution only 50 percent of the contracted hours in general medicine, pediatrics, pharmacy, and medical records had been completed.[a] Some doctors worked less than eight hours a day, yet were paid for as many as twenty hours a day of work. In fact, the total number of reimbursed medical hours surpassed the physical limits of the INSS clinics.

Since the revolution, doctors have been pressured to fulfill their contracted time and increase their scheduled public practice to at least six hours a day. Salaries for public service at each professional level have been standardized and a maximum salary level has been established. The one-year social service requirement for medical graduates has been increased to two years. Its uniform implementation has greatly increased the number of doctors in rural areas.

Well over half of the physicians still have private practices. Private practice is absent only in outlying areas, where foreign volunteers and recent Nicaraguan graduates providing social service have brought modern medicine for the first time. Fol-

*Excerpts from *American Journal of Public Health,* 74 (1984).

[a])Unpublished study. Oficina de Informatica e Estadistica, MINSA 1980.

lowing two years of social service, doctors are guaranteed the right to go into private practice. Even some MINSA personnel maintain private practices.[b,1] Although many hope that private practice will diminish, no legal mechanisms exist to encourage this. Many discussions at the medical school today revolve around preferences for private or public practice, with those advocating one side or the other attempting to win the hearts and minds of the next generation of physicians.

Prior to 1979, each of the four major hospitals in the capital city of Managua functioned as the personal domain of its medical director, a Somoza appointee. Long-standing feuds and fears of a progressive influence from medical students at the country's one medical school meant that students had only limited access to these hospitals for clinical rotations. By 1981, with the opening of a second medical school and the firing of Somocista hospital directors, routine student rotations in Managua were begun.[2]

All health career training programs have been greatly expanded and new ones added since the revolution. About three times as many nursing aides (600, in courses increased to one year in duration) and six times as many professional nurses (380) are being trained. Nine allied health careers for about 300 students have been developed. There are more than ten times as many medical students now (900); 146 physicians are in sixteen new residency training programs.[3,4] In the next few years, almost twice as many doctors as nurses will be graduated. Although MINSA's policy is to establish a more appropriate physician to nurse ratio, the imbalance inherited from the past will continue for the present period.[c,2–7]

One of the earliest MINSA programs trained independent volunteer paramedical health aides called *brigadistas*.[4] *Brigadistas,* selected primarily from the Sandinista Youth Organization, received several months of training and were supposed to be sent to isolated rural areas. They were to serve for two years, after which they would be eligible for professional training. Pressure from doctors who feared losing power led to a deemphasis of this program and an expanded enrollment in medical schools. In fact, many of these volunteers went on to become health educators, medical students, or health *brigadistas* in the revised volunteer program described below.

Although some emigration occurred in 1980, doctors have not left Nicaragua in large numbers. Any deleterious effects of the trickling exodus of doctors have been offset by foreign health workers, numbering about 800 at present.[9] Most of these *internacionalistas* come from Western Europe and Latin America, especially Mexico and Cuba; there are also some physicians from the United States. Many of these doctors provide services to populations never reached by the departing physicians, especially in rural areas. The absence of emigrated physicians is felt most acutely in anesthesiology, ophthalmology, and internal medicine subspecialties.

---

[b])This is found in many Latin American countries.

[c])Unpublished data from MINSA, DINEI, 1983.

Financing of Health Services

Government funds directly related to the provision of health care jumped from 200 million córdobas[d] in 1978 to 1,050 million córdobas in 1981[8] and reached an estimated 1,593 million córdobas in 1983.[e] Despite inflation, a general rise in government spending, and the national austerity program, the proportion of the government budget devoted to health rose from 7.5 percent in 1977 to 12 percent of all public spending in 1981.[e,3,10–12] While health funding continued to rise in 1984, the escalating war increased the Nicaraguan military budget from 18 percent in 1982 to 25 percent in 1984, thus slowing health development.

About 30 percent of all funds for health care since the revolution has come from the INSS.[10] In effect, the salaried sector subsidizes care for the much larger group of poor and unemployed in the sector served by government, through the transfer of funds to MINSA. "This represents the principle of solidarity between different social sectors, which represents a positive mechanism for income redistribution."[9] Before INSS makes its monthly contributions to MINSA, it deducts for sickness, occupational hazards, maternity compensation benefits, reimbursement for emergency treatments in private clinics or hospitals, and administrative costs. These deductions amount to about 15 percent of the total INSS contribution.

When they lost preferential access, salaried workers who had been covered by the INSS agitated for changes in the system. This agitation was only partially successful. The largest single group of workers covered by INSS were government workers.[13] Opposition to the integration of the INSS system into MINSA was weakened by the fact that so many of its members depended on the government for their livelihood. A large educational campaign to encourage workers to "share the wealth" with those outside of the social security system may also have helped reduce potential opposition.

Health expenditures in 1983 passed 500 córdobas per capita. A large but decreasing proportion of the health budget (53 percent in 1981, 47 percent in 1982, and 43 percent in 1983) was devoted to hospital care.[e,3] During these same years, malaria control,[14] health education, and rural sanitation increased their respective shares of the health budget. Thus, unification of the health system after 1979 has not resulted in a deemphasis of preventive activities as was feared when the policies of the Somoza dictatorship were dominant. This may reflect decreased corruption, the assistance of international organizations, improved administration, community participation in the development and execution of health policy, and a political commitment to care for underserved population sectors.

---

[d])The official rate of currency exchange was 7 córdobas to $1 (US) until 1978, when it changed to 10 córdobas to $1. The current rate of exchange in banks is 28 córdobas to $1. Because of the variability in the real value of Nicaraguan currency, values mentioned in this article should only be considered estimates.

[e])Unpublished data from MINSA, Area de Finanzas, 1983.

[f])Unpublished data from Area de Control y Erradicacion de la Malaria, MINSA, 1983.

Social Security

The social security system is expanding rapidly. Since 1979, the percentage of the working population covered by social security has doubled, from 16 percent to 32 percent. Perhaps more importantly, most of the newly covered groups work in the formerly neglected agricultural sectors in outlying parts of the country. INSS coverage provides retirement insurance and workers' compensation among other nonmedical benefits.

Where there had been separate hospitals and clinics for insured workers under the social security system, these facilities were opened to the entire population following the revolution. A general belief that former INSS centers provided better care led the general population to crowd these sites when they became available to the public in 1979, and a Ministry of Health study in 1980 found that their waiting times were much longer. Regionalization and the expansion of primary care resources have since reduced this problem. A nominal fee for filling prescriptions of non-INSS insurees has also been implemented in some areas.[1]

The integration of INSS and MINSA services has permitted primary health units to take responsibility for occupational health at nearby work centers. In the afternoons, when patient demands on the health centers are lessened, work-site visits are made by the medical staff. This has been found to be an efficient system of coverage.

Although there are no data on this point, it is believed that many insured workers go to private physicians because of reduced waiting times or preferred treatment modalities. Thus, the goal of a single national health service is tempered by the reality of resource limitations, causing continued although greatly reduced differentials in access to health care between those who can afford private care and the rest of the population.

Availability of Services

In addition to increasing the number of people who qualify for INSS coverage, public programs for rural medicine, maternal and child health, and occupational medicine have been greatly expanded. It is estimated that more than 80 percent of the population now has some regular access to medical care.[15] Since 1977, hospitalizations and surgical procedures have risen more than 50 percent, outpatient medical visits per capita have nearly tripled, and the number of vaccinations administered has had more than a fourfold increase. There are two and a half times more primary care units, while the number of hospital beds has risen only slightly. It is especially notable that the services most lacking before for the general population—outpatient care and prescription—have had the largest increase.

Community participation helps to explain the rapid growth in primary health care since 1980. Nurse-provided primary health programs established since the revolution are rapidly growing. These provide: prenatal visits, puerperal checkups, growth and development checkups, and oral rehydration for infants with diarrhea. The shortage of trained nurses at this time limits more rapid growth of these services.

Equity has also improved. In 1980 there was a 4:1 ratio between areas with the highest and lowest rates of outpatient visits per capita. By 1982 this was reduced to a 3:1 spread. In the same period, the variation in hospitalization rates was reduced from 2.5:1 to 2:1. In 1980 the variation in doctors per capita between the best and worst served areas was 16:1, while for nurses it was 5:1. By 1982 these had been reduced to 3:1 and 2.5:1, respectively. In general, the greatest improvements in distribution of health resources have occurred in the availability of health workers and numbers of medical visits. The least improvement has occurred in the availability of hospital beds among the different regions of the country.

Nonetheless, cities (especially Managua) still take the largest share of health resources. Residents of Managua in 1982 had 55 percent more medical consults per capita than people in the rest of the country.[16] The national average in 1982 was 2.06 consultations per capita; a region with a large indigenous population and economically important mines had the highest rate with more than three consults per capita, while several areas had between one and two consults per capita. Within five years, this situation could change considerably. About 800 beds, in five hospitals and 200 health centers, are currently under construction; most new construction is in rural and underserved areas.[c]

Health Campaigns

During 1980, periodic health campaigns to mobilize large portions of the general population were planned. Immunization, malaria prophylaxis, and sanitation campaigns were launched in 1981. The campaigns included massive short-term training courses and a heavy dose of public health education. So successful were these campaigns that up to 10 percent of the people in the country were mobilized as health volunteers.[14] The campaigns helped solidify the social role of mass organizations from which many of the volunteers came. They also promoted the formation of local, regional, and national community health councils which are now active throughout the country.

The structure of the health campaigns is currently being changed to promote permanent, ongoing activities. Activists are still volunteers, but receive more extensive training in maternal and child health, occupational health, first aid, or general health assistance. There are now 25,000 of these permanent *brigadistas,* comprising about 1 percent of the total population. This program appears more like the original *brigadista* program, discussed earlier, and will be supplemented by mass participation in short-term campaigns.

Perhaps the most successful health campaigns have been those held four times a year to provide immunizations. The 1983 immunization campaign concentrated on measles, leaving tetanus toxoid vaccinations for a special campaign among pregnant women. Reported cases of measles, pertussis, and diphtheria have decreased sharply and no polio cases have been reported since 1981.

Developments in health services, prevention activities, and education may be related to rapid improvements in the population's health status since 1979. It is estimated that, between 1978 and 1983, infant mortality decreased from 121 to 80.2 per 1,000 live births, life expectancy at birth rose from fifty-two to fifty-nine years. The number of reported malaria cases has decreased by 50 percent, polio cases have not been reported for two years, no measles cases were reported in the first half of 1984, and most other immunization preventable diseases are considerably reduced. Diarrhea has fallen from the first to the fourth most common cause of hospital mortality.

Effects of War

The war along Nicaragua's borders adversely affects the development of primary health services. At the time of this writing, sixteen health workers (including one French and one German physician) have been killed, twenty-seven others have been seriously wounded, and thirty have been kidnapped and tortured along the country's northern border. In addition, three health educators, seven medical students, and at least forty health volunteers have been killed by the *contras*. At least two hospitals and nineteen health centers and posts have been destroyed.[17] The Nicaraguan response has been to remove foreign health workers from border areas, organize mobile health teams to make up for the closed medical centers, and further promote community participation. In at least some fields, this strategy has been successful. Immunization coverage, for example, was higher in a war zone than in neighboring areas, due to the methods used to reach the population. Rather than one volunteer per community, a large group of *brigadistas* entered the war zone on unannounced days to reach all houses quickly. Immunization rates of 95 percent among children under five years old in the war zone helped to protect the country from a polio epidemic occurring in neighboring Honduras during the summer of 1984.

Nevertheless, the destruction of infrastructure and the increasing danger of travel in the war zones is taking a toll on the population's health. Some areas report decreases in the number of hospitalizations and visits to physicians due to the war, in spite of continued increases in the provision of health services in the country as a whole.[18] In hospitals near the fighting, up to 25 percent of the patients have war-related injuries, lessening the number of beds available for routine care. Construction of more than half of the health posts planned for 1983 was abandoned because of the war. Oral rehydration and nutrition programs for children and the supervision of births are decreasing in some war zones as a result of the attacks. The *contras'* strategy seems to be to terrorize the dispersed rural population and limit its integration into the social programs of the revolutionary government. Among other effects, this has caused the destruction or closing of 153 rural schools and 125 social service centers, the deaths of 158 adult education teachers and students, halting of construction of 2,000 homes, and the paralysis of some rural sanitation, water, and road improvement projects.

As of this writing, about 1,000 peasants have been killed and more than 100,000 made refugees within Nicaragua by *contra* troop attacks. In 1983, in the country as a whole, MINSA provided about 79 percent of all medical visits, the army provided

6 percent, and physicians in private practice provided about 15 percent. With MINSA unable to provide for the growing health needs of the civilian population in the war zones, the army is significantly expanding its provision of services to civilians in those areas. Refugee concentrations have led to malaria epidemics.[f] Outside of the war zones, some health centers and posts are understaffed due to the mobilization of Nicaraguan physicians to serve in the militia or at MINSA health posts in the war zones. This personnel gap is being filled in part through an influx of foreign volunteers. Health workers on long-term assignment in Nicaragua come from more than thirty countries and are supplemented by short-term volunteers from Western Europe and the United States who work in teams for periods of three months.[19]

Given the economic and military attacks on the health system, maintaining the formidable achievements of the last four years may be considered a success. The massive increase in access and utilization of health services since the revolution will lead to new demands on private medicine and public sector curative care. Continuing efforts to reorient private medical practice toward preventive care and rural medicine may provide important examples for other developing countries in coming years.

Notes

1. La Prensa: Fundan una Nueva Clinica en Managua. Managua, June 10, 1982; 1.
2. El Nuevo Diario: Aprueban Escuela de Medicine para Managua. Managua, Oct. 30, 1980; 6.
3. MINSA: Plan de Salud 1982. Division de Planificacion, Managua 1982.
4. MINSA: Plan de Salud 1983, DIPLAN, Managua, 1983.
5. MINSA: Boletin Estadistico #3, Series Historicas, 1974–1978. Division de Planificacion, Managua, Junio de 1981.
6. MINSA: Actividades de Salud en el Primer Año de la Revolucion Sandinista, Boletin Estadistico #2, Oficina de Informacion y Estadistica, Managua, Noviembre 1980.
7. MINSA: Informe 1981, Managua, 1982.
8. Amador C: Informe de la Situacion de Salud de Nicaragua. MINSA, Managua, 1980.
9. Barricada: 768 Medicos Internacionalistas en Nicaragua. Managua, March 22, 1981; 1.
10. Instituto Nicaraguense de Seguridad Social y Bienestar: Cuatro años de Revolucion en el INSSBI: Managua, 1983; 5–47.
11. Ministerio de Hacienda y Credito Publico; Presupuesto General de Ingresos y Egresos de la Republica. Nicaragua, 1977.
12. El Nuevo Diario: Managua, Aug. 30, 1983; 20.
13. De Kayzer B, Ulate J: Education, Participacion en Salud e Ideologia; Nicaragua Pasado y Presente. Revista Centroamericana de Ciencias de la Salud 1980; 6:143–157.
14. Garfield RM, Vermund S: Changes in malaria incidence after a mass drug administration in Nicaragua. Lancet 1983; 2:500–503; Garfield RM, Vermund S: Malaria in Nicaragua: an update. Lancet 1984; 1:1125.
15. Barricada International: Managua, Dec. 19, 1983; 1.
16. Barricada: Se Inicia Jornada Cientifica de Salud. Managua, Sept. 24, 1982; 5.
17. MINSA: Repercusion de la Agresion en la Situacion de Salud del Pais. Nuevo Diario, August 13, 1983; 12–13.
18. Lezama MA: Agression Prejudico Programas de Salud. Barricada, Managua, Dec. 29, 1983; 5.
19. Links: Central American Health Rights Network: Health Brigades to Nicaragua. New York, April 1984; Vol. 1, No. 2, p. 5.

Acknowledgments

The authors wish to gratefully acknowledge the assistance of the Ministry of Health in the collection of information, including Dr. Ivan Tercero, Vice-Minister of Health for Medical Attention, Dr. Carlos Lopez, and Enrique Morales, Director of the Division of Statistics and Information. We would also like to thank Dr. Sophia Perez and Dr. Sten Vermund for their assistance. Dr. Taboada, who worked in the Nicaraguan Ministry of Health from March 1980 until May 1981, is a graduate of the Nicaraguan National University Medical School and did internship, residency, and social service in that country. Mr. Garfield worked in the Nicaraguan Ministry of Health from April 1981 to December 1981 and from June to November of 1983. He is supported by a fellowship from the InterAmerican Foundation, with additional support from the Health Research Training Program of the New York City Department of Health.

Chapter III:

Problems and Conflicts

Editor's Introduction

The preceding chapter dealt with Nicaragua's generally acclaimed revolutionary policies. This chapter attempts the far more difficult task of analyzing aspects of government programs that remain problematic. The challenge, of course, is to understand the origins and underlying bases of these problems and conflicts.

The political debating positions are, as usual, predictable. Supporters of the Reagan administration claim that problems demonstrate the failures of the Sandinista-led system, while supporters of Nicaragua claim that they result from U.S. aggression. In fact, there is some truth to each side: both Sandinista policy and the U.S.-backed war are partly to blame. Even though no one can objectively evaluate the success and failure of Sandinista policy until the war is over, contrasting points of view on four of these problematical areas are presented in this chapter.

The first, having to do with church-state relations, is exceedingly complicated in Nicaragua. Taken to the extreme, both opposing views are wrong: the Sandinistas are not in any sense against religion, nor does the Catholic Church uniformly oppose the Sandinistas. The Church-state debate has to be understood in its historical and international context, especially with regard to the worldwide challenges to the traditional Catholic church. This international context is explored in the first selection. Following this are contrasting articles by the White House staff and Father Miguel d'Escoto, Nicaragua's foreign minister. Finally, Andrew Reding briefly reviews both sides of the major questions at issue in the debate over liberation theology and the role of the Church in the revolution.

Fundamental to the Sandinista commitment to the poor is the need to end hunger. From the start, the government has struggled with the problems of food shortages.

In the next article, noted food and development policy expert Joseph Collins reviews this problem from the perspective of increasing demand coupled with severe constraints on supply. Anthropologist Phillipe Bourgois then tackles one of the most controversial issues in the Nicaraguan revolution: the question of the ethnic minorities on the Atlantic Coast. This is followed by a discussion of the role of women in the revolution. Nicaragua is often held up as an example of women's participation in a revolutionary process. Yet as both Comandante Tomás Borge and sociologist Maxine Molyneux point out, there is still a long way to go. Last is an article by Minister of Agriculture Jaime Wheelock on Nicaragua's plans for economic development.

*71. Ideological Struggle in the Nicaraguan Church**

By the Michigan Interchurch Committee on Central American Human Rights

"The Nicaraguan church used to be divided horizontally," a Jesuit who works at the Central American Historical Institute told me when I was visiting his Managua office. Drawing what looked like a pie with several small slices and one very large piece, he explained: "The only real divisions were between the Catholic and various Protestant churches, each competing with the others for the allegiance of the people. The basic struggle was for amassing the greatest membership.

"The real division now is a vertical one," he explained while feverishly sketching social pyramids on the scrap of paper. "There are leaders among all the churches who continue to be allied with the very few who are rich, the big businessmen and landowners, who seek to keep the nation's power and wealth to themselves. But there is also a growing number of church leaders, both Catholic and Protestant, both lay and cleric, that believe that the church must make a preferential option for the vast majority who are poor. They believe the power and wealth should be shared by all. Theirs is a struggle for justice and liberation."

A Polarized Church

On the one side is the traditional church, centered around Managua's Archbishop, Miguel Obando y Bravo. Most of the country's Catholic bishops and many of the priests closely follow the archbishop's lead. Despite the obvious differences in formal theology and worship style, Nicaragua's growing movement of small, fundamentalist, Protestant churches constitutes another important component of this traditional church. What joins these diverse sectors together is an outspoken opposition to the Sandinista-led popular revolution. Happy that the Somoza period marked by extreme

*Excerpted from *A Voice of the Voiceless,* vol. 4, no. 1 (January 1983).

corruption and repression has ended, the traditional church leaders are nevertheless fearful of the Sandinista attempts to place economic and political power in the hands of the masses of the poor. Rather, the traditional church leaders envision Nicaragua as a Western-style capitalist democracy, encompassing reforms that benefit the poor, but maintaining the real economic and political power firmly in the hands of the small minority of wealthy landowners and industrialists. Although the fundamentalists have made some inroads into the country's impoverished majority, the major following of the traditional church are the very rich (about 5 percent of the population) and a growing percentage of the small middle class.

On the other side is the "popular church," a name shunned in public to avoid fears of an impending schism, but the term commonly used by the people among themselves. The popular church has its center in the growing movement of grass-roots Christian communities, both Catholic and Protestant. Also a part of the popular church are the lay and cleric leaders who either work directly with the grass-roots communities, or in any of a number of ecumenical institutions that espouse the theology of liberation. They believe that it is their obligation as Christians to help develop a new society in which the needs of the poor come first. Believing that the Sandinista-led revolution shares these same basic aspirations, the popular church works actively within the revolutionary process: as members of the various popular organizations; as volunteers in government programs for adult literacy, health care, and civil defense; and as officials in all levels of the government itself. The popular church claims the adherence of the great majority of Nicaragua's poor who comprise 80 percent of the population, and a decreasing percentage of the middle class.

A Church of the Poor Is Born

SUPPORTING THE STATUS QUO

This polarization of the Church along ideological lines is a new phenomenon in Nicaragua. For centuries, the Nicaraguan Catholic Church (to which 90 percent of the population belongs) was firmly and undividedly allied with the landed elite and their military protectors. Most bishops and priests were members of very wealthy families themselves, and they lent their considerable power to bless the system that was so good to them. They preached to the impoverished masses that they should accept their current state in life as the will of God, and that their hope for a better life should be focused on heaven, to which the sacraments were the only path. Worldly concerns, such as widespread poverty and the absence of political freedoms, were largely ignored.

The close alliance between the Catholic leadership, the landed elite (and the newly emerging industrialists), and the military regime continued well into the Somoza era. The Church appointed chaplains to serve the repressive National Guard. High Church authorities regularly participated in government ceremonies, lending their moral support to the dictatorship. The Somozas were even sworn into power by the Catholic bishops.

GRASS-ROOTS COMMUNITIES: LIBERATION THEOLOGY

The firm support of the Catholic Church in Nicaragua and most of Latin America began to erode in the 1960s. Early in the decade, a program was begun in Brazil to initiate small Bible study groups where priests were scarce. People began to discuss scriptural stories and teachings in the light of their everyday experience of poverty and oppression. This was a radical break from the top-down model of traditional Catholicism where priests alone were charged with spiritual interpretation. With the help of progressive-minded priests and religious, lay leadership was fostered in order to facilitate these discussion groups and help conduct religious services. This was the beginning of the *comunidades de base* movement (base, or grass-roots, communities) which has since spread throughout Latin America.

The reforms of the Second Vatican Council, held between 1962 and 1965, served as an important impetus to this movement. The most important statements the council made with respect to Central America were assertions of the Church's fundamental responsibility to care for oppressed social classes, and to declare explicit support of human rights to a decent standard of living, adequate education, and political participation. Vatican II also emphasized the need for greater lay participation in Church affairs, demystifying and deemphasizing the role of the clergy.

The council's teachings were strengthened and given direction at the gathering of Latin American bishops held at Medellín, Colombia, in 1968. Some priests had written about the new theological ideas emerging from the grass-roots communities, but it came as a great surprise when the Bishops' Conference, traditionally the most conservative element of the church, embraced the new theology of liberation. The bishops called on the Church to make "a preferential option for the poor," and to work for their liberation from all forces of oppression and injustice. The traditional Church alliance with the wealthiest families and the military regimes was dealt a stunning blow.

The Medellín Conference coincided with the beginning of the *comunidades de base* movement in Nicaragua. A program was initiated by Nicaraguan clergy to train lay "delegates of the Word" to form rural communities. In addition to these communities operating outside of the traditional Church structure, another Church organization, the Center for Agrarian Promotion and Education, was founded by the Jesuits in 1969 to give agricultural training and socially oriented religious education to community leaders in rural areas. These leaders were then to transfer what they had learned to their communities. Spurred on by this new religious/social movement among their Catholic neighbors, many Protestants began to form grass-roots communities as well.

In the communities, many people began to discover for the first time that life had other possibilities, and that through a commonly shared Christian faith they could actively participate to improve their living conditions. Some communities succeeded in building schools and other community improvements. In 1976 Committees of Agricultural Workers, formed by the "delegates of the Word" on coffee estates on the Pacific Coast, organized economic protests over working conditions and wages. In the atmosphere of extreme government repression which existed at the time, to attempt to form unions and rural community organizations on an independent basis was to risk death, and the Church was the only institution through which people were able to effectively organize.

THE CHURCH JOINS THE REVOLUTION

Grass-roots Christian communities attempting to improve the conditions which marginalized them soon came to be viewed as subversive by the Somoza dictatorship and its National Guard. Peasants belonging to base communities were kidnapped, tortured, and killed. Members began to realize that they could no longer remain silent, hoping the National Guard would pass by their houses; instead, they began to organize for their common defense. As a joint statement of Nicaraguan Catholic and Protestant organizations said:

> It was very difficult for many Christians to choose armed struggle, but it was the last and only alternative which was left to them in order to stop the terror and genocide.

By the mid 1970s, the grass-roots strength of the Church had grown to unprecedented proportions in Nicaragua. The FSLN had recognized the importance of religion as a basis for community action, and church leaders involved in rural organizing became allied with or joined the FSLN. Notable among priests who joined the Sandinistas were Ernesto Cardenal, whose religious community at Solentiname had been destroyed by the National Guard, and Gaspar García Laviana, a Spanish priest who was later killed in battle. By 1978, as the political and military victories of the FSLN turned massive popular sentiment against Somoza, many churches began to stockpile medicines and food for those fleeing the violence and bombings of the National Guard. Throughout the final insurrection, the Catholic Church provided food, medicine, and shelter to those fighting with the FSLN, many of whom were Christians who had decided they had no alternative but to take up arms in the defense of their people. National Guard attacks on religious processions and demonstrations led to the formation of solidarity committees and parish support of armed defense by citizens against the National Guard.

*72. Persecution of Religious Groups in Nicaragua**

By the White House Office of Media Relations and Planning

History has shown us that Communist regimes inevitably seek to either eradicate the Church or to subvert it. Ideologically, the Church's existence is repugnant to them. Allegiance to God prevents total allegiance to and subjugation by the State,

*Reprinted from *White House Digest,* February 29, 1984.

which, according to Marx, is the salvific vehicle for the secular transformation of man into god.

The Communists cannot tolerate this limitation on their absolute power. Thus, in the Soviet Union all but a tiny percentage of churches have been closed and religious affiliation routinely brings the loss of precious privileges and sometimes brings more serious persecution.

In Nicaragua, the self-admitted Marxist-Leninist leaders of the government are following the same path. They are seeking to turn the Catholic Church, by far the largest in Nicaragua, into an arm of the government.

A small number of Catholic clergy have the government's official approval and sponsorship. They are used to generate support for the government, to spread the idea that only Marxists are true Christians, and to defame and divide the mainstream Church.

Meanwhile, the Sandinistas have harassed, persecuted, and defamed legitimate Church leaders, including Pope John Paul II. Church telecasts are subject to prior censorship and the Sandinistas seek to isolate the Church leadership from the people.

The Church vs. Somoza

Under the Somoza dictatorship, which was overthrown in 1979, the Catholic Church had been in the forefront of those forces calling for reform. Indeed, in 1979 the prelate of Nicaragua, Archbishop Obando y Bravo, took the extraordinary step of announcing that the Somoza regime had become intolerable and that Christians could in good conscience revolt against it.

At that time, the revolution against Somoza was broad based and included most of the mainstream leadership of Nicaragua. The revolution was publicly committed to democracy and pluralism. But, shortly after Somoza's ouster, the Communist faction—with the control of the military—began to consolidate its power.

Despite early danger signals, the Catholic hierarchy was initially supportive of the revolutionary government.

The First Step

But, in October of 1980, the Sandinistas took their first real step toward the dual Communist goal of a) limiting the Church's influence, and b) co-opting what is left of that influence for the government.

In a publicly promulgated policy on religion, the Sandinistas declared that Christians were not permitted to evangelize within Sandinista organizations. Moreover, only those religious who fully accepted the objectives of the revolution, as put forth by the Sandinista leadership, were to be permitted to take an active role in public affairs.

The bishops responded swiftly and firmly, saying that such attempts to limit the influence of the Church were "totalitarian." Totalitarian systems, the bishops argued, seek to turn the Church into an ''instrument'' by tolerating only those activities the government finds convenient.

Priests and Politics

In 1981, responding to Pope John Paul II's desire to keep the Church free of political entanglements, the Nicaraguan bishops called on all Catholic clergy to limit their political activities to something less than full-time devotion to the regime, or to any political faction.

A long controversy ensued. The Sandinista clergy refused to leave their posts. The bishops, stymied, agreed that the Sandinista priests could temporarily remain in government as long as they did not exercise their priestly functions.

These high-ranking Sandinista priests that chose to discontinue their priestly functions while continuing to occupy political office are: Miguel d'Escoto, minister of foreign affairs; Fernando Cardenal, director of Sandinista youth organizations; and his brother Ernesto, minister of culture.

Since that time, the Sandinistas campaign to rigorously support Church factions responsive to its interests steadily intensified. Priests who have expressed a desire to leave the regime have been told by the junta that they cannot resign from their posts.

The ''People's Church''

The first step was to co-opt and expand a unique Latin American institution called the Christian base community.

The base community is a neighborhood group of Catholics who meet for prayer and religious services but who also work together for social and political reform. Over the years, most of these groups have not been Marxist, but have worked for reforms that most Americans would recognize as basic.

However, the bishops had long recognized that the base communities have had the potential to become ''prisoners of political polarization or fashionable ideologies which want to exploit their immense potential.''

The Sandinistas began to exploit that potential. Many base communities have remained loyal to the Catholic hierarchy, but many have been made instruments of the revolution, part of what the Sandinistas refer to as ''the people's church,'' a church subservient to the government.

The Sandinistas began to speak openly of two churches, one, the ''popular church'' which is the friend of the people, and the other which oppresses the people.

In reference to the traditional and ''popular church,'' Sandinista junta member Sergio Ramírez stated that one of these ''churches'' was not revolutionary, but the other church was:

> [A] church of change. This church became the people's ally. This church boosted the revolution and committed itself to this revolution. This church is

participating in the revolutionary process and is incorporating the patriotic and revolutionary priests of whom we are very proud into the government.''

In response, Archbishop Obando y Bravo has condemned ''those who are trying to divide the Church'' and spread the idea that there is ''one bourgeois church and another church for the poor.'' The Vatican has become so alarmed at the attempt of the Sandinistas to divide the Church in Nicaragua that the Pope issued a pastoral letter on June 29, 1982, which criticized advocates of the ''popular church'' for their

> . . . infiltration of strongly ideological connotations along the lines of certain political radicalization of the class struggle, of acceptance of violence for the carrying out of political ends. It is not through a political role, but through the priestly ministry that the people want to remain close to the Church.

*73. Nicaragua: Unfinished Canvas**

By Father Miguel D'Escoto

Father Miguel D'Escoto is a Maryknoll priest and is the foreign minister of Nicaragua.

When a revolution takes place, people look for the ideology that guides the building of the new society. Sometimes revolutions can be embarked upon rather hastily, and people may think the essence of a revolution is to overthrow a government. That is not the revolution. That is something that has to happen prior to the revolution.

If, due to political myopia, the people decide that the revolution is the overthrowing and they do not carefully consider beforehand what they will do after the overthrow, they may run in haste to the international supermarket of ideological formulas to see which best fits their situation. Well, thank God, in Nicaragua, in the varying trails of our mountains and valleys and in our cities there has been in gestation for more than half a century a true Nicaraguan ideology, which we call Sandinismo.

Sandino was not a philosopher; he did not sit down to explain in a systematic way his political thought. He was a person endowed with a great amount of popular wisdom, and although he was without formal education, he synthesized the common denominator or the end result of Nicaraguan political thought, the result of our experience.

Sandinista thought rests on four fundamental pillars. The first is nationalism. We are not talking about chauvinism here, but about a nationalism that is manifested in

*Reprinted from *Sojourners,* March 1983. Reprinted with Permission from *Sojourners,* Box 29272, Washington, DC 20017

the will of our people to regain sovereignty, to determine our own destiny, even to have the right to make our own mistakes and learn from them—and to determine what system of government we will opt for to best meet the needs of our people.

Sandinismo is not nationalistic in any sense that leads us to believe that we have discovered a formula that is good for any other country. We believe that, just as we are looking for our own way, every other country has to look for its own way. This is why for us it seems strange that we might be intent on exporting our revolution.

A revolution is not an exportable item. Revolutions can take place only when a people decides to make it possible, as happened in Nicaragua. Without broad popular participation, our revolution would not have been possible. And this participation was not only because of antagonism to Somoza. Many political groups during this half century tried to change the established order, but they never got wide popular support.

The natural wisdom of the people wants more than a negative plan to overthrow; the people want to know what we are going to do afterwards. Therefore, it was only when the Sandinista Front emerged that the popular support was captured that was indispensable in the overthrow of Somoza.

Another of these four pillars of Sandinista thought is a democratic aspiration. Now, you ask, why should we aspire to democracy if we never had it? Well, it is natural to humankind. We believe that humanity has been created in the image and likeness of God, created to be a cocreator with God in the unfinished task of making this a world after God's own design.

I am reminded of a marvelous painting of the baptism of Christ in a gallery in London. It was painted by Leonardo da Vinci's teacher, Verrocchio. In it you see John the Baptist pouring water over our Lord in the river. An angel stands by the side holding the garments of our Lord.

Verrocchio had great love and admiration for Leonardo, his young disciple, and he wanted him to participate in this masterpiece. So he asked Leonardo to paint the angel. Of course, the disciple was better than the teacher, and what is most interesting in that picture is the angel, although the whole work is very good.

And so our Lord also made us cocreators, wanting us to participate and share in the canvas. God initiated a process, and in his great love for humankind, decided not to do it all. Having been given that orientation, we cannot accept being reduced to the level of simple spectatorship in a game in which only a few play. We have a built-in need to actively participate with our God-given lights in the common task of searching for a more human and just society.

This democratic aspiration is not to be confused with an aspiration to have just the formality of democracy; we are talking about real participation. We are quite aware that democracy entails social democracy, economic democracy, political democracy, and many rights, such as the right to work, to a family wage, to learn, to read, to write—all those different rights that provide us with an opportunity to participate and not be manipulated.

We are moving in every direction to develop our new democratic Nicaragua. We are not going to fall to what Somoza did. He tried to give a shellac of democracy by having controlled elections from time to time, so that the United States could say that his regime was democratic. The United States is saying this about El Salvador and a great many other governments it wants to support.

The third pillar of Sandinista thought is its Christian element. Despite many deficiencies in the work of evangelization in Nicaragua, Christian evangelical gospel values have permeated down deep, and they are reflected in one of the main characteristics of Sandinismo.

I first realized this years back reading the things that Sandino wrote. In spite of the fact that he was fighting in the mountains of Nicaragua against interventionist American marines and that the United States had imposed a National Guard on Nicaragua, which from the very beginning was the tool of American domination, Sandino always manifested love for the American people. He had a Christian attitude and did not wrap up in one package the people of the United States.

As much as two years before the triumph, we were afraid that after Somoza was overthrown there would be a popular reaction that we could not control and that the people would take justice into their own hands, taking revenge for the many grievances they had suffered for such a prolonged time. So we created a slogan and repeated it all the time: "Relentless in the struggle, but generous in victory." The Front was trying to prepare the people so that they would look upon generosity as a virtue. Few revolutions do that. Many would try to get people to understand why you should have mass killings or mass executions.

This reservoir of Christian values became apparent to the world after the revolution, when a great amount of forgiveness was manifested. Immediately after the overthrow, Comandante Tomás Borge decided to free every one of the former national guardsmen in Matagalpa. Of course, we had to pay dearly for this because they went to the other side of the border and formed the nucleus of those who from Honduras are working against the revolution.

Soon after the overthrow I went with Tomás to visit the jail. The jail had a special area where former Somozan torturers were held, including the man who had tortured Tomás and who was most notorious.

Tomás said to him, "Remember when I told you I would take revenge when I was free? I now come for my revenge. For your hate and torture I give you love, and for what you did I give you freedom." And the man went free.

The fourth pillar of Sandinista thought is a further clarification of the second, which I said was a democratic ideal: We aspire to a system of social justice. This is a revolution that is being made to create a democratic system that has meaning and consequence for the people. And by "the people" I mean everyone, not just an elite, but everyone.

Sandinismo is not static. It develops and is enriched by new generations of Sandinistas.

As a twentieth-century revolution, we are definitely influenced by Marxist thought. I certainly am, as many modern people are—maybe they don't know it—but they are influenced too. For example, the emphasis on conceptualizing the present as an historical trend to better understand it is one of the contributions of Marxism.

But also our understanding of capitalism is a contribution of Marxism. History will condemn the Catholic Church for this particular myopia or blindness: We were never able to detect, until now, that there has never been in the history of Christianity anything more diametrically opposed to Christian values than liberal philosophy.

The underlying anthropological conception of liberalism is that humanity is fundamentally selfish, and if you want to have people working and producing you must cater to that selfishness. Anything else is unrealistic and idealistic. The liberal believes therefore that humanity is doomed to suffering.

The other terrible thing about liberalism is that it splits the person. It says that there are three separate realms: political, economic, and religious. Our Christian philosophical tradition says that the person is a whole and responsible agent. But the liberals say that if we go to church on Sunday, we are religious animals for that day. But on the next day, I may be a political animal or an economic animal.

So don't come to me, the owner of an enterprise, you priests, and tell me that I have to pay just wages. Don't intrude with your theological discipline into something that is autonomous—theology is a different realm. Don't talk to me about justice; that is an intrusion. The slogan is, "The business of business is business," which is to say, profit. Liberalism then supports capitalism with values that are certainly not Christian.

Every human being has to have ambition; ambition cannot be condemned. On the contrary, we Christians ought to be the most ambitious of all, because our Lord said that we should love one another as he loved us. That is quite an ambition, to love as Christ loved. Lest we miss the point, our Lord also said that we must be perfect as our heavenly Father is perfect. In other words, always aspire to be more. But the question is, to what do we aspire?

Because capitalism is the economic expression of liberalism, when it comes to getting people to work, capitalism develops systems only for material incentives. People can be motivated materially, but we have two buttons, and if we only push the material incentive button, we will atrophy the moral incentive button. The liberal thought of being more through having more instead of being more through loving more which is the Christian position, constitutes the greatest contradiction to Christianity.

When we develop a social situation in which we foment the idea that being more is having more, we are producing a cirrhosis of the heart. In time the heart becomes so hardened that the Word of God will not be able to permeate it; so much so that sometimes I ask myself, will it be possible to be Western and to be Christian? Oh, I could keep the mitre and the cross and the incense, but there will be no Christianity if we continue on this terrible course.

From a philosophical perspective, of course, Marx helps us understand the connection between liberal philosophy, capitalism, and imperialism, and the connection between liberal thought, capitalism, and racism. Sure, no one really believes that someone is inferior because of color, but a different pigmentation helps you justify exploitation.

So in the Sandinistas, we have been very much aided by Marxist thought to understand some great problems. But we have been equally or more influenced by Christian thought.

In Latin America the Church had been for so long identified with the powers that be, with an established order that was not a Christian established order. We had been preaching resignation and helping the rich to continue exploiting, telling the people that later they would be rewarded if they accepted this exploitation. We were preaching a kind of idolatry toward the system just because it was.

To preach resignation indiscriminately is very dangerous. Resignation in the face of the inevitable is oftentimes a virtue, but some types of resignation are sinful. To resign yourself to the point that you become an accomplice with crime, with exploitation, is a total refusal to do the will of God and become a leavening and transforming agent in society.

A process of renewal in the Catholic Church began after Vatican II permeated our reality through the historic meeting of Latin American bishops in 1968 in Medellín, Colombia. It filtered down and reached Catholic schools, where they began to have qualms of conscience that they were educating only the elite and helping them to live in a bubble separate from the rest of their brothers and sisters.

The schools began to foment the idea that young students should voluntarily help out in the poor *barrios,* in the poor neighborhoods, with parish priests who were working among the poor. That's how the students discovered the plight of their brothers and sisters and began to search for what to do. From there they went to the mountains and joined the Sandinista Front. Very many of these students who are in high government positions today are very young, because this all happened in the early seventies. The great growth in the Sandinista Front occurred when the Church began this process of renewal in Nicaragua and consciences began to open. Comandante Daniel Ortega publicly has said that he went to the revolutionary struggle because he understood that was what was demanded if he was to be faithful to Christ.

Do you know the apostle Thomas? Most people are like Thomas. They can't simply accept that the Lord was resurrected, and so the Lord says to them, "Come and put your finger in my wounds." Christ wanted to show Thomas his credentials, because Thomas demanded to inspect them.

We preach the message of our Lord. But the people want credentials. Where are our wounds, what are we suffering? In every Gospel you will see what our Lord is promising you: persecution. The inevitable consequence of doing the Father's will is the cross. And the Father's will is that we proclaim the brotherhood and sisterhood of all of us under God and therefore necessarily denounce whatever stands in the way of achieving this brotherhood and sisterhood. Do that, and our Lord says that we will be persecuted as he was persecuted; the disciple is no greater than the master.

Eight years before the insurrection, after the earthquake, I talked to the archbishop. And I said, "Archbishop, don't you see how this is going to explode?" To me it seemed inevitable that sooner or later in spite of the great patience of our people—everything human is limited—that patience would run out. I said, "Bishop, it is going to be terrible, there will be so many dead people, so much destruction and death. Why don't we go into the streets? You lead us, armed with the rosary in our hands and prayers on our lips and chants and songs in repudiation for what has been done to our people. The worst that can happen to us is the best, to share with Christ the cross if they shoot us.

"If they do shoot us, there will be a consciousness aroused internationally. And maybe the people in the United States will be alerted and will pressure their government so that it won't support Somoza, and then maybe we can be freed without the destruction that I see ahead."

And the archbishop said, "No Miguel, you tend to be a little bit idealistic, and this destruction is not going to happen." And then when it did happen, the Church insisted on nonviolence.

To be very frank with you, I don't think that violence is Christian. Some may say that this is a reactionary position. But I think that the very essence of Christianity is the cross. It is through the cross that we will change.

I have come to believe that creative nonviolence has to be a constitutive element of evangelization and of the proclamation of the Gospel. But in Nicaragua nonviolence was never included in the process of evangelization.

The cancer of oppression and injustice and crime and exploitation was allowed to grow, and finally the people had to fight with the means available to them, the only means that people have found from of old: armed struggle. Then the Church arrogantly said violence was bad, nonviolence was the correct way.

I don't believe that nonviolence is something you can arrive at rationally. We can develop it as a spirituality and can obtain the grace necessary to practice it, but not as a result of reason. Not that it is antireason, but that it is not natural. The natural thing to do when somebody hits you is to hit them back.

We are called upon to be supernatural. We reach that way of being, not as a result of nature, but of prayer. But that spirituality and prayer and work with people's consciences has never been done. We have no right to hope to harvest what we have not sown.

Our Lord never said that we should take our cross and walk. He said, "Take your cross and follow me." Our Lord was the first to be nailed, spat upon, and crowned with thorns. He led as Martin Luther King led. That is why I always look upon King as the Christian who most exemplifies what it means to follow our Lord today.

No one has influenced my own life more than Martin Luther King. For years and years it was his book *The Strength to Love* that I used in chapel for meditation. I gave a copy to many priests. And it was Martin Luther King's picture that hung in my office when I was in New York. But I used to look upon the picture with a certain amount of guilt or shame, because I admired him so much and wanted to follow what he had done, but I was afraid.

And then it came to me one day as we were preparing for Lent and I was alone in my office thinking, "Well, another Lent, and the same old mediocre me. What am I to do? You may say you are not going to eat hot dogs or do a particular thing; well, that doesn't help anyone. So what am I going to do for this Lent?"

I stayed there for a long time oblivious to everything, and then a prayer formulated: "Lord, help me to understand the mystery of your cross. Help me to love the cross and give me the guts to embrace it in whatever shape or form it comes."

And everything was different all of a sudden because the cross became to me a symbol of life, the beginning of life. I began to see it inseparable and indistinguishable from resurrection. Why? Because we come to understand in John that life is love, and greater love has no one than to give his or her life. The cross is the greatest act of love, and therefore the greatest manifestation of life.

During the revolution I was greatly uplifted by the experience of praying and offering the sacrifice of the Mass, celebrating the Eucharist with people who were in the struggle. It was a wonderful experience because for the first time I realized that we were not only repeating the words of Christ, "This is my blood, this is my body, which is shared, which is offered for all." Our Lord didn't want us only to repeat those words, he wanted us to repeat them after we had made them our own. The people who were participating in those prayers were making them real, because we didn't know if at that celebration or immediately afterwards, we would share our own blood and give our life—and many people did.

I remember that one day, late in the evening, I came to a camp where some combatants for the revolution were sitting in the grass under a tree having a conversation. They saw me coming and asked me to celebrate the Eucharist. I had no bread or wine, but I was able to respond to their request to "give us some uplifting words from the Gospel of our Lord."

As I talked I noticed that one young man was fidgeting and seemed very uneasy. Finally I said, "Hernand, it looks to me as if you want to say something."

"You are always talking about the Lord," he replied. "Who is this Lord? The Lord People?"

"No, not the Lord People," I answered, "although he is identified with the people and is the Lord of many."

At this point an older man broke in, "Father, don't be upset with this young *compañero*. He is a good boy, he's just very revolutionary and has gotten himself confused by reading a book written by that Spaniard."

"What Spaniard?" I asked.

"Karl Marx."

No one laughed, and the man continued, "I don't know how to read. But I can tell this little fellow who the Lord is, because my grandfather used to tell us about him."

At that everyone hushed, because they knew that the older man's grandfather had been a lieutenant with Sandino. The man continued, "I don't want to brag, but I remember what my grandfather said. He said it was all in the book—the Bible. There it says that God is the Father of all of us and that Christ is his Son and is both God and man. We are all brothers and sisters, and we must be willing to give our lives for one another.

"So that's why when I was at home in my little town near Honduras and we heard on the radio that we must go to free our people, all of us Christians knew that we were supposed to be willing to risk our lives. And so we went in obedience to the Lord."

My father died three months before the triumph. He knew he was dying, because his heart was getting bigger and bigger and this was making it difficult for him to breathe.

I was living clandestinely at the time and couldn't visit him. But I heard that a bomb had been placed in his house, and it exploded where he usually sat. Somoza's people were looking for me, and after the bomb exploded, thirty-six armed men came and threw my father to the floor and demanded to know where I was.

After the men left, my father called me because he was afraid that news of this event would weaken me, make me worried. And he said, "I want you to know that your mother and I wanted to call and tell you not to worry about us because no one can really kill us." This is a new understanding of death: They can shoot our bodies but they cannot kill us.

And he said, "Don't be afraid yourself to die. I am praying with your mother one more rosary." (By now they were up to about six, because for everything that I got involved in he was praying another rosary.) "I am praying with your mother that you have the Christian guts to accept Calvary, if that is what the Lord wants."

But our struggle didn't end with the overthrow of Somoza, because we are still working for *Patria Libre o Morir,* a free country or death—free from internal tyranny, from external oppression, domination, and control; free to do what we believe is in the best interest of our people and will result in a social situation that will be certainly compatible with our Christian faith and belief. And in that commitment we continue.

Lopez Portillo, the former president of Mexico, met with Reagan not too long ago, and he said to me after the meeting that he told President Reagan he should not make a mistake in evaluating Nicaraguans. He said to Reagan, "You have to understand that those people in Nicaragua are just crazy enough to mean it when they say 'a free country or death.' They are not afraid to die for the sake of keeping this freedom."

In fact, that freedom began when the inner shackles of fear were broken, by the grace of God. All liberation must be first spiritual and internal. A free people can then proceed to free a nation, with freedom to do what it feels is the right and the just thing to do, regardless of the consequences.

What we are striving to do is to create a new Nicaragua, a Nicaragua that is really a Nicaragua of all of us, not just of a certain class. One doesn't choose the cradle; one chooses only the alliances that one makes.

I happened to be born into a class that enjoyed everything, which the majority of my brothers and sisters in Nicaragua did not. We could not continue to pray the Our

Father because the hypocrisy of saying it became very repugnant. I can only say Our Father if I am concerned for the lot of every individual as if he or she really were my brother or sister, I could not honestly pray or go to communion. Then I realized that "I" was "we," we Nicaraguans, because this is a collective experience that led us to assume this position that took us to where we are now and for which we are being penalized. Pray that we can embrace the cross and endure being penalized for doing the Father's will, for proclaiming in word and deed the universal brotherhood and sisterhood of all of us.

Nicaragua has embarked on a project destined to secure for the first time real autonomy, sovereignty, and independence for our nation so that we can create a social, political, and economic situation that would allow us to live as brothers and sisters and respect the God-given dignity of each individual. Now we are confronted with this very aggressive attitude from people and governments that prior to this time were able to get along so well with the system that oppressed our people and condemned us to a most inhuman existence.

In their effort to discredit Nicaragua, some in the United States have tried to manipulate a presumed bad situation between Church and state, and have launched allegations of religious persecution. Not that they ever cared much for religion, but if they can make these allegations to the people of their country, they can reduce any resistance to their political objectives against Nicaragua. This is why it is for us vital that our Christian brothers and sisters in the United States and elsewhere actively protest against this manipulation of the religious feelings of the people at home.

The triumph over Somoza has come, and we can begin, as patriots and Christians, to build this new country. It is only natural for the Church to participate by developing the inner spiritual disposition among the people, so that their generosity would be up to par with what the revolution demands. The revolution demands that we abandon ideas of only ourselves becoming better off. It demands a great amount of brotherhood and sisterhood and sharing and thinking not only of myself but of *us*.

But soon after the revolution I saw that unfortunately there were some members of our Church in very high and prominent places who opted to side with the small minority, who could not be satisfied by a popular revolution because they could not retain the privileges and prerogatives that they had enjoyed of old. And we had some inner Church conflicts, which not only involved us as priests sympathetic with the revolutionary process, but at this point in time, as those exercising positions of responsibility within our government. It was alleged that we were doing something not in keeping with our responsibility as priests. It was even pretended that our actions were somehow against our Christian and priestly commitment.

But thank God we have the Gospels and the parables and the many ways in which our Lord tried through different means to clarify his message. When these conflicts arose I began to think more and more about the good Samaritan, because, like him, and the priest who went ahead and the other religious man who followed him, I was on the way to Jericho. My life had a very specific agenda. I had my work cut out for me, but all of a sudden the unexpected happened. There was my fellow countryman bleeding by the roadside, and I had to get off the beast and forget, for the time being, going to Jericho.

We go and we do, not what the priest did or the second man, but the one whom the Jews said could not be saved—the Samaritan. And so, we must be obedient to the Lord who calls us in many ways, and sometimes through events in which you, all of a sudden, find yourself immersed.

I am a man, a Nicaraguan, a Christian, and a priest, all of which demand of me certain things, but not contradictory demands. Being a Christian and being a priest means that I have to fulfill even more abundantly and completely the demands made upon a man and a citizen of a country. And I would never, by the grace of God, for fear of any reprisals, betray the people, who must be always the most important thing—the people for whom our Lord became incarnate, lived, died, and was resurrected.

And if, in trying to be faithful to what I believe is what our Lord demands of us in unusual circumstances, I suffer consequences, I will accept them. I have been told that I cannot celebrate the Holy Eucharist in public or private because somehow I'm supposed to be a scandal. It was the very center of my life. Well, I accept that. But when I was told that, I cried the whole night.

So, we go back to prayer: only to understand it, to love it, and to embrace it. You must join me in prayer that I will never betray the people, that I will accept the consequences of solidarity with the people who hunger for justice and for peace and for brotherhood and sisterhood.

*74. Debate Topic: The Church's Nature and Mission**

By Andrew Reding

Marianismo

Archbishop Miguel Obando y Bravo of Managua and conservative clerics argue that liberationist clerics have lost sight of the importance of Mary in Catholic theology. The conservatives equate Jesus with the biblical message of justice and Mary with that of peace and reconciliation. These times, they insist, call for special attention to Mary in the interest of social peace. It is in connection with this theme that the "sweating virgin" made her appearance.

Liberationist clerics respond by reminding the conservatives of the powerful social justice content of Mary's Magnificat. (The use of a verse from it on a banner at the celebration I saw in Estelí was no coincidence.) Through frequent textual refer-

*Reprinted from *Christianity and Crisis*, November 12, 1984.

ences and reflections, they suggest that the conservatives' dichotomy between Jesus and Mary is less than faithful to the biblical witness.

Church Unity

The hierarchy, led by Archbishop Obando and Bishop Pablo Vega of Juigalpa, insist that the unity of the Church is founded on strict obedience to the leadership of, well yes, the hierarchy. The bishops are particularly nervous about the *comunidades de base,* and look anxiously to the Pope to rein in the decentralist, participatory, often revolutionary tendencies set in motion by "the preferential option for the poor."

The liberationists counter that, biblically speaking, unity emerges from adhering to Jesus' evangelical call to solidarity with the poor and the weak. They look to a unity not of the Church thought of as synonymous with its clergy but rather, in accord with the reconceptualizations of Vatican II, of the Church as the broader community of the faithful. And they remind the bishops of the Christian model of leadership set up by Jesus himself, wherein those who would lead must humbly place themselves and their material interests last. In this vein they point to Oscar Romero, martyred archbishop of San Salvador, as model.

The conservatives respond by accusing the liberationists of trying to split the Church in two with conceptions of "hierarchical" and "popular" churches. They insinuate, sometimes explicitly, that the liberationists are really Marxists in clerical clothing, seeking to neutralize the Church and pave the way for atheistic communism to infect Central America.

Liberationists ridicule the charges, indicating they are born of the close connections some hierarchs have made with their counterparts in the upper and middle classes (witness Obando's recent dealings with W. R. Grace), and calling attention to the long, sordid history of collaboration between Catholic hierarchs and Latin American tyrants. They insist they have no desire to found a separate church, but that on the contrary they hope to persuade more of the hierarchy to return to the fold of leadership through servanthood in conformity with the guidelines of St. Augustine and the dictates of Jesus Christ (*"La Funcion del Obispo en la Comunidad Cristiana." Amanecer,* May-June 1984).

Preferential Option for the Poor

Conservatives further accuse liberationists of fomenting "class hatred" by so militantly championing the cause of the poor. The Church, they say, is church of all, not just the poor. That means there can be no talk of class struggle among Christians. Christian love must be extended to rich and poor alike, though the rich need to be persuaded to be more compassionate in their treatment of the poor.

Yes indeed, reply the liberationists, but to love the rich is not the same as letting them persist in wrongdoing. Noting that Jesus was particularly severe in his treatment of the rich, they insist that to love the sinners one must attack their sins, not just through generally ineffectual appeals to stop worshiping Mammon, but also through political reforms that rescue them from the soul-killing institutional arrangements by which they abuse fellow human beings.

The Amado Pena Affair

A major controversy erupted between Archbishop Obando and the government in June when a right-wing priest close to the archbishop was placed under what amounted to house arrest in a seminary (with the option of leaving the country), after the Ministry of the Interior claimed it had irrefutable evidence of his participation in a CIA conspiracy. Abscam-type videotapes of the priest conversing and drinking with men who later confessed to having been CIA operatives were repeatedly aired on television. In these tapes, Pena is observed to say, among other incriminating things, "We have to say, for the time being passive resistance, but when the hour comes we know that here there is nothing peaceful," and "God wants that it not be bla bla bla. Here what's needed is four bullets in one of those sons of bitches, believe me, there will be more deaths of certain of those *jodidos* [literally, "fucked-up ones"], and with two or three [of those deaths] I will set out to sow horror."

Pena claimed to have been framed. Obando immediately endorsed him on his word, refusing even to investigate the government's charges in spite of their seriousness. The videotape, he said, could have been doctored. Interior Minister Tomás Borge countered by offering to turn the tapes over to him for professional analysis, an offer that was rarely mentioned in international dispatches, and to which Obando did not reply.

Church and State

The unresolved questions in the Pena affair in turn bear upon the case of the ten foreign-born priests expelled from the country shortly thereafter. They were put on a plane for Costa Rica immediately after joining Obando in a solidarity march for Padre Pena. The government claimed that as foreign citizens they were meddling in domestic politics by demonstrating on behalf of someone accused of conspiring to overthrow the government.

Obando pointed to this incident as conclusive evidence of persecution of the Church by the Sandinistas. In response, *El Nuevo Diario* (July 13) cautioned him against hypocrisy, publishing an even longer list of priests and nuns banished from the country by Obando and his allies for their support of the revolution. As if to further underscore the point, still another priest was shortly thereafter transferred to Guatemala, because, in a funeral mass for militia killed by the *contras,* he condemned the CIA for supporting the war against Nicaragua. Again, little of this has been reported outside the country. Nor has the larger Central American context been conveyed. Why do Washington and Rome exhibit shock and horror when a handful of foreign-born priests are expelled from Nicaragua, but not physically harmed, and yet at the same time continue to support governments in El Salvador and Guatemala that are known to have connived in the removal of priests and an archbishop by means of murder? Why was it all right for Catholic priests to serve as chaplains in Somoza's National Guard but a scandal for them now to condemn the CIA for its semiclandestine war on Nicaragua?

Liberationism and Marxism

Opponents of the revolution and of liberation theology charge that the "popular church" is a mere tool of Marxist totalitarianism, misusing Christianity to try to legitimize what is at base an atheistic and repressive reality. Interestingly, the presidential candidate of the Nicaraguan Socialist party (the Moscow-line Communist party) similarly denounces the Sandinistas for misusing Marxism while handing the country's education over to devout Catholics. Just what is the relationship between the FSLN and radical Christians?

To begin with, it should be noted that liberationist Christians have not been mere cheerleaders in the revolutionary process. Many have taken up arms, many have risen to important positions in the FSLN, others run key government ministries. In so doing they have played a major role in shaping the very character of this revolution.

Historically, revolutions have not been dominated by mercy and moderation. What makes the Nicaraguan revolution so distinctive is that in spite of the mass horrors of the Somoza years, the lives of even the most sadistic torturers have been spared. There is no death penalty, and the maximum prison term is thirty years: Somoza himself, tried *in absentia,* was sentenced to only twenty-six years. Offers of amnesty with grants of land have been extended to all but the leadership of the *contras*. Even more remarkably, in view of more than a century of U.S. intervention in Nicaragua, the revolution (unlike its Iranian counterpart) had welcomed thousands of U.S. citizens in a spirit of friendship and reconciliation. Interior Minister Tomás Borge attributes this "revolutionary generosity" to the leadership role played by revolutionary Christians.

Naturally, there is less inclination to criticize when one is given a significant role in shaping policy. Yet liberationist Christians do engage in what they see as constructive public criticism of the government. Padre Uriel Molina, who heads the *Centro Ecumenico Antonio Valdivieso,* deplored the government's "dirty" handling of the Bismarck Carballo Affair (see "Are Nicaragua's Churches Free?" September 20, 1982 issue). Carballo, a priest closely associated with the archbishop, was photographed naked with a female parishioner in what the Church charges was a setup. Though the truth is hard to come by, the government indecently turned over the pictures to *Barricada* and *El Nuevo Diario* after *La Prensa* accused it of a frame-up.

More recently the Centro Valdivieso, the Ecumenical Axis, the Community of Christians in the revolution, the weekly *El Tayacan,* the Christian base communities, and other groups of revolutionary Christians joined in denouncing the government's expulsion of the ten foreign-born priests. In a letter published in *El Nuevo Diario* (July 17), they likewise deplored the confrontational attitude of the archbishop, and concluded: "We appeal to the revolutionary government that it pursue by all possible means the use of resources of persuasion. The path of dialogue is difficult, but we see it as indispensable to the good of our people."

75. The Food System: Expanding Demand, Sabotaged Supply*

By Joseph Collins

Joseph Collins is an internationally renowned hunger expert. Together with Frances Moore Lappé (Diet for a Small Planet) *he coauthored* Food First, *and cofounded the Institute for Food and Development Policy in San Francisco. He travels often to Nicaragua as an unpaid advisor on food policy.*

In many Third-World Countries (and also in the United States), people go hungry not because there is not enough food, but because they are deprived of the economic resources they need either to grow or to buy food. Often farmers complain about mounting surpluses and shopkeepers tell of food thrown out because no one buys it. In economists' terms, the problem is *effective* demand, not supply.

In Nicaragua, by contrast, the effective demand for food has greatly increased since the revolution. The reason is simple: many more Nicaraguans now have the money to buy food. Nicaragua's food crisis is rooted precisely in the country's increased demand for food. The increased demand has become ever more difficult to meet due to serious food-production obstacles.

In addition to setting low controlled prices for staple foods, the revolution increased effective demand through a number of early measures. These included: interventions in wholesaling and marketing by ENABAS, the National Basics Food Corporation; steeply subsidizing consumer food prices; establishing a "guaranty card" system; opening thousands of workplace commissaries and cafeterias; and establishing special nutrition programs for the most vulnerable Nicaraguans.

Let's take a look at how these measures have fared over the past two years.

ENABAS

ENABAS has attempted to guarantee low food prices by undermining speculation on shortages. The goal is to maintain reliable stocks of whatever basics might be in short supply even if imports become necessary. The Sandinistas hoped to use ENABAS to avoid direct government control of marketing.

In the past two years the government has become increasingly active in whole-

---

*Excerpts from *Nicaragua: What Difference Could a Revolution Make? Food and Farming in the New Nicaragua* (Institute for Food and Development Policy, 1985).

saling. Expanded storage facilities, the wider use of production contracts (whereby farmers are guaranteed seeds, fertilizers, etc., if they sell to ENABAS), and higher producer prices helped ENABAS "capture" an ever greater share of each harvest of the staple food crops. In 1983 ENABAS purchased 23 percent of the corn crop, 60 percent of the beans, and 95 percent of the rice and sorghum. (Because rice and sorghum are large-scale, highly mechanized crops with few producers, it is relatively easy for the government to coordinate their purchase and marketing. This contrasts with corn and beans which are produced on as many as 90,000 individual farms and cooperatives.) Taking into account substantial corn imports in 1983, ENABAS controlled 60 percent of the wholesale corn market.

ENABAS also expanded its "network" of stores to over 8,500 by 1984. Almost half are the privately owned *expendios populares* (people's outlets), neighborhood stores that agree to sell the controlled basic goods at official retail prices in return for a guaranteed supply from ENABAS at official wholesale prices. That so much of the network is privately owned speaks to the continued efforts of the Sandinista-led government to work with the private sector (and benefit from small merchants' know-how).

We talked with one such "franchised" store owner in Ciudad Sandino, Doña Mercedes, in March 1984. She was glad the CDS approved her shop being in the ENABAS network. "It's an honor because it means my neighbors think I'm honest." She also thought her ENABAS contract would mean good business. As the basics become increasingly scarce, her store would become the most popular place to shop for everything, including some noncontrolled items. "A guaranteed, though modest, profit is something. Empty shelves don't make a profit."

SUBSIDIZED FOOD PRICES

The government froze most official food prices throughout 1982 and 1983. While overall inflation rose to an annual rate of 40 percent in 1983, prices for salt, cooking oil, sugar, rice, beans, corn, and milk were the same as in 1981 at supermarkets and other official distribution outlets. In 1983 ENABAS was buying corn from local producers for 1.80 córdobas per pound (and paying dollars for imported corn) yet selling it to consumers for 1.00 córdoba. The government absorbed the entire difference in addition to all the costs of drying, packaging, storing, and transport. Official prices for some other foods, such as eggs, chicken, cheese, and pork, were raised somewhat but much less than rising costs. Subsidized food prices, of course, helped make it possible for many Nicaraguans to afford more food. (And controlled, subsidized prices for many nonfood basics, ranging from soap to public transportation, left Nicaragua's poor majority with more to spend on food.)

THE "GUARANTY CARD" SYSTEM

The idea behind the guaranty card was to ensure everyone's right to the food he or she needs. The card offered each Nicaraguan who so desired a formal guarantee of a monthly quota of particular staples at the affordable official prices.

Guaranty cards were introduced in early 1982 in order to distribute sugar more equitably. Previously, spot shortages of sugar, an important food for Nicaraguans, had touched off widespread hoarding and speculation. Then, in the aftermath of the severe flooding caused by tropical storm Aleta in May 1982, a wave of speculation—and widespread outcries against it—convinced government leadership that the guaranty card system should be expanded. The Ministry of Internal Commerce (MICOIN) added rice, cooking oil, and soap to the card in early 1983.

As with sugar, households received their cards from their CDS neighborhood organization. Guaranty cards entitled each household to purchase up to official monthly limits of each item: four pounds for sugar and rice, one liter of cooking oil, and two large bars of laundry soap for each member. The expansion of the guaranty-card system appreciably undercut speculation and regularized the sale of these key goods at official prices, most importantly in low-income neighborhoods.

The government emphasized without qualification that no one need belong to a neighborhood CDS organization to obtain a guaranty card; furthermore, to deny anyone a card for his or her views is a punishable offense. Those who wish to paint a picture of Nicaragua as a "totalitarian dungeon" (to cite a phrase from President Reagan) have claimed that the guaranty cards are used to force political compliance. We have been close to this situation and have found no credible evidence to support these charges.

Beans and corn were not brought onto the card at this point because producers are so numerous and scattered that it would be exceedingly difficult to organize and control their marketing. Also corn is a special case since most Nicaraguans consume their daily corn in the form of tortillas which they buy ready-made from thousands of small-scale tortilla makers. It is these corn processors, often among those very poor people the revolution most wants to help, and not the final consumers, who most need to have a reliable and stably priced supply of corn.

In many isolated rural areas, a guaranteed supply of refined sugar and cooking oil tended to increase consumption of these products. In fact, before the guaranty-card system, such industrially processed foods had never been available. In some places they were seen for the first time during the 1980 literacy campaign when middle- and upper-class urban youths and their visiting parents brought them. This difference in the countryside escapes the notice of many of the better-off residents of Managua and of all those journalists whose knowledge of Nicaragua comes from "Western diplomatic sources."

In Managua and the other urban areas, the guaranty-card system expanded effective demand, rather than curbing it, as a rationing system might have. Those in jeopardy of being cut out by speculators' prices generally had their minimal consumption needs protected by the guaranty card. At the same time these four items could still be purchased in unlimited quantities, although at much higher prices, on the "parallel" or black market. While shopping on the black market was technically illegal, no buyers, as far as we know, have ever been arrested.

Of course, these goods—cooking oil, sugar, rice, and soap—come from a handful of factories either owned by the government or supposedly selling all their production to it. How could these staples end up for sale on the black market? This was a question raised in some CDS neighborhood meetings in Ciudad Sandino. It seems the sources of free-floating goods varied. Much was secretly siphoned off at the production site and sold illegally on the side. In some cases, goods were "leaked" by corrupt MICOIN officials out for some quick money. At other times, MICOIN actually distributed the controlled items, usually sugar, to small vendors for resale on the black market—a political decision taken to improve the livelihoods of the small vendors and to allay the grumblings of sweet-toothed consumers for whom the official quota (one pound per person per week) was not enough.

COMMISSARIES

Workplace commissaries were set up to sell the food staples and the other basic items to workers at official prices. These outlets were primarily located in factories, government agencies, and on the large farms. We heard frequent complaints about shortages and the limited variety of goods in many of the commissaries.

WORKPLACE CAFETERIAS

By 1984 almost 2,000 *comedores populares* were providing substantially subsidized hot lunches in state-owned farms and factories as well as in some private enterprises.

NUTRITION PROGRAMS

In 1982 the Ministry of Health began providing weekly allotments of milk, flour, cooking oil, and other products to some 60,000 preschool children and pregnant and lactating women throughout the nation. The same year the Ministry of Education started sponsoring a program providing primary school children a morning glass of milk and noontime meal free of charge. Initially serving 30,000 children in two provinces, the program was expanded throughout the country, despite—or perhaps, because of—the deepening economic crisis. Partly as a result of these programs, health workers have suggested that the revolution's greatest nutritional improvements have been made by low-income mothers and infants.

In addition to these policies that *directly* concern food distribution, other factors have resulted in increased demand for food. Among them are wage hikes and enforcement of minimum-wage regulations, as well as expanded free health services and other items in the "social wage." Government policies have led to a greater number of people employed and mushrooming public expenditures, putting more money into more people's hands. The amount of money in circulation more than doubled in the first five years.

Another factor, often overlooked, is that Nicaragua's population has been growing at a very rapid rate. Although the birth rate has been high for years and good statistics are hard to come by, there is a widespread sense that the revolution has triggered a baby boom—as well as a significant decline in infant mortality. Rough calculations suggest that by the revolution's fifth anniversary there were over a half million more Nicaraguans than in 1979—a 22 percent increase. This is a legion of new consumers who are, needless to say, too young to produce or pay for their own food. The baby boom also brings an increased demand for special foods, notably powdered milk. Postrevolutionary Nicaragua has also seen an appreciable and steadily growing influx of foreign visitors. Before the revolution, Nicaragua was never a tourist mecca. There have also been tens of thousands of resident ''internationalists'' working in Nicaragua. Unquestionably foreigners up the effective demand for food. (The Intercontinental Hotel still offers its world-class, all-you-can-eat buffet to tourists.)

Food Supply: Not Keeping Up

Nicaragua's heightened demand for food makes for a volatile mix with its deepening food-supply problems. By 1983, major obstacles such as the war and the foreign-exchange crisis were also starting to have a negative impact on getting food supplies to market.

By the end of 1983, one-third of ENABAS' fleet of grain-transport trucks was paralyzed for lack of spare parts. More than half the trucks used to transport food in and out of Matagalpa are off the road for lack of tires. The defense effort required the mobilization of scores of civilian trucks, which aggravated an already serious shortage of vehicles needed for the delivery of farm inputs and the marketing of farm produce.

Even when trucks were available, deliveries to the cities were held up by the mining of northern country roads, the bombing of bridges, and attacks by *contra* commandos on trucks hauling food. It was not long before ENABAS found it difficult to find drivers willing to transport farm produce from the war zones. In June 1984 Minister of Internal Commerce Dionisio Marenco told the Council of State: ''Right now, the beans that are being eaten all over Nicaragua came from the winter harvest of Nueva Guinea. It cost the lives of six *compañeros* to get those beans out of the mountains. It is very common now to talk about the war and its effects on the food supply and so forth. But when you have to go to the house of a dead man's mother and say, 'Here, I've brought your son's body. He died driving a truck to bring beans to the people,' it's a more painful and difficult task which brings the whole security question down to earth.''

The *contras,* recognizing the importance of food supplies, have targeted storage facilities wherever they attack. In 1983 alone, they destroyed 8 percent of the national grain storage capacity. In June 1984 *contra* commandos attacked the northern town of Ocotal, destroying all six of the region's main grain silos. Twelve hundred tons of rice, corn, beans, and sorghum were set afire, and four workers were killed. American Maryknoll sisters living in Ocotal told us that the next day the townspeople sifted through the charred rubble gleaning whatever grain they could.

The severity of the military war's impact on basic food supplies really sank in when a top official told us in September 1984 that the government had just cut in half its estimates for the year of how much corn and beans ENABAS would be able to buy from producers in the northern provinces. Moreover, he commented, the food situation will be even more critical next year. He anticipated that the war will make it impossible next spring to bring out anything from the winter harvests in Nueva Guinea and much of the rest of northern Nicaragua.

The Reagan administration's economic warfare, by exacerbating the foreign-exchange shortage, has seriously sabotaged Nicaragua's food distribution. Key items such as cooking oil and powdered milk, even when produced from local sources, are processed and packaged with materials that must be imported. Understandably, priority in the allocation of foreign exchange has gone to agricultural inputs. Yet the lack of enough foreign exchange to also import such items as waxed cartons and tin sheets for cans and bottlecaps has increasingly resulted in food-supply bottlenecks. There is plenty of wheat, donated by a wide political range of countries (too much in fact, leaving no room to store the sorghum crop). But no one donates yeast, and with more pressing priorities, Nicaragua has a hard time coming up with the money to import it. There is also a shortage of plastic bags for selling flour.

The Managua Problem

As U.S.-supported counterrevolutionary offensives grew ever more fierce and frequent, the government was forced to shift its long-standing priority favoring Managua in the distribution of consumer goods. In order to bolster civilian morale in the face of enemy attacks and efforts at internal subversion, Nicaragua's supply priorities now favor the defense forces and the war regions. In mid-1984, the Sandinistas launched an educational campaign on the supply crisis in Managua with the slogan: "Everything for the combatants, everything for the war fronts!"

Managua, with somewhat less than a third of the national population, has long been accustomed to consuming more than half the country's food. The capital has taken an even greater share of processed foods. In the past, more than 70 percent of canned powdered milk—a much-sought-after item in Nicaragua, especially with the baby boom—was sold in Managua; in 1984, less than 30 percent. And there is less powdered milk produced, period. (In September 1984 we were told powdered-milk production would plummet still further: in addition to the shortage of milk and of tin cans, half of the personnel of the factory had been mobilized for combat.)

To many in Managua, the war is unreal: There has been no combat, no sound of mortar fire, no schools burned to the ground. Foreign visitors are often struck that their anticipated sense of militarization is absent from the capital. Yet at the same time Managua is increasingly pressed by the war's economic brunt. As an agricultural technician in Jinotega put it, "Up north, you don't have to remind people that there's a war going on. They see it, hear it, breathe it, in some places every day. In Managua it's very different. People grumble and grumble because they're only told about the war. Some even think the war is just the government's excuse."

The "Managua problem," as one top government strategist referred to frustrated consumer demand, is exacerbated by Nicaragua's daily doses of U.S.-style consumption messages. People in Managua can receive radio and television broadcasts from Costa Rica. In the north they get it from Honduras. And it seems every Nicaraguan family has relatives abroad—Los Angeles, Miami, San Francisco, Panama, Mexico. "Everyone knows what the latest is and they want it," commented the government strategist.

Many of us might at first take a certain satisfaction in learning of a country where the tables are reversed—where the countryside gets priority in consumption over the capital city. But the deteriorating level of consumer goods in Managua undoubtedly spells a growing political handicap for the revolution.

*76. Nicaragua's Ethnic Minorities in the Revolution**

By Philippe Bourgois

Philippe Bourgois is a doctoral candidate in anthropology at Stanford University. He has conducted extensive fieldwork on the Atlantic Coast of Central America.

By the end of the fifth year, tensions with ethnic minorities had become an Achilles heel of the Nicaraguan revolution: 1) militarily, the Atlantic Coast region where the minorities lived had exploded into an arena of bitter fighting; 2) politically, accusations of human rights violations against the indigenous population had damaged the revolution's international image; and 3) morally, the inability to incorporate minorities—the most marginalized sector of Nicaraguan society—into a full participation in the revolutionary process had contradicted Sandinista political principles. Although the Nicaraguan government committed errors in its policies toward the coastal—*costeño*—population, the crisis can best be understood from a historical perspective, as the outcome of several hundred years of tension between ethnic minorities and the Mestizo national majority. In the final analysis, the responsibility for the conversion of these historic tensions into a fratricidal war lies with the United States, which armed, trained, and provided international legitimation for the counterrevolutionary *(contra)* forces, thereby preventing a peaceful solution from emerging based on dialogue and compromise.

Ethnic minorities at the time of the revolutionary triumph represented less than 5 percent of the national population and were all located in the Atlantic Coast province of Zelaya, the poorest, most isolated region in the nation.[1] The Miskitu Amerindians numbering 67,000 were the largest minority group and lived, along with some 5,000 Sumu Amerindians, in the northeast near the Honduran border. Together they comprised 25 percent of their province's total population. The Creoles were the second

*Reprinted from *Monthly Review*, January 1985.

largest minority group, an English-speaking, Afro-Caribbean population of just under 26,000 concentrated mostly in the southern coastal port of Bluefields. Also in South Zelaya were 1,500 Garifuna, a people of Afro-Amerindian descent, and some 600 Rama Amerindians. Finally Mestizos, the product of European, Amerindian, and some African admixture were the dominant ethnic group, both at the regional and national levels, constituting over 180,000 or 65 percent of the Atlantic Coast population.

From the outset, the revolution encountered problems on the coast. Prior to the triumph of the revolution there had been almost no fighting or clandestine organizing in Zelaya. Consequently, especially in the Miskitu-dominated north, there was no indigenous revolutionary leadership forged in struggle. The first major Sandinista/Amerindian tension arose when the Miskitu demanded the recognition of an ethnic-based mass organization. Although the Sandinistas initially thought the fundamental interests of minorities could be represented in the class-based mass organizations that operated at the national level, out of revolutionary principle, they acceded. Misurasata, the new indigenous mass organization, was given political legitimacy, logistical support, and a seat on the National Council of State by the new government.[2]

Misurasata seized the democratic opening provided by the revolution in order to mobilize militantly throughout the northeast on a platform of indigenous rights devoid of class content. Although the organization lobbied for concrete economic gains, its central thrust was to stress the dignity—and indeed, it turned out later, the superiority—of Amerindian identity. Furthermore, the Amerindian nationalist tone of the organization struck a responsive chord in most of the over 300 impoverished Miskitu agricultural communities. A full-fledged indigenous revitalization movement caught hold and Misurasata emerged as a powerful force in northern Zelaya to the point of challenging Sandinista political influence.[3]

Relations between Misurasata and the FSLN were confrontational from the outset. Misurasata leaders lacked a class consciousness and FSLN cadre, most of whom were from the Pacific provinces, were unprepared to deal with the historical patterns of interethnic domination and tension that they encountered in the Atlantic. In practice, however, in response to minority demands during the first year and a half, the Nicaraguan government passed more legislation favorable to the indigenous population than has any government in the history of Central America. Most notably, a bilingual education law was passed in the Council of State and a literacy campaign was launched in Miskitu, Sumu, and English. The government also commissioned Misurasata to prepare a study on indigenous land rights stating its willingness to grant communal land titles to the indigenous communities.

In South Zelaya, on the other hand, the ethnic organization purporting to represent the Afro-Caribbean population, known as the Southern Indigenous Creole Community (SICC), was not recognized by the FSLN as a mass organization since it was openly against the government from its inception, and it never emerged as a powerful movement. Tensions, however, exploded in the south in late September and early

October of 1980 with street demonstrations and the paralyzation of economic activity in Bluefields. The crowd, which was multiethnic but largely Creole, was protesting the presence of "Communist" Cuban primary school teachers and doctors in the town. Through a process of dialogue, compromise, and flexibility the FSLN sensitized itself to local concerns, and tensions in Bluefields were slowly dissipated. Nonetheless, although few Creoles took up arms and joined the *contra,* they tended to remain apathetic toward the revolutionary process.

In the Miskitu-dominated territory in the northeast, however, the process of confrontation, negotiation, and compromise did not defuse Sandinista/Amerindian tensions. February 1981 marked the turning point when the leadership of Misurasata was detained (thirty-three individuals) and accused of fomenting "separatism."[4] All those arrested were released within two weeks with the exception of the main leader, Steadman Fagoth. The Ministry of Interior released documents found in the Somoza government's abandoned files demonstrating that Fagoth had been an informer in Somoza's secret service.[5]

During the arrests in the community of Prinzapolka eight people, including four Sandinista soldiers, were killed when a Misurasata leader was being detained for questioning. News of the arrests and the deaths, enhanced by grossly inaccurate rumors of mass assassinations, swept the isolated communities of the Coco River, and up to 3,000 young Miskitu men crossed the Coco River into Honduras, declaring themselves to be refugees. Blood had been spilled and the Miskitu movement assumed a millenarian mystique; rumors abounded that the young Miskitu men were arming to return, and that the United States was going to recognize "secret" nineteenth-century treaty provisions between the Miskitu king and the British Crown guaranteeing nationhood for the Miskitu people.

The *costeños* had not suffered repression from Somoza's National Guard, and consequently, to the surprise of the Sandinistas, the Miskitu were indifferent to the evidence of Fagoth's Somocista attachments. The Nicaraguan government was unprepared for the militance of the continued support for Fagoth, who had by this time become, in the eyes of many Miskitu, a revered leader ordained to bring them redemption. In response to Miskitu popular pressure, the government, evidently hoping that dialogue and compromise were still possible, granted Fagoth conditional release one month later. Fagoth, however, promptly crossed into Honduras to join with former national guardsmen and Somoza supporters and began emitting tirades in Miskitu against the "Sandino-Communists" on the Somocista clandestine radio station "15th of September."[6]

By August 1982 most of Misurasata's leaders had joined Fagoth in Honduras, including Brooklyn Rivera, another principal leader. Misurasata was renamed Misura and integrated into the National Democratic Force (FDN) with economic, military, and logistical aid, as well as political legitimation and international media support from the United States' Central Intelligence Agency. Rivera later broke with Fagoth in 1982 to form a rival *contra* organization (which he called Misurasata), affiliated with the Revolutionary Democratic Alliance (ARDE) based in Costa Rica. In a January 11, 1984, interview, Rivera accused Fagoth of having allied himself with "the dirtiest, most assassinating right wing elements of the Honduran army . . . [choosing] . . . the dirtiest Somocistas, expelled from the FDN for thievery and murder, as his protective godfathers."[7]

Misura's first major military offensive, "Red Christmas" began in November 1981 with attacks on the Miskitu border communities along the Coco River.[8] Within less than two months sixty civilians and Sandinista military had been killed. Faced with this military crisis in January of 1982 the Nicaraguan government ordered the evacuation of the civilian population from the war zone to a region approximately fifty miles inland, in a new settlement called Tasba Pri. At this point the Sandinistas were responding essentially to military exigencies: 1) to defend the civilian population supportive of the revolution from *contra* reprisals; 2) to prevent the Somocista-Misura alliance from establishing a civilian base of support along the Coco River; and 3) to prevent civilians from being caught in government-*contra* crossfire.

Less than half of the Coco River population, some 8,500 Miskitu and Sumu, were relocated to Tasba Pri; another 10,000 chose instead to cross into Honduras where they became refugees. The emergency evacuation under war conditions of such a large number of people on short notice was a profoundly traumatic experience for all involved. Human rights organizations, however, while critical of aspects of Sandinista policy toward the Miskitu, stated that there was no evidence of systematic abuse on the part of the FSLN.[9]

Beginning in July 1982, simultaneously with the joint U.S. and Honduran military maneuvers underway in the Atlantic region only a few miles from the Nicaraguan border, there was a sharp intensification of Miskitu *contra* activity. Large numbers of government troops, most of whom were Mestizos from the Pacific, were sent to defend the zone. According to an investigation by the Center for Information and Documentation of the Atlantic Coast (CIDCA), an autonomous research institution affiliated with the National Council on Higher Education (CNES), there was a lack of sufficient control over the military commanders in Zelaya from July through September of 1982, resulting in cases of "reprehensible" behavior by government troops, ranging from "cultural disrespect—a function of historic racism" to actual "physical abuse" and "bodily harm."[10] CIDCA noted that this resulted in cases of civilian loss of life.[11]

The FSLN publicly condemned these excesses and over forty-four soldiers, including officers, were prosecuted and given prison sentences.[12] By 1984, 70 percent of local security forces were *costeños,* and Pacific Coast recruits received seminars before being assigned to Zelaya.[13] In an attempt to restore lost trust, the Sandinistas granted a general amnesty to virtually all the Miskitu arrested for counterrevolutionary activity, releasing 307.[14] Indeed in the introduction to an April 1984 report on Nicaragua, Americas Watch, a U.S.-based human rights organization, noted:

> The most important improvement has taken place in relations with the Miskito Indians.
>
> We have previously said that human rights violations in Nicaragua most se-

verely victimized the Miskito population. Accordingly, Americas Watch is very pleased by the positive developments affecting them.[15]

Just as the human rights record of the Sandinistas improved from late 1982 through 1984, that of the Miskitu *contra* deteriorated. All "collaborators" of the "Sandino-Communist dictatorship" were considered fair military targets by the anti-Sandinista guerrillas. The result was the assassination of school teachers, literacy trainers, and even peasants trained as volunteer health workers in the government's new "barefoot doctor" program. It was against their fellow Amerindians, however, that the Miskitu *contra* were cruelest. For example, Myrna Cunningham, a Miskitu doctor (the only one that existed) and Regina Lewis, a Miskitu nurse, were kidnapped during Red Christmas in 1981 and gang-raped by a squad of Fagoth's men who were singing religious hymns.[16]

Brooklyn Rivera, who described himself as having been "very intimate" with Fagoth—"closer than a brother"—claims that by 1982 Fagoth had become "psychopathic," with a "persecution trauma," and was "totally blinded and sick with power and personal ambition." He states that Fagoth tortured and killed young Miskitu men in the refugee camps when they refused to join Misura.[17] Indeed, by 1983, press reports began surfacing that Misura was using force to conscript Miskitu refugees.[18] Similarly, officials at the United Nations High Commission for Refugees in Honduras made private declarations that Misura was the greatest security problem faced by refugees in Honduras.

Although somewhat more careful with their public image, Rivera's troops—like Fagoth's—also engaged in human rights abuses against the civilian population in 1983–84. The most dramatic of these documented cases was the kidnapping of Thomas Hunter, a Creole who headed an artesanal fishing cooperative in the coastal community of Tasbapaunie in southern Zelaya. Rivera's troops took Hunter to their camp in nearby Punta Fusil and after protracted torture finally killed him, but not before cutting off his ears and forcing him to eat them.[19]

From 1982 to 1985 the heartland of Miskitu territory was a war zone. The goal of the *contra* was to declare a provisional government in the northeast, where they could subsequently "invite" a U.S. "peacekeeping force." Even though local FSLN cadre were showing greater sensibility to the complicated issues of racism and indigenous rights, there were no short-term perspectives for definitive reconciliation. As long as the United States continued to fund and train the *contras,* the situation remained fundamentally a military problem. Indeed, the continuous deepening of the war had reduced the area within which civilians could live safely in North and Central Zelaya, resulting in further, smaller-scale population relocations out of the war zones inside Nicaragua and an increase in the number of Amerindian refugees in Honduras. The exigencies of defense and the violent instability caused by guerrilla warfare hindered the emergence of a working relationship between the Amerindians and the Sandinistas based on dialogue, peaceful confrontation, and compromise. The question remains, however, as to why it was so easy for the Central Intelligence Agency to find thousands of young Miskitu men willing to engage in violent armed struggle. To grapple with this question, first the profound historical roots of the conflict must be examined.

Historical Roots of the Conflict

There are historical reasons why militarist Amerindian nationalism would strike a responsive chord among so many Miskitu. During the sixteenth and seventeenth centuries, the Miskitu became the first Amerindian people on the Central American littoral to obtain firearms through trade with the European buccaneers preying on Spanish shipping in the Caribbean. With their superior fire power, the Miskitu not only resisted Spanish conquest, but also "conquered" almost 700 miles of the Atlantic seaboard from Trujillo, Honduras, through Chiriqui Lagoon in Panama.[20]

Gradually, British "alliance" with the Miskitu became valuable to Britain's strategy of undermining Spanish power, as well as trade, on the Caribbean mainland. In 1687 the governor of Jamaica formalized the alliance by crowning a Miskitu leader "King of the Mosquitia." Indeed the British systematically promoted the concepts of Miskitu national sovereignty and militarism in order to legitimize their own colonial expansion into the region: "[We] . . . mounted . . . [the fort] . . . with cannon, hoisted the Royal flag and kept garrison to show that this independent country of the Mosquito Shore was under the direct sovereignty and protection of Great Britain."[21]

Ironically, therefore, the Miskitu have long been at the center of international power struggles. In the 1700s it was Spain versus Great Britain; in 1984 it was the United States versus Nicaragua. The manipulation of the Miskitu *contra* by the United States, therefore, is analogous to the Miskitu-British relationship noted by a historian in 1774:

> [The Miskitu] . . . have always been, and still are, in the place of a standing army; which, without receiving any pay, or being in any shape burthensome to Great Britain, Maintains the English in firm and secure possession [of the region], protects their trade, and forms an impenetrable barrier against the Spanish, whom they keep in constant awe.[22]

Modern-day Miskitu have mystified the former existence of an Amerindian king into a symbol of nationalist aspirations. For example, in the 1970s under Somoza there were repeated rumors that the Miskitu king had returned and was circulating throughout the lower Coco River preparing his people for secession. Similarly when Misurasata was in its early formative stage in 1980, elderly Miskitu sometimes talked of "working for the return of the king."[23] On a more neutral level, the Miskitu could still point out descendants of the "royal family"; they used to argue over the true location of the cache holding the defunct monarch's scepter and crown jewels. In this context, debates over whether or not the Miskitu are a national minority become academic. The Miskitu do not fulfill the objective requisites necessary to constitute a sovereign nation state; at the same time, however, Amerindian nationalist ideology is a part of their ethnic identity and the *contra,* especially Fagoth, succeeded in distorting these nationalist aspirations in order to provoke confrontation with the new Nicaraguan government.[24]

The tensions between ethnic minorities and the Nicaraguan revolution were not limited to being merely a "Miskitu problem" and a "black problem," or even strictly an ethnic problem. Even the Mestizos from the coast were less enthusiastic about the revolution than those living in the Pacific provinces.

Nicaragua, like almost all Central American nations, faced an Atlantic Coast region that had been integrated historically into a different social formation from that of the national mainstream. The entire Atlantic seaboard of Central America was penetrated by U.S. multinational corporations beginning in the late 1800s. Because of the physical isolation of these zones, the foreign companies established an unparalleled level of control. The classic examples, of course, are the banana companies which established mini-nation-states on the Atlantic Coast of every single nation in Central America (except for El Salvador which only has a Pacific Coast).[25]

In Nicaragua the most important North American companies extracted minerals, lumber, and bananas strictly for export to the United States. The coastal economy had no linkage with that of the rest of the country. There was more regular transport and commerce from Bluefields to the United States than to the interior of the country. Indeed, it was easier to get to the Atlantic Coast from New Orleans than from Managua.

This economic domination was reflected culturally and politically in the consciousness of the local population and even affected the actual ethnic composition of the region. For example, most of the Afro-Caribbean people in Central America arrived as migrants at the turn of the century seeking wage work in the burgeoning North American companies. The extensive U.S. investments also repeatedly attracted U.S. Marines to protect them, and from 1912 through 1933 North American troops occupied the country with but a brief respite in 1925–26. The marines spent a disproportionate amount of their time on the Atlantic Coast.[26]

Out of this protracted period of economic and military domination by the United States there developed a profoundly anti-Communist, pro-North American political ideology among the Creole, Miskitu, and to a lesser extent Mestizo *costeños.* This was exacerbated by the conservative and likewise fervently anti-Communist and pro-North American tenor of the Moravian church, the strongest ideological influence on the Miskitu and Creole peoples. The rigidity of the ideological template of the local population—especially the older generation—resulted, for example, in complaints by elderly folk in Bluefields over the "spread of communism" when they mistook a group of visiting North American tourists for Soviet military advisers.

The FSLN was largely unaware of this stark contrast in political identity between the Pacific and Atlantic populations. In the first years the FSLN, for example, mechanically introduced the same political symbolism (slogans, songs, heroes, chants, etc.) which had been effective in the Pacific. In contrast, Voice of America and the *contra* radio stations were skillfully responsive to local ideological prejudices. This was exacerbated by the war emergency which focused revolutionary slogans more on nationalistic, patriotic themes such as defense of the homeland, rendering them less flexible or adaptable to local ways of thinking.

Another legacy of the North American enclave on the Atlantic Coast was a history of internal colonialism. The previous regimes had not bothered to administer or develop the region. There had been a minimal local presence of petty bureaucrats who contented themselves with minor taxes and kickbacks from the foreign corporations which were busily extracting the region's natural resources. Along with the Moravian church, North American corporations and aid agencies had provided the few social services available, confirming to the local populace the superiority of North America and its institutions. Five years after the revolution, many *costeños* insisted that the Atlantic Coast still contributed more to the national economy than it received in government services and investments, despite the fact that the reverse was actually the case. Furthermore, with the massive expansion in government welfare services following the revolution, the local population was sensitive to overrepresentation of Pacific Coast functionaries in these new desirable jobs.

The ethnic composition of the FSLN prior to the revolutionary triumph reflected the marginality of the Atlantic Coast to national politics. There were no FSLN members of Sumu, Rama, or Garifuna descent, only a handful of Miskitu descent, a slightly larger number of Creole revolutionaries, and not many Mestizo *costeño* cadre. The Sandinistas, therefore, lacked representatives who spoke the same language as the ethnic minorities or who were familiar with the problems of the region. Once again South Zelaya had an advantage over the north since the commander and "delegate minister"—roughly equivalent to governor—of the zone was an English-speaking Creole and the majority of the FSLN's limited number of *costeño* cadre were from the Bluefields area. Significantly, in June 1984 a Miskitu woman was appointed "governor" for North Zelaya. Consequently, by the fifth year of the revolution, the two highest political administrative posts in the regions of ethnic minority concentration were held by minorities themselves.

Another legacy confronting the FSLN was the historically entrenched pattern of ethnic and class domination. Nicaragua's ethnic minorities, unlike the majority of workers and peasants in the rest of the country, suffered a dual form of domination: class exploitation *and* ethnic oppression. The Miskitu, Sumu, and Rama were at the bottom of this local class-ethnic hierarchy, performing the least desirable, most poorly paid jobs.[27] In the gold mines in Bonanza, for example, the Miskitu and Sumu were usually relegated to the most dangerous, strenuous tasks in the pits, where they suffered from the highest rates of silicosis, a permanently debilitating lung disease.[28]

Above the Amerindians but below the Creoles came the Mestizo population, many of whom were landless laborers, recent migrants from the Pacific provinces. Like the Miskitu, they engaged in poorly remunerated agricultural wage labor and had a high level of illiteracy and alcoholism.

The Creoles dominated the skilled jobs. Because of their superior education they tended to obtain white-collar employment in disproportionate numbers. Since the decline in activity of the foreign corporations in the region over the last fifty years, many Creoles had withdrawn from the local labor market, relying instead on income earned as seamen on foreign vessels or on cash remittances from family members in the United States. Above the Creoles there was a stratum of upper-class Pacific-born Mestizos, usually of lighter complexion than the poorer Mestizos, who held administrative and political-appointee positions. Finally, until the triumph of the revolution this ethnic-class hierarchy was capped by a miniscule layer of North American and European whites who owned or ran the few companies still operating on the coast, such as the gold mines or the lumber export firms.[29]

This class hierarchy was accompanied by acute racial prejudice. Mestizos and Creoles presented the "inferiority" of the Miskitu and other Amerindians as a matter of common sense. In turn, the working-class and peasant Mestizos looked down upon the Creoles for their dark complexion while the Creoles—whether dark or light complexioned—insisted upon their superiority over the *Pañias* (Spaniards).[30]

It would be ahistorical to expect it to be possible to eradicate quickly these patterns of interethnic domination, so solidly rooted in local class inequalities. Indeed, these patterns of ethnic-class hierarchy existed with local variations throughout all the nations of the Central American Atlantic littoral. Racism was an integral part of the social formations spawned by the multinational enclaves.[31]

By the end of the fifth year of the revolution, theoreticians within the revolutionary process were beginning to publish analyses of the dual nature of ethnic/class domination in Zelaya. For example a CIDCA document noted that there was an inherent tendency for class-conscious movements composed of the dominant ethnic group of a country to subordinate the struggle against ethnic oppression to that of economic exploitation. The document concludes that in the case of Nicaragua "class exploitation and ethnic oppression are inextricably interconnected both in history and in the present. Therefore, one form of domination cannot be successfully eradicated without a conscious, simultaneous struggle to eliminate the other."[32] Ironically the *contras,* for all their indigenous rights rhetoric, had evidently not learned this lesson. In fact, in mid-1984, a prominent member of ARDE resigned from the organization, citing racism against the Miskitu as one of his primary motives.[33]

Perhaps the most explosive psychological legacy of this history of dual domination was the neurosis of internalized racism on the part of the Amerindians at the bottom of the hierarchy. This explains why so many Miskitu could be mobilized into a virtually suicidal war. The Miskitu *contras* appealed to these deeply ingrained sentiments of heartfelt injustice and humiliation. Through Misurasata and later Misura, Fagoth offered the Miskitu people, who had always been ridiculed and exploited by the surrounding ethnic groups, an illusion of racial superiority. For example, he advocated the expulsion of the Mestizo population from the northeast and the relegation of Creoles to the status of second-class citizens.

Such racial, ethnic-nationalist revival movements, often combined with a messianic and millenarian mystique, are a sociological phenomenon common to ethnic minorities suffering from social and economic discrimination throughout the world. Comparable examples of mass mobilization include the Ghost Dance movement among North American Indians in the 1870s and 1890s, the numerous cargo cults of the Melanesian islands, and the Mamachi religion of the Guaymi Amerindians in Panama during the 1960s.[34] These movements unleash energies that have been distorted by decades or even centuries of oppression and alienation.

The Atlantic Coast and the Sandinista Revolution

Ironically, it was the revolution itself which initially mobilized the Miskitu. The Sandinistas introduced not only a genuine democratic opening into Nicaraguan political and social life, but also an infectious sense of hope and omnipotence. Daily the radio urged everyone, including the Miskitu, to organize, to be proud of being poor, and above all, to demand their just rights. Rivera, a Miskitu *contra* leader who ironically recognized his debt to the Sandinistas, stated: "Of course the revolution made this whole movement possible. The fervor of the revolutionary triumph injected into the soul, heart, and atmosphere that everybody could express themselves and participate. Before there was no incentive . . . we were just asleep."[35]

The original strategy of the revolution had been to integrate the ethnic minorities into the revolutionary process by providing concrete solutions to their material needs. Subsidies were established for farm implements and inputs; technical aid was dispensed free of charge; crops were purchased at guaranteed prices; credit was made accessible and cheap; electricity was brought to the countryside; and schools and health clinics were built in even the most remote communities. An all-weather road from the Pacific was completed in 1982 and telephone and television connections were extended. This campaign to reactivate the economy and build infrastructure, however, was offset by the initial disruption caused by the revolutionary transition and then later, more dramatically, by the *contras*' campaign of economic sabotage. Millions of dollars worth of economic infrastructure was destroyed. Constant ambush of transport routes resulted in food shortages in the isolated rural communities and prevented the delivery of social services, since nurses and agricultural extension agents were often targeted by the *contras*. Furthermore, the de facto economic embargo on the country by the United States further exacerbated the already tenuous economic situation, as precious fishing and transport craft as well as other productive machinery were paralyzed for lack of spare parts and foreign exchange.

Significantly, in the south, where the military situation was somewhat less critical, the rural communities received more of the benefits of the revolution: schools, health clinics, artesanal fishing cooperatives, subsidized river transport, among other things. These communities, many of which were largely Garifuna and Creole, were noticeably more appreciative of the revolutionary process.

However, the principal economic problems faced by the urban-based Creoles, especially in Bluefields, were not poverty and unemployment. The Creoles participated, to a certain extent, in a miniature consumer economy, receiving much of their income from cash remittances or savings from previous out-migrations. The revolution's emphasis on meeting the needs of the poorest sectors therefore actually lowered their standard of living. The Central Bank was channeling scarce foreign currency to build schools in the countryside rather than to assure adequate supplies of toothpaste and toilet paper in urban centers.

While many Creoles were disaffected by their inability to purchase consumer goods, a significant sector of the Creole intelligentsia accepted jobs in the expanded local government ministries, and some became revolutionaries. This was not the case, however, with the Miskitu equivalent of the Creole intellectuals, namely, the dozen university-educated Miskitu and the more numerous community-level Miskitu Moravian ministers. The generally lower literacy level of the Amerindians, their limited skills in interethnic interaction, and the more antagonistic status of Amerindian/Mestizo ethnic relations resulted in relatively few Miskitu being selected for employment in white-collar government jobs. In contrast to the Creoles, therefore, most of the educated Miskitu "elite" were not incorporated into the public service sector and instead became the backbone of the Miskitu *contra* movement. Although not wealthy by any standard, this Miskitu intelligentsia did not share the impoverished semiproletarian class position of the majority of their people. Consequently, they failed to appreciate the progressive economic changes being promoted by the revolution. Instead they reacted most strongly to the continued manifestations of ethnic oppression, since that is what affected *them* most directly on the personal level.[36]

Ultimately, the factor which most obstructed reconciliation between the Sandinistas and alienated *costeños* was the war itself. The war disrupted more than just the economy; it reduced the space for politically acceptable dialogue. The Sandinista leadership repeatedly recognized the revolution's errors in the Atlantic Coast, and specifically cited heavy-handedness and cultural insensitivity on the part of FSLN cadre. The war, however, forced military defense rather than flexibility and self-criticism into the foreground.

U.S. Intervention

This takes us full circle to the core of the problem: U.S. intervention. If Fagoth and the Misurasata leaders had not been provided with sophisticated military hardware, intensive military training, and millions of dollars of spending money, they could not have engaged in protracted armed struggle. There would have been serious conflicts between the ethnic minorities and the Sandinistas, but it would not have escalated into a bloody war; it could have been resolved through a nonviolent—albeit tensely charged—process of negotiation and accommodation.

Minorities suffering from ethnic oppression feel their injustice deeply and have a tremendous potential for militant mobilization. The FSLN leadership had not been aware of the complexity of the situation in the Atlantic Coast. Few Sandinistas had ever been to the region; no systematic analysis of the indigenous minority question existed. Tragically this was not the case for the United States. The Defense Department and the Central Intelligence Agency have spent millions of dollars analyzing ethnic minorities throughout the Third World.[37] The manipulation of indigenous peoples with historical grievances has become a recurrent pattern in North American interventions. The most spectacular example of this strategy was the military mobilization of the Hmoung in Southeast Asia (the Thailand/Laos border) behind United States objectives.[38]

In the particular case of Nicaragua, the real fear of the Central Intelligence Agency and the U.S. State Department, therefore, was not that the Sandinistas might mistreat their ethnic minorities, but rather the reverse. The Sandinista attempt to dismantle in a democratic—although sometimes clumsy and insensitive—fashion the historical patterns of interethnic domination and class exploitation on the Atlantic Coast threatened to set a "subversive" precedent for other multiethnic nations. By promoting armed struggle and prolonging an agonized bloodbath, therefore, the United States hoped to prevent, or at least to retard, the emergence of that liberating example.

Notes

1. Because of the isolation of the Atlantic Coast no definitive census of the Amerindian populations exists. For the most accurate population estimates, as well as an excellent demographic history of the Coast, see Centro de Investigaciones y Documentación de la Costa Atlántica (CIDCA), *Demografía Costeña: Notas Sobre la História Demográfica y Población Actual de los Grupos Etnicos de la Costa Atlántica Nicaragüense* (Managua: CIDCA, 1982). CIDCA arrived at its figures by counting the number of houses appearing in aerial photographs of the Atlantic Coast.
2. Misurasata stood for Miskitu, Sumu, Rama, and Sandinistas working together, but the Miskitu dominated the organization. Previous to the revolution there had been an indigenous organization named ALPROMISU (Alliance for Progress of the Miskitu and Sumu), but its leadership had been largely co-opted by Somoza. In June 1984 the first meetings were held in North Zelaya to found a new Miskitu mass organization, Misatan.
3. See Philippe Bourgois, "The Problematic of Nicaragua's Indigenous Minorities," in Thomas Walker, ed., *Nicaragua in Revolution* (New York: Praeger, 1982), pp. 303–18.
4. CIDCA, *Trabil Nani: Historical Background and Current Situation of the Atlantic Coast* (Managua: CIDCA, 1984; available from the Riverside Church Disarmament Program), p. 15; and Roxanne Dunbar Ortiz, "Miskitus in Nicaragua: Who is Violating Human Rights?" in Stanford Central America Action Network, ed., *Revolution in Central America* (Boulder, Col.: Westview, 1983), pp. 466–70.
5. *Barricada,* February 25, 1981; and *El Nuevo Diario,* February 25, 1981.
6. *Foreign Broadcast Information Service* VI, no. 099 (1981): 25; *Diario las Américas* (Miami), July 11, 1981.
7. In this same January 11, 1984, tape-recorded interview in Tibás, Costa Rica, Rivera accused Fagoth of forcing the Miskitu "into a fratricidal war . . . [converting them] . . . into cannon fodder in the hands of the Somocistas, the CIA and all those kinds of people." He also admitted that "It might be true that I'm playing Imperialism's game"; nevertheless, his troops were coordinating their military actions with those of Fagoth. See CIDCA, *Trabil Nani,* pp. 28–29; and Americas Watch, *Human Rights in Nicaragua* (New York: Americas Watch, April 1984), p. 43.
8. See CIDCA, *Trabil Nani,* pp. 19–24; and Americas Watch, *On Human Rights in Nicaragua* (New York: Americas Watch, May 1982), pp. 56–59.
9. Americas Watch, *On Human Rights,* pp. 58–71; Americas Watch, *Human Rights in Nicaragua,* pp. 9–11; and *San Francisco Examiner,* March 1, 1982, citing a U.S. Ecumenical Rights Commission report.
10. CIDCA, *Trabil Nani,* p. 38.
11. CIDCA, "The Atlantic Coast: A Policy of Genocide?" *Envio* 3, no. 35 (June 1984): 8b. See also Americas Watch, *Human Rights in Central America: A Report on El Salvador, Guatemala, Honduras and Nicaragua* (New York: Americas Watch, June 1984), p. 18.
12. For example, a sublieutenant in Lapán, Zelaya, was sentenced to eighteen years for rape. See Americas Watch, *Human Rights in Central America,* p. 23; CIDCA, *Trabil Nani,* p. 40; and "Condena a

Sub-Teniente del EPS que Abusó en Lapán,'' *Avances* (Zona Especial 1, Zelaya Norte, Nicaragua) 2, no. 15 (May 1984): 3.

13. Charles Hale, ''Ethnopolitics, Regional War, and a Revolution's Quest for Survival: An Assessment of the Miskitu Question in Nicaragua,'' *Alternative Newsletter* (Committee on Native American Struggles of the National Lawyers' Guild, June 1984): 19, reprinted in *Nicaraguan Perspectives,* Summer 1984.
14. Americas Watch, ''Human Rights in Nicaragua,'' p. 12.
15. Ibid., p. 3.
16. *Philadelphia News,* December 10, 1982. For further details of *contra* atrocities against civilians see ''A Public Forum: Human Rights Violations and Violence in Nicaragua and El Salvador,'' chaired by Senator Edward Kennedy (Washington, D.C.: Transcript of Proceedings, Miller Reporting Company, May 25, 1984), pp. 25–63.
17. Tape-recorded interview with Brooklyn Rivera, January 11, 1984, Tibás, Costa Rica. Journalists who interviewed Fagoth in 1983 and 1984 likewise stated that Fagoth appeared ''genuinely, certifiably, clinically insane.''
18. ''Evening News,'' Cable News Network Television, June 1, 1984; *El Tiempo* (Tegucigalpa), May 21, 1984; and *El Nuevo Diario,* February 2, 1984.
19. Information based on interviews with officials in charge of the artesanal fishing project in Bluefields, October 1983. Also documented in Americas Watch, ''Human Rights in Nicaragua,'' p. 47, and CIDCA, *Trabil Nani,* p. 28.
20. See John Holm, ''The Creole English of Nicaragua's Miskito Coast: Its Socio-Linguistic History and a Comparative Study of its Lexicon and Syntax'' (Ph.D. diss., University of London, 1978); and Troy Floyd, *The Anglo-Spanish Struggle for the Mosquitia* (Albuquerque: University of New Mexico Press, 1967).
21. Robert White, *The Case of the Agent to the Settlers on the Coast of Yucatán;* and *The Late Settlers on the Mosquito Shore* (London: T. Cadwell, 1789), p. 45.
22. Floyd, *The Anglo-Spanish Struggle for the Mosquitia,* p. 67 citing Edward Long, *The History of Jamaica,* vol. 3 (London: 1774), p. 320. In fact the Miskitu became so trusted by the British that on several occasions in the late 1600s and early 1700s they were brought to Jamaica to quash slave revolts.
23. Tape-recorded interview with Brooklyn Rivera, January 11, 1984, Tibás, Costa Rica.
24. Fagoth, for example, climaxed a speech in early 1981 with visions of a not-too-distant future when Mestizo Nicaraguans would have to show passports in order to enter Miskitu territory. See CIDCA, *Trabil Nani,* p. 15.
25. For example, a French consul in Costa Rica complained to his superiors in 1904: ''With elements of penetration such as the United Fruit Company and the Panama Canal Company, the United States have thereby as of now become the masters of the entire Atlantic Coast of Central America. The complete absorption of this part of the world is just a question of days barring a European intervention.'' Taken from: Foreign Affairs Archives of the Quai d'Orsay, (FAA) Paris, France, Nouvelle Série Tome 1, ''Depêche de M. Emile Joré, Consul de France à San José,'' March 27, 1904: 15 (courtesy of research notes of Dr. Isabel Wing-Ching, University of Costa Rica).
26. For an account of military interventions in Bluefields at the turn of the century see Lester Langley, *The Banana Wars: An Inner History of American Empire 1900–1924* (Lexington: University Press of Kentucky, 1983), pp. 53–72.
27. In fact, the Sumu and Rama are below the Miskitu in the ethnic-class hierarchy.
28. Tani Marilena Adams, ''Life Giving, Life Threatening: Gold Mining in Atlantic Nicaragua. Mine Work in Siuna and the Response to Nationalization by the Sandinista Regime'' (Masters thesis, University of Chicago, 1981), pp. 69–71.
29. In fact, right up to July 19, 1979, nonwhites—indeed even upper-class Mestizos—were forbidden from frequenting the housing compound reserved for management.
30. There was considerable variation in phenotype within the Creole population. Although they conceived of themselves as a unified ethnic group, it was considered ''better'' to have Caucasian physical features and straight hair.

31. For an examination of the historic role racism and ethnic group differentiation played on the United Fruit Company plantations on the Atlantic Coast of Costa Rica and Panama, see Philippe Bourgois, "Racismo, División y Violencia," *Diálogo Social* (Panama) XVII, no. 164 (February 1984): 18–25; for a slightly modified English translation see Working Group on Multinational Corporations in Central America, "Racism and the Multinational Corporation: The Ethnicity of the Labor Force on a Subsidiary of the United Fruit Company in Limon, Costa Rica, and Bocas del Toro, Panama," *Indigenous World/El Mundo Indígena* 111, no. 2 (1984): 7–10.
32. Edmundo Gordon Gitt (CIDCA), "La Labor del CIDCA y Aproximación Teórica a la Problemática de la Costa Atlántica de Nicaragua," in Carmen Murrillo and David Smith, eds., *Memoria del Seminario Costa Atlántica de Centroamérica* (San José, Costa Rica: Confederación Universitaria Centroamericana, 1983), pp. 148 and 151.
33. Hugo Spadafora, "Errores de Edén Pastora," *La Nación Internacional,* June 7–13, 1984, p. 11.
34. See Bernard Barber, "Acculturation and Messianic Movements," in William A. Lessa and Evon Z. Vogt eds., *Reader in Comparative Religion* (New York: Harper and Row, 1958), pp. 512–15; Peter Worsley, *The Trumpet Shall Sound: A Study of 'Cargo' Cults in Melanesia* (New York: Schocken, 1968); and Philip Young, *Ngawbe: Tradition and Change Among the Western Guaymi of Panama* (Chicago: University of Illinois Press, 1971).
35. Tape-recorded interview with Brooklyn Rivera, January 11, 1984, Tibás, Costa Rica.
36. With the case of Nicaragua in mind, Edmundo Gordon Gitt in "La Labor del CIDCA," p. 150, discusses the tendency of intellectuals with upwardly mobile aspirations to dominate ethnic movements, thereby distorting their class orientations.
37. See Eric Wolf and Joseph Jorgensen, "Anthropology on the Warpath in Thailand," *New York Review of Books,* no. 9 (December 17, 1970): 26–35. A good example of a study "designed to be useful to military and other personnel" is Kensington Office of the American Institutes for Research, *Ethnographic Study Series: Minority Groups in North Vietnam* (Washington, DC: GPO, 1972).
38. See Roxanne Dunbar Ortiz, *Indians of the Americas: Human Rights and Self-Determination* (New York: Praeger, 1984), pp. 229–39.

Acknowledgments

This article could not have been written without the assistance of the Center for Investigation and Documentation of the Atlantic Coast (CIDCA), especially that of its director, Galio Gurdián, who made the documentation at CIDCA available to me and included me in several theoretical discussions on the coast organized by the Center. Edmundo Gordon, the CIDCA director in Bluefields, prepared the outline for this article and much, if not most, of the analysis is his. Marc Edelman, Judy Butler, and Charles Hale supplied helpful comments on an earlier draft; theoretical discussions on ethnicity with Eric Wolf were also extremely useful. Finally I would also like to thank Commander Lumberto Cambell and the Regional Government for Special Zone Number 2 for having facilitated my brief period of fieldwork in South Zelaya in 1983. I take full responsibility, however, for any errors in interpretation and analysis presented in this article.

77. *Women and the Nicaraguan Revolution**

By Tomás Borge

Dear *compañeras,* in the world of today, profound changes are taking place. New offspring of history are being born in the midst of grief, anguish, and heroic splendor. Social revolution is the order of the day in Africa, Asia, and Latin America. Central America is being rocked with social earthquakes. Poor people of all latitudes are demanding—each time more vigorously—profound transformations in the old and rotting structures of class exploitation and imperialist domination.

And in Nicaragua, land of volcanoes and wildcats, we are winning national liberation through the Sandinista revolution.

Therefore it's normal, absolutely logical that we now speak of a new revolution—that is, a revolution of women, a revolution that will complete the process of national liberation.

The woman question is nothing more than an aspect of social reality in its totality. The definitive answer to the liberation of women can emerge only with the total resolution of the class contradictions, of the social diseases that originate in a society like ours—politically liberated but with the rope of economic dependence still around our neck.

Nevertheless, we must have patience to deal with the woman question in an independent and concrete manner.

Before the revolutionary triumph, the incorporation of women in productive work was minimal. The great majority of women were condemned to slavery in the home. When women could sell their labor power, in addition to fulfilling their obligations on the job, they had to fulfill their duties in the home to assure the upbringing of their children. All of this in a regime of political oppression and misery imposed by a dependent capitalist society. And subjected, on the other hand, to exploitation by man—the male of the species—who placed on the woman's shoulders the fundamental weight of household chores, thereby endlessly prolonging her working day.

Did this end with the triumph of the Sandinista People's Revolution, we ask ourselves?

The triumph of the Sandinista People's Revolution eliminated terror and opened the way for the process of national liberation, initiating at the same time economic and social transformations that represented a qualitative advance in the conquest of freedom and development.

It can't be said, therefore, that the situation of women in Nicaragua has in no way changed.

Nevertheless, all of us have to honestly admit that we haven't confronted the struggle for women's liberation with the same courage and decisiveness.

Independently of the fact that women, in this stage, continue to bear the main

*Reprinted from a 1982 pamphlet published by Pathfinder Press, New York.

responsibility for reproduction and the care of children, the burden of housework and discrimination still relentlessly weighs down upon them.

From the point of view of daily exertion, women remain fundamentally in the same conditions as in the past.

Of course, behind this objective reality there is an economic basis. Workers' living conditions continue to be difficult and incompatible with the political will of the revolution. For reasons that are well-known to you and because barely three years have passed [since the revolution], it has not been possible to meet legitimate expectations for improvement in workers' general living conditions.

This explains why many times women are still compelled to do work that pays no wages, that is not taken account of anywhere, that is not credited toward social security.

Independently of the fact that women often receive the help of men, the truth is that the customs and level of development of our society impose this superexertion on women. And it is in this sense that women are not only exploited—they're superexploited. They are exploited in their workplaces, if they work. They are exploited by lower wages and exploited in the home. That is, they are triply exploited.

What can be done to eliminate this dramatic plight of women?

There is no other alternative except to change the basic economic structure of society. There is no alternative but to develop an economy that guarantees the satisfaction of the fundamental needs of our people. There is no alternative but to create a productive apparatus whose rationale is not individual profit, but rather satisfaction of the demands of the entire society, the demands of the workers—whose rationale is to reaffirm and emphasize the potential of man and woman to live together socially as human beings.

This process of change, *compañeras,* is complicated, difficult, and will take place over time. But are we going to wait until economic development and social transformation have reached their culmination before we begin to think out the woman question? This would certainly be an inconsistency.

How can we fail to seriously consider the equality of women if we are to be elementally just to their struggle, their sacrifice, and their heroism? How can we not guarantee their participation in social life, in work, and in the political leadership of the country? How can we not guarantee that a woman can be both a mother and a worker, both a mother and a student, both a mother and an artist, both a mother and a political leader, both fulfill all the tasks the revolution demands of her and at the same time fulfill the beautiful work of a self-sacrificing, capable, and loving mother?

A concrete answer to these questions will be possible only to the extent that the individual tasks of women are socialized. It is society that has to provide the necessary day-care centers, laundries, people's restaurants, and other services that will, in effect, free women from household work. This is not easy.

So far, the revolution has only been able to build twenty CDIs [childcare centers]—obviously an insufficient number. The problem is that the cost of construction, equipment, and maintenance is very high. With all the economic difficulties that are holding our country back, it's impossible for us to move forward to the massive creation of these centers. And yet we must do it—not only to enable women to dedicate themselves to productive, social, and cultural tasks, but also to assure that the overall education of our children is as rich as possible.

How can we do it? How can we overcome this contradiction between the possible and the necessary?

We must look for audacious answers, I believe—answers based not so much on purely budgetary considerations but on the initiative, organization, and strength of the masses. Here AMNLAE should be the leading force and catalyst of these initiatives, fundamentally in coordination with the CDSs [Sandinista Defense Committees].

This is possible in a revolutionary society. There is no task that wouldn't be possible for the revolutionary masses and there is no task that wouldn't be possible for Nicaraguan women.

However difficult a task may be, the challenges that are being put forward now can hardly be compared with what Nicaraguan women faced and conquered in the past when they were capable of participating in the trenches with rifles in hand.

On the other hand, the revolution must guarantee equal pay for men and women and at the same time open the doors of production to women's participation in new fields of development—in industry as well as in agriculture.

We have already taken the first step to guarantee this equal participation. To assure the effectiveness of the principle, "equal pay for equal work," we enacted decrees 573 and 583 for the rural sector. These decrees for the first time established norms governing agricultural labor in coffee and cotton, and provided that everyone above fourteen years of age, man or woman, will be paid directly. Because before the victory, only the head of the household received the wages for the family—the young ones and women were not treated as real workers.

But the important thing is that we watch over the execution of laws the revolution has created to guarantee equality between men and women.

Just as workers gained consciousness of the exploitation they suffered and of their vanguard role in the revolution, women must also gain full consciousness of the discrimination they are still subjected to and of their role in the revolutionary struggle. We said that women were triply exploited, which means that women should be revolutionary in three different dimensions, seeking a single objective—the total liberation of our society.

It's good to remember, however, that economic development by itself will not accomplish the liberation of women, nor will simply the organization of women be sufficient.

We have to struggle against the habits, customs, and prejudices of men and women. We have to embark upon a difficult and prolonged ideological struggle—a struggle that equally benefits men and women.

Men must overcome a multitude of prejudices. We know *compañeros* who are revolutionaries in the street, in their workplaces, in their militia battalions—everywhere—but they're feudal *señores,* feudal lords in the home.

Right now, if we consider the path traveled by AMNLAE from the moment of its founding, it's evident that the self-sacrificing activity of the *compañeras* has achieved quantitative advances, and in some aspects qualitative advances. With respect to the present tasks, and above all regarding the state of emergency, women's participation has noticeably increased. The work of the Committees of Mothers of Heroes and Martyrs in denouncing the enemy's crimes and plans of aggression against Nicaragua has been outstanding.

However, in the militias, for example, the presence of women varies geographically. In Managua, women are 14 percent of the militia members, but in places like León, their participation is very low. León ranks twelfth in the incorporation of women into the militia, after having been first in the revolutionary struggle in combat against the dictatorship. It's a contradiction that perhaps they will explain to me later.

The participation of women has been important in the People's Health campaigns. In relation to organizational tasks, we can see a greater stability in leadership cadres, a greater coordination among the various mass organizations, and an advance in the consolidation of the Provincial Executive Committees—and therefore in overseeing the carrying out of tasks in the provinces.

In the field of international relations, it's correct to single out AMNLAE's participation in the Continental Meeting of Women as marking a considerable advance in establishing relations with different political and women's groups worldwide.

It would be an error, however, if we considered these accomplishments satisfactory. The revolution demands that we confront with dedication the deficiencies that limit the development of AMNLAE. The links between the leadership of the association and the ranks are not sufficient. At times general lines of action are put forward without being followed by specific concrete tasks. Adequate forms and mechanisms to assure the active participation of women in the work of the association do not exist.

All this results at times in improvisation and amateurish work habits.

Of course this is not just AMNLAE's problem but a problem of all the mass organizations and forms a part of the process of development of our revolution.

But our revolutionary society has to begin from a fundamental premise—the active, conscious, and permanent participation of each man and woman not only in aspects solely concerned with daily life but also in determining the course of our revolution.

If the masses participate in their workplaces, in their neighborhoods, in their schools, and in their organizations, then this revolution will advance toward a revolutionary society where the dignity of man will be counterposed to the alienation of man.

And we must take into account that analyzing this concrete problem means not only gaining knowledge of one particular aspect, such as legislation, but advancing the process of women's politicization as a whole.

If we don't do this our men and women will not be able to carry the process of liberation to its completion.

Right now AMNLAE should be more a great movement than an organization—a great movement that encourages the participation of women in the various mass organizations, in the CDSs, in the Sandinista Youth, in the ATC [Rural Workers Association], in the CST [Sandinista Workers Federation]—and that at the same time groups women together in their common bond, which is their status as women.

The central task of AMNLAE should be the integration of all women into the revolution, without distinction. It should be a broad and democratic movement that mobilizes women from the various social sectors, so as to provide a channel for their political, social, economic, and cultural demands and to integrate them as a supporting force in the tasks of the Sandinista People's Revolution.

AMNLAE should become a broad propagandistic, educational, and agitational movement that encourages women to play an active role in the economic, political, and social transformations of the country.

The peasant woman, for example, is a peasant and as such has specific demands. But she is also a woman—just like the woman worker, the woman militia member, the woman who is a housewife, the woman student, the professional woman, and so forth.

Being clear on this dual role is key to the development of AMNLAE.

Another immediate task of AMNLAE, we believe, is to deepen the analysis of the status of the Nicaraguan woman, to fight to massively incorporate women in productive work, to reclaim women's right to participate more fully in production, to participate more fully in leading the government, the mass organizations, and the Sandinista National Liberation Front. And to make sure that in scholarship awards, a considerable number are given to women, which in large measure is already happening.

Compañeras: Our National Directorate salutes Nicaraguan women with profound respect and affection. We can assure you we are not going to consider anyone a revolutionary who is not ready to fight the oppression of women. We would not be Sandinistas if in the new society we did not make women an essential pillar of this new society. If we are revolutionaries, even if we are men, we should be with AMNLAE.

From Conchita Alday and Blanca Aráuz to Luisa Amanda Espinoza, women have blazed a path of fire and tenderness that has given life and color to this revolution. Nicaraguan women have not only given the country the fruit of their bellies but also their enthusiasm and courage—selflessly, without limitations.

A revolution with these women is a revolution that will not be defeated by anyone—that will march invincibly into new dawns.

It's important that the imperialists know, that the National Guard murderers know, that the nation's traitors know, that in Nicaragua they will be confronted not only by men but by the women as well. And these women! Women that leave the fragrance of flowers for the fragrance of gunpowder—women who are as fertile in their wombs as they are in revolutionary consciousness.

78. *Women: Activism without Liberation?**

By Maxime Molyneux

From AMPRONAC to AMNLAE

Two months after the revolutionary triumph, in September of 1979, the existing women's association AMPRONAC *(Associación de Mujeres ante la Problemática Nacional)* became the revolutionary mass organization AMNLAE *(Asociación de Mujeres Nicaragüenses Luisa Amanda Espinoza),* named after a fallen fighter. AMNLAE immediately began to develop its political program concerning the problems faced by women. Its early slogan was, "Without women's liberation there is no revolution; and without revolution there is no women's liberation."

Yet in the first major speech by an FSLN leader on the role of women (reading *77*), Tomás Borge said that, although there have been advances, "all of us have to honestly admit that we haven't confronted the struggle for women's liberation with the same courage and decisiveness" with which the revolution itself was achieved. "From the point of view of daily exertions," he continued, "women remain fundamentally in the same conditions as in the past."

FSLN Policy toward Women

The 1969 Historic Program of the FSLN (reading *26*) stated that "the Sandinista People's Revolution will abolish the odious discrimination that women have been subjected to compared to men," and "will establish economic, political, and cultural equality between woman and man." Ten years later the Fundamental Statute of the new Nicaraguan state put into law the equality of all Nicaraguans, "without discrimination by race, national origin, creed, or sex." The statute further decreed that "the State must use all means at its disposal to overcome whatever obstacles remain in the path of achieving this equality." This furnished the legal basis for the future political and legal steps that would be taken.

Within this framework AMNLAE established its official program, based on the following objectives or principles:

- the defense of the revolution.
- the promotion of greater political and ideological participation and achievement by women in the social, political and economic life of the revolution.
- the struggle against legal and institutional inequality.
- the promotion of cultural and technical achievement by women, especially in fields traditionally reserved for men.
- the struggle for the recognition of housework as labor.

---

*Reprinted from *Pensamiento Propio,* vol. 3, no. 24 (Managua: June/July 1985). Translated from the Spanish by Peter Rosset.

- the creation of day care centers for working women.
- the strengthening of international women's solidarity.

Social Gains

In practice the largest gains by women have been in the areas of welfare and legal reform. There has also been growing and militant participation by women in the political movement of the revolution.

In general women have benefited more than men from the new policies of health care, education, social programs, housing, and agrarian reform. This is because these programs are oriented toward the poor, and women represent 60 percent of the poorest stratum of the Nicaraguan population. This is particularly evident in Managua, where the lowest income category contains 3.5 times more women than men. Many of these women are heads of households.

The new laws concerning family life—the Alimony Law and the Law on Relations between Mother, Father, and Children—have emphasized strengthening the institution of the family by promoting cohesion and discouraging sexual inequality. Several factors, including the high rate of family desertion by men, migration, and the common male practice of polygamy, have contributed to a situation in which many women are the only source of financial support for their children. In fact 34 percent of all Nicaraguan households are headed by a woman, of which 60 percent are found in Managua. The Alimony Law makes all adult members of the extended family, through three generations, legally responsible for the maintenance of the family unit, including the sharing of housework.

In addition to these changes, workplace conditions of occupational health and safety, and job security, have improved for women. Whereas traditionally only the man was paid when the whole family did farm work, the law now mandates a separate paycheck for each family member who works.

In terms of the political participation of women, there are now more women organized than at any point in Nicaraguan history. AMNLAE reported 85,000 members in 1984, and women make up 22 percent of the membership of the FSLN while occupying 37 percent of the leadership positions in the party. As the national crisis has worsened, the participation of women in other mass organizations and in defense has increased. At least half of the CDS membership is composed of women. The same is true for the militias.

Inequality Remains

The advances made by women have not been uniform. While employment opportunities for women in the formal sector of the economy have increased, they remain restricted in number and in level. Day care and the sharing of housework have affected only a minority of women. By mid-1984 there were forty-three day-care centers that cared for about 4,000 children, but because of the economic crisis no new centers were planned. The new laws protecting women in the family, passed in 1982, were supposed to promote a new concept of the family that would incorporate greater democracy, equality, and mutual responsibility. Yet these laws were never widely enforced, and public discussion of these issues petered out in 1983.

The policies of the revolution did respond, at a certain level, to the "practical" needs of women. But this did not always imply a response to the "strategic" interests of women; that is, the progressive abolition of inequality, discrimination, and oppression.

What caused these limitations? In addition to the obvious explanation of a lack of time for changes to take effect, there are several important factors that have played a role.

In the first place, there are practical limitations to the capacity of the state to promote social transformation. These are economic limitations, due to the general level of underdevelopment and to the effects of the war. Among the social programs affected by war-related cutbacks were several that directly affect women, such as the construction and staffing of day-care centers and the expansion of employment opportunities.

Furthermore, the constitutional commitment of the FSLN to the principles of political pluralism and a mixed economy has left political space for more reactionary forces like the Church to operate. This has carried a real cost for the women's movement. For example, deference toward the private sector has allowed certain business owners, particularly those with small, nonunion enterprises, to evade labor legislation and continue discriminatory hiring practices.

Pressure from the Catholic Hierarchy

The hierachy of the Catholic Church has offered ever more implacable resistance to Sandinista policies concerning women. The extensive institutional presence of the Church and its access to the media make it a formidible opponent. The conservative wing of the clergy has actively opposed reforms in the areas of family life and education. They have maintained the religious prohibition against work on Sundays, making community volunteer work difficult. They have opposed the participation of women in military service, and have argued strongly for traditional family life with its characteristic sexual division of labor.

The Church has also obstructed reform of the divorce law and insisted on adherence to the papal cyclical making contraception a sin. Finally, the opposition of the hierarchy to the legalization of abortion has forced thousands of women to resort to semiclandestine and dangerous practices.

Another factor that has conditioned the successes and failures of policies geared toward women has been the level of opposition or resistance among the general population, including women themselves. Although there has been no systematic study made of the extent of these attitudes, AMNLAE has nevertheless been deemphasizing feminist themes so as not to jeopardize its base of popular support.

Finally, we have to consider the priority that has been assigned to women's issues relative to other goals of the revolution. In this respect we can conclude that the

FSLN has been able to achieve, with great popular support and little resistance, those parts of the women's program that coincide with the broader goals of the revolutionary process, such as social welfare, development, social equality, and mobilization in defense of the revolution. On the the other hand, advances toward overcoming the specific problems of women have been far more relative, increasingly having to take second place.

*79. A Strategy for Development: The Agroindustrial Axis**

By Jaime Wheelock

Comandante Jaime Wheelock Roman is Nicaragua's minister of agricultural development and agrarian reform, and is a member of the FSLN's nine-person National Directorate.

The Search for a New Development Model

Nicaragua must base its development on the industrial transformation of its own natural resources, with the agricultural sector as its framework. While industrial transformation must also include forest resources, fisheries, and mining, agroindustry must be its main axis. With this perspective it will be possible to eliminate dependency and advance the struggle against backwardness and underdevelopment.

Producing primary materials like coffee, cotton, or lumber does not permit the internal development of other areas of the society. The result of our participation in the international division of labor is that we have assumed the production of consumable goods, while other countries have specialized in the production of means of production, such as tractors or factories. The production of factories symbolizes the production of the potential to transform other things. It signifies the creation of the tools necessary for the transformation of natural resources for the benefit of humankind. But we have been assigned the role of producing consumption goods, the production of which transforms nothing. We thus are a country which does not have the tools of transformation in our hands.

In our struggle against backwardness and dependence, the first thing we intend to do is modify the role Nicaragua has played in the international division of labor. We intend to stop being a country that sells its raw materials—the old agroexport model—and advance toward the industrialization of these original raw materials, putting them on the market with a value augmented by a secondary industrial transfor-

*Excerpts from *Entre la Crisis y la Agresion: La Reforma Agraria Sandinista,* by Jamie Wheelock, trans. by John Vandermeer (Managua: Editorial Nueva Nicaragua, 1985).

mation. In a word, the industrialization of our own natural resources must be the primary strategy of national development. Thus, instead of selling logs, we will sell manufactured wood products and substitute for the many wood products that we currently import. In place of selling cotton we have the potential to industrialize this resource and sell cloth or clothing; with leather, we can do the same. With all the products of this country, we can do the same.

A second crucial consideration is hunger and the potential for its solution by the end of the century. In the year 2000 there will be more than six million inhabitants who will have to consume more than triple that which is consumed today, and with certain products, such as meat and milk, consumption will increase more than five or ten times. It is obvious that we can neither convert to food importers nor die of hunger. Thus we are obliged to find an agricultural solution to this problem. In this respect our strategy of an agricultural axis is perfectly understandable.

The Three Reforms: Property, Land Use, and Technical Development

First we have to modify the land tenure system. The implementation of this goal will confer domestic stability and peace, create a rational distribution of land, and establish a relationship between humans and land that will be more advantageous for production.

Second, in addition to agrarian reform, we must have a reform in the *use* of the land. For reasons outside of our control, our crops are not necessarily where they should be. A majority of those that are indispensable for life have been displaced to low-quality lands by crops that serve to feed the needs of other countries.

The best lands of Nicaragua, those that are optimum for the production of corn, beans, and sorghum, were occupied by agroexport crops until the triumph of the revolution. The indigenous farmers, who traditionally occupied the best lands in Nicaragua, were displaced by the large landlords. The latter, stimulated by the profit motive, were dedicated to the production of coffee, sugar, or cotton, depending on the epoch. The profits went to purchase luxury goods, which had to be imported.

The landlords—more intensively since the 1950s—removed the small farmers from the Pacific plains and forced them to farm along roadsides, on steep hillsides, on the coast, or simply pushed them to the agricultural frontier. Thus the best lands of Nicaragua are not now devoted to the crops that are most important to the country's development. In some cases, the land may be well utilized from a strictly agronomic point of view, but not from the point of view of the country's basic needs. Nicaragua in time had been converted into a producer of exports and an importer of manufactured products, to the extent that even food was imported.

The new strategy that we are implementing, from the point of view of agriculture, must reserve the lands of the Pacific lowlands for the production of food, employing intensive technology with annual row crops. The mountainous regions, with the exception of some of the larger valleys, are not suitable for this type of agriculture.

The third reform, in addition to reforms in land tenure and land use, is the use of modern technology.

Nicaragua has limited resources for the production of row crops. Only the littoral zones of the Pacific region can be used for this purpose. A little more than a million hectares are suitable for the production of corn, beans, cotton, sesame, and sorghum. Furthermore, where we have the most fertile soils, we have inadequate precipitation. Considering what Nicaragua will consume over the next twenty years, we realize that we will need the entire Pacific region just to maintain the Nicaraguan diet at its present level. But what would we export in such a situation? If we assume that agriculture is the main axis of development (i.e., producing foreign exchange as well as food), and if we remember that our whole infrastructure (e.g., roads, energy) exists in the Pacific region, we must think, at least at the beginning, of the agricultural base in the Pacific region. Thus, we must plan to produce both food and foreign exchange in the Pacific region. But such a plan would necessitate a doubling of the available land. And here it occurs to us that, in fact, it is possible to double the land base—through the use of irrigation.

We need irrigation to produce cotton and corn in the same land in the same year. This is not only to increase the production of corn, but also to relocate its zone of production away from the mountainous regions where soil erosion has become a large problem. We are also bringing bean production into the Pacific region, similarly to stop the destruction of the fragile soils on which much of the production had been concentrated. We must produce these basic grains in the Pacific lowlands, but in order to do so we must introduce irrigation. We are going to have, year by year, the development of more irrigated croplands to produce both export goods and goods for internal consumption, the latter in terms of food for direct use of the population and in terms of inputs for agroindustry.

In the Pacific plains we will produce cotton, corn, sorghum, sesame, tobacco, and beans, following the principles of intensive land utilization. We are going to relocate the production of corn, eliminating it from the humid mountainous north-central zone. We are going to encourage the production of more suitable products there, such as coffee, cattle, and fruits and vegetables. Finally, in the Atlantic zone we are going to plant crops more adequately suited to the humid tropics and also develop rational uses for the forest products. The only way to rationally exploit the humid Atlantic zone is to cultivate appropriate species: oil palm, coconut, rubber, cacao, spices, bananas, root crops, etc.

Many people will say, "This road is not correct," or "From the point of view of technology, it is a fragile road." But nevertheless, no one has indicated a better route that we could take. All routes contain their contradictions and we know the contradictions that are present in the route we choose. It is possible that in our contingency plan we will not get the yields we expect. Possibly we will get less, or the same that a cooperative in Masaya could have obtained without irrigation. That's possible. It is the cost of taking an unknown route. But we are going to learn little by little. Our idea is to go forward now with some clear ideas, assisted with a strategy that appears to us correct. In this way, we believe that we are contributing, in the first place, to the economic independence of the country.

The agrarian reform, the rationalization of land use, the application of technology, and industrialization is the route we choose to gain food self-sufficiency and control over our natural resources. We are going to go in stages. Selling tomatoes is not the same as processing them and selling the paste. Selling cotton fiber is not the same as producing and selling textiles. The important point is to industrialize our natural resources, principally those of agriculture. This attitude signals a shift in the international division of labor. We will change from a country that produces consumables and raw materials to a country that industrializes its natural resources and sells products manufactured from its own resources.

80. *Table of Basic Economic Indicators*

By the Editors

Basic Economic Indicators for Nicaragua

	Nicaragua: Yearly Figures									Comparative Figures: 1979–1983			
	1976	1977	1978	1979	1980	1981	1982	1983	1984	Nicaragua	Costa Rica	Central America	Latin America
Gross Domestic Product (percent growth)	5.0	6.3	−7.2	−25.1	10.7	8.7	−1.2	5.3	0.0	22.5	−6.49	−5.7	2.8
Exports (millions $)	542	637	646	567	503	500	408	411	380				
Imports (millions $)	485	704	553	326	930	999	776	819	790				
Trade deficit (millions $)	−57	67	−93	−241	427	499	368	408	410				
Foreign debt (millions $)	653	867	964	1101	1290	2163	2789	3400	3939				
Terms of trade[a]	100	127	113	100	98	92	83	76	N.A.	−17.3[b]	N.A.	0.0[b]	−22.3[b]
Consumer Price Index (percent inflation)	6.3	10.2	4.4	70.3	24.8	23.2	22.2	37.3	40.0	101.1	345.1	78.8	329.6

[a]Changes in the price of imports relative to the price of exports, in other words Nicaragua's exports in 1983 had only 76 percent of the purchasing power of the 1976 exports.

[b]1981–1983 only

SOURCES: United Nations Economic Commission for Latin America (ECLA). Michael E. Conroy, "Economic Legacy and Policies: Performance and Critique," in *Nicaragua: The First Five Years*, T. W. Walker, ed. (New York: Praeger, 1985). Joseph Collins, *What Difference Could a Revolution Make?* (Institute for Food and Development Policy, 1985). *Business Latin America*, March 13, 1985. Marc Edelman, "Back from the Brink," *NACLA*, November/December, 1985.

Selected Bibliography

Books and Pamphlets about Nicaragua or Central America

Aldaraca, Bridget; Baker, Edward; Rodriguez, Ileana; and Zimmerman, Marc. *Nicaragua in Revolution: The Poets Speak. Studies in Marxism* vol. 5. Minneapolis: University of Minnesota Anthropology Department, 1980.

Barry, Tom; Wood, Beth; and Preusch, Deb. *Dollars and Dictators: A Guide to Central America.* New York: Grove Press, 1983.

Barry, Tom, and Preusch, Deb. *The Central America Fact Book.* New York: Grove Press, 1986.

Berryman, Phillip. *Inside Central America.* New York: Pantheon Books, 1985.

———. *The Religious Roots of Rebellion: Christians in Central American Revolutions.* Maryknoll, New York: Orbis Books, 1984.

Black, George. *Triumph of the People: The Sandinista Revolution in Nicaragua.* London: Zed Press, 1981.

Black, George, and Butler, Judy. *Target Nicaragua. NACLA Report on the Americas.* New York: North American Congress on Latin America, 1982.

Booth, John A. *The End and the Beginning: The Nicaraguan Revolution.* Boulder, Colo.: Westview Press, 1981.

Borge, Thomás; Fonseca, Carlos; Ortega, Daniel; Ortega, Humberto; and Wheelock, Jaime. *Sandinistas Speak.* New York: Pathfinder Press, 1982.

Brody, Reed. *Contra Terror in Nicaragua: Report of a Fact-Finding Mission: September 1984–1985.* Boston: South End Press, 1985.

Burbach, Roger, and Draimin, Tim. *Nicaragua's Revolution. NACLA Report on the Americas.* New York: North American Congress on Latin America, 1980.

Butler, Judy, ed. *Central America—Guns of December? NACLA Report on the Americas.* New York: North American Congress on Latin America, 1982.

Cabestrero, Teófilo. *Blood of the Innocent: Victims of the Contras' War in Nicaragua.* Maryknoll, New York: Orbis Books, 1985.

———. *Ministers of God, Ministers of the People: Testimonies of Faith from Nicaragua.* Maryknoll, New York: Orbis Books, 1983.

Cabezas, Omar. *Fire from the Mountain.* New York: Crown Publishers, 1985.

C.A.H.I. *Chronology of U.S.-Nicaraguan Relations: Policy and Consequences* (covers January 1981–January 1983.) Washington, D.C.: Central American Historical Institute, Georgetown University, May 1983.

Cardenal, Ernesto. *The Gospel of Solentiname,* 4 vols. Maryknoll, New York: Orbis Books, 1976.

———. *Zero Hour and Other Documentary Poems.* New York: New Directions, 1980.

Center for Research and Documentation of the Atlantic Coast (CIDCA). *Trabil Nani: Historical Background and Current Situation on the Atlantic Coast of Nicaragua.* New York: The Riverside Church Disarmament Project, 1985.

Chomsky, Noam. *Turning the Tide: U.S. Intervention in Central America and the Struggle for Peace.* Boston: South End Press, 1985.

Christian, Shirley. *Revolution in the Family.* New York: Random House, 1985.

Collins, Joseph. *What Difference Could a Revolution Make? Food and Farming in the New Nicaragua.* San Francisco: Institute for Food and Development Policy, 1985.

Debray, Regis. *The Revolution on Trial.* London: Penguin, 1978.

De Nogales, Rafael. *The Looting of Nicaragua.* New York: Robert M. McBride & Co., 1928.

Dilling, Yvonne, and Wheaton, Phillip, eds. *Nicaragua: A People's Revolution.* Washington, D.C.: EPICA, 1980.

Diskin, Martin. *Trouble in our Backyard: Central America and the United States in the Eighties.* New York: Pantheon Books, 1983.

Dixon, Marlene, ed. *On Trial: Reagan's War Against Nicaragua.* San Francisco: Synthesis Publications, 1985.

Dixon, Marlene, and Jonas, Susanne, eds. *Nicaragua Under Siege.* San Francisco: Synthesis Publications, 1984.

Dozier, Craig L. *Nicaragua's Mosquito Shore: The Years of British and American Presence.* University, Alabama: University of Alabama Press, 1985.

Eich, Dieter, and Rincon, Carlos, eds. *The Contras: Interviews with Anti-Sandinistas.* San Francisco: Synthesis Publications, 1985.

Ellman, Richard. *Cocktails at Somozas: A Reporter's Sketchbook of Events in Revolutionary Nicaragua.* Cambridge, Mass.: Applewood Books, 1981.

EPICA Task Force. *Nicaragua: A People's Revolution.* Washington, D.C.: EPICA Task Force, 1980.

EPOCA (Environmental Project on Central America). *Green Paper No. 1: Environmental Policy in Nicaragua.* San Francisco: Earth Island Institute, 1986.

Everett, Melissa. *Bearing Witness, Building Bridges: Interviews with North Americans Living and Working in Nicaragua.* Philadelphia, Penna.: New Society Publishers, 1986.

Fagen, Richard R., and Pellicer, Olga, eds. *The Future of Central America: Policy Choices for the U.S. and Mexico.* Stanford, Calif.: Stanford University Press, 1983.

Fagen, Richard. *The Nicaraguan Revolution: A Personal Report.* Washington, D.C.: Institute for Policy Studies, 1981.

Grossman, Karl. *Nicaragua: America's New Vietnam?* Sag Harbor, New York: The Permanent Press, 1984.

Hackel, Joy, and Nagle, Ellen, et. al. *Deceit and Illegality on Central America.* Washington, D.C.: Institute for Policy Studies, 1985.

Hirshon, Sheryl, and Butler, Judy. *And Also Teach Them to Read.* Westport, Conn.: Lawrence Hill & Co., 1983.

Jones, Jeff, ed. *Brigadista: Harvest and War in Nicaragua.* New York: Praeger, 1986.

Kornbluh, Peter. *Nicaragua: The Price of Intervention.* Washington, D.C.: Institute for Policy Studies, 1985.

Lappé, Frances Moore, and Collins, Joseph. *Now We Can Speak: A Journey through the New Nicaragua.* San Francisco: Institute for Food Development Policy, 1983.

Lernoux, Penny. *Cry of the People: United States Involvement in the Rise of Fascism, Torture, and the Persecution of the Catholic Church in Latin America.* New York: Penguin, 1980.

Macaulay, Neill. *The Sandino Affair.* New York: Quadrangle Books, 1967.

McGinnis, James. *Solidarity with the People of Nicaragua.* Maryknoll, New York: Orbis Books, 1985.

Meiselas, Susan. *Nicaragua* (photography). New York: Pantheon Books, 1981.

Millett, Richard. *The Guardians of the Dynasty: A History of the U.S.-Created* Guardia Nacional de Nicaragua *and the Somoza Family.* Maryknoll, New York: Orbis Books, 1977.

Murguia, Alejandro, and Paschke, Barbara, eds. *Volcan: Poems from El Salvador, Guatemala, Honduras, Nicaragua.* San Francisco: City Lights Books, 1983.

Omang, Joanne, and Neier, Aryeh. *The CIA's Nicaragua Manual: Psychological Operations in Guerrilla Warfare.* New York: Vintage Books, 1985.

Pearce, Jenny. *Under the Eagle: U.S. Intervention in Central America and the Caribbean.* Boston: South End Press, 1982.

Poelchau, Warner. *White Paper, Whitewash: Interview with Philip Agee on the CIA and El Salvador.* New York: Deep Cover Books, 1981.

Randall, Margaret. *Christians in the Nicaraguan Revolution.* Vancouver: New Star Books, 1983.

———. *Sandino's Daughters.* Trumansburg, New York: Crossing Press, 1981.

Rosset, Peter, and Vandermeer, John, eds. *The Nicaragua Reader: Documents of a Revolution Under Fire.* New York: Grove Press, 1983.

Ryan, John Morris, et. al. *Area Handbook for Nicaragua.* Washington, D.C.: U.S. Government Printing Office, 1970.

Selser, Gregorio. *Sandino.* New York: Monthly Review Press, 1981.

Stanford Central America Action Network. *Revolution in Central America.* Boulder, Colo.: Westview Press, 1983.

Swezey, Sean, and Daxl, Rainer. *Breaking the Circle of Poison: The IPM Revolution in Nicaragua.* San Francisco: Institute for Food and Development Policy, 1983.

The Resource Center. *Low Intensity Warfare: The New Battlefield in Central America.* Albuquerque, N.M.: The Resource Center, 1986.

———. *New Right Humanitarians.* Albuquerque, N.M.: The Resource Center, 1986.

Tijerino, Doris. *Inside the Nicaraguan Revolution* (As told to Margaret Randall). Vancouver, Wash: New Star Books, 1978.

U.S. Central Intelligence Agency. *The Freedom Fighter's Manual.* New York: Grove Press, 1985.

Vilas, Carlos. *The Sandinista Revolution: National Liberation and Social Transformation in Central America.* New York: Monthly Review Press, 1986.

Walker, Thomas W. *Nicaragua: The Land of Sandino*. Boulder, Colo.: Westview Press, 1981.
Walker, Thomas W., ed. *Nicaragua in Revolution*. New York: Praeger, 1982.
———. *Nicaragua: The First Five Years*. New York: Praeger, 1985.
Weber, Henri. *Nicaragua: The Sandinist Revolution*. Translated by Patrick Camiller. London: Verso Editions and NLB, 1981.
Weissberg, Arnold. *Nicaragua: An Introduction to the Sandinista Revolution*. New York: Pathfinder Press, 1981.
Wheelock Roman, Jaime. *Nicaragua: The Great Challenge*. An interview with Marta Harnecker. Managua, Nicaragua: Alternative Views, 1984.
White, Steven F. *Poets of Nicaragua: A Bilingual Anthology 1918–1979*. Greensboro: Unicorn Press, 1982.
Zimmerman, Marc, ed. *Nicaragua in Reconstruction and at War: The People Speak*. Minneapolis: MEP Publications, 1985.
Zwerling, Phillip, and Martin, Connie. *Nicaragua: A New Kind of Revolution*. Westport, Conn.: Lawrence Hill & Co., 1985.

Publications with Regular Coverage of Nicaragua

Barricada Internacional (available in English or Spanish), Apartado Postal 576, Managua, Nicaragua. Weekly.

Censa's Strategic Reports, Center for the Study of the Americas, 2288 Fulton St., No. 103, Berkeley, Calif. 94704. Five issues/year.

Central America Report, Infor Press CentroAmericana, 9A Calle (A) 3-56, APDO, 2823 Zona One, Guatemala City, Guatemala. Weekly.

Christianity and Crisis, 537 W. 121st St., N.Y., N.Y. Bimonthly.

Counter Spy, P.O. Box 647, Ben Franklin Station, Washington, D.C. 20004. Bimonthly.

Covert Action Information Bulletin, P.O. Box 50272, Washington, D.C. 20004. Bimonthly.

Envio, Instituto Histórico Centroamericano (available in English, Spanish, German, and French), Apartado Postal A-194, Managua, Nicaragua. Monthly.

Food First Action Alert. Institute for Food and Development Policy, 1885 Mission St., San Francisco, Calif. 94103.

Latin American Perspectives, Box 792, Riverside, Calif., 92502. Quarterly.

Latin American Weekly Report, 91-93 Charterhouse St., London, EC1M 61N, England. Weekly.

Latin American Update, Washington Office on Latin America (WOLA), 110 Maryland Ave. N.E., Washington, D.C. 20002. Bimonthly.

Legislative Update, Coalition for a New Foreign and Military Policy, 120 Maryland Ave. N.E., Washington D.C. 20002. Irregular.

Maryknoll Magazine, Maryknoll, N.Y. 10545. Monthly.

Mesoamerica (English), Apartado 300, San José, Costa Rica. Monthly.

NACLA Report on the Americas, 151 W. 19th St., New York, N.Y. 10011. Bimonthly.

Nicaraguan Perspectives, Nicaragua Information Center, P.O. Box 1004, Berkeley, Calif. 94704. Quarterly.

The Alert! Focus on Central America, U.S. Committee in Solidarity with the People of El Salvador (CISPES), 19 W. 21st, 2nd floor, New York, N.Y. 10010. Monthly.

Third World (Tercer Mundo) (available in English or Spanish), Apartado 20572-01000, Mexico D.F., Mexico. Monthly

Update, Central American Historical Institute, Intercultural Center, Georgetown University, Washington, D.C. 20057. Weekly.

Index

N